FROM *Collective Security*
TO *Preventive Diplomacy*

FROM *Collective Security* TO *Preventive Diplomacy*

Readings IN INTERNATIONAL ORGANIZATION
AND THE MAINTENANCE OF PEACE

Edited by
JOEL LARUS
Brandeis University

JOHN WILEY & SONS, INC.

New York   London   Sydney

To R.R.L.

Preface

This anthology results from the belief that an appreciation of the complexities of containing aggression by collective action and maintaining peace with a permanent international organization needs to be understood in its historic setting and must never be isolated from the case histories that give it form and substance. Students who seek to arrive at an appreciation of Man's eternal search for a peaceful and secure universe should begin by taking Al Smith's advice and "look at the record." Guided by this philosophy, I have designed this book as a supplementary text with a sufficiently detailed body of historically oriented material so that the undergraduate or graduate student will better realize the dangers and pitfalls in relying on either collective security or preventive diplomacy as an approach to peace.

The book incorporates two stylistic features which reflect my thinking concerning the teaching of international organization. First, I believe that such courses should draw heavily from original source material, that is, the actual record of peacekeeping by the League and currently in the United Nations. Consequently, the learned essays that are customarily included in readers of this type have been interspersed with speeches, debates, and reports from the records of the two organizations. By combining these two bodies of complementary material, the ever-changing dynamics of organizing a politically realistic approach to peace in the twentieth century can be examined and discussed in the classroom with greater precision.

Second, I am of the opinion that case histories are one of the most revealing ways to study the peacekeeping record of both international organizations. At periods of political crisis the student best appreciates these organizations' capabilities and limitations. Did they succeed in restoring the peace because of bold action and determination or fail because of structural misconceptions, vascillation, or faulty basic premises? Four political crises from the League era and four from the United Nations experience have been included in this book. Considered collectively, they offer a cross section of the evolving history of the two leading contemporary peacekeeping approaches to peace.

Footnotes that originally appeared in some of the books and articles cited have been omitted. A few explanatory editor's notes have been inserted.

I wish to express my appreciation for many kindnesses to Professor James Barros of Dartmouth College and Dr. Gabriella Rosner Lande of the Center of International Studies, Princeton University. My research assistant was William Schneider of Brandeis University, and he was immeasurably helpful. A number of research librarians gave most generously of their time and skill. These include Mrs. Ivon Mills and Mrs. Karl Girshmann of Goldfarb Library, Brandeis University; Miss Marion Kanaly and Mr. Richard Chamberlin of the Wellesley College Library; and Mrs. Kaye Jaffe of Bapst Library, Boston College. Brandeis students provided any number of incisive and fruitful criticisms when using earlier versions of the text.

J. L.

Waltham, Mass.
August 1965

Contents

FROM *Collective Security*
TO *Preventive Diplomacy*

INTRODUCTION
The Myth Is Born

The hope of establishing peace based on collective security was not an idea that burst unannounced onto the twentieth century political stage. Many in the past had dreamed of a general association of sovereign states pledged by treaty to act jointly to check aggression, each participant promising to come to the assistance of any victim of aggression and giving up the right to use armed force save in the common interest. Peacekeeping schemes incorporating the collective security principle are scattered throughout the political literature of the West. Some were introduced by philosophers and scholars; others by eminently practical statesmen. Woodrow Wilson and his World War I associates did not dream an original dream, but were heirs of an approach to peace whose roots are deeply implanted in the political history of Western civilization. Long before the League of Nations era began, a collective response to aggression was held out as a politically realistic arrangement to terminate the unilateral use of armed force, eliminate balance of power politics, and end entangling alliances. Such high hopes in the light of history were an illusion based on the myth of the collective security approach to peace.

Even a cursory review of the history of the collective security idea shows how long it has been politically attractive. Traces and suggestions of plans for pooling power for mutual advantage are present in a number of Europe's earliest privately sponsored peace schemes. A number of ratified treaties also relied on collective coercion to maintain the continent's public order. These plans applied exclusively to European states; no one suggested guaranteeing the territorial integrity of all political communities that fell victim of aggression, irrespective of location.

The geographical limitation found in the earliest versions of collective security arrangements was not without good reason. To Europe emerging from the Middle Ages, the continent was co-extensive with the world. Asia and Africa were considered to be outside the family of civilized states. The Middle East was held by infidels, beyond the pale of Christian concepts of law and justice.

The political purist may raise questions concerning terminology. Is it proper to characterize as adumbrations of the collective security idea peacekeeping arrangements that were so geographically restricted? Does the collective approach to peace not imply something more than local arrangements for the joint defense of sovereign nations? We believe that the publicists of the fourteenth to eighteenth centuries who drafted plans requiring the European monarchs to support each other and who sought to align all

1

continental powers against an offending or war-making state were championing an inchoate version of the collective security idea. They are the originators of our contemporary variant of universal peacekeeping under the aegis of a permanent international organization. Generally speaking, their proposals were based on the assumption that if the continent was not to experience repeated instances of naked aggression, all aggression must be rigorously opposed. The invader had to be confronted with the combined resources of the remaining states, that were expected to be ready and willing to apply sanctions. To implement such security systems, policy decisions were to be determined jointly. In some instances provisions were made for an international body to control the multinational armed force that was to be employed in restoring the continent's peace and tranquility. These features, if accompanied by a worldwide guarantee insuring the political integrity of all states, epitomizes our contemporary version of the collective security idea. There is no question that the League's universal extension of the earlier arrangement is an important landmark in the history of man's quest for a more orderly world, but the beginning of the concept ought not to be denied because originally only European states were permitted to participate.

The Holy Roman Empire was a viable political association when the continent was offered its first group of proposals calling for collective action in defense of peace and tranquility. In 1306 Pierre Dubois, a French jurist and minor advisor to Philip the Fair, published a detailed plan for winning Palestine back from the Moslems. Whatever aggrandizement would incidentally accrue to France and its monarch as a result of his suggestion was not unattractive to the shrewd, politically ambitious Dubois. The main section of his treatise, *The Recovery of the Holy Land*,[1] dealt with the formation of a league of Catholic European sovereigns who had to agree to settle all inter-state disputes by arbitration. In the event that a signatory waged war in violation of the terms of the agreement, Dubois' plan called for a joint coercive response. There was to be a common economic boycott of the offending state. Provisions for joint military action were also spelled out in considerable detail. Articles 4 and 5, the sections most pertinent to the history of collective security movements, read as follows:

IV . . . The whole commonwealth of Christian believers owing allegiance to the Roman Church must be joined together in the bonds of peace. United in this way, all Catholics will refrain from making war upon one another. . . .

. . . Let no Catholic rush to arms against Catholics; let none shed baptized blood. If anyone wishes to make war let him be zealous to make war upon the enemies of the Catholic faith, of the Holy Land, and of the places made sacred by the Lord. . . .

Let the lord pope punish those who make war and those who knowingly in any way give aid and comfort to the warmakers or associate with them by furnishing them with any provisions, water, fire, or other necessities of life. . . .

[1] For complete text see Pierre Dubois, *The Recovery of the Holy Land*, Walter I. Brandt, trans. (New York: Columbia University Press, 1956), pp. 69-198.

V . . . The question next arises whether the warmakers can easily be subjugated, and whether it will be advantageous to exile them to the Holy Land. Let us suppose that the duke or court of Burgundy makes war on the king of the French, his overlord. The king . . . will at once take steps to prevent anyone from bringing into their territories provisions, arms, merchandise, or any other supplies, even though due them for any reason. By decision of the council . . . this prohibition will be made to apply to all Catholics under like penalty. . . .[2]

The military exploits of the Muslim Turks were responsible for another important collective security proposal. In 1462 George Podebrad, newly elected King of Bohemia, circulated a draft treaty which called upon all European Catholic rulers to join with him in a "cult of peace." Since the 1453 fall of Constantinople, Europe had watched with growing dismay the steady advance of the Turks on the eastern flank of Christendom. As infidel troops moved through Asia Minor and went on to secure a number of Balkan bridgeheads, the continent's leaders had good reason to fear a general Muslim offensive. When Mohammed II seized a number of key Venetian possessions around the Aegean, the Slav states of central Europe began to prepare for the impending clash. In his Bohemian capital, George Podebrad, a Hussite involved in a bitter quarrel with the Holy See, attempted to organize a Europeanwide, anti-Muslim coalition. He called for an organization of Catholic nations, functioning through an Assembly, that would have authority to initiate collective military action to block deeper Turkish penetration of Eastern Europe.[3]

Article 13 of Podebrad's idea dealt with specific procedures that were to be initiated whenever the Turks, "the severest enemy of the Christian name," attacked or oppressed any signatory to the treaty.

We, the above kings and princes [it stated] pledge and swear to our Lord Jesus Christ . . . that we shall defend and protect the Christian religion and all the oppressed faithful against the vilest princes of the Turks with our joining forces and means which will be proportionately determined and declared.

The following article describes in some detail how the proposed organization would remove Muslim armed forces from Europe.

We hereby resolve that our whole assembly or its majority shall determine when it is suitable to attack the enemy or what land and naval forces should be used to conduct the war, or under which generals this should be done, what machines or instruments of war should be used, and at what place all the land forces should assemble that will march against the Turks. Also, in what manner it would be possible to obtain at decent prices victuals and billets in towns, villages and other suitable places. Also, in what manner a common coin should be provided so that the troops would not find themselves in difficulties on the march, when billeting and on their return.[4]

[2] *Ibid.*, pp. 74-76.
[3] See *The Universal Peace Organization of King George of Bohemia: A Fifteenth Century Plan for World Peace 1462/1464* (Prague: Publishing House of Czechoslovak Academy of Sciences).
[4] *Ibid.*, pp. 86-87.

The plan was rejected, but the idea of collective European action to maintain peace persisted. By the early seventh century it became increasingly attractive and influential. *The Great Design* of the Duke de Sully has been called "the most famous of the many projects advocating a federation of states in order to secure and to maintain peace between nations." [5] Believed to have been written sometime between 1635-38, it called for a General Council of sovereigns acting in concert to maintain the established religious balance of the continent, namely, that between Roman Catholics, Protestants, and Calvinists. "Each of these three religions being now established in Europe in such a manner that there is not the least appearance that any of them can be destroyed," the duke noted, "the best therefore that can be done is to preserve and even strengthen all of them. . . ." [6]

The heart of Sully's proposal is what he designates as a "military confederacy" of European princes. The General Council was to enforce peace by committing, when needed, a multinational army consisting of about 300,000 troops, 200 pieces of artillery, and more than 120 ships or galleys. A quota system determined the military contribution of each member state. Once used to recast the political map of Europe, the international force was then available for overseas duty. "After they had conquered with it whatever they would not suffer any stranger should share with them in Europe," the duke wrote, "they would have sought to join to it such parts of Asia as were most commodiously situated, and particularly the whole coast of Africa, which is too near to our own territories for us not to be frequently incommoded by it." [7] *The Great Design* today is interpreted by historians both as a scheme for uniting all Europe against the Hapsburgs and also a project for the political organization of Europe. It was not adopted by Europe's sovereigns, but did arouse the interest of many succeeding generations to the idea of collective peace enforcement.

As earlier noted, adumbrations of the concept are not limited to the theoretical suggestions of continental philosophers and scholars, but can be found in very early multilateral treaties. The Treaty of Westphalia is customarily regarded as marking the establishment of the modern territorial nation-state. It was concluded only after three decades of exasperating negotiations, but once implemented, irretrievably altered the continent's entire political system. For our purposes what is instructive about the Treaty of Westphalia, or more precisely the Treaty of Osnabrück and the Treaty of Munster, are not the specific details concerning religious freedom, commerce, or boundaries. More noteworthy are the clauses in each agreement which were to operate in the event of a breach of the peace. According to

[5] James Brown Scott, Introduction to William Ladd, *An Essay on a Congress of Nations for the Adjustment of International Disputes without Resort to Arms* (New York: Oxford University Press, 1916) and quote in Sylvester John Hemleben, *Plans for World Peace through Six Centuries* (Chicago: University of Chicago Press, 1943), p. 31.

[6] *The Great Design of Henry IV*, Edwin D. Mead, ed. (Boston: Ginn and Company, 1909), p. 21.

[7] *Ibid.*, p. 25.

Article 17 of the Osnabrück treaty, ". . . all and each of the contracting parties . . . shall be held to defend and maintain all and each of the dispositions of this peace, against whomsoever it may be. . . ." [8] It was this authorization for collective European action, incidentally, that was used as legal justification by the great powers in 1789 to prevent the spread of the revolutionary doctrine of the French extremists. The clause in the Treaty of Munster providing for a collective European response against unilateral lawlessness is more detailed. It stated:

Each and every party of this transaction shall be held to guard and protect each and all the terms and laws of this peace against anyone whomsoever regardless of religion, and if it happens that some clause be violated, the offended first of all shall urge the aggressor from the path of his action by submitting the cause to either a friendly composition of the processes of law, and if in the space of three years these differences are not ended by one or the other of these means, then each and every one of the parties to this transaction are bound to join themselves to the wounded party and to help with all their advice and arms to redress the injury.[9]

This is not the place to continue the historic parade of European pioneers who called for collectivized responsibility to deter aggression or to cite additional multilateral agreements that incorporated the same pattern. The commentaries and proposals of such men as William Penn, the Abbé Saint-Pierre, Jean Jacques Rousseau, and Gustave de Molinari have been reported widely and evaluated painstakingly.[10] Each writer in his own fashion advanced the cause of collective security. It also seems unnecessary to call attention to additional treaties that relied on post-war collaboration and cooperation to maintain the peace. All students of world affairs are familiar with the 1814 Concert of Europe and the ill-fated attempts of the great powers to preserve jointly the tranquility of Europe. These two sources—the philosophical expressions of early European political theorists and also multilateral treaties—have contributed to the growth of the modern version of the collective security idea.

Before turning to the contemporary origins of the concept, one additional feature of collective security needs to be mentioned and that is its parochialism. It is an approach to peace that is exclusively of Western origin. An examination of non-Western political literature, that is, Chinese, Hindu, Islamic, and African, reveals that the collective security idea was never proposed by early writers from these civilizations. Other political concepts and schemes to maintain peace that are generally associated with Western

[8] Quoted in Inis L. Claude, Jr., *Power and International Relations* (New York: Random House, 1962), pp. 106-107.

[9] Translated by and quoted in Gerard J. Mangone, *A Short History of International Organization* (New York: McGraw-Hill Co., 1954), p. 32.

[10] For a useful general survey see Edith Wynner and Georgia Lloyd, *Searchlight on Peace Plans* (New York: E. P. Dutton and Company, 1949), or Sylvester John Hemleben, *Plans for World Peace Though Six Centuries* (Chicago: University of Chicago Press, 1943).

statecraft can be found in ancient non-Western political writings.[11] Early Asians were familiar with the theory and practice of balancing power with power, and they knew how to apply this idea to the formulation of foreign policy. Muslims developed an inchoate legal code to help regulate the affairs of nations. Diplomatic techniques were known. Gauging a state's power, coupled with sophisticated power capability analyses, were commonplace occurrences in classical India. Disarmament proposals were not only introduced, but one noteworthy Hindu king actually carried out such a plan. The collective security idea, however, is missing from the premodern political literature of the non-Western world.

This observation is not meant to denigrate the political record of non-Western statesmen and scholars. China, India, and Arabia had both utopian visionaries and agile diplomats working to resolve power conflicts and contain aggressive warfare. Collective guarantees to maintain peace, similar in approach to the geographically restricted European examples that have been mentioned, are not part of the diplomatic legacy of these regions. Collective security must be considered as a uniquely indigenous Western political idea, one that in time was exported to Asia, the Middle East, and Africa.

During the nineteenth century the collective security approach to peace lost much of its appeal in Europe and the United States. There was no lessening in the search for ways to conduct the international affairs of sovereign nation-states in a less bellicose fashion. In fact, the tempo of the search quickened. As novel ideas emerged for reconciling nationalistic power and international order, the dream of a viable collective security arrangement was relegated to a secondary status. The shift from collective security to arbitration and mediation, international law, functionalism, and disarmament was the result of a combination of factors. Resolution of the *Alabama* claims encouraged many Americans and Englishmen to believe that all international conflicts could be judicially resolved. The establishment of various multilateral economic, social, and humanitarian unions, such as the Universal Postal Union, the Danube Commission, and the International Telegraphic Union, led others to work for peace through functionalism. The Permanent Court of Arbitration was hailed as a notable advance. Many peace leaders worked tirelessly to make international law more responsive to the stresses and strains of the times. And, of course, another group of humanitarians would settle for nothing less than a disarmed world.

Distinguishing many of these nineteenth century peace proposals is the failure to provide for collective coercion in the event of insoluble aggression. Proposal after proposal neglected to incorporate any provision for bringing the combined power of the signatory states to bear against a nation that refused to comply with the court's decision or one that committed an aggressive act in defiance of its pledged word. True internationalism, many seem to have believed, had to be divorced from the problem of sanctions and

[11] See Joel Larus, ed., *Comparative World Politics: Readings in Western and Premodern Non-Western International Relations* (Belmont, Calif.: Wadsworth Publishing Company, 1964).

enforcement. They based their plans on the hope that an enlightened public, aided by high-minded statesmen, would bring about a revolution in international politics. Typical of such thinking, but certainly not the only example that could be mentioned is the 1896 report by the editors of *The Christian Register*. They announced that "a new order of facts, indicating that the era of peace and goodwill for men and nations, is not far away." Their confidence in a pacific world order rested on ten points, a program for peace that intentionally eliminated any provision for collective action. World peace was at hand because:

(1) The sense of justice, the disposition to treat one's fellow-men in a way that is right and fair, has grown remarkable and become widely prevalent since the century began. . . . Righteousness is the foundation of peace.

(2) Equally marked has been the expansion of the spirit of benevolence. . . . Love in united service is the creator of peace.

(3) Universal education, with its humanizing influences, had its origin in this same expanded spirit. Science has had a new birth. . . . Education and science are cosmopolitan. They know no race, nor national boundary, nor prejudice. They are the messengers of peace.

(4) Liberty and free government have made great strides. Slavery and the slave trade have practically disappeared. . . . Liberty is the handmaid of peace, and free governments will not long endure militarism.

(5) Increased commerce and travel . . . have brought peoples into contact, made them acquainted, removed prejudices, created common interests, modified law, internationalized capital, opened world-wide opportunities for labor. Commerce and travel demand peace.

(6) . . . The union of labor the world over is one of the giants who are to pull down all the pillars of militarism. Labor hates war and loves peace.

(7) [Woman's] advancement is accompanied by a corresponding decline in the supremacy of the law of might. She is the queen of peace, which is sure to follow in the footsteps of her elevation.

(8) Our century has substituted law for the fist and the revolver, in the settlement of private disputes. The duel . . . has been outlawed in all but one or two countries calling themselves civilized and is on the point of outlawry in these.

(9) The special philanthropy of peace has been permanently organized. . . .

(10) The growing peace sentiment has also expressed itself in the numerous international arbitrations of the last hundred years. . . . No dispute now arises between civilized nations without the question of arbitration being raised in connection with it. No fact could be more significant.[12]

Others characterized such programs for what they in fact were: high-minded yet quite utopian dreams. Only after a group of more politically sophisticated men became interested in the various peace movements of the period did the collective security idea re-appear. When its renaissance took place, all geographical limitations effecting a joint response to aggression

[12] Benjamin F. Trueblood, *The Development of the Peace Idea and Other Essays* (Boston, 1932), pp. 197-201.

were removed. These men believed that all states of the world, but particularly the major powers, would join together in preventing or halting any incident that might disturb the peace of the world, irrespective of location.

Alfred Nobel was a man who considered his peace ideas to be sound and practical. Excessive idealism or pious hopes were no substitute for realistic programs to eliminate aggression, he believed. The inventor of dynamite refused to be carried away by myopic visions of a disarmed world, although his sympathies unquestionably were with those who were seeking ways to curb the unilateral use of a nation's military armed might. After attending a number of peace congresses and deciding that many of the anti-war schemes being suggested were quite fanciful, Nobel began to consider with great seriousness his own role in the movement. Careful reflection led him to write to a Belgian pacifist:

I am beginning to believe that the only true solution would be a convention under which all the governments would bind themselves to defend collectively any country that was attacked.[13]

In the United States there was also a reawakened interest in collective security as an approach to peace. In 1904 Andrew Carnegie cabled the Thirteenth Universal Peace Congress being held in Boston that the time was propitious to take "the next possible and necessary step forward" in the campaign for a more orderly world. His message to the delegates implied that their program would be faulty if it failed to incorporate some mechanism for collective enforcement. Specifically, he requested the Congress to consider the possibility that the preservation of peace required cooperative action, at least by the major powers. Carnegie's telegram was brief, first posing a hypothetical question and then going on to offer his proposal:

Suppose that Britain, France, Germany and America, with such other minor states as would certainly join them, were to take that position, prepared, if defied, to enforce peaceful settlement, the first offender (if there ever were one) being rigorously dealt with, war would at one fell swoop be banished from the earth. For such a result, surely the people of these four countries would be willing to risk much. The risk, however, would be trifling. A strong combination would efface it altogether. I think that this one simple plan most likely to commend itself to the intelligent masses. A committee might be formed to consider this. If a body of prominent men of each nation agreed to unite in urging the cooperation of their respective countries in the movement, I think the idea would soon spread.[14]

It is generally accepted that Carnegie's suggestions caused considerable debate among the delegates, although the committee that he advocated was never formed. More appealing to the delegates was the Congress' Model Treaty for a Pacific Alliance of States. A recital of two sections of the

---

[13] Ragnar Sohlman and Henrik Schück, *Nobel: Dynamite and Peace* (New York: Cosmopolitan Book Corporation, 1929), p. 231.

[14] *Official Report of the Thirteenth Universal Peace Congress* (Boston: The Peace Congress Committee, 1904), p. 53.

proposed multilateral agreement points up the wide divergence in the thinking of those who had begun to champion the collective security concept and those who adjured all force in international relations.

The high contracting powers pledge themselves to refer to the Permanent Arbitral Tribunal . . . every dispute which may arise between them that cannot be solved by diplomacy, or some other amicable method agreed upon, whatever the cause, nature or object, of the disagreement may be; and further pledge themselves not to engage in any warlike action, directly or indirectly, with respect to each other.

In case an acute contention shall threaten to break out between two or more powers, the other high contracting powers shall immediately, by a collective note, remind them that the permanent tribunal is open to them.[15]

Other prominent world leaders besides Nobel and Carnegie had begun to speak publicly in favor of collective security. In the United States Theodore Roosevelt as early as 1902 had declared that it was "incumbent on all civilized and orderly powers to insist on the proper policing of the world."[16] After his retirement from the Presidency, the man who had been so instrumental in moving the United States to the center of the world's political stage, many times deplored the traditional unilateral resort to armed force to settle political disputes. In his acceptance speech at the 1910 Nobel Peace Prize convocation, Roosevelt made an impassioned plea for such traditional ideas as further development of arbitration procedures, strengthening the international judicial system, and even disarmament. Reaching the climax of his remarks, Roosevelt offered his listeners a vague yet enticing formula for the elimination of wars. It was this section of his speech that *The New York Times* the following day called "undoubtedly the most striking and impressive of the suggestions of Mr. Roosevelt at Christiania."[17]

Finally [Roosevelt said] it would be a master stroke if those great powers honestly bent on peace would form a League of Peace, not only to keep the peace among themselves, but to prevent, by force, if necessary, its being broken by others. The supreme difficulty in connection with developing the peace work of The Hague arises from the lack of any executive power or any police power to enforce the decrees of the court.

. . . Each nation must keep well prepared to defend itself until the establishment of some form of international police power, competent and willing to prevent violence as between nations. As things are now, such power to command peace throughout the world could best be assured by some combination between those great nations which sincerely desire peace and have no thought themselves of committing aggression. . . . [T]he ruler or statesman who should bring about

[15] *Ibid.*, pp. 196-197.

[16] Quoted in Inis L. Claude, Jr., *Power and International Relations* (New York: Random House, 1962), p. 107.

[17] *The New York Times*, May 7, 1910, p. 8.

such a combination would have earned his place in history for all time and his title to the gratitude of all mankind.[18]

In this country and throughout Western Europe the beginning of World War I greatly accelerated interest in the collective security approach to peace. F. P. Walters in his *History of the League of Nations* notes that a few general ideas "reappeared again and again in the speeches of statesmen, and had been widely accepted as a necessary basis for the future organization of the world." [19] Among the principles that the author lists is the view that "any country guilty of attempting to gain its ends by war should be forced to desist by the economic and military action of all the rest." It would be quite beyond the scope of this introductory chapter to enumerate in detail the many, many suggestions that were made in the immediate pre-League period for a permanent organization that would ultimately rely on collective sanctions to maintain peace. The activities of the so-called Lord Bryce group deserve mention, however, because their conclusions regarding peacekeeping in the post-war world were of singular importance among pro-League men and women. In 1917 this group of distinguished British scholars and public leaders published their program. Among the concepts that they found attractive was one that called for collective enforcement of peace in the event that any state should resort to war without first using the machinery that was to be established. Specifically, the Bryce plan called for the signatory states to take joint action, economic or military, against any law-breaking power. The willingness of all the rest to assume the burdens of collective peacekeeping arrangements, they argued, insured compliance and cooperation.[20]

When elaborated by such distinguished public figures as President Wilson, Colonel House, M. Bourgeois of France, or Lloyd George of Great Britain, the collective security approach to peace seemed so eminently feasible, so fundamentally sound and timely. In all sections of the globe, the non-Western world as well as the Western, universal peace by collective action promised to assure unbelievable rewards if all states would but adopt the League's formula. Aggression was to be opposed universally so that it would not spread. Each state was to guarantee the security of all others because the Covenant said the maintenance of universal peace was a fundamental common responsibility. The heart of the League's system of collective security was Article 10, oftentimes called the Article of Mutual Guarantee. It read:

The members of the League undertake to respect and preserve as against external aggression the territorial integrity and existing political independence of all members of the League.

[18] *The New York Times,* May 6, 1910, p. 4.
[19] F. P. Walters, *History of the League of Nations* (London: Oxford University Press, 1960), p. 21.
[20] See Henry R. Winkler, *The League of Nations Movement in Great Britain 1914-1919* (New Brunswick, N.J.: Rutgers University Press, 1952), pp. 16-23.

When negotiations for the establishment of the League system were being conducted, however, too little attention was given to the political reasonableness of basic assumptions implicit in the collective security approach to peace. Looking back, many men seem to have been too anxious to believe that the threat of collective coercion would act as a deterrent. But how politically sound is a peacekeeping arrangement that relies on sovereign states acting in concert, especially the great powers with their primary military strength, whenever and wherever aggression occurs and the peace is threatened? Can the national interests of nation-states ever be so adjusted that a common program of sanctions will be agreed upon? Is it not short-sighted to expect that states not directly involved in a power conflict and whose security is not directly jeopardized to expend their resources in a collective peacekeeping action?

In theory, the Covenant's collective security system seemed such a progressive step forward. In practice, as the record of both the League of Nations and the United Nations will make clear, the concept was a noble idea that turned out to be a utopian dream.

Following the post-Korean demise of the collective security approach to peace, a new peacekeeping concept has begun to be formulated. Preventive diplomacy, the late Dag Hammarskjold said, is the system to "which the efforts of the United Nations must thus be to a large extent [now] directed." [21] It is a more limited security arrangement and applies to situations that permit the application of very special rules for stopping violence and preventing local aggression from widening into a more general conflict. By interposing a United Nations presence in select situations, the leaders of the United Nations who fathered the concept hoped to establish a more realistic technique to maintain peace and security. On the basis of its record to date, it is impossible to say with any assurance how or if preventive diplomacy will develop. As the organization continues to adjust to the realities of political conditions in the Age of Nuclear Missiles, preventive diplomacy, if used with imagination and if permitted to evolve according to the needs of the times, could help meet the requirements of a world plagued by conflicting ideologies and competing interests.

[21] See *infra*, p. 402.

INTRODUCTION TO PARTS
ONE, TWO, AND THREE

The Life and Death of the Myth: Phase I

The birth of the League was hailed as an event of almost unparalleled political importance. At the first meeting of the Council, the newly elected chairman, M. Léon Bourgeois of France, announced that "January 16, 1920 will go down in history as the date of the birth of the new world."[1] On the day following the initial meeting of the organization, *The New York Times* began its feature story by reporting the start of "the most ambitious experiment in government man has ever essayed." The lives of untold millions of humans for centuries to come, the *Times* continued, would be influenced by the events about to unfold.[2]

Today such powerful expressions seem to be examples of political and journalistic license, but millions of people throughout the world believed that General Jan Christian Smuts was correct when he said that "mankind is once more on the move."[3]

The League's period of soaring expectations and exaggerated hopes soon passed. "Died at the age of twenty," later wrote Marcel Hoden, one-time Principal Private Secretary to the Secretary-General, was an incorrect epitaph because "the League of Nations did not live even that long."[4] Looking back, the date of the organization's birth was also the beginning of its demise. When the Council held its opening session in the Clock Room of the French Foreign Ministry, it was popularly believed that the absence of the United States, although most regrettable, was certainly only temporary. The comments of M. Bourgeois, Lord Curzon, and other League dignitaries, with which we introduce the chapters on the League, indicate the high hopes for eventual American participation. The United States, opting for international irresponsibility and political laissez-faire, declined to share the burdens of collective peacekeeping. By failing to live up to the principles that we had introduced at Paris and not supporting others that we had so

[1] See *infra*, p. 25.
[2] *The New York Times*, January 17, 1920, p. 1.
[3] J. C. Smuts, *The League of Nations—A Practical Suggestion* (New York: The Nation Press, Inc., 1919), p. 63.
[4] Marcel Hoden, "Europe Without the League," *Foreign Affairs*, Vol. 18, No. 1 (October 1939), p. 13.

13

vigorously championed, this country must bear great responsibility for the initial defects that atrophied the organization's peacekeeping machinery, although certainly not the total blame. The leadership that the United States might have given to the organization, especially in its formative stages, and the economic and military support that we could have provided in periods of political crisis were never forthcoming. Deprived of much needed power and leadership, the Council and Assembly were unable to initiate the Covenant's program for basic security arrangements. A truncated version of the collective security system was improvised but was a shabby substitute for the version so lavishly praised by early League enthusiasts.

Walter E. Rappard's selection, "The Refutation of Articles 10 and 16," portrays the despair and terrible concern that existed in a number of leading capitals once the Senate had rejected the Treaty of Versailles. Washington's policy reversal caused Ottawa to be anxious that someday it might be called upon to take action that the United States opposed. Canadian worries, in turn, had political repercussions in the three Scandinavian capitals, which resulted in considerable distress in Havana, Vienna, and Montevideo. In Geneva additional League members became concerned. The key articles concerning collective security were re-interpreted and the League's plan for an effective security system collapsed. By divorcing itself from the center of post-war political debate, the United States helped frustrate the organization's capacity to protect its members from aggression.

The conceptually defective and operationally wanting League debated and attempted to resolve approximately sixty political crises jeopardizing the interwar peace. We have selected four cases which we feel are representative of the major problems and issues that confronted the membership. Professor James Barros' analysis of the Greek-Bulgarian dispute is the lead-off piece. Students of international organization repeatedly have designated the 1925 quarrel as being the League's greatest political success. Led by an energetic and determined Council president who had the unanimous support of all the great powers, the League in remarkably short time settled peacefully the Balkan dispute. Professor Barros analyzes the intricate moves of individual governments and how, when, and why they coordinated policies within the League régime.

The next three political crises that are examined had a less sanguine outcome. In Manchuria, Ethiopia, and Finland, the three major disputes considered by the Council and Assembly, a great power was the initiator of aggression and resolutely determined to prevail militarily no matter what the cost to League power and influence. As mentioned earlier, the League's role in world peace heavily depended upon extensive and active cooperation among all member states, but the powers in positions of predominance had to be united on policy. The consequences that followed when Japan, Italy, and the Soviet Union disregarded their League obligations and carried out programs of military conquest illustrate the varied problems of trying to enforce peace in a world of sovereign states.

Japan was the first to defy the organization successfully. The events in Manchuria found Great Britain, France, and Italy unable to agree on a united program of action that would stop the Japanese. In all three capitals political leaders found it expedient to disregard the frantic appeals of China for aid. Attempts by the United States to cooperate with the League and to encourage forceful action were disappointing. Japanese tactics all but paralyzed the Council. The Assembly vaingloriously attempted to deal with the incident but with even less success. Quincy Wright's essay, "The Manchurian Crisis," presents an analysis of the first stage of the Far Eastern dispute. At the time that Professor Wright's essay appeared (February 1932) there was considerable hope that the Commission of Enquiry, which he discusses, would help restore peace to the Pacific. Geneva awaited its report with deepening concern as the military situation worsened for the Chinese defenders. Nine months after its formation, the Commission reported their findings to the Council. Even today the lengthy background sections of the report, which have been omitted, are considered a notable and impartial record of the events that lead up to the Pacific situation and the reasons why great power conflicts disturbed the peace of the area. The section of the Lytton Commission's report that is offered contain their program for resolving the issues damaging Sino-Japanese relations. Both disputants were called on to accept a negotiated settlement of their disputes; new treaties were to be concluded that would fix their rights and responsibilities in Manchuria. Generally acclaimed to be proposals offering a reasonable basis for compromise solutions, the report was approved unanimously by the Council, save for the Japanese who resigned from the League.

Many League enthusiasts found the Japanese position unbelievable. *The Economist,* for example, called the Lytton Report "one of those documents which a government can reject only at its peril." Their November 26, 1932 editorial continued:

> The Japanese Government has now taken this perilous course. But is it possible for the other Governments to do likewise? Will the Americans, British, French, German and Italian Governments have the face to declare before their own people and before the world: 'We believe, like you, that the Lytton Report gives a fair statement of the facts and a statesmanlike suggestion for a settlement; but we are going to pretend all the same that we do not believe this . . . because we are determined at any price not to fall foul of Japan?'
>
> We do not think that even the diplomatic vocabulary contains phraseology that is capable of glozing such a *baseness* as this. We do not believe that it is morally possible for the Great Powers to take this line; and we know very well that it will not be taken by any of the sixty smaller countries of the world, which are desperately anxious for the maintenance of the collective system of international security and order. What is the Council going to do?

The answer to *The Economist's* question and some of the background reasons for the Council's vacillation is provided in the next selection by Sean Lester, who, during the Manchurian affair, was the Irish Free State's Permanent Delegate to the League. As a member of the Council, he had witnessed at close hand the first major League surrender to political expediency. Joined by other representatives from small states, Lester had tried to preserve the territorial integrity of China, but was unable to prevail in the face of big power intransigence. In his essay, "The Far East Dispute from the Point of View of the Small States," Lester, who in the final years of the League was its Secretary-General, argued for the impartial application of the Covenant. It had to apply against any powerful aggressor as assuredly as it was put into operation against a small member. The author employed the language of diplomacy in his remarks, that is, guarded phrases, nonprovocative statements, and understated emphasis, but his serious warning about the League's future could not have been more prophetic. Especially trenchant were Lester's comments concerning the responsibilities of all member states: "The Covenant cannot be disregarded in China or South America and remain a guarantee for the small States of Europe."

The 1935-36 Italo-Ethiopian war offered the League the opportunity to regain some of the influence that it had lost in the Far Eastern situation, perhaps to rebuild the collective security system that had been so widely discredited after Manchuria. Again in Africa, the organization's peace-keeping apparatus failed, and the second surrender to aggression destroyed the League entirely. The next group of essays discuss the Italian invasion of Ethiopia from three different points of view, but all have a common meeting ground, namely, the crucial importance of the League's first and only attempt to apply economic sanctions against an aggressor state. Sir Alfred Zimmern's article was written with the author's characteristic optimism. To this early and dedicated supporter of the League, the Italo-Ethiopian affair, if circumspectly and courageously handled, could place the organization at the threshold of what might be the greatest success for the idea of collective security. The organization was at a momentous crossroad. "Never since the Armistice has it been so difficult to foresee the turn which events will take, even in the immediate future," Sir Alfred wrote in early 1936. In the hearts and minds of the people of the leading member states, the League "is not merely a piece of machinery . . . but a reality." The League had to take advantage of the bold spirit, avert catastrophe, and go "forward."

Less than six months later, Haile Selassie, Emperor of Ethiopia, appeared in the Assembly and gave one of the most poignant speeches ever presented before the organization. Catastrophe had not been averted, and the League was in full retreat. His Majesty's small African empire was being overrun by the invader and his people had experienced treatment at the hands of the Italians so barbarous that it seemed inconceivable in the twentieth century. The king fled his capital and came to Geneva to plead that the Covenant's promises faithfully be kept. His speech stands as the most dramatic expression of the tragic emptiness of League collective security ideals.

The press reported that many of the Assembly delegates appeared to be ashamed and were experiencing acute embarassment as Haile Selassie concluded speaking. Those present generally knew that Ethiopia was to be abandoned to her fate. Great Britain was no less firm than France in her resolve not to provoke Italy militarily. The concluding words of the king are not easily forgotten.

> I ask the great Powers, who have promised the guarantee of collective security to small States . . . : What measures do they intend to take? Representatives of the world . . . What answer am I to take back to my people?

Had England followed a less pusillanimous Ethiopian policy, had France been less eager to come to terms with the aggressor because of Paris' anxiety over Nazi Germany, had meaningful oil sanctions been imposed, political events in Europe and Africa might have been less frightful. The League's Ethiopian failure was a grave blow, which is doubly regrettable because the economic sanctions that were imposed came remarkably close to stopping Italian aggression. As Adviser on International Economic Affairs in the Department of State, Herbert Feis was in an unusually good position to see the Italian-Ethiopian crisis develop and observe the economic consequences of the sanctions. His essay, "The United States and the Italo-Ethiopian War," underlines even today the need for big power unanimity in security actions. The American refusal to support wholeheartedly the League's decision to employ sanctions contributed to the success of the Italian armies. Mr. Feis argues that every government, including our own, should have been willing to accept "some restraints on its action to renounce some advantage, and to risk its fate for others."

Whether by acting collectively in Africa the great powers might have gained security without war and have demonstrated the reliability of the League's peacekeeping system became academic as the rush of new political crises led to World War II. After 1936 the League was *in extremis*. Collective security as an approach to peace was thoroughly discredited. Geneva gave up even the pretense of being a key center where the world's major disputes could be negotiated and where all states were assured of collective assistance if they were a victim of aggression. Yet the League was offered one final opportunity to act courageously. In the fall of 1939 Germany declared war on Poland. England and France began their five year struggle to crush the Nazi military might. In early December the Soviet Union, hoping to secure its borders, invaded Finland. A desperate Helsinki government turned to the League, although F. P. Walters comments, "It did not at first sight appear probable that Finland would appeal to Geneva." He then asks rhetorically, "If no move had been made to submit to the League the issues which had led to war between Germany and Poland, France, and Britain, what result could be expected from its intervention in this new conflict?"[5]

When the League took up Finland's appeal, the Assembly and later the

[5] F. P. Walters, *A History of the League of Nations* (London: Oxford University Press, 1960), pp. 804-805.

Council seized the occasion to repay old debts and soothe festering political wounds. The tone of the debate was set by the Argentine's delegate who said, "We need not be restrained, as in other cases, by the desire to act cautiously and to weigh our responsibilities with a view to the preservation of peace. Peace no longer exists."

In Chapter 3 the League's entire experiment in collective security is assessed by two distinguished students of international organization, who represent the extreme judgments of its peacekeeping record. Gilbert Murray, as he notes in his piece, was an early proponent of the League idea and continued to believe in the soundness of its fundamental premises. After witnessing from unusually close range the sundry trials of checking aggression by collective action, he is impressed with how close the League came to success. The late Professor Walter Schiffer also seeks to discover the political errors that the drafters of the Covenant committed, but his analysis is not colored by years of lobbying on behalf of the organization. After painstaking scrutiny, he finds that the League's entire security arrangements were based on inherently contradictory ideas. In providing these dissimilar analyses we believe that we have presented two hard-hitting arguments relevant to past and present peacekeeping organizations.

The Life and Death of the Myth: Phase II

World War II scarcely had begun when the peace planners set to work again, dreaming of an organization of peace that would avoid a third global conflict. In a number of capitals, but primarily in Washington, scholars and statesmen worked diligently to meet the needs of the future while avoiding the mistakes of the past. As negotiated, the Charter makes the Security Council the primary organ for the maintenance of peace and security. The Council was to decide if collective measures were needed and what they should be. Chapter VII of the Charter (Articles 39-51) assumes that the permanent Security Council members would never experience irreconcilable disagreement concerning the maintenance of peace and security. If great power conflicts did materialize in the post-war period (and when have victor states maintained their wartime singleness of purpose?), the United Nations would be unable to keep the peace, but the Charter's sponsors believed the calculated risk was worth taking. As the definitive *A History of the United Nations Charter* by Ruth B. Russell explains the quandary of San Francisco:

No terms of agreement, or particular procedures and machinery could guarantee that the permanent members of the Security Council would achieve this degree of cooperation. A framework of appropriate constitutional provisions could be erected, however, on which a complete system of international enforcement might be built if cooperation was forthcoming. The prize, in this event, was worth the effort.[6]

[6] Ruth B. Russell, *A History of the United Nations Charter* (Washington, D.C.: The Brookings Institution, 1958), p. 960.

When the Charter was first published, some commentators attempted to exaggerate the points of difference between the United Nations and the League. Professor Leland N. Goodrich's essay ended all such baseless speculations. Rather than being divorced from its predecessor, the Charter did not contain novel peacekeeping ideas that emerged *ab initio* from wartime experiences, but represented still another attempt to implement Man's dream of collective security. The United Nations, like its predecessor organization, is founded upon the concept that a league of sovereign states pledged to unite their power and resources can prevent war. As Professor Goodrich's article shows, the police powers of the United Nations were believed to be more potent than those of the League, but nevertheless the security arrangements of the two organizations were remarkably similar.

The General Assembly delegates at their first meeting used considerably more restraint in introductory remarks than their League predecessors. The ghosts of Geneva were present in London's Central Hall when Dr. Zuleta Angel opened the meeting. Only indirectly did he call attention to the past and refer to the great responsibilities that had been placed on the organization. "We cannot, therefore, with impunity, fail mankind again," Dr. Angel soberly concluded. Mr. Clement Attlee, British Prime Minister, was more he said, "we can trace the origins of the late war to acts of aggression, the significance of which was not fully realized at the time." The formalities ended, the United Nations began debating whether Trygve Lie or Paul-Henri Spaak should be the first President of the General Assembly.

In order for the system of collective security designed at San Francisco to operate effectively, a military arm of the United Nations had to be established. The Security Council in early 1946 asked all five permanent members to direct their Chiefs of Staff to appoint representatives to the important Military Staff Committee. The recommendations of the Committee were to provide the Council with the basic principles that should govern the formation of a United Nations force, the *sine qua non* of collective coercion under the Charter. The essay on the hopeless deadlock that followed is the theme of "The Rise and Fall of the Military Staff Committee." The failure to implement Article 43 recalls the League's disappointment with Articles 10 and 16.

Again a conceptually defective and operationally wanting international organization was called upon to maintain the peace. Approximately five years to the day after the Charter was signed at San Francisco, the United Nations' collective security system received a most important test. From the moment that the news flashed that the North Koreans had invaded South Korea, men and women throughout the world looked to the organization to prevent the military subjection of Seoul by its aggressor neighbor. Those old enough to recall the successive defeats of the League were determined that the United Nations' system of collective action had to triumph. President Harry Truman has written of his thoughts as he flew back to Washington after being informed that hostilities had broken out in the Pacific:

In my generation, this was not the first occasion when the strong had attacked the weak. I recalled some earlier instances: Manchuria, Ethiopia, Austria. I remembered how each time that the democracies failed to act it had encouraged the aggressor to keep going ahead. Communism was acting in Korea just as Hitler, Mussolini, and the Japanese had acted ten, fifteen, and twenty years earlier. I felt certain that if South Korea was allowed to fall Communist leaders would be emboldened to override nations closer to our own shores. . . . It was also clear to me that the foundations and the principles of the United Nations were at stake unless this unprovoked attack on Korea could be stopped.[7]

Three years later peace returned to the two Koreas. Was the application of an international army a success or a failure? Was Korea an example of collective security in operation or did it represent something decidedly different? Dr. Arnold Wolfers has provided one of the most seasoned attempts to assess whether the Korean episode demonstrated the practicality of collective enforcement of world peace under the Charter. Specifically, he asks whether or not "intervention in Korea represents a radical break with the traditional foreign policy of nation-states and, as a consequence, fulfills the expectations widely held for 'collective security.'" He thinks that there are two types of collaborative peacekeeping operations. The first is a genuine collective security operation, but the second is better designated as a collective defense action. Indicating why the Korean war never can be properly called an application of the former, Dr. Wolfers shows why the American response is more accurately evaluated as an example of containment under the convenient rationale of a United Nations' police action.

During the Korean conflict the United Nations experienced its first great constitutional crisis, as the remaining selections of the chapter illustrate. The fortuitous absence of the Soviet delegate from the Security Council in June and July 1950 permitted a condemnation of North Korea as the aggressor, but Mr. Jacob Malik's return on August 1 stopped all further efforts to set up a unified operation. The need for more dependable arrangements to deal with the Korean situation, as well as any future aggression, seemed plain. Mr. Dean Acheson's speech to the General Assembly explains why the United States believed that its "Uniting for Peace" proposal deserved approval from the organization. In Korea there was a United Nations' army fighting to enforce peace, but it was highly unlikely that a similar combination of circumstances would again occur. If the United Nations was not to atrophy, the Secretary of State believed, the General Assembly would have to decide whether or not to interpret the Charter in the light of conditions that had developed since 1945.

Whenever a legal document must be interpreted, whether it be a multilateral treaty such as the Charter or the constitution of a nation-state, there is bound to be considerable difference of opinion. Generally speaking, one side will favor a literal interpretation of the instrument while another fac-

---

[7] Harry S. Truman, *Memoirs by Harry S. Truman*, Vol. II (Garden City, N.Y.: Doubleday & Co., Inc., 1956), pp. 332-333.

tion will argue for a less restricted, more liberal reading. The American proposal to strengthen the General Assembly so as to be able to deal more efficiently with aggression signaled such a soul searching United Nations' debate. On one side, the Russians and their allies vigorously urged a strict interpretation of the Charter while on the other hand John Foster Dulles led the fight for constitutional liberalism as the way to insure the United Nations' future viability. It may fairly be said that the debate showed that the Charter was flexible enough to be adapted to a bipolar world. This virtue was at the same time a great hazard because subsequent peacekeeping operations approved by the General Assembly under authority of the "Uniting for Peace" resolution have demonstrated the need for big power unanimity. We have included a portion of a longer essay by Professors Myres S. McDougal and Richard N. Gardner to illustrate some of the canons of interpretation of legal instruments.

Once the Korean armistice was negotiated, the idea of collective security within the United Nations' régime underwent scholarly analysis. If Korea represented such a major victory for collective coercion, many asked, why was the operation so largely an American one and so feebly supported by most United Nations members? Was it reasonable to continue placing reliance in an approach to peace that could not marshal a greater measure of collectivism? Continuing the pattern that we have set earlier, we offer a pair of essays by two skillful advocates of their respective positions. We hope that the article by Professor Roland N. Stromberg and also Professor Kenneth W. Thompson's well-known essay provide the student of international organization with a clear frame of reference within which to come to his own conclusions concerning the efficacy of the collective security approach to peace.

PART ONE

Collective Security and the League

Extracts of Addresses: First Meeting of the Council (Feburary 16, 1920)*

M. Bourgeois, having been elected Chairman, thanked the Council for the great honour conferred upon him. . . .

M. BOURGEOIS continued as follows: The High Contracting Parties, in order to promote international co-operation, and to achieve international peace and security by the acceptance of obligations not to resort to war, by the prescription of open, just and honourable relations between nations, by the firm establishment of the understandings of International Law as the actual rule of conduct among Governments, and by the maintenance of justice and the scrupulous respect for all Treaty obligations in the dealings of organised peoples with one another, have agreed to the Covenant of the League of Nations. . . .

To-day, Gentlemen, we are holding the first meeting of that Council, convened by the President of the United States on January 13, 1920.

The task of presiding at this meeting and of inaugurating this great international institution, which opens so wide a field of hope for humanity, should have fallen to President Wilson.

We respect the reasons which still delay the final decision of our friends in Washington, but we may all express the hope that these last difficulties will soon be overcome, and that a representative of the great American Republic will occupy the place which awaits him among us. The work of the Council will then assume that definite character and that particular force which should be associated with it. . . .

Even if under these conditions the machinery of the League remains incomplete until a later date, the meeting of to-day bears nevertheless the character of a first and solemn act.

January 16, 1920, will go down to history as the date of the birth of the new world. The decision to be taken to-day will be in the name of all States which adhere to the Covenant. It will be the first decree of all the free nations leaguing themselves together for the first time in the world to substitute right for might. . . .

We do not forget the impatience with which our decisions are awaited. We are well aware of the doubts of some and the ardent enthusiasm of others, but we are here to represent responsible Governments, and while realising the grandeur of the work, we cannot ignore the inevitable difficulties of the enterprise we are serving.

* League of Nations *Official Journal*, Vol. 1, No. 1 (February 16, 1920), pp. 18-24.

Animated by deep conviction, supported by the public opinion of the world and by the numerous manifestations of those great associations, which in all free countries have undertaken the education of the people in the precepts of the League of Nations, and determined to prevent, by every means in our power, the recurrence of these terrible disasters, which have imperilled civilisation and drenched the world in blood, we shall proceed by the only sure method—that of attaining practical and successive results. With eyes fixed on the distant future, but with our feet on the solid ground of political and social realities, we will create a world in which the League can develop in the spirit of justice and the will for peace.

LORD CURZON spoke as follows: Born a year ago, amid great hopes, though not without anxious symptoms, the League of Nations to-day enters upon its active existence, and on behalf of the British Empire I desire to express the loyalty of my Government, and of the external Dominions of the British Crown, to the spirit which underlies the Covenant of the League, our intention by every means in our power to ensure its practical efficacy, and our firm belief that through its instrumentality alone we can hope to ensure that such horrors and miseries as the world has experienced during the past five years shall not be repeated, and that a new era of international relationships shall dawn.

The League of Nations is the expression of a universal desire for a saner method of regulating the affairs of mankind. It is not a mere expression in platonic language of the necessity for international friendship and a good understanding. It provides the machinery by which practical effect may be given to these principles. The doctrine of community of international interests is now for the first time provided with an instrument endowed with formidable powers, fortified by the allegiance of Governments, and supported by the public opinion of the civilised world.

The Council which meets for the first time to-day is the forerunner of many similar gatherings at which the Statesmen of the nations, great and small, will meet together to promote this co-operation and to exchange views. In the League of Nations an organ is thus created which will bring together those who are chosen by their people to represent them. Should disputes unhappily arise, the disputants will find themselves in an assembly of impartial and unbiassed Councillors, whose sole aim will be to remove misunderstandings which may have arisen and to point the way towards an amicable solution.

It has sometimes been said that the League of Nations implies the establishment of a Super-State, or a Super-Sovereignty. The very title "League of Nations" should be sufficient to dispel this misconception. The League does not interfere with nationality. It is upon the fact of nationhood that it rests.

The League is an association of sovereign States whose purpose is to reconcile divergent interests and to promote international co-operation in questions which affect—or may affect—the world at large. . . .

The peoples of all countries have now learnt that foreign affairs are their vital concern, and they are demanding, with ever-increasing insistence, that international obligations shall not be incurred without their knowledge and behind their backs. Their eyes have been opened to the necessity for co-operation between all nations, but they ask that it shall be open co-operation.

There is another and more important result which it is to be hoped that the habit of mutual confidence may bring about. It is this, that great national armaments will in time automatically disappear. We shall not perhaps see this come about in the immediate future, but the present weight of armaments is so oppressive to the nations and peoples concerned, that we should at once resort to the measures indicated in the Covenant to bring relief. . . .

Whilst I am in entire agreement with all that Monsieur Bourgeois has said, I should wish especially to express my full concurrence in his observations as regards the United States of America. The decision must be her own, but if and when the United States elects to take her place in the new Council Chamber of the Nations, the place is vacant for her and the warmest welcome will be hers.

In conclusion, I have to thank my colleagues for having given me the opportunity to utter these few words on an occasion of so much importance in the history of the spiritual progress of mankind.

M. MAGGIORINO FERRARIS spoke as follows: Upon me has fallen the honour of confirming in the name of the Italian Government the eloquent words of our illustrious Chairman, M. Léon Bourgeois. . . .

Italy did not hesitate to take her place of danger by the side of her valiant Allies at the most serious and perilous moment of the war. Italy does not hesitate to-day to give her confident and unreserved reply to the invitation of President Wilson, and the great American people. In full agreement with the Allied States and with all enlightened nations, our sole aim is to have done with that past in which countries impoverished their existence through distrust and suspicion, and to strive instead for the relief of suffering humanity, for the reconstruction of homes destroyed, for the ideal of universal brotherhood of Governments and peoples, for social peace and for progress, security and well-being of States and their citizens.

That illustrious Statesman, who brings back to us memories of the teachings of ancient Greece, carries with him the imperishable traditions of his country, our friend and neighbour.

Throughout the centuries Italy has been ready to embrace the ideal of the League of Nations. It has been the fundamental principle inherited from doctrines of Roman Law handed down through the teachings of jurists and students of the middle ages, to the philosophers and Statesmen of the last century. . . .

It would neither be just nor sincere to hide from ourselves the fact that the League of Nations is born to-day in a certain atmosphere of scepticism.

Together with our eminent President, we do not consider that this scepticism is justified, but we must neither exaggerate nor ignore it. After all their suffering so heroically borne, the world to-day is still awaiting many of the benefits of peace. Here lies the task for the League of Nations to fulfil. On the conduct of the Governments and on the wisdom of their representatives in this Assembly depends the success of the League of Nations. . . .

The world knows that the solution of these problems is a heavy task, which can only be accomplished through the solidarity of all nations, great and small, rich and poor. It looks to the League of Nations for the practical realisation, within the limits of possibility, of the sincere co-operation of Governments and of peoples. Thus only will it be possible to overcome the difficulties of the present day, to create a better world for generations yet unborn, and to convince the suffering nations how real and durable is the value of this noble and glorious institution, which we lay to-day upon the altar of History and consecrate to the triumph of justice over brute force, and the advancement of Social Peace.

Address of President of Swiss Confederation: First Plenary Meeting of the Assembly (November 15, 1920)*

M. HYMANS, Delegate of Belgium: The Covenant of the League of Nations, in Article 5, lays down that the first Assembly of the League of Nations shall be summoned by the President of the United States of America.

On May 19th last, the Council of the League of Nations asked the President of the United States of America to convene the Assembly of the League of Nations. On July 17th, the President of the United States of America sent to the Secretary-General of the League of Nations the following telegram, which was transmitted to all Members of the League of Nations:

"At the request of the Council of the League of Nations that I summon a Meeting of the Assembly of the League of Nations, I have the honour, in accordance with the provisions of Article 5 of the Covenant of the League of Nations, to summon an Assembly of the League to convene in the City of Geneva, the seat of the League, on the fifteenth day of November, 1920, at eleven o'clock."

It is in answer to that invitation that you are gathered together to-day in this Hall.

* League of Nations *Records of the Assembly,* Vol. 1, No. 1 (November 15, 1920), pp. 24-29.

Consequently, I have the honour to declare the first Session of the Assembly of the League of Nations to be open.

Gentlemen, I believe I shall be interpreting correctly the desire of the Assembly and of the President of the Swiss Confederation if I invite him to take the Chair and to address the Assembly.

M. MOTTA (Switzerland): On behalf of the Swiss people and Government, and as President of the Swiss Confederation, I cordially welcome this distinguished Assembly which has been summoned for the first time, and is meeting at the official seat of the League of Nations.

If I make no attempt to conceal the emotion which I feel, it is because I am trying to realise the unprecedented greatness and the significance of the event now taking place upon my native soil. A great honour is thus conferred upon Switzerland, and I feel overwhelmed by the privilege, which attaches to my official position, of being the first to address you in the name of my country. . . .

I would add to this message of thanks a hope, or rather a keenly-felt desire, that the United States of North America may before long take its rightful place in the League.

The country which is a world in itself and is blessed with all the riches of the earth—the glorious democracy which has absorbed members of all races and given them a common language and Government—the people which is influenced by the highest ideals and is affected by every advance made in material progress—the State which threw the decisive weight of its resources and armies into the scales, and thus decided the future of continents, and of Europe in particular—the native land of George Washington, father of liberty, and of Abraham Lincoln, champion and martyr in the cause of brotherhood; this country, I say, cannot, and surely does not, intend for ever to turn its face against the appeal made to it by nations, which, while retaining their independence and their sovereign rights, intend to co-operate for the peace and prosperity of humanity.

What a task this is for humanity on the morrow of the upheaval which has attacked it at the heart with fire and sword! We can find no tragedy in history which can be compared with the great struggle in which we have been actors or spectators. The tremendous but gradual collapse of the Roman Empire is a small matter in comparison.

Courage, self-sacrifice, patriotism, genius for military organisation never reached such heights. Heroism has passed all the bounds which man's imagination, nourished by previous tales of brave deeds, had hitherto compassed. In this direction, the War has brought out the really great qualities of man, the master, yet victim, of nature. But at the same time the shock of armies has never been so formidable, the earth has never drunk so deep of blood and tears, the work of destruction has never been more grievous or more savage.

True, the War was not entirely destructive. It has helped some peoples to achieve their national unity. It has repaired injustice; it has broken chains. In some cases it has been the leaven of the resurrection of peoples. But was it really the one and only way of achieving these results? Can it be said that its results are in any way proportionate to the destruction it has caused?

There were times when we all asked ourselves if the higher conquests of civilisation—the law of love, the virtue of pity, the sense of right, the bonds of fraternity, and the arts of beauty—were not about to sink and to disappear for ever in the catastrophe.

It was in these circumstances that the idea of the League of Nations— which was, indeed, no new idea, but one which had hitherto appeared to float in vague Utopian realms—appealed to all generous hearts and to all discerning minds with a force hitherto unknown. Experience had shown us that war was the worst of all the plagues which scourge humanity; fatal to the vanquished, but terrible also for the victors. We could already see in the distance visions of future wars more sinister and more horrible than the last. It was essential at all costs to make them impossible or less frequent; this was to be the principal aim of the League of Nations.

Our respect and gratitude are due to the benefactors of humanity, to those who came before us—the philosophers and statesmen, the philanthropists, those who worked in churches, in parliaments, in peace societies, in international congresses, who never despaired and who brought a lofty ideal down from the clouds to the world of tangible reality.

We must also bow before the touching procession of weeping women, who, transfigured by their sacrifice and ennobled by a new consciousness of their duties and their political rights, have stretched out their arms above the tombs to their companions, imploring them to end the reign of brutality and to use force as the weapon of justice alone.

The day which witnessed the birth of the League of Nations witnessed an event whose consequences will have a permanent influence on the evolution of nations. This fact cannot be affected by the obvious omissions and inevitable imperfections of the first Covenant. Once the seed is sown, the earth can never be completely barren. Even if this first edifice, which so many States have helped to build, were destined to collapse—an impossible hypothesis which I must apologise for advancing—the foundations would still remain. The ruins would cry aloud and would summon new workmen to the task of rebuilding.

Among the millions of soldiers whom the war destroyed, even in the neutral countries, there were countless men of the finest moral fibre. They sacrificed themselves for their countries, but they laid down their lives for humanity also. They had before them a vision of a great human family from which force should be banished, and where justice should reign by sovereign right. At the supreme moment, when they heard the mysterious appeal from above, they were able to fuse in a perfect harmony the idea of humanity and the idea of country. I salute you, heroes of all countries, heroes known and unknown, wise men and simple, you whose bodies lie beneath the triumphal arches, in the cathedrals, in your native earth and in foreign lands. I salute you with infinite tenderness and an emotion which I cannot restrain, for you are the divine seed of future harvests, the witnesses of the world to be.

The League of Nations will live. Already it would be impossible to think of the world without it. But it would be childish to expect miracles. Individuals are impatient because their spell of life is short. Collective bodies develop slowly, because their life endures indefinitely.

The Treaties of Peace would, in some respects, be impossible of execution if the League of Nations did not exist. Its material sanctions are perhaps at present and possibly for a long time yet of doubtful power, but it already possesses the penetrating moral energy which we call international consciousness. Coercion will be within its sphere of action, but it will rule above all by moral force. If the first Assembly sets up the Permanent Court of International Justice, it will have opened wide the door to the solution of disputes between States.

The more universal the League of Nations becomes, the more its authority and impartiality will be guaranteed. The victors will not for ever be able to dispense with the collaboration of the vanquished. Such collaboration, one with another responds to a vital necessity. Hatred is a curse. Peoples are great when they are great by their generosity or by their repentance. I should fail in my duty as the interpreter, I fear the inadequate interpreter, of Swiss sentiment if I had not the courage to proclaim this belief within these walls.

Moral, economic and financial brotherhood will survive all disasters; notwithstanding all national indignations, even the most righteous and the most legitimate. This first Assembly, which will have to consider the admission of new States, will have the opportunity and the duty of preparing the means by which the League of Nations may attain its ideal of universality and hence also of reconciliation and final peace.

The day will come—and I pray for it—when Russia herself, cured of her madness and delivered from her misery, will seek in the League of Nations that mutual help, order and security which are indispensable for her reconstitution.

The League is not an alliance of Governments; it is an association of nations. Hence it has included within the sphere of its main activities questions of disarmament, of communications, of transit and of commerce, of health, of financial reconstruction and, above all, the labour question. States cannot possibly continue to be weighed down by the crushing burden of military expenditure; if these burdens are to continue, the sorrows of the war have taught us nothing. No longer will States erect against each other insurmountable barriers. All countries will have free access to the sea. No longer will those countries which produce raw materials—and especially metals and coal—exploit their wealth as a monopoly. The Financial Conference at Brussels has shown us the remedies by which the ills of public finance may be healed; but the gulf between theory and practice will not, alas, be bridged so soon. Conditions of labour will continue to be ruled by the needs of production. The dignity of the worker will, however, be respected, as will his sacred right to happiness both for himself and for his home.

Even the most superficial observer knows that the structure of human society has already been profoundly changed. The brotherhood of the trenches has not only destroyed the disruptive fanaticism which arises from opposing habits of thought; it has at the same time destroyed that cold and paltry pride which once divided class from class: it has become rooted in the fields and has gained a footing in the workshops. New classes of society, the most numerous and consequently the least prepared, are aspiring to take into their hands the guidance of the State. Political freedom is no longer an individual ideal, but a potent means of reducing inequality at the very outset of the struggle for life, if indeed it is not a means of realising a permanent equality in the conditions of life, which is judged in the interests of humanity to be but a foolish dream. Democracy stands forth as the most solid obstacle in the path of violence, disorder and the dictatorship of a minority. But democracy will not fulfil its essential duty as educator and peacemaker unless it first opens and broadens the road to the widest collective aspirations and the boldest social evolution. It is in this respect—and I may even say through this moral kinship—that democracy and the League of Nations are allies.

We do not wish the democracies to remain motionless and silent. Their silence would be a delusion, and inaction for them would mean stagnation. Let us be thankful for democracies even when they rail, for their trend is upward! Though they still display some suspicion towards the new international organisation, they are none the less our common hope. A century ago, the Holy Alliance believed that it could bridle them. The League of Nations looks upon them as its indispensable collaborators. The oldest democracy in the world, which alone decided to enter the League of Nations by means of a free plebiscite, salutes through me all the others, great and small, with impulsive gladness, and a brotherly heart. . . .

The official correspondence between the Federal Council and the Governments of the Swiss Cantons always ends with this venerable formula (if you will allow me the quotation), which we have inherited from our fathers: "We commend you, dear and faithful confederates, as we commend ourselves, to the protection of the Almighty."

The League of Nations will live, because it is a work of fraternity and love. Illustrious representatives of diverse civilisations, races and tongues, distinguished personages assembled from all quarters of the globe, enlightened disciples of all philosophies and faithful followers of all religions, let me place the new city under the guard of Him Whom Dante has called in that sublime verse which completes and sums up his sacred poem: "L'Amor che muove il sole e l' altre stelle." Love which moves the sun and the other stars.

The Refutation of Articles 10 and 16 *

William E. Rappard

Collective Security in the United States

In considering the quest for organized peace at the Peace Conference, we saw how decisive was the part played by President Wilson in the drafting of Article 10. We saw also how readily he supported the British in defending Article 16, of which they were the authors. The idea of the League of Nations as an association for the protection of its members, by its members and for its members was essentially American, or at least Wilsonian.

This circumstance alone would have sufficed to explain the reaction against this conception of collective security which the refusal of the United States to ratify the Covenant immediately brought with it. The debates before the Foreign Affairs Committee of the American Senate and in the Senate itself had been closely followed in Europe. It had not escaped the attention of careful observers that the very article which alone in the whole Covenant was purely Wilsonian in origin was the one on which the opposition in America had concentrated its attacks. Nor did they fundamentally disagree with President Wilson who held the American guarantee essential for European peace. The following words he had addressed to the Quadrennial Jackson Day Dinner on January 8, 1920, made ominous reading in Europe at the beginning of 1920. He had said:

The maintenance of the peace of the world and the effective execution of the treaty depend upon the whole-hearted participation of the United States. I am not stating it as a matter of power. The point is that the United States is the only Nation which has sufficient moral force with the rest of the world to guarantee the substitution of discussion for war. If we keep out of this agreement, if we do not give our guarantees, then another attempt will be made to crush the new nations of Europe.

* William E. Rappard, *The Quest for Peace Since the World War* (Cambridge: Harvard University Press, 1940), pp. 208-243. Reprinted by permission. William E. Rappard (1883-1958) was the Director of the Graduate Institute of International Studies at the University of Geneva and a member of the Permanent Mandates Commission of the League of Nations. His publications include *International Relations as Viewed from Geneva* (1925), *Uniting Europe* (1930), and *The Government of Switzerland* (1936).

The Destiny of Article 10

Disavowed by its parents, Article 10 lost many of the sympathies it had before enjoyed as their child. But the United States, by their negative attitude, weakened the idea of collective security for another and still more potent reason. As a consequence, Article 10 seemed not only less effectively to protect the possible victims of aggression, but also more dangerously to expose those whom it obliged to come to their assistance. Disavowed by its American father, the child had forfeited something of its social standing. Unsupported by him, it threatened to become a public charge.

It was not from Europe, however, but from America, that the first attack on Article 10 was launched. On December 4, 1920, when the first session of the Assembly of the League of Nations was more than half over, a Canadian delegate, Mr. Doherty, suddenly tabled a motion calling for an amendment to the Covenant to the effect "that Article 10 of the Covenant of the League of Nations be and is hereby struck out." That Canada should take such a step was not in the least surprising. Already at the Peace Conference, Sir Robert Borden, the Canadian Prime Minister, had, in a memorandum of March 13, 1919, submitted to the Commission on the League, proposed the deletion of Article 10. He had criticized the mutual guarantee of territorial integrity mainly on the ground that it might lead to an impossible attempt to prevent the modification of unjust and untenable frontiers.

Since then, Article 10 had served to estrange from the League, of which Canada was a loyal member, her mighty and only immediate American neighbor. Thereby she was forced into a most embarrassing position. The Canadian proposal of 1920 was therefore not unexpected. However when, instead of being adopted, it was, together with all the other suggested amendments to the Covenant, referred for further consideration to a special committee to be set up by the Council, Mr. Doherty yielded, "as gracefully as may be, to the inevitable."

In June of the following year, the Canadian Government again presented its case to that committee. In a further memorandum they added to the objections already put forward in 1919 those based on the hostility of the United States. In 1921 the Assembly had before it a recommendation of the special Committee on Amendments which had considered the Canadian proposal in the light of this memorandum. In accordance with these recommendations, the following resolution, in which Canada again, although somewhat impatiently, concurred, was adopted by the Second Assembly on October 4, 1921:

Whereas a motion has been submitted by the Canadian Delegation for the striking out of Article 10 of the Covenant;
Whereas widely different opinions have been expressed with regard to the legal bearing of this Article and its relationship to the other Articles of the Covenant, especially to Articles 12 to 17;

And whereas the legal and political arguments made both in favour of and against the striking out of Article 10 are of great weight;

The Assembly postpones the continuation of the examination of the proposal and the decision until its next Session, and recommends that this proposal be decided before any other amendment.

When the Assembly met for its third session on September 4, 1922, there had been a change of government in Canada. Mr. Lapointe, the new Canadian delegate, no longer pressed for the deletion of Article 10, as Mr. Doherty had done from the start. Realizing no doubt that even such a drastic measure could hardly bring the United States back into the fold of the League, but no less anxious than his predecessor about the consequences which a strict application of Article 10 as it stood might have for the whole world and particularly for his country, he proposed to amend it on two important points. The draft amendments he put forward took the shape of two additions to the original text.

In the first place, while maintaining the mutual guarantee against external aggression, he proposed to add to the second sentence of Article 10, which reads:

In case of any such aggression or in case of any threat or danger of such aggression the Council shall advise upon the means by which this obligation shall be fulfilled,

the words: "taking into account the political and geographical circumstances of each State."

Secondly he proposed the addition of a new paragraph to read as follows:

The opinion given by the Council in such cases shall be regarded as a matter of the highest importance, and shall be taken into consideration by all the Members of the League, which shall use their utmost endeavours to conform to the conclusions of the Council; but no Member shall be under the obligation to engage in any act of war without the consent of its Parliament, Legislature or other representative body.

In this amended form, the Canadian proposal was open to less objections on the part of the determined friends of the principle of collective security, who had formerly opposed the deletion of Article 10. And Article 10 thus amended would also have been open to less objections on the part of the no less determined foes of the unconditional and automatic sanctions to which a strict application of its terms would seem to oblige all the States Members of the League. However, it was again found impossible to reach unanimous agreement. The Third Assembly, like its two predecessors, was therefore once more obliged to postpone the consideration of the matter. It did so by adopting, on September 23, 1922, the following resolution:

The Assembly decides that the Canadian proposal with regard to Article 10 of the Covenant shall be adjourned until the fourth Assembly, in order that the subject may be considered in all its bearings. The Assembly leaves it to the Council to decide on the steps to be taken to provide for a detailed study of the Canadian proposal before the meeting of the fourth Assembly.

In an almost desperate attempt once and for all to settle this difficult matter, the Council, on January 29, 1923, addressed a circular letter to the Governments of all the States Members of the League, requesting their views on the Canadian amendment. The answers to this circular, as well as the debates which took place at the Fourth Assembly in September of the same year, afford an exceptionally interesting insight into the state of mind prevailing on the general question of collective security in the various capitals nearly five years after the end of the World War.

The first observation suggested by an analysis of the official documents is that, as might well be expected, the question attracted much more attention in Europe than in the rest of the world. Of the twenty-five replies to the circular of the Council, eighteen were sent in by European Governments. It is noticeable that no Member of the British Commonwealth of Nations except Canada took any part in this written consultation.

The replies were overwhelmingly negative. The only three European States which welcomed the Canadian proposals were, characteristically enough, Hungary, Austria and Bulgaria. But whereas the three Members of the League which had belonged to the group of the defeated Powers in the World War thus indicated their assent, all the former victors and all the new States, which felt their territorial integrity threatened by a possible war of revenge, were hostile to what they obviously looked upon as a weakening of the general guarantee. Quoting from the replies of the States which have since lost either their territorial integrity or their political independence, or which today feel imperilled in either, we note that: for Albania, Article 10 was the "cornerstone of the Covenant and the very foundation of the League"; for Finland, it was the "cornerstone of the whole structure of the League"; for Greece, "one of the foundations of the League of Nations" constituting "one of the most essential guarantees for world peace"; for Denmark, "an essential part of the system established by the Covenant"; Latvia attached "special importance to the retention of Article 10 in its present form"; the Chinese Government declared itself in favor "of maintaining this article exactly as it stands"; Roumania declared it to be "the most effective guarantee against all attempts at aggression with the object of modifying the territorial position established under the Treaties of Peace"; the reply of Jugoslavia, which was then still known as the Kingdom of the Serbs, Croats and Slovenes, was briefer but clearly negative; that of Poland, finally, contained the following interesting conclusions:

It is indisputable that the Covenant of the League of Nations imposes upon its Members certain obligations which *de facto* constitute important restrictions upon the exercise of their sovereign rights. . . . The States which constitute the League of Nations would probably never have consented to all these restrictions if they had not believed that they would find a compensation and a makeweight in the mutual guarantee of their territorial integrity and political independence.

Do not these notes tragically remind one of the above-quoted words of President Wilson, according to which "if we do not give our guarantees, then another attempt will be made to crush the new nations of Europe"?

The only answer favorable to the Canadian proposal, besides her own and those of the three vanquished States of the World War, was a laconic note from Uruguay. As a matter of fact, several other States, doubtless also the other Members of the British Commonwealth of Nations, were not all opposed to the interpretation which Canada wished to see put upon Article 10. But, for one reason or another, they felt it unnecessary or unwise to carry the public discussion of this troublesome matter any further. Unnecessary, because, in the existing state of international solidarity, it seemed only too obvious that the very ambitious construction placed upon Article 10 by those who hoped that it implied an automatic and mutual guarantee would inevitably be disproved by practical experience. Unwise, because, as real agreement was out of the question, nothing was to be gained and something might well be lost by repeated debates serving only to reveal and to stress the existing disagreement on fundamentals prevailing among Members of the League of Nations.

At the Fourth Assembly, the same opposition of views was again obvious. The States which felt threatened and which counted on the protection of the League for their security were opposed to any step which might weaken the guarantee of Article 10. They of course would not hear of its deletion nor even of its amendment. As Canada was, however, both extremely tenacious in her desire to clear up the uncertainties of the article and no less conciliatory in her methods of discussion, everyone felt, in the autumn of 1923, that, after four years of persistent argument, she was entitled to some measure of at least verbal satisfaction.

When, therefore, on September 12, 1923, Sir Lomer Gouin, the new Canadian Minister of Justice, who had been sent to Geneva to represent his country, again submitted the proposal his predecessor, Mr. Lapointe, had put forward in 1922, he met with a very sympathetic reception. To be sure, as the answers to the circular of the Council had shown irrefutably, the great majority of the Members of the League were opposed to the Canadian draft amendment. He recognized it himself in his opening speech before the First Committee. But the wish to spare his country a new disappointment led to the suggestion that the main idea of his draft be embodied in an interpretative resolution. This suggestion, which had already been contained in the reply of the Belgian Government to the circular of the Council, was renewed by M. Henri Rolin, its delegate, to the First Committee of the Fourth Assembly. As, at the first meeting of that Committee, it found the support of the Greek, Dutch, Chilian and other delegates, it was adopted by a sub-committee of that body. Sir Lomer Gouin himself, realizing that he could not put through his draft amendment and hoping to secure, if not an unanimous, at least a majority vote in favor of the interpretative resolution, supported it. He declared in the Assembly of September 25, 1923, just before the final vote was taken:

. . . we should have preferred an amendment, but we bow before the decision of the First Committee and we shall accept that of the Assembly. . . . We were asked to give time for reflection, and we agreed with a good grace.

As a loyal Member of the League we call upon you to give us, after four years of discussion, a clear interpretation of Article 10, in order that we may know what obligations we have undertaken by signing the Covenant which has united us.

We have been open to reason, but our opinion remains unchanged. We have exercised patience, but at the same time we have shown tenacity and perseverance in the pursuit of our object.

The resolution which the Assembly was called upon to adopt, after undergoing several alterations, was finally couched in the following terms:

It is in conformity with the spirit of Article 10 that, in the event of the Council considering it to be its duty to recommend the application of military measures in consequence of an aggression or danger or threat of aggression, the Council shall be bound to take account, more particularly (notamment), of the geographical situation and of the special conditions of each State.

It is for the constitutional authories of each Member to decide, in reference to the obligation of preserving the independence and the integrity of the territory of Members, in which degree the Member is bound to assure the execution of this obligation by employment of its military forces.

The recommendation made by the Council shall be regarded as being of the highest importance and shall be taken into consideration by all the Members of the League with the desire to execute their engagements in good faith.

Comparing this resolution with the Canadian draft amendment, one readily recognizes the reasons why it could be deemed acceptable by the authors of the latter. What actuated the Canadian Government, once it had abandoned its original idea of striking out Article 10, was the wish to be freed from any obligation of sending troops abroad to preserve the territorial integrity and political independence of any European State against aggression. This result its draft amendment was calculated to achieve by two methods. First, the Council was to be expressly invited to take into account the political and geographical conditions of each State in advising upon the means of securing the execution of the international guarantee. Secondly, it was to be made obvious that the Council could do no more than advise, that is, recommend, and not command or order, so that the final decision would clearly rest with the constitutional authorities of each Member State.

On the first point, Canada received almost complete satisfaction under the terms of the interpretative resolution. On the second, her satisfaction was only partial. It would be difficult to put the point at issue more clearly than was done by M. Rolin in a speech he delivered on September 17, 1923, as Rapporteur of the sub-committee. He said:

It was stated in Article 10: 'The Members of the League *Undertake*' . . . , and a little further on: 'In case of any such aggression or in case of any threat or danger of such aggression, the Council shall advise upon the means by which this *obligation* shall be fulfilled.' Article 10 thus implied both undertakings and international obligations.

The text submitted by the Sub-Committee emphasised the legal nature of these international obligations.

On the other hand, it had been repeated many times that the League of Nations was not a super-State, and that its Members had not surrendered their sovereignty. It followed, therefore, that the Members of the League who had, in virtue of the Covenant, contracted various engagements were, in accordance with the tradition of international law, the proper judges of those engagements. Unless any special exception was made, they retained the right to estimate the extent of their obligations.

The text submitted was thus clearly a compromise between those whom we might call the minimalists and the maximalists of collective security. As a minimalist, Canada would have preferred to minimize its international obligations and to stress the right of its national parliament to judge of the nature of these obligations. The maximalists, on the other hand, who favored the idea of an automatic, unconditional mutual guarantee, would have preferred not to mention the rights of national parliaments and to emphasise the absolute character of the international obligations.

When it finally came to a vote, at noon on September 25, 1923, the minimalists were all in favor of the resolution, which gave them a large measure of satisfaction. As minimalists could be counted such States as the Members of the British Commonwealth of Nations, Austria, Bulgaria, Hungary, Sweden and Switzerland. The maximalists, on the other hand, were divided. Some, such as France, Belgium, China, voted with the minimalists in the hope that unanimity might thereby be secured. This view was vividly expressed for France by her delegate, Professor Joseph-Barthélemy, who, in explaining the vote he was about to deliver, declared:

At the third Assembly, I had the honour, on behalf of the French delegation, of urging that Article 10 should remain intact. I pointed out that this article was an essential and fundamental part of our constitution. I illustrated my views with a number of metaphors, which though, perhaps, mutually inconsistent, none the less presented a profound truth. Article 10 is, I said, the standard, the pediment, the pillar, the foundation of the League of Nations. It is the cornerstone, the signpost which shows the way to be followed by the new international law which is most nobly and most completely realised in the League of Nations.

France has not abandoned the convictions which she expressed here last year. From the outset she has consistently endeavoured to give practical force to the decisions of the League and to ensure their execution. . . .

Speaking quite frankly, France would have preferred that there should have been neither amendment nor interpretation. If to-day she accepts an interpretation, it is because certain new facts have arisen of which I propose to give you an account.

The end of this speech is a eulogy on Canada and the Canadians, of which it would be disobliging both to France and to her delegate to admit that it was the expression of any new fact! The simple truth was that, for reasons of general policy, the French Government had instructed its delegate not to antagonize Canada and her friends and to accept what was obviously a rather painful compromise.

Most of the maximalists, on the other hand, expressed their dislike of the compromise by abstaining from voting for it. Among them were Albania, Czechoslovakia, Esthonia, Finland, Latvia, Lithuania, Poland. Jugoslavia and most of the Latin-American States.

Persia alone, as the most maximalist of the maximalists, voted against the resolution. Her delegate, the Emir Zokaed-Dovleh, clearly defined her position and her reasons when he said:

Why is it that Persia cannot accept any modification of this article? . . . She is surrounded by States such as Russia, Turkey and Afghanistan, which are not yet Members of the League.

She entered the League to safeguard her independence and the integrity of her territory, and to co-operate in the work of civilisation and peace, in order that a neutral country like ours should not again suffer the consequences and evils of such a scourge as the late war.

The result of the voting was as follows: for the resolution, 29; against the resolution, 1; absent or abstaining, 22.

Technically the resolution was therefore lost on account of Persia's negative vote. As an expression of opinion, it showed that Article 10, in its original form, still commanded the loyalty of many and perhaps even of most Members of the League. But after this vote, its authority as a constitutional provision could of course no longer be regarded as intact.

The Whittling Down of Article 16

As I recalled when considering the quest for organized peace at the Peace Conference, collective security is provided for by two distinct articles of the Covenant of the League of Nations. We have just seen how the Fourth Assembly dealt with Article 10, the Wilsonian contribution. The destiny of Article 16, the British contribution, was different, but the general outcome of the first debates to which it gave rise before the Council and the Assembly of the League was appreciably the same. The League had hardly been organized that efforts set in successfully to relieve its members of part of the burden which Article 16, as Article 10, placed upon them as guarantors of the general peace. We have now to consider how and why this came about.

At its eighth session, in the summer of 1920, the Council of the League had before it a memorandum by the Secretary-General entitled "Preparatory measures to give effect to Article 16 of the Covenant of the League." The purpose of this memorandum and the spirit in which it was prepared are well shown by the following preliminary paragraph, in which we read:

Many people think that the League is founded more upon good intentions than upon a cool consideration of the stern realities of international trouble. It is, therefore, desirable on general grounds that while the first meetings of the Council and of the Assembly should give the world the positive hope of removing misunderstandings and promoting international co-operation, they should also show quite clearly that the Members of the League as a whole are determined, if necessity arises, to enforce their will by effective action on any particular country which, in the circumstances contemplated by the Covenant, defies the general verdict of the world.

In order to provide for this "effective action," the Secretary-General suggested "that an International Blockade Commission . . . be appointed under the authority of the first Assembly for the purpose of studying the problem and settling the general plan of action, the organisation of the more permanent machinery required and the principles on which it should work." On the basis of this memorandum, a report was presented by Signor Tittoni, the Italian representative on the Council, and adopted on August 3, 1920. Especially in view of the fact that the only attempt at wielding the so-called "economic weapon" of the League was made in the Ethiopian dispute and bitterly resented by the country of him who first forged it, it is interesting to note his remarks on the subject. He declared in his report to the Council:

The application of this weapon is intended to safeguard the peace of the world, and the League of Nations may have recourse to this means of coercion without employing other means of constraint or it may at the same time employ military force.

As soon as the League has decided, in principle, to have recourse to the application of Article 16 of the Covenant, the various measures should be taken immediately by all the States, and the question, therefore, is rather one of a series of similar measures to be taken simultaneously than of collective and united action.

From what precedes, it is clear that the measures to be taken must, in order to be efficacious, in the first place be decided by common agreement, and applied simultaneously in all the different countries. In the second place, they should be closely co-ordinated, and this co-ordination can only be realised if the States come to a previous agreement as to the necessary legislative and executive steps which must be taken.

Thirdly, organisations must be established which can ensure this immediate and perfect co-operation between the different countries, as soon as the measures laid down in Article 16 have to be taken. . . .

In the fourth place, these organisations should be able to take all useful steps to enable the Members of the League to give each other mutual support in the general interest, and at the same time to minimise the loss and inconvenience which the blockade might entail for each of them. . . .

In my view, it should be clear that the States Members of the League of Nations who declare the blockade have the right to render it effective against all States, including those who are not Members of the League, but they have not the right to force the States who do not form part of the League to declare the blockade themselves.

Further, this question will no longer be of importance when all the States, without exception, belong to the League of Nations. This is the final end which we endeavour to attain and which will give to us all the moral authority which should be our principal strength and of which measures of coercian should only constitute an auxiliary and strengthening support.

It is obvious that all the measures to be taken and the means of putting Article 16 into execution must be considered in advance. If the line of action to be taken is considered in advance, without waiting for the moment when action becomes necessary, the measures to be taken will clearly be more efficacious, and will have a speedier effect. Since, however, the solution of the problem which I have thus briefly outlined is of supreme general interest for all the States Members of the League of Nations, I think that the Assembly would be better qualified than the Council to deal with this question, and I have the honour to submit to you the following proposals:—

The Council decides to place upon the Agenda of the first Assembly of the League of Nations the consideration of the necessary measures to ensure the application of Article 16 of the Covenant. With this aim in view, it will propose to the Assembly that, as a preliminary measure, an International Blockade Commission should be appointed under the authority of the first Assembly for the purpose of studying the problem and settling the general plan of action, the organisation of the more permanent machinery required and the principles on which it should work.

The Council proposes that a Committee composed of an equal number of Members of the Council and of the Assembly be set up to examine the question of the constitution of this international Commission and its duties.

In accordance with the recommendation contained in this report, the topic was placed on the agenda of the First Assembly under the title "Preparations required to enable the economic weapon of the League to be used in case of necessity." In the Sixth (Political) Committee of that Assembly, to which it was referred, the matter was first considered on November 27, 1920. At the request of the chairman, Mr. Branting, Lord Robert Cecil, who as former British Blockade Minister had had practical experience of economic warfare, submitted a brief report.

This report, entitled "Notes on economic pressure," makes extremely interesting reading today. It reveals the optimism with which the possibilities of Article 16 were considered on the morrow of the World War. Had not the Entente Powers achieved victory largely through the application of economic pressure on the enemy? Had they not succeeded in spite of their lack of technical preparation, in spite of the difficulties created by the existence of troublesome neutrals, and in spite of the size, composition and might of the coalition of Central Powers arrayed against them? Now that everything was to be arranged beforehand, that there were to be no more neutrals and that the enemy, if ever there was again to be an enemy, could only be an occasional misled and isolated aggressor, was not the problem to be solved by the League of Nations infinitely simpler? This is how Lord Robert Cecil considered it. He wrote:

It is only where one of the neighbours of the blockaded State is not a Member of the League that any great complication arises, apart from questions of indirect financial pressure, which are much more difficult. It seems, therefore, that there is no reason why a very considerable amount of economic pressure could not be applied by the League to almost any offending State, even as things stand, without the creation of an International Commission. All that seems necessary is machinery by which the Members of the League can be informed that an occasion for the exercise of economic pressure has arisen, and that they are, in consequence, bound to take the necessary measures for that purpose, and this machinery might be, as far as I can see, of the simplest kind. For instance, take the case of one Member making war upon some other State in defiance of its obligations under Article 15. As soon as that fact actually occurs the obligation arises for each of the other Members of the League to prevent its nationals having any intercourse with those of the Covenant-breaking State. All that is required, therefore, is to create sufficient machinery to enable the Members of the League to know that such an emergency has arisen.

For this purpose it would not seem to be necessary to do more than charge a special department or even a special official of the Secretariat with the duty of watching for the occurrence of such an emergency, and to entrust him with the duty of immediately calling the attention of the Members of the Council to the fact that it had arisen.

The Council would then hold a meeting summoned with the least possible delay, and if they were satisfied that the emergency had arisen, they would be bound so to inform the Members of the League, and call upon them to fulfill their obligations under Article 16.

Whether this particular machinery will be thought by the Committee to be all that is wanted or not it is for them to decide, but I certainly hope that they will take this aspect of the question suggested to them into their consideration, because if they agree with the general line of this reasoning much can be done to put the economic weapon into a condition for effective action, without waiting for the creation of any such complicated machinery as an International Commission with its reports and so on.

The simple optimism reflected in these words was, however, not shared by all the States represented even in the Assembly of 1920, which as yet included none of the defeated Powers. The three Scandinavian neutrals had already submitted draft amendments to Article 16. In favor of such Members of the League "for whom the application" of economic sanctions "might entail serious danger," they proposed that certain facilities and exceptions be provided. In submitting its draft amendment to that effect, the Swedish Government added a note in which it observed:

The economic blockade, which by virtue of this Article threatens any State which violates the Covenants of the League constitutes the most effective coercive weapon of the League; and it is clearly of the utmost importance that the blockade should be enforced in the most rapid and effective fashion possible. In the view of the Swedish Government, however, the fact should not be ignored that, for certain States of secondary importance—whose situation owing to the vicinity of other and more important States, is specially exposed—a complete rupture of economic relations with such powerful neighbours would present grave dangers.

It can, indeed, be imagined that in such a case the Great Power in question might be tempted to occupy the territory of the smaller Power, so as to protect the very important economic interests which, as a result of the blockade, would be at stake. For this reason the Swedish Government is of opinion that it would be desirable in cases of this nature to leave to the Council the option of modifying in some measure the obligation upon a Member of the League to take part in the blockade.

In presenting his above-mentioned report, on November 27, 1920, Lord Robert Cecil, who therein had made no reference to these draft amendments, added in an oral statement:

. . . that there were two other matters which would have to be considered by the proposed International Commission:—

(1) The case of those countries which would incur grave danger by enforcing a blockade, and the support to be given by Members of the League to one another in financial and economic measures to minimise the loss and inconvenience resulting from such action.

(2) The question of how far it would be possible to issue licences to certain Powers allowing them to derogate from the duties imposed upon them by the Covenant.

The discussion which followed already showed that the problem of collective security to be realized through the application of economic sanctions was not quite as simple as it at first appeared. Mr. Millen, of Australia, pointed to "the danger of discrepancies in legislation on this subject between individual States." Mr. Lange, of Norway, "drew attention to the word 'nationals' in Article 16 of the Covenant, and asked what measures were to be taken in the case of nationals of the blockading State domiciled in the blockaded territory." M. Motta, of Switzerland, observed that his country "would be ready to participate in a blockade provided that it . . . did not prejudice her military neutrality." Mr. Fock, of the Netherlands, "insisted that every State should have the right to decide for itself whether the facts were really such as to justify the Council in instituting economic measures, and to refuse to take part in such measures if they appeared to be unjustifiable."

These objections and observations, as yet very timidly formulated, brought forth energetic replies from the representatives of France, Great Britain and Italy. Of these, the latter, Signor Schanzer, went furthest by declaring "that there was some danger in allowing each State to decide for itself whether or not to carry out the blockade, when ordered by the Council to do so."

That the Council could "order" a State to take part in a blockade which seemed unjustifiable and which, even if justified, might imperil its very national existence, was an entirely novel conception of the League of Nations.

After this preliminary skirmish, a sub-committee was set up which reported to the Political Commission, which in turn reported to the plenary Assembly on December 10, 1920.

The debates to which the preparation and the presentation of these reports gave rise immediately revealed that the complexities and difficulties of the problem were far greater and more numerous than Lord Robert Cecil seemed to have suspected.

The most important point of conflict was one relating to the interpretation of Article 16. Here, exactly as in the case of Article 10 and for exactly the same reasons, there were disagreements between maximalists, who stressed the powers of the League represented by the Council, and minimalists, who minimized those powers in order to safeguard the rights of national sovereignty. We have already seen Signor Schanzer advocating the power of the Council to order the States not represented on it to participate in the blockade. His view was shared, with certain reservations, by Lord Robert Cecil and more unqualifiedly by M. Léon Bourgeois and Mr. Benes, of Czechoslovakia. The latter, on December 7, 1920, declared that "the Council alone had the authority to decide whether a breach of the Covenant had taken place, and to order the Members of the League to resort to a blockade." Against this maximalist view, minimalists, such as Mr. Fock of the Netherlands, held "that the Members of the League should be free to judge for themselves whether a violation of the Covenant had taken place." This opinion, which was shared by M. Motta of Switzerland, also received the support of Mr. H. A. L. Fisher, who happened to be the spokesman in this debate of the Lloyd George Government, far less international in its outlook than the South African administration of General Smuts, which Lord Robert Cecil was representing.

Again, as in the case of Article 10, a compromise agreement was reached and on the same basis. Each State Member of the League was to be regarded as the final judge of the emergence of the *casus foederis*. But it was not free to withhold its cooperation if it recognized that a violation of the Covenant had taken place. The relevant passage of the report adopted by the plenary Assembly of December 10, 1920, reads as follows:

(a) It shall be the duty of the Secretary-General to call the attention of the Council to any facts which in his opinion show that a Member of the League has become a Covenant-breaking State within the meaning of Article 16;

(b) Upon receiving such an intimation, the Council shall, on the request of any of its Members, hold a meeting with the least possible delay to consider it, and shall send a copy of the procès-verbal of the Meeting to all the other Members of the League;

(c) As soon as a Member of the League is satisfied, in consequence of the communication of the procès-verbal of the Council, that a breach of Covenant within Article 16 has occurred, it is its duty to take measures for the purpose of carrying out the first paragraph of Article 16.

Another point on which agreement proved difficult was that raised by the Scandinavian amendments. In the plenary Assembly, M. Lafontaine, of Belgium, made a speech specifically to attack these proposals. On behalf of his delegation he said:

Denmark, Sweden and Norway ask that those countries which will find themselves endangered should they take part in the blockade should not be obliged to do so.

Belgium thinks, that, however great the peril which a country might have to undergo under the system which we seek to establish here, that country ought to do its duty. It was thus that Belgium understood her obligations in 1914, and she has resolved to adopt the same attitude in future, whatever the danger may be to which she may find herself exposed. (*Applause.*) We think that all countries should interpret their duty in this manner. We think, too, that here is the duty of international solidarity, a duty before which every interest, whatever it may be, must give place.

We fully admit that, in circumstances of this nature, powerful countries may take certain general measures, but in our opinion it would be impossible, on the pretext that they would suffer more than others, for some countries to hold aloof from the sacred task of defending justice, even at the peril of their own existence. *'Fais ce que dois, advienne que pourra.'*

The matter was not settled by the First Assembly. It merely decided to refer the question for further consideration to the International Blockade Committee which it requested the Council to set up. It did so in the following terms:

It is . . . desirable to consider, in accordance with the proposals made by Denmark, Norway and Sweden, what measures, if any, should be taken in the case of Members of the League which, from smallness of their resources and their geographical position, might be in serious danger if they carried out to the full their obligations under the first paragraph of Article 16 as against a powerful Covenant-breaking State. This is a matter which may have to be considered at any moment from a practical point of view if the necessity for coercion of a Covenant-breaking State should arise. In that case the Council would have to take whatever measures it thought suitable for the emergency.

On the whole, the First Assembly did not do much more than open the discussion on the possibilities of the practical application of Article 16. In the course of this discussion, certain difficulties had become apparent which seemed to have escaped the attention of the framers of the Covenant or at least to have been underestimated by them. The feverish atmosphere which had prevailed in Paris during the first months of 1919, the absence of the defeated Powers and of the neutrals and the recent memories of the final success of the inter-Allied blockade had all contributed to create certain illusions as to the ease with which even an incomplete League of Nations could organize and work an effective scheme of collective security.

Since then, the difficulties had begun to be appreciated. Furthermore, they had in themselves of course very appreciably increased by reason of the negative attitude of the United States. It is therefore not surprising that, after a fortnight's discussion at Geneva, Lord Robert Cecil should, in his final speech on the subject, have adopted a much more cautious tone than in his above-quoted preliminary notes. On December 10, 1920, in submitting the report of the Sixth Committee to the plenary Assembly, he declared:

The present position in the Covenant is not very satisfactory. You have that provision in Article 16. It is indeed one of the vital, the cardinal, provisions in the whole Covenant, without which you would not have the final material guarantee which in human society is no doubt necessary for the enforcement of even the most beneficent code. Thought you have got that solemnly enacted in the Covenant, no means, no machinery is provided for carrying it into execution.

It was with a view to the setting up of such machinery that the Assembly, following the lead of the Council, recommended the institution of an International Blockade Committee.

On February 22, 1921, the Council acted on these recommendations. It decided to request the Governments of Great Britain, France, Italy, Japan, Cuba, Spain, Norway and Switzerland to appoint experts to constitute the International Blockade Committee. At the same time the Secretary-General was instructed to secure from all the States Members of the League the official information considered necessary for the work of that Committee.

It was not before June 15, 1921, however, that the Secretary-General was in a position to make known the final composition of that body. The States which were to be represented thereon had been selected by the Council with a view to allowing the most divergent national interests to be considered. In asking Spain, Cuba, Norway and Switzerland to participate in a preliminary discussion on economic sanctions, the Council was obviously animated by the desire to be informed of the feelings and of the wishes of those Members of the League who had the least to expect and the most to fear from an international blockade. Of these four States, three had been neutral throughout the World War. For them, to participate in a system of collective security was therefore to abandon a régime of complete national independence, which had protected them against the worst effects of the international catastrophe in the past, in favor of an untried experiment which might well, in the future, involve them in dangerous complications. Furthermore, these three States, and to no less a degree Cuba also, were geographically so located, politically so weak and economically so dependent upon their neighbors that, while inevitably pacific themselves, they felt extremely vulnerable in case of general hostilities. In the balance sheet of their national security,

Article 16, strictly interpreted, might therefore well be listed as a liability more than as an asset.

Thus constituted, the International Blockade Committee met for a week's session at the end of August 1921 in Geneva. The information with which it had been supplied by the Members of the League was scanty. Most of the latter had not replied at all to the Secretary-General's request and even the material sent in by the nineteen States which had, did not contain much that proved useful.

The report of the Committee was transmitted by the Council to the Second Assembly, which referred it to its third Committee. It was found so involved by the members of this latter body that, on its first consideration on September 9, 1921, Lord Robert Cecil moved

That the members of the International Blockade Committee who are also members of this Committee, be requested to formulate and submit to this Committee the definite recommendations contained in the report of the International Blockade Committee.

Accordingly Messrs. Schanzer, of Italy, Oka, of Japan, de Aguero, of Cuba, and Max Huber, of Switzerland, who had represented their countries in the Blockade Committee and to whom were added representatives of France and of Belgium, were constituted into a sub-committee. Three days later this sub-committee presented to the Third Committee a document entitled "The Conclusions of the Report of the International Blockade Committee."

It was on this document that all the ensuing discussions were to be based and it was through this channel that the principal suggestions of the Blockade Committee finally came to be embodied in the resolutions of the Assembly.

Before quoting these resolutions, the general tendency of which is so clear that they call but for very little comment, let us see how they came to be adopted.

When the conclusions of the International Blockade Committee were submitted to the third Committee of the Second Assembly, it was very obvious that they were deeply to disappoint the staunchest friends of the principle of collective security. Lord Robert Cecil, who was at the head of these, who had not been called upon to cooperate with the Blockade Committee, but who was present at the Second Assembly as a delegate from South Africa, did not disguise his feelings. At the very first meeting of the Third Committee, when the question of the publicity of its debates arose, he spoke in favor of complete publicity and declared:

The Committee had very difficult questions to consider, and since a satisfactory solution of them was opposed by the official classes, it was essential that the Committee should be supported by public opinion. On the other hand, certain problems would perhaps prove insoluble, and it was desirable that the public should realise the real obstacles in the way of the success of the efforts made for their solution. Finally, if recommendations were made by the Committee, they would only be of value in so far as they were supported by the public opinion of the world.

As no one opposed this suggestion, it was immediately adopted. Thanks to this circumstance, we are able to follow the debates of the Committee in all its details.

After Lord Robert Cecil had presented his first remarks on the work of the Blockade Committee, remarks which, in spite of their diplomatic form, were unmistakably critical, Signor Schanzer replied. This Italian delegate, who had played a leading part in the work of that Committee, was to interpret and to defend its work before the Second Committee as rapporteur both of the sub-committee and of the Third Committee:

In reply to Lord Robert Cecil, he stated, first, that the International Blockade Committee realised that Article 16 constituted an effective weapon, but one which might be turned against the nation which applied it; it was for this reason that it had thought necessary to interpret it with certain reservations, and to leave certain questions unanswered.

According to the Blockade Committee's interpretation, Article 16 referred particularly to economic pressure for the purpose of avoiding war, and not to the traditional naval blockade. The Blockade Committee wished, above all, to put forward two fundamental principles: respect for the sovereignty of each State in the interpretation of facts which might give rise to the application of Article 16, and the centralisation, by the Council, of the measures employed in the use of the economic weapon.

As to the possibility of conceding to certain States the right to apply this measure only in a partial degree, M. Schanzer recalled the fact that this question was settled by the Blockade Committee in such a way as to exclude all exemptions, except in specific cases.

As regards the case of a Blockaded State neighbouring on a State which was not a Member of the League of Nations, M. Schanzer admitted that the Committee had not arrived at any definite solution.

These opening remarks suffice to show how Signor Schanzer, who a year before had spoken of the Council's "ordering" States not represented on it to take part in the blockade, had been led to temper his views. The latter, which were those of the Blockade Committee itself, differed from those of the original authors of Article 16 on four main points. Before considering them in turn, it may be useful here to recall the exact terms of the first paragraph of Article 16 on which the discussions were principally to turn. This paragraph is worded as follows:

Should any Member of the League resort to war in disregard of its covenants under Articles 12, 13 or 15, it shall *ipso facto* be deemed to have committed an act of war against all other Members of the League, which hereby undertake immediately to subject it to the severance of all trade or financial relations, the prohibition of all intercourse between their nationals and the nationals of the covenant-breaking State, and the prevention of all financial, commercial or personal intercourse between the nationals of the covenant-breaking State and the nationals of any other State, whether a Member of the League or not.

The first observation which an unprejudiced reading of these provisions seems to suggest is that in the intention of their framers, a violation of Articles 12, 13 or 15 of the Covenant by any Member of the League was automatically to create a state of war between that Member and all others. On this point, the comment of the Blockade Committee was to the effect that

The unilateral action of the defaulting States does not create a state of war; it merely entitles the other Members of the League to declare that a state of war exists between them and the Covenant-breaking State.

This interpretation, whether faithful or not, was undoubtedly wise, as it prevented, to use M. Motta's words in the Assembly of September 26, 1921, "the Covenant-breaking State" from letting "loose, by its action, a general state of war in the world."

On the second point, of still greater importance, there is no doubt that the proposals of the Blockade Committee were not in full harmony with the text of Article 16. In the case of a resort to war in violation of the Covenant by a Member of the League, this Article called for action on the part of "all other Members of the League, which hereby undertake immediately to subject it" etc. To this the Blockade Committee remarked:

All States alike must apply the measures of economic pressure, with the following exceptions:

(a) It may be necessary to assign certain special duties to States whose territory immediately adjoins the defaulting State, and to States in a position to contribute the forces necessary for taking naval, military, or air measures.

(b) The Council may, at the request of a Member, which can show that the facilities demanded are essential for its economic or political security, grant such exemptions as in the opinion of the Council will not conflict with the aims of Article 16. . . .

Financial measures should, above all, include the forbidding of all access to the money markets in countries of the League, subject to exception, if facilities subsequently as good could be obtained on some market of a country not a Member of the League.

We have here an echo of the draft amendments presented by the Scandinavian States to the First Assembly in favor of those for whom the application of sanctions "might entail serious danger." But Sweden, Denmark and Norway were not the only Members of the League who felt threatened by a drastic application of Article 16. On September 16, 1921, Mr. Pflügl, the representative of Austria,

stated that immense difficulties would supervene for Austria if she were forced rigidly to apply Article 16 of the Covenant. Owing to her peculiar geographical situation, she was unable to exist without her neighbours. In particular, she was entirely dependent upon foreign sources for her coal supply. M. Pflügl therefore supported the amendment of the Scandinavian countries, which laid down that certain derogations in the application of Article 16 of the Covenant should be allowed.

Mr. de Aguero, on behalf of Cuba, added that "he, like the Austrian Representative, had been instructed by his Government to support the amendment of the Scandinavian countries."

On behalf of Canada, Sir George Perley made similar reservations. The most outspoken of all delegates on this point was Mr. Manini Rios, the representative of Uruguay, who before the plenary Assembly declared, on September 26, 1921:

We all know that the Scandinavian amendments were actuated by quite legitimate considerations. My country is also one of those which is the neighbour of nations far more powerful and consequently it is inevitably bound to them from an economic point of view while enjoying cordial and friendly relations in the political and moral fields.

Uruguay is situated in a corner of South America, hemmed in between the Argentine Republic and Brazil; it is separated from the former by a narrow river, and it has an almost open frontier of 500 kilometres contiguous to the latter; and it would be unable to carry out its duties as a Member of the League of Nations, and maintain a blockade against either the Argentine or against Brazil should either of these countries fail in their international duties.

M. Motta, of Switzerland, while alluding to his own country only by inference, stated in general terms what was the obvious truth and one to which Signor Schanzer had already alluded in his first reply to Lord Robert Cecil, namely that:

One of the indispensable conditions for rendering the blockade really effective is the universality of the League of Nations. It is, indeed, difficult to imagine how a blockade could operate completely as long as the United States do not participate in it, or have not recognised it.

This principle of the universality of the League is, in theory, proclaimed by everyone; unfortunately, it has not yet taken root in the conscience of the whole world. It is important to note that the Inernational Blockade Committee has understood that this universality is of vital importance, and that it is not only a postulate of pure reason, but, above all, a postulate of practical reason.

Article 16 called for "the severance" and the "prevention of all financial, commercial or personal intercourse between the nationals of the covenant-breaking State" and the nationals of all other countries. Nothing could more explicitly define complete ostracism than the terms deliberately used by the authors of that article. The Blockade Committee, on the contrary—and that was the third very important point of difference—were very reserved and very discriminating in their recommendations on this point. Thus we read in their conclusions:

. . . those relations, the severance of which is not provided for by Article 16, may continue to exist between the defaulting State and the other Members of the League. Measures which would not be calculated to exercise a decisive influence on the economic resisting power of the defaulting State should not be included among the measures which have to be taken by virtue of this Article. . . .

For the same reasons, the Committee considers that the cutting off of the food supplies of the civil population of the defaulting State should be regarded as an extremely drastic measure which should only be applied if the other measures employed have been found to be inadequate.

Although the Third Committee of the Second Assembly, at the insistent demands of Lord Robert Cecil, M. Reynald, of France, and M. Poullet, of Belgium, finally consented to show less leniency to the Covenant-breaking State than the Blockade Committee, the measures it recommended were far less drastic than those contemplated by the framers of Article 16 in 1919. The texts which they proposed were less intended to secure the complete isolation and blockade of the aggressor than to exercise upon him a gradual restraining pressure. Here also the reluctance of the former neutrals and of other States to be drawn into a general struggle, combined with the lack of universality of the League, led to a distinct blunting of the teeth of Article 16, if that expression be allowed. Here as elsewhere, therefore, the desire to reassure the law-abiding Members of the League as to the nature and extent of their obligations suggested concessions which were at least equally reassuring for any would-be aggressor.

Fourthly and finally, the automatic and therefore immediate action contemplated under Article 16 made way, in the conclusions of the Blockade Committee, for a policy of eclectic, gradual and consequently often deferred intervention by the League. It is in the following terms that that Committee outlined the procedure which it recommended against the Covenant-breaker:

It is the duty of the various Members of the League to decide whether violation of the Covenant has been committed, and whether they ought, in consequence, to adopt the measures laid down in the Covenant.

All cases of violation of the Covenant should be referred to the Council as a matter of urgency, at the request of any Member of the League. The Secretary-General would communicate to the Members events which might possibly lead to a violation of the Covenant. Upon receipt of such communication, the Council would convene. When convening, the Council would summon representatives of the parties to the conflict, and all States which are neighbours of the defaulting State, or which normally maintain close economic relations with it, or whose co-operation would be especially valuable for the application of Article 16. The selection of the States which would have to be summoned would be made provisionally by the Acting-President of the Council, subject to the decision arrived at by the Council.

The Council's decision that there has been a violation of the Covenant shall be immediately communicated to all the Members of the League, with a statement of reasons, and with an invitation to the Members to give it their support. It should be made public.

In decisions of the Council as to whether the Covenant has been violated, the votes of the States which are parties to the conflict shall not be counted.

The Council should be assisted by a Technical Committee at the moment when Article 16 has to be applied, and in view of the putting into force of the sanctions. The composition of this Committee, which will sit permanently as soon as the action decided on has been taken, will be subject to modification, and will include, as the case may require, representatives of the States most especially affected.

The Council should fix a date on which the measures are to be taken, and should intimate that date to all the Members of the League, without prejudice to the right for any State to take preliminary measures.

On this point, the advice of the Blockade Committee was followed by the Third Committee and by the Assembly itself. After prolonged debates, the latter finally, on October 4, 1921, recorded its views on the economic weapon of the League by adopting four draft amendments to Article 16 and nineteen interpretative resolutions which "shall so long as the amendments have not been put in force in the form required by the Covenant, constitute rules for guidance which the Assembly recommends, as a provisional measure, to the Council and to the Members of the League in connection with the application of Article 16."

As the draft amendments in question have never secured the ratifications which would have been required in order to put them into force, we shall be content here to quote the most significant of the nineteen interpretative resolutions. They read as follows:

3. The unilateral action of the defaulting State cannot create a state of war: it merely entitles the other Members of the League to resort to acts of war or to declare themselves in a state of war with the Covenant-breaking State; but it is in accordance with the spirit of the Covenant that the League of Nations should attempt, at least at the outset, to avoid war, and to restore peace by economic pressure.

4. It is the duty of each Member of the League to decide for itself whether a breach of the Covenant has been committed. The fulfilment of their duties under Article 16 is required from Members of the League by the express terms of the Covenant, and they cannot neglect them without breach of their Treaty obligations.

5. All cases of breach of Covenant under Article 16 shall be referred to the Council as a matter of urgency at the request of any Member of the League. Further, if a breach of Covenant be committed, or if there arise a danger of such breach being committed, the Secretary-General shall at once give notice thereof to all the Members of the Council. Upon receipt of such a request by a Member of the League, or of such a notice by the Secretary-General, the Council will meet as soon as possible. The Council shall summon representatives of the parties to the conflict and of all States which are neighbours of the defaulting State, or which normally maintain close economic relations with it, or whose co-operation would be especially valuable for the application of Article 16.

6. If the Council is of opinion that a State has been guilty of a breach of Covenant, the Minutes of the meeting at which that opinion is arrived at shall be immediately sent to all Members of the League, accompanied by a statement of reasons and by an invitation to take action accordingly. The fullest publicity shall be given to this decision.

7. For the purpose of assisting it to enforce Article 16, the Council may, if it thinks fit, be assisted by a *technical* Committee. This Committee, which will remain in permanent session as soon as the action decided on is taken, may include, if desirable, representatives of the States specially affected.

8. The Council shall recommend the date on which the enforcement of economic pressure, under Article 16, is to be begun, and shall give notice of that date to all the Members of the League.

9. All States must be treated alike as regards the application of the measures of economic pressure, with the following reservations:

(a) It may be necessary to recommend the execution of special measures by certain States;

(b) If it is thought desirable to postpone, wholly or partially, in the case of certain States, the effective application of the economic sanctions laid down in Article 16, such postponement shall not be permitted except in so far as it is desirable for the success of the common plan of action, or reduces to a minimum the losses and embarrassments which may be entailed in the case of certain Members of the League by the application of the sanctions.

10. It is not possible to decide beforehand, and in detail, the various measures of an economic, commercial and financial nature to be taken in each case where economic pressure is to be applied.

When the case arises, the Council shall recommend to the Members of the League a plan for joint action.

11. The interruption of diplomatic relations may, in the first place, be limited to the withdrawal of the heads of Missions.

12. Consular relations may possibly be maintained.

13. For the purposes of the severance of relations between persons belonging to the Covenant-breaking State and persons belonging to other States Members of the League, the test shall be residence and not nationality.

14. In cases of prolonged application of economic pressure, measures of increasing stringency may be taken. The cutting off of the food supplies of the civil population of the defaulting State shall be regarded as an extremely drastic measure which shall only be applied if the other measures available are clearly inadequate.

15. Correspondence and all other methods of communication shall be subjected to special regulations.

16. Humanitarian relations shall be continued.

17. Efforts should be made to arrive at arrangements which would ensure the co-operation of States non-Members of the League in the measures to be taken.

Commenting on these resolutions, which were adopted practically unchanged, the Third Committee, in its report of September 21, 1921, declared:

There is no doubt that Article 16 is one of the most important and fundamental Articles contained in the Covenant. As Lord Robert Cecil pointed out, in the speech which he made on this question at the First Assembly, the most powerful weapon possessed by the League of Nations is the public opinion of the world, which will force the Members of the League to respect the Covenant. In the domestic affairs of States, however, it is sometimes necessary to use force in order to compel certain individuals to respect the law, and in the same way it may, in certain cases, be necessary to resort to the economic weapon in order to compel Members of the League to fulfil their obligations.

It follows, therefore, that Article 16 is one of the principal elements of the legal system embodied in the Covenant, and this system would be altogether incomplete were no provision made for the enforcement of effective sanctions against States which did not fulfil their obligations.

On the other hand, there is no doubt whatever that the application of Article 16 involves many complicated questions which it is very difficult to solve.

The starting point of the argument and of the conclusions arrived at by the Blockade Committee has been as follows:—The authors of the Covenant had considered the League of Nations as an organisation embracing all or nearly all States, and capable of prompt action in the event of breach of the Covenant. In the view of the International Blockade Committee, the application of Article 16, even had the League been universal, might have formidable consequences either for the League of Nations in general or for some of its Members. But the afore-mentioned Committee was of the opinion that as the League of Nations had not yet attained a world-wide or nearly world-wide character, a very rigid application of Article 16 would not only meet with very great obstacles, but might also place the States Members of the League in very difficult situations. That is why the International Blockade Committee has seen fit to recommend solutions which, in the present stage of the League of Nations, will, so far as possible, make allowance for the facts as they are.

Your Committee, therefore, considered that it must proceed cautiously and by degrees; hence the texts which it ventures to submit to you.

The report of the Third Committee was finally adopted by an unanimous vote of the Assembly. As has often been the case in the League of Nations, this formal unanimity was, however, anything but a true indication of the real sentiments of the various delegations. Those States, such as the former neutrals, the British Dominions and others, which looked upon Article 16 as a liability more than as an asset, were relieved when the Assembly interpreted it almost into insignificance. But those, such as France and Belgium, for instance, who felt threatened and would have been happy to place their trust in collective security, either openly deplored the action taken or pretended to favor it by putting upon it a most misleading construction. Thus, for example, M. Poullet, of Belgium, who had throughout struggled for a stringent interpretation of Article 16, declared in the plenary Assembly, when the report of the Third Committee was presented:

I wish to register the complete agreement of my delegation with the thorough, lucid and complete report submitted by M. Schanzer, and with the draft resolutions which follow it.

Indeed, Committee No. 3 had only one aim, which directed all its work—that was, not to weaken the scope of Article 16.

It would be difficult to imagine a more perfect example of official optimism or of wishful thinking. In fact, it was generally recognized that, after the Assembly of 1921 had ended its labors, the sanctions provided for in Article 16 of the Covenant had been seriously limited in their possible efficacy. Confidence in collective security, which had never been complete anywhere, especially since the United States had decided to remain aloof from the League, was so shaken by these decisions that international disarmament was rendered impossible. Lest I be accused of misreading these developments and of judging them less in the light of the contemporaneous situation than in that of later happenings which clearly showed the frailty of Article 16, I may perhaps be allowed to recall the opinion I ventured to express on them as far back as 1925. Speaking on the then recent history of Articles 10 and 16 before the much lamented Williamstown Institute of Politics, I declared, in the late summer of that year:

By the various interpretations adopted, these articles have been so appreciably weakened, that to-day no responsible European statesman would venture to stake his reputation and the security of his country on the potential protection of the League in case of international disturbance.

CHAPTER 2 *Security Disputes Before the League:*
Four Case Histories

I THE GREEK-BULGARIAN INCIDENT OF 1925

The Greek-Bulgarian Incident of 1925 *

James Barros

A Border Incident

. . . The autumn of 1925 appeared to have ushered in a new Europe. On
. . . October 16, after long negotiations the Locarno Pacts had been signed,
establishing the Franco-Belgian-German frontiers and readmitting Germany
once more into the family of nations. For the moment Europe was at peace.
Even in the Balkans, that cockpit of European politics, there was peace.

Thus the border incident that occurred on the early afternoon of October 19, at the Greek-Bulgarian frontier near Demir-Kapu, for a while went
unnoticed by the Allied representatives in Sofia.

Conflicting accounts make it difficult to pinpoint responsibility for the
incident. The only facts definitely established by subsequent investigation
were that on the early afternoon of October 19, in an exchange of shots, a
Greek border sentry was killed and a Greek officer arriving at the scene
ostensibly to effect a cease fire was also killed. Shooting along the border
became general and the Greek troops were forced to evacuate their exposed
border post.

First news of the skirmish reached Athens in the early morning hours
of October 20. In retrospect, this dispatch was important for it stated that
the "incident was premeditated by the Bulgarians," thus establishing the
atmosphere of mistrust that was to pervade the Greek Ministry of War that
morning. In an earlier report from Demir-Kapu the Intelligence Officer of
the covering battalion had communicated to his commanding officer that,
"according to information, Bulgarian forces *amount to one battalion,"* and
that the Bulgars were equipped with machine guns. This news, however,
was transmitted to the War Ministry in an altered form so that it read that
"Bulgarians have *attacked"* in battalion strength and were occupying the
hilltop. Unfortunately, no attempt was made by the ministry to verify this

* James Barros, "The Greek-Bulgarian Incident of 1925: The League of Nations and the
Great Powers," *Proceedings of the American Philosophical Society,* Vol. 108, No. 4 (August 27,
1964), pp. 354-385. Reprinted by permission of the author and the *American Philosophical
Society.* James Barros is an Assistant Professor of Government at Dartmouth College and is
author of *The Corfu Incident of 1923: Mussolini and the League of Nations* (1965).

information. Doubtlessly feeling that this was a premeditated Bulgarian attack in considerable strength, and nervous over its communications with Thrace which were precarious in that area (the railway line ran parallel to the Bulgarian frontier at a distance less than 6.25 miles) receipt of this message propelled the Ministry of War to order the 3rd and 4th Army Corps to prepare an advance into Bulgaria by way of the Struma Valley.

What started out as a simple frontier incident had, because of faulty intelligence and distorted messages, escalated into a situation of serious proportions. Events during these early hours had moved with such breathtaking speed that they sealed beforehand the fate of the diplomatic moves that would unfold between Athens and Sofia.

Bulgarian Proposals in Sofia and Athens

On the Bulgarian side, news of the firing at Demir-Kapu reached the General Staff at about 5 P.M. on the afternoon of October 19. Considered as merely another border incident, instructions were transmitted to terminate the skirmish and no more thought was given it by the Staff.

In the case of the Royal Bulgarian Ministry of Foreign Affairs, information of what had transpired at the border was received only at 2:30 P.M. the following day. Arrival of the news prompted the Secretary-General of the Ministry, Constantine Minkoff, to request an interview with the Greek chargé d'affaires, Raoul Rosetti-Bibica. On Rosetti's arrival at the Foreign Ministry, Minkoff explained the occurrences at the frontier and requested that the Greek Government and the military authorities at Salonika be immediately informed in order that the Greek troops cease fire. He also requested that the Greeks contact the Bulgarians at the border in order to ascertain the causes and responsibilities for the incident. Instructions in this sense were also forwarded to the Bulgarian Legation in Athens. In an urgent message to the Greek Foreign Ministry the chargé recounted his discussion with the Secretary-General and added that, according to Minkoff, though Bulgarian officers had repeatedly raised the white flag to effect a cease fire, the Greek troops had continued shooting. Concluding his report, Rosetti begged that Athens give immediate orders to the military in the sense desired by the Bulgarian Foreign Ministry. At 8 P.M. that night, after filing his message to Athens, and undoubtedly attempting to reassure the Bulgarians, Rosetti informed the Foreign Ministry by telephone that he had telegraphed to his government in the sense desired by Minkoff.

At the same time that Rosetti's message was speeding its way towards Athens other messages on the same subject were making their way to the Bulgarian Legation in the Greek capital. These messages from Sofia, after describing the incident and Minkoff's interview with Rosetti, instructed the legation to make *démarches* to the Greek Government similar to those made to Rosetti, insisting that the Greek authorities receive orders to establish contact with their Bulgarian counterparts at the frontier. Acting on these instructions, the Bulgarian chargé d'affaires, Ivan Dantcheff, on the morning of October 21 requested an interview with the Greek Foreign Minister, Admiral Alexandros Hadjikyriakos. The interview took place at noon. As arrangements for the interview were being made the Bulgarian Legation submitted to the Foreign Ministry a very urgent *note verbale* in line with the instructions it had received from Sofia. The note pointed out that though the incident had broken out two days before, firing continued in spite of the efforts of the Bulgarian authorities, who had hoisted the white flag a number of times in an attempt to contact their opposite number. The legation asked therefore that the Foreign Ministry intervene immediately so that orders could be transmitted without delay to the Greek border authorities to effect a cease fire and to contact quickly their Bulgarian counterparts. In ending, the legation reserved the "right to make further *démarches* in connection with the responsibilities springing from the . . . incident."

In his interview with Hadjikyriakos, Dantcheff repeated the Bulgarian requests and pointed out that the "continuation and the eventual extension of the shooting could complicate the situation and lead to results contrary to the interests of the two countries." The Foreign Minister ignored this comment and observed that the situation was grave because the attack appeared "premeditated and prepared for long since," and had been executed by an unusual number of regular troops comprising about a battalion of the Bulgarian Army. He felt that the assault had not been provoked from the Greek side, and that the Bulgarian assailants, after having killed the Greek sentry and the Greek officer who had advanced under a white flag, had penetrated and occupied a large area of Greek territory. If it had merely been an armed attack perpetrated by "irregulars and irresponsibles" (i.e., comitadjis), the event would have been far less serious. However, in view of the gravity of the situation and given the over excited state of mind of the troops in the threatened region, the Greek Government thought itself obliged to "give full powers to the military authorities of the region in question to undertake all measures which could be judged necessary in order to assure their security and that of the national territory."

At this point Hadjikyriakos enumerated the demands that would form the basis of Greece's subsequent note to Bulgaria. He stressed that the Greek Government, feeling that its national honor had been injured and that it was just to grant indemnities to the families of the slain men, hoped that the Bulgarian Government would consent to the following: to inflict an exemplary punishment on the military commanders responsible; to express its regrets to the Greek Government; and lastly, to pay an equitable indemnity of three million French francs to the families of the men killed. To these demands the Greek Government desired an immediate response. Almost as an afterthought he added it was possible that the Greek troops in the Salonika region, unaware of the "designs and the intentions of the

Bulgarian troops," might deem it necessary "to proceed to the occupation of certain strategic points of Bulgarian territory," so as to assure their own security which had been put in danger by the Bulgarian attack.

In reply, Dantcheff maintained that on the basis of the information which he had received from Sofia "it was a question of a simple frontier incident" and that a mixed commission of inquiry could easily establish the causes and the responsibilities involved. Besides, he observed, in many cases of a similar nature, his government had always insisted on the need to proceed with preliminary inquiries in order to establish responsibility and that this was the way indicated for the settlement of the border incident which had arisen. Though he would of course communicate the Greek view to his government, he insisted again on the need to effect an immediate cease fire on the Greek side and to order the competent authorities to establish contact with the Bulgarian officers at the border.

Concluding the interview, the Foreign Minister promised Dantcheff to transmit to the Prime Minister, General Theodoros Pangalos, the requests of the Bulgarian Government and to contact him accordingly.

While this discussion was going on in Athens, in Sofia Rosetti once more appeared at the Bulgarian Foreign Ministry. It was his second interview with Minkoff within twenty-four hours. He was informed by the Secretary-General that shooting on the frontier had subsided and that the Bulgarian Government had appointed officers and begged that the Greek Government do likewise so that responsibility for the incident could be settled "in [a] spirit [of] complete sincerity." Later in the day Rosetti was again recalled to the Foreign Ministry. In the interval the situation had worsened. According to Minkoff, since two o'clock that afternoon Bulgarian officers had been waiting at the border to meet with their Greek opposites. Unfortunately, shooting had again broken out and become general. Because of this Sofia wanted settlement of the incident by an investigatory committee. Minkoff assured Rosetti that the Bulgarian military had been given strict orders to avoid any friction with the Greeks and to maintain only a defensive position. In ending the meeting he again begged that the Greek military be given orders to restore peace on the border in order to make possible a settlement of the incident.

Late that night Rosetti was visited by the British chargé d'affaires, Ralph C. S. Stevenson. Informed of the resumption of fire at the frontier he had called seeking further information. The only additional details that Rosetti could offer were those he had dispatched to Athens. His English colleague then desired to know what "official information" he had reflecting Greek views. Rosetti explained that he lacked instructions, but "attempted to explain and convince" Stevenson that the incident, as always, derived from Bulgarian responsibility because of the continued efforts of comitadji bands to cross the Greek frontier. During the present period many such crossings had been reported, with the comitadjis then committing murder on Greek territory. On this occasion, this was precisely what had happened.

Though Stevenson "accepted this interpretation," he observed that among foreign correspondents in Sofia the belief was circulating that the Greek Government, finding itself in internal difficulties, had invited the border clash for the "diversion [of Greek] public opinion." This story Rosetti characterized as "vile fancy," denying it categorically.

Stevenson appeared convinced by Rosetti's denials, but did not hide the fact that the story about Greek internal difficulties, if circulated abroad, would likely be believed. In leaving, he added that he would communicate about the incident to London and to the British Legation in Athens.

While this discussion was taking place in Sofia, proposals similar to those made to the Greek chargé by Minkoff were being repeated to Dantcheff in Athens. According to his instructions he was to propose the nomination of a Greek-Bulgarian mixed commission of inquiry with a view to ascertaining the responsibilities for the incident and punishing the guilty. He was also charged to bring to the attention of the Greek Foreign Ministry that, until the evening of October 21, no Greek officer had presented himself at the border to put an end to the shooting in conjunction with the Bulgarian officers there. Regardless of the absence of the Greek officers, the Bulgarian military had received strict instructions not to fire and to defend themselves only in case of attack.

Simultaneously, the Bulgarian Missions in Belgrade, Bucharest, London, Paris, and Rome were ordered to inform their respective governments of the *démarches* and propositions made by the Bulgarian Government to Athens. The dispatch of these orders perceptibly widened the international scope of what had until this point been solely a Greek-Bulgarian affair.

The Greek Note

During this period events were also unfolding in the Greek Foreign Ministry where the desire for moderation was mirrored in the Secretary-General, Lysimachos Caftanzoglou. His attitude was to be symptomatic of the attitude of his colleagues serving in Berne, Paris, and Sofia, who during the coming days would plead with Athens for moderation and for a policy based on the realities of Greece's weaknesses and international position. Though Caftanzoglou, it appears, only with difficulty was able to convince the Prime Minister of the dangers of an ultimatum and felt that his insistence on moderation had avoided one, the note delivered late on the evening of October 21 to the Bulgarian Legation was for all intents and purposes still an ultimatum. This note was also forwarded to Rosetti for delivery to the Bulgarian Government with copies to the Greek Missions in Belgrade, Berlin, Bucharest, London, Paris, and Rome.

The note sent from the Foreign Ministry to the legation protested in the "most energetic fashion" the incident for which Bulgaria was held entirely responsible. To the Greeks the incident was an "unqualified aggression." The note then quickly recounted the Athens version of the incident: that on the nineteenth, Bulgarian border posts "unexpectedly and without provocation" had commenced fire, killing a Greek sentry; that firing along the line became general and when the officer of the covering company arrived to effect a cease fire, under a flag of truce, he too was killed; that Bulgarian troops estimated at battalion strength with machine guns and automatic weapons had then advanced and occupied positions on the ridges in Greek territory endeavoring thereby to gain the advantage of the ground. Furthermore, from "information carefully collected on the part of authorized and competent authorities," it appeared clearly, according to this note, that the Bulgarians had by "surprise and without provocation" opened fire. With "premeditation" they had concentrated troops "disproportionate" to those required under such circumstances. Though the Greeks had ceased fire, the Bulgarians had not and thereby killed the officer of the covering company.

The continued violation of Greek territory, the note observed, and its occupation by Bulgarian forces had been verified by reconnaissance. Thus orders had been issued to the "military commander to repulse the invasion by taking all measures that he will judge *á propos* for the integrity of the national territory and its security, until satisfaction is given." Then repeated were the demands that Hadjikyriakos had made to Dantcheff at their noon meeting. Concluding, the note maintained that, because of the "gravity of the incident," the Athens Government expected to receive from Sofia "satisfaction with the least possible delay."

Arriving at the Foreign Ministry the next day, October 22, after receipt of the Greek note, Dantcheff arranged an interview with Hadjikyriakos for noon. At this meeting the chargé reiterated the request for a cease fire and transmitted the proposal of his government for the nomination of a mixed commission of inquiry. Dantcheff's proposals, however, were not accepted. The Foreign Minister persisted that inquiries were useless, given the incontestable responsibility falling on Bulgaria for the incident. Dantcheff, however, insisted a number of times to Hadjikyriakos on the necessity of preventing a simple frontier incident from degenerating into a serious conflict, as well as on the usefulness of delegating to a mixed commission of inquiry the task of establishing responsibilities. He pointed out that in previous border incidents, many of them more serious, "where the responsibility of superior organs of Greek authority was gravely engaged," his government "instead of losing patience," had proffered the nomination of a mixed commission of inquiry; and that in these instances Sofia had proposed the nomination of two arbiters to fix in common with Athens the amount of the indemnity to be granted to the families of the slain Bulgarian soldiers. Hadjikyriakos was not moved by Dantcheff's pleadings and his formal refusal to accept any of the Bulgarian proposals compelled the chargé to request an immediate confrontation with the Prime Minister, General Pangalos, so he might present personally at the highest level the Bulgarian proposals and insist on their acceptance. The meeting was fixed for one o'clock.

In his half hour meeting with Pangalos, Dantcheff was no more success-ful than he had been with Hadjikyriakos. Greek fears, real or imagined, of Bulgarian intentions had come to fruition. To the chargé's pleas Pangalos objected that Athens was in no position to accept them, "as long as Bul-garian troops, belonging to the regular army and commanded by Bulgarian officers, trampled on Greek territory and continued the struggle." Dantcheff observed that his government had "affirmed categorically" that there was no Bulgarian advance into Greek territory and that the military had received "strict orders to avoid all provocation" and not to reply to any Greek fire. Pangalos, however, was not persuaded by the chargé's words. There had been an invasion of Greek territory by Bulgarian forces and the Greek Government was unable to consent to a mixed commission of inquiry while the invasion continued. Dantcheff retorted that the very inquiry demanded by his government would establish in a "positive and indubitable manner" the absence of any such invasion. Pangalos ignored the remark that the conditions stipulated by Athens removed all possibility of verifying the allegations of the Greek authorities as to a Bulgarian invasion. He instead requested that the chargé contact Sofia for a withdrawal of the Bulgarian troops from Greek territory expressing the fear that the Commander of the Salonika Army Corps (the Third), forced to defend his area, may have "already advanced his troops into Bulgarian territory" with the intention of forcing the invading Bulgars by a flanking movement to evacuate Greek territory. With these words the meeting terminated. The interview obviously got nowhere. Dantcheff's role, foredoomed before it began because of events at the frontier and the Greek Ministry of War, had ended. Unknown to him, at six o'clock that morning, Greek troops had entered Bulgarian territory via the Struma Valley.

Events in Sofia

While Dantcheff's fruitless efforts were grinding away in Athens, events were also developing in Sofia. There, that same morning, the American chargé, Philander L. Cable, was asked by the French Minister, Émile Dard, whether he had "heard of a grave frontier incident, which might develop into serious trouble." According to Dard, he had received instructions from the Quai d'Orsay "to hold the Bulgarians in check as far as possible." Though he had read of the sentry killed on the nineteenth, Dard could not believe that Paris' anxiety could have been caused by that occurrence. This doubt was quickly dispelled with the arrival of the British chargé, Steven-son, who informed both Dard and Cable that he had learned from the Foreign Office in London that the Greeks had thrust into Bulgaria on a thirty-two kilometer front and had penetrated to a depth of about six kilo-meters. Both Dard and Stevenson "evidently decided to act in concord" since both "had received similar instructions concerning the matter, i.e., that the Bulgarians should retire before the Greek advance and not offer resist-ance."

Dard and Stevenson now hurried to consult with the Italian chargé d'affaires, Weill Schott Leone. In line with his orders from the Quai d'Orsay, Dard explained to Leone that it was necessary to advise the Bulgarian Government not to oppose the Greek advance. Simultaneously, the three Powers would intervene in Athens to settle quickly an incident which otherwise could have the "gravest consequences." This view was also shared by Stevenson. The Italian chargé agreed, believing there were no obstacles involved in giving the Foreign Minister, Kristo Dimov Kalfoff, advice to be "calm [and] persuading him to defer [the] work [of] peace-maker to the Great Powers." In accord, the three diplomats went separately to the Bulgarian Foreign Ministry to talk with Kalfoff.

In his interview with the Foreign Minister, Leone, as agreed, advised calm. Kalfoff appeared to "welcome the recommendation," assuring the chargé that his government would make every effort "not to disturb the peace."

Virtually demilitarized under the Treaty of Neuilly, Bulgaria was really in no position to resist a Greek advance. Therefore, her first reaction was to make a general appeal and her second to ask for specific assistance. To her missions in Belgrade, Bucharest, London, Paris, and Rome, orders were issued requesting intervention with the government in Athens so that the military operations might be stopped. She declared at the same time that she was prepared to submit the incident to investigation by an impartial commission of inquiry.

As to specific assistance, Leone was asked personally by Kalfoff whether he would contact Mussolini to support a Bulgarian request that Rome intervene in Athens to stop the Greek advance. He was also asked whether Lieutenant Colonel Scanagatta, President of the Military Organ of Liquidation, could go immediately to the invaded zone to verify occurrences. A similar proposal to authorize the sending of the French and British delegates of the Military Organ of Liquidation was made to Dard and Stevenson. Further moves along these general lines were made the next day, October 23, when contact was established with the German Legation.

As the German Minister, Eugen Rümelin, explained to Berlin, Raschko Madjaroff, the Minister of Justice and an influential member of the Bulgarian cabinet, had addressed him by way of a third party and asked his personal advice as to what the government should do. Rümelin tendered the same advice as his British, French, and Italian colleagues: withdraw the Bulgarian troops in order not to spoil the present favorable impression held of Bulgaria abroad. Because of her demilitarization, military superiority was clearly on the Greek side, and therefore Sofia should concentrate on an "energetic political and press campaign abroad." Madjaroff, Rümelin added, was especially interested in ascertaining Chancellor Stresemann's personal interpretation of the whole situation. Stresemann agreed completely with Rümelin's advice to Madjaroff and felt that, despite Germany's friendship with Bulgaria, it was inadvisable to tender advice at this moment in view of the impending intervention of the League of Nations, which by this time had been appealed to by Sofia. Bulgarian cabinet feelers towards the Wilhelmstrasse had been stymied.

Unaware of the Greek advance on the morning of October 22, Rosetti was contacted by Minkoff "unofficially" by means of a "personal communication." The Secretary-General informed the chargé of the Greek action and relayed to him word that the Bulgarian Army had orders to withdraw five kilometers from the frontier in order to avoid any collision with the oncoming Greek Army. As to the demands of the Athens Government, which, telegraphed by Dantcheff, had now been received at the Foreign Ministry, Minkoff "considered [them] personally very severe."

A little later British chargé Stevenson, calling on Rosetti, revealed that he had advised the Bulgarian Government to issue orders to its military not to oppose the Greek advance, so as to avoid a pitched battle. By doing so, the Bulgarians would place themselves in an "advantageous position" vis-à-vis the Greeks in any subsequent settlement of the dispute. The Britisher also thought that by afternoon the Bulgarian Government would appeal to the League of Nations, asking its intervention for settlement of the question.

Rosetti's own reactions were immediately telegraphed to Athens following the dispatch of this message. Like Caftanzoglou, he too pleaded for moderation. He felt that since the Bulgars had already been taught a lesson and the border areas reoccupied, it would be good to stop the Greek advance and remain on the line retaken. Any further advance would perhaps weaken the Greek case and give the impression that another aim was being pursued: when provoked, Greece needed to occupy a portion of Bulgarian territory till it was given satisfaction.

Desirous of learning more about the Greek position, Rosetti was then visited by Lieutenant Colonel Scanagatta. The colonel divulged that he had had an interview that morning with the Minister of War, Colonel Ivan Volkoff. The latter, according to Scanagatta, had been very "uneasy" and had expressed to him his surprise at the events which had taken place. He was "grieved" that the incident occurred during a period when Greek-Bulgarian relations appeared to have improved. He then informed Scanagatta that he had given orders to the Bulgarian military to retreat without offering any resistance to the advancing Greeks. Scanagatta noted to the Greek chargé that though the army would obey he did not know what would be the "position [of the] powerful Macedonian organizations" (i.e., comitadjis), which the government in Sofia could not control. The Italian colonel feared that the Bulgars would ask the Allied Powers for increased military measures (i.e., mobilization). In an undoubted reference to Article 66 of the Treaty of Neuilly, he pointed out that the Bulgarian Army was assigned to border security but once that was violated, as the Greeks were violating it that very moment, the Bulgarian Government would be in a position to ask for increased military measures. Thus Scanagatta appeared to be saying that violation of the Bulgarian borders by the Greeks could perhaps justify a Bulgarian request for mobilization, though this was expressly forbidden under Article 68 of the Treaty of Neuilly. His own personal view was that the Greek invasion could perhaps provoke Yugoslav interference which in turn could produce "other general complications." Rosetti thought that the latter comment was an oblique hint of possible Italian intervention.

No sooner had Scanagatta departed than the Greek note, dispatched the previous night from Athens, arrived at the Greek Legation. Rosetti immediately hurried to the Foreign Ministry and presented a copy of the note, the contents of which were subsequently described by Sofia as *"quasi-ultimatifs,"* to the Foreign Minister. By this point it was 6:15 in the afternoon. It was Rosetti's first encounter with Kalfoff since the inception of the incident. The latter expressed his "sorrow" for what had occurred and reassured the chargé that from the beginning it was the desire of his government to settle the issue. When no reply, however, had been received from Athens to Sofia's proposals, but on the contrary it was learned that the Greek Army was advancing into Bulgarian territory on a 30 kilometer front, penetrating to a depth of 10 kilometers, and was bombarding Petrich, his government had turned to the League of Nations, whose decisions it would faithfully carry out. Since Petrich was an unfortified city, Kalfoff begged that the Greek Government order a cessation of fire. On these words the interview ended.

Dispatching his last message for the day, Rosetti related the *démarches* of the Allied representatives at the Bulgarian Foreign Ministry and made it clear to Athens that the decision of the Greek Government to advance into Bulgaria had "caused [an] unfavorable impression" among these representatives. He therefore repeated his opinion that it would be good to order a cease fire so as not to alienate the support of the Great Powers who might "come out diplomatically against us." He also revealed that Kalfoff had reassured the British chargé, Stevenson, that Bulgaria would continue its passive attitude, but if the Greeks enlarged their present position it would reconsider that attitude. At any rate, he promised to make no decisions without notifying the Allied representatives beforehand. With the filing of this message Rosetti's busy day had come to an end. The Bulgarians, demilitarized, without allies, and therefore defenseless, had turned to the League of Nations—the one organization they felt could offer them succor.

Kalfoff's message to the Secretary-General of the League of Nations, Sir Eric Drummond, first sketched Sofia's version of the incident and then noted that Bulgarian proposals for a mixed commission to establish responsibilities had remained unanswered by Athens. On the contrary Greek troops had advanced into Bulgarian territory, whose military had received orders not to resist. His appeal therefore protested "with all possible vehemence against the flagrant invasion" by the army of a League Member, of a country known to be disarmed. Thus, in virtue of Articles 10 and 11 of the Covenant, Kalfoff requested that Drummond convene the League Council "without delay to take the necessary steps." Convinced that the Council would do its duty, Sofia would maintain its orders to the Bulgarian troops not to resist the Greek advance.

Reactions in Geneva

The Greek note and the subsequent advance into Bulgaria as well as Kalfoff's appeal to Geneva had produced, like a pebble thrown into a calm pool, waves in concentric circles whose ripples touched cities and washed shores, until then unaffected by the events unfolding between Athens and Sofia.

The first city to manifest its anxieties was Geneva. On October 21, at a time the Dantcheff-Hadjikyriakos discussions were taking place and the Greek note was being drafted in the Foreign Ministry, the Greek chargé d'affaires in Berne, Vassili Dendramis, was telegraphing Athens that he observed "restlessness in League of Nations circles . . . regarding [the] Greek-Bulgarian border incident." He requested therefore that the Foreign Ministry immediately telegraph him the "dimensions" of the occurrence and whether the ministry foresaw any "serious consequences."

That night, Dendramis was telephoned from Geneva by Arthur Salter, Director of the Economic and Financial Section of the Secretariat, on orders from the Secretary-General, Sir Eric Drummond. This overture, it should be noted, was made well before Kalfoff's appeal to the League. According to Salter, information had reached the Secretariat via London that the Greek Government had handed the Bulgarians an "ultimatum" demanding a reply within forty-eight hours. The Secretary-General, however, asked that Athens be informed that he had every conviction that Greece wanted to "conform with [the] provisions [of the] Covenant [of the] League of Nations."

Athens' first reply was to the latter report and was dispatched on October 22, the very day Greek forces crossed the Bulgarian frontier. It informed Dendramis that no ultimatum had been sent to Sofia, but only a diplomatic note, "moderate" in tone, a copy of which had been forwarded to him.

In answer to Dendramis' first report, a second message was sent on October 23, a full day after the advance into Bulgaria. The Greek Government, the chargé was curtly informed, hoped the border incident would have no serious repercussions, "provided that Bulgaria accepts the terms of the diplomatic note delivered."

While these messages were heading towards Berne, Dendramis was urgently telegraphing Athens that the League's Secretary-General felt the "greatest disquiet" over the incident. The Director of the League's Political Section, Paul Mantoux, had telephoned him that Council members and especially Sweden's representative, Foreign Minister Östen Undén, had telegraphed the Secretary-General asking for information, so in case a threat or disturbance of the peace took place the Council would be in a position to take those "measures dictated by the Covenant."

The following day, October 23, at a time Kalfoff's appeal had not yet reached Geneva, Dendramis was reporting that the prevailing opinion in the League Secretariat was that, if the incident were not solved by diplomatic means and if Greek forces continued their advance to "enforce by arms [the] terms [of the] diplomatic note" sent to Sofia, Bulgaria or perhaps another power like Sweden would act in order that the Council urgently undertake the question under Articles 11 and 15 of the Covenant. In that case it would undoubtedly decide to send to the frontier an investigation committee. Dendramis then emphasized to Athens the most serious consequences that would arise should any Greek actions be contrary to the provisions of Articles 10 and 12 of the Covenant. He also warned that Athens "take into consideration [that] any invasion and occupation [of] Bulgarian territory without [a] previous appeal to [the] League of Nations will weaken [the] international position of Greece." Should Greece ignore the League, she would place herself in opposition to all other League Members. For the above reasons, the chargé opined, if the Bulgars refuse to satisfy Athens and if all means of settling the difference diplomatically are exhausted, then Greece should undertake the initiative and appeal to the League asking adjustment of the question on the basis of the terms proposed in Greece's note to Sofia.

The arrival of Kalfoff's appeal at Geneva prompted Dendramis urgently to contact Athens once again. If Athens desired, he telegraphed, to make Greece's position before the League Council strong and not have fall on its shoulders all "moral responsibility" for the incident and thus be found by the Council as having broken the Covenant, it was necessary that the Greek Army withdraw immediately to the Greek frontier. This would make it possible for the Greek representative to declare in any future Council debate that no Greek troops were to be found on Bulgarian territory.

To strengthen his case in Athens, Dendramis telegraphed soon after that an "English friend of ours [a] higher official" of the League Secretariat had recommended that the Greek Army withdraw from Bulgarian territory. Simultaneously, the Secretary-General was to be informed that the Greek Army, after reoccupying areas seized by the Bulgarian Army and safeguarding the national territory, had received orders to withdraw to Greek territory. The Secretary-General was also to be informed that the Greek Government would be represented at the next meeting of the League Council at Paris by a person to be soon designated. Only in this manner, Dendramis ended, could Greece's diplomatic position before the Council be strengthened.

Further impressions were reported by Dendramis soon after the dispatch of this last message. The Assistant Secretary-General, Joseph Avenol, in a conversation with Thanassis Aghnides, a senior Secretariat colleague, had "cautioned wisdom" to the Greek Government. Avenol noted that during the Corfu Incident two years before, a great deal of sympathy had been shown for Greece. He stressed that many dangers encircled her which had to be taken into consideration. He thought that Athens must "not think only for today but for tomorrow." If a tragic event were to occur to Greece the following day and resort were made to Geneva, it would be difficult for the League "to move international public opinion" in her favor if in the present situation it could not show an adjustment of the Greek position "toward [the] letter and the spirit [of the] Covenant of the League of Nations."

Consultations Among the Great Powers

Dendramis' advice, the anxieties of the Secretary-General, and the counsel of Avenol apparently made less of an impression on Athens than the words and admonitions of the Great Powers. During the first days, however, because of lags in communication the Powers were put in the unenviable position of merely reacting to events that had already occurred in Athens and Sofia.

On the morning of October 22, when news of the Greek advance into Bulgaria was yet unknown at the Foreign Office in London, the Foreign Secretary, Sir Austen Chamberlain, was visited by the Swedish Minister, Baron Erik-Kule Palmstierna. The minister had come to the Foreign Office on instructions from his government to express to Sir Austen the warmest congratulations of the Swedish Government and people for the success of the Locarno Conference. Chamberlain was gratified that the accomplishments of Locarno were as warmly approved by other nations as those which had been directly involved.

On instructions, Palmstierna then asked Sir Austen his views on the Greek-Bulgarian "quarrel" and whether he "proposed to bring the matter before the Council of the League of Nations, especially in view of the news of an ultimatum by Greece."

Sir Austen replied that his "information was at present too meager" to enable him to "take a decision." Such information as he had had from Greece led him "however to hope that the incident would not have dangerous results."

Palmstierna then asked whether Sir Austen thought that Stockholm should take action. Chamberlain could not reply until he had fuller information, but for the moment he did not "advise immediate reference to the League." Closing the interview, the minister asked that he be kept informed of Sir Austen's views. Chamberlain promised that the Foreign Office would keep in touch with him.

Words in a similar vein were expressed that same day to the Italian Ambassador, Marchese Pietro Tomasi della Torretta, by the Under-Secretary of the Foreign Office, Sir William Tyrrell. Torretta, who had gone to the Foreign Office ostensibly to elicit information on the occurrences between Greece and Bulgaria, was told by Tyrrell that no news had arrived at the

Foreign Office from Sofia and that the British Legation in Athens attached scarce importance to the event hinting in no way at an ultimatum and military measures. Sir William dismissed the frontier incident "as one of the many that are in the habit of taking place in Balkan countries." He added, however, that, if further information changed the picture, "he would propose to Chamberlain to enter into relation[s] immediately with the Cabinets [of] Rome and Paris in order to proceed to [an] exchange of ideas."

That same day the Foreign Office was visited by the Greek Minister, Demetrios Caclamanos, who appeared after news of the Greek advance into Bulgaria had reached London. He was attempting to forestall the effect of any Bulgarian communications to the Foreign Office. On arrival, he submitted a formal statement of the incident extracted from Greece's note addressed to Sofia the previous day.

Caclamanos' impression was that official English circles "recognized the responsibility" of Bulgaria for what had occurred and even the "justification" of the "decision to remove from the national territory these violators." Greece's military action, however, raised the fear that complications might arise, and there was agitation that the peace was being jeopardized. He feared that the Bulgars had deemed the moment opportune and the situation in the Balkans uneasy, and had initiated their attack against the Greek border at a spot near the Yugoslav border with the hope that complications would arise from which they could benefit. This fear, he added parenthetically, was not exclusively his. The minister also reminded Athens that the internal Bulgarian situation was "not at all pleasing." All these facts he was sure had not escaped the attention of the British Government. In London, it was generally thought that the solution of the incident could be to "bring [the] friendly intervention [of the] League of Nations," a thought being echoed in the articles of the evening newspapers.

Shortly after his departure from the Foreign Office, he was followed by the Bulgarian Minister who, as expected, gave the Bulgarian version of what occurred during the preceding days. Caclamanos, continuing his message, added that the British chargé d'affaires in Sofia had informed the Foreign Office that the Bulgars had proposed a commission of inquiry but no reply had been received from Athens. Lastly, he noted, newspaper correspondents in Sofia were maintaining that the Bulgarian Government would appeal to the League and that in order to protect its territory permission to mobilize had been asked from the Allied Powers.

Though accounts conflicted on which side responsibility rested, the question for the British Government was "to prevent what was apparently a frontier incident from developing into definite hostilities." Therefore, the British Legations in Athens and Sofia were instructed to offer "counsels of moderation to both sides" and urge them "to call an immediate truce in order that an enquiry may be held and time given for passions to cool." Requests were also made to Paris and Rome that similar instructions be given to the French and Italian Legations in Athens and Sofia and that they act in concert with their British colleagues in these two cities.

Thus the next morning, October 23, when Caclamanos returned to the Foreign Office to communicate a note from the Greek Foreign Ministry explaining the Greek advance into Bulgaria, he was informed that telegrams had been sent to the British representatives at Athens and Sofia. These instructions ordered them to take urgent steps with both governments advising "moderation" and recommending an immediate agreement for a cessation of hostilities. These steps, it was explained to him, would give time for passions to cool and an impartial investigation of the incident to take place. He was also told that a peaceful arrangement of the question coincided "not only with the desire of the Powers," but also with the interests of Greece. According to the Foreign Office, the Bulgarian Government would be advised to order the immediate evacuation of its troops from Greek territory as one of the important preconditions to help calm spirits.

At almost the same time in Rome, while Caclamanos was visiting the Foreign Office, the French Ambassador, René Besnard, appeared at the Italian Foreign Ministry. The purpose of his visit was to discuss with the Secretary-General, Salvatore Contarini, Italian participation in the projected measures of collectivizing the actions of the Powers towards Athens and Sofia.

In Paris, however, these measures of collectivization were being slightly altered because of unexpected events. The French Foreign Minister, Aristide Briand, in a conversation with the Italian Ambassador, Baron Camillo Romano Avezzana, related the steps being taken in Rome and London on the of the French Government towards a settlement of the dispute. At the same time Avezzana was informed by Briand that, as Acting President of the League Council, he might have to convene the Council at Paris for that coming Monday, October 26, "for the purpose of taking measures on the case." It would therefore appear that even *before* the arrival of Kalfoff's appeal, Briand was thinking of convening the League Council to help handle the question. Hence, the arrival of the appeal later that day requesting a convening of the Council seems to have coincided with Briand's own unannounced desires.

Briand's message to the Greek and Bulgarian Governments was short and to the point. The Secretary-General, he informed them, acting under Article 11, had convened a special session of the Council for Monday, October 26, at Paris. The question would be examined during that meeting, with Bulgarian and Greek representatives present. In the meantime, he reminded both Athens and Sofia of their solemn obligations as League Members under Article 12 of the Covenant, not to resort to war and the "grave consequences which [the] Covenant lays down for breaches thereof." Thus he exhorted both governments to give immediate orders that, pending examination of the dispute by the League Council, "not only no further movements shall be undertaken, but that troops shall at once retire behind their respective frontiers."

With the League now actively involved in the whole question, it was necessary to alter slightly the instructions sent to the French Ambassador, Besnard, in Rome. The new orders imparted by the Quai d'Orsay were that Besnard was to ask the Italian Government that its representatives at Athens and Sofia intervene collectively with their French and English colleagues in order "to stop immediately the hostilities and to entrust to the League of Nations the settlement of the conflict." Besnard explained to the Secretary-General, Contarini, that, though the Bulgars had asked that the French delegate on the Military Organ of Liquidation be sent to the invaded area to verify the facts, his government had decided against it. The French Government, according to Besnard, considered it preferable to entrust to the League any inquiry it might deem useful.

He further revealed that from information reaching him, it appeared that the Bulgarian Government would not send any reinforcements to the frontier until it had received replies from the Powers and the League of Nations. The French Minister in Sofia, however, feared that the Bulgarian military might not conform with these orders.

Besnard's overtures were not relayed by Mussolini to the Italian Missions until the following day, October 24. According to the Duce the formula proposed by the French Ambassador was in line with instructions already issued by the Italian Foreign Ministry and therefore acceptable. Because of the French decision declining to send their delegate on the Military Organ of Liquidation into the invaded zone, and Mussolini's desire undoubtedly to coordinate policies, the Italian chargé in Sofia was informed that the Bulgarian request to send Lieutenant Colonel Scanagatta to the invaded zone did not appear useful and would in fact be harmful.

Soon after Briand, as Acting President of the League Council, had sent his message to the Greek and Bulgarian Governments as well as new instructions to Besnard in Rome, he summoned the Greek Minister in Paris, Alexandros Carapanos, to the Quai d'Orsay. When Carapanos arrived, Briand recommended that in the interests of both countries "hostilities cease in the zone of conflict," orders having been given to the Bulgarians to withdraw their troops from Greek territory. He insisted on the profound impression caused by the bombardment of Petrich, which, according to news he had received from London, sharply moved the Foreign Office and the British public. In response, Carapanos emphasized the declarations of "pacific intentions" of his government, reserving to transmit Briand's recommendations to Athens; replying to him accordingly. Closing the interview, Briand inquired who would be designated to represent Greece at the Monday meeting of the League Council called to handle the frontier incident. Since Carapanos was in no position to answer, he turned to Athens for instructions.

Later that day, Carapanos charged the first secretary of the Greek Legation, Léon Melas, to communicate to the Director of Political Affairs, Jules
Laroche, and to the Director of Balkan Affairs, Charles Corbin, a note from
the Greek Foreign Ministry explaining the reasons for the Greek advance.
Melas was to explain the situation arising from the Bulgarian attack and
was to stress the peaceful intentions of his government. In the discussion
that followed, Laroche and Corbin did not conceal from Melas the "preoccu-
pation and uneasiness caused to the French Government [by the] alarming
situation provoked by the frontier incident which could involve very serious
consequences." They stated that "instead of recourse to pacific means for
settlement of the incident the Greek Government had [had] recourse to
force." Such procedure was surprising "on the morrow of the Locarno
Conference which had affirmed the pacific desire of the West." Thus the
French Government, faithful to its policy, followed with the greatest attention the development of events. "Deeply interested" in maintaining the
peace and desiring to prevent an armed clash between Greece and Bulgaria,
the Quai d'Orsay had "immediately arranged a common plan of action with
the English and Italian Governments in order that they charge their representatives at Athens to support the *démarche*" issued to the French Minister
at Athens. In Paris, it was explained to Melas, Briand had taken the initiative and immediately convened the League Council which would meet there
that coming Monday. This action of the French Foreign Minister had been
taken *before* the Bulgarian Government's appeal had brought the question
to the League of Nations.

Carapanos observed to Athens that considering what had been told
Melas, and despite the assurances of the Greek Government, the attitude of
the French Government remained "unfavorable to us."

A similar atmosphere prevailed in London. To underscore the concern
attached to the whole question by the Foreign Office, Caclamanos later that
day informed Athens that Sir Austen Chamberlain, the Foreign Secretary,
would go in person to the forthcoming Council session at Paris as England's
representative. This somewhat unusual step must have impressed Athens
and Sofia with the seriousness with which the situation was viewed by the
British Government and especially the Foreign Secretary.

This telegram was immediately followed by another from Caclamanos.
According to information given to him at the Foreign Office, the English
Government, desiring to prevent a simple frontier incident from degenerating into serious hostilities, had asked Paris and Rome that their representatives "intervene at Athens and Sofia in the same sense as the English
representative[s]." Thus the Great Powers, after a momentary delay, began
to coordinate their policies, which because of similar interests fortuitously
coincided. As Torretta subsequently and succinctly expressed it to the Foreign Office, he was satisfied, "for [the] identity of views and action existing
between the Cabinets [of] London and Rome."

Démarches in Athens and Sofia

While these events were transpiring between London, Paris, and Rome from the afternoon of October 22 until the following afternoon, other actions were taking place in Athens and Sofia.

On the morning of October 23 in Athens, the French Minister, Count Charles de Chambrun, and the British chargé d'affaires, Sir Milne Cheetam, called at the Italian Legation on the chargé d'affaires, Domenico de Facendis. Undoubtedly acting on orders sent the previous night they informed Facendis of their governments' instructions: for each to contact his two other colleagues in order to take joint steps towards the Greek Government, advising "moderation" in the current dispute with the Bulgars.

They asked Facendis therefore whether he had received instructions along these lines and whether he were inclined to act in a similar sense. Facendis replied that he had not yet received orders from Rome, but interpreting Mussolini's thoughts which were always directed towards peace, he found no difficulty in associating himself with his French and English colleagues, advising "calm and moderation" to the Greeks in their present dispute.

Apparently satisfied with Facendis' reply, Chambrun and Cheetam hurried together to the Foreign Ministry, with the Italian chargé following soon after. While waiting for the Foreign Minister, Hadjikyriakos, Facendis met Dantcheff who explained that he had come to inform the Foreign Minister that, following the Greek advance into Bulgaria, his government had turned to the League of Nations.

Facendis' interview commenced immediately upon Cheetam's exit from Hadjikyriakos' office. As expected, the Foreign Minister repeated the Greek case made in Athens' note to Sofia, and explained that to dislodge the Bulgarians from Greek territory, the military had decided to avoid a frontal attack which would have resulted in great loss of life, and instead chose to skirt the Bulgarian line thus forcing the Bulgars to retire or be surrounded.

Facendis observed that he had learned of the government's moderation in drawing up its note to Sofia and had been favorably impressed by this action. He had no doubts, he added, that the government would continue to be inspired by a desire for "moderation of action" and for the "serenity of judgment necessary" in order not to disturb the peace, which was ardently desired by all. Hadjikyriakos assured Facendis that his government wished nothing from Bulgaria and asked only to be allowed to live in peace. It did not wish to be molested repeatedly by the troops of the regular Bulgarian Army, much less by comitadjis—actions for which the government in Sofia was responsible. He felt that Greece had suffered an unexpected aggression and invasion of its territory and was obligated to defend itself. According to the Foreign Minister, Athens had a right to ask for a modest indemnity for the lives of the Greek soldiers unjustly murdered and his government would not fail to defend itself before the League of Nations, if it were asked by Geneva to state its reasons for invading Bulgaria.

In Sofia that same day somewhat similar moves were unfolding. Perhaps aware that negotiations were still proceeding in Rome for Italian participation, the British and French representatives did not call on their colleague as they had in Athens. As the Secretary-General, Minkoff, explained to the Italian chargé, the Anglo-French representatives had invited the Bulgarian Government "to abstain in [a] positive manner from any resistance or act that will complicate more the already grave situation." Minkoff ominously warned Leone that though the Cabinet had confirmed the orders to the military to retire without offering resistance, the Great Powers had to convince themselves that the Bulgarian troops would not continue to endure passively the Greek advance. In fact, the Macedonian population of the invaded region could at any moment revolt against the Greeks, provoking a conflict of greater proportions. The Cabinet, he revealed, had also refused to discuss with Athens its ultimatum as long as Greek troops had not evacuated Bulgarian territory. According to Minkoff, the government entrusted a solution of the conflict to the League and the Great Powers. The latter could help by immediately intervening at Athens in order to make the Greeks halt their advance.

The decision of the Bulgarian Government to continue its passive position was immediately relayed to Athens by the Greek chargé, Rosetti. Ever watchful of events as they developed in Sofia, he also divulged that his English colleague, Stevenson, had learned from the Foreign Office that the "English Government [had] telegraphed [to] Rome [and] Paris [in order] that [the] three Powers intervene [collectively at] Sofia [and] Athens. In line with their orders the Allied representatives had that afternoon, the twenty-third, called on the Foreign Minister, Kalfoff, and transmitted their governments' views. The Foreign Minister informed them that Bulgaria's stance would change only if the Greek Army attempted to attack with greater force. The Yugoslav chargé, Rosetti also telegraphed Athens, who had spoken with Kalfoff, had the impression that the Bulgarians would maintain their passive position "if we stop our advance." The Yugoslav's personal view was that, since Greece had already given the Bulgars a lesson, any further military action would only "impair Greece's diplomatic position." He also revealed to Rosetti that in conversation with the representatives of the Great Powers they had "adversely" criticized the Greek attitude.

Later that same day after all these messages had been dispatched to Athens, Rosetti received from the Bulgarian Foreign Ministry a reply to the Greek note of the previous day. As expected, the Bulgars denied in the "most categorical manner" the origins of the border incident as developed in Athens' note. Taking into consideration, however, that between both governments there was dispute as to fact, the Bulgarian Government had proposed from the very first that a commission *ad hoc* be instituted to proceed with an impartial inquiry. This proposition was proffered twice to the Greek chargé d'affaires at Sofia and once to the government in Athens by the Bulgarian chargé d'affaires. Simultaneously, the government in Sofia had requested that "categorical orders" be given to both sides in order to stop the firing along the frontier. Unfortunately, this proposition had never been answered. Instead, Greek troops in considerable numbers had crossed the Bulgarian frontier attacking on a 32 kilometer front and penetrating to a depth of about 12 kilometers. This invasion of the territory of a friendly nation, a League Member and a country well known to be disarmed, "was accompanied by veritable acts of war"; including the use of infantry, artillery, and aircraft.

Because of the situation that had developed, the Bulgarian Government thought it necessary to appeal to the League of Nations, invoking Articles 10 and 11 of the Covenant, and asking for an immediate convening of the Council to deal with the situation. While waiting for the Council's decision and because the Greek Army continued to occupy Bulgarian soil, the government in Sofia, to its great regret, found it impossible to "enter into direct negotiations with the Greek Government." On these grounds, to wit, the impossibility of direct talks between Greece and Bulgaria because the League was considering the issue, Sofia refused to reply to subsequent notes from Athens tendered by Rosetti on October 23, 24, and 25.

Greece's Reply to Geneva

Thus, Bulgarian acceptance of Briand's appeal the following day, October 24, was a foregone conclusion. Kalfoff expressed "deep gratitude" on behalf of his government for the speed with which the League Council and Secretariat had acted. His own government, conscious of its obligations as a League Member, had from the inception of the incident "given the strictest orders" to the Bulgarian military to "take no action which might make the situation worse." "Fresh instructions" in this sense had been immediately repeated in accordance with Briand's communication, though Greek territory had not been violated by the Bulgarian Army. Concluding, Kalfoff pointed out that Greek troops were still on Bulgarian soil and their artillery was bombarding the open city of Petrich. Protesting against this behavior he begged Briand to "intervene as soon as possible."

The Greek reply of that same day, in spite of the *démarches* of the Great Powers, was not a complete acceptance of Briand's appeal. Hadjikyriakos felt that Sofia's version was in contradiction with the actual facts and that "the sudden and unprovoked character of the Bulgarian aggression" was obvious. His government therefore had to "allow its military command to take all measures considered necessary for the defence and, if necessary, the clearance of its national territory," at that very moment still occupied by Bulgarian forces. Orders at the same time had been issued that bloodshed should be avoided and the population safeguarded if the defensive measures of the Greek Army led to military operations on Bulgarian territory. However, Hadjikyriakos noted, at that very moment Bulgarian fire continued "with the purpose of preventing us from re-occupying our two frontier posts." When these posts have been re-occupied and the whole area freed, "our troops will withdraw on to our frontier lines, provided that no fresh intervention of regular troops or [comitadjis] bands takes place." The Greek Government therefore felt that the measures undertaken by its military were nothing more than "measures of legitimate defence and could not be considered as hostile acts likely to lead to a rupture in accordance with the terms of Article 12 of the Covenant."

Because of this, Article 12 could not be invoked in the present question. Nevertheless, Hadjikyriakos ended, Athens, "strong and confident in the justice of its cause and in deference to the League of Nations, will . . . accept the competence of the Council in this matter."

Later that same day in Paris, Jules Laroche in a discussion with the Greek Minister, Carapanos, recommended that Athens accept a solution by the League Council. He pointed out that the Bulgarian declaration not to oppose the advance of the Greek forces as long as they did not exceed their present line of occupation, had produced among "official circles [a] good impression." Replying to Laroche, Carapanos limited himself merely to re-iterating the reports of his government refuting the Bulgarian charges. The minister's own impression was that the interview had been dictated by Geneva which felt "uneasiness" over Hadjikyriakos' unclear reply.

From London, the Greek Minister was also reporting important and interesting information. According to the general notions prevailing in the British capital, Caclamanos telegraphed Athens, the League Council would insist on both nations withdrawing their forces across their respective frontiers. Simultaneously, a neutral zone would be fixed and a neutral military committee appointed to investigate the incident. The question of damages, he explained, would be examined only after the report of the committee had been issued. His second telegram, however, contained an ominous warning. A member of the Cabinet, Lord Robert Cecil, Caclamanos reported, had given a speech in Scotland touching on the dispute. According to Cecil, both were honorable countries and League Members. He was convinced that in the desire to fulfill their obligations—accepting discussion or arbitration before the League of Nations—they would never resort to war. However, if war did come, the League was duty bound to "take measures against the attacker." The first measure would be the breaking of diplomatic relations with the attacking state by all fifty-two members of the League. If the attacking state still did not yield, the next step would be to halt all commercial relations. Lord Robert hoped and believed that neither Athens nor Sofia would "break the Covenant [of the] League of Nations," but if this were done, the League would quickly apply Article 16 of the Covenant. Since the speech had been made by one of Greece's staunchest supporters during the

Corfu Incident of two years before, English determination to use the League machinery if matters further deteriorated could only have impressed Athens and the Greek Foreign Ministry.

Advice that the Greeks submit completely to the League Council was also reported by Rosetti from Sofia. The French Minister, Émile Dard, in conversation with him, had maintained that the interests of Greece unquestionably were to "conform" with Briand's appeal, "establishing thus her diplomatic position." These same thoughts had also been echoed by the British chargé, Stevenson. Rosetti further reported that his Yugoslav colleague had expressed the view that once the League undertook the question, the continuation of military measures by Greece was harmful to her interests and galvanized world public opinion against her. Moreover, in Sofia's diplomatic circles, Greek actions were being criticized "adversely" especially after Hadjikyriakos' evasive telegram to Briand. As to the internal Bulgarian situation, Rosetti anxiously noted that according to information reaching him, King Boris had appealed to the Macedonians to listen to the orders of the government as Bulgaria went through this "critical hour."

While Rosetti was reporting to Athens, across the city his Italian colleague, Weill Schott Leone, was communicating with Rome. He revealed to Mussolini that both Dard and Stevenson were keeping him abreast of the instructions and reports that they received from their respective governments, and that for his part he was maintaining continuous contact with them.

The arrival of Mussolini's earlier instructions of that day, to act in concert with the French and British representatives, propelled the Italian chargé to seek an immediate interview with Minkoff at the Foreign Office. On arrival Leone repeated his previous "counsel for moderation." He explained that Rome, in company with Paris and London, while requesting the Bulgarian Government to maintain an attitude of calm, had also turned to Athens in order to resolve the incident in a just manner. Replying, Minkoff stated that his government had gone the limit in showing calm. He revealed to Leone that an hour before he had received notice from the Bulgarian General Staff that the Greeks had that morning resumed the bombardment of Petrich and other villages. He pointed out that Sofia responding to the message sent by Briand "had once again manifested its deep desire for peace and its trust in [the] work of the League of Nations." Ending his report to Rome, Leone noted that Minkoff gave great prominence to the fact that the resumed artillery fire was concentrated on defenseless villages and territory.

In Athens, Facendis like Leone also received his instructions dispatched earlier that day and informed his French and English colleagues accordingly. He felt that the advice for moderation collectively recommended by the Great Powers to the Greeks had not been without effect and that the incident could be said to have passed the "critical and disquieting stage." He reported that acts of hostility had ceased and that by Hadjikyriakos' telegram to Briand the question had been "deferred to the examination and judgment of the League of Nations."

Facendis' optimistic predictions, however, were premature as events on the Greek-Bulgarian frontier, as well as between London and Sofia, revealed.

Ominous Warnings from Sofia

At Whitehall that afternoon, the Bulgarian Minister, Pontcho Hadji Misheff, appeared at the Foreign Office with a telegram from Sofia dated the previous night, October 23. In effect the telegram alleged that Greek forces were still moving forward, east of the river Struma. Under these circumstances the Bulgarian Government was afraid of incidents developing for which they would have to disclaim all responsibility. Sofia therefore begged that the British Government pressure Athens to suspend all forward movement of its troops. The Foreign Office, however, in reply cautioned Misheff that previous orders to the Bulgarian military not to resist, should not be rescinded. These instructions, provided they were reported correctly, had strengthened the Bulgarian position. He was reminded that in Sofia's original appeal to Geneva, it had been emphatically stated that the orders of non-resistance had been affirmed. Thus, any modification of these orders would be "most unfortunate." In reply, the Bulgarian Minister denied that any such action was intended.

It was also pointed out to Misheff that the whole question was now in the hands of the League Council and therefore it was difficult for "an individual Government to take further action as suggested by the Bulgarian Government." Briand had reminded both nations in his telegram of their obligations as League Members under Article 12 of the Covenant not to go to war and the grave consequences that would result from any violations under the terms of the Covenant. Moreover, the "British, French and Italian representatives both at Athens and Sofia had general instructions to exercise such restraining influence upon both sides as was possible." Because of the above reasons, the Foreign Office thought it unnecessary to dispatch further instructions to Athens as desired by Sofia.

Some hours after Misheff's interview at the Foreign Office, further information was received from Stevenson in Sofia "indicating a danger that, if the Greek troops were to advance further, the local situation might get out of hand and a general conflict be precipitated."

It seems that at eight o'clock that morning "all desultory firing as the Bulgarians had been engaging in totally ceased." Later in the afternoon "the Greeks were observed to be packing up," and the Bulgarian Foreign Ministry was reporting that the incident was over. However, at 5:30 in the late afternoon Greek artillery fire was resumed. It appeared after examination by the Yugoslav military attaché in Sofia, Colonel Milkovitch, that the Bulgarians were preventing the Greeks from occupying their frontier posts until a neutral commission could examine the spot to ascertain on which side of the frontier line the corpse of the Greek sentry originally killed, was to be found.

Stevenson's fears were well justified on at least two counts: first, the fear of a Macedonian uprising mirrored in the apprehensions of King Boris and Minkoff, and secondly, the continuing military preparations of the Bulgarian Army as well as the movements of comitadjis bands towards the area of conflict. The arrival of Stevenson's telegram spurred the Foreign Office to send new instructions to Cheetam, its chargé d'affaires in Athens, "instructing him to see his Italian and French colleagues at once and to tell them of the information received by His Britanic Majesty's Government" and of the request made by Misheff in London. Cheetam was also "instructed to ask for the support of his Italian and French colleagues in warning the Greek Government of the folly of any forward movement of their troops" pending a decision by the League Council. In the opinion of the British Government, Athens had to realize that any contravention of the provisions of Article 12 of the League Covenant "might well have the most serious consequences for them."

On the following day, October 25, similar information of the deteriorating situation was urgently flashed to Rome by the Italian chargé, Leone. According to Leone he had been informed both by the Bulgarian Foreign Ministry and the General Staff at 6:30 in the morning that Greek forces were still holding all positions and maintaining their artillery fire. Minkoff reassured the chargé that the Bulgarian military continued their passive posture. Nevertheless, Leone reported to the Palazzo Chigi that information had come to his attention that further Bulgarian reinforcements were on their way to the place of conflict. He therefore thought it necessary to act at Athens with the greatest speed, "since the situation could from one moment to the next become worse."

Later that day, Dard, Stevenson, and Leone trooped once again to the Bulgarian Foreign Ministry to ascertain the intentions of the Bulgarian Government. According to the Greek chargé, Rosetti, the collective step of the three representatives were due to the initiative of the British chargé, Stevenson. The Foreign Minister, Kalfoff, declared to the threesome that his government would quickly order the withdrawal of Bulgarian troops from the two posts firing on the abandoned Greek border station. This would be done, however, as soon as verification by a neutral party could be made of exactly which side of the border the body of the slain Greek sentry lay.

This declaration by Kalfoff was immediately telegraphed by the French Minister, Dard, to Briand, requesting that it also be brought to the attention of Chamberlain and Italy's League delegate, Vittorio Scialoja. Dard's proposal was that Lieutenant Colonel Scanagatta, the President of the Military Organ of Liquidation, and another person might be designated by the League of Nations as the neutrals desired by Kalfoff.

Late that evening in a conversation with Leone, Dard opined that in case the conflict worsened the League of Nations would be in a position to exert "pressure" on Greece by "granting the mandate to a Great Power of blockading an Aegean port" or perhaps an island like Mytilene. As to the Bulgars, Yugoslavia or Rumania could be entrusted to occupy some "important point of Bulgarian territory." However, no penetration by Yugoslavia in the direction of Salonika was envisaged.

Somewhat analogous sentiments were expressed by Stevenson, who informed his American colleague "that should the Greeks refuse the arbitration of the League his Government stood ready to utilize their Mediterranean Fleet in order to bring them to their senses." He felt that if no definite understanding could be quickly arrived at, "all the work of the Locarno Conference would appear futile, and Britain had no idea of allowing that to take place."

Fortunately for Athens, these threats never evolved into physical actions even though the following day the League Council convened and the pressures on Athens increased. This time, however, the pressures of the Great Powers were channeled through the League of Nations and disguised as the intended actions of the world organization. It was to these pressures that Greece inevitably succumbed.

The Council Convenes

The Council's first meeting dealing with the incident was held, as scheduled, in Paris on Monday, October 26, at 6 P.M. The meeting was public. As Acting President of the Council, Briand dominated the discussions. His proposal was that the Council should hear from the Greek and Bulgarian representatives as to what actions their respective governments were taking "with regard to the cessation of hostilities and the withdrawal of troops and what is the present situation?"

The reply of the Bulgarian delegate, the ambassador in Paris, Bogdan Marfoff, was that "at no moment and at no point has Greek territory been invaded or occupied" by Bulgar forces. Furthermore, Sofia was ready to submit to an inquiry on this point.

Greece's delegate was also its ambassador in Paris. Carapanos was in an unenviable position. Though his government agreed without hesitation in complying with Briand's invitation to Athens to evacuate Bulgarian territory, it would do so "as soon as the Bulgarians have quitted Greek territory" —a major qualification.

At this point Briand called a private meeting of the Council to examine the situation, Chamberlain being invited to act as rapporteur. After an exchange of views between the different delegations, Carapanos and Marfoff were invited to the Council's private session, at which a draft resolution drawn up by Chamberlain was approved. The same resolution was later adopted in a public meeting of the Council which immediately followed.

Chamberlain's resolution began by approving Briand's prior communication to both countries. However, the Council was not satisfied that military operations had ceased and that the troops had been withdrawn behind their respective national frontiers. It therefore requested Carapanos and Marfoff to inform the Council within twenty-four hours that unconditional orders had been given to their forces to "withdraw behind their respective national frontiers." Within sixty hours all forces were to be withdrawn within their own frontiers, all hostilities to have ceased and all troops warned that resumption of firing would be severely punished.

To assist the Council and the two States, it was requested that the Governments of London, Paris, and Rome direct their officers who were within reach to proceed quickly to the area of conflict and to report directly to the League Council as soon as the troops of both States had been withdrawn and hostilities had ceased. Lastly, Athens and Sofia were requested to afford to these officers all facilities that would be required for the execution of their mission.

Asked by Briand whether he had any objections to raise, Marfoff replied that he was authorized to declare that Sofia was ready to comply with the terms of the resolution passed. Carapanos unfortunately was not in a position as secure as his Bulgarian colleague. Though he had no objections to the terms of the resolution, he was bound to forward the terms to Athens, "which would, he was convinced, comply with them."

Before closing the meeting Chamberlain made the point which was agreed to by his Council colleagues, that the time limit stipulated in the resolution would begin from the present session.

To cover all loopholes Briand made it clear both to Carapanos and Marfoff that the essential point was to stop the firing, which meant that the troops upon their withdrawal across the frontier had to cease "all acts of hostility." The adjournment of the Council prompted Carapanos to send an urgent telegram to Athens requesting that immediate instructions be forwarded to him so that he would be in a position to "reply within [the] time [limit] allowed."

Rumanian and Turkish Attempts at Mediation

While the Council was convening in Paris, attempts to solve the dispute were also undertaken that same day in Athens and Sofia by the Rumanian Government. At the inception of the dispute it had been explained to the Greek Minister in Bucharest, Constantine Collas, that the Rumanian Government desired that the incident be regulated peacefully and as quickly as possible in order that the "peace of the Balkans may not be troubled."

In line with this desire the Secretary-General of the Foreign Ministry outlined to Collas in a subsequent conversation the attitude and opinions of the Rumanian Government. According to the Secretary-General the frontier incident "had not been dictated by [Bulgarian] sentiments of enmity" towards Greece. He was certain that Sofia "had no interest in troubling the peace" at the very moment it was striving to consolidate its own position.

Because of these reasons, Bucharest, anxious that all incidents originating in the Balkans be regulated in a friendly manner so that the peace not be disturbed, had "given instructions to its Ministers at Sofia and at Athens to mediate before the respective Governments in order to make known [the] point of view [of the] Rumanian Government and to arrive [at a] pacific settlement of the frontier incident."

Toward this end the Rumanian Minister in Athens, Langa Rascano, on the morning of October 26, approached the Greek Government. The three propositions tendered by Rascano to General Pangalos, the Prime Minister, and Caftanzoglou, the Secretary-General of the Foreign Ministry, were accepted with alacrity. They were also communicated to the Bulgarian chargé, Dantcheff, as well as to Bucharest and Paris.

Rascano's proposals stipulated that a Greek and Bulgarian staff-officer proceed the following day at four in the afternoon to Demir-Kapu to place the Greek frontier guards at their respective posts. This action accomplished, the Greek forces occupying Bulgarian territory would commence their withdrawal into Greek territory as quickly as possible. Finally, during the withdrawal of the Greek forces the Bulgarian military facing them would not advance until the Greeks had crossed the frontier.

In Sofia, attempts to solve the dispute were advanced by the Turkish Government which wanted to know whether there were a possibility of arranging the incident "by a mixed commission of inquiry." Kalfoff's reply was that since the League Council was considering the issue, the Bulgarian Government found it impossible to enter into direct negotiations with the Greek Government. A similar reply was transmitted by Minkoff to the Rumanian Minister who had inquired whether Rascano in Athens could not intervene to help in settling the dispute. However, since Rascano had already made his overtures and the Greek Government had dispatched a senior officer to Demir-Kapu to effect a meeting with a Bulgarian officer, Sofia, out of courtesy, ordered on October 27 a Bulgarian senior officer, Colonel Zlateff, also to proceed to the border. In the presence of foreign journalists Zlateff made it clear to his Greek counterpart that he could not negotiate with him since the whole question was in the hands of the League Council and would be regulated by that body.

Discussions of Sanctions

Disclosure of Rumania's endeavors by Carapanos at the Council's Tuesday morning session prompted Briand to observe that the situation had not changed in any way, and hope that Athens would reply to the Council's communication. He noted that in its agreement with the Rumanian Government, Greece "had made certain reservations which appeared to attach conditions and which were in contradiction with the text of the decision of the Council." Briand undoubtedly was referring to the phrase in Hadjikyriakos' telegram to Carapanos that Greece had stipulated "as a *sine qua non* that it [would] evacuate Bulgarian territory only after the Bulgarians had retreated from the Greek post [of] Demir-Kapu which they continued to occupy."

In reply, Carapanos observed that an agreement had been concluded between the two interested parties to which conditions had been added. However, these conditions were agreed to by both sides. Therefore, they "were not conditions in the precise sense of the word, but rather methods proposed for carrying out the evacuation." Briand had no objection to a bilateral agreement. But the problem at the moment, regardless of any desire to come to an agreement, was that the firing continued. As long as this situation persisted nothing could be achieved. Thus, it was hoped that later news would be "entirely satisfactory." In the meantime he invited statements from both Marfoff and Carapanos.

Marfoff's talk was merely a long reiteration of the Bulgarian version of the events of the past week. Carapanos' remarks which followed, dictated by instructions from Athens, were also a mere repetition of all previous Greek arguments. In one respect, however, they proved to be of greater interest. Carapanos insisted that there had not been on the side of Athens "any hostile act 'likely to lead to a rupture' within the terms of Article 12 of the Covenant." This argument, though at first glance questionable, appears on closer examination to be valid. Certainly, diplomatic relations between the Greeks and Bulgars had not been severed and Carapanos, if he had wanted to, could have pointed to the Corfu Incident of two years earlier where an analogous situation had developed between Greece and Italy and yet relations had continued undisturbed.

In his report to Athens describing the day's events, Carapanos found it necessary to stress that the "atmosphere" at the Council session was not friendly towards Greece's position. He again begged for instructions, warning that the time limit stipulated by the Council the previous day would elapse that evening. In conclusion, he felt obliged to accent the "important consequences" that could develop, should Athens either reject the Council's request or reply to it tardily.

If Carapanos had been aware of the private and informal meeting of the Council members held at 5 P.M. that afternoon, his report to Athens would perhaps have been even more pressing. At this meeting, Vittorio Scialoja, Italy's Council representative, asked his colleagues to consider what action they could take in the dispute under Article 16 of the Covenant. Replying, the Secretary-General, Sir Eric Drummond, pointed out that the League Assembly had proposed in 1921 that under Article 16, the first action should be the withdrawal of diplomatic representatives. Briand contended that the mere withdrawal of ambassadors would appear "too feeble." As he expressed it, "if the leak were not stopped up at once there might be a flood." To Briand, Rumanian intervention was merely an attempt "to mask the League's action." If Greece's attitude were to continue "it was essential for the Council to act at once and to act strongly." Though Chamberlain agreed that at the proper moment the Council should act with vigor and dispatch, he felt it should do so according to the Covenant.

As to specific details, Scialoja asked whether economic or military measures should be applied. Undoubtedly with Greece's extended coast line and innumerable islands in mind, his own inclination was for the latter alternative in the form of a naval demonstration which he thought would be most effective.

Briand felt that the objection to a blockade was that it would affect both innocent and guilty. However, if the Council did act under Article 16, its action had to be quick, strong and decisive. He noted that one of the greatest arguments against the world organization was that its enforcement machinery was slow and clumsy. Regardless of his colleagues' arguments, Sir Austen was not moved. He believed a Greek decision rejecting the Council's overtures to be impossible. At any rate, if there were a rejection, he felt that a blockade was an unnecessarily large action in such a situation. Meanwhile, he thought it unnecessary to take a decision. After some closing remarks by Briand, the Council members agreed, at least for the moment, that it would make no moves with regard to possible action under Article 16 of the Covenant.

Nevertheless, the possibility of a naval demonstration against the Greeks led the League Secretariat to engage in "unofficial discussions as to the form, and legal authority, under which, if the need arose, such action should be taken." These discussions, however, proved to be in vain. For as Chamberlain had prophesied, the Greeks soon gave in to Council pressure.

Athens' surrender took place at the Council's morning session the following day, Wednesday, October 28. The Bulgarian representative, Marfoff, as was to be expected, communicated a telegram he had received from Sofia the previous day agreeing to the Council's resolution. According to Kalfoff's message, "strict orders" had been given to the Bulgarian military to cease all military action "either within Bulgarian territory or along the frontier." At the same time renewed orders had been sent to the Bulgarian Army to "withdraw immediately any Bulgarian troops which may be on Greek territory."

Diplomatically isolated and with the threat of sanctions looming on the horizon, the Greek Government was in no position to resist. Thus, according to Carapanos, the Government in Athens, after receipt of the Council's resolution, had only repeated and confirmed its previous instructions to the Greek military to evacuate Bulgarian territory. These orders had been given in conformity with the Rumanian offer of mediation communicated to the League previously.

Wishing assurance that there was no misunderstanding, Briand turned and asked Carapanos whether this meant "that the Greek Government had given orders that all hostilities should cease?" Carapanos replied affirmatively. Did the telegram also imply, Briand asked, that Athens would facilitate the task of the officers proceeding to the area of conflict. Undoubtedly, responded the Greek delegate. Noting with satisfaction that the first part of the Council's resolution had been accepted by Greece and Bulgaria, Briand observed that the second part of the resolution "allowed a period of 60 hours within which the orders had to be not only issued but also carried out."

Doubtlessly fearing that the second part of the Council's resolution might not be executed, Carapanos, in an urgent and detailed telegram to Athens describing the day's events, warned that in such a situation the League might "adopt against Greece Article 16 [of the] Covenant calling for [a] complete economic blockade [of the] country."

What followed was an anti-climax. Heeding Carapanos' appeal, Hadji-kyriakos the following day informed Briand that Athens, desiring to conform to the Council's decision, had "repeated its definite orders" hastening the withdrawal of Greek forces toward the frontier in spite of harassment by armed Bulgarian bands. Most important, it would "neglect no steps to ensure that the [sic] Bulgarian territory is evacuated by the hour laid down." During this session, and the following session, verification by the Allied military attachés dispatched from Belgrade, that the Greeks were evacuating Bulgarian territory, brought the Greek-Bulgarian Incident to a close.

Conclusions

The uniqueness of the Covenant of the League of Nations over all previous attempts at international organization was its provision for collective security. This aspect of the world organization strongly appealed to people of good will and was often cited to justify the very establishment of the organization.

To many, collective security was attractive because it seemed a great improvement over the anarchic system of alliances and coalitions which had previously flourished and which were viewed by many as largely responsible for the First World War. It was argued that since collective security was directed against no specific power, it was friendly to all, and especially to the weak. However, . . . there were difficulties in implementing the League's collective security arrangements; difficulties that stimulated discussion during the Greek-Bulgarian Incident and caused hardships during the Ethiopian Crisis a decade later.

Though collective security was the most important feature of the League and its weapon of last resort, the organization in practice attempted to circumscribe and restrict the traditional right of a state to resort to war—a right which prior to the First World War was perfectly legal under accepted norms of international law. The actions and procedures of the League thus resembled regulations rather than interdictions. It tried to limit a nation's right to war by compelling initial recourse to the measures of pacific settlement stipulated in the Covenant: arbitration, conciliation, and judicial settlement.

The founders of the League of Nations did not establish a super-state; they established a super-association. The basic unit of organization in the League—as in the United Nations—was the state which surrendered not one iota of its sovereignty. The organization was not established to change the world. Its primary task was to make the League machinery for peaceful settlement readily available to all nations; secondly, it was to assist these nations in the task of peaceful settlement; finally, by the creation of permanent rather than *ad hoc* institutions for peaceful change, it was to help build a system of international cooperation and so maintain the peace of the world.

The underlying assumption, however, on which this whole edifice for peaceful settlement rested, was that all nations—and particularly the Great Powers—would be willing and desirous of using the machinery of the League in disputes directly involving them. They would do this because disinterested foreign policies would be followed, in which nations would be guided by community interests rather than power considerations. In actual practice, though nations realized the value and possibilities of cooperation through the League of Nations and attempted whenever possible to integrate the world organization into their policies, they did not do this at the expense of what they considered their vital national interests. Unfortunately, the feeling of a world community was too abstract to warrant sacrifices for nations close by or far away. This feeling was particularly noticeable when discussions in the Council and Assembly of the League centered around the problem of applying the organization's enforcement machinery against an aggressor state. In these discussions, unless the interests of the powers—and especially the Great Powers—coincided; unless there were a direct and immediate interest among the major powers to thwart an aggressor state, League action was doomed to failure. . . .

Thus, when Great Power cooperation was not forthcoming decisive action against any nation proved virtually impossible. The requirement that substantive Council action be unanimous only increased the difficulties of the world organization and made Great Power agreement imperative.

The League could therefore be no more successful than the Great Powers were willing to make it. If there were disagreement among the Great Powers outside the League, it would almost automatically be reflected within the organization. . . .

The Corfu Incident of 1923 was the first occasion during which it became clear that the League could not operate successfully without Great Power agreement. Mussolini's bombardment and occupation of this defenseless Greek island found Anglo-French policy divided. Though the English were willing to bring the matter to the Council, the French were not. The feeling in the Quai d'Orsay was that if the Greek appeal over Corfu could be allowed to come to the League Council, a precedent would perhaps be established for a German appeal concerning the French occupation of the Ruhr; an occupation which had commenced in January of that same year.

Subsequent realization by the British that they were militarily overextended in the Mediterranean, plus the rejection of Foreign Office overtures in Paris for a joint British-French naval demonstration, forced Whitehall to compromise the issue outside the League.

The Greek-Bulgarian Incident therefore offers an excellent contrast and insight into the possibilities of collective security and peaceful settlement under the League of Nations and international organization in general.

The ingredients lacking in the Corfu Incident for collective Great Power action, and found in the Greek-Bulgarian Incident, were two in number. First, the nations directly involved in the Greek-Bulgarian dispute were merely minor powers in the configuration of European politics. Economically, Greece was reeling under the impact of over a million refugees who had flooded the country after the exchange of populations with Turkey, agreed to at the Lausanne Conference several years before. Politically, the country was seething with unrest due to the dictatorial government of General Theodoros Pangalos. Though these conditions partially help explain the Greek decision to obey dictation by the Great Powers, undoubtedly the most important consideration was its military weakness and susceptibility to naval blockade and harassment; a condition not lost sight of by the decision-makers in Athens. Likewise, a demilitarized, friendless, and isolated Bulgaria was more than happy to comply with any and all demands made by the Great Powers. The fact that neither nation was tied to one of the Great Powers in any alliance formal or informal, expedited the task of the powers and made collective action possible.

Secondly, and perhaps most important, the signature of the Locarno Pacts by all the Great Powers only days before the incident erupted, provided that immediate and direct interest which was so important in galvanizing and collectivizing Great Power action. The desire to consolidate the new European *status quo* legalized by the Locarno settlement, and make sure that no action by any state jeopardize this settlement, propelled all the powers to act in unison and with dispatch.

This certainly can be the only explanation for Briand's quick actions both as Foreign Minister and Acting President of the League Council. His actions are of even greater significance if one keeps in mind that to the French, the League was viewed as only one more instrument among many others, to be used against any future German menace, and that French interests inevitably began to lapse when discussions of sanctions against a nation other than Germany took place.

The same may be said for the actions of Sir Austen Chamberlain; of his hurried return to Paris only days after his triumphal return from Locarno. It was an action out of step with British views of the League, which, after the American Senate's rejection of the Covenant, looked upon the organization as a sort of great world debating society where nations might meet to air their grievances, rather than as an organ for political settlement. Like the

French and British, the Italians also saw greater advantage in united Great Power action than in allowing a dangerous situation to develop which might jeopardize the Locarno settlement. Though Italy had never been one of the League's most enthusiastic supporters, Mussolini was willing to act jointly through the world organization which only two years before during the Corfu Incident he had openly flaunted. The fact that Italian actions would in the long run assist Bulgaria, a country with which Mussolini was attempting to establish closer relations, made the Italian decision undoubtedly easier.

Direct pressure with increasing intensity was applied by the powers to both sides and later continued by using the machinery of the world organization. This pressure in the long run, as Sir Austen Chamberlain saw, would be enough to make the Greeks succumb to the desires of the powers. Thus the avoidance of sanctions through the League of Nations, as desired by Sir Austen, was probably for the better, for the application of sanctions and force against the Greeks posed dangers for the League at this time. Legal and political problems of the first order would have had to be faced when the League was still trying, after its failure in the Corfu Incident two years before, to establish itself as a viable instrument for peaceful settlement.

In passing, the activities of the Secretary-General, Sir Eric Drummond, should also be noted. From the beginning of the incident the Secretary-General, behind the scenes, took a very active role in attempting to moderate Greek actions. This initiative is extremely interesting since the position of the Secretary-General under the League was far less political than that same position under the United Nations. Nevertheless, even though Sir Eric's appeals were ignored in Athens, it clearly shows that, provided the Secretary-General is aware of his limited power position, he can still play an important and active role for the world organization. Though Drummond was aware of his limited powers in the Greek-Bulgarian Incident as well as in other situations, he astutely and discretely used his position and the prestige of his office to tender advice and to act as a mediator.

It would appear from this investigation of the Greek-Bulgarian Incident, that, provided the Great Powers can agree to act collectively because of a mutuality of interests, pressure to achieve peaceful settlement can and will be applied by the powers. If diplomatic pressure proves insufficient, direct physical pressure will be considered and inevitably supplied either within or outside the organization. But this situation leads to certain questions, for if collective action by the powers is a tenuous proposition at best, why institutionalize it within international organization at all? Are not greater risks presented by having it within the structure of the organization? For example, if institutionalized and unable to operate because of Great Power disagreement outside the organization, causing a paralysis of the organization, does not the prestige of the organization decrease and disillusionment set in? Do not these adverse reactions in turn hinder, if not destroy, the attempt to construct an atmosphere in which peaceful change may prove possible, especially through the procedures established by the organization?

Perhaps in the League, and for that matter in the United Nations, it would have been better to have restricted the organization's jurisdiction to only social and economic fields of endeavor, until such time as the actions of the powers, the feelings for a world community, and the desire to co-operate, would permit a greater assumption of responsibility by the organization. By tackling and solving economic and social problems considered by many to be important contributors to the tensions that rack the international community, the organization could contribute to producing an atmosphere in which expansion of its powers might take place. At the same time the organization could still play an important political role, being the meeting ground where competing states might always make contact. By doing so the organization would be divorcing itself from areas of conflict which experience shows are unlikely to be settled by international organization unless there is a manifestation of Great Power collaboration. In situations where the Great Powers can agree outside the organization, the organization appears to serve no necessary function and becomes superfluous. On the other hand, an organization narrower in scope is not harmed if there is disagreement by the Great Powers outside the organization.

The assumptions made at Paris in 1919 about the value of international organization as a political instrument within international politics were never seriously questioned at San Francisco in 1945. Yet experience seems to show that there are more advantages to keeping the purview of international organization narrow in scope rather than broad. Though the Greek-Bulgarian Incident, because of collective Great Power action, increased the prestige of the League of Nations, subsequent Great Power disagreement outside the League reflected itself within the organization, especially in important political episodes like Manchuria, the Chaco War, as well as the Ethiopian debacle, causing a great loss of prestige to the organization. Disillusionment with the League quickly set in, all of which in turn decreased the effectiveness of the League as an instrument for maintaining the peace.

An international organization like the League or the United Nations can be no more effective as an instrument of peace than the nations using it wish it to be. How they use or misuse the organ will in large measure decide the effectiveness of the organ. The appreciation of an institution like the League or the United Nations depends first on realizing its limitations in a world dominated by power. To view international organization in any other light is to be myopic to the realities of the international community where power is the omnipresent weapon of all states and particularly the great.

II THE SINO-JAPANESE DISPUTE OF 1931-1933

The Manchurian Crisis*

Quincy Wright

The bombardment of Mukden by Japanese forces on September 18, 1931, followed by the occupation of a large part of the three eastern provinces of China, i.e., Manchuria, by the Japanese, followed by the expulsion of the Chinese authorities, has brought to a head the long-standing disagreement between China and Japan in regard to their respective rights and policies in that territory, and has presented the League of Nations, the signatories of the Nine-Power Washington Treaty, and the signatories of the Kellogg Peace Pact with an opportunity to illustrate the meaning of these instruments.

The Background

With the underlying legal controversies between China and Japan in respect to Manchuria, it will be impossible to deal in this article beyond stating that it is recognized that Japan fell heir to certain legal rights of Russia in Manchuria as a result of the treaty of Portsmouth between Russia and Japan, and the treaty of Peking between Japan and China in 1905. Beyond this, there is perhaps little that is accepted by all parties interested. . . .

Although it is necessary to have these background problems in mind for any consideration of the international procedure initiated by the Chinese appeal to the League of Nations on September 19, 1931, it is with the latter that the states of the world other than China and Japan are mainly concerned. This interest is not merely humanitarian, but a legal interest resulting from the ratification by almost every state of some treaty which may be called into operation by the Manchurian incidents. The League of Nations Covenant, to which fifty-five states, including China and Japan, are parties, is clearly involved. Under Article 11, which has been invoked by China, "any war or threat of war, whether immediately affecting any of the members of the League or not, is hereby declared a matter of concern to the

* Quincy Wright, "The Manchurian Crisis," *The American Political Science Review*, Vol. XXVI, No. 1 (February 1932), pp. 45-69. Reprinted by permission of the author and *The American Political Science Review*. Quincy Wright is Professor Emeritus of International Relations at the University of Chicago and Professor of International Relations at the University of Virginia. He is the author of *A Study of War* (1942), *Problems of Stability and Progress in International Relations* (1954), and *Study of International Relations* (1955).

whole League, and the League shall take any action that may be deemed wise and effectual to safeguard the peace of nations." It has been suggested during the discussion that occasion may arise for invocation of Article 10 of the Covenant, by which the members of the League undertake "to respect and preserve as against external aggression the territorial integrity and existing political independence of all members of the League," and Article 12, by which "the members of the League agree that if there should arise between them any dispute likely to lead to a rupture, they will submit the matter either to arbitration or judicial settlement, or to inquiry by the Council, and they agree in no case to resort to war until three months after the award by the arbitrators or the judicial decision, or the report by the Council."

It has also been suggested that the Kellogg Peace Pact and the Nine-Power Washington Treaty relating to China may be involved. By the Kellogg Pact, which has now been ratified by fifty-nine states, including China, Japan, Soviet Russia, and the United States, the parties "solemnly declare in the names of their respective peoples that they condemn recourse to war for the solution of international controversies, and renounce it as an instrument of national policy in their relations with one another." They also agree "that the settlement or solution of all disputes or conflicts of whatever nature or of whatever origin they may be, which may arise among them, shall never be solved except by pacific means." By the Nine-Power Washington Treaty, to which China, Japan, the United States, the British Empire, France, Italy, Belgium, the Netherlands, and Portugal are parties, "the contracting powers other than China agree: (1) to respect the sovereignty, the independence, and the territorial and administrative integrity of China; (2) to provide the fullest and most unembarrassed opportunity to China to develop and maintain for herself an effective and stable government;" and "that whenever a situation arises which in the opinion of any one of them involves the application of the stipulations of the present treaty, and renders desirable discussion of such application, there shall be full and frank communication between the contracting powers concerned."

The Resolutions of the Council

The consideration of the Manchurian problem under these treaties has taken place in the Council of the League of Nations, and at the present writing (December 10, 1931) the third phase of the Council's discussion has just been completed.

The first phase, from September 19 to 30, resulted in two unanimous resolutions, one on September 22, and the other on September 30. By the first, the Council authorized the president

(1) To address an urgent appeal to the governments of China and Japan to abstain from any acts which might aggravate the situation or prejudice the peaceful settlement of the problem; (2) to seek, in consultation with the representatives of China

and Japan, adequate means whereby the two countries may proceed immediately to the withdrawal of their respective troops, without compromising the security of life of their nationals or the protection of the property belonging to them. [The Council also] decided to forward, for information, the minutes of all the meetings of the Council, together with the documents relating to this question, to the government of the United States of America.

The second resolution was approved on September 30 in the following form:

The Council (1) Notes the replies of the Chinese and Japanese governments to the urgent appeal addressed to them by its president and the steps that have already been taken in response to that appeal; (2) Recognizes the importance of the Japanese government's statement that it has no territorial designs in Manchuria; (3) Notes the Japanese representative's statement that his government will continue as rapidly as possible the withdrawal of its troops, which has already been begun, into the railway zone in proportion as the safety of the lives and property of Japanese nationals is effectively assured and that it hopes to carry out this intention in full as speedily as may be; (4) Notes the Chinese representative's statement that his government will assume responsibilty for the safety of the lives and property of Japanese nationals outside that zone as the withdrawal of the Japanese troops continues and the Chinese local authorities and police forces are reëstablished; (5) Being convinced that both governments are anxious to avoid taking any action which might disturb the peace and good understanding between the two nations, notes that the Chinese and Japanese representatives have given assurances that their respective governments will take all necessary steps to prevent any extension of the scope of the incident or any aggravation of the situation; (6) Requests both parties to do all in their power to hasten the restoration of normal relations between them and for that purpose to continue and speedily complete the execution of the above mentioned undertakings; (7) Requests both parties to furnish the Council at frequent intervals with full information as to the development of the situation; (8) Decides, in the absence of any unforeseen occurrence which might render an immediate meeting essential, to meet again at Geneva on Wednesday, October 14, 1931, to consider the situation as it then stands; (9) Authorizes its president to cancel the meeting of the Council fixed for October 14 should he decide after consulting his colleagues, and more particularly the representatives of the two parties, that in view of such information as he may have received from the parties or from other members of the Council as to the development of the situation, the meeting is no longer necessary.

The second phase of the discussion, from October 14 to 24, resulted in a resolution unanimous, with the exception of Japan, on the latter date and in the following words:

The Council, in pursuance of the resolution passed on September 30; Noting that in addition to the invocation by the government of China of Article 11 of the Covenant, Article 2 of the Pact of Paris has also been invoked by a number of governments; (1) Recalls the undertakings given to the Council by the governments of China and Japan in that resolution, and in particular the statement of the Japanese representative that the Japanese government would continue as rapidly as possible the withdrawal of its troops into the railway zone in proportion as the safety of the lives and property of Japanese nationals is effectively assured, and the statement of the Chinese representative that his government will assume the responsibility for the safety of the lives and property of Japanese nationals outside that zone—a pledge which implies the effective protection of Japanese subjects residing in Manchuria; (2) Recalls further that both governments have given the assurance that they would refrain from any measures which might aggravate the existing situation, and are therefore bound not to resort to any aggressive policy or action and to take measures to suppress hostile agitation; (3) Recalls the Japanese statement that Japan has no territorial designs in Manchuria, and notes that this statement is in accordance with the terms of the Covenant of the League of Nations, and of the Nine-Power Treaty, the signatories of which are pledged 'to respect the sovereignty, the independence, and the territorial and administrative integrity of China'; (4) Being convinced that the fulfillment of these assurances and undertakings is essential for the restoration of normal relations between the two parties, (a) Calls upon the Japanese government to begin immediately and to proceed progressively with the withdrawal of its troops into the railway zone, so that the total withdrawal may be effected before the date fixed for the next meeting of the Council; (b) Calls upon the Chinese government, in execution of its general pledge to assume the responsibility for the safety of the lives and property of all Japanese subjects resident in Manchuria, to make such arrangements for taking over the territory thus evacuated as will ensure the safety of the lives and property of Japanese subjects there, and requests the Chinese government to associate with the Chinese authorities designated for the above purpose representatives of other Powers in order that such representatives may follow the execution of the arrangements; (5) Recommends that the Chinese and Japanese governments should immediately appoint representatives to arrange the details of the execution of all points relating to the evacuation and the taking over of the evacuated territory so that they may proceed smoothly and without delay; (6) Recommends the Chinese and Japanese governments, as soon as the evacuation is completed, to begin direct negotiations on questions outstanding between them, and in particular those arising out of recent incidents as well as those relating to existing difficulties due to the railway situation in Manchuria. For this purpose, the Council suggests that the two parties should set up a conciliation committee, or some such permanent machinery; (7) Decides to adjourn till November 16, at which date it will again examine the situation, but authorizes its president to convoke a meeting at any earlier date should it in his opinion be desirable.

The third phase of the discussion, from November 16 to December 10, resulted in the passage by unanimous vote of the following resolution on the latter date:

The Council, (1) Reaffirms the resolution passed unanimously by it on September 30th, 1931, by which the two parties declare that they are solemnly bound; it therefore calls upon the Chinese and Japanese governments to take all steps necessary to assure its execution, so that the withdrawal of the Japanese troops within the railway zone may be effected as speedily as possible under the conditions set forth in the said resolution; (2) Considering that events have assumed an even more serious aspect since the Council meeting of October 24, notes that the two parties undertake to adopt all measures necessary to avoid any further aggravation of the situation and to refrain from any initiative which may lead to further fighting and loss of life; (3) Invites the two parties to continue to keep the Council informed as to the development of the situation; (4) Invites the other members of the Council to furnish the Council with any information received from their representatives on the spot; (5) Without prejudice to the carrying out of the above mentioned measures, desiring, in view of the special circumstances of the case, to contribute towards a final and fundamental solution by the two governments of the questions at issue between them: decides to appoint a commission of five members to study on the spot and to report to the Council on any circumstances which, affecting international relations, threaten to disturb peace between China and Japan, or the good understanding between them, upon which peace depends. The governments of China and of Japan will each have the right to nominate one assessor to assist the commission. The two governments will afford the commission all facilities to obtain on the spot whatever information it may require. It is understood that should the two parties initiate any negotiations, these would not fall within the scope of the terms of reference of the commission, nor would it be within the competence of the commission to interfere with the military arrangements of either party. The appointment and deliberations of the commission shall not prejudice in any way the undertaking given by the Japanese government in the resolution of September 30th as regards the withdrawal of the Japanese troops within the railway zone. (6) Between now and its next ordinary session, which will be held on January 25th, 1932, the Council, which remains seised of the matter, invites its president to follow the question and to summon it afresh if necessary.

Procedure of the League

The League of Nations Covenant provides for three quite distinct types of procedure in case of hostilities between two participating states: (1) that for stopping hostilities, (2) that for settling the dispute, (3) that for applying sanctions. The precedents have well established that the procedure for stopping hostilities should precede and, so far as possible, be isolated from the procedure for settling the dispute. This distinction is important because the determination of facts and responsibilities necessary for settling the dispute is by its nature a long process, while effective action to stop hostilities must necessarily be taken with the greatest possible expedition. Every day that warfare is allowed to continue increases the difficulty of stopping it. This separation has the added advantage that in recommending the cessation of hostilities the Council can treat both parties on a precise equality. No problem of defining the aggressor arises. Prior to the investigation of the merits, it would clearly be improper to impute illegal conduct to either. At the same time, resolutions suggesting a cessation of hostilities are more likely to be effective if they avoid any such implication.

The League Council has become equally insistent upon separating the problem of stopping hostilities from the problem of applying sanctions.

Under the Covenant, sanctions are applicable only when territorial integrity or political independence have been violated (Art. 10), or when war has begun contrary to Articles 12, 13, and 15 (Art. 16)—both very difficult matters to determine. Usually war in the legal sense would not exist, and the question of justifiable defense measures short of war would involve an examination of the facts in regard to incidents and the merits of the controversy for which data would generally not be available. On the other hand, the conservatory measures and mediatorial functions of the Council contemplated by Article 11 are authorized not only on the outbreak of war, but upon every "threat of war," or even upon the development of "any circumstances whatever affecting international relations which threaten to disturb international peace or the good understanding between nations upon which peace depends." Thus the Council's competence under this article could hardly be questioned. It is recognized that the most important data for determining the liability of a state to sanctions would be its own attitude and actions *after* the League has been seised of the matter. In other words, the very determination of aggression depends upon a somewhat protracted discussion before the Council while that body is acting without any presumption that either party is guilty of illegal conduct and with the sole objective of stopping hostilities.

These distinctions were emphasized in the report of the Committee of the Council on Article 11, approved by the Council and the Eighth Assembly in 1927. This report was divided into two sections, one of which dealt in detail with the procedure for settling disputes "where there is no threat of war or it is not acute," and the other dealing with the stopping of hostilities "where there is an imminent threat of war." The latter, in turn, was divided into seven paragraphs, only the last two of which dealt with sanctions which might arise "should any of the parties to the dispute disregard the advice or recommendations of the Council."

The importance of these distinctions is further emphasized by the existence of the Kellogg Pact, which forbids hostilities in the settlement of disputes, but specifies neither a procedure for settlement nor sanctions. Thus, if action is to be kept within the terms of the Pact, it must be confined to the prevention or stopping of hostilities. In fact, it seems probable that members of the League which have ratified the Pact are obligated, even when acting through League of Nations organs, to refrain from any consideration of the merits of disputes, except in the course of arbitral or judicial proceedings, until hostilities have been stopped. Participation by such states in discussion of the merits with a view to settlement by political agreement in the Council, or support by them of bilateral negotiations between the parties, while one of the parties is invading or occupying the territory of the other, or otherwise bringing military pressure upon it, would appear to abet such party in seeking the settlement of its dispute by other than pacific means, contrary to Article 2 of the Pact.

These distinctions in League procedure have been well illustrated by the Council's consideration of the Manchurian dispute. The Council has devoted its attention up to the time of writing solely to the problem of stopping hostilities and restoring the *status quo ante*. Its care in this regard can be seen by studying its treatment of all suggestions arising in discussions looking toward consideration of the merits of the dispute between China and Japan.

The First Phase

In its original formal appeal on September 21, 1931, China "requested that in pursuance of authority given to it by Article 11 of the Covenant, the Council take immediate steps to prevent the further development of a situation endangering the peace of nations; to reëstablish the *status quo ante;* and to determine the amount and character of such reparations as may be found due to the Republic of China." In presenting this appeal, the Chinese representative, Mr. Alfred Sze, added that "it is of course with reference to the first and second steps that immediate action is imperatively required." The Japanese representative, Mr. Yoshizawa, replied by suggesting that the Japanese military movements were necessitated as a defensive measure, and asserting that he had been informed that "a proposal has been made from the Chinese side that the solution should be sought by direct negotiations between the two governments," and that "the Japanese government had welcomed this proposal." The Chinese representative at once declared that "the *status quo ante* must be restored before negotiations are possible." The British representative, Viscount Cecil, endorsed this position by pointing out that "no question has yet arisen of any settlement of the merits of the dispute between the two parties," and that "the settled procedure" of the League in cases of this kind required, first, that "the Council through its president issue an earnest appeal to both sides not to do anything to aggravate the position and to avoid further fighting of all kinds," and second, "where it has been established that the troops of either party have entered the territory of the other, it has been customary for the president to issue an earnest appeal to the troops of both sides to withdraw from the territory of the other party and to avoid anything which might lead to a clash." He recognized that certain "precautions" might sometimes be necessary, but quoted as the *locus classicus* of League policy and procedure in cases of this kind a statement by M. Briand in connection with the Greco-Bulgarian dispute of 1925, agreed to at the time by the representatives of Great Britain, Italy, Japan, and other members of the Council, that

It was essential that such ideas [that hostilities were justified by defensive necessities] should not take root in the minds of nations which were members of the League and become a kind of jurisprudence, for it would be extremely dangerous. Under the pretext of legitimate defense, disputes might arise which, though limited in extent, were extremely unfortunate owing to the damage they entailed. These disputes, once they had broken out, might assume such proportions that the government which started them, under a feeling of legitimate defense, would be not longer able to control them. . . . The League of Nations through its Council and through all the methods of conciliation which were at its disposal offered the nations a means of avoiding such deplorable events. The nations had only to appeal to the Council.

On the following day, Lord Cecil's suggestion was approved by unanimous vote in the first resolution already referred to.

On September 25, the Japanese representative informed the Council that his government, in replying to the president's telegram, was "profoundly desirous of ensuring the peaceful settlement of this problem as rapidly as possible by negotiations between the two countries and has the firm intention not to depart from this line of conduct." Furthermore, that "the Japanese forces are being withdrawn to the fullest extent which is at present allowed by the maintenance of the safety of Japanese nationals and the protection of the railway," and "intended to withdraw its troops to the railway zone in proportion as the situation improves." He added that, in his opinion, with respect to the method to be selected for settling the dispute, "it is necessary to respect the wishes of the parties. If the latter or one of them clearly expresses their views as to the choice of procedure, it seems to me it is the duty of the Council—which is moreover confirmed by practice—to respect these desires and to allow the parties in conflict the time necessary to achieve the proposed object, which is the settlement of the problem." The Council, therefore, "would do well not to intervene prematurely, as by so doing it might run the risk of adversely affecting the situation, which actually shows signs of improvement."

The Chinese reply to the telegram sent by the president of the Council drew attention to orders sent by the Chinese government to its army "to avoid all possibility of clash with the invader" and willingness to "assume full responsibility for the protection of life and property as soon as it regained control of the areas evacuated by the Japanese troops." The Chinese representative suggested that a "commission of neutral members should be appointed by the Council and empowered to observe the modes in which, and the time at which, the troops are withdrawn and report thereon to the Council." He reiterated the Chinese government's refusal to negotiate bilaterally while its territory was occupied, and informed the Council that the initial approval by the Chinese finance minister, T. V. Soong, of the suggestion by the Japanese minister Shigemitsu for such negotiations had been withdrawn upon discovering that Chinese territory was actually invaded. Mr. Sze also suggested that unless Japan withdrew her troops immediately

Japan will place herself in opposition to the categorical obligations assumed by her under the first paragraph of Article 15 of the Covenant, to submit to the Council disputes which are likely to lead to a rupture and which are not submitted to arbitration or judicial settlement, and it need hardly be observed that, if Article 15 is brought into operation, the procedure to be taken by the parties to the dispute and by the Council or the Assembly, if the question is referred to them, is no longer a matter of discretion, but is stated definitely and with particularity.

This statement clearly had reference to consideration both of the merits of the dispute and of sanctions.

Lord Cecil, however, immediately professed inability to understand this reference to Article 15, "which could be invoked, as the Chinese representative was aware, by the proecdure indicated therein, but which had not been invoked in the present case." The duty of the Council under Article 11 was "not to settle the dispute or pass judgment on the action of the parties, or indeed to do anything but safeguard the peace of nations. It was only when peace had been safeguarded, for that was primarily the duty of the Council, that any question as to the settlement of the actual dispute could arise." He agreed with Japan that the question of the dispute could only be a matter for the parties at this stage; the Council, however, "to preserve the peace of nations" would desire—and the Japanese government too, he hoped—that those troops should be withdrawn as rapidly as possible.

On September 28, the Japanese representative reiterated that complete withdrawal was impossible until security to Japanese lives and property was assured, and the Chinese representative, referring to his earlier proposal of a neutral commission to examine this question on the spot, said that to be conciliatory "he proposed that the Council should help the parties to reach an agreement as to arrangements on the spot, which would make it possible to fix an early date for the completion of the withdrawal of troops and render it unnecessary for the Council to send a commission of enquiry from Geneva." He, however, thought that the Council should appoint neutral observers in the Far East to meet with representatives of the parties. Lord Cecil supported this proposal on the supposition that it concerned only negotiations on the question of evacuation and similar questions. When it appeared that the Chinese and Japanese representatives were contemplating a negotiation of wider scope, which, however, the Chinese would accept only if under League auspices and the Japanese only if entirely bilateral, Lord Cecil thought "the Council would be unable to carry the matter further at the present stage."

At its meeting on September 30, the Council unanimously adopted the resolution already quoted, which the president of the Council (who at this time was Señor Lerroux, Spanish minister of foreign affairs) explained was in pursuance of the duty of the Council under Article 11 "to take such action as may be deemed wise and effectual to safeguard the peace of nations." He added that the Council, "in viewing the actual situation before it in the light of this injunction, has singled out one object as being of immediate and paramount importance—namely, the withdrawal of troops to the railway zone. Nevertheless, it could not but admit that, in the special circumstances, a certain time had to be allowed for the withdrawal, particularly in order to ensure the safety of life and property."

The Second Phase

The situation in Manchuria actually became worse, and, upon Chinese request, the Council reassembled on October 13, a day earlier than the time set. The Chinese representative, citing statements of Señor Lerroux, the president of the Council, of Lord Cecil, and of M. Briand, insisted that the restoration of the *status quo ante* "is the first and preliminary step which it is imperative should be taken at once, and it is one which does not involve questions of fact existing prior to September 18, nor should it be confused with the later distinct steps which will need to be taken in order that satisfactory relations between China and Japan may be fully reëstablished and maintained." After a brief adjournment, the Japanese representative made a long statement emphasizing the danger to Japanese lives and property in Manchuria, the rise of anti-Japanese agitation in China through meetings attended in some instances by Chinese officials, and to the history of Chinese violations of Japanese rights in Manchuria:

In the face of the situation created by the systematically vexatious manner in which the Chinese authorities deal with our essential rights and interests, the command of the Japanese troops considered it indispensable after the incident of September 18 to take legitimate defensive action with a view to averting at any cost the imminent danger which threatened the very existence of the Japanese in Manchuria. It is from this point of view that the operations undertaken by our troops over a relatively wide radius should be considered.

He thought too great importance should not be attributed to theoretical arguments and possibilities. "Vital realities of the international situation" must be the basis of action, which meant that the Council should "look first of all for means of calming the minds of the public and creating a moral disarmament between the two nations." "The public of my country," he said, "excited beyond measure by the proceedings of the Chinese authorities, cannot be calmed until it is convinced that the perpetual menace to our rights and opportunities in Manchuria has ceased." Therefore,

If the Chinese government were to make serious efforts to check the anti-Japanese agitation and to arrive in common accord with us at a preliminary basis for the reëstablishment of normal relations between the two countries, it would do much (I am convinced) to promote the relaxation and pacification which is so eminently desirable, thus removing the most serious obstacle to the withdrawal of our troops. The withdrawal of our troops is not conditional on the realization of such an understanding. It is, I repeat, conditional on the security and protection of our nationals.

The Chinese representative, referring to the allusions to anti-Japanese agitation in China, "knew of no accepted principle of international law whereby a government, however strong, powerful, or autocratic, can compel its people to buy from persons whom they do not like," and in regard to the proposed bilateral negotiation, declared that "China will never agree to such a course so long as Japanese troops are illegally upon her soil and while satisfactory arrangements have not been made for compensating China for the wrongs done to her since September 18."

Indeed [he added] Japan herself first rejected direct negotiations. After the occurrences of September 18, she did not limit her action to meeting the precise local condition (whatever that was) by localized action, and dealing with the immediate need for defense (if there was such a need). Without waiting for direct negotiations, she sent large numbers of troops into China, established military occupation in important places over a wide area of China, and carried on military operations which resulted in the loss of many Chinese lives and the destruction of much Chinese property. Thus Japan herself abandoned any possible resort to direct negotiations and made it necessary for China to appeal to the League to prevent further acts of violence and to help her to obtain relief and reparations for the injuries already committed. Surely it is not now right or reasonable for Japan to claim that the adjustment of the whole controversy should be effected through direct negotiations.

The Japanese representative then said, while "it is essential to reach agreement on certain principal points as a basis for negotiation," his government's intention was that these negotiations "shall not include details relating to the settlement of the conditions resulting from the incident of September 18, but shall only deal with the bases of negotiation, with a view to reach an agreement with China on the matter of evacuation, and so on. Without such preliminary negotiation, it is impossible for us to withdraw our troops into the railway zone in view of past experience in analogous cases." The president of the Council, now the French foreign minister, M. Briand, interpreted this as meaning that "he had not in mind negotiations on the situation as a whole, but simply the possibility of conversations on questions relating directly to the problem of the occupation."

At the meeting of the Council on October 22, after the collaboration of an American observer had begun, the president notified the Council that telegrams had been sent by most of the parties to the Kellogg Pact, recalling to China and Japan their obligations, particularly under Article 2 of that instrument. He then submitted a draft resolution which called for evacuation by Japanese troops before the next Council meeting, set for November 16, for Chinese protection of the lives and property of Japanese subjects in Manchuria, and recommended a Sino-Japanese conference to arrange for the evacuation, and "as soon as the evacuation is complete, the beginning of direct negotiations on the questions outstanding between them."

At the meeting on October 23, a communication from Japan in response to the appeals under the Kellogg Pact was read. In this Japan suggested that "activities of the anti-Japanese organizations are acquiesced in by the Chinese government as a means to attain the national ends of China. The Japanese government desire to point out that such acquiescence by the

Chinese government in the lawless proceedings of their own nationals cannot be regarded as being in harmony with the letter or the spirit of the
stipulations contained in Article 2 of the Pact of Paris." This effort of Japan
to present the Chinese boycott as a more serious means of coercion than the
Japanese invasion of Manchuria continued throughout the discussion.

Debate then proceeded upon the proposed resolution, and the Chinese
representative expressed his government's willingness to accept it, adding

Any attempt to make the military invasion of Manchuria the occasion for
pressing for the solution of other claims would be contrary to the spirit of the
Covenant and a violation of Article 2 of the Pact of Paris. China will not discuss
any subject with any power under the pressure of military occupation of her
territory, nor, what amounts to the same thing, under the pressure of accomplished
facts resulting from the use of force during such occupation. This point is vital
and goes to the root of the whole controversy before the Council; it is, indeed, the
basic principle on which the Covenant and the Pact of Paris are founded. It is
because, in the view of the Chinese government, this point is vital and fundamental
that I have stressed it, and it is for the same reason I add that the Chinese government is assured that, in adopting this attitude, it has, as a matter of course, the
full and unqualified moral support of every member of the League and signatory
of the Pact of Paris.

The Japanese representative then proposed a substitute resolution
"noting the statement by the representative of Japan made on October 13 to
the effect that the Japanese government would withdraw those of its troops
still remaining in a few localities outside the said zone as the present atmosphere of tension clears and the situation improves, by the achievement of a
previous understanding between the Chinese and Japanese governments as
regards the fundamental principle governing normal relations—that is to
say, affording an assurance for the safety of the lives of Japanese nationals
and for the protection of their property;" and "recommending the Chinese
and Japanese governments to confer together at once with a view to arriving
at the understanding mentioned" in the above statement. Although the
Japanese representative said there was "no question of an attempt to wrest
concessions and privileges from China," Lord Cecil felt that more explanation of these "fundamental principles" was necessary. The Japanese representative said that "the purpose of the fundamental principles is merely to
make that security and that protection [mentioned in the resolution of
September 30] effective."

The president, M. Briand, then distinguished between negotiations on
police, administrative, and military measures relating to withdrawal, on
which the parties were in agreement, and negotiations on "questions on
which, for a long time past, the two countries have been unable to agree. If,
before evacuation, matters which have not been settled for months, and even
for years, must be discussed between the two governments, obviously the
time limit contemplated by the Council is far too short to enable results to

be achieved. On this point there is complete disagreement between the two parties. The Chinese view is that negotiations of this nature must be postponed to a date when military pressure no longer exists. They are rejected as a condition of evacuation." Did the "fundamental principles" mentioned by Japan relate to the first or second category?

At the next meeting, on October 24, the Japanese representative said that they "related only to questions coming within the first category," to which Lord Cecil replied that in that case it would be better to omit so ambiguous a term. The Japanese representative declined, saying, "as regards the fundamental principles, my government holds certain views, but I cannot communicate these views officially to the Council until my government has authorized me to do so." The Spanish representative, now Señor Madariaga, noticed "a danger in allowing anyone to claim the right to remain on the spot when that party has invaded a territory in which it has no right to be, by stating that there is no security, particularly as in certain respects at least the party is partially responsible for the state of insecurity." He found himself perplexed by the Japanese proposal, which seemed to be "that evacuation depends on security, security depends on pacification, and pacification depends on the settlement of a number of questions which have nothing to do either with security or with evacuation." He thought, however, that "the rule of the League—which is to separate the nations so as to enable them to discuss peacefully—and the interests of Japan and of China" could both be accommodated by advance agreement to begin negotiations immediately upon evacuation of Chinese territory.

Lord Cecil then referred to reports that "Japanese official circles were very disappointed and resentful as a result of the League's apparent intention to override Japan's insistence on Chinese recognition of treaty commitments as a *sine qua non*." He thought

There can be no question of the League desiring to override the sacredness of treaties. Of course it is quite possible that there may be a dispute between the parties to treaties as to the validity of a treaty or as to the interpretation of a treaty. Fortunately, any such dispute as that can now be settled authoritatively by an appeal to the Permanent Court of International Justice at The Hague, over which, as it happens, a Japanese national at the moment presides. It is certain that any such question would be discussed with absolute fairness and impartiality at The Hague. The League could, at any moment, obviously express the view that all treaties ought to be carried out; but that is not the question before us. The treaties hold; but to discuss up to what point they bind the contracting parties would seem to me to be definitely reversing the order of things. Evacuation must take place first, discussion of the treaties may follow. It is an important matter, but is not one which would directly affect the safety of the nationals of Japan, and therefore is not one which ought to be discussed before the Japanese troops retire from the territory which they occupy.

The president, M. Briand, referred to the resolution of September 30, agreed to by Japan, in which no mention was made of negotiations upon "fundamental principles" before evacuation. Then, referring to Article 10 of the Covenant and Article 2 of the Kellogg Pact, he said:

This is a dispute which has been laid before the Council. There can be no question of dealing with it by other than pacific means. Japan, who always so scrupulously honors her obligations, could not dream of adopting any other means. I do not wish to dwell unduly on this point; but public opinion would not readily admit that a military occupation under these circumstances could be regarded as coming under the heading of pacific means. To prolong this situation would be to perpetuate a state of anxiety which has already lasted too long.

M. Briand admitted "uneasiness" if the Japanese representative intended by his proposal "to begin negotiations concerning the substance of certain delicate problems which have long existed," but this intention had been denied. He hoped, therefore, there would be agreement. The Japanese representative, however, was unmoved, and Señor Madariaga asked for a clarification of the "fundamental principles," calling attention to the preamble of the Covenant prescribing "open, just, and honorable relations between nations." The Council adjourned, to meet in the afternoon, when it voted down the Japanese substitute proposal, 1 to 13, and voted for the president's proposal 13 to 1. The president, M. Briand, declared that "the draft resolution which has been adopted after a long discussion is now on the Council table," and the meeting adjourned until November 16.

The Third Phase

The Japanese government, holding that this resolution had not achieved the unanimity required under Article 11 of the Covenant, declined to recognize it as a binding obligation, and when the Council reassembled on November 16, far from being withdrawn, the Japanese occupation of Manchuria had been extended. In opening the discussion, M. Briand drew attention to events which had occurred since the closing of the last session, including receipt of a communication from China (October 24) by which she "undertook to settle all disputes with Japan as to treaty interpretation by arbitration or judicial settlement as provided in Article 13 of the Covenant," and receipt of a communication from Japan (October 26) setting forth five "basic principles" relating to "(1) mutual repudiation of aggressive policy and conduct; (2) respect for China's territorial integrity; (3) complete suppression of all organized movements interfering with freedom of trade and stirring up international hatred; (4) effective protection throughout Manchuria of all peaceful pursuits undertaken by Japanese subjects; (5) respect for treaty rights of Japan in Manchuria." He had replied (October 29) that the first four points seemed to be fully covered by the draft resolution of October 24 and, although the Japanese representative in agreeing to the resolution of September 30 had given "no indication whatever . . . that matters such as an agreement on treaty rights of Japan in Manchuria were in any way connected with the safety of lives and property of Japanese nationals," yet solution of the fifth point could be sought along the lines suggested in the Chinese note. He had also several times, on the occurrence of incidents in Manchuria, reminded the parties of their obligations under the resolution of September 30.

The Council met formally only four times during this session, but labored continuously in private conversations to arrive at a formula which would gain the consent of both China and Japan. On November 21, the Japanese representative, referring to "the openly declared policy of the Chinese Nationalist party" of "unilateral repudiation of treaties," and to its encouragement of "disregard in practice" of treaty clauses and of "anti-foreign campaigns," which had led in Manchuria "to a long series of vexatious acts, of acts of hostility and provocation, and to cases of denial of justice," until "the Japanese people had been forced to realize that China was seeking in every way to take from the Japanese nation its legally acquired rights and to deprive the Japanese and Koreans residing in Manchuria of the fruits of their hard and patient labor," declared that "Japan's right to live and her very existence are today at stake." He considered that "the essential condition of a fundamental solution of the question is a real knowledge of the situation as a whole, both in Manchuria and in China itself," and accordingly proposed that the League send a commission of inquiry to the spot, which, however, "would not be empowered to intervene in the negotiations which may be initiated between the two parties, or to supervise the movements of the military forces of either."

The Chinese representative insisted that the "military occupation of Chinese territory by Japanese forces in violation of solemn treaties and of the Covenant was the crux of the situation," and that his government could not "bargain for withdrawal." Nevertheless, he was ready to accept "reasonable arrangements involving neutral coöperation under the auspices of the League." Discussion proceeded in regard to the Japanese proposal, although the members of the Council wished to make it clear that the dispatch of a commission with such a wide competence prior to evacuation could be justified only by the "exceptional character" of the situation. Thus Señor Lerroux of Spain said: "The important point is not the history of the relations between China and Japan, nor the validity of the treaties and protocols in which these relations are defined," nor even the "nature of the dispute," but only "the methods employed to remedy the position and the question whether these methods can be reconciled with the principles" of the Covenant and the Pact. He even thought the resolution of September 30, "by making evacuation of Chinese territory by Japanese troops depend upon the security of Japanese nationals and their property," had "reversed the rôle which the desire for security should play" and would be "dangerous" to take as a precedent. In any case, "safety and protection should be understood in their obvious and direct sense," and should not include "the settlement of certain questions relating to the disputed treaties."

It was evident during the two weeks of private conversations which ensued—partly consumed by an effort to stop the threatened hostilities about Chinchow—that a conciliatory policy by either government was opposed by increasingly vociferous elements of home public opinion. Nevertheless, under immediate danger of forced resignation, both governments instructed their representatives at Geneva to approve the resolution which had been drafted on December 10. This reiterated the duty, recognized in the resolution which both had accepted on September 30, of Japan to withdraw her troops "as speedily as possible," and of both states "to adopt measures necessary to avoid any further aggravation of the situation." In addition, the resolution provided for dispatch to Manchuria of a commission of five, with an assessor from China and one from Japan. The competence of this commission was stated, in the words of the second sentence of Article 11 of the Covenant, to report to the Council "on any circumstance which, affecting international relations, threatens to disturb peace between China and Japan or the good understanding between them on which peace depends." This suggests a broad survey of "all matters in dispute" between the two parties in Manchuria, and such was the interpretation given by M. Briand in presenting the resolution, and by President Hoover in his message delivered to Congress on the same day. This seems to depart from the League's previous position that all consideration of the merits must be deferred until military pressure is ended.

It is to be observed, however, that while the commission might report to the Council on all elements of the situation prejudicial to peace and good understanding, any negotiation between the parties was expressly excluded from "the scope of the terms of reference," as was "any interference with the military arrangements of either party." As the utilization of the text from Article 11 of the Covenant indicated, the commission's labors were to be contributory to the peace-preserving functions of the Council under that article, and to avoid any direct consideration of the merits of the controversy or of sanctions. However, the members of the council seemed to feel that it suggested some lapse from principle, and the representatives of Great Britain, France, Spain, Poland, Venezuela, Peru, and Panama emphasized in individual speeches that the situation was exceptional and could not serve as a precedent for the future. M. Briand attributed this special character to "the exceptional nature of the treaty or customary relations existing in normal times between the two countries," and to the fact that the "political status of one of the countries was governed by the international obligations of the nine-power convention. . . . which it was not within our competence to interpret here." He insisted, however, that the resolution "in no way affected the doctrine of the Council of the League of Nations" that:

Except in the case of an express stipulation in treaties in force, the Covenant of the League of Nations does not authorize a state, however well founded its grievances against another state, to seek redress by methods other than the pacific methods set forth in Article 12 of the Covenant. For members of the League that is a fundamental principle, in the same way as the 'scrupulous respect for all treaty obligations,' on which such stress has rightly been laid in the preamble of the Covenant. These two principles are of equal value. Any infringement of either lays a grave responsibility on members of the League. This responsibility was reaffirmed in the Pact of Paris, whose signatories assumed or renewed the undertaking to resort to pacific means alone for the settlement of international disputes.

Lord Cecil emphasized that, under Article 11, the Council could act only by unanimity, and that its "task was not one of arbitration and decision but mediation and persuasion," and must be judged in that light. He added that the work of conciliation could easily be destroyed by either party, but such party "would bear a heavy load of responsibility before the public opinion of the world. . . . In no case nowadays must a nation take the law into its own hands." The representatives of the Latin American states (Venezuela, Peru, Panama) particularly emphasized the compromise character of the resolution due to exceptional circumstances, and insisted that in voting for it they in no way receded from the basic principles of international law expressed in the League Covenant and, in a more limited manner, in the Second Hague Convention of 1907 based on the Drago Doctrine, that military occupations are not justified "to insure the execution of certain treaties" or "to impose direct negotiations on questions that are pending" or "to collect debts," and that the right of a state "to ensure the protection of the lives and property of its nationals must be limited by respect for the sovereignty of the other state; no state being entitled in order to provide such protection to authorize its military forces to penetrate into the territory of the other for the purpose of carrying out police operations." The representative of China observed in reference to the "special character of the question" that "China cannot be expected to admit that the operation of treaties, covenants, and accepted principles of international law stops at the border of Manchuria."

This discussion indicates the importance which the Council attaches to deferring discussion, or even investigation of the merits of a dispute, until military pressure has ended. In this phase, as in the two preceding ones, allusion to possible sanctions was considerably veiled. It is clear, however, that if the application of sanctions should be considered at a later time, the proceedings before the Council since September 19 will furnish important evidence as to the aggressor. Under Article 12 of the Covenant, a state that goes to war without utilizing the pacific machinery suggested by this article is liable to sanctions, particularly to the economic blockade provided in Article 16. In the resolution of 1927, already referred to, other sanctions, such as the withdrawal of diplomatic representatives and display of force, were suggested. The League's proceedings themselves should make it clear which state has declined to utilize the pacific machinery suggested, and which would consequently be liable to sanctions should war eventuate. For this decision, no examination of the events before September 19, 1931, would be necessary. . . .

Principles and Conditions of Settlement. Report of the Commission of Enquiry (The Lytton Commission)*

Review of Previous Chapters

In the previous chapters of this Report, it has been shown that, though the issues between China and Japan were not in themselves incapable of solution by arbitral procedure, yet the handling of them by their respective Governments, especially those relating to Manchuria, had so embittered their relations as sooner or later to make a conflict inevitable. A sketch has been given of China as a nation in evolution with all the political upheavals, social disorders and disruptive tendencies inseparable from such a period of transition. It has been shown how seriously the rights and interests claimed by Japan have been affected by the weakness of the authority of the Central Government in China, and how anxious Japan has shown herself to keep Manchuria apart from the government of the rest of China. A brief survey of the respective policies of the Chinese, Russian and Japanese Governments in Manchuria has revealed the fact that the administration of these Provinces has more than once been declared by their rulers to be independent of the Central Government of China, yet no wish to be separated from the rest of China has ever been expressed by their population, which is overwhelmingly Chinese. Finally, we have examined carefully and thoroughly the actual events which took place on and subsequent to September 18th, 1931, and have expressed our opinion upon them.

Complexity of the Problem

A point has now been reached when attention can be concentrated on the future, and we would dismiss the past with this final reflection. It must be apparent to every reader of the preceding chapters that the issues involved in this conflict are not as simple as they are often represented to be. They are, on the contrary, exceedingly complicated, and only an intimate knowledge of all the facts, as well as of their historical background, should entitle anyone to express a definite opinion upon them. This is not a case in which one country has declared war on another country without previously exhausting the opportunities for conciliation provided in the Covenant of

* League of Nations, *Political Publications,* VII (1932), pp. 126-131. Doc. No. C.663.M.-320.1932.VII.

the League of Nations. Neither is it a simple case of the violation of the frontier of one country by the armed forces of a neighbouring country, because in Manchuria there are many features without an exact parallel in other parts of the world.

The dispute has arisen between two States, both Members of the League, concerning a territory the size of France and Germany combined, in which both claim to have rights and interests, only some of which are clearly defined by international law; a territory which, although legally an integral part of China, had a sufficiently autonomous character to carry on direct negotiations with Japan on the matters which lay at the root of this conflict.

Conditions in Manchuria Unparalleled Elsewhere

Japan controls a railway and a strip of territory running from the sea right up into the heart of Manchuria, and she maintains for the protection of that property a force of about 10,000 soldiers, which she claims the right by treaty to increase, if necessary, up to 15,000. She also exercises the rights of jurisdiction over all her subjects in Manchuria and maintains consular police throughout the country.

Diversity of Interpretations

These facts must be considered by those who debate the issues. It is a fact that, without declaration of war, a large area of what was indisputably the Chinese territory has been forcibly seized and occupied by the armed forces of Japan and has, in consequence of this operation, been separated from and declared independent of the rest of China. The steps by which this was accomplished are claimed by Japan to have been consistent with the obligations of the Covenant of the League of Nations, the Kellogg Pact and the Nine-Power Treaty of Washington, all of which were designed to prevent action of this kind. Moreover, the operation which had only just begun when the matter was first brought to the notice of the League was completed during the following months and is held by the Japanese Government to be consistent with the assurances given by their representative at Geneva on September 30th and December 10th. The justification in this case has been that all the military operations have been legitimate acts of self-defence, the right of which is implicit in all the multilateral treaties mentioned above, and was not taken away by any of the resolutions of the Council of the League. Further, the administration which has been substituted for that of China in the Three Provinces is justified on the ground that its establishment was the act of the local population, who, by a spontaneous assertion of their independence, have severed all connection with China and established their own Government. Such a genuine independence movement, it is claimed, is not prohibited by any international treaty or by any of the resolutions of the Council of the League of Nations, and the fact of its having taken place has profoundly modified the application of the Nine-Power Treaty and entirely altered the whole character of the problem being investigated by the League.

It is this plea of justification which makes this particular conflict at once so complicated and so serious. It is not the function of our Commission to argue the issue, but we have tried to provide sufficient material to enable the League of Nations to settle the dispute consistently with the honour, dignity and national interest of both the contending parties. Criticism alone will not accomplish this: there must also be practical efforts at conciliation. We have been at pains to find out the truth regarding past events in Manchuria and to state it frankly; we recognise that this is only part, and by no means the most important part of our work. We have throughout our mission offered to the Governments of both countries the help of the League of Nations in composing their differences, and we conclude it by offering to the League our suggestions for securing, consistently with justice and with peace, the permanent interest of China and Japan in Manchuria.

Unsatisfactory Suggestions of Settlement

Restoration of the *status quo ante*. It must be clear from everything that we have already said that a mere restoration of the *status quo ante* would be no solution. Since the present conflict arose out of the conditions prevailing before last September, to restore these conditions would merely be to invite a repetition of the trouble. It would be to treat the whole question theoretically and to leave out of account the realities of the situation.

The Maintenance of "Manchukuo." From what we have said in the two preceding chapters, the maintenance and recognition of the present regime in Manchuria would be equally unsatisfactory. Such a solution does not appeal to us compatible with the fundamental principle of existing international obligations, nor with the good understanding between the two countries upon which peace in the Far East depends. It is opposed to the interests of China. It disregards the wishes of the people of Manchuria, and it is at least questionable whether it would ultimately serve the permanent interests of Japan.

About the feelings of the people of Manchuria towards the present regime there can really be no doubt; and China would not voluntarily accept as a lasting solution the complete separation of her Three Eastern Provinces. The analogy of the distant province of Outer Mongolia is not an entirely pertinent one, as Outer Mongolia is bound to China by no strong economic or social ties, and is sparsely inhabited by a population which is mainly non-Chinese. The situation in Manchuria is radically different from that in Outer Mongolia. The millions of Chinese farmers now settled permanently on the land have made Manchuria in many respects a simple extension of China south of the Wall. The Three Eastern Provinces have become almost as Chinese in race, culture and national sentiment as the neighbouring Provinces of Hopei and Shantung, from which most of the immigrants came.

Apart from this, past experience has shown that those who control Manchuria have exercised a considerable influence on the affairs of the rest of China—at least of North China—and possess unquestionable strategic and political advantages. To cut off these provinces from the rest of China, either legally or actually, would be to create for the future a serious irredentist problem which would endanger peace by keeping alive the hostility of China and rendering probable the continued boycott of Japanese goods.

The Commission received from the Japanese Government a clear and valuable statement of the vital interests of their country in Manchuria. Without exaggerating the economic dependence of Japan on Manchuria beyond the limits ascribed to it in a previous chapter, and certainly without suggesting that economic relationship entitles Japan to control the economic, still less the political, development of those provinces, we recognise the great importance of Manchuria in the economic development of Japan. Nor do we consider unreasonable her demand for the establishment of a stable Government which would be capable of maintaining the order necessary for the economic development of the country. But such conditions can only be securely and effectively guaranteed by an administration which is in conformity with the wishes of the population and which takes full account of their feelings and aspirations. And equally is it only in an atmosphere of external confidence and internal peace, very different from that now existing in the Far East, that the capital which is necessary for the rapid economic development of Manchuria will be forthcoming.

In spite of the pressure of increasing over-population, the Japanese have not as yet fully utilised their existing facilities for emigration, and the Japanese Government has not hitherto contemplated a large emigration of their people to Manchuria. But the Japanese do look to further industrialisation as a means to cope with the agrarian crisis and with the population problem. Such industrialisation would require further economic outlets and the only large and relatively sure markets that Japan can find are in Asia and particularly in China. Japan requires, not only the Manchurian, but the whole Chinese market, and the rise in the standard of living which will certainly follow the consolidation and modernisation of China should stimulate trade and raise the purchasing power of the Chinese market.

This economic *rapprochement* between Japan and China, which is of vital interest to Japan, is of equal interest to China, for China would find that a closer economic and technical collaboration with Japan would assist her in her primary task of national reconstruction. China could assist this *rapprochement* by restraining the more intolerant tendencies of her nationalism and by giving effective guarantees that, as soon as cordial relations were re-established, the practice of organised boycotts would not be revived. Japan, on her side, could facilitate this *rapprochement* by renouncing any attempt to solve the Manchurian problem by isolating it from the problem of her relations with China as a whole, in such a way as to make impossible the friendship and collaboration of China.

It may, however, be less economic considerations than anxiety for her own security which has determined the actions and policy of Japan in Manchuria. It is especially in this connection that her statesmen and military authorities are accustomed to speak of Manchuria as "the life-line of Japan." One can sympathise with such anxieties and try to appreciate the actions and motives of those who have to bear the heavy responsibility of securing the defence of their country against all eventualities. While acknowledging the interest of Japan in preventing Manchuria from serving as a base of operations directed against her own territory, and even her wish to be able to take all appropriate military measures if in certain circumstances the frontiers of Manchuria should be crossed by the forces of a foreign Power, it may still be questioned whether the military occupation of Manchuria for an indefinite period, involving, as it must, a heavy financial burden, is really the most effective way of insuring against this external danger; and whether, in the event of aggression having to be resisted in this way, the Japanese troops in Manchuria would not be seriously embarrassed if they were surrounded by a restive or rebellious population backed by a hostile China. It is surely in the interest of Japan to consider also other possible solutions of the problem of security, which would be more in keeping with the principles on which rests the present peace organisation of the world, and analogous to arrangements concluded by other great Powers in various parts of the world. She might even find it possible, with the sympathy and good-will of the rest of the world, and at no cost to herself, to obtain better security than she will obtain by the costly method she is at present adopting.

International Interests

Apart from China and Japan, other Powers of the world have also important interests to defend in this Sino-Japanese conflict. We have already referred to existing multilateral treaties, and any real and lasting solution by agreement must be compatible with the stipulations of these fundamental agreements, on which is based the peace organisation of the world. The considerations which actuated the representatives of the Powers at the Washington Conference are still valid. It is quite as much in the interests of the Powers now as it was in 1922 to assist the reconstruction of China and to maintain her sovereignty and her territorial and administrative integrity as indispensable to the maintenance of peace. Any disintegration of China might lead, perhaps rapidly, to serious international rivalries, which would become all the more bitter if they should happen to coincide with rivalries between divergent social systems. Finally, the interests of peace are the same the world over. Any loss of confidence in the application of the principles of the Covenant and of the Pact of Paris in any part of the world diminishes the value and efficacy of those principles everywhere.

Interests of U.S.S.R.

The Commission has not been able to obtain direct information as to the extent of the interests of the U.S.S.R. in Manchuria, nor to ascertain the views of the Government of the U.S.S.R. on the Manchurian question. But, even without sources of direct information, it cannot overlook the part played by Russia in Manchuria nor the important interests which the U.S.S.R. have in that region as owners of the Chinese Eastern Railway and of the territory beyond its north and north-east frontiers. It is clear that any solution of the problem of Manchuria which ignored the important interests of the U.S.S.R. would risk a future breach of the peace and would not be permanent.

Conclusions

These considerations are sufficient to indicate the lines on which a solution might be reached if the Governments of China and Japan could recognise the identity of their chief interests and were willing to make them include the maintenance of peace and the establishment of cordial relations with each other. As already stated, there is no question of returning to the conditions before September 1931. A satisfactory regime for the future might be evolved out of the present one without any violent change. We offer certain suggestions for doing this, but we would first define the general principles to which any satisfactory solution should conform. They are the following:

Conditions of a Satisfactory Solution

1. *Compatibility with the interests of both China and Japan.* Both countries are Members of the League and each is entitled to claim the same consideration from the League. A solution from which both did not derive benefit would not be a gain to the cause of peace.

2. *Consideration for the interests of the U.S.S.R.* To make peace between two of the neighbouring countries without regard for the interests of the third would be neither just nor wise, nor in the interests of peace.

3. *Conformity with existing multilateral treaties.* Any solution should conform to the provisions of the Covenant of the League of Nations, the Pact of Paris, and the Nine-Power Treaty of Washington.

4. *Recognition of Japan's interests in Manchuria.* The rights and interests of Japan in Manchuria are facts which cannot be ignored, and any solution which failed to recognise them and to take into account also the historical associations of Japan with that country would not be satisfactory.

5. *The establishment of new treaty relations between China and Japan.* A re-statement of the respective rights, interests and responsibilities of both countries in Manchuria in new treaties, which shall be part of the settlement by agreement, is desirable if future friction is to be avoided and mutual confidence and co-operation are to be restored.

6. *Effective provision for the settlement of future disputes.* As a corollary to the above, it is necessary that provision should be made for facilitating the prompt settlement of minor disputes as they arise.

7. *Manchurian autonomy.* The government in Manchuria should be modified in such a way as to secure, consistently with the sovereignty and administrative integrity of China, a large measure of autonomy designed to meet the local conditions and special characteristics of the Three Provinces. The new civil regime must be so constituted and conducted as to satisfy the essential requirements of good government.

8. *Internal order and security against external aggression.* The internal order of the country should be secured by an effective local gendarmerie force, and security against external aggression should be provided by the withdrawal of all armed forces other than gendarmerie, and by the conclusion of a treaty of non-aggression between the countries interested.

9. *Encouragement of an economic* rapprochement *between China and Japan.* For this purpose, a new commercial treaty between the two countries is desirable. Such a treaty should aim at placing on an equitable basis the commercial relations between the two countries and bringing them into conformity with their improved political relations.

10. *International co-operation in Chinese reconstruction.* Since the present political instability in China is an obstacle to friendship with Japan and an anxiety to the rest of the world (as the maintenance of peace in the Far East is a matter of international concern), and since the conditions enumerated above cannot be fulfilled without a strong Central Government in China, the final requisite for a satisfactory solution is temporary international co-operation in the internal reconstruction of China, as suggested by the late Dr. Sun Yat-sen.

Results Which Would Follow from the Fulfilment of These Conditions

If the present situation could be modified in such a way as to satisfy these conditions and embody these ideas, China and Japan would have achieved a solution of their difficulties which might be made the starting-point of a new era of close understanding and political co-operation between them. If such a *rapprochement* is not secured, no solution, whatever its terms, can really be fruitful. Is it really impossible to contemplate a new relationship even in this hour of crisis. Young Japan is clamorous for strong measures in China and a policy of thoroughness in Manchuria. Those who make these demands are tired of the delays and pin-pricks of the pre-September period; they are impetuous and impatient to gain their end. But, even in Japan, appropriate means must be found for the attainment of every end. After making the acquaintance of some of the more ardent exponents of this "positive" policy, and those especially who, with undoubted idealism and great personal devotion, have constituted themselves the pioneers of a delicate undertaking in the "Manchukuo" regime, it is impossible not to realise that, at the heart of the problem for Japan, lies her anxiety concerning the political development of modern China, and the future to which it is tending. This anxiety has led to action with the object of controlling that development and steering its course in directions which will secure the economic interests of Japan and satisfy strategic requirements for the defence of her empire.

Japanese opinion is nevertheless vaguely conscious that it is no longer practicable to have two separate policies, one for Manchuria and one for the rest of China. Even with her Manchurian interests as a goal, therefore, Japan might recognise and welcome sympathetically the renaissance of Chinese national sentiment, might make friends with it, guide it in her direction and offer it support, if only to ensure that it does not seek support elsewhere.

In China, too, as thoughtful men have come to recognise that the vital problem, the real national problem, for their country is the reconstruction and modernisation of the State, they cannot fail to realise that this policy of reconstruction and modernisation, already initiated with so much promise of success, necessitates for its fulfilment the cultivation of friendly relations with all countries, and above all with that great nation which is their nearest neighbour. China needs, in political and economic matters, the co-operation of all the leading Powers, but especially valuable to her would be the friendly attitude of the Japanese Government and the economic co-operation of Japan in Manchuria. All the other claims of her newly awakened nationalism—legitimate and urgent though they may be—should be subordinated to this one dominating need for the effective internal reconstruction of the State.

Notification by the Japanese Government of Its Intention to Withdraw from the League of Nations*

TELEGRAM FROM THE MINISTER FOR FOREIGN AFFAIRS
OF JAPAN TO THE SECRETARY-GENERAL

Tokio, March 27th, 1933.

The Japanese Government believe that the national policy of Japan, which has for its aim to ensure the peace of the Orient and thereby to contribute to the cause of peace throughout the world, is identical in spirit with the mission of the League of Nations, which is to achieve international peace and security. It has always been with pleasure, therefore, that this country has for thirteen years past, as an original Member of the League and a permanent Member of its Council, extended a full measure of co-operation with her fellow-Members towards the attainment of its high purpose. It is,

* League of Nations *Official Journal*, Parts I-VI (1933), pp. 657-8.

indeed, a matter of historical fact that Japan has continuously participated in the various activities of the League with a zeal not inferior to that exhibited by any other nation. At the same time, it is and has always been the conviction of the Japanese Government that, in order to render possible the maintenance of peace in various regions of the world, it is necessary in existing circumstances to allow the operation of the Covenant of the League to vary in accordance with the actual conditions prevailing in each of those regions. Only by acting on this just and equitable principle can the League fulfil its mission and increase its influence.

Acting on this conviction, the Japanese Government, ever since the Sino-Japanese dispute was, in September 1931, submitted to the League, have, at meetings of the League and on other occasions, continually set forward a consistent view. This was that, if the League was to settle the issue fairly and equitably, and to make a real contribution to the promotion of peace in the Orient, and thus enhance its prestige, it should acquire a complete grasp of the actual conditions in this quarter of the globe and apply the Covenant of the League in accordance with these conditions. They have repeatedly emphasised and insisted upon the absolute necessity of taking into consideration the fact that China is not an organised State; that its internal conditions and external relations are characterised by extreme confusion and complexity and by many abnormal and exceptional features; and that, accordingly, the general principles and usages of international law which govern the ordinary relations between nations are found to be considerably modified in their operation so far as China is concerned, resulting in the quite abnormal and unique international practices which actually prevail in that country.

However, the majority of the Members of the League evinced, in the course of its deliberations during the past seventeen months, a failure either to grasp these realities or else to face them and take them into proper account. Moreover, it has frequently been made manifest in these deliberations that there exist serious differences of opinion between Japan and these Powers concerning the application and even the interpretation of various international engagements and obligations, including the Covenant of the League and the principles of international law. As a result, the report adopted by the Assembly at the special session of February 24th last, entirely misapprehending the spirit of Japan, pervaded as it is by no other desire than the maintenance of peace in the Orient, contains gross errors both in the ascertainment of facts and in the conclusions deduced. In asserting that the action of the Japanese army at the time of the incident of September 18th and subsequently did not fall within the just limits of self-defence, the report assigned no reasons and came to an arbitrary conclusion, and in ignoring alike the state of tension which preceded, and the various aggravations which succeeded, the incident—for all of which the full responsibility is incumbent upon China—the report creates a source of fresh conflict in the political arena of the Orient. By refusing to acknowledge the actual circumstances that led to the foundation of Manchukuo, and by attempting to challenge the position taken up by Japan in recognising the new State, it cuts away the ground for the stabilisation of the Far-Eastern situation. Nor can the terms laid down in its recommendations—as was fully explained in the statement issued by this Government on February 25th last—ever be of any possible service in securing enduring peace in these regions.

The conclusion must be that, in seeking a solution of the question, the majority of the League have attached greater importance to upholding inapplicable formulæ than to the real task of assuring peace, and higher value to the vindication of academic theses than to the eradication of the sources of future conflict. For these reasons, and because of the profound differences of opinion existing between Japan and the majority of the League in their interpretation of the Covenant and of other treaties, the Japanese Government have been led to realise the existence of an irreconcilable divergence of views, dividing Japan and the League on policies of peace, and especially as regards the fundamental principles to be followed in the establishment of a durable peace in the Far East. The Japanese Government, believing that, in these circumstances, there remains no room for further co-operation, hereby give notice, in accordance with the provisions of Article 1, paragraph 3, of the Covenant, of the intention of Japan to withdraw from the League of Nations.

(*Signed*) COUNT YASUYA UCHIDA,
Minister for Foreign Affairs of Japan.

REPLY BY THE SECRETARY-GENERAL

Geneva, March 27th, 1933.

The Secretary-General of the League of Nations has the honour to acknowledge the receipt of the telegram of the Minister for Foreign Affairs of Japan, dated March 27th.

At the conclusion of that telegram, the Japanese Government gives notice of the intention of Japan to withdraw from the League of Nations in accordance with the provisions of Article 1, paragraph 3, of the Covenant, which runs as follows:

"Any Member of the League may, after two years' notice of its intention so to do, withdraw from the League, provided that all its international obligations and all its obligations under this Covenant shall have been fulfilled at the time of its withdrawal."

The Secretary-General will not fail to communicate immediately the telegram from the Japanese Government, together with his reply, to the Members of the League.

(*Signed*) DRUMMOND,
Secretary-General.

The Far East Dispute from the Point of View of the Small States*

Sean Lester

I have been asked to speak on the point of view of the small States with regard to the Sino-Japanese dispute. If there is a separate point of view, and, unfortunately, it can be argued to exist, it is shared and encouraged very whole-heartedly by many people who are distinguished and loyal citizens of the great States. That point of view [of the small states] is perfectly simple: it is that the Covenant must be applied as completely and firmly against a powerful aggressor as against any small country which tries to take the law into its own hands. The organization of peace is not a question of sentimentality nor even of abstract justice but of vital concern, perhaps of life or death, to the States which are not militarily strong.

It is not necessary to recount the history of the dispute nor of the efforts made at Geneva to find a solution—to persuade a great Power that its plighted word, its honour, and, indeed, its permanent interests were involved in carrying out the Pact of which it had itself been one of the authors. . . .

I shall, therefore, confine myself to exposing to you some of the motives which actuated the representatives of certain small States up to the present stage in the Sino-Japanese conflict.

Imperialists have always found plenty of arguments in support of the conquest and seizure of territory belonging to weaker peoples. Japanese diplomacy did not fail to produce such arguments and excuses, but in that case, as in others, the aggressor relied on its military strength as the final argument. Japanese action in Manchuria was, except in one respect, no more immoral than the action of other Powers in the past. They may, therefore, feel themselves unfortunate in being treated on a different basis because their action took place in 1931 and not in 1901; and, no doubt, recognition of this fact made the position of States which had already built empires by the same methods a somewhat delicate one. The outstanding difference in the Japanese case was, of course, the existence of the Covenant, a solemn contract between Japan and fifty-six other nations. The maintenance of the

* Sean Lester, "The Far East Dispute From the Point of View of the Small States," in *Problems of Peace,* Eighth Series (London: George Allen & Unwin, Ltd., 1933), pp. 120-135. Reprinted by permission. Sean Lester (1888-1959) served in the League of Nations as Irish Free State's Permanent Delegate (1929-34). He later served as the organization's Deputy Secretary-General (1937-40) and then as its Secretary-General (1940-47). In 1945 he was recipient of the Woodrow Wilson Foundation Award.

principles of that Pact is of personal importance to every man and woman in the world, though millions may not even have heard of it, and most of the others regard it as a matter only for their Minister for Foreign Affairs. It is of importance to all countries, whether they are great or small, but, not unnaturally, it means more to the smaller and weaker States than to the wealthy and powerful nations.

It must be understood that, during discussions which lasted about eighteen months, there were changes in the attitude of the various Powers, and it would be foolish to imagine that small States as such make any exclusive claim to virtue and consistency; but I think it will also be evident to students of the question that small States did maintain more vigorously that the strength and size of an indicted State must not be allowed to affect the action of the League.

I am afraid it must also be said that it was felt from time to time that too much energy and time had to be spent, often fruitlessly, in endeavouring to convert those who should themselves have been missionaries. If by the process of time, by the exhaustion of argument, the patient and indeed tragic learning of experience, the representatives of some small States were found in the role of advocate for the defence of the League it was not by any desire of their own; it was rather by the failure of leaders who would not lead. Voices which should have been authoritative and firm were, at best, silent; and sometimes when they had been heard it might have been better otherwise. A few small States with no axe to grind, independent, and with some courage, did, I believe, save the League from complete bankruptcy. Of that history must judge. Their task was not pleasant nor easy but they realized that behind them, not quite as articulate but equally convinced, stood dozens of others, many of them most anxious and seriously concerned for the fate of the League idea.

The New Responsibility of the Small States

The League of Nations has presented, for the first time I think in history, an opportunity for the small States to take part in the settlement of world affairs, in which, in other circumstances, their intervention would have been regarded as an impertinent interference with the affairs of their betters. But it would be foolish and childish to exaggerate the extent of this influence, just as it would be foolish to under-estimate it. While the theory of equality between States is clearly accepted, certain and inevitable physical factors must be recognized.

Progress of international co-operation has already imposed certain limits to the exercise of sovereignty; but there is yet a long way to go before nations will assent to the making and application of majority law in all international affairs as it is understood within national frontiers. Curiously enough it is usually the governments of powerful nations, whose influence in the making and shaping of international law would naturally give them additional safeguards, which seem most nervous of development on these lines. Again and again during the long period of discussions about the Far Eastern question, the representatives of small States were reminded that their greater brethren had greater responsibilities. Their colonies, their wide-spread commercial interests, the very fact that they possessed military power, made their decisions of very much greater import to their peoples than those States whose contacts, interests, and resources, and also whose distance from the scene of war, made the consequences of their decisions appear less direct and less menacing. The force of these arguments was fully admitted, though at times they seemed rather irrelevant and no answer to the cold print which registered the articles of the League's Charter.

It will, as I have said, be realized that even in the League questions of important policy cannot always be decided merely by the equal votes of States most unequal in other respects. It must be accepted that in many League matters—that is to say in many international affairs—effective decisions can rarely be secured against the wishes of the Great Powers or against the wishes of one or more of them; and certainly in no matter which they consider to be of vital interest. The difference between the new and the old procedure is that the League provides the means of discussion and of compromise in a way previously impossible, and above all of publicity, which in itself gives the small States an invaluable tactical advantage. . . .

The influence of a small country depends upon its disinterestedness, its reputation for impartiality, its courage, combined with some skill and a balanced judgement, and that influence may in the League be something undreamt of under the old system. The representative of such a country has behind him no battleships or battalions, no great coercive power in commerce or finance. His influence is a moral one and nowhere but in the League of Nations can it be really exercised. The reason for this is that, if the Covenant is very far from being a perfect instrument, certain invaluable principles for the future of the world have been therein declared and attested, and if States, great or small, which have so attested, fail to apply those principles either through weakness or through greed and self-interest, they can at least be pilloried, they can be put into the dock, they can be denounced before their own people and before the world, and the world can bring in its formal and solemn verdict of guilt. It is also true that the Covenant provides the possibility of retribution for grave offences, but to deal with that question alone in its legal and other aspects would require much longer time than is at my disposal. In the end, it depends upon the will of the various governments, for the League of Nations is only as powerful as those governments wish to make it. It will, however, be clear to you that it is easier to enforce judgement against a little offender than a great, although it will be realized that in the present circumstances, when national interests are so interwoven, it may not always be easy to secure agreement to compel even the small offender to rectitude.

Their Interest More Than Academic

Emphasis has been laid in many quarters on the responsibility of the Great Powers; not quite so much emphasis has been laid upon the fact that the type of responsibility referred to is necessarily accompanied by another responsibility: the greater the power, the more insistent is the duty of seeing that the Covenant is respected.

And is the responsibility of the small State so much less? It is true that in the case of a distant conflict their frontiers may be safe, and the proportion of immediate economic disturbance may be much less; but if the principles of the League, to the extent to which they are the principles of international morality, are to be any protection in any part of the world, they must be respected and, if necessary, enforced (with all the factors of each case duly considered) in every part of the world. The Covenant cannot be disregarded in China or South America and remain a guarantee for the small States of Europe. The interest of the small States in such affairs is therefore by no means an academic interest, although it is true that they are also in a special way called upon to maintain and to advocate the maintenance of those principles and of that organization which contain at least a promise for the establishment of peace and justice and the replacement of the principle of force as the unquestioned arbiter by the reign of law. Small States which cherished their liberty might fight against absorption or conquest to their last man, and yet be comparatively easily overwhelmed by a great Power. The world has always condemned such crimes, but very rarely has anything been done to prevent them unless such action threatened the interests of another great Power. Small States believe they have now in the Covenant got a promise of something more than a little moral indignation in such circumstances; they want to be assured that that promise is a reality, capable of development, and certain to be applied, and this responsibility and this interest are to them as important as the responsibilities and interests of the Great Powers of the earth. In seeking to protect this interest, they are not acting contrary to the real interests of the big nations. The common people of the world, whether they are peasants in Spain or Ireland, mill-workers in Japan or England, have in reality the same interests. They want their children or their children's children to grow up freed from the threat of the cruel and brutal waste of life and wealth which war entails. They want the whole force of the Nations to be used, both within their frontiers and in co-operation with others, to enrich the lives of the common people. The directors of the foreign policies of great powers may sometimes realize this common interest, but they are still faced with and often blinded by the old, persistent rivalries and trickery and distrust and ambitions. You will recall the saying that it is easier for a camel to pass through the eye of a needle than for a rich man to enter the kingdom of Heaven. The rich Powers of the world certainly need sympathy and help and persuasion to enable them to reach the kingdom of Peace and some modest help can be given by small States which do not suffer from all their disabilities.

League as Third Party to Disputes

This brings me to another consideration. Early in the dispute between the two great countries in the Far East, it was pointed out that there were not merely two parties to that dispute; that the League of Nations itself was a third party, and that it was not merely a question of establishing the facts or of comparing the actions of either party, or of assessing the blame or of speaking at Council or Assembly on behalf of one's own State and its interests. The League of Nations was as much a party to the dispute as either China or Japan. It, too, was attacked; the League had its obligations and its rights as well as the two peoples engaged in battle. This argument did not presuppose the League as a super-State, but there is, or should be, in the policies of all its Members at least an element which is based on the integral maintenance of the principles of the Covenant and the sum-total of these elements does create something greater than and different to its component parts. It would be unfair to suggest that this point of view was entirely overlooked by the great States. Once again I would emphasize that at one time or another throughout the long discussions, the representatives of the more active of the small States found themselves in agreement with one or another of the great States, and occasionally with them all. But so far as the Council is concerned, I think it is not incorrect to emphasize that small States which are elected by the Assembly have a special mandate. It has been maintained that their selection gives them a special duty to guard the interests which are common to their electors, and for this reason the position of the League as third party to the dispute was frequently raised by the representatives of small States. Japan, instead of following the procedure laid down in the Covenant, had assumed the right to be the sole judge in her own case and had used force to settle it to her own satisfaction; the law did not apply to her in the special circumstances, a plea that, if admitted, would have re-enthroned anarchy where the infant Law was feebly grasping the Sceptre. This was not merely an attack, therefore, upon a weaker and disorganized neighbour but a direct assault upon the League. Here again, perhaps only re-stated in another form, was one of the motives which led certain small States to participate actively in the consideration of the dispute and the search for a just solution. Japanese friends, personally as honourable as they were able, were told that if one had to choose between old friendship and respect for Japan on the one hand and the League on the other there would be no doubt of the choice: that it was no longer a question between China and Japan, but also a question between Japan alone and the League of Nations.

It will be recalled that for about four or five months the Council considered this dispute under Article 11 of the Covenant under which the action of the Council is restricted, as it can propose no solution, according to a widely accepted legal theory, unless the Council, including both parties to the dispute, are unanimous. The power of veto was thus given to either of the disputants. Every resolution which the Council wished to pass required to be negotiated with both the Chinese and Japanese representatives. The Council has been criticized for not taking more energetic measures during that period, and I am certainly not going to undertake the defence of the Council. . . . [N]o one who had not participated in those discussions could fully realize the situation and the difficulties which any such proposal encountered. I would also recall, however, that the Council received many assurances which unfortunately proved to be unreliable. In September the Japanese representative joined in a resolution recognizing his country's obligation to withdraw her troops as speedily as was compatible with the safety of the lives and property of Japanese subjects. In October, Japan rejected a resolution fixing a time limit for that withdrawal—fourteen votes to one, and yet legally it was said to be an ineffective resolution! In December she reaffirmed the undertaking. There was a conflict of view as to the circumstances in which hostilities opened and as to the circumstances in which they were continuing. A League Commission was therefore organized to report to the Council. But it was made clear that the Japanese withdrawal was not dependent upon and not to be delayed on account of the Lytton Commission inquiry.

The Lytton Report Cleared the Way

Then, early in 1932, Article 15 was invoked by the Chinese Government, thus permitting the possibility of recommendations without the assent of the parties, and the matter was transferred to the Assembly. The Assembly found itself faced with similar difficulties, although it was now in a position to exercise greater powers, but statements made at the Special Session showed that the Assembly also demanded the immediate restoration of a situation compatible with the Covenant. It was pointed out that the final settlement might take some time, but that the dispute must not merely be settled, but must be settled only in accordance with the principles of the Covenant. The Committee of Nineteen continued the watching and exhortations which had been the duty of the Council, but the next really important stage was when the Lytton Commission's epoch-making report was received. In the meantime, the Japanese Government had steadily extended its conquest and had set up a puppet Government in Manchuria which it formally recognized. It is no small gratification to me that by happy accident the leader of the Irish Delegation made the first declaration at the Special Assembly when the report came under consideration and, recognizing to the fullest degree the justice of giving complete satisfaction to all legitimate Japanese interests in the territory, was the first there formally to declare that his Government would refuse to recognize a 'State' set up under the conditions which had operated in Manchuria. The declarations by the representatives of other small States were also very firm and helped to make it clear that the report of the League Commission having been received, the Assembly was not merely in a position to take action, but that many Governments were determined it would do so.

This attitude was crystallized in a draft resolution presented by the representatives of Czechoslovakia, Sweden, Spain, and Ireland. That incident might be compared to the hoisting of a flag; an intimation that now that the League had received not only a report but very important recommendations from its Commission, the time for patience and exhortation was approaching an end and that some States-Members at least were determined to make their position and that of the League of Nations perfectly clear. A great English newspaper, the *Manchester Guardian,* commenting on the incident declared: 'When the crisis comes we must look to the smaller Governments, like those of Spain, Sweden, and the Irish Free State, with whom liberty is more than a platform phrase. It was not, however, until some weeks later that the Assembly adopted the report (concurred in by the United States of America, which had collaborated with the League from the beginning) laying down the principles on which the settlement must be based and calling upon all members of the League to refuse to recognize in any way the existence of the so-called State of Manchukuo. Since then, steps have been taken to co-ordinate and guide the action of governments in this direction. No one can tell what the outcome will be. Hostilities have ceased between the Japanese and Chinese people, but Japan remains in unlawful occupation of Chinese territory. In consequence of the Assembly's verdict that she had violated the Covenant, Japan has resigned her membership of the League.

The Balance Sheet Is Not Yet Drawn Up

To many people the outcome of the conflict up to the present represents a setback to the League of Nations. The States composing the League have failed to prevent a Permanent Member of the Council from seizing by military force the territory of another Member of the League, and diplomatic, trade, and financial relations continue almost undisturbed. The balance sheet, however, has not been finally drawn up. The Japanese Government has placed its great nation in a position of at any rate moral isolation, condemned solemnly in public session by the Assembly and by the unanimous opinion of the world. No Member of the League can by any action, or omission to act, acquiesce in her possession of Manchuria without violating its own honour.

There are critics who say that all this should not have been done, and that China should have been left to pay for what were described as the consequences of her weakness and disorganization. There are other critics who say that much more should have been done by the Governments composing the League. Whatever one's views may be on this there seems to be a fairly general opinion that in so far as the Covenant has been vindicated, the small States have taken an honourable share. In doing so, they have not, I

think, at any time, divested themselves of a sense of realities, as has sometimes been said, but have shown appreciation of the fact that in the world
to-day the League of Nations, while still far from being all that it can and
may be, is also a reality.

Small States and the Future

It has been said that in the case of the big Powers they must move
slowly, with the greatest deliberation, and with the anticipation that the
brunt of any international action may fall upon them. All this may be true.
One of the great questions in international affairs to-day is, however,
whether or not the Governments of the Permanent Members of the Council will be in fact prepared in future to act, though it may be slowly and
with all deliberation. Upon the answer depends the future of the League of
Nations. Great Powers in the League may say that that answer in turn also
depends in some cases upon the extent to which non-Member States will be
prepared to co-operate to maintain peace and the inviolability of the Kellogg
Pact. But those Great Powers who have accepted the privileges and duties of
League membership cannot justly shelter behind any State which has not, as
they have, solemnly bound themselves. That situation must be cleared up,
and the other members of the League are entitled to know exactly at what
value to assess the guarantees of the Covenant. . . .

III THE ITALO-ETHIOPIAN DISPUTE OF 1935-1936

The Testing of the League*

Sir Alfred Zimmern

On October 7 and 10 last [1935], at meetings of the Council and Assembly of the League of Nations, fifty members of the League, acting
according to their individual judgment upon the facts of the case, registered
their decisions that a fellow-member, Italy, had violated Article XII of the
Covenant by resorting to war against Ethiopia. As a result, Article XVI of
the Covenant, which declares that a League member resorting to war in
violation of Article XII "shall *ipso facto* be deemed to have committed an

* Sir Alfred Zimmern, "The Testing of the League," *Foreign Affairs,* Vol. 14, No. 3 (April
1936), pp. 373-386. Reprinted by permission of the Council on Foreign Relations, New York.
Sir Alfred Zimmern (1879-1957) was Professor of International Relations at Oxford from
1930-1944. His numerous publications in both classical and international studies include *The
Greek Commonwealth* (1911), *The League of Nations and the Rule of Law* (1939), and
Modern Political Doctrines (1939).

act of war against all other Members of the League," was brought into force; and a special diplomatic conference known as the "Coördination Committee" was set on foot in order to watch over the execution of the measures undertaken by League members in virtue of that Article.

To the diplomatic world which frequents Geneva and to the officials of the League the events of those few days seemed little less than a miracle. Had they not become inured to the notion that Article XVI was a dead letter? Had not the whole question of implementing it been pigeon-holed since the Assembly of 1921, which had itself adopted a set of resolutions involving a considerable watering-down of the original text? And had not the League's handling of the Sino-Japanese and the Chaco disputes induced amongst Geneva *habitués* a mood of defeatism—not to say cynicism—which reached its height during the steady transport of Italian troops to Eritrea and Italian Somaliland in the course of the past summer? True, the problem of sanctions had been disinterred in April and referred to a committee; but this action had been taken in pursuance of the policy of the "Stresa Front" and seemed therefore to have little relevance to the African policy of the nation acting as host at the Stresa meeting. Moreover, the committee in question, or rather its legal subcommittee (on which Italy was of course represented), had soon become embogged in juridical subtleties which augured ill for any practical results.

But for the man in the street, whether in Great Britain, the Northern countries, the Netherlands, Belgium, Czechoslovakia or any other democratic country, the adoption of sanctions or punitive measures against Mussolini's government after its flagrant attack upon a fellow-member of the League seemed the natural and obvious course to be pursued. The prevailing sentiment on receipt of the news was not one of astonishment that the Geneva machine was really functioning, but rather of impatience because a week had been allowed to elapse between the outbreak of hostilities and the registering of the aggression in the Assembly. If a German army had invaded Alsace, men asked, or a Hungarian army had marched into Transylvania, would not the days have been shortened to hours?

The divergence between these two mentalities—that of the diplomatic world and that of the general public which believes in the League—is a measure of the extent of the task on which the League thus found itself engaged. It constitutes also one of the principal reasons why its success, after four months of common action in the Coördination Committee, is still relative rather than absolute.

The object of the following pages is to examine, in the light of this experience, the nature of the problem confronting the League and to analyze the degree and quality of its achievement to date.

II

First let us ask two preliminary questions of a hypothetical character. What would have happened in regard to Ethiopia if there had been no

League of Nations? And, alternatively, what would have happened if the League, whilst continuing to function, had failed to intervene to restrain Italy in her designs?

It is impossible to give a direct answer to the first question. The "might-have-beens" of history, on which Mr. Winston Churchill and others so much enjoy indulging their speculations, cannot be submitted to scientific analysis. But we can at least recall the fact that when in 1898 an attempt was made by France to extend her power eastwards from her existing African possessions to the basin of the Upper Nile, it met with the determined resistance of the British Government of the day. Lord Salisbury, indeed, as the records reveal, was always particularly concerned to safeguard British interests in that region. And he was equally concerned to keep the Concert of the European Great Powers from what he would have considered an undue interference in a matter which concerned Great Britain and France alone. If the League of Nations had not come into existence, we are perhaps justified in assuming that the pre-war British policy in that region would have been maintained. It would have been more difficult for British statesmanship to steer clear of outside interference; and there would have been less chance than there is today of arriving at a settlement taking genuine Italian needs and aspirations into account. That is perhaps all that can be said on this very hypothetical subject.

Let us now take the other hypothesis and assume that the League, constituted as it was in the summer of last year, had on one pretext or another failed to take action on behalf of Ethiopia. This, so far as a non-Italian observer can judge, is the hypothesis on which Signor Mussolini proceeded when he planned his invasion. He seems to have depended on Geneva not merely not to obstruct his "Colonial War," but even to facilitate it. For him, Geneva did not stand for the Covenant, with its rules and safeguards "for great and small alike," as President Wilson conceived it: it was simply a diplomatic metropolis and market-place where the three Great Powers in the League—Great Britain, France and Italy—dominated the scene and imposed their will, by appropriate forms of pressure, upon the smaller fry. In other words, in case it proved necessary to keep Great Britain in check, he relied on his understanding with M. Laval, dating from their meeting at Rome in January 1935, together with the complicated Geneva machinery with its inexhaustible opportunities for intrigue and delay. One can imagine Lord Salisbury turning in his grave as Signor Mussolini employed one Genevan artifice after another in order to promote an aggressive national policy of his own, whilst the much-vaunted Covenant, "the sheet-anchor of British policy," not only itself failed to protect the integrity and independence of Ethiopia, but also effectually prevented Britain from taking individual action to safeguard her own legitimate interests. If the Italian calculation had proved correct, the Italo-Ethiopian war would not simply have been acquiesced in by the League: the very existence of the League would have made the war "practical politics" for Italy. The League would thus have performed, in its own peculiar way, the part played by pre-war power diplomacy when it cleared the way for Italian occupation of Tripoli and, in an earlier generation, for the French occupation of Tunis.

Such a League would clearly have been very useful to Italy. On a short view, it would also have been very useful to France; for it would have meant that Africa, always a region of secondary importance in French eyes, would have been withdrawn from the political orbit of the League and that the whole of the attention and effective authority of the League would have been concentrated upon the Continent of Europe.

In this way, the Ethiopian crisis would have carried to a logical conclusion a movement which had been in progress during the preceding four years—if not since the Pan-European campaign of M. Briand in 1929 and 1930. For Geneva had been witnessing a steady process of what can be called "dis-annexation." Ths Far East was politically dis-annexed from the League through the events of 1931 and 1932, in Manchuria and Shanghai, when the French Government of the day was—to say the least—no more anxious than Lord Reading and Sir John Simon to set the machinery of sanctions in motion. Later on, Latin America was at least morally dis-annexed through the war of attrition which was allowed to be waged in the Chaco—a disgraceful episode which must awaken equally disagreeable memories at Geneva and Washington, if not at Buenos Aires. Here again the French Government, if one may judge from the attitude of its representative in the Advisory Committee, was not amongst the foremost in seeking to apply the procedure of Article XVI to the Covenant-breaking state: it left the championship of strict League principles to the watchful care of Czechoslovakia and Soviet Russia. With Africa equally withdrawn from the League's orbit, and in the continued absence of the United States, all that would have been left to the supervision of Geneva would have been Europe and the Near East. The League would thus have become, for political purposes, what many Americans have regarded it as being from the first, a predominantly European body. Indeed, the area over which its effective authority would have been exercised or projected would have corresponded almost exactly with that which enjoyed the intermittent attention of the Concert of the European Great Powers under the pre-war system.

What figure would such a League have presented in British eyes? Merely to put this question is sufficient to bring out the shortsightedness of the French conception, if indeed it was entertained in the responsible quarters in Paris. A League of Nations limited to the European Continent would not have been for Great Britain—still less for the British Dominions —a League of Nations at all. It would have been idle for French or other European partisans of the League to attempt to interest the British people in the application of the Covenant to European problems alone. Britain is indeed unalterably tied to the European mainland. But Sir Samuel Hoare was rightly interpreting the sentiment of his countrymen when he declared, at the conclusion of his famous speech on September 11, that the failure of the League in the crucial Ethiopian test would break down the "main bridge" between Great Britain and the Continent. Thenceforward, British statesmanship would have pusued national interests according to what seemed the most opportune methods, as it did throughout the eighteenth and nineteenth centuries. The League would no doubt have continued to exist, as the Norwegian Foreign Minister, Professor Koht, speaking after Sir Samuel Hoare in the afternoon of the same day, significantly pleaded that it should be allowed to do in such an eventuality. But it would have degenerated into little more than a clearing-house for information and a coördinating center for non-political activities—a sort of glorified Postal Union. The Wilsonian League would have passed into history.

III

Let us now turn to the actual record of the League in the Italo-Ethiopian affair.

The first fact which confronts us is that a war is actually in progress between two members of the League. The League did not succeed in preventing war from breaking out. That is—and whatever may happen later, will always remain—an unhappy page in its history. Moreover, the war broke out under circumstances particularly humiliating to the League. The Assembly had only just been in session, with its members deeply interested in the dispute. The Council was actually in process of dealing with it. The eyes of the whole world were on Geneva when the Italian dictator, at the opening of the campaigning season in East Africa, rudely interrupted the business of the diplomatic talking-shop and resorted to arms in violation of four treaties. That this could occur at all is a severe reflection upon the authority of the League and indeed of the whole system of international right. It ought no more to have been able to occur than a violation by some organized group in the United States of a decision of the United States Supreme Court. If a member of the League can thus take the law into his own hands, what is there left of the law? The Covenant of the League of Nations, the Kellogg Pact, the Italo-Ethiopian Treaty of 1928, the Tripartite Treaty of 1906 (still valid, within the terms of Article XX of the Covenant) become merely so many pieces of waste paper. Why not put an end to the whole machinery of treaty-making if that is all that its results are worth? Such must have been the reflections of many on hearing the news that the Italian army had crossed the Ethiopian border whilst the Committee of Five was engaged on drawing up its report for the Council.

Why was the League unable to prevent the war from breaking out?

It was not, as in the case of the organization of sanctions, for want of previous discussion and preparation on the subject. During the fifteen years of the League's life an immense amount of time and trouble had been devoted to precisely that problem. It had been prominent in the debates on the Geneva Protocol and in the Preparatory Committee for the Disarmament Conference as well as in the Council and the Assembly. In 1930, on the impulsion of the British Labor Government, the Assembly actually gave its approval to a "Model Treaty for Strengthening the Means to Prevent War" which, if it had been signed and observed by League members, would have enabled the Council to intervene on the spot at an early stage of the Italo-Ethiopian dispute. Under the "Model Treaty" the members of the League who had agreed to be bound by it were pledged to accept certain actions taken by the Council for the prevention of war. But even without this pledged acquiescence by the parties, the Council was authorized, as the result of a report dating from 1927, to adopt any of a number of specified measures in the event of an "imminent threat of war." Amongst the measures thus enumerated by what is known as the Cecil-de Brouckère-Titulesco Report, we find the mention of "naval demonstrations" such as "have been employed for such a purpose in the past." Would not a joint naval demonstration on the part of the Mediterranean Powers in the Red Sea and the adjacent Indian Ocean have given pause to the Italian Government in its transportation of troops to the borders of Ethiopia?

Why were no such measures adopted? Why, indeed, was there no suggestion throughout the eight months during which the dispute was before the League of action by the Council on the lines of the Report of 1927? Here we come back to the point from which we started. It was because Italy is a Great Power. To set in motion measures of this kind against a Great Power involved, for the diplomatic world, a revolution in international politics. To begin with, it would have been argued, it was not practicable: and, even if it were, it would not be desirable, for it would fail in its object. So far from preventing war, it would precipitate war.

Let us probe into this reasoning a little more deeply, for it brings us to the heart of our subject. Why was it not "practicable" for the Council or Assembly of the League to organize a joint naval demonstration in the Red Sea?

There was, of course, one immediate and insuperable difficulty—the attitude of France under the Laval Government. But to regard this as the sole objection is to evade the real problem. Even if French opinion had been less favorable to Italy and more favorable to the League than it actually was, the adoption of preventive measures against Italy would have been considered last summer to be outside the range of practical politics.

Why should this be so? For two reasons. First, because of the risks to which the individual Powers taking part in these measures would have exposed themselves at the hands of an aggrieved Great Power. It requires a very high degree of courage and public spirit in the statesmen and peoples of smaller states for them to be willing, above and beyond their obligations under the Covenant, to incur the displeasure of a Great Power. *Nemo me impune lacessit* embodies a Latin sentiment which is not yet extinct in Rome; and its natural counterpart in the foreign offices of smaller states is "Leave it to George"—in other words, leave it to Geneva or to the other Great Powers. Why must *we* be brought in?

The second general reason why preventive measures against Italy were not practical politics was that Italy, being a Great Power, would have been exasperated rather than restrained by their adoption. She would have considered them a blow to her prestige. Great Powers may be negotiated with; they may be privately warned; they may even be subjected to pressures of various kinds behind the scenes; but they must not be coerced or intimidated in public. Let the reader, whether he be American or British, transpose the situation and apply it to his own country. He will realize that the problem thus revealed is not a problem affecting only the Italian people, still less the present ruler of Italy. Prestige, or "face" as it is called in the East, is an element which cannot be ignored in dealing with any Great Power. It is the counterpart or inseparable shadow of something that is of supreme importance and value in international politics—something without which the political system of the world would disintegrate into atoms—the sense of responsibility for world affairs. To accept the position of a Great Power is to accept certain obligations—not definite contractual obligations such as are embodied in the Covenant and the Kellogg Pact, but obligations of a more intangible but no less binding character. They are perhaps best summed up in the old French watchword *noblesse oblige*. But if a Great Power has obligations arising out of the greatness of its station, it is part of the same order of ideas that it cannot be coerced or publicly rebuked by others of a lower or lesser station. *Noblesse ne se laisse pas intimider*. That is the psychological reason, with its roots deep in European history, why it was not considered either at Geneva or in the Chancelleries as "practical politics" to adopt preventive measures against the Italian war preparations in the spring and summer of last year. That is why, in spite of the elaborate armory of such measures provided in the 1927 Report, the Council set prevention on one side and devoted all its energies to "conciliation."

It is worth adding, however, that the League's effort at conciliation, which did not begin in earnest until the first week in September, was accompanied by a naval demonstration carried out on its own responsibility by a single Power—Great Britain. This measure was in part a response to the concentration of Italian troops near the Egyptian border in Libya and to the persistent anti-British propaganda carried on by the Italian Government in the Near East and through Italian wireless stations. But it was no doubt also hoped that it would sober the mind of the Italian Government and so act as a preventive against the outbreak of war in Ethiopia.

In so far as this was its object, it proved unsuccessful. The Italian transports made their way past the British warships in the Eastern Mediterranean, threaded the Canal, emerged to meet more British craft in the Red Sea, and discharged their human cargoes at Massaua, Assab or Mogadishu. Just so, a few weeks later, the vessels conveying arms and other forms of assistance to the Ethiopians braved the Italian warships, which might have held them up for carrying contraband of war, and landed their consignments safely at Jibuti.

IV

If the record of the League has been a failure so far as the prevention of war is concerned, what are we to say of its record in restraining the aggressor whom it had failed to deter?

There are two answers to this question, one in the practical realm, the other in the psychological.

The practical answer is that the members of the League, other than Italy and a few dissentients and absentees, set machinery on foot against Italy within ten days of the breach of the Covenant and had by October 19 adopted four measures, the combined scope of which is very considerable: (1) the prohibition of the export of arms, ammunition and implements of war; (2) the prohibition of loans, credits, issues of or subscriptions to "shares or other capital flotations for any public authority, person or corporation in Italian territory;" (3) the prohibition of the importation of Italian goods; (4) an embargo on certain exports to Italy, including transport animals, rubber, bauxite, aluminium, iron ore, chromium, manganese, nickel, tungsten and certain other key-minerals together with tin and tin-ore.

These measures had, of course, to be referred to the various governments. Most if not all of these, in the absence of a study of Article XVI at Geneva, had made no previous arrangements for carrying out their obligations in the economic and financial sphere under that Article. When the replies received by the governments were classified on December 11 for the Committee of Eighteen, which is a kind of Executive Committee for the larger Conference, the result was as follows:

Four states, Albania, Austria, Hungary and Paraguay, were taking no action under Article XVI. Of these, Paraguay had given notice of resignation from the League in the previous February: the other three were—if one may so put it—not wholly their own masters. It is, however, worth while pointing out that none of the three, in their speeches in the Assembly in October, contested the *facts* on which the Council Committee based its conclusion that Italy had "resorted to war in disregard of its covenants under Article XII of the Covenant of the League of Nations." In other words, they admitted by implication that they had decided, or felt themselves compelled, to go back upon their obligations under the Covenant. Of the other members, Guatemala, whilst accepting the proposals "in principle," had taken no definite action on any of them, while Salvador had only taken action on the third.

For the rest, the record stood as follows:

Fifty states had adopted measures putting in force Proposal I, forty-seven states had acted on Proposal II, forty-three states on Proposal III, and forty-five states on Proposal IV. The four lists include all the more important members of the League, the absentees being chiefly among the Latin-American states. The chief practical difficulty amongst League members has occurred in connection with the application by Switzerland of the third proposal. The Swiss Government has not prohibited the import of goods from Italy, owing to the existence of an open alternative route through Austria; but it has arranged to prevent any transfer from Switzerland of funds derived from Italian exports and also to keep down to the 1934 level the total value of imports from and exports to Italy.

In addition, the Committee of Eighteen at its meeting on November 6 submitted to the governments a proposal which, in view of the controversy which it aroused, should be cited textually:

It is expedient that the measures of embargo provided for in Proposal IV should be extended to the following articles as soon as the conditions necessary to render this extension effective have been realized:

Petroleum and its derivatives, by-products and residues;

Pig-iron; iron and steel (including alloy steels), cast, forged, drawn, stamped or pressed;

Coal (including anthracite or lignite), coke and their agglomerates, as well as fuels derived therefrom.

December 12 was set as the date for discussing this proposal in the light of the replies from the governments and "the conditions necessary to render" it "effective." That date found the League in the midst of the political crisis provoked by the Hoare-Laval proposals, and no action was therefore taken. On January 22, however, the Committee of Eighteen recurred to the subject and, concentrating on the subject of oil, decided "to create a committee of experts to conduct a technical examination of the conditions governing the trade in and transport of petroleum and its derivatives, by-products and residues, with a view to submitting an early report to the Committee of Eighteen on the effectiveness of the extension of measures of embargo to the above-mentioned commodities." At the moment of writing, this expert Committee is in session at Geneva.

How effective the measures in operation are proving to be, what result they would have if reinforced by an oil embargo, it is impossible for any one outside Italian government circles to estimate. A thick curtain hangs between Italy and the outer world. It would be asking too much of political human nature to expect the statements or official statistics of the Italian government to be taken at their face value. But that the "siege" of the peninsula is causing grave material and moral discomfort is certain. How could it be otherwise? For it is not so much the actual pressure of the League action at the present time which has to be taken into account and must be weighing upon the minds of all thoughtful and responsible Italians. It is the vista of the future.

The Geneva machine is no doubt a ponderous and rusty apparatus which proceeds on its path with a great deal of creaking and spluttering. But if it is difficult to roll it forward, it is equally difficult—perhaps even more difficult—to roll it backwards. The four measures now in force may fall far short of the total suspension of intercourse contemplated by the framers of Article XVI. They may be entailing for Italy, not an intense and urgent crisis in her economic life, but something resembling rather a severe and wasting form of pernicious anæmia. And what hope is there of relief—to say nothing of cure? It was difficult enough to bring to an end the Great War after the principal allies had bound themselves not to make a separate peace. How much more difficult will it be, Italians must be asking themselves, especially after the Hoare-Laval fiasco, to bring to an end sanctions voted by fifty states united by a bond of common principle, as also by the very considerable sacrifices involved for each in the diminution of its trade?

Perhaps we may leave this part of our subject with a single further reflection. There are four sanctions at present in force against Italy. Two of them are economic—the action taken by the League of Nations and the sanction—for it is a sanction—involved for the Italian people by the cost of the war itself. A third is the climate and the other physical conditions in the war-zone. A fourth is the military resistance of the Ethiopians. It is impossible for anyone not in the secrets of the Italian Government to assess the relative intensity of these four forms of pressure. But who can doubt that their cumulative effect is very considerable or that the imponderables represented by the action taken at Geneva form a very substantial accretion to the total burden?

V

Let us now turn to the psychological aspect of the question—to the effect upon public opinion throughout the world, and especially amongst the peoples included in the League, of the application of sanctions and of the common effort and enterprise which it represents.

Here we come upon what is undoubtedly the principal event not merely in the unhappy Italo-Ethiopian conflict, but (it is no exaggeration to say) in the history of the League up to the present time. For the last few months have witnessed the emergence of a new political force—a force the existence of which was proclaimed in past years by some and suspected by others, but which had never yet revealed itself as an element with which the democratic governments were bound to reckon and which it would be perilous, indeed suicidal, for them to ignore. The prompt, complete and determined rejection of the Hoare-Laval proposals by the people of Great Britain and other countries, leading to the departure from office of the two statesmen responsible for framing them, marks a turning point in the history of the democratic control of foreign affairs—one might go further and say of democracy itself. It showed that, of the two forces or agencies or bodies of opinion contrasted at the outset of this article, that embodying the opinion of the plain citizen could prove itself irresistible on a clear issue of principle. It showed also that the plain citizen did not intend that the issue of principle on which he had definite views (and on which in Great Britain at any rate he had recently expressed his opinion at the polls) should be obscured either by diplomatic verbiage or by power-politics bargaining of the pre-war type or, what is still more important, by threats of violence. What happened in December, so far as the British voter is considered, is simple. The British Government, or at least the Foreign Secretary—it is difficult to speak as definitely on this point of the former as of the latter—did not feel justified in continuing a policy which involved a risk, uncertain in degree, of involving Great Britain in war with Italy. The people of Great Britain showed unmistakably that they were prepared to take that risk in preference to the alternative course which would have involved the end of the League system as they conceived it.

The consequences of this decision by the British people are momentous. For the first time since the League machinery was set up in Geneva in 1920 the League is known and felt to be a power. For the first time, to use the familiar American expression, it has teeth—not teeth in the sense of elaborate provisions drawn up in treaties, such as the Geneva Protocol, but in the sense that the plain citizen is known to be ready to assist the public authority in the restraint of violence. Once sure of that support, the public authority can grapple with its task in an entirely new spirit. The only real sanction, as President Wilson repeatedly declared, and as many, including not a few defeatists, have declared since, is public opinion, "the organized opinion of mankind." In the present instance this opinion organized itself in less than a week.

With the marching order thus clearly given, the rest ought to be comparatively easy. The problem of security, insoluble so long as the element of public opinion remained in doubt, has been transformed into a matter of practical adjustment. Truly it was a great day's work which was performed at the Quai d'Orsay on Sunday, December 8, 1935. To General Göring and to M. Pierre Laval must be awarded twin prizes as educators of the British people. The former had already purged it of insular habits of thought which had resisted all previous physicians. Now came the latter, and by dint of a treatment as sudden and almost equally violent fixed the new habits firmly in the groove of collective security. It rests now for British statesmen to continue at home, on constructive lines, the rude education thus supplied from abroad.

For the moment the prospect is obscure, not only in the battle-zone and in Italy, but over the whole of Europe. Never since the Armsitice has it been so difficult to foresee the turn which events will take, even in the immediate future. But one thing seems clear. The demonstration that the League is not merely a piece of machinery at Geneva but a reality in the hearts and minds of the people in the leading member-states, great and small alike, both in Europe and overseas, is an immense addition of strength to the League and to the governments associated together in upholding the Covenant. How best to make use of this newly revealed force, how to bring together the plain man's sense of responsibility and grasp of principle with the experience and technique of the Chancelleries, how to prevent Geneva from relapsing once more into the paralyzing cynicism of last summer—all this is on the knees of the gods. But the gods, who in the past have loaded Geneva with so many disappointments, have shown themselves of late not too unkind. No one would say that the sky is clear; but the watchword is "Forward."

Address of Haile Selassie Before Assembly (June 30, 1936)*

THE PRESIDENT: His Majesty the Negus Haile Selassie, first delegate of Ethopia, will address the Assembly.

H.M. THE NEGUS HAILE SELASSIE (Ethiopia), speaking in French: [Translation] I ask the Assembly to excuse me if I do not speak in French as I should have wished. I shall express myself better, with all the strength of my heart and mind, if I speak in Amharic.

H.M. HAILE SELASSIE continued in Amharic: I, Haile Selassie I, Emperor of Ethopia, am here to-day to claim that justice that is due to my people, and the assistance promised to it eight months ago by fifty-two nations who asserted that an act of aggression had been committed in violation of international treaties.

None other than the Emperor can address the appeal of the Ethiopian people to those fifty-two nations.

There is perhaps no precedent for a head of a State himself speaking in this Assembly. But there is certainly no precedent for a people being the victim of such wrongs and being threatened with abandonment to its aggressor. Nor has there ever before been an example of any Government proceeding to the systematic extermination of a nation by barbarous means, in violation of the most solemn promises made to all the nations of the earth that there should be no resort to a war of conquest and that there should not be used against innocent human beings the terrible weapon of poison gas. It is to defend a people struggling for its age-old independence that the Head of the Ethiopian Empire has come to Geneva to fulfil this supreme duty, after having himself fought at the head of his armies.

I pray Almighty God that He may spare nations the terrible sufferings that have just been inflicted on my people, and of which the chiefs who have accompanied me here have been the horrified witnesses.

It is my duty to inform the Governments assembled in Geneva, responsible as they are for the lives of millions of men, women and children, of the deadly peril which threatens them, by describing to them the fate which has been suffered by Ethiopia.

It is not only upon warriors that the Italian Government has made war.

* League of Nations *Records of the Assembly* (18th Plenary Meeting, June 30, 1936), 1936, XVI, pp. 22-25.

It has, above all, attacked populations far removed from hostilities, in order to terrorise and exterminate them.

At the outset, towards the end of 1935, Italian aircraft hurled tear-gas bombs upon my armies. They had but slight effect. The soldiers learned to scatter, waiting until the wind had rapidly dispersed the poisonous gases.

The Italian aircraft then resorted to mustard gas. Barrels of liquid were hurled upon armed groups. But this means too was ineffective; the liquid affected only a few soldiers, and the barrels upon the ground themselves gave warning of the danger to the troops and to the population.

It was at the time when the operations for the encirclement of Makale were taking place that the Italian command, fearing a rout, applied the procedure which it is now my duty to denounce to the world.

Sprayers were installed on board aircraft so that they could vaporise, over vast areas of territory, a fine, death-dealing rain. Groups of nine, fifteen, eighteen aircraft followed one another so that the fog issuing from them formed a continuous sheet. It was thus that, from the end of January 1936, soldiers, women, children, cattle, rivers, lakes, and fields were constantly drenched with this deadly rain. In order to kill off systematically all living creatures, in order the more surely to poison waters and pastures, the Italian command made its aircraft pass over and over again. That was its chief method of warfare.

The very refinement of barbarism consisted in carrying devastation and terror into the most densely populated parts of the territory, the points farthest removed from the scene of hostilities. The object was to scatter horror and death over a great part of the Ethiopian territory.

These fearful tactics succeeded. Men and animals succumbed. The deadly rain that fell from the aircraft made all those whom it touched fly shrieking with pain. All who drank the poisoned water or ate the infected food succumbed too, in dreadful suffering. In tens of thousands the victims of the Italian mustard gas fell. It was to denounce to the civilised world the tortures inflicted upon the Ethiopian people that I resolved to come to Geneva. None other than myself and my gallant companions in arms could bring the League of Nations undeniable proof. The appeals of my delegates to the League of Nations had remained unanswered; my delegates had not been eyewitnesses. That is why I decided to come myself to testify against the crime perpetrated against my people and to give Europe warning of the doom that awaits it if it bows before the accomplished fact.

Need I remind the Assembly of the various stages of the Ethiopian drama?

For twenty years past, as Heir-Apparent, Regent of the Empire, and as Emperor, I have been directing the destinies of my people. I have ceaselessly striven to bring to my country the benefits of civilisation, and especially to establish relations of good-neighbourliness with adjacent Powers. In particular, I succeeded in concluding with Italy the Treaty of Friendship of 1928, which absolutely prohibited the resort, under whatsoever pretext, to force of arms, substituting for force the procedure of conciliation and arbitration on which civilised nations have based international order.

In its report of October 5th, 1935, the Committee of Thirteen recognised my efforts and the results I had achieved. It stated as follows:

"The Governments considered that the entry of Ethiopia into the League would not only afford her a further guarantee for the maintenance of her territorial integrity and independence, but would help her to reach a higher level of civilisation. There does not appear to be more disorder and insecurity in Ethiopia to-day than was the case in 1923. On the contrary, the country is better organised and the central authority is better obeyed."

I should have procured still greater results for my people had not obstacles of every kind been put in the way by the Italian Government, which stirred up revolt and armed the rebels.

Indeed, the Rome Government, as it has thought fit to proclaim openly to-day, has been ceaselessly preparing for the conquest of Ethiopia. The treaties of friendship it signed with me were not sincere; their only object was to hide its real intention from me. The Italian Government asserts that for fourteen years it has been preparing for its present conquest. It therefore recognises to-day that, when it supported the admission of Ethiopia to the League of Nations in 1923, when it concluded the Treaty of Friendship in 1928, when it signed the Pact of Paris outlawing war, it was deceiving the whole world. The Ethiopian Government for its part saw, in these solemn treaties, only fresh guarantees of security, enabling it to achieve further progress along the pacific path of reform upon which it had entered and to which it had devoted all its strength and all its heart.

The Walwal incident in December 1934 came as a thunderbolt to me. The Italian provocation was obvious. I did not hesitate to appeal to the League of Nations. I invoked the provisions of the Treaty of 1928, the principles of the Covenant; I urged the procedure of conciliation and arbitration.

Unhappily for Ethiopia, this was the time when a certain Government considered that the European situation made it imperative at any price to obtain the friendship of Italy. The price paid was the abandonment of Ethiopian independence to the greed of the Italian Government. This secret agreement, contrary to the obligations of the Covenant, has exerted a great influence over the course of events. Ethiopia, and the whole world, have suffered and are still suffering to-day its disastrous consequences.

This first violation of the Covenant was followed by many others. Feeling itself encouraged in its anti-Ethiopian policy, the Rome Government feverishly made war preparations, thinking that the concerted pressure which was beginning to be exerted on the Ethiopian Government might perhaps fail to overcome the resistance of my people to Italian domination. Time had to be gained; so all kinds of difficulties from all sides were placed in the way, so as to protract the procedure of conciliation and arbitration.

Every kind of obstacle was placed in the way of that procedure. Certain Governments tried to prevent the Ethiopian Government from finding arbitrators amongst their nationals. When once the arbitral tribunal was set up, pressure was exercised to ensure an award favourable to Italy. All was in vain. The arbitrators—two of whom were Italian officials—were forced to recognise unanimously that in the Walwal incident, as in the subsequent incidents, no international responsibility was attributable to Ethiopia.

After this award, the Ethiopian Government sincerely thought that an era of friendly relations might be opened with Italy. I loyally offered my hand to the Rome Government.

The Assembly was informed by the report of the Committee of Thirteen, dated October 5th, 1935, of the details of the events which occurred after the month of December 1934 and up to October 3rd, 1935. I need only quote a few of the conclusions of that report:

"The Italian memorandum [containing the complaints made by Italy] was laid on the Council table on September 4th, 1935, whereas Ethiopia's first appeal to the Council had been made on December 14th, 1934. In the interval between these two dates, the Italian Government opposed the consideration of the question by the Council on the ground that the only appropriate procedure was that provided for in the Italo-Ethiopian Treaty of 1928. Throughout the whole of that period, moreover, the despatch of Italian troops to East Africa was proceeding. These shipments of troops were represented to the Council by the Italian Government as necessary for the defence of its colonies menaced by Ethiopia's military preparations. Ethiopia, on the contrary, drew attention to the official pronouncements made in Italy which, in its opinion, left no doubt 'as to the hostile intentions of the Italian Government.'

"From the outset of the dispute, the Ethiopian Government has sought a settlement by peaceful means. It has appealed to the procedures of the Covenant. The Italian Government desiring to keep strictly to the procedure of the Italo-Ethiopian Treaty of 1928, the Ethiopian Government assented; it invariably stated that it would faithfully carry out the arbitral award, even if the decision went against it. It agreed that the question of the ownership of Walwal should not be dealt with by the arbitrators, because the Italian Government would not agree to such a course. It asked the Council to despatch neutral observers and offered to lend itself to any enquiries upon which the Council might decide.

"Once the Walwal dispute had been settled by arbitration, however, the Italian Government submitted its detailed memorandum to the Council in support of its claim to liberty of action. It asserted that a case like that of Ethiopia cannot be settled by the means provided by the Covenant.

"It stated that, 'since this question affects vital interests and is of primary importance to Italian security and civilisation,' it 'would be failing in its most elementary duty, did it not cease once and for all to place any confidence in Ethiopia, reserving full liberty to adopt any measures that may become necessary to ensure the safety of its colonies and to safeguard its own interests.' "

Such are the terms of the Committee of Thirteen's report. The Council and the Assembly unanimously adopted the conclusions of that report and solemnly proclaimed that the Italian Government had violated the Covenant and was in a state of aggression.

I unhesitatingly stated that I did not want war, that it was imposed upon me, that I should struggle solely for the independence and integrity of my people, and that in that struggle I was defending the cause of all small States exposed to the greed of a powerful neighbour.

In October 1935, the fifty-two nations who are listening to me to-day gave me an assurance that the aggressor would not triumph, that the resources of the Covenant would be implemented in order to ensure the rule of law and the failure of violence.

I ask the fifty-two nations not to forget to-day the policy upon which they embarked eight months ago, and on the faith of which I directed the resistance of my people against the aggressor whom they had denounced to the world.

Despite the inferiority of my weapons, the complete lack of aircraft, artillery, munitions and hospital services, my trust in the League was absolute. I thought it impossible that fifty-two nations, including the most powerful in the world, could be successfully held in check by a single aggressor. Relying on the faith due to treaties, I had made no preparation for war, and that is the case with a number of small countries in Europe. When the danger became more urgent, conscious of my responsibilities towards my people, I tried during the first six months of 1935, to acquire armaments. Many Governments proclaimed an embargo to prevent my doing so, whereas the Italian Government, through the Suez Canal, was given all facilities for transporting, without cessation and without protest, troops, arms and munitions. On October 3rd, 1935, Italian troops invaded my territory. Not until a few hours later did I decree a general mobilisation. In my desire to maintain peace, I had, following the example of a great country in Europe on the eve of the great war, caused my troops to withdraw thirty kilometres back so as to remove any pretext of provocation.

War was then waged in the atrocious conditions which I have laid before the Assembly.

In that unequal struggle between a Government commanding more than forty-two million inhabitants, having at its disposal financial, industrial and technical means which enabled it to create unlimited quantities of the most death-dealing weapons, and, on the other hand, a small people of twelve million inhabitants, without arms, without resources, having on its side nothing but the justice of its own cause and the promise of the League of Nations, what real assistance was given to Ethiopia by the fifty-two nations who had declared the Rome Government guilty of a breach of the

Covenant and had undertaken to prevent the triumph of the aggressor? Has each of the State Members, as it was its duty to do in virtue of its signature appended to Article 16 of the Covenant, considered the aggressor to have committed an act of war personally directed against itself?

I had placed all my hopes in the fulfilment of these undertakings. My trust had been confirmed by the repeated declarations made in the Council to the effect that aggression must not be rewarded, and that, in the end, force would be compelled to bow before law.

In December 1935, the Council made it quite clear that its sentiments were in harmony with those of hundreds of millions of people who, in all parts of the world, had protested against the proposal to dismember Ethiopia.

It was constantly repeated that there was not merely a conflict between the Italian Government and Ethiopia, but also a conflict between the Italian Government and the League of Nations.

That is why I refused all proposals to my personal advantage made to me by the Italian Government if only I would betray my people and the Covenant of the League. I was defending the cause of all small peoples who are threatened with aggression.

What has become of the promises made to me? As early as October 1935 I noted with grief, but without surprise, that there were three Powers which regarded their undertakings under the Covenant as absolutely valueless. Their connections with Italy impelled them to refuse to take any measures whatsoever to stop Italian aggression.

On the other hand, it was a profound disappointment to me to note the attitude of a certain Government which, whilst tirelessly protesting its scrupulous attachment to the Covenant, has equally tirelessly striven to prevent its observance. As soon as any measure which was likely to be rapidly effective was proposed, pretexts in one form or another were devised, to postpone even consideration of that measure. Did the secret agreements of January 1935 provide for this tireless obstruction?

The Ethiopian Government never expected other Governments to shed their soldiers' blood to defend the Covenant when their own immediately personal interests were not at stake. Ethiopian warriors asked only for means to defend themselves. On many occasions I asked for financial assistance for the purchase of arms. That assistance was constantly denied me. What, then, in practice, is the meaning of Article 16 of the Covenant and of collective security?

The Ethiopian Government's use of the railway from Jibuti to Addis Ababa was in practice obstructed as regards the transport of arms intended for the Ethiopian forces. Yet at the present moment this is the chief, if not the only, means of supplying the Italian armies of occupation. The rules of neutrality should prohibit transports intended for the Italian forces; but in this case there is not even neutrality, since Article 16 lays upon every State Member of the League the duty not to remain neutral, but to come to the aid, not of the aggressor, but of the victim of aggression. Has the Covenant been respected? Is it being respected to-day?

Finally, statements have just been made in their respective Parliaments by the Governments of certain Powers, the most influential Members of the League of Nations, that, since the aggressor has succeeded in occupying a large part of Ethiopian territory, they propose not to continue the application of any of the economic and financial measures decided upon against the Italian Government.

These are the circumstances in which, at the request of the Argentine Government, the Assembly of the League of Nations meets to consider the situation created by Italian aggression.

I assert that the issue before the Assembly to-day is a much wider one. It is not merely a question of a settlement in the matter of Italian aggression. It is a question of collective security; of the very existence of the League; of the trust placed by States in international treaties; of the value of promises made to small States that their integrity and their independence shall be respected and assured. It is a choice between the principle of the equality of States and the imposition upon small Powers of the bonds of vassalage. In a word, it is international morality that is at stake. Have treaty signatures a value only in so far as the signatory Powers have a personal, direct and immediate interest involved?

No subtle reasoning can change the nature of the problem or shift the grounds of the discussion. It is in all sincerity that I submit these considerations to the Assembly. At a time when my people is threatened with extermination, when the support of the League may avert the final blow, I may be allowed to speak with complete frankness, without reticence, in all directness, such as is demanded by the rule of equality between all States Members of the League. Outside the Kingdom of God, there is not on this earth any nation that is higher than any other. If a strong Government finds that it can, with impunity, destroy a weak people, then the hour has struck for that weak people to appeal to the League of Nations to give its judgment in all freedom. God and history will remember your judgment.

I have heard it asserted that the inadequate sanctions already applied have not achieved their object. At no time, in no circumstances, could sanctions that were intentionally inadequate, intentionally ill-applied, stop an aggressor. This is not a case of impossibility, but of refusal to stop an aggressor. When Ethiopia asked—as she still asks—that she should be given financial assistance, was that a measure impossible to apply? Had not the financial assistance of the League already been granted—and that in time of peace—to two countries, the very two countries which in the present case refused to apply sanctions against the aggressor?

In presence of the numerous violations by the Italian Government of all international treaties prohibiting resort to arms and recourse to barbarous methods of warfare, the initiative has to-day been taken—it is with pain that I record the fact—to raise sanctions. What does this initiative mean in practice but the abandonment of Ethiopia to the aggressor? Coming as it does on the very eve of the day when I was about to attempt a supreme effort in the defence of my people before this Assembly, does not this initiative deprive Ethiopia of one of her last chances of succeeding in obtaining the support and guarantee of States Members? Is that the guidance that the League of Nations and each of the States Members are entitled to expect from the great Powers when they assert their right and their duty to guide the action of the League?

Placed by the aggressor face to face with the accomplished fact, are States going to set up the terrible precedent of bowing before force?

The Assembly will doubtless have before it proposals for reforming the Covenant and rendering the guarantee of collective security more effective. Is it the Covenant that needs reform? What undertakings can have any value if the will to fulfil them is lacking? It is international morality that is at stake, and not the articles of the Covenant.

On behalf of the Ethiopian people, a Member of the League of Nations, I ask the Assembly to take all measures proper to secure respect for the Covenant. I renew my protest against the violations of treaties of which the Ethiopian people is the victim. I declare before the whole world that the Emperor, the Government and the people of Ethiopia will not bow before force, that they uphold their claims, that they will use all means in their power to ensure the triumph of right and respect for the Covenant.

I ask the fifty-two nations who have given the Ethiopian people a promise to help them in their resistance to the aggressor: What are they willing to do for Ethiopia?

I ask the great Powers, who have promised the guarantee of collective security to small States—those small States over whom hangs the threat that they may one day suffer the fate of Ethiopia: What measures do they intend to take?

Representatives of the world, I have come to Geneva to discharge in your midst the most painful of the duties of the head of a State. What answer am I to take back to my people?

The United States and the Italo-Ethiopian War*

Herbert Feis

The behavior of the United States was of little importance during the period of dissolution at Geneva which has just been reviewed. But it contributed to the outcome and made it more excusable. And the final failure at Geneva left a permanent impression on American policy.

In the United States the Hoare-Laval incident caused a deep shock in the subsoil of the spirit, where the longing that nations might act justly had preserved itself. Only a faint mark was permitted to show on the surface of American official utterances. The caution that had been used in their formulation proved now to be a comfort to their authors; the assertion that American action had always been independent and governed solely by the wish to stay out of war was newly useful. If faith in the power of aspiring phrases flew out of the window, few openly mourned. If Americans decided that this country must prepare to ward off against the evil will that was making itself plain in Rome and Berlin, the conclusion expressed itself in action only after a long lag.

The enemies of the League claimed their proof that this organization was nothing but a lure for the United States. The supporters of Italy gloated. The isolationists in Congress felt refreshed for their next foray; from then on they talked to an even more responsive audience when they preached the avoidance of entanglement with other nations. The advocates of rigid "neutrality" legislation became more convinced that they were on the right road to peace.

Thus, during the first two months of 1936, while the hand of the League turned for the last time towards the valve that might shut off oil to Italy and then drew back again, American debate ignored the situation. It centered on the terms of a new statute intended to establish a uniform rule of behavior towards all nations at war—for all the future.

The administration made an effort to assume leadership in the framing of this legislation with the thought that it might thereby retain a certain freedom of action. The legislative proposal that it sponsored (introduced into Congress by the Senator from Nevada, who was Chairman of the

* Herbert Feis, *Seen from E.A.* (New York: Alfred A. Knopf, 1947), pp. 276-283 and 297-308. Reprinted by permission. Herbert Feis has been advisor on American industrial relations to the League of Nations, an economic advisor to the Department of State, and a member of the Policy Planning Staff of that department. He received the Pulitzer Prize for history in 1960. His books include *The Road to Pearl Harbor* (1950), *The Diplomacy of the Dollar* (1950), *The China Tangle* (1953), and *Japan Subdued* (1961).

Committee on Foreign Relations, on January 8, 1936) would have given the President discretionary power to control the export to belligerents of "articles and materials used for war purposes" in excess of normal amounts. The President affirmed in an address of the same date that in wars that did not directly concern the Americas he would maintain a "twofold neutrality," (*a*) no sales of weapons and ammunitions to belligerents would be permitted; (*b*) he would seek to discourage the sale of any other products above and over peacetime exports if they served war purposes.

This was the offer, then, that the American government wished to put forward during the final period of faltering at Geneva. It would not cease to import from Italy as most of the League members had; it would not end all sales of war materials to Italy if the League members did. But it would, if Congress gave authorization, restrain American trade within ordinary limits, and so not undo what the League might still attempt to do. This was the weary compromise upon which the President and the Secretary of State fell back as the League was falling back. In doing so, the State Department disavowed any lingering aspiration for any other course. As expressed by the Counsellor of the Department in testimony before the Foreign Relations Committee on January 17, "The State Department has interred the aggressor theory."

Only the stinging words with which the President lashed the dictatorships showed that the retreat could not leave at rest a spirit deeply immersed in the ideals of American justice and independence. The experienced politician who dealt with other possessors of political power and was confronted with caution and mistrust in every cable file expressed himself in the official recommendations. The youthful, aspiring figure that had been assistant Secretary of the Navy during the first struggle against Germany found expression to suit his just anger only in 1940. The words he then spoke to Mussolini—who had just sent his army into the prostrate land of the French, "The hand that held the dagger has stuck it in the back of its neighbor," must have long burned in the spirit.

Mussolini had little to fear from the proposals sponsored by the Executive but he squirmed with hatred at the words with which they were accompanied. The Italian press showed new talents in abuse. But, at the same time, the Italian Foreign Office apparently had the idea that any disapproval that the American people might feel of Italian conduct could be soothed by a chance to do more business. The officials of the State Department, while still fingering cabled reports of Italian press abuse, received an offer from Italy to negotiate a new trade agreement with the United States. The memorandum that the Ambassador presented promised that Italy would grant to American exports full most-favored-nation treatment in the Italian market— a concession that up to that time had been stubbornly refused. The agreement would have made it easier for us to sell Italy products that members of the League were currently refusing to sell. In Rome, apparently, it had been concluded that both our dislike of Fascism and our lingering belief in the ideal of international co-operation would succumb to the chance to grab other nations' trade. The offer was put aside with irritated silence.

The proposals of the Executive regarding neutrality legislation were no more pleasing to the extreme group of isolationist senators. This group definitely opposed granting the Executive any discretion. The strength of the opposition to any policy that would make possible even indirect co-operation with the League was shown by a vote of the House Committee on Foreign Affairs on January 26. This Committee approved a clause to be inserted in the neutrality legislation which would have compelled the President, before curbing trade with any belligerent, to secure the revision of any commercial treaty that might be construed as banning such action. This meant acceptance of the argument of the supporters of Italy that any restriction of our trade with Italy was a violation of our treaty of commerce and amity with that country.

The advocates of direct co-operation with the League also found the Administration's proposals poor; for they fell far short of the steps members of the League would have to take to be effective, and side-stepped responsibility if a graver crisis followed.

And, to complete the circle of dissent, supporters of the view that the United States should maintain and defend what they considered our rights, under international law, to carry on all ordinary commerce with belligerents, disliked the White House suggestions. They regarded voluntary restriction as stupid weakness.

In short, the proposed line of compromise pleased no one—not even its authors.

To recall the details of the legislative battle that dragged on through January and February 1936, while the Italian armies were advancing, would now serve no purpose except further to illustrate the confusion and division in the American judgment. The determined advocates, both inside and outside of Congress, of neutrality legislation thought they were engraving in stone. The State Department officials who found themselves engaged in shaping the phrases thought they were writing in ink—which might or might not fade. Only a small minority proclaimed with certainty that the law was being written in chalk which would be washed out in the next great rain.

It proved impossible to compose the jangled differences. Therefore Congress finally decided merely to extend—with two amendments—the life of the Neutrality Resolution for some fourteen months. The President signed the revised statute on February 29. This curtailed even the small measure of discretion he had possessed under the original resolution in regard to the sales of arms. He was placed under a mandatory command to extend the arms embargo to *additional* states if they became involved in war. This meant that if Great Britain and other members of the League found themselves at war with Italy the United States would not sell them arms. The fatigued and demoralized committees at Geneva saw one more reason for not taking risks. This provision, it may be noted, was carried over into later neutrality legislation, where, no doubt, it figured pleasantly in the reckoning of Germany.

Thus the President was granted no legal authority to control trade with countries at war—except the trade in arms. But the League sanctions were still in force and Proposal 4A was still before the Committee of Eighteen. American sales of oil and similar products to Italy continued to exceed normal. With or without legal authority, it seemed necessary to renew the attempt to discourage them or suffer shame.

The President, therefore, upon signing the extension of the Neutrality Resolution, declared:

It is true that the high moral duty urged on our people of restricting their exports of essential war materials to either belligerent to approximately the normal peacetime basis has not been the subject of legislation. Nevertheless, it is clear to me that greatly to exceed that basis, with the result of earning profits not possible during peace, and especially with the result of giving actual assistance in the carrying on of war, would serve to magnify the very evil of war which we seek to prevent. This being my view, I renew the appeal made last October to the American people that they so conduct their trade with belligerent nations that it cannot be said that they are seizing new opportunities for profit or that, by changing their peacetime trade, they are giving aid to the continuation of war.

This was the last American attempt to restrain trade with Italy. Few of the readers of the President's words believed that the sanctions program of the League would be maintained. To the Secretary of State the chapter seemed at its end, and any attempt to affect its ending pointless. So it proved—for the Committee of Eighteen at its subsequent meeting remained inert. Germany's resurgence soon dimmed American interest in the fate of Ethiopia. The American gaze followed Haile Selassie into exile, through the newsreels, as though he were a figure in a historical novel. Italy reduced its purchases of American oil as danger vanished.

Other questions regarding the behavior of the United States in the event that decisive sanctions had been employed remained unanswered to the end. If, in order to prevent the Italian forces from being supplied with oil from the United States or elsewhere, the League had supplemented sanctions by a blockade, would the United States have accepted that action passively? If Britain and France had closed the Suez Canal, would we have insisted on the right of American ships to traverse it? If the members of the League had found themselves at war with Italy (and perhaps Germany), would we have maintained our refusal to sell them arms?

The answers cannot be guessed. But it seems likely that, because of the confusion in American thinking and feeling during those days, and the caution of the officials who were contained in this confusion, we would have assumed no positive position. We would have been likely to argue and to reprimand, to have let trade continue but refused to protect it, to have pawed the air until some event took the power of decision out of our hands.

None of the teetering measures by which the United States weathered the Italian-Ethiopian episode could have been of much use in safeguarding our future national security. That could have been done only by participating in a collective effort to deal with Italian aggression. Had we done so, a union of forces between ourselves, Great Britain, France, and the USSR might have been born that even Hitler might have not been mad enough to challenge.

But where, in 1936, anywhere in the world, was there enough trust, understanding, and intelligence between nations to create that union of forces? Trust between the victors of the last war was gone. Quarrels and injustices, real or imagined, had destroyed understanding. Without these, intelligence became perverted. The fact that the security and independence of all countries devoted to peace and personal liberties could only be preserved if they stood together dropped out of sight. Life entered into a dark tunnel down which Goebbels launched his corrosive words.

SUPPLEMENTARY NOTE ON THE EFFECTIVENESS OF THE
SANCTIONS EMPLOYED AGAINST ITALY, AND THE
PLAYED BY AMERICAN TRADE

(1) Italy was distinctly vulnerable to economic sanctions. It was dependent upon foreign countries for many raw materials essential to the maintenance of its economic life and to the conduct and implements of war —among them oil, coal, copper, cotton, lead, nickel, chrome, tungsten, tin, and rubber. Furthermore, its capacity to manufacture the machinery needed in the munitions industries, to make armor steel and many instruments and parts of instruments used in modern warfare, was far less than would have been necessary in a sustained war against a strong enemy.

But the sanctions that were put into force did not seriously interfere with the Italian conquest of Ethiopia nor deeply disturb its economic life. They were neither universal, extensive, nor prolonged enough to do so.

(2) The four economic sanctions voted by the Committee of Eighteen were not universally put into force.

The record of the Members of the League was summarized by Litvinov on July 1, 1936, as follows: "Four members of the League, from the very beginning, refused to apply any sanctions whatever. One member of the League bordering on Italy refused to apply the most effective sanction—namely, the prohibition of imports from Italy; while, of those countries which raised no objection in principle to sanctions, many did not in fact apply several of them, pleading constitutional difficulties, the necessity of 'study,' etc. Thus, even the embargo on arms was not applied by seven members of the League, financial measures by eight countries, and prohibition of imports from Italy by thirteen countries—that is, 25 per cent of the total membership of the League."

No less important than the defections of the members of the League was the fact that three large countries—the United States, Germany, and Japan—were not members of the League and did not join in the sanctions program of the League.

The importance of American and German absention from the ban on *importing* from Italy is indicated by the fact that, in 1934, the United States and Germany alone bought over 23 per cent of Italian exports. They continued, during the sanctions period, to purchase Italian goods in at least previous quantities. This, of course, lessened the rate at which Italian external purchasing power was drained; and therefore softened both the possible economic disturbance caused in Italy by this ban and lengthened the potential period of Italian power to carry on the war.

The nonparticipation of these important countries in the League program affected the measures taken to end the *export* of goods to Italy even more substantially. The effect was evident in several ways:

(*a*) The League had to recognize that, if non-member states continued to supply Italy with products that League members refused to supply, the ban would injure the countries applying sanctions rather than Italy. The League concluded that it would be unsatisfactory to prevent the sale to Italy of products which Italy imported, or could import, in large or growing measure from countries not participating fully in the sanctions program. Or, as expressed by the Subcommittee on Economic Measures of the Committee of Eighteen on October 15, "When the Subcommittee came to study measures of embargo, it would soon be found that a number of the most important products were not entirely controlled by the States' Members of the League, and that, consequently, the latter would have at first only have been able to impose an embargo on a limited number of articles, the others being reserved until it was known whether the countries not members of the League, which were also producers, would consent to join the League Members."

The fact that countries that had not obligated themselves to participate in the League program were important or chief sources of world supply of oil, coal, cotton, and copper contributed to the hesitation of the League to shut off the flow of these vital raw materials to Italy.

(*b*) The failure of many countries to participate in the sanctions program increased the possibility that Italy would be able to substitute manufactured products for any raw materials that were being denied to it. Thus, if the League had prohibited the sale of iron ore and scrap iron, Italy might have been able to substitute manufactured iron and steel products. If the sale of copper metal had been prohibited, Italy might have been able to import brass tubes or strips. If the sale of cotton had been prohibited, Italy might have been able to substitute imported cloth.

This problem of substitution could only have been met by prohibiting the sale to Italy of manufactured products made from any raw material that was banned. But, and this is the point, countries not obligated to participate in the League program were exceedingly important sources of supply for virtually all manufactured products. This left a possibility not only of natural substitution of manufactured products for raw materials, but of contrived substitution. As the Canadian delegate pointed out at the October 15th meeting of the Subcommittee on Economic Measures of the Committee of Eighteen, "An embargo might be put on a very important raw material, and another country might buy that raw material, make it up into tools, and sell these to the country against which the embargo of the raw material had been placed. The greatest care must be taken to prevent such materials from being taken by a third state, worked up and sold to the belligerent country. Otherwise a sense of injustice would be created and the system might break down."

(c) The nonparticipation of some countries in the sanctions program increased the possibility that Italy could secure forbidden imports indirectly. These are often extremely hard to forestall. For example, Holland was obligated under treaty to sell coal to Germany; it might, in conformity with the sanctions program, both refuse to sell coal to Italy and secure a promise from Germany that the coal that Holland sent to Germany was not passed on to Italy; but the addition to German coal supplies derived from or through Holland would make it easier for Germany, a nonparticipant in the sanctions program, to increase its exports to Italy of coal produced in Germany.

The vexing problems of indirect trade led to the suggestion that the participating countries should ration their exports to nonparticipating countries. It was feared, however, that such a measure would be resented, particularly by Germany and the United States.

In these and various other ways the fact that some countries were not participants in the sanctions program constrained the League in the formulation of the program, increased its hesitation to include many products, and lessened the hindering effect of the sanctions that were applied.

The lack of universality, in short, added to the risk that economic sanctions could only wound, not kill; and that the countries applying them would be obliged to resort to more severe and direct measures of force to achieve their purpose.

(3) Bearing these facts into account, it is of interest to review the effect on Italian trade of the two main sanctions employed: (a) the ban on the purchase of Italian exports; (b) the ban on the sale to Italy of certain goods. This will give only a rather superficial indicative measurement of the actual effect of the sanctions upon the Italian economy and war efforts. A more thorough investigation would require study of the substitution and adjustments made by Italy, the stocks accumulated, the effect upon the actual course of production, standard of living, and military operations.

The four critical months were November 1935 to February 1936, inclusive, for sanctions were only placed into effect in November and gradually began to lose effect in March.

The comparative size of *total Italian exports* in each of these four months as compared with the same month of the preceding year is as follows (using the old gold dollar as the unit of valuation):

Millions of Old Gold Dollars

November	1934—31.0	November	1935—32.0
			To 69 countries
December	1934—30.5	December	1935—21.9
			To 68 countries
January	1935—26.8	January	1936—15.2
			To 67 countries
February	1935—27.7	February	1936—16.8
			To 38 countries

It will be seen that, mainly because of the large amounts that were afloat and because the execution of various types of outstanding contracts was permitted at the commencement of sanctions, Italian exports were affected little during November 1935. An increasingly serious drop in the size of Italian export trade—approximately some forty per cent—took place in the following months. There is little doubt but that this sanction would have grown still more effective had it remained, with unimpaired authority, in prolonged force.

The imports from Italy of all countries that employed this sanction against Italy declined. German imports remained about what they had been in previous years. Austrian and Hungarian imports of Italian goods rose decidedly. Statistics of American imports are given in another section.

(4) The record of total *imports* into Italy during this four-months period was as follows:

Millions of Old Gold Dollars

November	1934—21.8	November	1935—26.0
			From 69 countries
December	1934—21.9	December	1935—17.4
			From 68 countries
January	1935—19.4	January	1936—10.1
			From 67 countries
February	1935—19.7	February	1936—8.6
			From 62 countries

During November 1935 Italian imports were abnormally great. This shows the heavy buying of war materials that Italy carried out before November. The effect of the ban on shipments to Italy did not become serious until January. By February 1936, Italian import trade had been reduced to less than half.

Statistics are not available for an analysis of the extent to which the decline in Italian imports consisted of those commodities which were banned by the League. The record seems to show that imports from Germany rose but little, imports from Austria and Hungary greatly.

(5) Trade with the United States was a substantial fraction of Italy's total trade. In 1933, the United States purchased 8.7 per cent of Italy's total exports; and in 1934, 7.4 per cent. In 1933 the United States provided 15.0 per cent of Italy's total imports; and in 1934, 12.5 per cent. Total American trade with Italy, and particularly with Italian Africa during 1935, the year in which League sanctions were initiated, was greater than either the year previous or the year following.

Total American Trade with Italy
(Millions of Current Dollars)

	Exports to Italy	Imports from Italy
1934	64.6	35.7
1935	72.4	38.7
1936	59.0	40.3

Total American Trade with Italian Africa
(Thousands of Current Dollars)

	Exports to I.A.	Imports from I.A.
1934	276	213
1935	4558	214
1936	771	224

A clearer story is told by the record of trade conducted with Italy and the Italian colonies during the four critical months (October 1935-January 1936).

American Exports to Italy
(Thousands of Current Dollars)

Oct.	1934—6226	Oct.	1935—6529
Nov.	1934—8445	Nov.	1935—9125
Dec.	1934—4821	Dec.	1935—7944
Jan.	1935—6257	Jan.	1936—5420

Imports from Italy during these months also rose well above normal.

American Imports from Italy
(Thousands of Current Dollars)

Oct.	1934—2943	Oct.	1935—4401
Nov.	1934—4179	Nov.	1935—6108
Dec.	1934—5207	Dec.	1935—4740
Jan.	1935—2424	Jan.	1936—3170

The rise in exports to Italian Africa was concentrated in the second half of 1935 and plainly was for Italian military operations.

Exports to Italian Africa
(Thousands of Current Dollars)

Aug. 1934—11	Aug. 1935—1704
Sept. 1934—29	Sept. 1935— 508
Oct. 1934—45	Oct. 1935— 363
Nov. 1934—18	Nov. 1935— 590
Dec. 1934— 4	Dec. 1935— 374
Jan. 1935—20	Jan. 1936— 22

The gradual decline after November may have been caused in part by the moral appeal of the American government.

(6) The experts at Geneva, reached the conclusion that the one economic sanction most certain to check Italy would be to refuse to supply it with *petroleum and petroleum products*. The proposal to do so was the issue on which the League program faltered and failed. Always, when the subject was before the League, the question arose as to whether any such step would be defeated by the importation into Italy of oil procured in the United States and Venezuela. The United States government resorted to appeals to avoid an increase in petroleum shipments above previous peace-time amounts. How important a supplier Venezuela might have become no one could guess; throughout this period it was without a strongly established government; however, production of oil in Venezuela was controlled by American, English, or English-Dutch companies, and was refined outside of the country—mainly in the Netherlands East Indies.

On February 12, 1936, an Expert Subcommittee of the Committee of Eighteen reported upon the United States as a factor in the oil sanction question. The main points of its report were that, during 1931-4, the United States had supplied on the average the following parts of Italy's total importation: of crude oil—14.9 per cent, of petrol—9.4 per cent, of fuel oil—3.5 per cent, of lubricating oil—48.3 per cent. Grouping all types of petroleum products together in terms of gross quantities, during 1934 the United States had supplied 6.4 per cent of total Italian imports, Rumania—32.2 per cent, the USSR—27.8 per cent, Latin America—17.4 per cent, Iran—10.3 per cent, other countries—5.9 per cent. It reported further that during the final months of 1935 and the beginning of 1936 American shipments of these products to Italy had grown far beyond their usual amounts. It estimated that a *total* embargo by all countries would result in an exhaustion of Italian stocks in something like three to three and one-half months.

It concluded that, if the embargo on oil shipments to Italy were applied by all member-states represented on the Committee of Coordination and the United States limited its exports to the normal prior to 1935, the ban would still be effective; Italy's ability to supply its needs would have been prolonged a month or so. But an unrestrained flow of oil from the United States could cause a ban by other suppliers to have little or no effectiveness.

The course of Italian imports of petroleum products was affected by the war and the sanctions as follows: Total Italian imports (excluding bunker oil bought by Italian ships in foreign ports) was around 3 million tons in 1934. It increased to 3.8 million tons in 1935; most of this increase took place during the fourth quarter of 1935, when the question of repressing Italy was before the League. Of the increase of 800 thousand tons, about 300 thousand represented an increase in imports from the United States.

The average *monthly* average value of American exports of all petroleum products to *Italy* and *Italian Africa* during 1932-4 had been $480,000. In October 1935, the United States exports to these points was $1,084,000; in November 1935, $1,684,000; in December 1935, $2,674,000. Total American exports during these three months were $5,442,000, as compared with $6,062,-000 during the whole of the year 1934. Included in our shipments during the last three months of 1935 was $828,000 sent directly to Italian East Africa—that is, directly supplied for the use of the Italian Army and Navy and Merchant Marine.

American monthly shipments for 1936 were: During January—$1,658,-000; during February—$1,798,000—then, in March, a decline to normal of $663,000. The preceding figures do not include such shipments of American oil as may have found their way to Italy indirectly.

The growth of American sales of oil, which at the time was known to the public only vaguely, gave genuine ground for the fear that a League ban could not work without participation by the United States. The American officials who were working on this matter at the time had the impression that the increase of American oil shipments to Italy during the first months of sanctions reflected special orders that had been placed by Italy in the United States in preparation for the invasion of Ethiopia. Then the later shipments were largely arranged for by new groups who were attracted into the trade by the chance to make money swiftly or a wish to support Italy. The large companies established in the trade conformed, on the whole, to the moral appeals that the government addressed; but new merchants and brokers were ready to seize any business that was going.

The record proves that profitable trade will cease only under command.

IV THE FINNISH-RUSSIAN CONFLICT OF 1939

Appeal of the Finnish Government (December 3, 1939)*

TELEGRAM, DATED DECEMBER 3RD, 1939, FROM THE SECRETARY-GENERAL TO THE MEMBERS OF THE COUNCIL AND THE MEMBERS OF THE LEAGUE OF NATIONS

Geneva, December 3rd, 1939.

I have received the following letter of December 3rd, 1939, from the Permanent Delegate of Finland accredited to the League of Nations:

"The Union of Soviet Socialist Republics, with which Finland, since the signature of the Treaty of Peace at Tartu in 1920, has maintained neighbourly relations and signed a Pact of Non-aggression which should have expired only in 1945, unexpectedly attacked on the morning of November 30th, 1939, not only frontier positions but also open Finnish towns, spreading death and destruction among the civilian population, more particularly by attacks from the air. Finland has never engaged in any undertaking directed against her powerful neighbour. She has continually made every effort to live at peace with her. Nevertheless, alleging so-called frontier incidents and adducing Finland's alleged refusal to acquiesce in the strengthening of the security of Leningrad, the Union of Soviet Socialist Republics first denounced the above-mentioned Pact of Non-aggression and then refused the Finnish Government's proposal to have recourse to the mediation of a neutral Power. In consequence, acting on instructions from my Government, I have the honour to bring the foregoing facts to your knowledge and to request you, in virtue of Articles 11 and 15 of the Covenant, forthwith to summon a meeting of the Council and the Assembly and to ask them to take the necessary measures to put an end to the aggression. I shall forward to you in due course a complete statement of the reasons and circumstances which have led my Government to request the intervention of the League of Nations in a dispute which has brought two of its Members into conflict with one another.—RUDOLF HOLSTI."

In accordance with Article II, paragraph I, of Covenant, I request Members of Council to meet at Geneva on Saturday, December 9th, at noon. Am submitting to President of Assembly proposal convoke Assembly on Monday, December 11th. Shall confirm date.

AVENOL, *Secretary-General.*

* League of Nations *Official Journal*, Annex 1756 (1939), Parts VII-XII, pp. 509-515.

TELEGRAM, DATED DECEMBER 5TH, 1939, FROM THE
GOVERNMENT OF THE UNION OF SOVIET SOCIALIST
REPUBLICS TO THE SECRETARY-GENERAL

Moscow, December 5th, 1939.

In accordance with instructions from the U.S.S.R. Government, I have the honour to inform you that that Government considers unjustified proposal to convene December 9th Council League of Nations and December 11th Assembly League of Nations on the initiative of M. Rodolphe Holsti and in virtue of Article II, paragraph I, of the League Covenant.

The U.S.S.R. is not at war with Finland and does not threaten the Finnish nation with war. Consequently, reference to Article II, paragraph I, is unjustified. Soviet Union maintains peaceful relations with the Democratic Republic of Finland, whose Government signed with the U.S.S.R. on December 2nd Pact of Assistance and Friendship. This Pact settled all the questions which the Soviet Government had fruitlessly discussed with delegates former Finnish Government now divested of its power.

By its declaration of December 1st, the Government of the Democratic Republic of Finland requested the Soviet Government to lend assistance to that Republic by armed forces with a view to the joint liquidation at the earliest possible moment of the very dangerous seat of war created in Finland by its former rulers. In these circumstances, appeal of M. Rodolphe Holsti to the League cannot justify convocation of the Council and the Assembly, especially as the persons on whose behalf M. Rodolphe Holsti has approached the League cannot be regarded as mandatories of the Finnish people.

If, notwithstanding considerations set out above, Council and Assembly are convened to consider the appeal of M. Rodolphe Holsti, U.S.S.R. Government would be unable to take part in these meetings. This decision is also based on the fact that the communication from the Secretary-General of the League concerning convocation Council and Assembly reproduces the text of the letter from M. Rodolphe Holsti, which is full of insults and calumnies against the Soviet Government, this being incompatible with the respect due to the U.S.S.R.

MOLOTOV.

LETTER, DATED DECEMBER 7TH, 1939, FROM THE FINNISH
GOVERNMENT TO THE SECRETARY-GENERAL

Geneva, December 7th, 1939.

With reference to the last paragraph of the letter which I addressed to you on the 3rd instant, I have the honour to communicate below the promised statement of the reasons and circumstances which have led my Government to request the intervention of the League of Nations in the conflict that has broken out between Finland and the Union of Soviet Socialist Republics.

When, on December 6th, 1917, the Government of Finland declared its independence, it appealed to all the Powers, including Soviet Russia, to recognise its independence *de jure*. The Soviet Government, indeed, was among the first to assent. But no sooner had the Soviet Government, on January 4th, 1918, announced its recognition of Finland's independence, than it hastened, before the end of that same month, to open hostilities against an almost entirely unarmed Finland. Nevertheless, the fighting ended in less than four months with a Finnish victory. Peace was concluded between the two countries at Tartu on October 14th, 1920.

Thereafter, relations between Finland and Russia developed on normal lines. In order to strengthen the ties of neighbourly relations, a Treaty of Non-aggression and Pacific Settlement of Disputes was signed on January 21st, 1932, and, on April 22nd of the same year, a Conciliation Convention which forms an integral part of that Treaty. . . .

[T]he two contracting parties declare[d] in the most conclusive terms that they will settle any disputes of whatever nature or origin which may arise between them, and will resort exclusively to pacific means of settling such disputes.

Attention must also be drawn to Article 8, which provides that: "The present Treaty is concluded for three years. If it is not denounced by either of the High Contracting Parties after previous notice of not less than six months before the expiry of that period, it shall be deemed to be automatically renewed for a further period of two years." Actually, the Treaty was renewed by a Protocol signed on April 7th, 1934, in which the two parties noted "that the conclusion of the Treaty signed on January 21st, 1932, . . . between Finland and the Union of Soviet Socialist Republics has had a beneficent influence on their relations." According to that Protocol, the Treaty was to remain in force until the end of 1945, no provision being made for denunciation before that date. This last clause assumes a quite special importance in the present circumstances.

The Soviet proposals of 1933 concerning the definition of the aggressor should likewise be borne in mind.

Again, on September 17th last, the Soviet Government, in a note to the Finnish Legation at Moscow, gave an assurance that, war having broken out between certain European Powers, it would pursue a policy of neutrality in Finno-Soviet relations. In consequence, M. Erkko, Minister for Foreign Affairs of Finland, issued the following statement to the Press: "As the official announcement states, the Government of the Union of Soviet Socialist Republics, when it informed the Finnish Legation at Moscow that it had declared war on Poland, intimated at the same time that it would maintain relations of neutrality with Finland. That intimation has been received in Finland with great satisfaction, and is in harmony with the spirit of the peaceful and friendly relations that Finland has maintained with the Commissariat for Foreign Affairs of the Union of Soviet Socialist Republics."

Notwithstanding the foregoing facts, the Soviet Government informed the Finnish Government on October 5th last that an exchange of views between the two Governments on political questions was desirable; no explanation of the nature and scope of the negotiations was given by the Soviet Government. The Finnish Government, however, ever ready to furnish proof of its sincere desire to maintain neighbourly relations, accepted the invitation and sent delegates to Moscow.

In the course of the negotiations, it soon became apparent that the Soviet Government's intention had been to induce Finland to agree to the cession of Finnish territories to the Union of Soviet Socialist Republics, either permanently or on lease. Although the Soviet Government's proposals, some of them in particular, were of such a nature as to threaten the fundamental conditions of national security, Finland continued the negotiations in the hope that a solution answering fully to the interests of the two countries would finally be found.

The negotiations between the two Governments were suspended on November 13th last, and the Finnish delegates returned to Helsinki for further instructions. On that same day, when receiving the representatives of the international Press, M. Erkko, Minister for Foreign Affairs, expressed his firm conviction that, given good-will, it was possible to find a solution that would satisfy both parties, and that, in any case, so far as concerned its attitude towards the Union of Soviet Socialist Republics, the Finnish Government was still anxious to bring the matter to a successful conclusion.

Having regard to the fact that the Finnish Government had agreed to institute these negotiations on such a vague basis, it is understandable that it should have wished to reconsider the situation as soon as it knew the Soviet Government's real intentions. In accordance with democratic principles, the Finnish Government also desired to consult Parliament.

These consultations were in progress when suddenly, on Sunday, November 26th, an explosion took place on the Karelian Isthmus, on the Russian side of the frontier, causing, as the Soviet Government alleged, the death of some Russian officers and soldiers. The Soviet Government at once stated that guns had been fired on the Finnish side. An exhaustive investigation carried out by the Finnish authorities, however, showed that no shots had been fired across the frontier from the Finnish side. The Soviet Government, nevertheless, continued to accuse Finland of violating the integrity of Soviet territory.

But on the Finnish side of the frontier there were only the ordinary frontier-guard troops, who had no artillery of any kind. The field artillery was twenty kilometres and the heavy artillery fifty kilometres behind the frontier. It is obvious that in those circumstances Finland could not have been responsible for the accident in question.

As for the Soviet assertion that some Finnish soldiers crossed the frontier near the Arctic coast, the investigations of the Finnish authorities have shown that, on the contrary, Russian soldiers had entered Finnish territory, destroying a Finnish frontier-guard post and carrying off three Finnish soldiers as prisoners.

To show its unshakeably pacific spirit, the Finnish Government at once proposed to the Soviet Government an exhaustive investigation of the foregoing charges and other even more trifling allegations put forward on the Soviet side. The Soviet Government was less conciliatory. In its view, Finland was to withdraw her troops unilaterally on the Karelian Isthmus for such a distance—twenty-five kilometres from the frontier—as would have endangered Finland's own security. For its part, the Soviet Government did not see its way to accept the Finnish proposal that the troops of both Powers should be withdrawn for the same distance.

In answer to this note, the Finnish Government, on November 29th, sent its reply to the Soviet Government with the utmost despatch through its Minister at Moscow. In this note . . . it proposed the conciliation procedure provided for in the Treaty of Non-aggression, to which resort was to be had, in particular, for the purpose of ascertaining whether the obligation of non-aggression had been violated. As an alternative, the Finnish Government intimated its readiness to submit the dispute to neutral arbitration.

For reasons unknown to the Finnish Government, the telegraphic transmission of this note was delayed in Soviet territory. At the same time, the Finnish Minister was summoned at midnight to the Commissariat for Foreign Affairs, where he was informed that the Government of the Union of Soviet Socialist Republics was no longer willing to maintain diplomatic relations with Finland. He had therefore no opportunity of transmitting the note to the Soviet Government. In a note of the same date the above-mentioned Treaty of Non-aggression had already been denounced by the Soviet Government.

Although the Treaty of Non-aggression could not be denounced before 1945 without six months' notice, and although both countries were bound by the provisions of the Peace Treaty of Tartu, the Covenant of the League of Nations, the Kellogg-Briand Pact, and various other treaties and conventions of similar effect, on November 30th, at 8 A.M. (Central European time), hostilities were opened against Finland by the Union of Soviet Socialist Republics.

The Government of the United States hastened to offer its good offices to the two Governments with a view to a peaceful settlement of the dispute. The offer was immediately accepted by the Finnish Government, but the Soviet Government rejected it.

At the same time, a further attempt was made by the Finnish Government, through the intermediary of the Swedish Government, to secure the continuance of the above-mentioned negotiations with the Union of Soviet Socialist Republics, notwithstanding the fact that hostilities had already begun, but once again the Soviet Government refused its consent.

All these attempts having failed, the Finnish Government decided to submit the dispute to the League of Nations. With this object, the under-signed was instructed to hand you a note requesting you, under Articles 11 and 15 of the Covenant, forthwith to summon a meeting of the Council and the Assembly with a view to putting a stop to the aggression.

In compliance with this request, you were good enough to summon a meeting of the Council and the Assembly.

In reply to your invitation, the Soviet Government sent you a telegram, the tendencious character of which is obvious. In this telegram, M. Molotov, Commissar for Foreign Affairs of the Union of Soviet Socialist Republics, ignores the existence of the Finnish Government, and declares that the Soviet Union maintains peaceful relations with the Democratic Republic of Finland, whose government is alleged to have signed a pact of assistance and friendship with the Union of Soviet Socialist Republics on December 2nd.

As for the so-called democratic government of the Finnish Republic, referred to by M. Molotov, it is only a puppet government set up by the Soviet Government itself, and it consequently has no right to represent the Finnish people. In point of fact, it represents only a number of Finnish refugees who took refuge in Russia after the civil war in 1918 and became Soviet citizens. At the same time, they are regarded in Finland as criminals accused of high treason against their native land.

M. Molotov considers that the request addressed to the League of Nations by the Permanent Delegate of Finland for the convening of the Council and Assembly is unjustifiable, on the ground that that delegate possesses no mandate from persons who are authorised to speak in the name of the Finnish people.

It should, however, be observed that, on July 1st-2nd, 1939, elections were held in Finland, and that the Finnish people freely elects its representatives to Parliament. This expression of the will of the people is of special significance in view of the fact that since 1906 the vote has also been extended to women, who form the majority of the population and whose love of peace is beyond all doubt.

The Government which had started the negotiations with the Union of Soviet Socialist Republics in October had obtained a unanimous vote of confidence from Parliament at the very moment when the Soviet Government broke off diplomatic relations with Finland. Nevertheless, that Government resigned to enable a Government to be formed which would include all the larger parties, from the Conservatives to the Social Democratics. There is no communist party in Finland.

It should be specially emphasised that the Minister for Foreign Affairs of the new Government, M. Tanner, who was Finance Minister in the Government which resigned and one of the delegates taking part in the Moscow negotiations, is the leader of the Social Democratic Party. Even before the opening of hostilities, that party, which is the largest in the country, and the General Labour Confederation, had expressed their full confidence in M. Tanner. As soon as the Union of Soviet Socialist Republics set up the so-called "Democratic Government of Finland" on the 2nd instant, these two Finnish Labour organisations immediately issued a solemn declaration once again affirming their patriotism and their firm resolve to defend the country together with all other parties against this treacherous act of aggression. These facts afford the best proof of the unanimous determination of the whole Finnish people to fight to the end for the independence of their country.

It is in pursuance of the legitimate Government's request that the Council and Assembly of the League of Nations have been convened.

Since the 3rd instant, when I had the honour to send you my note, the Union of Soviet Socialist Republics has continued its ferocious attacks on Finland. The land, naval and air forces of the Soviet Union are in full action, spreading death and destruction among the civilian population and in open towns. According to the latest news, the Soviet army is even using poison gas.

Such are the facts which it is my painful duty to bring, with your kind assistance, to the knowledge of all States Members of the League. . . .

I therefore have the honour, without prejudice to the rights of the Council, and acting on behalf of my Government under the optional right conferred upon it by Article 15, paragraph 9, of the Covenant, to request the Council to refer to the Assembly without delay the dispute which has arisen between my country and the Union of Soviet Socialist Republics, in order that the Assembly may deal with it forthwith.

(*Signed*) RUDOLF HOLSTI.

Extracts from Assembly Debate of "Appeal of the Finnish Government" (December 11-14, 1939)

SECOND PLENARY MEETING OF THE ASSEMBLY[*]

Appeal of the Finnish Government

THE PRESIDENT informed the Assembly that the Council, at its meeting on December 9th, considered the Finnish Government's request to the effect that its appeal should be submitted to the Assembly in virtue of Article 15 of the Covenant. The Council decided to request the Assembly to place the question on its agenda and instructed the Secretary-General to take the necessary steps for that purpose. The Council took that decision in conformity with the second sentence of paragraph 9 of Article 15, which states that

[*] League of Nations *Records of the Twentieth Ordinary Session of the Assembly*, 1939, Second Plenary Meeting, December 11, 1939, pp. 7-11.

"the dispute shall be so referred" (*i.e.*, to the Assembly) "at the request of either party to the dispute."

M. HOLSTI (Finland) made the following statement: A week ago, the Finnish Government requested the Secretary-General of the League of Nations to summon the Council and the Assembly in order to deal with the sudden Soviet aggression of which Finland was the victim. You are met here to-day to consider this request after the decision, taken by the Council on December 9th, to the effect that the appeal of Finland should be brought before the Assembly.

On behalf of Finland, I have the great honour to offer my warm thanks to you and, through you, to your respective Governments, for the celerity with which you have answered that appeal. This constitutes a clear proof to the whole world that, notwithstanding the enormous political difficulties of the present moment, the fundamental idea of the League of Nations is still living enough and strong enough to be converted into practical energy. . . . You have been in a position to get to the very root of the conflict. I do not wish, therefore, to go over all the details again, but I should like to deal with the question more particularly from the moral standpoint and to deduce the practical consequences.

We have all seen the wave of indignation aroused throughout the world by the Soviet aggression against Finland. This is, above all, a moral reaction against an unprecedented act of violence. I desire to express here the profound gratitude of the whole Finnish people for this expression of world conscience. No judgment is sterner than that pronounced against oneself. It sometimes happens that an individual or a nation in the first place voices opinions that bear witness to a high moral level, and then subsequently becomes the first to act in complete contradiction to its own principles. In the present conflict, we should recall what the Soviet Union has said in the League of Nations and observe how it passes judgment on itself in regard to its aggression against Finland.

At the Assembly meeting of September 21st, 1937, the first delegate of the U.S.S.R. said, in the course of his speech:

"I think the time has come to make an end of this dangerous propaganda weapon of aggression; that it is time for those to whom the interests of peace are really dear to tell the parrots in high places that nonsense repeated day by day does not cease thereby to be nonsense; that a spade should be called a spade and aggression aggression, with whatever slogan it decorates itself; . . . there is no international justification for aggression, armed intervention, invasion of other States and breaches of international treaties which it cloaks.

"It is time also to tell these avowed preachers of hate that it is not for them to profess concern for the interests of humanity; that they who have resurrected the most savage and long-dead theories of the heathen and dark ages may not dare to speak in the name of modern Europe; that they who burn the finest creations of the human spirit, who persecute the most brilliant representatives of art, science and literature, they who are despised by the entire world of culture, only make themselves ridiculous when they prate of saving civilisation, and use that plea to preach a crusade against other peoples."

The Soviet representative continued:

"Yet I am firmly convinced that a resolute policy pursued by the League of Nations in one case of aggression would rid us of all the other cases. Then—and only then—would all States become convinced that aggression does not pay, that aggression should not be undertaken . . . and then will be attained our common ideal of a universal League, preserved as an instrument of peace. But we shall attain that ideal, not by the circulation of questionnaires, but only by collectively repelling the aggressor, by collectively defending peace, which we all need and the fruits of which we all shall enjoy."

It was with these thoughts, expressed by the Soviet delegate, that the Assembly closed its discussions in the hall which had up till then served as its meeting-place. A week later it was sitting for the first time in this magnificent setting, the new headquarters of the League of Nations. The delegate of Finland had the honour to be the first to speak there. Deeply conscious of the importance of that historic moment, I then said:

"I am sure that I shall be faithfully interpreting the feelings of all the delegations here present when I express the earnest hope that this new building will remain for ever the home in which all noble ideas and humanitarian intentions will find a warm and generous welcome. May all the peoples of the world realise that their true enemies are not neighbouring nations, but the miseries and sufferings of mankind. . . .

"Since earliest times, man has sought to satisfy his false ambitions in devastation and oppression. The voice of the mothers, who by their sufferings have created new generations, has, alas, found too little echo. Yet, women have their own conception of honour—I would even say the most noble conception: love which sacrifices itself for creative life. The more this vibrant voice, borne aloft by a sentiment of honour and duty, is heard in this hall the more strongly will the maintenance of peace be guaranteed in the world and the more highly will creative work be esteemed in all branches of life." . . .

We must not forget these principles and this attitude of the Soviet Union during recent years when we are passing judgment from the moral standpoint on the way in which the Soviet Union has acted towards Finland since October 5th last, the date on which my Government was invited to enter into negotiations which led up to hostilities.

During the last fortnight, the Soviet army, fleet and air force have sown death and destruction throughout our country, have terrorised the civilian population and have done everything in their power to break down the resistance of our defence forces; but the whole Finnish people remains faithful to its Government.

Nothing could afford better proof of the moral baseness of the Soviet Government than this attempt to prevent Finland from making her voice heard in this, the most important meeting-place of the world, the League of Nations. In a little frontier village, the Soviet Union has created a self-styled democratic Government composed of traitors in Soviet pay. . . .

[T]he Soviet Government has sought to use international methods of a yet more scandalous character. After the rupture of diplomatic relations between Finland and the U.S.S.R., the Finnish Government having requested Sweden to administer its affairs in Moscow, the Soviet Government refused to accept such representation. The Finnish Government then turned to the United States, which had offered it their good offices; but the U.S.S.R. again refused. . . .

But, greatly as the Finnish people are touched by the sympathies of the whole civilised world, strongly as they are convinced of the political hypocrisy of the Soviet Government, demonstrations of friendship, marks of encouragement, and the passing of judgment on the aggression are not enough. To be able to stand up against this treacherous aggression, the Finnish people have need of every possible practical support and assistance, and not merely of words of encouragement. The world's tears of indignation have gone to our hearts; Finland herself has shed tears enough in these last days. But we cannot protect the Finnish people from the bullets, the bombs, the shrapnel, and the gas of the aggressor by international resolutions.

With an energy and endurance that call forth the admiration of the entire world, Finland is fighting for nothing less than her life. But everywhere throughout the world where, in these terrible days, there is a feeling of profound disgust at the action of the Soviets, it is perfectly well known that Finland is fighting also for the highest political ideals of all the nations. . . .

When the Finnish Government asked you to meet, it thought that you would find means to transform the world's sympathy into practical help. Finland asks only to live in peace and to secure her own existence by contributing her humble share to the creation of a happier future for mankind.

Gentlemen, bring back peace to Finland, and all the peoples and individuals who, in these tragic days, will hearten the Finnish people with their sympathy in its struggle for life, will bless you as the upholders of the highest ideals of the League of Nations.

Gentlemen, do your duty! The Finnish people is doing its duty to the civilised world and paying the cost with its most precious possession, its own life.

THE PRESIDENT said that the General Committee proposed that the discussion should be adjourned for the present, and that a special Committee should be appointed to consider the Finnish appeal. . . .

The General Committee's proposal was adopted.

THIRD PLENARY MEETING OF THE ASSEMBLY*

Appeal of the Finnish Government (continued): Proposal of the Argentine Delegation

The PRESIDENT read to the Assembly the telegram dated December 11th, 1939, sent to the Government of the Union of Soviet Socialist Republics by the Special Committee set up to study the Appeal of the Finnish Government, and the reply received by M. Caeiro da Matta, Chairman of the Special Committee, on December 12th, 1939:

"Geneva, December 11th, 1939.

"Narcomindel, Moscow.

"The Committee set up by the Assembly, which is seized in virtue of Article 15 of the Covenant, addresses an urgent appeal to the Government of the Union of Soviet Socialist Republics and the Finnish Government to cease hostilities and open immediate negotiations under the mediation of the Assembly with a view to restoring peace. Finland, which is present, accepts. Should be grateful if you would inform me before to-morrow (Tuesday) evening if the Government of the Union of Soviet Socialist Republics is prepared to accept this appeal and cease hostilites forthwith.

José CAEIRO DA MATTA,
Chairman of the Committee."

"Moscow, December 12th, 1939.

"José Caeiro da Matta, President Assembly
Committee, Nations, Geneva.

"The Government of the Union of Soviet Socialist Republics thanks you, Monsieur le Président, for kind invitation take part discussion Finnish question. At the same time the Government of the Union of Soviet Socialist Republics begs to inform you that it is not able to accept this invitation for the reasons set out in the telegram of December 4th from the Commissariat for Foreign Affairs sent in reply to M. Avenol's communication.

MOLOTOV."

THE PRESIDENT said that . . . after the Assembly had heard the delegate of the Argentine, he would suggest that the Argentine proposal should be referred to the Special Committee. . . .

M. RODOLFO FREYRE (Argentine): Some people no doubt consider that, having regard to the present state of the world and the international situation, the voice of the League should certainly not be heard and that this tribune erected in honour of right and justice placed at the service of peace among nations should remain empty. . . .

The Argentine Government—on whose behalf I have the honour to

* League of Nations *Records of the Twentieth Ordinary Session of the Assembly,* 1939, Third Plenary Meeting, December 13, 1939, pp. 13-18.

speak—is not of that opinion. My country entered the League inspired by the strongest faith and the most fervent hopes, and it has taken part in the work of this institution with a desire to uphold the principles on which it was founded and which constitute its real value. On the contrary, it considers that in reaffirming once again these ideals in support of an international law which has been ignored and the elementary duties formerly regarded as sacred for humanity, it is both fulfilling an inescapable duty and rendering a further service to the League.

We are determined to oppose the decay of moral values by defending moral rights against the brutal rule of force. We are faced with a fact which is capable of only one interpretation: A State which is a Member of the League, in flagrant violation of the Covenant of that institution and of the Pact of Non-aggression it has concluded with another Member State, has unexpectedly attacked the latter, invading its territory and spreading death and destruction. Having regard to the forces employed, its character and the explanations furnished by the Soviet Union in the guise of justification, this twofold violation constitutes a veritable challenge to the League and is an insult to all the Governments of which it is composed.

It is by no means a question of ideology or of regime. Countries have the government they choose or the Government which is imposed upon them. That is their right. The question now before us is whether we are going to continue to allow the perpetrator of this act of aggression to sit among us. My Government considers this impossible.

True, it is not the first time that a State which is a Member of the League has been unjustifiably attacked. But the present case is attended by circumstances such as to compel my Government to pass the most severe judgment. On this occasion the aggression was committed by a Member of the League. The State which was the victim of this aggression has appealed to the League and has already shown, during the days that have elapsed since it was invaded, its heroic determination to live and to fight.

Disdaining even the outward form of legality, the aggressor has denied that it is at war, and to this end has referred to the normal relations which it maintains with a puppet government set up by itself on the eve of the aggression on its own territory. The Soviet Union has thus placed itself outside the Covenant.

In these circumstances, what is the duty incumbent upon the League? The League has already had experience of sanctions. We must admit that purely moral sanctions—the only ones possible—are meaningless, unless they are preceded by the exclusion of the guilty Government. We need not be restrained, as in other cases, by the desire to act cautiously and to weigh our responsibilities with a view to the preservation of peace. Peace no longer exists. We are faced with a state of war. This being the case, the duty and attitude of the Argentine Republic are imposed upon it by its own tradition at Geneva and elsewhere. . . .

[A] new case arose on the international plane, which brought the League face to face with a clear-cut situation, devoid of all ambiguity. Countries and peoples, whether Members of the League or non-members, have thrown into the scale against the aggressor the weight of their moral condemnation. This case, which has been tried and judged already by the tribunal of the world's conscience, has placed the Argentine Government under the imperative necessity of demanding the expulsion of the Soviet Union from the League of Nations. We have already considered the particular circumstances which characterise this new international case and which place it in an altogether special category.

We now have to consider the consequences which this necessarily involves for the League of Nations. The Covenant of the League contains, in so far as the political part is concerned, a triple undertaking: that of non-aggression, that of conciliation and that of mutual assistance. . . .

The League no longer possesses the strength it would require for the application of the economic and military sanctions necessitated by the undertaking in regard to mutual assistance. As to the passing of judgment, this is conceivable, simply from the point of view of its moral effect, only if the intention is to reach non-member States. How, indeed, could we apply a sanction of this kind to a State which is a Member of the League, while continuing side by side with that State—notwithstanding the fact that it is a rebel and notwithstanding the gravity of the international offence of which it is guilty—while continuing, I say, to fulfil those duties in regard to common action which the League imposes on us? What sort of international league or society would this be, if, despite the solemn undertaking in the matter of non-aggression by which it is conditioned, it allowed one of its Members to indulge in acts of aggression against another with absolute impunity? Again, what moral bond would be conceivable that would still unite the other Members in the face of the aggressor?

The League has no doubt lost all coercive force, but there is still one gesture that it has to make, one gesture that it cannot refuse to make, unless it is prepared to resign its functions in a spirit of truly suicidal defeat. That gesture consists in excluding from its midst those who, after having proclaimed themselves the defenders of the essential principles for whose establishment this institution was founded, have repudiated those same principles without exhibiting the slightest scruple, without giving their reasons, thus placing themselves outside what still remains of the League's heritage—the honour we hold dear.

Mr. President, Gentlemen, if we are to save the world from the abyss which is opening before it, if we are to bring about the rebirth of international law, it behooves us to realise that the time has come to set aside material considerations and rally those moral forces which have fallen into oblivion. International law—nay, all law—demands for its proper functioning the existence of a moral atmosphere, and this moral atmosphere cannot exist without the sentiment of honour. . . .

In view of all these considerations and in the light of these observations,

I find it my duty to state with the greatest regret, but voicing my Government's unalterable decision, that the Argentine Republic can no longer consider itself a Member of the League of Nations as long as the Soviet Union is able to claim that title.

THE PRESIDENT proposed that the discussion should be adjourned and that the Assembly should refer to the Special Committee the speech and the proposal of the delegate of the Argentine, at the same time inviting all delegations which had proposals or suggestions to make to be present at the proceedings of the Special Committee. . . .

The President's proposal was adopted by a majority vote.

FOURTH PLENARY MEETING OF THE ASSEMBLY*

Appeal of the Finnish Government (continued): Report of the Special Committee

(At the invitation of the President, M. CAEIRO DA MATTA (Portugal), Chairman of the Special Committee, came to the platform.)

THE PRESIDENT observed that, on Monday, December 11th, the Assembly, after having heard the statement of the delegate of Finland, had decided to set up a Special Committee, composed of fourteen members, to study the appeal of the Finnish Government. The Committee had had referred to it a number of written and verbal proposals and declarations, including that of the Argentine delegation at the plenary meeting on December 13th. After extremely arduous work, the Committee had, on the previous day, adopted a report accompanied by a draft resolution, which had been circulated to delegations.

The President then called on the Chairman of the Special Committee, M. Caeiro da Matta.

M. CAEIRO DA MATTA (Portugal): I do not propose to speak in my capacity as Chairman of the Special Committee appointed to study the Appeal of the Finnish Government, whose report is now under discussion. I am speaking on behalf of the Portuguese Government and as its delegate to this Assembly.

The Government of the Argentine Republic was the first to protest formally before the League of Nations against the aggression of which the Soviet Union has been guilty in respect of Finland, in violation not only of the principles of the League but also of the most elementary dictates of justice and humanity. In the opinion of the Government of the Argentine Republic, this violation justifies the immediate expulsion of the Soviet Union from the League.

The Portuguese delegation cannot but support—and it does so wholeheartedly—the views expressed by the Argentine Government. I would even

* League of Nations *Records of the Twentieth Ordinary Session of the Assembly*, 1939, Fourth Plenary Meeting, December 14, 1939, pp. 24-37.

add that, if the proposal to expel the Soviets from the League had not been made by the Argentine Republic, a proposal for their expulsion would have been submitted by the Portuguese delegation, in the name of international justice and morality, the strengthening of which is to-day more than ever felt by the noblest minds to be most essential.

The aggression against Finland constitutes a crime against right and against humanity, a crime for which there can be no excuse. Unprovoked aggression cannot be recognised as a normal method of conducting policy. The worldwide indignation provoked by Russia's action against a small neighbouring State clearly proves that world conscience is not deceived as to the duplicity and perfidy of Soviet policy, and as to the grave threat and danger which it implies for all nations in direct contact with Communist Russia. And this threat and this danger are not confined to those nations alone: the struggle which for two-and-a-half years drenched with blood one of the noblest nations of Europe—Spain—was at bottom the work of the propaganda and action of the agents of Soviet Russia.

So far as Portugal is concerned, the attitude of the Soviets in the present conflict, which they themselves have provoked, has occasioned neither surprise nor disappointment because it was what we had been led to expect. When Switzerland, the Netherlands and Portugal voted in 1934 against the admission of the Soviets to the League, they merely expressed the feelings of millions of human beings who still had a belief in the triumph of spiritual values. Those values are ignored by Communist Russia. . . .

After helping to crush Poland—and we certainly ought not to forget that other victim—Soviet Russia is preparing to crush Finland. For the Soviet Union, international commitments are meaningless. Once again we find that no words are strong enough to describe its deep designs, its greed and its psychological realism.

[T]here is only one course open to us. We must have the courage to purify the League so that it may subsist worthily.

We cannot collaborate with Moscow. Collaboration calls for a minimum of common thoughts; the very social structure of the Soviet Union is opposed to this. A vote of condemnation is therefore essential and, in order to uphold the prestige of the League Assembly, this vote should be unanimous. It is for the Council to pronounce exclusion, in application of Article 16, paragraph 4, of the Covenant. That is the hope that I express on behalf of the Portuguese Government. The Soviet Union has, moreover, by its own action, already placed itself outside the Covenant; it must also be placed outside the League.

In conclusion, I should like to express my country's solidarity with Finland, which has already given a moving example of courage to all nations that are not resigned to servitude and that still attach due value to those moral forces which are the pride of our civilisation and can alone save it from total and final ruin. . . .

MR. BUTLER (United Kingdom): The report, accompanied by a resolution, now before the Assembly, has the full support of the United Kingdom delegation. It enables us to carry out our responsibilities. An examination of its contents reveals practical suggestions for aiding Finland, while the pages in which the guilt of the aggressor is set forth constitute an indictment which could not be more formidable or more conclusive. . . .

The case which we are considering to-day is the latest link in the chain of aggression in Europe. It follows hard upon the attacks made by Germany upon her weaker neighbours, the Czechs and the Poles, of whose cause we are not and shall not be forgetful.

The resolution sets out the various solemn international and bilateral pacts or treaties other than the League Covenant which have been broken by the Soviet Union in its attack upon Finland. This assault has aroused the sympathy and indignation not merely of the Members of the Assembly but of almost every country in the world, and it is significant that the resolution authorises the Secretary-General to consult non-member States, in order to enlist their co-operation in the aid which we now promise. It is no wonder that there has been such a demonstration of public sympathy for Finland. Though a small country, its whole record since it achieved independence has proclaimed a devotion to the cause of peace and to those ideals of social progress for which the League has always stood. The Finnish people have attained their spiritual and material well-being and their political stability entirely through their own exertions.

The paragraphs of the resolution promising aid to Finland seem, to the United Kingdom delegation, to follow the principles which they advocated before the Sixth Committee in September 1938. Among other things, we then declared that, even in the case where a breach of the Covenant had been established, there would be no automatic obligation to apply either economic or military sanctions. There would, however, be a general obligation to consider, in consultation with the other Members, whether and, if so, how far, they were able to apply the measures provided in the Covenant and what steps, if any, they could take to render aid to the victim. In the course of such consultation, each State would be the judge of the extent to which its own position would allow it to participate in any measures which might be proposed.

The Assembly may rest assured that, despite the heavy burden which we in the United Kingdom, in common with other nations of the British Commonwealth and our Allies, are bearing at the present time in the major struggle for right and law in which we are engaged, His Majesty's Government in the United Kingdom will not excuse themselves from giving the greatest assistance in their power to Finland. We are indeed already taking certain steps to enable the Finnish Government to obtain in the United Kingdom material required for their defence. . . .

BARON DE VOS VAN STEENWIJK (Netherlands): The Netherlands delegation is instructed by its Government to state that it interprets the text of the fifth paragraph of the first part of the draft resolution—that is to say, the authorisation given to the Secretary-General to lend the aid of his technical services—in the sense that the aid in question should in no way be considered as collective action of the League of Nations, but solely as assistance on the part of its technical services to such individual Members as might wish to help Finland.

Subject to this interpretation of that paragraph, the Netherlands delegation is authorised to vote for the draft resolution.

In the fourth paragraph of the second part of the draft resolution, it is stated that the Union of Soviet Socialist Republics has placed itself outside the Covenant. The Netherlands delegation is instructed to point out that the Netherlands Government does not greatly favour this expression, which has no basis in the articles of the Covenant; but as the sense of the resolution is clear, it does not wish to raise any difficulties in that connection.

COUNT CARTON DE WIART (Belgium): The Belgian delegation understands that the authorisation given to the Secretary-General to lend the aid of his technical services does not imply any collective action on the part of the League. In its opinion, this refers to aid which might be given by the services of the Secretariat to such of the States Members as might wish to help Finland.

Subject to this observation, we shall vote for the draft resolution of the Special Committee of the Assembly. . . .

THE PRESIDENT requested the delegates in favour of the adoption of the report and of the resolution to remain seated and those opposed thereto to rise.

The Assembly took note of the statements made, approved the report and unanimously adopted the accompanying resolution.

Resolution of the Assembly*

REPORT OF THE ASSEMBLY, PROVIDED FOR IN ARTICLE 15, PARAGRAPHS 4 AND 10, OF THE COVENANT, SUBMITTED BY THE SPECIAL COMMITTEE OF THE ASSEMBLY

Introduction

The first duty of the Assembly, which is seized in virtue of Article 15 of the Covenant, is to endeavour "to effect a settlement of the dispute" referred to it. . . .

* League of Nations *Official Journal,* Doc. No. A.46.1939.VII (December 13, 1939), pp. 531-541.

In view of the absence of a delegation of the Government of the U.S.S.R. and as a result of the examination of the reasons it adduces in explanation of that absence, it is unfortunately clear that to attempt at the present time to obtain the cessation of hostilities and the restoration of normal peaceful relations between Finland and the U.S.S.R. through mediation and conciliation would be fruitless. . . .

Resolution

The Assembly:

I

Whereas, by the aggression which it has committed against Finland, the Union of Soviet Socialist Republics has failed to observe not only its special political agreements with Finland but also Article 12 of the Covenant of the League of Nations and the Pact of Paris;

And whereas, immediately before committing that aggression, it denounced, without legal justification, the Treaty of Non-aggression which it had concluded with Finland in 1932, and which was to remain in force until the end of 1945:

Solemnly condemns the action taken by the Union of Soviet Socialist Republics against the State of Finland;

Urgently appeals to every Member of the League to provide Finland with such material and humanitarian assistance as may be in its power and to refrain from any action which might weaken Finland's power of resistance;

Authorises the Secretary-General to lend the aid of his technical services in the organisation of the aforesaid assistance to Finland;

And likewise authorises the Secretary-General, in virtue of the Assembly resolution of October 4th, 1937, to consult non-member States with a view to possible co-operation.

II

Whereas, notwithstanding an invitation extended to it on two occasions, the Union of Soviet Socialist Republics has refused to be present at the examination of its dispute with Finland before the Council and the Assembly;

And whereas, by thus refusing to recognise the duty of the Council and the Assembly as regards the execution of Article 15 of the Covenant, it has failed to observe one of the League's most essential covenants for the safeguarding of peace and the security of nations;

And whereas it has vainly attempted to justify its refusal on the ground of the relations which it has established with an alleged Government which is neither *de jure* nor *de facto* the Government recognised by the people of Finland in accordance with the free working of their institutions;

And whereas the Union of Soviet Socialist Republics has not merely violated a covenant of the League, but has by its own action placed itself outside the Covenant;

And whereas the Council is competent under Article 16 of the Covenant to consider what consequences should follow from this situation:

Recommends the Council to pronounce upon the question.

Extracts from Council Debate of "Appeal of the Finnish Government" (December 14, 1939)*

Appeal by the Finnish Government

THE PRESIDENT: The Assembly has to-day adopted, in virtue of Article 15 of the Covenant, its report on the appeal by the Finnish Government. At the end of this report, there are two resolutions, the second containing a recommendation by the Assembly to the Council. . . .

As, in this second resolution, the Assembly has stated that the Union of Soviet Socialist Republics has not merely violated a covenant of the League but has by its own action placed itself outside the Covenant, and as it has recommended the Council to pronounce upon the question, I would remind you of the provisions of Article 16, paragraph 4: "Any Member of the League which has violated any covenant of the League may be declared to be no longer a Member of the League by vote of the Council concurred in by the representatives of all the other Members of the League represented thereon."

Article 16, paragraph 4, of the Covenant, which I have just read to you, provides for a vote by the Members of the League represented on the Council. I accordingly submit for the Council's approval the following draft resolution:

"The Council,

"Having taken cognisance of the resolution adopted by the Assembly on December 14th, 1939, regarding the appeal of the Finnish Government;

"1. Associates itself with the condemnation by the Assembly of the action of the Union of Soviet Socialist Republics against the Finnish State; and

"2. For the reasons set forth in the resolution of the Assembly,

"In virtue of Article 16, paragraph 4, of the Covenant,

"Finds, that, by its act, the Union of Soviet Socialist Republics has placed itself outside the League of Nations. It follows that the Union of Soviet Socialist Republics is no longer a Member of the League."

* League of Nations *Official Journal* (107th Session of the Council, December 14, 1939), 1939, pp. 501-508.

I now invite you to discuss this draft resolution. . . .

M. PAUL-BONCOUR: I think, indeed I hope, that none of our colleagues will have misunderstood the reasons for the extreme discretion that France, like the United Kingdom, has observed in the course of this debate. . . .

France is here, although she has many other preoccupations, because, whatever States might be involved, she has always answered "present" when it was necessary to defend principles of which I may fairly say that, had they been defended a little sooner and a little more firmly, we should not perhaps be having to defend them to-day, at the price of immense material sacrifices and of the personal sacrifices of the whole younger generation massed on our frontiers, by tearing an entire nation away from its peaceful labours and mobilising it to wage a war that it will continue to the end, until the causes that led to it have ceased to exist.

France is here to impose by her vote a sanction, in the most categorical and painful form, for the breach of the Covenant brought about by the violation of the territory and sovereignty of free and democratic Finland, by an associated State which we were accustomed of late years to see in the front rank of the defenders of those principles in whose name we are constrained to pass judgment upon it to-day.

But I should be failing in my duty to the great country that I have the honour to represent here if I did not say to you that, as we see it, this condemnation would not have its full meaning or its full scope if the aggression that has led to it were not shown to be closely and indisputably linked with all those previous aggressions that have made it possible. . . .

And so you see that, beyond the present aggression on which alone we have to pronounce to-day, that truth appears which lies at the very foundation of the League of Nations, which is the reason of its existence, and to which it must return—indeed, it is already doing so, as witness the speed and the plainness of our decisions in the present conflict—if it wishes that the great hope that must emerge from this new conflict shall still bear its name: collective security, indivisible collective security.

I seem to remember—not in irony, but with real grief—that it was M. Litvinoff who, here and in the Assembly, so often dwelt upon the indivisible character of collective security. He it was who most persistently propagated that conception, and who deduced its consequences in the definition of the aggressor—the clearest and completest of all the definitions that resulted from labours in which I had too large a share to forget them—which was signed in London by Russia and her neighbours.

It is in the name of that very definition of aggression, which covered everything, even, alas, the circumstances and methods of the present case; it is in order to associate myself, on behalf of my country, with this somewhat tardy awakening of the universal conscience which it is for the League of Nations to turn to account to prevent the list of victims from lengthening, that, without absolving the first and chief author of the present European upheaval, without forgetting the previous aggressions that have made this new aggression possible, I shall vote for the resolution which is submitted to the Council.

MR. BUTLER: . . . These responsibilities have already been in a large measure discharged by the Assembly. But the Council has now to perform a duty which is laid upon it by the Covenant. Once the issue which we have to decide has been raised—and you will all remember the manner in which it was raised—the Council has in my view no alternative but to accept the resolution before it. . . .

The Council is not, in my view, in a position to reach any other decision without stultifying itself and compromising those principles of which it is the guardian. I should like to endorse the words which M. Paul-Boncour used about the re-awakening and the new life which we have evidenced here at this meeting of the Council. Should we fail to discharge the duty laid upon us by the Assembly, the whole world will doubt the reality of our convictions, and the structure which in the present world crisis we are striving to maintain will be dangerously shaken. . . .

THE PRESIDENT: The Council will take note of the statements that have just been made and, as abstentions do not count in establishing unanimity, if there are no other observations I shall take it that the draft resolution has been adopted.

The resolution was adopted.

CHAPTER 3 *"The Cause of Death Was . . ."*:
Two Post-Mortems

A League of Nations: The First Experiment (1939)*

Gilbert Murray

I feel to-day rather like an ancient Greek magistrate, summoned before the Assembly to hand in his 'Accounts' and stand his trial for having 'given false advice to the people,' on the ground that his policy has obviously failed. I was in the League of Nations movement from the beginning, I had some share in the preliminary discussions which led to the Covenant; I have been for twenty years either Chairman or Vice-Chairman of one of the official committees of the League at Geneva, and of the largest unofficial League of Nations Society in the rest of the world; and have always been one of those who insisted that for English foreign policy, in Lord Cecil's phrase, the League must be all or nothing. You can tell me that the League has failed; my answer, of course, is that the League has failed because the Covenant was not carried out. Step by step it has been the betrayal, or at least the non-fulfilment, of the pledges of the great European nations that have led to the disaster of this war.

The project in 1918 was, as stated in the Royal Charter of the League of Nations Union, to build up some great international organization which would secure international justice, maintain international order, and 'eventually rid the world of war and the effects of war.' War had become incompatible with modern civilization. One looks back with a smile at Gibbon's statement about the development of war, that the art of war itself had come to be civilized. It was dependent on mathematics, chemistry, mechanics, and architecture; and 'the European forces were exercised by temperate and indecisive contests,' which did little harm but served to keep alive the manly spirit of the civilized peoples. It is indeed dependent on mathematics, chemistry, mechanics, and architecture—but otherwise Gibbon's prophecy has proved the reverse of truth. War does not less harm, but infinitely more harm than it used: and that not merely through the increased destructiveness of weapons. Another cause is the vastly increased power of govern-

* Gilbert Murray, "A League of Nations: The First Experiment (1939)," Ch. IV in *From the League to U.N.* (London: Oxford University Press, 1948), pp. 65-83. Reprinted by permission of George Allen & Unwin Ltd. Gilbert Murray (1866-1957) was a member of the Committee of Intellectual Co-operation of the League of Nations and worked for the League of Nations Union. His publications include *The Ordeal of This Generation* (Halley Stewart Lectures, 1928) and *Liberality and Civilization* (Hibbert Lectures, 1937).

ments, who can now search out every source of strength from every stratum of their population to throw into the all-absorbing effort of destruction: another is the highly complex structure of modern industrial communities, which cannot easily be rebuilt when once it has been destroyed.

To put an end to war—a recurrent disaster, and to the fear of war—a permanent poison: that was our purpose. What was to be the method? The simplest and most direct method would have been a *Pax Romana,* peace imposed upon the world by a dominant nation of overwhelming strength; but that was clearly impossible. There is no modern State capable of enforcing its will on the rest of the world. The only practicable method, therefore, was some system of voluntary international organization. The world, which was growing more and more of a unity both in economics and culture, was still administered, as it were, in fragments, by some sixty-two sovereign independent States, each one a law to itself, each claiming the right to make war on any neighbour at any time for any cause. Of course this sovereignty was not absolute; it was modified by every treaty that was made; it was modified in fact, if not in form, by the advance of public opinion or conscience, and, at that particular time, by a realization that the past war had threatened universal ruin, and that the common interest was permanent peace. We had to seek some general agreement; an agreement which would be effective in preventing war, yet an agreement which these stubborn sovereign States, eager for peace at the moment but still full of national feeling and pride in their independence, would be willing to sign. We had to demand at least one vital reduction of sovereignty; the nations must agree in the first place to renounce war among themselves, and, in the second place, to use their united strength to defend any unoffending member against an aggressive attack. It was no use agreeing to live in peace unless that peace was to be defended.

I remember the surprising progress made in the years 1916, 1917, and 1918, and the growing hopefulness with which I found this general conception of a Society of Nations welcomed in the year 1916 by both the Presidential candidates in America, Mr. Hughes and Mr. Wilson; by Conservative as well as Liberal and Labour statesmen in England; by delegates or voluntary societies in different countries of Europe. I remember particularly the thrill with which I first heard Lord Phillimore read in the Foreign Office the proposed text of Article XI . . . and the almost incredulous joy with which we early League workers found the Covenant of the League unanimously accepted by all Members of the Peace Conference and afterwards by some four-fifths of the world.

They accepted the pledge. But, so I am told by those who worked on the League Committee at Versailles, it was hard work to persuade them to make such a sacrifice of sovereignty. The United States presently backed out altogether. The others found their Covenant very hard to live up to. Three eventually broke it: most others, in course of time, tried to explain it away.

Yet the sacrifice that was asked of them was, I still think, an irreducible minimum. The continuance of absolute sovereignty, together with the prevailing emotion on which it rested, was what made permanent world order impossible.

As I wrote many years ago in one of the Open Letters of the Committee of Intellectual Co-operation:

The reason is that while the civilized world is growing more and more a Unity this Unity has no organ of government. It is ruled by some sixty or more independent sovereign states each of whom had till a few years ago . . . and therefore has still in the minds of its average citizens . . . no duty whatever towards its neighbours.

In all countries—in dictatorships and monarchies as well as in democracies—statesmen depend for their power and office not on the goodwill of the world but on the favour of their own countrymen.

This is the clue to our tragedy. The safety of civilization depends on the great world issues being settled in accordance with the interests of the world: yet, under the system of national states, any statesman who attempted so to settle them would be facing great danger. For it is not the votes of other nations by which he stands or falls, but only the votes of his own people.

This same consideration shows the futility of the numerous proposals which were then made for making the League more 'democratic,' a League of peoples, not of governments. Democracy is the right remedy for injustices inside a country; when one class oppresses another class the appeal should be made to the whole people. But when one nation is pitted against another nation, it is no help at all to stir up the feelings of the whole people on each side. The appeal should be to some supreme international authority, as far removed as possible from political passions. Experience at the League has shown that even difficult questions can be settled if they can be removed from a political atmosphere to a judicial disinterested atmosphere; even easy questions become insoluble when they are left to the mercy of nationalist politics. Furthermore, it soon became clear that neither this country nor any other could impose its own constitution upon the rest. Each member of the international society must be free to choose its own form of government and its own method of appointing its delegates.

Another suggestion, or set of suggestions, which proved to be impracticable was that of an international Parliament, making decisions by a majority vote. How were the votes to be counted? Was Norway with 3 million inhabitants to count as equal to Germany with 66 million? Clearly not. Then was the voting to be by population? If so, to say nothing of the smaller countries, would even Britain and France commit their whole future destinies to the decision of a vast foreign assembly in which they had some 40 votes each, Germany 60, the United States 120, Russia 180, and China 400? It soon became clear that no nation would even contemplate a coercive World Parliament, deciding policy by majority vote. Even with individuals we are often confronted by the state of mind expressed in the saying: 'If I must, I won't; if I needn't, I don't mind.' And nations are far more stubborn than individuals.

Meantime all difficulties were increased by the intensification of national feeling due to the Great War. The newly emancipated nations especially were intoxicated by the ideal of independence; the ideal of international co-operation, so much more necessary at the time, left them cold. People now talk much about the harshness of the Treaty of Versailles. But at the time the treaties only expressed, and expressed in a more mild and reasonable form than popular rage would have liked, the prevalent public feelings. The more Liberal elements, typified by President Wilson, were struggling not against kings and diplomats, but against democratic statesmen dependent upon furious peoples.

War had, as usual, taught the two contradictory lessons between which nations could make their choice: to some it taught that war is so vast an evil that it should be avoided at almost any cost; to others that no instrument is so effective as war or the threat of war for extorting from your peace-loving neighbours any demand you choose. It is always to be remembered that the first aggressors against peace were not victims of the peace treaties, but two of the conquerors, Japan and Italy.

Looking back and trying to reflect on one's mistakes, I think perhaps we failed here to recognize as a danger what was the most immediate danger of all, the profound war-weariness of England, France, and all the law-abiding or progressive nations. They longed for peace, and they longed in a selfish way. No public injustice which did not directly strike their national interests could goad them into facing trouble or risk. Consequently a free path lay open to all ambitions that were bold enough. Mustafa Kemal was first. He roused his people against the Treaty of Sèvres; England and France were too tired to take the trouble of stopping him; it was easier to abandon the Armenians. The war party in Japan came next. Neither Britain nor America nor Russia cared to check them. Mussolini, baffled in his attempt to seize Corfu in 1923 by the personal energy of Lord Cecil, was more successful in his next aggression; and we know how Ribbentrop assured Hitler time after time that, however France and England might grumble, they would never fight. War weariness was the main motive, but, speaking of this country in particular, it was reinforced by two curiously unrelated currents of opinion. Entrenched in high places were the old traditional diplomatists, who thought always in terms of 'British interests,' disliked the whole conception of the League, and resented the intrusion of moral ideals into politics. On the whole they sought the friendship of the aggressors rather than the victims because the aggressors were usually the stronger, and a strong friend is better than a weak. These people received the support not only of the pacifists, who were opposed to any armed resistance whatever, but also of a wider class who were troubled in conscience about the supposed harshness of the peace treaties, and were anxious to show penitence for their own sins—or more often for those of their political opponents—by a belated and often excessive indulgence towards Germany. The Germans, and even the Italians and Japanese, might be behaving rather badly; but, after all, had they all had a fair deal?

The makers of the Covenant had, of course, imagined it as working in a normal world, and the world in which it had to work was utterly abnormal. The surprising thing, and a thing which gives great comfort for the future, is that, in spite of all, the League very nearly succeeded. It is a cheap and facile error to which we are all prone, to explain as the fault of your own national government, or of some party opposed to your own, a failure that is due to the weakness of a whole civilization. Still, in looking back, one feels that many grave things went wrong through our ungenerous treatment of the Weimar Republic; many through the unreasonableness of France and the Little Entente, and many through our British unwillingness to give the firm assurances that would have made them reasonable.

And, looking at British politics alone, it seems as if a few very little changes might have made for the peace cause all the difference between success and failure. If at the first start, in the early twenties, we had had in the Foreign Office a statesman like Grey or Cecil, who understood and cared for the League, instead of Lord Curzon, who was steeped in the old diplomatic tradition; if at the time of the Disarmament Conference we had had as Foreign Minister Arthur Henderson, who believed in disarmament, instead of Ramsay MacDonald, who preferred that it should fail; if in the Manchurian crisis we had had Eden or Lord Lytton instead of Sir John Simon; if in the early stages of the Abyssinian crisis we had had Sir Austen Chamberlain, the whole course of history would have been different. We might well have had a disarmed world, probably backed by some international air force; the Manchurian aggression would probably have been settled by negotiation, the Abyssinian aggression have been nipped in the bud. It was not till after the Abyssinian failure that a British Prime Minister announced in despair that no single small nation in Europe could expect to be defended by the League of Nations. The great experiment had failed. The hope of a peaceful world order was gone.

Here many critics will stop me. 'Do you mean to say,' they will ask, 'that in these cases your friends wished this country and the rest of the League to go to war?' Our answer is clear. I do believe, first, that you cannot prevent war by simply running away from it. It was our duty under the Covenant not merely to avoid war but to prevent war. And the obvious way to prevent war in a world where the vast majority of mankind wants peace is for the Peace Forces to be ready to deal in time with every threat of war, whether due to genuine grievance or to mere ambition; and, if all else fails, to show that they will by united action protect any nation unjustifiably attacked. As the Article I have already quoted explains: 'Any war or threat of war is a matter of concern to the whole League; and the League shall take'—beforehand, when the war is still only a threat in the future—'whatever measures'—remedial or preventive; diplomatic, financial, or economic—

'may be deemed wise and effectual for safeguarding the peace.' But, in the last resort, there must be the possibility of coercion. A great many plans for world peace were put forward in the years 1916, 1917, and 1918, by the American League to Enforce Peace, by the British League of Nations Society, by the League of Free Nations Association, as well as by various individuals, official and unofficial; but all, I think, without exception were based on the idea of a League or group of nations willing, first, to settle all disputes among themselves peacefully, and, secondly, to defend every member against aggressive attack. A formula which occurs time after time with slight variations in the various drafts of that date runs thus:

Members of the Society . . . shall make provision for mutual defence, diplomatic, economic or military, in the event of any of them being attacked by a state which refuses to submit the case to an appropriate tribunal or council.

That was the hardest duty which members of the League undertook; it was indispensable; and they failed in it. Had they been ready to act in time, there would have been no talk of force: had they been ready to use force, there would have been no need for it. It was because the aggressor could always count on the Great Powers not being ready to face a risk of war that he felt free to do his worst against smaller victims.

Take, as examples, the two cases I have mentioned. In the case of Manchuria, we clearly could not have gone to war against Japan without the active support of America. I omit the disputed question whether America offered us that support or not; Mr. Stimson and Sir John Simon have given different accounts; I suspect that both parties were about equally anxious to shirk such dangerous responsibilities. But, apart from that, there were two things which the League Governments could have done had they been true to their principles. The Council proposed that a Commission of Inquiry should go to the spot to consider the best solution of the problems between Japan and China and the relief of Japanese grievances. The Japanese Government agreed. A Commission was appointed—a first-rate Commission, with Lord Lytton as the Chairman—but there were needless delays in appointing it and further needless delays in sending it out, so that, excellent as its proposals were, they came far too late. The war they might have prevented was almost finished. And why had the Japanese ventured not merely to break their treaties but to defy the resolution of the League Council? Probably they cared little for what the Council of the League might say; they cared greatly what England and France and the other great nations might say. When resolutions from the Council of the League were duly sent from Geneva to Japan, Lord Lytton tried in vain to get the Governments of the great nations each to send its own Ambassador to hand in the League resolution. To do that would have shown that the Governments were in earnest; and the path for negotiation would have been laid down. The Governments preferred to show that they were not in earnest; the Germans and others secretly encouraged Japan, and Sir John Simon proclaimed openly his rejection of the fundamental principle of the League: 'The object of my policy,' he said in the House, 'is to keep my own country out of trouble.' The aggressor might do as he liked.

In the Abyssinian case, the same Foreign Minister proclaimed the same rejection of principle. He 'would not risk losing a single British ship for the sake of Abyssinia.' With a sincere and resolute policy there would have been no need to risk ships; our Government and the French Government knew well beforehand, certainly as early as 1934, of Mussolini's project for a war against Abyssinia. They knew it when it was only an idea; when Mussolini was in no sense committed. They had time to stop it without danger in 1934; they had time to stop it even at the Stresa Conference in April 1935. That conference was specially called in order to settle all existing points of difference between England, France, and Italy; yet Abyssinia was never mentioned at it. Mussolini was allowed to assume, and did assume, that his aggression upon Abyssinia constituted no 'point of difference'; that Great Britain, like France, was ready to stand aside, break her treaties, and give friendly connivance to his international crime. When it was already too late for effective action, Sir John Simon resigned, Sir Samuel Hoare tried an unsuccessful compromise, Mr. Eden did goad the unwilling governments into imposing economic sanctions on Mussolini; but, do what he would, he could not make them impose the one sanction that would have settled the war in a month—the refusal of petrol for Mussolini's aeroplanes. It appeared afterwards that certain governments had given Italy the assurance that they would not agree to any sanctions being imposed which would effectively hamper Italian arms. The whole story should be read in the annual *Survey* published by Chatham House. A clear case had been put before the civilization of western Europe, the Liberal Christian civilization under which we live; that civilization was asked whether it would or would not, in a case where success was certain, be faithful to its Covenant and protect a backward member of the League against utterly unprovoked aggression; and the great nations had turned in their sleep and been unwilling to move. As Mr. T. E. Water, on behalf of the South African Government, stated in the Assembly on 1 July 1935: 'Fifty nations, led by three of the most powerful nations in the world, are about to declare their powerlessness to protect the weakest in their midst from destruction.' He went on to point out that there was no lack of power to fulfil the trust; only a lack of will 'to bear the sacrifices necessary for the fulfilment of their obligations.'

Our civilization had announced to the world and to history that it had not the necessary sense of corporate duty, not the necessary strength of mind, to defend itself.

One could write a sort of Sunday-school story, showing how this deadly failure at the last was only the climax of a series of actions showing slight incorrectness, slight bad faith, and an increasing neglect of international obligations. In July 1934 the Nazis murdered President Dollfuss. The matter ought instantly to have been brought before the League; but Mussolini, always an enemy of world order, offered to protect Austria himself on condition the League was not brought in; and Britain and France assented. Britain made a naval treaty with Germany, contrary to the Treaty of Versailles and without the consent of France. M. Laval made a private understanding with Mussolini, without the knowledge of England. The re-militarization of the Rhineland, the overrunning of Austria, the hideous persecution of the Jews, which soon assumed an international and not merely a domestic significance, the preposterous hypocrisies of non-intervention in Spain, the invasion and persecution of Czechoslovakia, followed in gradually ascending scale, till at last, with the League broken and the collective security that had once existed thrown away, England and France found themselves alone, clinging together for mutual protection and ready for almost any sacrifice if only they might be left in peace. It was not to be. At last they are forced in mere self-preservation to face alone a peculiarly dangerous war on behalf of the vital interests of the whole civilized world: the very war which the League was intended to prevent, and would have prevented if it had not been betrayed!

'True enough,' you may say, 'but is not this confession of failure a condemnation of your whole scheme? Why did the member nations fail to support the League? Because you were asking too much of them. The Governments were mostly supported by their own peoples in their refusal to take these risks. No nation will face war or the risk of war for the sake of another.' If that is so, I can only say again that civilization is doomed. It is exactly like the situation in Chicago in the palmy days of Al Capone and Bugs Moran. The peaceful citizens of Chicago hated the gangsters, they were infinitely stronger than the gangsters, they could have put the gangsters down at any time they liked; but the man who was first to interfere with them ran the risk of being shot, and no individual apparently, in the police or out of it, cared to take that risk. So the gangsters did what they liked. In the case of Chicago, the town was saved by a God from the Machine in the shape of the U.S. Government, which was far away out of the gangsters' power and proceeded to arrest Al Capone not for his Chicago murders, but for certain errors in his Federal income tax. There is no *deus ex machina* to save our civilization. It must save itself or perish.

Apologists for these betrayals spoke in Parliament and wrote in *The Times* saying that what they wanted was a League without sanctions. I always wondered if they knew what the words meant. It was a League of Nations intended to preserve peace, and the condition they required was that every member of it should be free to make war; there should be no obligation on the rest of the League either to stop the aggression or even to refrain from helping the aggressor. The League might indeed intercede with him, it might express its moral condemnation; but it must on no account cease to trade with him or refuse to supply him with such materials of war as he might need. The other members should, in fact, say to the aggressor: 'We condemn your action; you are committing a crime against God and man; and now, that point being clear, what would you like us to sell you—oil, arms, iron, anything else to help your crime? We are all ready for a profitable trade.' This notion that nations should form a society or League for co-operating in other matters, in putting down the opium traffic or the white slave traffic, in making arrangements about posts and currencies and railways, but at the same time be perfectly free to use their sovereign right of war, is surely both in fact and principle an absurdity. The very first result would be rival groups of armed alliances, treating war or peace not as a matter of public right and wrong, but as a pure question of self-interest. War would be no longer a crime: it would be re-established as the recognized and respectable *ultima ratio* of politics.

Let me turn to an opposite criticism. Did we perhaps, on the contrary, ask too little? We certainly asked for as much as ever we could get. Free nations cannot be compelled to sign agreements against their will; if they are cajoled into doing so the agreements are not practically enforceable. Any organization of world order which could be relied upon had to be one accepted by voluntary agreement.

Two great societies of nations already existed, and might to some extent be used as a model, the British Commonwealth and the United States; the one with no binding constitution at all except a common allegiance to the person of the king; the other with a particularly precise and rigid constitution, which it had as a matter of fact outgrown. Neither was a very apposite example to the League-makers, because both were held together by a community of laws, traditions, history, and language and for the most part also by common interests. Our task was far harder: to make a new society out of nations among whom no such community existed, a society in which potential enemies should sit in peace at the same table and gradually learn to cooperate. The League-makers followed on the whole the British precedent, though they did put in the Covenant one or two obligations which were not in the constitution of the British Commonwealth, but which have as a matter of fact now become the chief constitutional bond between its parts. (See the Report of the Commonwealth Conference at Toronto, 1933.) It was impossible to go farther. It is surprising indeed how far the nations, under the impact of the World War, were willing to go in the limitation of their sovereignty.

Consider what the makers of the Covenant got them to resign. First, they accepted an International Court for the settlement of all justiciable disputes. True, at first it was only a voluntary court; but soon all the greater nations were persuaded to sign the so-called Optional Clause, and thus to accept without qualification the third-party judgement of the Court on all justiciable disputes. This was a great achievement. I remember M. Motta, then President of the Swiss Republic, saying to me that the first Great Power which should sign the Optional Clause would be followed by all the lesser nations like a guiding star! There remained of course the disputes that were not justiciable, where there was no problem of legal right and wrong, but only of interests or what is called 'national honour.' On these the nations are bound to go to arbitration; to submit to any unanimous decision of the Council; and if the Council is not unanimous at least to submit to long delays before going to war.

The Right of War, the very citadel of sovereignty, if not absolutely abolished, was reduced almost to vanishing point. A genuine attempt to abolish it was made in the Geneva Protocol, which failed to find acceptance in 1924 owing to British opposition, but soon afterwards it was resigned altogether in the Kellogg Pact. As far as mere treaties could do it, the Right of War was given up.

The surrender would have been made practically effective had the disarmament clauses of the Covenant been carried out. By Article VIII the nations agreed to accept whatever limitation an international body should impose on them, and agreed further not to arm beyond that limit afterwards. International inspection was an obvious corollary; another corollary, in my opinion, must have been some kind of international policing to prevent illegal armament. Had this Article of the Covenant been carried out, it would, I think, practically speaking, have been impossible for any member of the League, or even for a rebel against the League like Japan, Italy, or Germany, to make war in defiance of the League.

Why did the Disarmament Conference fail? It was a long struggle, and ended very nearly in success. Years of thought were spent on the technical problems, that is, the problem of so reducing armaments that every nation shall be secure, and no nation capable of a successful invasion of another. Much nonsense was talked about the words 'aggressive' and 'non-aggressive'; people delighted in proving that a lead pencil was an aggressive weapon if properly jabbed into your neighbour's eye, or arguing that nations could fight as bitterly with spears and arrows as with gas and machine guns. The problem was not to put all nations on an equality of armament, but to make sure that no nation could have the weapons which would enable it successfully to invade a neighbour; and I can quote Sir John Simon himself for the judgement that towards the end of the Conference every technical problem had been solved, and only the political problems remained. In other words it was lack of will, and almost exclusively lack of will among the Great Powers, which prevented the success of that great Conference; lack of will based on lack of mutual trust, and on the knowledge of Germany's widespread secret rearmament in factories outside her own borders.

A third surrender of sovereignty was far harder to bring about, at any rate so long as armaments remained national and not international. It is not so very difficult for a law-abiding nation to give up its so-called 'right of war,' and agree not to use war as an element of national policy; it is far more difficult, as experience has shown, for it to agree actually to use war as an instrument of international authority to protect not itself but some other member of the society. But of that I have already spoken. The engagements of the Covenant on this point are both hesitating and obscure. When Article XVI was drafted, all nations were strongly impressed by the immense effectiveness of the economic blockade, while they hated the very thought of war. This reluctance to accept any obligation to fight runs through the whole Article. Nations agree to apply a boycott, and even a blockade; but no clear provision is made for the possibility that the boycotted aggressor might fight to resist the boycott. No account is taken of the obvious fact that a boycott, to be effective, has to be practically unanimous; unless it is so, it breaks down. No adequate distinction is drawn between the respective obligations of nations which are really able to enforce a blockade or use military measures and those which could not do either. I think the obligations of this Article should in some ways be more limited: but at all costs should be made clear and definite. Nations have not much scruple in evading a loosely expressed obligation; they do not like to be seen publicly breaking a perfectly specific pledge.

There was another problem, even more elusive, which the Covenant for the first time in history attempted to face. No treaty known to me has ever made provision for future changes in the world to be effected by peaceful agreement among nations. Article XIX attempted this; the Assembly was given the power of considering and reconsidering any treaty which had grown obsolete or any international condition whatever which threatened the peace of the world. The Article has never been actually used, though its existence as a threat in the background has had some effect, and very large changes have as a matter of fact been brought about. The cause that prevented Peaceful Change is the same that has wrecked the other hopes of mankind, the constant threat of war lurking in the background. Nations living under the shadow of that threat will never agree to any change that weakens their military security.

So far, in running through the main limitations of sovereignty imposed by the Covenant, we have found in each case that the limitations were great but imperfect. . . .

[T]he League is not dead. Its roots are too deep and far-reaching to be torn up. . . . The first experiment has failed. Certain men of my generation, under the guidance of a great and inspired leader, Lord Cecil, have done what we could towards facing a gigantic task which was never likely to be solved in the twenty-odd years which we have given to it, nor likely ever to be solved within the lifetime of those who started the movement. We die, but the movement cannot die; for to let it die would be to despair of civilization.

The Idea of Collective Security*

Walter Schiffer

Article 11 of the League Covenant contained the following statement: "Any war or threat of war, whether immediately affecting any of the Members of the League or not, is hereby declared a matter of concern to the whole League." These words expressed the progressive thinkers' assumption that any disturbance of the peace is prejudicial to all nations alike and that all peoples of the world have an equal interest in general peace. This was one of the reasonable, natural interests which were supposed to keep the various peoples of the world together and to unite them within a global community. It was now proclaimed that the reasonable, natural interests, which in the past had often been disregarded, were the actual interests of the member states of the League. This proclamation meant that the League existed as a unit with concerns of its own. For in the absence of a central authority of the type existing within states the solidarity of interests was the uniting element of the organization. The situation cannot be compared to that existing within a national community when a matter previously unregulated is made the subject of a new statute and thus becomes a matter of general concern. In this case the national community is already in existence and simply adds a new provision to the set of rules which constitute its legal order. Neither is the situation similar to the formation of a federal state. In this case the unity of the new entity finds expression in a central authority; the common interests here only provide the motives which lead to the creation of the federal bond. In the case of the League, the solidarity of reasonable interests was and remained the only basis of the community's legal order, which consisted of rules creating rights and duties for independent states. The legal order could be regarded as effective only if that solidarity existed. But since, in the past, states had been guided by considerations of narrowly interpreted national advantages, and since there was to be no fundamental change in the external situation which had produced this evaluation of national interests, the declaration contained in Article 11 was more than the statement of a fact. The international solidarity appeared as a goal which was still to be attained and which the states were obliged to

* Walter Schiffer, *The Legal Community of Mankind* (New York: Columbia University Press, 1954), pp. 202-223. Reprinted by permission. Walter Schiffer (1906-1949) after having served as Research Associate at the Geneva Research Center, was associated with the Institute for Advanced Study at Princeton from 1943-48. His publications included *Repertoire of Questions of General International Law before the League of Nations* (1942) and *The Quest for Peace* (1944).

reach. From now on each state was expected to act on the assumption that its reasonable interests—that is, the general interests of the community— actually were its real interests and that all the other members of the community regarded their respective interests in the same light.

In accordance with the principle that any war was a matter of general concern, Article 11 provided that in a situation threatening the peace of the world the League should take any action that might be "deemed wise and effectual to safeguard the peace of nations." The most important rule laid down in the following articles was the provision that a state, going to war against another, without submitting the dispute to arbitration or judicial settlement or to the Council, or without waiting until three months after the award of the arbitrators or the judicial decision or the report of the Council, should be deemed to have committed an act of war against all other members of the League. These were immediately to break off all relations with the guilty state and resort, if necessary, to the use of armed force against the lawbreaker. The same sanctions applied if a state resorted to war against a state complying with an arbitral award, a judicial decision, or the recommendations concerning the settlement of the dispute which were agreed upon by all members of the Council not parties to the dispute.

The Covenant did not prohibit war in all circumstances. But the League was established to make another general conflagration impossible. The provisions of the Covenant could be considered appropriate to achieve this purpose if certain assumptions were made. The first assumption was that blind, unreasonable passion was the main source of wars. If this view were correct, the delay which the members of the League had undertaken always to observe before going to war could be expected at least considerably to diminish the danger of armed conflicts by giving the parties to a dispute the opportunity to consider the case more calmly—that is, in the light of reason. The idea that war resulted from unreasonable passions implied the further assumption that all international conflicts could find a reasonable, generally acceptable, solution through peaceful means. The Covenant offered to the members of the League such peaceful methods of settlement. Disputes likely to lead to a rupture between two states, which were not submitted to arbitration or judicial decision, could be brought by one of the parties before the Council of the League which was to try to end the dispute by an agreement between the parties. The Council had no power to impose a settlement. But if its efforts to bring about an agreement were unsuccessful, this organ was to make a report containing, besides a statement of the facts, "just and proper" recommendations with regard to the settlement of the dispute, and, if this report should be adopted by the delegates of all members of the Council not parties to the conflict, a war against the party complying with the recommendations was prohibited. The Covenant took account of the possibility that the delegates of the states not directly involved in the dispute could not adopt a unanimous report on its settlement. But it was hoped, of course, that this case ordinarily would not occur.

Unanimity was required in principle for all decisions of the main League organs, the Council and the Assembly; this requirement of unanimity, which safeguarded the sovereignty and equality of the member states of the League, was not expected to create serious practical difficulties. The official British Commentary to the Covenant declared in this regard: "Granted the desire to agree, which the conception of the League demands, it is believed that agreement will be reached, or at least that the minority will acquiesce." The conception of the League indeed demanded not only the desire to agree, but also the certainty of an agreement which existed only if a reasonable, "just and proper," and therefore generally acceptable, solution were available for every dispute. A satisfactory working of the League regime obviously required that it generally appeared clearly who was right and how a dispute was to be settled, and that an organ composed of the impartial representatives of states not involved in the dispute generally would be able to find this solution. This requirement again could be fulfilled only if mankind, whose just opinions the League organs were supposed to express, was united by a general spirit of justice and reasonableness undisturbed by considerations of national power and politics. Otherwise an open discussion of international conflicts by a conference of state representatives could not only not produce the expected beneficial effects, but even result in a further complication of the international situation. The opportunity to bring their grievances before an international forum could induce states to magnify their quarrels and to provoke an international discussion of cases which otherwise might not have arisen at all or might have been settled quietly between the parties directly concerned. In a politically divided world such a discussion could lead to the extension of isolated conflicts and to the accentuation of existing general differences between opposing blocs of states.

Under such circumstances the League obviously could not fulfill its task. Without a fundamental unity of opinion and will, it was also impossible to enforce the Covenant's provisions concerning the prevention of war. If, however, that unity existed, it could be expected that the sanctions provided for in Article 16 would generally not be necessary.

Within a world governed by evident common standards of reason and justice, breach of the law, always easily recognizable as such, necessarily was an isolated phenomenon. If in an exceptional case a violation of the peace of the international community occurred, it could be expected always clearly to appear as the result of irrationality and bad faith. The maintenance of peace thus was considered to be essentially a matter of reason and good will. The moral cohesion of the world was believed to be so strong that even a state which, under the influence of irrational passion, contemplated going to war against another would not be entirely insensitive to the voice of reason, especially if it were clearly expressed by an impartial international organ, but would be prevented from executing its plans by the moral disapproval of the global community. In this sense President Wilson said at the Plenary Session of the Peace Conference of February 14, 1919: "throughout this instrument [the Covenant] we are depending primarily and chiefly upon one great force, and that is the moral force of the public opinion of the world, the cleansing and clarifying and compelling influences of publicity." He expected that sinister designs, if drawn into the open, would be "promptly destroyed by the overwhelming light of the universal expression of the condemnation of the world." Wilson went on to say: "Armed force is in the background in this programme, but it is in the background, and if the moral force of the world will not suffice, the physical force of the world shall. But that is the last resort because this is intended as a constitution of peace, not as a League of War."

It was hoped, of course, that the fear of collective action would generally discourage a state contemplating a resort to war in violation of the Covenant. But even use of the physical force of the world against the lawbreaker did not necessarily mean war. In its first paragraph, Article 16 provided for economic sanctions, for a complete economic isolation of the disturber of the peace; the experience of the World War seemed to have demonstrated the irresistible power of this weapon. It was assumed that it would be "as terrible a weapon as was the papal excommunication in the Middle Ages." Like excommunication, boycott was supposed to produce a profound spiritual effect on the lawbreaker. Here again the idea of the moral bond uniting mankind appeared very clearly. It was believed that it was especially the moral isolation resulting from it which made the economic sanction irresistible.

The second paragraph of Article 16 mentioned military sanctions. But according to an opinion which soon became dominant, there existed no legal obligation to take part in them. As the British Commentary stated, the contingents to be used against the law-breaker actually were to be settled by agreement; according to the Commentary, this procedure was necessary if the spirit of the Covenant were to be preserved and if joint action were to be efficacious. Participation in the economic sanctions was considered compulsory in the case of a breach of the Covenant. But it was left to each member of the League to decide whether such a breach actually had occurred. Also, this principle, that the states were free to decide for themselves whether the case had arisen in which they were obliged to apply the sanctions, seemed to be in agreement with the spirit of the Covenant; to invest the Council with the power to give a decision binding on all members of the League would not have been consistent with these members' sovereign rights. It was assumed, of course, that the members of the League would always arrive at the same conclusion with regard to the fact of a breach of law, which was expected generally to be evident to all reasonable persons, and that they would fulfill their obligations arising from that fact. Only on this condition was an effective combined action certain, and only the certainty of such action could have the effect of deterring from the execution of his plans the prospective disturber of the peace who was not amenable to reason.

The sanctions provided for in the Covenant were intended to make the global community similar to a state insofar as the enforcement of the legal order was concerned. The obligation of all League members to participate at least in the economic sanctions seemed to be an important element in this transformation of the global community. When previously a combined action of the members of this community against a disturber of the peace was contemplated, participation in this action generally appeared as the exercise of a right. The use of combined force against a violator of the legal order was regarded as a war waged for just cause. Christian Wolff's concept of a common action undertaken in the interest of universal security was an example of this view. [O]ppenheim spoke of a right of intervention which, he supposed, belonged to all states in case the award of an international tribunal was not accepted by one of the parties. It was assumed that the states would exercise this right because their reasonable interests would induce them to do so. Although the Covenant of the League seemed to introduce a fundamental modification of the concept of collective law enforcement, the change was more apparent than real. According to Article 16, a member of the League that resorted to war in disregard of the provisions of the Covenant was *ipso facto* deemed to have commited an act of war against all other members of the League. This formula expressed the idea that every unlawful war, although immediately directed against a single member of the community, also directly affected the interests of all others. The act of war committed against them entitled all the states to use force against the lawbreaker. There existed no means of forcing them to exercise this right, and there was in this respect no distinction between economic and military sanctions. The distinction made between these two kinds of sanctions became still less important if, as was the case according to Wilson's interpretation of the Covenant, the members of the League were not legally but morally obliged to take part in the combined action of a military character, and if, as Wilson explained in this connection, a moral obligation were superior to a legal obligation and had "a greater binding force." Whether the members of the League applied the economic as well as the military sanctions ultimately depended on their good will, and this good will could be expected to exist only if the members were reasonable enough to regard their interests as directly affected by a war in which they were not immediately involved.

If it were possible generally to rely on the good will and reasonableness of states, then the provisions of the Covenant could seem to be sufficient for an effective prevention of war. It could even appear doubtful whether so detailed provisions were necessary for the achievement of this purpose. It should have been possible to expect, if the world were in the condition which alone enabled it to preserve general peace, that it would always be easy in a case of emergency to convene a conference for the consideration of a dispute not submitted to arbitration or judicial settlement, and that a state contemplating war without laying its case before an international organ or in defiance of the decision or recommendation of such an organ would be restrained from executing its plans by the fear of the collective action in which all the states, motivated by their own reasonable interests, would certainly participate. If, on the other hand, that condition did not exist, no additional undertakings of the member states could possibly make the League better qualified to fulfill its task of preventing war. No greater security would have been achieved if war, or at least offensive war, had been entirely prohibited, if the Council had been given the right to issue a binding decision instead of a mere recommendation, if the unanimity principle had been abandoned, if there had been precise clauses providing for the execution of the decisions of international organs, and if the member states had been obliged to make military contingents available to the League for the enforcement of its legal order. The maintenance of the legal order of the League thus "strengthened" would in the last resort also have depended on the good faith of the member states. The idea of "strengthening" the Covenant was clearly inconsistent with its basic premise. On the one hand, this idea presupposed the necessity of imposing more rigid obligations on states which otherwise could not be trusted to live together peacefully; on the other hand, it had to be assumed that the same states would generally be willing to fulfill heavier duties with regard to the enforcement of those obligations without any possibility of enforcing the enforcement.

For the same reason it was impossible to regard the League Covenant as a first phase in the development of international organization. A greater perfection in the machinery of the League was not necessary if the moral conditions existed on which its functioning depended, and, if these conditions were not fulfilled, no machinery was likely to give the world greater security. Therefore, the League could appear as initiating a new phase in the development of international relations only in the sense that the new era was to be one of increased rationality and morality. But unless a high degree of rational and moral conduct were already reached, the League could not be expected to work at all. Its functioning presupposed that the behavior of the member states was ordinarily motivated by considerations of reasonable interest rather than by considerations of power and politics. Of particular interest in this respect is a statement of the official British Commentary to the Covenant which is to be found in a passage dealing with the Permanent Court of International Justice set up under Article 14 of the Covenant. The League Covenant did not impose on the member states any binding obligation to have their conflicts decided by arbitral or judicial organs. But in Article 13 they agreed to submit to such organs any disputes which they recognized to be suitable for this kind of settlement, and the same article enumerated certain classes of disputes which were to be regarded as generally suitable for submission to arbitration or to the Permanent Court of International Justice. In this connection the British Commentary expressed the following opinion: "As things now stand, the political rather than the judicial aspect of the settlement of disputes is prominent in the Covenant, but 'political' settlements can never be entirely satisfactory or just. Ultimately and in the long run, the only alternative to war is law, and for the enthronement of law there is required such a continuous development of international jurisprudence, at present in its infancy, as can only be supplied by the progressive judgments of a Permanent Court working out its own traditions." The concept of the ideal condition of the world which appears in this passage obviously is very similar to the idea of the unpolitical sphere which was expressed by progressive writers before the first World War. The author of the Commentary must have considered the political settlement of a dispute—that is, especially the settlement through the action of the League Council—to be more satisfactory and reasonable than its decision by war. But he regarded such a settlement as still imperfect, and the existing situation, in which the political aspect of international conflicts was prominent, appeared to him as not entirely consistent with the ideal of a League of Nations governed by law. Since political settlements were the natural consequence of political disputes, it appears that the ideal League was to be free from conflicts of this type.

It was, however, precisely the existence of such conflicts which had led to the idea that a League of Nations was required for the maintenance of peace between states. Such an organization seemed indispensable, just because the ideal situation, characterized by peaceful intercourse and voluntary compliance with international law, was not realized. The passions of the world were not dead. By providing for the creation of an international legal court, the Covenant fulfilled an old hope of progressive thinkers. But its characteristic new feature was the machinery which it set up for the settlement of political disputes and the prevention of war. To prevent the outbreak of hostilities between states, the provisions of the covenant seemed generally sufficient, although the right to go to war was not entirely eliminated but only restricted. But by simply limiting that right, the Covenant obviously admitted that war was a method normally used by states to enforce their claims. In fact, the primary reason for not prohibiting war entirely was that such a prohibition seemed impracticable under the existing circumstances. According to General Smuts, the utmost that it seemed "possible to achieve in the present conditions of international opinion and practice" was "to provide for a breathing space before the disputants are free to go to war." He expressed what he declared to be the general opinion in the following words: "states will not be prepared to bind themselves further; and even if they do, the risk of their breaking their engagements is so great as to make the engagement not worth while and indeed positively dangerous." The situation thus described considerably differs from that which seemed required for a satisfactory working of the League. This difference is made still clearer by Smuts's observation concerning the political disputes— that is, the conflicts from which wars had generally resulted and for which the Covenant attempted to find a peaceful solution. In cases of this kind, according to Smuts, the issues "are generally vague, intangible, and spring from special grounds of national psychology. They involve large questions of policy, of so-called vital interests, and of national honor." When political disputes arose, passions ran high, "not only among the disputants, but also their partisans among other states." The global community here appeared as at least potentially disrupted into hostile blocs composed of states which considered their vital, essential interests as opposed to those of other states. From the progressive point of view this situation might have seemed to result from the fact that the states had not yet reached that highest degree of reasonableness which would have enabled them to realize that there was no antagonism between their real interests and especially that they had in common the most vital interest, that of peace. But it was this fact which made it necessary to create a machinery for the prevention of war. On the other hand, as seen before, the satisfactory working of this machinery presupposed the existence of a community characterized by an essential unity of reason and good will, a unity at worst occasionally broken by isolated cases of unreasonable behavior. With this concept of unity, which was a fundamental element of the League of Nations idea, conflicted the other equally essential concept that there was a special category of political disputes.

Smuts's idea of political conflicts corresponded to that expressed in a number of prewar arbitration treaties by which the contracting parties agreed to settle by arbitration all such differences of a legal nature as did not affect their vital interests, their independence, or their honor. Lord Robert Cecil, who together with General Smuts represented the British Empire at the League of Nations Commission of the Peace Conference, obviously shared this concept. In his opinion even the interpretation of a treaty, which apparently was a matter most suitable for decision by judicial procedure, could involve the honor or the essential interests of a country and thus become the subject of a political dispute which could not be settled by legal decision. According to this view, there existed no precise distinction between legal and political disputes. This difficulty was one of the reasons for which it seemed impossible to establish in the Covenant the principle of compulsory jurisdiction for disputes in themselves susceptible of legal decision. [O]ppenheim thought it unreasonable to exempt from judicial settlement questions involving essential interests. The state practice of the period after the first World War followed him insofar as it no longer used the concept of political conflicts that at the end of the war had still been maintained by Lord Robert Cecil and General Smuts. The reservations concerning the vital interests and the honor of the countries no longer appeared in the instruments by which states obliged themselves to have their disputes settled by a legal decision, and they were especially absent from the undertakings of a considerable number of them to accept the compulsory jurisdiction of the Permanent Court of International Justice. But compulsory jurisdiction generally was accepted for legal disputes only, and in this respect the regime differed from that envisaged by Oppenheim, who had hoped that ordinarily all international differences would be submitted to judicial organs. The distinction between legal and other disputes still was maintained. But it still proved impossible to arrive at a precise definition of the two categories. If, as was supposed, the global community were united under a global system of law, it should have been possible to solve every question in accordance with a legal rule. If extralegal considerations could give a conflict such a character as to exclude the possibility of judicial settlement, there was no objective legal criterion left according to which the question could be answered as to whether the obligation to submit all legal disputes to a judicial organ applied to a particular case. But whatever definition of nonlegal or nonjusticiable disputes might have been attempted, it was usual to refer to them as political conflicts or conflicts of interests, and the controversies which could not be brought under the control of law were regarded as those which were most likely to disturb the peace of the world. Since a state ordinarily does not use force in cases of minor importance, it was therefore still true that nonlegal disputes were those involving "large questions of policy" or "vital interests." Thus the distinction between legal and nonlegal conflicts meant that states still generally had essential political interests of their own which could bring them into conflict with other states. This condition, however, was hardly compatible with the assumed existence of a fundamental unity of interest which guaranteed the maintenance of peace through the machinery of the League and under the guidance of a uniform public opinion.

Progressive thinkers believed that the expansion of international administration of justice and the corresponding contraction of the sphere of politics was simply a question of increasing and perfecting the body of international law. The League appeared to be particularly qualified to further this development. It was supposed to perform its task of promoting international cooperation and achieving international peace and security "by the firm establishment of the understandings of international law as the actual rule of conduct among nations." It seemed possible to expect that the new organization would help to bring about a comprehensive codification of international law and that the existence of a complete system of rules which precisely defined the legal rights and duties of states would facilitate lawful conduct within the global community and decrease the sphere of politics. But international legislation—that is, the process of establishing rules by consent—could be expected to lead to the creation of such a complete system only if it were possible to assume that their essential interests would be regarded by all the states as generally coinciding. This assumption was contradicted, however, by the recognition of the fact that states had, at least in their own opinion, essential interests of their own, which were not necessarily in agreement with those of other states and which could not even be defined precisely enough to make the establishment of a purely legal sphere possible. As long as this situation prevailed, it could hardly be expected that a complete codification of international law would be possible and that the elimination of the political element would be achieved by the process of lawmaking. If it had been possible to eliminate it, the League's war-preventing machinery would have become correspondingly unnecessary.

In fact, the political element and the power factor were so important in the League that it appeared necessary to take account of them in the composition of the Council. On this organ, which particularly was concerned with the task of preventing war, the Great Powers were permanently represented while other states, selected for membership on that body by the Assembly, occupied their seats only for limited terms of office. As the British Commentary explained, the Council had to represent "the actual distribution of the organized political power of the world" if it were to "exercise real authority." Although in form the Council's decisions were only recommendations, it seemed likely to the author of the Commentary that recommendations made unanimously by a body of delegates of states including those of the Great Powers would be "irresistible." There the importance of the relative political strength of the members of the League was openly recognized to an extent which to some seemed incompatible with the principle of state equality. It may be recalled that Oppenheim had considered the hegemony of the Great Powers as a political fact without legal significance. As far as the composition of the League Council was concerned, the preponderance of the Great Powers was not, as had been the case previously, merely a matter of political practice; it was confirmed by a rule embodied in an international treaty. As a body deriving its authority at least partly from the representation of the Great Powers, the Council was particularly qualified to function as an instrument of collective mediation and dictatorial interference in the conflicts arising between weaker states. Pufendorf had conceived of an action of this type as a method of maintaining peace. This concept seemed somewhat out of place in that writer's theory, in which the world appeared as a wholly unpolitical community of free and equal persons coexisting under the exclusive rule of the law of nature and reason. In the League of Nations, which was supposed to represent the combined moral and physical power of the whole world and to exclude political combinations supported by the power of particular states, the recognition of the predominant power of some states should also have seemed incompatible with fundamental concepts. It is true that the Great Powers represented on the Council were supposed to act in the interest of the whole world community. The power of the strong was to maintain the right of the weak. Moreover, the delegates of the Great Powers were not alone sitting on the Council, and that body was expected to fulfill its tasks under the general control of the Assembly, in which all members of the League were represented. Nevertheless, the special position which the Covenant granted to the Great Powers by making them permanent members of the Council could easily appear as a concession made to existing political conditions and thus involving a deviation from the pure League of Nations idea.

But such a concession could hardly be considered to be an expression of sound realism if the primary purpose of the League were kept in mind. In this regard the following remarks by D. H. Miller, the legal adviser to the American Commission at the Peace Conference, are significant: "To suppose the existence of a League of Nations and at the same time a war between its members is to suppose an unreal impossibility. Of course, I am speaking of serious things. Haiti and the Dominican Republic might, I suppose, go to war and a League go on. But a world war, a war of Great Powers and a League of Nations of these same Powers with the rest, are contradictory in their essence." The significance of this statement will become clear if one considers the general opinion with regard to the condition of the world as it existed during the nineteenth century after the close of the Napoleonic Wars. This period appeared as generally peaceful; the political situation then prevailing seemed to justify the hope of progressive thinkers that the institution of war was becoming obsolete. There were, however, wars throughout the nineteenth century; some of them involved even Great Powers. But there was no general conflagration of the type of the Napoleonic Wars or the first World War. The League was established primarily in order to prevent the recurrence of catastrophes of such dimensions. They resulted from the antagonism between Great Powers which finally led to the disruption of practically the whole world into two hostile blocs. But the League seemed not to be qualified for dealing with such emergencies. Its functioning depended on a constant agreement of the Great Powers—that is, on a condition the absence of which would have made its working particularly necessary. It certainly was a success when the Council prevented a border incident between two small states from developing into a real war. But it can hardly be said that by effecting a success of this kind the League achieved the main purpose for which it was created. This purpose clearly was the prevention of another World War. The struggle of 1914 to 1918 was to be the last of its kind. It was hoped, of course, that general agreement on international problems would exist not only between the Great Powers but throughout the world, and this hope could seem justified because of the changes in the general situation which were to take place after the war. If, as was expected, the war resulted in eliminating once and for all the conditions which in the past had provoked international conflicts, then it seemed possible to believe that in the future the peoples' reasonable interests, and especially their natural interest in peace, would be free to assert themselves. In this respect there appeared, therefore, to exist a certain relationship between the peace treaties which created new conditions and the League whose Covenant formed the first part of those treaties. But here again the idea that the international community organized through the League was united by a bond of common reason and good will conflicted with considerations of a political nature.

The new territorial settlement was to be based on the principle of self-determination—that is, on the rule that every nation's reasonable desire to live together in a separate independent unit was to be respected. In doubtful cases the plebiscite was considered to be the appropriate method of ascertaining the wishes of the population of a given territory. The creation of the League of Nations seemed to make it possible to realize the principle of self-determination to the fullest extent. Without this institution it might have appeared necessary to establish boundaries between states in such a way as to facilitate their defense. But in Article 10 of the Covenant the states belonging to this organization undertook to respect and preserve, as against external aggression, the territorial integrity and existing political independence of all members of the League. Supplemented by the provisions regarding the peaceful settlement of disputes and the prevention of war, this article was supposed to give security even to those states whose boundaries, drawn in accordance with the nationality principle, were unfavorable from a strategic point of view.

It is not intended here to decide whether the peace treaties were just or to what extent the establishment of European frontiers actually was determined by the rigid application of the pure principles of nationality and self-determination. But it must be observed that even if it had been possible objectively to determine what absolutely just conditions were, such conditions could be created only at the expense of the conquered states and could, therefore, hardly be equally acceptable to the whole world. The guarantee against aggression, which the League provided for its members, was therefore bound to appear as a guarantee of the results of victory, and the common interest on which the League's functioning depended became an interest of the victorious powers not so much in peace as such as in the maintenance of the concrete political situation created by the peace treaties. The war had led to entirely new political conditions, especially insofar as the position of Germany in Europe and in the world was concerned. Germany had lost her ally, the Austro-Hungarian Monarchy, which completely disappeared through dismemberment, and was herself decisively weakened. This effect of the war could appear as justified in the light of the progressive concept on which the League of Nations idea was based. The Austro-Hungarian Monarchy had to disappear because its existence was incompatible with the principle of self-determination, and Germany was to be weakened because she seemed to have proved her innate tendency toward aggression and conquest and her disregard for the rights of other peoples. If this judgment of the German character were correct, if a strong Germany were a menace to the security of other states, then it could have seemed that a policy designed to keep Germany in a position of comparative weakness and to maintain a certain power situation as a safeguard against future German attacks was not in itself inconsistent with the League's ideals of peace and order in the international domain. It is irrelevant here whether the premises of such a policy were correct or whether it could have been carried out successfully. The fact is important, however, that when member states tried to use the League as an instrument of maintaining the political conditions created by the peace treaties, their policy could be criticized, not because it was bad, but because it was a policy. It was possible for critics of the institution simply to denounce it as the "Entente League of Nations" without investigating the merits of "Entente" policy. Writers could demonstrate their moral and intellectual boldness merely be revealing to a startled public the fact that political activities still were carried on in the world. From the point of view of the pure League idea, it seemed difficult for states which, as League members, had a policy of their own to answer this kind of criticism. According to this idea, the League had no policy of its own and was not compatible with a policy of its members based on particular interests and special power combinations, although this organization seemed to be required because of the danger to world peace resulting from political conflicts which could arise only if there existed a diversity of essential interests.

The Covenant itself contained a provision which clearly showed that the League was not intended to be connected with any particular political situation. This provision was Article 19 which ran as follows:

The Assembly may from time to time advise the reconsideration by Members of the League of treaties which have become inapplicable, and the consideration of international conditions whose continuance might endanger the peace of the world.

According to the British Commentary, this provision made it plain that the Covenant was "not intended to stamp the new territorial settlement as sacred and unalterable for all times, but, on the contrary, to provide machinery for the progressive regulation of international affairs in accordance with the needs of the future." The Commentary added that "absence of such machinery, and the consequent survival of treaties long after they had become out of date, led to many of the quarrels of the past"; the new regulation thus seemed "to inaugurate a new international order, which should eliminate, so far as possible, one of the principal causes of war." One of the main purposes of Article 19 was to provide for the readjustment of frontiers in such a way as to make it impossible that under Article 10 the members of the League should be obliged to defend against aggression boundaries which were drawn unjustly, especially in disregard of the wishes of the populations concerned.

This concept very clearly reveals the conflicting ideas underlying the League of Nations and its Covenant. The fact was recognized that territorial disputes frequently had caused wars in the past. The provision of the Covenant, designed to eliminate wars resulting from this source, was based on the assumption that the general opinion of the world, as expressed by the delegates of all the members of the League in the Assembly, would be sufficient to induce a state voluntarily to give up parts of its territory whenever its right to rule them appeared no longer compatible with the requirements of justice. The working of the new "machinery" depended on the possibility of objectively determining an unjust territorial settlement and on a change in the attitude of states with regard to territorial problems. The meaning of this change is illustrated by a clause which appeared in one of the several drafts of a Covenant prepared by President Wilson. Although this sentence was not inserted in the Covenant as finally adopted it nevertheless is characteristic of its spirit. It was said there: "The Contracting Powers accept without reservation the principle that the peace of the world is superior in importance to every question of political jurisdiction or boundary." In the framework of the Covenant, which guaranteed the territorial integrity of the member states against outward aggression, this clause could only mean that from now on the states would neither individually nor collectively defend at the risk of war boundaries which were obviously unjust. While, therefore, the new machinery seemed necessary since states were inclined to go to war because of a difference of opinion as to the justness of territorial settlements, the functioning of this machinery could be expected only when this condition no longer existed. The Covenant thus did not really provide for a solution of the problem which it intended to solve, but rather theoretically eliminated the problem by postulating its nonexistence.

It may be appropriate in this connection to point out the difference between the League of Nations idea and the progressive concept as it appeared before the first World War. In the prewar period, progressive thinkers who were convinced that in the international sphere a legal regulation of political problems was impossible had hoped that politics would eventually disappear from that sphere and that the common, unpolitical interests would unite the peoples of the world in a peaceful, legally ordered community. The observance of the nationality principle appeared as one of the essential conditions of the realization of the ideal situation. But it was not expected that this situation would be reached before that principle was generally applied nor that it would be possible to put the principle into effect by peaceful means. Revolutions and wars commonly were regarded as the inevitable results of oppressive governments—that is, of governments disregarding the right of nations to be united in an independent state—and revolutions and wars seemed the ordinary methods of compelling such governments to give up their unjust authority. During the World War the hope had arisen that the great struggle would result in a general reasonable and just situation as far as the nationality principle was concerned. The peace negotiations had demonstrated, however, the difficulty of finding a generally satisfactory solution in this respect, and it seemed even hardly possible to find a solution which would remain permanently satisfactory. The League, therefore, faced conditions which always had appeared as political and consequently as sources of war. But the working of this institution, which was created in order to exercise a control over these political conditions, presupposed the existence of the unpolitical legal community that progressive thinkers before the war had conceived of. Constant modifications of boundaries by agreement, arrived at under the guidance of a public opinion which was determined by principles of pure justice, were conceivable only when political considerations were of no importance at all. For such changes of frontiers were bound to affect the relative strength of the states concerned and could alter the whole power situation in the world, especially that

situation which had resulted from the World War and on which the observance of the peace treaties seemed to depend. But the idea that the League
had to prevent conflicts concerning territorial questions in itself implied that
the ideal of an unpolitical world was not yet realized.

Territorial problems formed the subject of political disputes. These
disputes frequently were defined as conflicts arising from the fact that one
party demanded a change in the existing law. This law was regarded as
expressed in the delimitation of the respective territorial spheres of the
different states. In this connection it was observed that within national
communities legislative procedure provided an opportunity for changing the
law in accordance with changing conditions of life, but that international
legislation was not developed enough to make possible such changes
through an orderly procedure. Here again appeared the connection between
political conflicts and international legislation; it seemed only necessary to
improve international legislation in order to enable the League effectively to
deal with political problems. It must be noted, however, that international
legislation, as conceived of by progressives before the first World War, was
not regarded as having the task which now it seemed required to achieve. In
the ideal situation as it was then expected to develop, international legislation was to lay down by consent rules required by reason for the regulation
of the common unpolitical interests of the various peoples which had united
in nation-states and had no longer any conceivable interest in territorial
changes or in any other political problems. The idea that states corresponded to individuals in their role of private citizens and that they lived
together under the rule of a law comparable to the private law of national
communities was at the basis of that concept of international legislation,
which, in the framework of progressive thinking, was the only one that
could consistently be maintained. Within national communities, however,
there existed besides the rules of private law those concerning the organization of the state and the acquisition and exercise of political power; the
operation of these rules within the state organization makes it possible
legally to control conflicting political activities out of which the policy of the
state itself emerges. The adaptation of the legal order to changed circumstances through legislation forms part of this process. By instituting international organs, the Covenant had not transformed the international community in such a way as to make it similar to a state; the League could not
fulfill in the international sphere the same tasks which the state performed
in the national community.

The international community remained essentially in the same condition in which it had been when Oppenheim suggested an unpolitical organization of the world based on the principle of state sovereignty and equality.
With these principles the existence of a political central authority standing
above individual states had seemed incompatible. Such an authority was still
nonexistent. The League could act only through individual actions of its
member states. Its functioning depended on the good will of these states, or

at least of their great majority. Under these circumstances the formulation of the common interest could be only a matter of calm reasoning, not of political activity. In the absence of a central authority as it existed within the states, such activity appeared as an element disrupting the community. The League organs were, therefore, essentially instruments for facilitating reasonable behavior, which consisted in the preservation of a supposedly natural harmony of interests. The Assembly and the Council were not supposed to formulate a definite League policy. The League Council especially was not, as might perhaps have been assumed, an organ determining the policy of the whole community in accordance with the political tendencies prevailing within that community. It was not quite clear in what sense the member states of the Council represented other members of the League. But it is evident that they were expected neither to represent currents of a political nature nor to promote any political program to be adopted by the League as a whole. The election by the Assembly of the nonpermanent members of the Council was not to be determined by considerations of this kind; nor were the Great Powers which occupied their Council seats permanently supposed to impose a certain policy on the League, although their privileged position was due to political considerations. So long as the League remained an association of independent states, it was impossible for legislation to fulfill in the international domain the same tasks with regard to political problems which it performed in national communities, and this situation could not have been altered by any attempts to improve the procedure of international legislation so long as this was an international procedure.

PART TWO

Geneva to New York
(via Washington and San Francisco)

CHAPTER 4 *The Charter and the Covenant*

From League of Nations to United Nations*

Leland M. Goodrich

On April 18, 1946, the League Assembly adjourned after taking the necessary steps to terminate the existence of the League of Nations and transfer its properties and assets to the United Nations. On August 1, this transfer took place at a simple ceremony in Geneva. Thus, an important and, at one time, promising experiment in international cooperation came formally to an end. Outside of Geneva, no important notice was taken of this fact. Within the counsels of the United Nations, there was an apparent readiness to write the old League off as a failure, and to regard the new organization as something unique, representing a fresh approach to the world problems of peace and security. Quite clearly there was a hesitancy in many quarters to call attention to the essential continuity of the old League and the new United Nations for fear of arousing latent hostilities or creating doubts which might seriously jeopardize the birth and early success of the new organization.

This silence regarding the League could well be understood at a time when the establishment of a general world organization to take the place of the discredited League was in doubt, when it was uncertain whether the United States Senate would agree to American participation, and when the future course of the Soviet Union was in the balance. Though careful consideration had been given within the Department of State to League experience in the formulation of American proposals, it was quite understandable that officers of the Department, in the addresses which they delivered and reports which they made on the Dumbarton Oaks Proposals, should have for the most part omitted all references to the League except where it seemed possible to point to the great improvements that had been incorporated in the new Proposals. Nor was it surprising, in view of the past relation of the United States to the League and the known antipathy of the Soviet Union to that organization, that Secretary of State Stettinius in his address to the United Nations Conference in San Francisco on April 26, 1945, failed once to refer to the League of Nations, or the part of an American President in the establishment of it. In fact, from the addresses

* Leland M. Goodrich, "From League of Nations to United Nations," *International Organization,* Vol. 1, No. 1 (February 1947), pp. 3-21. Reprinted by permission. Leland M. Goodrich is currently Professor of Public Law and Government at Columbia University. He is the author of *The United Nations* (1959) and co-author of *Charter of the United Nations: Commentary and Documents* (1959).

and debates at the San Francisco Conference, the personnel assembled for the Conference Secretariat, and the organization and procedure of the Conference, it would have been quite possible for an outside observer to draw the conclusion that this was a pioneer effort in world organization. Since the United Nations came into being as a functioning organization there has been a similar disinclination on the part of those participating in its work to call attention to its true relation to the League of Nations.

While the circumstances which make it necessary for those officially connected with the United Nations to be so circumspect in their references to the League of Nations can be appreciated, the student of international organization is free, in fact is duty bound, to take a more independent and objective view of the relations of the two organizations. If his studies lead him to the conclusion that the United Nations is in large measure the result of a continuous evolutionary development extending well into the past, instead of being the product of new ideas conceived under pressure of the recent war, that should not be the occasion for despair, as we know from the past that those social institutions which have been most successful in achieving their purposes are those which are the product of gradual evolutionary development, those which in general conform to established habits of thought but which nevertheless have the inner capacity for adaptation to new conditions and new needs.

While progress largely depends upon the discovery and application of new ideas and techniques, it has always been considered the test of practical statesmanship to be able to build on the past, adapting what has been proven to be useful in past experience to the needs and requirements of the changing world. Thus the framers of the American Constitution, while they created much that was new, did not hesitate to draw heavily upon the institutions and principles which were a part of their common background of experience in America and in England. At the time of the establishment of the League of Nations, the view was commonly held, certainly with more justification than today in relation to the United Nations, that something really unique was being created. However, we have come to recognize that even the League system was primarily a systematization of pre-war ideas and practices, with some innovations added in the light of war experience. Sir Alfred Zimmern has expressed this fact very well in these words:

. . . The League of Nations was never intended to be, nor is it, a revolutionary organization. On the contrary, it accepts the world of states as it finds it and merely seeks to provide a more satisfactory means for carrying on some of the business which these states transact between one another. It is not even revolutionary in the more limited sense of revolutionizing the methods for carrying on interstate business. It does not supersede the older methods. It merely supplements them.

We have come to recognize the various strands of experience—the European Concert of Powers, the practice of arbitration in the settlement of disputes, international administrative cooperation, to mention only a few—which entered into the fabric of the League. Should we be surprised to find that what was true of the League of Nations is even more true of the United Nations?

Those who have thus far attempted a comparison of the United Nations with the League of Nations have, generally speaking, been concerned with pointing out the differences. Furthermore, comparison has been made of the textual provisions of the Covenant and the provisions of the Charter, not taking into account actual practice under the Covenant. Such a basis of comparison naturally leads to an exaggerated idea of the extent of the gap which separates the two systems. If in similar fashion the Constitution of the United States as it existed on paper at the time it became effective in 1789 were compared with the Constitution as it is applied today, the conclusion undoubtedly would be that a revolution had occurred in the intervening period. Obviously, any useful comparison of the League and the United Nations must be based on the League system as it developed under the Covenant. If that is done, it becomes clear that the gap separating the League of Nations and the United Nations is not large, that many provisions of the United Nations system have been taken directly from the Covenant, though usually with changes of names and rearrangements of words, that other provisions are little more than codifications, so to speak, of League practice as it developed under the Covenant, and that still other provisions represent the logical development of ideas which were in process of evolution when the League was actively functioning. Of course there are many exceptions, some of them important. But the point upon which attention needs to be focused for the serious student of international affairs is that the United Nations does not represent a break with the past, but rather the continued application of old ideas and methods with some changes deemed necessary in the light of past experience. If people would only recognize this simple truth, they might be more intelligent in their evaluation of past efforts and more tolerant in their appraisal of present efforts.

Space does not permit a detailed analysis with a view to establishing the exact extent to which the United Nations is a continuation of the League system. All that is attempted here is to consider the more important features of the United Nations system, particularly those with respect to which claims to uniqueness have been made, with a view to determining to what extent in general this continuity can be said to exist. . . .

Basic Character of Two Organizations. The statement has been made that the United Nations is "potentially and actually much stronger" than the League of Nations. That statement might lend itself to some misunderstanding, particularly in view of the fact that it is only one of many statements that have been made suggesting that the United Nations inherently is a more powerful organization and therefore more likely to achieve its purpose by virtue of the specific provisions of its Charter than was the League of Nations.

We can start, I think, with the fundamental proposition that the United Nations, as was the League of Nations, is primarily a cooperative enterprise and falls generally within the category of leagues and confederations instead of within that of federal unions. Except in one situation, neither the United Nations nor its principal political organs have the authority to take decisions binding on Members without their express consent. Without this power, it is impossible to regard the organs of the United Nations as constituting a government in the sense of the federal government of the United States. The essential character of the United Nations is specifically affirmed in the first of the principles laid down in Article 2 of the Charter where it is stated that "the organization is based on the principle of the sovereign equality of all its members." This principle was not expressly stated in the Covenant of the League of Nations, but was, nevertheless, implicit in its provisions.

Since both the United Nations and the League of Nations are based primarily upon the principle of voluntary cooperation, the point that needs special consideration is whether, more or less as an exception to the general principle, the Charter contains provisions which give to the organs of the United Nations greater authority than was vested in the corresponding organs of the League. In this connection a great deal of emphasis has been placed upon the provisions of the Charter regulating voting in the General Assembly and the Security Council. It is, of course, true that under Article 18 of the Charter decisions of the General Assembly can be taken by a two-thirds majority of the members present and voting, instead of by unanimous vote of these present, as was the requirement for the League Assembly. It must be borne in mind, however, that on questions of policy the General Assembly can only recommend, and that consequently any decision taken is a decision to make a recommendation. Also, it is quite unfair to compare these provisions without taking into account the practice of the League Assembly under the Covenant. In several important respects the rule of the Covenant was interpreted so as to bring actual League practice fairly close to the provisions of the Charter. For one thing, it was provided in the rules of the Assembly that a state which abstained from voting was not to be counted as present, with the result that abstention was a means by which certain of the consequences of the unanimity rule could be avoided. More important, however, was the rule which was established in the first session of the League Assembly, that a resolution expressing a wish, technically known as a "voeu," might be adopted by a majority vote. This had the effect of making possible a whole range of Assembly decisions by majority vote which did not differ in any important respect from decisions which may be taken by the General Assembly by majority or two-thirds votes. Furthermore, it should be noted that the League Assembly early came to the conclusion that the decision to recommend an amendment to the Covenant under Article 26 might be taken by a majority vote, with the result that the power of the Assembly to initiate amendments actually could be exercised more easily than under the Charter of the United Nations. Thus it would seem erroneous to view the provisions of the Charter with respect to the power of the General Assembly to make decisions as representing any fundamentally different approach from or any great advance over the comparable provisions of the Covenant of the League of Nations as interpreted in practice.

When we turn our attention to the Security Council we find admittedly that an important change has been made. Under the League Covenant the Council was governed by the unanimity rule except in procedural matters, and this proved a serious handicap, particularly when the Council was acting under Article 11 of the Covenant. It was possible for a member of the Council, accused of threatening or disturbing the peace, to prevent any effective action under this Article by the interposition of its veto, has happened in the case of Japanese aggression in Manchuria in 1931 and the threat of Italian aggression in Ethiopia in 1935. Under the Charter it is possible for a decision to be taken binding Members of the United Nations without their express consent. Furthermore, this decision may require specific acts upon the part of the Members of the United Nations and it is not to be regarded as a simple recommendation as was the case with decisions taken by the League Council under Articles 10 and 16.

Nevertheless, there are important points to be kept in mind before we conclude that a revolutionary step has been taken. In the first place, a decision by the Security Council can only have the effect of a recommendation when the Security Council is engaged in the performance of its functions under Chapter VI, *i.e.* when it is seeking to achieve the pacific settlement or adjustment of a dispute or situation. Furthermore, while the decision of the Security Council with respect to enforcement action under Chapter VII is blinding upon Members of the United Nations, including those not represented on the Security Council, such decisions cannot be taken without the concurrence of all the permanent members of the Security Council. Consequently, in a situation comparable to that of Japanese aggression against China in Manchuria in 1931 and the threat of Italian aggression against Ethiopia in 1935, where the League Council admittedly failed on account of the unanimity principle, the Security Council would be prevented from taking any decision. Under the Charter the Security Council has power, which the League Council did not have, to take action against the small powers, but the experience of the past would seem to show that it is not the smaller powers, acting alone, who are most likely to disturb the peace. When dealing with threats by smaller powers acting alone the League Council was reasonably effective; it failed only when small powers had the backing of great powers. In spite of important changes in the technical provisions of the Charter, one is forced to the conclusion that so far as the actual possession of power is concerned, the United Nations has not advanced much beyond the League of Nations and that in comparable situations much the same result is to be anticipated. In the last analysis under either system success or failure is dependent upon the ability of the more powerful members to cooperate effectively for common ends. . . .

Basic Obligations of Members. . . . Enumerated in Article 2 of the Charter are certain basic obligations of Members of the United Nations. These include the obligation to settle disputes by peaceful means in such a manner that international peace and security are not endangered, the obligation to refrain from the threat or the use of force against the territorial integrity or political independence of any state, and the obligation to give assistance to the United Nations in any action taken under the terms of the Charter. Similar commitments phrased in somewhat different language and with somewhat different meanings were to be found in various Articles of the Covenant. From the point of view of form the Charter does represent a somewhat different approach in that these basic commitments are grouped together as Principles binding upon all Members. The phraseology of the Charter in certain respects undoubtedly represents improvement. For instance, the provision of Article 2, paragraph 4, by which Members are to refrain "from the threat or use of force against the territorial integrity or political independence of any state" represents an advance over the corresponding provisions of the Covenant which made it possible for members to take refuge in the technicality that an undeclared war in the material sense was no war and that therefore such use of armed force did not constitute a "resort to war." On the other hand, in one important respect, the basic obligations of the Members of the United Nations may prove to be less satisfactory since, in the matter of enforcement action, the obligation of the Members of the United Nations is to accept and carry out decisions of the Security Council and to give assistance to the United Nations in any action taken under the Charter, while under Article 16 of the Covenant, the obligation of members extended to the taking of specific measures against any state resorting to war in violation of its obligations under the Covenant. While this obligation was weakened by resolutions adopted by the Assembly in 1921, it nevertheless proved capable of providing the legal basis for important action against Italy in 1935. . . .

Like the League of Nations, the United Nations is a "general international organization" in the sense that its functions and actions cover the whole range of matters of international concern. Both the Preamble and the statement of Purposes contained in Article 1 of the Charter make this clear. In fact this generality of purpose and function is more explicitly stated in the Charter than it was in the Covenant, though in the practice of the League it came to be fully recognized. The Charter of the United Nations, in its general arrangement and substantive provisions, divides the major activities of the Organization into three categories: (1) the maintenance of international peace and security, by the pacific settlement of disputes and the taking of enforcement measures; (2) the promotion of international economic and social cooperation; and (3) the protection of the interests of the peoples of non-self-governing territories.

The Pacific Settlement of Disputes. The Charter system for the pacific settlement of disputes, while differing from that of the League in many details of substance and phraseology, follows it in accepting two basic principles: (1) that parties to a dispute are in the first instance to seek a peaceful settlement by means of their own choice; and (2) that the political organs of the international organization are to intervene only when the dispute has become a threat to the peace, and then only in a mediatory or conciliatory capacity.

The obligation which Members of the United Nations accept under Article 2, paragraph 3 is to "settle their international disputes by peaceful means in such a manner that international peace and security, and justice are not endangered." Under Article 34, paragraph 1, the parties to any dispute "the continuance of which is likely to endanger the maintenance of international peace and security, shall, first of all seek a solution" by peaceful means of their own choice. Furthermore, by the terms of Article 36 of the Statute of the Court, Members may by declaration accept under certain conditions the compulsory jurisdiction of the Court. Declarations made by Members of the United Nations accepting the compulsory jurisdiction of the Permanent Court of International Justice and still in force are declared to be acceptances under this Article.

The legal obligations which Members of the United Nations have thus assumed are substantially the same as the obligations of League members under the Covenant and supplementary agreements. The Covenant itself did not place upon members of the League the obligation to settle all their diputes by peaceful means. However, forty-six states accepted the compulsory jurisdiction of the Permanent Court by making declarations under Article 36 of the Statute. By Article 2 of the General Pact for the Renunciation of War of 1928 (Kellogg-Briand Pact), the signatories agreed that "the settlement or solution of all disputes or conflicts of whatever nature or of whatever origin they may be . . . shall never be sought except by pacific means."

The powers of the United Nations organs for the pacific settlement of disputes are substantially the same as those of the principal organs of the League. Under the Charter, as under the Covenant, the functions of political organs in this connection are limited to discussion, inquiry, mediation and conciliation. It is clear from the words of the Charter and from the discussions at San Francisco, that the Security Council has no power of final decision in connection with its functions of pacific settlement. The Charter does, however, seek to differentiate between the functions and powers of the General Assembly and the Security Council in a way that the Covenant did not do. More specifically it makes the Security Council primarily responsible for the maintenance of peace and security, does not permit a party to a dispute to have the matter transferred at its request to the General Assembly, and limits the power of the General Assembly in principle to that of discussion. This constitutes an important departure from the textual provisions of the League Covenant which gave the Council and Assembly the same general competence and expressly allowed a party, acting under Article 15, paragraph 9, to have a dispute transferred at its request to the Assembly. It is significant, however, that out of some 66 disputes that came before the League, only three were actually brought before the Assembly under this provision. It would thus appear, and this is the conclusion of a careful student of the Assembly, that actual practice under the Covenant resulted in a differentiation of function. This the Charter seeks to make obligatory.

In certain other respects the Charter system departs from the League pattern, but the importance of these differences can be greatly exaggerated. The elimination of the requirement of unanimity in voting theoretically increases the power of the Security Council, as compared with the League Council, in dealing with disputes and situations, but considering that the Security Council can only recommend, and that in League practice, agreement of the great powers was likely to result in the necessary agreement among all members of the Council, the practical importance of this difference is not likely to be great. Furthermore, under the Charter provision is made for the consideration by the Security Council and General Assembly of situations as well as disputes, but this does not mean any increase in the powers of the United Nations organs, particularly the Security Council, as compared with those of the corresponding organs of the League. In fact, it can be argued that the provisions of the Charter suffer somewhat in flexibility and capacity for growth, as compared with the corresponding provisions of the Covenant, because of the greater detail and consequent rigidity of certain of its terms. A comparison of experience under the Charter to date in the peaceful settlement or adjustment of disputes and situations with that of the League gives little basis for a confident conclusion that the Charter system is inherently better than, or for that matter, significantly different from, that which operated under the terms of the Covenant.

Enforcement Action. It is in respect to enforcement action that the provisions of the Charter seem to offer the most marked contrast to the provisions of the Covenant, but here again when we compare the Charter provisions with the way in which the Covenant provisions were actually applied the differences do not appear so great. The League system, as originally conceived, was based on the principle that once a member had restored to war in violation of its obligations under the Covenant, other members were immediately obligated to apply economic and financial sanctions of wide scope against the offending state. The Council was empowered to recommend military measures which members of the League were technically not required to carry out. As a matter of fact, in the one case where the provisions of Article 16 were given anything like a real test, the application of sanctions against Italy in 1936, acting under the influence of the resolutions adopted by the Assembly in 1921, the members of the League established a mechanism for the coordination of their individual acts, and proceeded to apply selected economic and financial measures. No recommendation was made by the Council for the application of military measures.

The Charter makes the Security Council responsible for deciding what enforcement measures are to be used to maintain the peace. Obligations arise for Members of the United Nations only when such decisions have been taken. This is a further development of the principle recognized in the 1921 Assembly resolutions and in the application of sanctions against Italy, that a central coordinating agency is needed to insure the taking of necessary measures with the maximum of effectiveness and the minimum of inconvenience and danger to the participating members. However, the provisions of the Charter go much further than did the Covenant in providing for obligatory military measures and advance commitments to place specific forces at the disposal of the Security Council. Even though certain members of the League, notably France, were insistent upon the need of specific military commitments, little was done in League practice to meet this need. The Geneva Protocol of 1924 was one notable attempt to meet this demand, by methods which in certain respects anticipated the Charter, but it never came into force. The framers of the Charter, no doubt recognizing this as a defect in the League system, sought to remedy the deficiency by providing in some detail for military agreements between members of the United Nations and the Security Council, and for a military staff committee to assist the Security Council in drawing up advanced plans and in applying military measures.

It can, however, be queried whether the Charter system will be more effective than the League system, in view of the requirement of unanimity of the permanent members of the Security Council. If we imagine its application in situations such as the Italian-Ethiopian and Sino-Japanese affairs, it is difficult to see how the United Nations would achieve any better results than did the League. Like the League, but for somewhat different technical reasons, the United Nations, in so far as its enforcement activities are concerned, is an organization for the enforcement of peace among the smaller states. If the permanent members of the Security Council are in agreement, it will be possible to take effective action under the Charter. It is not likely that such agreement will be reached to take measures against one of these great powers or against a protégé of such a great power. Consequently the sphere of effective enforcement action by the United Nations is restricted in advance, even more perhaps than was that of the League. Within the area of possible operation, the actual effectiveness of the United Nations system will depend upon political conditions which, if they had existed, would have also assured the success of the League of Nations. . . .

To the student of international organization, it should be a cause neither of surprise nor of concern to find that the United Nations is for all practical purposes a continuation of the League of Nations. Rather it would be disturbing if the architects of world organization had completely or largely thrown aside the designs and materials of the past. One cannot build soundly on the basis of pure theory. Man being what he is, and the dominant forces and attitudes of international relations being what they are, it is idle to expect, and foolhardy to construct the perfect system of world government in our day. Profiting from the lessons of past experience, we can at most hope to make some progress toward the attainment of a goal which may for a long time remain beyond our reach. The United Nations is not world government and it was not intended to be such. Rather it represents a much more conservative and cautious approach to the problem of world order. As such, it inevitably falls into the stream of institutional development represented by the League of Nations and its predecessors. Different names may be used for similar things, and different combinations of words may be devised to express similar ideas. There may be changes of emphasis, and in fact important substantive changes, deemed desirable in the light of past experience or thought necessary in order to meet changed conditions. But there is no real break in the stream of organizational development.

The student of international organization must recognize the United Nations for what it quite properly is, a revised League, no doubt improved in some respects, possibly weaker in others, but nonetheless a League, a voluntary association of nations, carrying on largely in the League tradition and by the League methods. Important changes have occurred in the world distribution of power, in the world's economic and political structure, in the world's ideological atmosphere. These changes create new problems and modify the chances of success or failure in meeting them, but the mechanics remain much the same. Anyone desiring to understand the machinery, how it operates, the conditions of its success, must look to the experience of the past, and particularly to the rich and varied experience of that first attempt at a general international organization, the League of Nations.

PART THREE
*Collective Security
and the United Nations*

CHAPTER 5 *Early Optimism: Initial Qualification*

Address of Chairman of First General Assembly (January 10, 1946)*

THE CHAIRMAN, DR. ZULETA ANGEL (Colombia): The meeting is open.

Determined to save succeeding generations from the scourge of war which, twice in our lifetime, has brought untold sorrow to mankind, and imbued with an abiding faith in freedom and justice, we have come to this British capital, which bears upon it the deep impress of a heroic majesty, to constitute the General Assembly of the United Nations and to make a genuine and sincere beginning with the application of the San Francisco Charter. That instrument, having been freely and democratically debated, has been unreservedly accepted by all in the knowledge that the machinery set up under its provisions will prove adequate to the achievement of its historic purpose; this, in a word, is the maintenance of peace and security by collective recourse, when needed, to the use of land, sea and air forces and the establishment, through cooperation in the economic, social, educational and humanitarian fields, of those conditions of stability and well-being which will ensure peaceful and friendly relations, based on the principle of equal rights and self-determination among the nations of the world.

It is an arduous and difficult duty, but one which we can and must discharge without delay, for the whole world now waits upon our decisions, and rightly—yet with understandable anxiety—looks to us now to show ourselves capable of mastering our problems. We cannot, therefore, with impunity, fail mankind again—to-day above all—in the face of the suffering which has supervened upon the most terrible and devastating of wars.

In this we shall not fail. An inner voice tells us that, animated by a broad and sincere feeling for humanity, we can lift up our hearts and bring to bear on the problems of peace the spirit of co-operation, the tenacity of purpose, the self-sacrifice and the technical effort which, when applied to the dramatic problems of war, led to the splendid triumph of the democracies that has enabled us to meet here to-day. We know that this is so from our memories of San Francisco, where the gravest difficulties were overcome in an atmosphere of goodwill lit up by the dying glare of the world conflagration. We feel it when we consider the ability shown and the harmony achieved by the Executive Committee and by the Preparatory Commission. It is evident in the interest which the great Powers have shown in the working of the organs of the United Nations. It is evident, above all, in

* General Assembly, *Official Records,* 1st year, 1st meeting (January 10, 1946), pp. 37-39.

217

the determination which animates each one of us to fulfil a task second to none in importance, nobility and grandeur, for there is no purpose to which leading statesmen can more readily apply their intellect and will than that of maintaining peace on the basis of full international co-operation, and so alleviating the ills which beset mankind.

In the achievement of this task, all of us, great and small, strong and weak, will give our unqualified and unhesitating support.

The five great Powers which, by virtue of Articles 24 and 27 of the Charter, and by the very nature of things, will shoulder the chief responsibility for the maintenance of peace and security, will bring not only the immense power of their military, financial and industrial resources, but something more important, without which their very power would be nothing but the prelude to an unthinkable cataclysm; I mean good will, divested of every shred of intrigue or trickery, and that spirit of co-operation which is vital in order to maintain among them of good understanding upon which our whole Organization rests.

In signing the Charter, the other Powers have already deposited as their first contribution to this great undertaking, a large part of that which they hold most dear and most precious, a large part, that is, of their sovereignty. They made this sacrifice with deep emotion, but without hesitation, in the belief that here was the beginning of a new era in which their security would be collectively guaranteed by adequate and effective means, and any aggression or attempt at aggression directed against them would be severely repressed.

They have, however, another obligation to fulfil, that of joining their efforts, in good faith, to maintain harmony amongst the great Powers, knowing full well that any ill-advised action or policy likely to endanger their unity would be suicidal.

In this Assembly which, to use a well-known phrase, is the Town Meeting of the world, the small Powers will be able, year in, year out, to make their voices heard in as free and democratic an atmosphere as that which prevailed at San Francisco and London.

We must not, however, lose sight of the fact that the weight that their voices will carry and the influence they will exert will depend less on the terms of the Charter, on the functions and duties of the Assembly, than on the wisdom, the judgment, the spirit of co-operation and sense of justice by which it is guided and inspired.

Founded on reason and actuated by a real love of peace and mankind, its pronouncements will not fail to command the attention and respect of the Security Council.

Under Article 2 of the Charter, the Organization is based on the principle of the sovereign equality of its Members; and this is not, after all, inconsistent with the self-evident fact that the chief responsibility for the maintenance of peace rests upon those nations which have the greatest resources for the purpose.

That this principle is not a dead letter in the Charter is evidenced by the fact, which may have occasioned some surprise, that the unique privilege of opening this Assembly of the United Nations, comprising so many eminent personalities, has fallen to the obscure representative of a small Spanish-American Republic which has no pretensions to military force or economic power, but which is none the less proud of its legal structure, its democratic organization and its love of freedom. . . .

The Rise and Fall of the Military Staff Committee*

Leland M. Goodrich and Anne P. Simons

Failure to Conclude Agreements under Article 43

The Security Council, on February 16, 1946, directed the Military Staff Committee, as its first task, to examine from the military point of view the provisions of Article 43 of the Charter. The committee decided that, as a first step, it should formulate recommendations to the Council on the basic principles that should govern the organization of the forces to be made available to the Council under that article. Later, the General Assembly, in the course of its consideration of the general principles governing the regulation and reduction of armaments, during the second part of its first session, recognized that the organization of collective security was closely related. Consequently, in the resolution that the Assembly adopted, it recommended that the Council accelerate as much as possible "the placing at its disposal of the armed forces mentioned in Article 43 of the Charter."

On February 13, 1947, the Council requested the Military Staff Committee to submit its recommendations not later than April 30. The report of the committee submitted on April 30 included recommendations on which the delegations were in agreement and others on which they were unable to agree. Their agreements for the most part were on propositions that were explicitly stated or clearly implied in the words of the Charter. Their disagreements were on questions of vital importance that had to be answered in order for the agreements to be concluded under Article 43. The Security Council examined the report between June 4 and July 15, 1947. But it was unable to resolve the deadlock that had developed in the Military Staff

* Leland M. Goodrich and Anne P. Simons, *The United Nations and the Maintenance of International Peace and Security* (Washington, D.C.: The Brookings Institution, 1955), pp. 398-405. Reprinted by permission. Anne P. Simons is currently Research Associate at the Washington Center of Foreign Policy Research. She is a former member of the General Political Division of the UN Secretariat; former Research Associate of The Brookings Institution; and former Editor of *National Studies on International Organization* for the Carnegie Endowment for International Peace.

Committee over general principles. Moreover, the committee reported on July 2, 1948 that it could not make any progress in establishing levels of strength until it received guidance from the Council on general principles. Discussions thus came to a standstill, and it became apparent that agreements under Article 43 could not be concluded, in the absence of a definite improvement in the political atmosphere. The General Assembly subsequently urged the Security Council to make efforts to implement Article 43, but the deadlock continued.

With respect to the strength and nature of armed forces to be made available to the Security Council, the views of the United Kingdom, France, and China appear to have been closer to those of the Soviet Union than to those of the United States; and from the discussions that took place in the Security Council, it was clear that a wide divergence existed between the views of the United States and the Soviet Union. The United States position was that since the problem facing the United Nations was that of enforcing peace "in all parts of the world, . . . the United Nations needs, first of all, a mobile force able to strike quickly at long range and to bring to bear, upon any given point in the world where trouble may occur, the maximum armed force in the minimum time." The United States appeared unwilling to admit that the armed forces made available to the Security Council might not be used against a permanent member. The estimates of strength that the United States delegation to the Military Staff Committee presented reflected an emphasis on mobile and striking weapons, such as air force and navy. Furthermore, the quantitative estimates were far in excess of those submitted by other delegations, especially the Soviet Union.

The Soviet position, on the other hand, was that the armed forces made available to the Security Council need not be "excessively numerous," considering that the "aggressor bloc" in the last war had been defeated and that former enemy states had been placed "under the control of the Allies." "In the present situation," argued the Soviet representative, "it would be sufficient for the Security Council to have at its disposal relatively small armed forces." The United Kingdom, France, and China also favored small forces, largely, no doubt, because of their inability to make large contributions. The Soviet view derived a measure of support from the assumption quite generally made from the beginning that these forces, by virtue of Article 27(3), would not be used against a permanent member. Furthermore, it appeared to find support in Article 5 of the Report of the Military Staff Committee, one of the articles on which there was unanimous agreement, which emphasized "the moral weight and the potential power behind any decision to employ the Armed Forces made available" as a factor influencing the size of the forces required.

The composition of armed forces to be made available to the Security Council proved to be one of the basic issues on which the Soviet Union and the other permanent members were in disagreement. The United States contended that in order to have a force of the mobility and striking power required, one utilizing the latest technical developments, it was necessary for each member to contribute those elements that it was best able to contribute. Said the United States representative, in the course of the discussion in the Council:

We consider that the contributions of the permanent members of the Security Council can be properly balanced and rendered roughly comparable without prejudice to the interests of individual nations by arranging that those nations which make available a lesser proportion of the new mobile components could put up a larger portion of other components or other forms of assistance and facilities.

Other members of the Council, with the exception of the Soviet Union and Poland, accepted this general view.

The Soviet position was that the contributions of the permanent members of the Council should be equal, both in over-all strength and composition. "The principle of equality," the Soviet representative argued, "is based on the provisions of the United Nations Charter which place the main responsibility for the maintenance of international peace upon these States," and it "preserves the equal status of the permanent members in respect of the decision on this important question." The principle of comparable contributions, he argued, would lead to a situation in which some members would enjoy "a predominant position as compared to others." It might lead to use of the armed forces "in the interest of individual powerful States and to the detriment of the legitimate interests of other countries." Soviet support of the idea of a small force was, of course, closely related to its support of the equality principle, because if the principle of equality were applied in all categories, the size of the resulting force would of necessity be small, because of the inability of certain permanent members to make substantial contributions in some categories. However, as a minor concession to reality, the Soviet Union proposed that the Council might excuse a permanent member, at its request, from making an equal contribution.

The positions of the Soviet Union and other permanent members were also completely at variance on the implementation of Article 45 of the Charter. The position of the Soviet Union was that requirements "of national air-force contingents . . . immediately available" should be determined after the conclusion of agreements provided for in Article 43 and within the framework of those agreements. The other permanent members took the view that the total strength, composition, and readiness of national air force contingents to be made available to the Council under Article 43 agreements should be determined in part by the special obligations arising from Article 45. This would justify a larger and more powerful force than the Soviet Union considered necessary.

All the permanent members of the Council were in agreement that initially they would contribute the major part of the armed forces to be made available to the Council. This would facilitate the early establishment of a force that would enable the Council to exercise its powers under Article 42.

In regard to the provision of Article 43 that members are to make available to the Council, in addition to armed forces, "assistance, and facilities, including rights of passage," the Soviet Union insisted on an interpretation that would exclude the provision of bases. In addition to pointing out that the article in question contained no mention of bases, the Soviet representative in the Security Council argued that "the provision of bases inevitably affects the sovereignty of nations." He claimed that "the acceptance of the proposal on bases would be utilized by some States as a means of exerting political pressure on other nations which provided such bases." The other permanent members, however, took the position that provision should be made in the agreements for the use of bases, and, with the exception of France, they felt that there should be "a general guarantee" of the use of such available bases of Member States as the armed forces operating under the direction of the Security Council might require. The Soviet Union also objected to "a general guarantee of rights of passage."

On the location of armed forces, again, the argument of the Soviet Union was that the presence of such forces of one state within the territory of another, even on the basis of agreement, would constitute a means of political pressure. The Soviet representative proposed that such forces should be stationed within the frontiers of the contributing Member, except in cases envisaged in Article 107 of the Charter. The position of China, the United Kingdom, and the United States, on the other hand, was that armed forces available to the Security Council, when not employed by it, might "be based at the discretion of Member nations in any territories or waters to which they have legal right of access." This was also in substance the French position.

On the question of the employment of armed forces, the members of the Military Staff Committee were in agreement that armed forces made available should be employed only by decision of the Security Council and only for the period necessary to fulfill the task envisaged in Article 42. It was also agreed that use of these forces, whenever possible, be initiated in time to forestall or to suppress promptly a breach of the peace or act of aggression.

There was disagreement, however, on the principle governing withdrawal of the forces, once their mission had been completed. All the permanent members except the Soviet Union were of the opinion that, after the armed forces made available to the Council had completed their tasks, they should be withdrawn "as soon as possible" in accordance with the provisions of the agreements governing the location of forces. This left considerable freedom of decision to the Council because the time and conditions of withdrawal were to be fixed by the Council. The Soviet Union objected, maintaining that strict time limits should be set for withdrawal. The Soviet argument was stated by the Soviet representative as follows:

The general formula providing for the withdrawal of armed forces "as soon as possible" is absolutely insufficient. It does not oblige the armed forces to leave the territories of other States when their presence is no longer necessary and when it is not called for in the interests of the maintenance of peace. This formula, if accepted, would be used as a pretext for the continuous presence of foreign troops in territories of other States, which is inadmissible from the point of view of the basic purposes of our Organization.

Under the Soviet proposal, a decision of the Council would be required to delay withdrawal beyond a certain time rather than to fix the time of withdrawal.

On the question of logistical support, all the permanent members of the Council were in agreement that Members should provide their respective forces with necessary replacements in personnel and equipment and with all necessary supplies and transport, and that they should maintain specified levels of reserves. China, the United States, and the United Kingdom proposed that in case Members could not discharge their responsibilities as defined in Article 29 of the Report, they might invoke the assistance of the Council, which would negotiate with other appropriate Member nations for the necessary assistance. The Soviet Union and France, on the other hand, proposed that deviations be permitted only in individual instances at the request of the Member and by special decision of the Council. Although the difference between the two positions does not appear to have been great, the Soviet representative, in the discussion in the Council, professed to see in the majority proposal another indication that certain powerful nations were prepared to exploit the weakness of some Members "for political benefits and advantages."

The divisions within the Military Staff Committee and the Security Council did not all follow the pattern indicated above. On the question whether national contingents might be used in case of self-defense and of national emergencies, France and China took an affirmative position, while the other three permanent members took a negative one. On the organization of command, China, the Soviet Union, and the United States favored a provision for an over-all commander, or over-all commanders, without any mention of service commanders, while the United Kingdom and France favored making provision for service commanders as well. These differences, however, were not of such a nature as to bar all possibility of agreement, as was true of the differences separating the Soviet Union and the other permanent members of the Council.

Failure of the Security Council to agree on principles governing the conclusion of agreements under Article 43 made it impossible for the Military Staff Committee to make any progress in establishing the levels of strength of the national contingents to be made available to the Council. This failure to reach decisions necessary to the implementation of Article 43 was not due primarily to technical difficulties. It was primarily the result of a political impasse. This was explicitly stated by the Soviet representative in the course of his argument for the principle of equal contributions when he said:

. . . I should like to draw the Security Council's atention to the fact that the whole question of armed forces being made available to the Security Council by the United Nations under special agreements is not only, and not so much, a technical question as a political one. It is a political problem and should be decided as such. Obviously, in the settlement of this problem there will also arise a number of technical questions, which the Security Council will decide in the course of negotiations with the States which make armed forces available to the Security Council. I think, however, that no one will deny that, as I have pointed out, this whole question is political. If we bear this in mind, we cannot take such a light view of the Soviet proposal of equal contributions as certain representatives on the Council do.

As a result of this impasse, the Council was never provided with armed forces that would enable it to discharge its responsibilities under Article 42 of the Charter. Furthermore, the fact that this had been a result of the inability of the permanent members of the Council to co-operate meant that there was little, if any, possibility of these same permanent members taking joint action under Article 106 to maintain or restore international peace and security.

Collective Security and the War in Korea*

Arnold Wolfers

The action taken by the United Nations in 1950 to halt the attack on South Korea has been heralded as the first experiment in collective security. The implication is that a radical break with the traditional foreign policy of nations has occurred; power politics, we are told, have been replaced by police action of the world community. It is quite likely that many who suffered in the Korean War on our side have been comforted by the thought that they have served the cause of law enforcement by community action, though others who believed that no vital interests of their country were at stake may have found the ordeal harder to bear. Whatever the emotional reaction, it is necessary to investigate dispassionately whether in fact a turning point in world politics was reached when the United Nations flag was unfurled in Korea. On the answer may depend what future policy we and others are entitled to expect of this country.

It may sound like quibbling to ask whether Korea was an example of "collective security." Obviously, the answer depends on the definition of the term. If one chooses to make it include every collective action undertaken for defensive purposes by a group of nations, then the Korean intervention by the United States and its associates falls under the term. Actually, it has become the habit of official spokesmen of our government to use the term in this way. For instance, they speak of NATO as a means of "collective security," although the treaty was legally justified by reference to Article 51 of the United Nations Charter, which explicitly permits "collective self-defense" in cases where the universal collective security provisions of the United Nations *fail* to protect a victim of aggression. But there is nothing new or revolutionary in nations' aligning themselves for purposes of defense against their common national foes. Except for countries pursuing a "go it alone" policy, such conduct has been traditional among the members of multistate systems.

This is not what exponents of the principle of collective security have in mind when they urge nations to change the customary direction of their

* Arnold Wolfers, "Collective Security and the War in Korea," *The Yale Review*, Vol. XLIII, No. 4 (June 1954), pp. 482-496. Reprinted by permission. Arnold Wolfers is Sterling Professor Emeritus of International Relations at Yale University and currently Director of the Washington Center of Foreign Policy Research, School of Advanced International Studies, of The Johns Hopkins University. He is the author of *Britain and France between Two Wars* (1940) and co-author of *The Anglo-American Tradition in Foreign Affairs* (1956).

defense policy. They call upon nations to go beyond aligning themselves with each other only to meet the threats emanating from common national enemies and to embrace instead a policy of defense directed against aggression in general or, more precisely, against any aggressor anywhere. Coupled with arrangements to name the aggressor by community decision, nations— instead of reserving their power to defend or enforce their national interests —would be lined up like a police force to strike against any country, friend or foe, that had been declared an aggressor. Such a policy would constitute a radical break with tradition.

Since there are fundamental differences between these two types of collective action, with only one of them constituting a break with traditional national foreign policy, to avoid confusion and misunderstanding the two should be distinguished by the use of different labels. And since "collective security" has become the symbol for a break with power politics, it should be reserved for action that meets this test. It will be used so in this discussion, while other types of multilateral defensive action will be called "collective defense." Aside from semantics then, the problem is whether intervention in Korea represents a radical break with the traditional foreign policy of nation-states and, as a consequence, fulfils the expectations widely held for "collective security."

How serious a break with tradition the policy of collective security would be becomes evident if one considers what risks and sacrifices nations would have to incur in order to make such a policy effective and meaningful. It stands to reason that provisions and commitments for police action would add nothing to the protection that victims of aggression have enjoyed under the old system unless such victims could expect more military assistance than they would have received otherwise. The exponents of collective security have stressed this point. They have assumed that under a system of collective security such as they advocate, overwhelming force would be placed behind the law and at the disposal of a victim of attack. As in municipal affairs, therefore, the power of the police would usually suffice to deter any would-be attacker and thereby serve to maintain the peace rather than merely to punish the offender.

In order that collective security add in this way to the strength of the defense and to the chances of deterrence, it must be assumed that some nations, including one or more of the great powers, will be prepared to resort to force—that is, for all practical purposes, go to war—when, if they had not been devoted to the principle of collective security, they would have remained neutral or fought on the side of the aggressor. Instead of being allowed to reserve their military strength for the exclusive task of balancing the power of countries considered a threat to themselves or their allies, nations committed to a policy of collective security must divert their strength to struggles in remote places or, worse still, take action against friends and allies on whom reliance had been placed for defense against common foes. In extreme cases, a nation might even be called upon to defend and strengthen a foe at the expense of a friend or ally, if the latter were condemned as an aggressor.

If these should seem to be far-fetched contingencies, French experience, as well as possibilities now facing this country, prove them to be anything but theoretical. When Italy attacked Ethiopia, the French were urged in the name of collective security to participate in sanctions, if need be military sanctions, against Italy, a country which had just become a virtual ally against Germany, then considered France's number-one opponent; in the Korean War, France came under pressure to divert more of her strength to the fight with the North Koreans and Chinese aggressors at a time when she already felt too weak at home even to dare consent to German rearmament. A more dangerous situation might arise for the United States if Syngman Rhee should ever make good his threat to seek unification of his country by force. To take police action against him—or even to agree to have the Soviet bloc take such action—would run directly counter to this country's primary defense interests.

In order to be able to assert, then, that collective security has become a living reality, it is necessary to show that one or more countries have in fact proved ready to run the risks and consent to the sacrifices that this radical break with traditional defense policy presupposes. In the instance of Korea, this means inquiring whether there is evidence that such a switch to defense against aggression *per se* was made by the United States and its associates. Before doing so, it may be worth while to ask whether it is possible to conceive of incentives that might be powerful enough to induce nations to change their habits in so radical a fashion.

Those who seek to make a case for collective security, either as having become a reality or as being a practical goal for the future, argue along two lines, one more idealistic, the other more realistic. Nations, it is said, might take up arms against any aggressor anywhere simply because the crime of aggression arouses their moral indignation. The fact that there is such indignation both here and abroad is not in doubt. The desire to see perpetrators of wanton attack stopped and punished is widespread in a world that has had so much experience of brutal attack on weak and peaceful peoples. Yet, it is one thing to be indignant; another to be prepared to plunge one's country into war, though it be called police action, and to do so in an age of increasing wartime horror and destruction. Even aside from narrow nationalist preoccupations which might lessen the ardor for punitive action on behalf of the world community, there is reason to doubt whether moral indignation alone can be relied upon to carry nations into military action when no vital national interests push them in the same direction. In order to have a chance, it would rather seem as if collective security itself would have to appeal to interests of the kind traditionally considered vital to the nation.

According to the more realistic argument, such an interest is in fact at stake, though nations may still often fail to realize it. The argument rests on what has been called the principle of "indivisible peace." If aggression is allowed to go unpunished anywhere, it is said, potential aggressors will be encouraged everywhere, and as a result no nation will be secure. Instead, if any aggressor anywhere is stopped or deterred by overwhelming police power, all other potential aggressors will understand the warning and cease to constitute a threat. Thus, by a kind of detour, nations which for reasons of collective security are forced to divert strength or to weaken alignments against specific opponents gain more security in the end, even against their national foes.

This second line of argument has been called realistic because it rests on security considerations of the kind which have customarily guided national governments. But the question remains whether the long-run advantage of deterrence (which is hard to evaluate) can win out against the very real short-run risks of diversion of strength and unbalancing of power. Unless it can be shown in the case of Korea that the United States and its associates actually chose the long-run advantage at the expense of immediate security, the war in Korea cannot be called an example of collective security.

In a discussion of Korea, it might appear as if attention would have to be focused on the United Nations rather than on its members. In a sense this is true. Had no world organization such as the United Nations existed in 1950, there could have been no question of police action on behalf of the world community. Collective security presupposes that the aggressor be named and condemned by means of some recognized procedure; resort to violence in defense of the law against such an aggressor must be authorized by an organization which can claim to speak for the community. Yet no provisions, resolutions, commands, or recommendations of a world organization of sovereign nations can suffice to make collective security a reality. It can become real only by the fact of military power being employed for police purposes; the decision rests with the members who possess such military power and can use it for collective security if they will. In regard to the United Nations, the question is merely whether it did its part in inducing members of the organization to take police action on its behalf and under its auspices.

This is not the place to investigate whether the Charter of the United Nations was aimed at collective security as defined here or offered the best means of inducing countries to act in accordance with this principle. The veto provision certainly allowed members to assume that they would never be expected to participate in police action which would seriously antagonize one or more of the major powers. Furthermore, Article 43 left the implementation of any commitment to participate in such action to subsequent negotiations which have not taken place. It is agreed, however, that when the members of the United Nations subscribed to the purpose of the organization as being "to take effective collective measures . . . for the suppression of acts of aggression," they accepted the principle of common defensive action against any aggressor anywhere. Their legal or at least moral obligation to do so whenever the competent organs of the United Nations order or recommend such action would seem to be beyond doubt, unless one were to assume that the "inherent right of self-defense" permits nations to beg out of any military action which would endanger their security. If one accepted this reservation, the Charter could not be said to create much legal embarrassment for members who wanted to avoid the risks of collective security. In the case of Korea, majorities sufficient to reach decisions both in the Security Council and in the General Assembly took all the steps for which they were competent to get police action under way.

The attack by the North Koreans occurred on June 25. On the same day, in the absence of the Soviet delegate, the Security Council determined that a breach of the peace had occurred. It called upon North Korea to withdraw its forces and proceeded to invite its members "to render every assistance to the United Nations in execution of this resolution." Some hours prior to the second meeting of the Council, on June 27, the United States Government announced that it had ordered American air and sea forces to go to the assistance of South Korea for the specific purpose of executing the June 25 resolution of the Security Council. If this was not enough to qualify American intervention as United Nations action, the Security Council identified itself with the action of the United States by voting on the same day that urgent military measures were required. The members were now called upon to furnish assistance of the kind necessary to repel the attack. From then on, the action of the United States and its associates was carried forward in the name of the United Nations, under the United Nations flag, and under a unified United Nations command set up by the United States in accordance with a resolution of the Security Council. Limited to recommendations, the United Nations continued to put what little pressure it could on its members to get them to participate or to make larger contributions; at the same time it sought to influence the United Nations command in the conduct and termination of the war, acting in this respect as a restraining factor.

Aside from this rather marginal though not unimportant role played by the United Nations itself, the character of the action in Korea must be judged by the decisions and acts of the United States and its associates. It would seem permissible, in fact, to concentrate on the conduct of the United States, because the other nations which made contributions to the defense of South Korea might conceivably have done so as friends and allies of the United States, whether this country was acting traditionally in what it considered to be its national interest and that of its friends or was conducting police action on the principle of collective security.

It is not a simple matter to discover whether or not United States intervention in Korea qualifies as collective security in the restricted sense in which the term is used here. The motivations of the chief architects of the policy are not decisive. The devotion of men like Mr. Truman and Mr.

Acheson to the idea of collective security as they conceived it is not in doubt, any more than their desire to prevent the United Nations from suffering the same dismal fate which befell the League of Nations at the time of Italy's aggression against Ethiopia.

What is being asked is whether the United States, even if it believed itself to be engaging in police action in conformity with the concept of collective security, did in fact break with traditional national defense policy by accepting the kind of risks which such a break presupposes. If the aggressor had been South Korea rather than North Korea, the answer could not be in doubt. To take up arms against South Korea would have meant siding with this country's chief national enemy, the Soviet bloc, and strengthening the Communist countries at the expense of a country on which the United States could have relied as an ally in the Cold War. No more striking proof could have been given of unqualified American support for police action against any aggressor anywhere. But, the aggressor was Communist North Korea backed by the Soviet Union. It becomes necessary therefore to investigate how intervention in these circumstances looked from the point of view of American security interests as interpreted in Washington at the time.

Speaking negatively first, the United States was obviously not taking up arms against a friend or ally. On the contrary, it was setting out to stop expansion by the Soviet bloc, thus serving what had long been proclaimed to be the major goal of American foreign policy. It might be argued, however, that in extending the "containment" policy to Korea, the United States was diverting military power from Europe, which was considered the chief danger area. As the war proceeded, and American involvement exceeded all early expectations, much fear of such diversion was in fact expressed in Europe. But in this country, the opinion continued to prevail that in terms of the Cold War it would have been much more dangerous even for Europe if Communist aggression had gone unpunished in Asia. Moreover, powerful groups in Congress had long pressed for a stronger stand against Communism in Asia. Thus while the sacrifices in men and resources, borne by the American people in the course of the Korean War, were far in excess of even the most pessimistic initial expectations, they did not include the sacrifice or diversion of defensive military power from the tasks of the Cold War. Instead, the rearmament effort provoked by Communist aggression in Korea led to a multiplication of this power.

The fact that no sacrifice in terms of national protection against a major enemy was involved is not enough, however, to explain why this country should have decided to resort to military force. Except for a radical break with tradition, nations are not expected to take up arms unless there are interests which they consider vital at stake. Accordingly, the apparent absence of any vital American interest in South Korea made it seem as if devotion to collective security alone could have induced the United States to intervene. It was known that our civilian and military leaders did not consider the defense of the 38th Parallel or the preservation of a free South Korea a matter of vital strategic importance to this country, despite the fact that loss of the area to the Communists would have rendered Japan more vulnerable to attack. The Joint Chiefs of Staff had reached this decision at the time American troops were withdrawn from the territory of the Republic of Korea, long before Secretary Acheson made his famous "perimeter" speech. It is also true that the United States was not bound by any treaty of alliance to go to the assistance of South Korea. However, this lack of what might be called a local strategic interest and the absence of any specific commitment to assist South Korea, other than that implied in the United Nations Charter, do not suffice to prove that vital interests were not at stake. The fact is that one can discern a threefold American interest of exactly the kind which, thinking along the lines of traditional power politics, governments would normally consider serious enough to justify military action or even to make it imperative.

In the first place, according to the views prevailing in both political parties at the time of the North Korean attack, any further expansion in any direction on the part of the Soviet bloc constituted a threat to American security. The "containment" policy was under attack not because it went too far in this respect but because it was thought too negative. As a matter of established policy, then, no area adjoining the Soviet Empire was held to be strategically nonvital; any addition to the territory behind the Iron Curtain would threaten to upset an already precarious world balance of power.

In the second place, the United States was vitally interested in proving to its European Allies that they could rely on American military assistance in case of a Soviet attack. NATO, this country's main bulwark against the threat from the East, was weakened by European fears of a resurgence of isolationism in this country. It was strongly felt, therefore, particularly by Secretary Acheson, that if South Korea were left at the mercy of the attacker, all of Russia's weak neighbors—and there were none but weak neighbors—would lose what confidence they had gradually gained that this country meant business when it promised to prevent further Soviet conquest.

As if this were not enough, there was a third reason for this country to be most seriously interested in not allowing a challenge by its number-one enemy to go without military response. The United States was engaged in a vast and strenuous effort to unite the entire free world in a common effort of defense against the Soviet and Communist menace. From most countries, particularly in Asia, it had not succeeded in obtaining commitments of mutual assistance of the kind customarily laid down in treaties of bilateral or multilateral alliance. Therefore, all other non-Communist countries were committed to common defense against Communist aggression only if they could be made to accept the United Nations Charter as such a commitment. Consequently, from the point of view of American security policy, it was of paramount importance that the United Nations be made to serve as a substitute for a formal alliance of the free world. If there was any chance of achieving this result—and subsequent events showed how slim the chance was—it could only be done by demonstrating that under the Charter the United States considered itself committed to take up arms against the North Korean aggressor.

If it be correct, then, to assert that strong American national interests, other than an interest in collective security, pointed in the direction of intervention in Korea, certain conclusions can be drawn concerning the character of this action. In order to avoid misconceptions, certain other conclusions which do not follow from what has been said must also be mentioned.

In the first place, because the resort to violence against North Korea served to maintain and in fact to strengthen this country's power position relative to its major national opponent, it cannot be considered the kind of break with tradition earlier defined as a prerequisite of effective collective security. However, this does not mean that the Korean action did not represent a drastic change—or call it a break—in United States policy. This country demonstrated its intent to stop Soviet and satellite aggression everywhere, thereby identifying its interests with those of the entire non-Communist world. This is a far cry from earlier isolationist policies which sought national security in withdrawal from areas of conflict. Moreover, the fact that American security interests were at stake does not prove that the Administration or the public would have considered them sufficiently vital to warrant a resort to force if defense of these interests had not coincided with the assertion of the principle of United Nations police action against aggression. Faith in this principle may at least help to explain the almost unanimous support Mr. Truman received at the start of the war.

In the second place, despite the popularity which collective security undoubtedly enjoyed in 1950 and may still enjoy, American military action against a member of the Soviet bloc cannot be taken as evidence that this country would be prepared to follow the same road in the case of an aggressor who was not a member of the Soviet bloc, or, in a particular instance, had attacked a member of that bloc. Here the national interest as traditionally understood and the interest in collective security would not coincide; instead, they might run directly counter to each other. One cannot help wondering whether the United States would resort to the same measures if at some future date a Syngman Rhee were declared the aggressor, though only the future can provide a definite answer.

It follows, then, that Korea has not established the practicability or reality of collective security in the sense in which the term is used here. Instead of being a case of nations fighting "any aggressor anywhere" and for no other purpose than to punish aggression and to deter potential aggressors, intervention in Korea was an act of collective military defense against the recognized number-one enemy of the United States and of all the countries which associated themselves with its action. If would-be aggressors have reached the same conclusion, they will not be deterred by the Korean War unless they belong to the Soviet bloc.

This is disheartening news to those who have placed their faith in deterrence through collective security, unless they should believe that aggression by non-Communist countries is out of the question anyway. Disappointment of the high hopes placed on the "first experiment in collective security" should be weighed, however, against possible advantages accruing to this country for not having committed itself by precedent to fight all aggressors everywhere.

While it will always remain a matter of controversy whether a certain commitment or course of action is or is not in the national interest, one may assume wide agreement on the proposition that in the present circumstances this country cannot afford to jeopardize seriously its ability to balance the power of the Soviet bloc. If this be so, any military action against an aggressor would run counter to the elementary rules of prudence if it threatened to tip the balance in favor of the Soviets. It need not do so in the case of every non-Communist aggressor. One can imagine cases of aggression by a non-Communist country against another non-Communist country in which this country would have more to lose from allowing such aggression to be successful than from weakening and antagonizing the aggressor and his friends. In some instances there might be grave danger in allowing violence to continue and spread. But it needs little imagination to see how rare the cases are likely to be in which military intervention against a non-Communist country would favor this country's security position in the Cold War. One need only think of the disastrous consequences which might follow from a resort to force against, say, one of the Arab countries, or against Yugoslavia, or against a member of NATO. These consequences would be particularly grave if a large part of American military strength had to be diverted to such an operation.

A commitment to intervene would be most serious if a non-Communist country launched an attack on a member of the Soviet bloc. While it is to be hoped that this will remain a theoretical contingency, recent fears about Syngman Rhee's intentions and French fears that the West Germans might set out some day to unify their country by force, indicate why it must be taken into consideration. Police action in such instances would necessarily favor the Soviet bloc if it did not lead to Soviet expansion; it would be hard enough for the United States to remain on the sidelines while one of its erstwhile allies was being defeated by Communist "police" forces. In the present situation, in which this country and the other members of the free world are having the greatest trouble mustering enough strength for their defense against the East, how could their statesmen risk destroying what non-Communist solidarity and common defense positions now exist, even if in doing so they were serving the cause of collective security and future deterrence?

This does not answer the moral question. Some insist that it is the duty of nations to participate in police action because peace and the establishment of the rule of law in the world require that aggressors be stopped or punished. This means placing higher value on such punishment than on national self-defense whenever the two conflict. Against this view it can be argued on moral grounds that when, as today, everything the American people and most free peoples cherish, from independence to their way of life, is in grave danger of Soviet and Communist attack, precedence must be given to the defense of these values. After all, even staunch supporters of collective security are apt to draw a line somewhere beyond which nations cannot be expected to go in their devotion to the cause of police action; they will not expect them to commit national suicide for the sake of serving the long-run interests of the world community.

But what about the world public opinion? Will people abroad not be shocked to learn that the United States cannot be counted upon to use force against all aggressors, Communist or non-Communist, and will this not make enemies for this country? Where the public stands on this issue is a matter of conjecture. Experience during the Korean War may be revealing, however. This country was given almost unanimous and in most cases enthusiastic moral support by articulate opinion throughout the non-Communist world when it first took up arms to stop the North Koreans. Yet, when the question of taking more forceful action against Red China arose, after that country had been declared an aggressor, condemnation of any such "adventurous" or "militaristic" move was hardly less widespread. Liberal opinion—which had always been most keen to see collective security applied—was now most vigorously opposed to any extension of the war. The reason for this apparent inconsistency is not hard to discover. Punishment of an aggressor is desired but not if it means plunging the nation into a major war, in this case a world war, not even perhaps if it means gravely endangering the immediate security of the nation. "Before the great powers can join in sacrifices of blood and treasure to keep the peace in regions where they have no real interest," wrote Samuel Flagg Bemis prior to the Korean War, "a great transformation of will must take place among the peoples of the nations." This would still seem to hold true, more so, of course, where intervention runs directly counter to these "real interests." Thus, however tempting a system of collective security may appear in the abstract, its implementation in the case of aggressors of considerable military power runs into serious objections on the grounds of morality as well as of prudence.

If it is doubtful, to say the least, whether this country will intervene against any aggressor anywhere, serious disadvantages will accrue to it if the popular label of "collective security" is applied to United States foreign policy. There is first the danger of future disillusionment. There has been some already, because Red China, found guilty of aggression by the United Nations, did not receive the same punishment as North Korea, the weaker country. If the expectation takes root that American military forces will be available against any aggressor anywhere and if in some future instance this expectation is disappointed, the bitterness of the victim of an attack and its friends might have embarrassing consequences.

A second disadvantage has also been borne out by the events. If the American people are made to believe that this country involved itself in a costly and in many ways inconclusive war for no other interest than to serve the cause of collective security, is it surprising that there is resentment against other members of the United Nations who failed to live up to a principle to which they were no less committed than the United States? Such criticism of our friends and allies may be silenced if it is understood that this country in fact did have what were then considered to be very pressing national interests in stopping the North Koreans. It will also be better appreciated that some of the other members of the United Nations, including India, went quite far in backing the United Nations when, in disregard of what they believed to be their interest in neutrality, they voted to authorize the actions of the United States and its associates and to condemn the North Koreans and Chinese as aggressors.

It may be objected that if Korea has not opened the way for a universal system of collective security against all aggression, it has merely served to demonstrate once more the tragic hold that "power politics" has on the nations even of the free world. The United Nations as a security organization, it will be said, can have no place in such a world. However, such conclusions are not warranted. The United States and its associates made good on a policy of "collective defense of the free world" carried out under the authority and control of the United Nations. While the control was weak, it nevertheless brought a restraining influence to bear on one of the world's greatest powers engaged in a bitter and costly defensive struggle. The one great contribution to the development of more lawful conditions in the world which this country can claim to have made in Korea consists therefore in its willingness to recognize the authority of the United Nations over actions which required sacrifices mainly from the American people. If some deplore the way in which the majority in the General Assembly exercised this control, believing that it would have been better for this country and the free world to have fought for victory at all costs, they give testimony thereby to the price countries may have to pay for the advantages of having collective defense operate according to the rules and with the approval of an international organization.

As to the United Nations itself, it has gained stature by the fact of having been able to be useful to the free world in its defense against Communist aggression without having to give up its universal character and its mediatory potentialities. Obviously, its role has been a more modest one than that contemplated by the exponents of collective security. Instead of being able to order the bulk of its members to fight aggressors whatever their relations to the aggressor, all the United Nations could do was to name the aggressor, to authorize and recommend action by its members, to lend its name to their action, and to seek to exert influence on the way it was carried out and terminated. This is exactly the role which would fall to the United Nations in cases in which collective self-defense was carried out under Article 51 and preceded action by the Security Council. The similarity is not accidental. If nations will resort to force only against national opponents when it accords with their national defense interests, as was true in Korea, the United Nations must limit itself to functions which are consistent with the needs of collective defense of likeminded countries. This has now been shown to be a practical and beneficial way of using an organization which, it should be added, has many important tasks to perform other than to stop or punish aggression.

Address of Dean Acheson before General Assembly (September 20, 1950)*

This session of the General Assembly is a session of decision.

Before us lies opportunity for action which can save the hope of peace, security, well-being, and justice for generations to come. Before us also lies opportunity for drift, for irresolution, for effort feebly made. In this direction is disaster. The choice is ours. It will be made whether we act or whether we do not act.

The peoples of the world know this. They will eagerly follow every word spoken here. Our words will reach them mingled with the sound of the battle now raging in Korea. There, men are fighting and dying under the banner of the United Nations. Our Charter, born out of the sacrifices of millions in war, is being consecrated anew to peace at the very moment of our meeting. The heroism of these men gives us this opportunity to meet and to act. Our task is to be worthy of them and of that opportunity.

We meet also with full knowledge of the great anxiety which clutches at the hearts of the people of this earth. Men and women everywhere are weighted down with fear—fear of war, fear that man may be begetting his own destruction.

But man is not a helpless creature who must await an inexorable fate. It lies within our power to take action which, God willing, can avert the catastrophe whose shadow hangs over us. That terrible responsibility rests upon every man and woman in this room. At the end of this meeting each of us must answer to his conscience on what we have done here.

* General Assembly, *Official Records*, 5th session, 279th meeting (September 20, 1950), pp. 23-27. Also in *Department of State Bulletin*, Vol. XXIII, No. 587 (October 2, 1950), pp. 523-529.

How have we come to this condition of fear and jeopardy? The lifetime of many here has seen the rise and fall of empires, the growth of powerful nations, the stirrings of great continents with newborn hope, the conquest of space, and great inventions, both creative and destructive. We have lived in a century of alternating war and hope.

Now, the foundation of our hope is the United Nations. Five years ago we declared at San Francisco our determination "to save succeeding generations from the scourge of war," our faith in fundamental human rights, our belief in justice and social progress. During the years that have intervened, some of us have worked hard to bring this about.

There is no longer any question: Will the United Nations survive? Will the United Nations suffer the fate of the League of Nations? This question has been answered. If by nothing else, it has been answered by United Nations action against aggression in Korea. Blood is thicker than ink.

But a pall of fear has been cast over our hopes and our achievements.

What is the reason for this fear? Why is it that we have been unable to achieve peace and security through the United Nations in these 5 years? Why has there not been the cooperation among the great powers which was to have buttressed the United Nations? Why have we not been able to reach an agreement on the control of atomic energy and the regulation of armaments? What has been the obstacle to a universal system of collective security?

We have been confronted with many and complex problems, but the main obstacle to peace is easy to identify, and there should be no mistake in anyone's mind about it. That obstacle has been created by the policies of the Soviet Government.

We should be very clear in our minds about this obstacle. It is not the rise of the Soviet Union as a strong national power which creates difficulties. It is not the existence of different social and economic systems in the world. Nor is it, I firmly believe, any desire on the part of the Russian people for war. The root of our trouble is to be found in the new imperialism directed by the leaders of the Soviet Union.

To be more explicit, the Soviet Government raises five barriers to peace.

First, Soviet efforts to bring about the collapse of the non-Soviet world, and thereby fulfill a prediction of Soviet theory, have made genuine negotiation very difficult. The honorable representative of Lebanon, Dr. Charles Malik, stated it precisely at our last Assembly when he said: "There can be no greater disagreement than when one wants to eliminate your existence altogether."

Second, the shroud of secrecy which the Soviet leaders have wrapped around the people and the states they control is a great barrier to peace. This has nourished suspicion and misinformation in both directions. It deprives governments of the moderating influence of contact between peoples. It stands in the way of the mutual knowledge and confidence essential to disarmament.

Third, the rate at which the Soviet Union has been building arms and armies, far beyond any requirement of defense, has gravely endangered peace throughout the world. While other countries were demobilizing and converting their industries to peaceful purposes after the war, the Soviet Union and the territories under its control pushed preparation for war. The Soviet Union has forced countries to rearm for their self-defense.

Fourth, the use by Soviet leaders of the international Communist movement for direct and indirect aggression has been a great source of trouble in the world. With words which play upon honest aspirations and grievances the Soviet leaders have manipulated the people of other states as pawns of Russian imperialism.

Fifth, the Soviet use of violence to impose its will and its political system upon other people is a threat to the peace. There is nothing unusual in the fact that those who believe in some particular social order want to spread it throughout the world. But as one of my predecessors, Secretary Adams, said of the efforts of an earlier Russian ruler, Czar Alexander, to establish the Holy Alliance, the Emperor "finds a happy coincidence between the dictates of his conscience and the interests of his empire." The combination of this international ambition and the Soviet reliance on force and violence—though it be camouflaged as civil war—is a barrier to peaceful relations.

This conduct conflicts with the Charter of the United Nations. It conflicts with the "Essentials of Peace" Resolution passed at our last Assembly. It has created a great and terrible peril for the rest of the world.

Even this conduct has not made war inevitable—we, for our part, do not accept the idea that war is inevitable. But it has lengthened the shadow of war. This fact cannot be obscured by propaganda which baits the hooks with words of peace and, in doing so, profanes the highest aspirations of mankind.

STRENGTH TO PREVENT AGGRESSION

There is only one real way the world can maintain peace and security in the face of this conduct. That is by strengthening its system of collective security. Our best hope of peace lies in our ability to make absolutely plain to potential aggressors that aggression cannot succeed. The security of those nations who want peace and the security of the United Nations itself demand the strength to prevent further acts of aggression.

One of the fundamental purposes of the United Nations, as expressed in article 1 of the Charter, is that it shall ". . . take effective collective measures for the prevention and removal of threats to the peace, and for the suppression of acts of aggression or other breaches of the peace . . ."

The action of the United Nations to put down the aggression which began on June 25 against the Republic of Korea was exactly the effective collective measure required. It marked a turning point in history, for it showed the way to an enforceable rule of law among nations.

The world waits to see whether we can build on the start we have made. The United Nations must move forward energetically to develop a more adequate system of collective security. If it does not move forward, it will move back.

Article 24 of the Charter gives the Security Council primary responsibility for the maintenance of peace. This is the way it should be. But if the Security Council is not able to act because of the obstructive tactics of a permanent member, the Charter does not leave the United Nations impotent. The obligation of all members to take action to maintain or restore the peace does not disappear because of a veto. The Charter, in articles 10, 11, and 14, also vests in the General Assembly authority and responsibility for matters affecting international peace. The General Assembly can and should organize itself to discharge its responsibility promptly and decisively if the Security Council is prevented from acting.

To this end, the United States delegation is placing before the Assembly a number of recommendations designed to increase the effectiveness of United Nations action against aggression.

This program will include the following proposals:

First, a provision for the calling of an emergency session of the General Assembly upon 24 hours' notice if the Security Council is prevented from acting upon a breach of the peace or an act of aggression.

Second, the establishment by the General Assembly of a security patrol, a peace patrol, to provide immediate and independent observation and reporting from any area in which international conflict threatens, upon the invitation or with the consent of the state visited.

Third, a plan under which each member nation would designate within its national armed forces a United Nations unit or units, to be specially trained and equipped and continuously maintained in readiness for prompt service on behalf of the United Nations. To assist in the organization, training, and equipping of such units, we will suggest that a United Nations military adviser be appointed. Until such time as the forces provided for under article 43 are made available to the United Nations, the availability of these national units will be an important step toward the development of a world-wide security system.

Fourth, the establishment by the General Assembly of a committee to study and report on means which the United Nations might use through collective action—including the use of armed force—to carry out the purposes and principles of the Charter.

The United States delegation shall request that these proposals be added as an item to the agenda. It is the hope of our delegation that the Assembly will act on these and other suggestions which may be offered for the strengthening of our collective security system.

In so doing, we must keep clearly before the world the purpose of our

We need this defensive strength against further aggression in order to collective security system, so that no one can make any mistake about it.

pass through this time of tension without catastrophe and to reach a period when genuine negotiation may take its place as the normal means of settling disputes. . . .

This perspective takes into account the possibility that the Soviet Government may not be inherently and unalterably committed to standing in the way of peace and that it may some day accept a live-and-let-live philosophy.

The Soviet leaders are realists, in some respects at least. As we succeed in building the necessary economic and defensive military strength, it will become clear to them that the non-Soviet world will neither collapse nor be dismembered piecemeal. Some modification in their aggressive policies may follow if they then recognize that the best interests of the Soviet Union require a cooperative relationship with the outside world.

Time may have its effect. It is but 33 years since the overthrow of the Czarist regime in Russia. This is a short time in history. Like many other social and political movements before it, the Soviet revolution may change. In so doing, it may rid itself of the policies which now prevent the Soviet Union from living as a good neighbor with the rest of the world.

We have no assurance that this will take place. But, as the United Nations strengthens its collective security system, the possibilities of this change in Soviet policy will increase. If this does not occur, the increase in our defensive strength shall be the means of insuring our survival and protecting the essential values of our societies.

But our hope is that a strong collective security system will make genuine negotiation possible and that this will in turn lead to a cooperative peace.

It is the firm belief of the people and the Government of the United States that the United Nations will play an increasingly important role in the world during the period ahead as we try to move safely through the present tensions.

I have already stressed the importance we attach to the United Nations as the framework of an effective system of collective security. The steps we take to strengthen our collective security are not only essential to the survival of the United Nations, but will contribute positively toward its development. The close ties of a common defense are developing an added cohesion among regional groups. This is a significant step toward a closer relationship among nations and is part of the process of growth by which we are moving toward a larger sense of community under the United Nations.

The United States also attaches importance to the universal character of the United Nations, which enables it to serve as a point of contact between the Soviet Union and the rest of the world during this period of tension.

As our efforts to strengthen the collective security system become more and more effective, and as tensions begin to ease, we believe that the United Nations will be increasingly important as a means of facilitating and encouraging productive negotiation.

The United States is ready and will always be ready and willing to negotiate with a sincere desire to solve problems. We shall continue to hope that sometime negotiation will not be merely an occasion for propaganda.

Solving the many difficult problems in the world must, of course, be a gradual process. It will not be achieved miraculously, overnight, by a sudden dramatic gesture. It will come about step by step. We must seek to solve such problems as we can, and endure the others until they too can be solved. . . .

Extracts from General Assembly Debate of "United Action for Peace" Resolution (October 9-10 and November 1-3, 1950)

354TH MEETING OF THE FIRST COMMITTEE*

United Action for Peace

1. MR. DULLES (United States of America) said that the authors of the joint draft resolution, of which his country was one, had been inspired by the United Nations action in Korea, which had proved that the Organization could be an effective instrument for suppressing aggression. Nevertheless, if aggressors were to be deterred by fear of the United Nations, certain organizational weaknesses would have to be remedied. It was only thanks to a series of adventitious and favourable circumstances that the United Nations had been able to take action against the aggressors in Korea.

2. It was doubtful, firstly, whether the Security Council would have acted if at the decisive moment, for extraneous reasons, one of the permanent members had not been absent; secondly, whether, if the General Assembly had not sent a commission to Korea three years ago, the Council would have had the information needed to justify prompt and decisive action; thirdly, whether United Nations forces could have saved the Republic of Korea if the United States had not stationed troops in Japan five years ago to enforce compliance with the terms of the armistice; lastly, whether the aggressor would have failed in Korea except for what amounted to, from his standpoint, extraordinarily bad fortune.

3. If potential aggressors were to be deprived of all hope of success, a reliable system would have to be created instead of matters being left to chance.

4. The need for collective resistance to aggression was as imperative today as it had been in March 1939. Then, Generalissimo Stalin had asserted that the non-aggressive States, primarily the United Kingdom, France and

* General Assembly, *Official Records,* 5th session, First Committee, 354th meeting (October 9, 1950), pp. 63-65.

the United States of America, had rejected the policy of collective resistance to aggressors in favour of non-intervention and neutrality, thus conniving at aggression and allowing the war to become a world war.

5. Generalissimo Stalin's prediction had been fulfilled. Since then, however, the peoples had progressed and they expected the United Nations to show them how to promote collective resistance to the aggressors. There were doubtless those who feared that such action would precipitate aggression. The United States, for its part, would not resign itself to tolerate repeated acts of aggression, or to take action outside the United Nations, or to revert to a condition of each for himself and the devil take the hindmost.

6. Fortunately, the Charter had provided for the three basic security needs: (*a*) prompt and dependable action; (*b*) reliable means of information; (*c*) a backing of adequate power ready for action. In those three respects, the Security Council had what the Charter referred to as "primary responsibility." . . .

7. Five years had elapsed and, while the Security Council had in many respects served admirably the purposes for which it had been set up, experience had shown that it was impossible to rely solely on the Council on the three points referred to above. The right of veto had already been used nearly fifty times; the Security Council had not established an adequate system of observation; it had not taken the initiative required of it in virtue of Article 43. On those three points, the facts were so well known that it was unnecessary to dwell on them.

8. But the Charter, which gave the Security Council "primary responsibility" for peace and which sanctioned the veto, also gave the General Assembly the right to make recommendations even in cases where the right of veto could be exercised. Apart from Articles 11 and 14, Article 10 gave the Assembly the right to make recommendations to the Members on any matters "within the scope of the present Charter" except in relation to disputes or situations with which the Security Council was dealing.

9. In fact, at San Francisco the small Powers had only agreed to the power of veto on condition that the General Assembly were granted the power to intervene and to make recommendations within the framework of Chapters VI and VII of the Charter in cases where the Security Council was unable to discharge its primary responsibility. As the delegation of the USSR had objected to the General Assembly having the right to overrule a veto, even by way of a recommendation, the United States had advised the Soviet Union on 19 June 1945 that, in view of the short time which remained before the ceremony of signing the Charter, the United States could wait no longer and that, in order to break the deadlock, it was going to negotiate alone with the small Powers. The following day, the Chairman of the Soviet Union delegation had informed the Secretary of State that his Government agreed to the extension of the scope of Article 10. The time had now come to use the right obtained that day.

10. Section A of [the] draft resolution provided that the General Assembly could promptly make a recommendation if Security Council action were blocked. Obviously, a recommendation by the General Assembly had not the force of a decision of the Security Council taken under the terms of Chapter VII of the Charter. But the history of the Korean question had shown that the voluntary response to a recommendation could be even more effective than obedience to an order; although the Security Council had not exercised its powers of action, fifty-three Members were carrying out its recommendation.

11. It was doubtless considered in some quarters that an amendment of the rules of procedure of the General Assembly to provide for emergency special sessions, although legally permissible, would be unwise, because the Assembly might be unable to act responsibly, and that if it could not be relied upon to act responsibly, it would be better to abandon all idea of United Nations action.

12. The United States delegation considered that the responsibility for maintaining peace was not the monopoly of the great Powers and that an informed world opinion was the factor most likely to affect the course of events. There was every reason to believe that the General Assembly, better than any other organ, would reflect world opinion on the question of what was right, in other words, the supremacy of law.

13. The Security Council, of course, should have the opportunity of exercising its primary responsibility, but in the unfortunate eventuality of its failing to do its duty, it was the right and the duty of the General Assembly to consider the situation without delay. The very fact that the General Assembly would stand ready to act if the Security Council failed to do so would stimulate the members of the Council to co-operate so that that organ might function as was contemplated by the Charter.

14. Section B of the joint draft resolution dealt with the establishment of a more adequate system of observation; a peace observation commission would be set up, its members to be chosen by the Assembly from among Member States other than the so-called great Powers. That commission, and any subsidiary organs and observers it might have, would be the eyes and ears of the United Nations and it would reduce the danger of aggression. As Generalissimo Stalin had said of the League of Nations in 1939, the existence of a forum in which the aggressors would be exposed might hinder the outbreak of war. If the Security Council—or, failing that, the General Assembly—nevertheless found itself obliged to deal with a breach of the peace, the observation commission would be able to supply prompt and reliable information. It was thus that, in Greece and Korea, commissions of the Assembly had in the one case perhaps prevented open war and in the other case made prompt action possible. In the present state of tension, all those who were innocent of aggressive intentions would welcome a development of the United Nations' system of observation.

15. Under section C of the draft resolution, certain elements of the armed forces of Member States would be brought into readiness to serve the United Nations. There was no question of binding commitments for the future, or even of the designation of particular forces, and each of the Member States would continue to be able to avail itself of all of its armed forces in virtue of its right of individual or collective self-defence, as recognized in Article 51 of the Charter. Finally, a panel of military experts under the authority of the Secretary-General would be put at the disposal of any Member State which so requested.

16. Since the Security Council had not taken the initiative prescribed by Article 43, the Member States, which under the Charter had assumed the obligation of putting armed forces at the disposal of the United Nations, should now be invited to undertake some first steps without awaiting further attempts at negotiation by the Security Council. Certain Member States had in fact expressed regret at not having had forces ready to act in Korea, where one nation had had to bear initially a great weight of sacrifice. Without giving orders to anyone, the General Assembly could thus make recommendations on the subject to Member States, which, it would seem, were awaiting such an initiative on the part of the Assembly.

17. Under section D of the seven-Power draft resolution, a collective measures committee would report to the Security Council and to the General Assembly on the whole problem of collective security.

18. Subject to further suggestions, the seven-Power draft resolution recommended no objectives or methods that were not in conformity with the Charter, into which new life should be breathed without further delay. For, verbal attacks and threats of violence had been succeeded by civil wars and then by an armed attack which had led many people to believe that a world war was inevitable. The United States of America, while not sharing that view, recognized that fear of war, if not allayed, created the conditions that made war more likely.

19. The fifth session of the General Assembly should therefore take "effective collective measures for the prevention and removal of threats to the peace." Already fifty-three Member States had responded in varying degree to the appeal made by the Security Council on 25 and 27 June, and the forces of eighteen Member States were then actually committed to serve in Korea under the United Nations flag, to achieve the aims of the United Nations. For the first time in history, humanity's dream of seeing a world organization repel an aggressor had come true. But now some people were wondering in retrospect whether the action taken in relation to Korea had not been only an accident, and whether aggressors would not still have an opportunity to succeed in the future; while others believed that if a new spirit were to animate the United Nations, it would be possible to avoid such local aggressions, which, as history had shown, were the prelude to general war.

20. The measures proposed did not involve acceptance of any particular theory as to the causes of the present tension, on which everyone had his own ideas, no doubt, without anyone being wholly right. The proposals were not based upon any finding of past guilt, but upon two general propositions that had been accepted ever since San Francisco: the first, that the dangers of aggression and of world war were ever present, and secondly, that effective collective resistance to aggression was an excellent preventive.

21. The representative of the USSR, who affected alarm at the alleged aggressive intentions of the United States, should welcome the protection offered under the draft resolution. For the nations which would principally implement the measures proposed therein would be precisely those nations whose devotion to the cause of peace could not be questioned and which could not possibly be considered as warmongers. Those were the nations which would constitute the proposed observation commission, and whose votes would make possible the two-thirds' majority needed for General Assembly recommendations.

22. Thus, the keys to peace now lay in the hands of the General Assembly.

357TH MEETING OF THE FIRST COMMITTEE*

. . . 15. MR. VYSHINSKY (Union of Soviet Socialist Republics) noted that the draft resolution submitted by seven delegations headed by the United States contemplated measures designed to ensure the solution of a problem of extraordinary importance, particularly in the present circumstances, namely the maintenance of peace and the removal of the threat of a new war. . . .

17. Mr. Vyshinsky said that it must be recognized that there were numerous hurdles to be overcome in the struggle for peace. Unless cognizance were taken of the nature of those hurdles, it would be impossible to find a method for removing them or to remove them.

18. The sponsors of the joint draft resolution apparently believed that they had found the answer to the question of the nature of those hurdles as well as to that of the ways and means by which they could be removed. Thus, Mr. Acheson, in his speech to the General Assembly on 20 September had said in effect that the principal obstacle on the path to peace had been created by policies of the USSR which were designed to bring about the destruction of the non-Soviet world and thus fulfil the predictions of Soviet theory. According to Mr. Acheson, the only thing which constituted a threat to the maintenance of peace was the desire of the Government of the USSR to use force to impose its will and political system on other nations. Mr. Acheson and later Mr. Dulles had outlined and analysed measures to be taken to counteract that threat and Mr. Dulles had analysed them for the First Committee in some detail.

* General Assembly, *Official Records,* 5th session, First Committee, 357th meeting (October 10, 1950), pp. 80-86.

19. Mr. Vyshinsky observed that the authors of the joint draft had found it convenient for themselves and their purposes to repeat all kinds of fairy tales about USSR policy, though he was convinced that they themselves did not believe what they propagated.

20. Mr. Vyshinsky said that the USSR delegation agreed to some parts of the joint draft resolution but at the same time had certain amendments to submit and objections to propound regarding some points. However, he wished to analyse some general considerations advanced by the advocates of the joint draft before stating his delegation's views on the draft itself.

21. According to its sponsors, the joint draft resolution was designed to strengthen the United Nations. Mr. Dulles had stated that the organizational weaknesses of the United Nations must be corrected if it was to be able to halt those who were preparing for aggression. Similar ideas had been expressed by other delegations, including the view that adoption of the joint proposal would be the best method of strengthening the United Nations, raising respect for it, and turning it into a mainstay of peace. Apparently the United Nations was not respected throughout the world and not the mainstay of peace but had to be turned into one. Mr. Vyshinsky said that his delegation must take exception to those premises.

22. However, the important element in the argument of the proponents of the joint draft resolution was the emphasis placed upon the necessity of strengthening the United Nations and removing organizational weaknesses which were supposed to have come to light. Unfortunately, those were only empty phrases. There could be no question of strengthening the United Nations by weakening the Security Council, which would be the inevitable result of the adoption of proposals like those contained in the joint draft resolution. The purpose of that draft was to relieve the Security Council of its primary responsibility, the maintenance of peace and security as stipulated in Article 24 of the Charter. There could be no strengthening of the United Nations if the cornerstone of the Organization, the organ which under the Charter had the exclusive right and power to fight against aggression, to forestall the threat of aggression, and to call upon forces not available to other organs under the Charter, was to be weakened. The proclaimed purpose of the sponsors of the joint draft resolution—the strengthening of the United Nations—would thus inevitably have a contrary result, through the implementation of measures which would weaken the Security Council.

23. Mr. Dulles' speech of 9 October had contained four implicit conclusions about the Security Council. They were that the Council was incapable of acting speedily or of acting at all; that the Council could not have the information required for the adoption of quick and decisive actions; that the Security Council, or the United Nations as a whole, could not have armed forces at its disposal; and that the Security Council, or the United Nations as a whole, was incapable of fighting against or forestalling aggression. The reason in each case had been ascribed to the principle of unanimity in the Security Council in connexion with action on non-procedural questions, or,

in other words, to the veto. The same spectre of the veto was discerned in every direction and the general conclusion to be drawn was that the principle of unanimity must be liquidated. However, if that was the conclusion reached by the sponsors of the joint draft resolution led by the United States, why was it that the constitutional method provided in the Charter for the revision and amendment of the Charter was not resorted to? If the establishment of a new method of operation to circumvent the Security Council was demanded, why was it that the sponsors of the joint proposal remained silent about the possibility of changing the Charter, which was what was actually proposed? The fact was that the seven-Power draft resolution would explode and crush the Charter.

25. Everything that had been said and that would be said in the future against the principle of unanimity, however, could not withstand criticism from the point of view of the implementation of those principles which formed the basis of a United Nations composed of sovereign States. The principal questions relating to implementation of measures for the maintenance of peace and security had remained unsolved, not because of the veto but because of the position taken in the Security Council by the Anglo-American bloc, which had consistently tried to foist decisions designed for its own benefit, on the Security Council, decisions which consistently failed to take into consideration the interests of the United Nations and were designed to favour the American monopolists. That had been done by dint of the Anglo-American bloc's majority in the Security Council. There was no use in the veto if a majority could always be commanded. The advantage was always on the side of the majority, particularly when it had reached an understanding and had set forth an objective to which all members of the majority must submit, though perhaps not all of them sympathized with it. When a country was completely in debt to another Power, it could not take an independent position. That was the situation in the Security Council.

27. Under such conditions, there might have been many more vetoes than there had been. The veto was a method of self-defence against pressure and dictation by those countries which regarded themselves as powerful, mighty and glorious and therefore entitled to implement their plans. An international organization could hardly have become viable if a sovereign State had been unable to rely on the veto to defend its interests. Such an organization could hardly have failed to become an alliance of groups of States, kept together by their own interests, rather than by the interests of mankind, which had guided the efforts of the States that had sponsored the United Nations five years previously.

28. Mr. Dulles had been wrong in ascribing the state of affairs in the Security Council to the principle of unanimity. The basis of every international organization was the obligation of each of its members to respect the governmental and national independence and equality of rights of all other members. The root of the evil was the use of the method of imposing one's will at any cost in international relations. . . .

30. Mr. Vyshinsky recalled that, at the very beginning of the Organization, the principle of unanimity had aroused discontent and protests, leading to various attempts to deprive the Security Council of its role. At San Francisco, there had been an argument over the question of the inter-relationship of the Security Council and the General Assembly and the rights and obligations of those two organs. Various amendments which had been submitted at that time could be divided into two categories, as follows: proposals for granting the General Assembly rights equivalent to those of the Security Council; and proposals to turn the General Assembly into the supreme organ of the United Nations with a view to subjugating the Security Council to the General Assembly. The motivation at San Francisco had been exactly the same as that which had been repeated before the Committee by Mr. Dulles when he said that more rights should be granted to the General Assembly because the Security Council might not be able to act on account of the veto. . . .

31. Mr. Vyshinsky recalled that when the Interim Committee had been established in 1947, over the objection of the delegation of the USSR, many hopes had been vested in that Committee by the opponents of the principle of unanimity in the Security Council. The Committee had then been called the Interim Committee on Peace and Security. In welcoming its establishment, the *New York Times* had indicated that the Interim Committee would be given various functions in the hope that it would be able to take rapid and effective measures if and when the Security Council found itself incapable of action. However, there had been some scandal in connexion with the establishment of the Committee and it had, therefore, been found necessary to change its name. It had been decided to make it a subsidiary organ of the General Assembly, since there would otherwise have been no constitutional justification for it. That attempt to counteract the Security Council had failed, but new attempts were now being made on the basis of the present political situation in Korea. Those new attempts were being made with a view to implementing a plan which had been consistently pursued year after year by certain delegations since the Dumbarton Oaks Conference in 1944.

34. Mr. Vyshinsky recalled that, on 14 October 1947, his delegation had exposed the tendency of the United States delegation to use all quibbles and excuses to transfer to the Interim Committee as many as possible of the powers and rights of other organs of the United Nations, particularly those belonging to the Security Council. Now that that had failed, it was proposed to endow the General Assembly with functions clearly vested in the Security Council under the Charter. The purpose of that proposal was to get the United Nations to do without the Security Council and allow the General Assembly to act in lieu of the Security Council, thus undermining the very basis of the joint, common and mutual responsibility of the five great Powers for the maintenance of peace.

37. Mr. Vyshinsky recalled that, on 6 November 1944, when the Charter of the United Nations was being drafted, Generalissimo Stalin had indicated that the actions of the proposed international organization would be effective if the great Powers that had borne on their shoulders the main burden of the war against Hitlerite Germany would act in the future in the spirit of unanimity and agreement. They would not be effective if that essential prerequisite were violated. Such were the principles on which the United Nations had been erected and must continue to stand in the future.

38. Now, however, another policy had been predicated, namely, the uprooting of the Charter. It had been proposed by the authors of the American draft resolution, who contemplated that the General Assembly would delegate to itself the function of acting in lieu of the Security Council.

39. To give that proposal the cloak of legality, Mr. Vyshinsky said, reference had repeatedly been made to Articles 10, 11 and 14 of the Charter. Those Articles had been cited to prove that the General Assembly had the right to deal with all questions that might be dealt with by any other organ of the United Nations. That was clear to anyone who read the Charter and could not be contested. Nor was it debatable that the General Assembly could submit, to all other organs of the United Nations, and to Member States, recommendations on any questions coming within the competence of the Assembly or of the other organs of the United Nations, within the framework of the Charter, except as provided in Article 12. But the representative of France had stated that Article 11, if taken in conjunction with Article 10, would even strictly forbid any discussion or consideration of a question. The representative of France had reached that conclusion because the last sentence of paragraph 2 of Article 11 stated that "any such question on which action is necessary shall be referred to the Security Council by the General Assembly either before or after discussion." It followed that, if action was necessary, the question must be referred to the Security Council. If the General Assembly wished to make a recommendation on that question, it could not do so because action must be taken by the Security Council alone.

40. Therefore, there could be no question of contradiction between the powers of the General Assembly and those of the Security Council, particularly since the last paragraph of Article 11 stated that Article 11 should not be construed as limiting the powers possessed by the Security Council under Article 10 of the Charter. But what kind of recommendations might be made to the Security Council by the General Assembly? Article 11, Mr. Vyshinsky explained, made it quite clear that if a recommendation were to involve some action, the General Assembly would have no right to take such action and, consequently, could not recommend what was to be done. In other words, the General Assembly could not arrogate to itself the right to take action that was incumbent on the Security Council. One could not

say that the General Assembly must make a recommendation and, therefore, there was a moral obligation for the Security Council, or for any other organ, or for the Members of the United Nations, to act. That would violate the provisions of Article 10, since only the Security Council could take action on questions falling within the scope of Articles 10 and 11.

41. Mr. Vyshinsky said that the representative of France had also committed a fallacy in contending that Article 11 was not applicable to Article 10 because Article 11 spoke of recommendations to the States concerned and not to Members of the United Nations in general, whereas Article 10 referred to Members of the United Nations rather than to States concerned, in particular. In fact, Mr. Vyshinsky explained, the beginning of Article 11 also made a reference to "Members" of the United Nations and not to States concerned. Furthermore, every Member of the United Nations was, of course, concerned and interested. There was no State Member of the United Nations which was not interested or not concerned in forestalling a threat of aggression, in counteracting a breach of the peace, and in acting against war or aggression. Therefore, Mr. Vyshinsky concluded, the argument advanced about the applicability of the last sentence of paragraph 2 of Article 11 to recommendations which might be made by the General Assembly under Article 10 was fallacious and lacking in legal meaning. In fact, all speakers other than the representative of France had deliberately omitted any reference to Article 11, paragraph 2, the meaning of which was of paramount importance. To say that the General Assembly could recommend action under the Charter to forestall aggression would be a flagrant violation of Article 11, paragraph 2, which clearly vested that prerogative in the Security Council. That was a very important prerogative whose fulfilment might be fraught with dire consequences for the peace of the world since it related to the kind of action which required the concurring votes of the five permanent members of the Security Council. Elimination of that requirement was the essential proposal of the seven-Power draft resolution.

42. Explaining the position of his delegation regarding the joint draft resolution, Mr. Vyshinsky stated that it had no objection to the provision contained in section A calling for extraordinary sessions of the General Assembly. Article 20 of the Charter had directly provided for such special sessions. However, his delegation could not agree to the proposal that such special sessions should be convoked at the request of seven members of the Security Council. According to the Charter, a decision to convoke a special session of the Assembly could not be made by any seven members of the Council; it must be a decision of the Council as legally constituted, which required the concurring votes of the permanent members. Moreover, the delegation of the USSR believed that, since a special session would be called in special circumstances, special preparation would be necessary. Obviously, such preparation would require more than the twenty-four hour period

proposed in the joint draft resolution. His delegation was of the opinion that a period of two weeks would be needed to allow Members to send specially prepared and qualified representatives.

43. Mr. Vyshinsky stated that his delegation also accepted the establishment of the peace observation commission proposed in section B of the joint draft resolution. The General Assembly had the right, under Article 22 of the Charter, to establish such subsidiary organs as it deemed necessary for the performance of its functions. Nevertheless, the USSR delegation wished to draw attention to the fact that the primary issue in connexion with this proposal was the question of the membership of the commission. His delegation believed that such a commission should be a representative-organ of the United Nations and not a mere tool in the hands of one group of States.

44. Section C, as well as some parts of the preamble to the joint draft resolution, contemplated the setting up of armed forces of the United Nations. The USSR delegation could not agree to the proposal because it constituted an attempt to usurp the rights of the Security Council and violated Chapter VII of the Charter, which provided for armed forces to be put under the control not of the General Assembly but of the Security Council through its Military Staff Committee. The proposal would call upon Member States to earmark armed elements to await orders. But whose orders? They would be subject to the orders not of the Security Council, as provided in the Charter, but of the General Assembly. Mr. Dulles had contended that the General Assembly would not order but would merely recommend. Various representatives, however, had pointed out in the Committee that a recommendation, morally speaking, was tantamount to an order. But where did the Charter endow the General Assembly with the function of recommending troop movements? Moreover, it was contended that the General Assembly had the right to recommend anything it wished. Mr. Vyshinsky begged to differ. The Assembly could recommend everything except that which Article 11 stated it could not do. Article 11 stipulated that any question on which action was necessary must be referred to the Security Council. The movement of armed forces obviously would be for the purpose of taking action. Therefore, Section C of the joint draft resolution was basically and fundamentally incompatible with the Charter. It short-circuited both the Military Staff Committee and the Security Council. Mr. Vyshinsky also objected to paragraph 9 of the joint draft resolution on the ground that it suggested that military experts and advisers would be under the orders of the Secretary-General.

45. The representative of the USSR declared that Mr. Dulles and Mr. Acheson had endeavoured to camouflage the question as to what authority would control the proposed armed forces. They had not specified the organ of the United Nations at whose disposal those armed elements would be placed. He would assume that the Security Council would act, in such a case, in the name of the United Nations since that was what the Charter

provided under Articles 23, 25, 47 and 48 and under Chapter VII. If that was so, it should be said.

46. It was further suggested, Mr. Vyshinsky continued, that in case of aggression, some steps preliminary to the measures stipulated in Article 43 should be taken. But the Charter did not leave a vacuum before the agreements referred to in Article 43 were concluded. Article 106 of the Charter stipulated that, pending the coming into force of such agreements, the parties to the Four-Nation Declaration, signed at Moscow on 30 October 1943, and France, should, in accordance with the provisions of paragraph 5 of that Declaration, consult with one another and, as occasion required, with other Members of the United Nations with a view to taking such joint action on behalf of the Organization as might be necessary for the purpose of maintaining international peace and security. Article 106 was in force since no agreements existed under Article 43; but thus far no one had even tried to act in accordance with the provisions of Article 106. The USSR delegation intended to submit a formal proposal in that connexion. There was no reason, therefore, for the establishment of panels of military experts which would encroach upon the exclusive province of the Security Council. Instead, the United Nations should endeavour to implement Chapter VII of the Charter, especially Article 43.

47. Finally, as to section D of the joint draft resolution calling for the establishment of a collective measures committee, Mr. Vyshinsky said that his delegation was of the opinion that that section was contradictory to Chapters V and VII of the Charter and would encroach upon the functions of the Security Council. The Soviet delegation was therefore opposed to section D.

48. In conclusion, Mr. Vyshinsky stated that the Security Council was faced with the task of elaborating measures to implement the provisions of Articles 43, 45, 46 and 47 of the Charter. The Council was also acutely faced with the adoption of measures for removing threats to peace, for dealing with aggression, and for the peaceful settlement of disputes likely to endanger the maintenance of international peace and security. It must take measures for the effective functioning of the Military Staff Committee. The Council and, in the first instance, its permanent members, must take all necessary steps to remove the obstacles which thus far had prevented the implementation of those measures, thus discharging the duties vested in them by the Charter of the United Nations.

299TH MEETING OF THE GENERAL ASSEMBLY*

United Action for Peace: Reports of the First Committee and the Fifth Committee

13. MR. THORS (Iceland), Rapporteur of the First Committee: The question now before the General Assembly for discussion and consideration bears the title "United action for peace." People all over the world will place great hope in any genuine united action for peace, and will wholeheartedly welcome any such action. Many will be encouraged by the unanimity achieved for the draft resolution of Iraq and Syria, recommending to the permanent members of the Security Council that they should meet and discuss all problems which are likely to threaten international peace and which are likely to hamper the activities of the United Nations, with a view to solving their fundamental differences and reaching agreement in accordance with the spirit and letter of the Charter. Let us hope that subsequent actions will not cause disappointment, and that the noble hopes of all people all over the world may come true.

14. THE PRESIDENT: In addition to the First Committee's report, the Assembly has before it the Fifth Committee's report on the financial implications of the draft resolutions submitted for its consideration. The report is self-explanatory: I do not think it is necessary to ask the Rapporteur of the Fifth Committee to present it. In addition to the reports of the First and the Fifth Committees, the Assembly has before it some amendments and a draft resolution submitted by the USSR.

18. MR. ARMAND UGON (Uruguay): The debates held in the First Committee on this important draft resolution were chiefly devoted to a discussion of legal problems bearing on the constitutionality or unconstitutionality of this proposal in terms of the Charter. Our delegation considers that that necessary and most useful discussion has demonstrated the complete conformity of the draft with the provisions of the Charter and with the distribution of powers set forth therein. Consequently we do not believe that it is necessary to dwell upon this legal discussion, but will confine ourselves to what we said in the First Committee. On the other hand, the legal discussion, although indispensable in view of the legal aspects of the draft resolution, has to a certain extent obscured consideration of the political and constitutional significance of the step about to be taken by the United Nations.

19. If we take a more general view, and consider the draft in a wider context, we find that this measure represents the most decisive progress yet made by man in the organization of peace and security. It is beyond any doubt the most constructive step taken since San Francisco. If the fourth

* General Assembly, *Official Records,* 5th session, 299th meeting (November 1, 1950), pp. 291-355.

session of the General Assembly of the United Nations could be called the "Peace Assembly," these reasons justify us in calling the fifth session the "Assembly of collective security," as its President, Mr. Entezam called it in a memorable speech.

20. This resolution, once it has been adopted, will empower the organized international community to take the enforcement measures indispensable to repel aggression, a power which the League of Nations never acquired. We have benefited from our experience in Korea and broadened its application to build a practical, realistic and world-wide system of collective security, the most advanced yet known.

21. This system is not a substitute for, but rather an addition to, the one already in existence. It is not designed to replace the security system envisaged at San Francisco and hinging on the Security Council. It is designed to operate in the event of a flaw or breakdown in the Security Council system of security. The Security Council retains the vast powers conferred upon it by the Charter. The big five Powers continue to bear the heavy weight of primary responsibilities conferred upon them by that document. The new system merely gives to the Assembly and the smaller States a responsibility for collective security in addition to that of the Council and the big five.

22. The new system will come into play whenever the Security Council is unable to act because of the veto, or the misuse of presidential powers, or any other hindrance due to disagreement among the great Powers.

23. No revision of the Charter is involved; what is proposed is a remedy, within the system of the Charter, for the inactivity of the Security Council. In the opinion of our delegation the essential part of this draft resolution is the provision for calling, for the first time in international history, upon the smaller States to take decisions on collective security and contribute towards it.

24. Hitherto the maintenance of collective security has been the affair of the great Powers, which arrogated to themselves the function of preserving peace in the Holy Alliance, in the Concert of Europe, in the Council of the League of Nations—as permanent members, in the Security Council—also as permanent members, and finally in the transitional system envisaged in Article 106 of the Charter and which was apparently intended to become permanent. Now, however, the smaller Powers are called upon to contribute, at the international level, to the maintenance of collective security.

25. We have here, for the first time in history, a system of collective security based on the contribution of all States, large and small, in proportion to their economic and military means.

26. As Uruguay pointed out at San Francisco, we are sure that this clarion call to the small States will be of fundamental importance and will serve to strengthen peace and security.

27. Lacking in strong military forces, but likewise lacking in designs for conquest and aggrandisement, the small countries represent an untapped force for peace and international justice, since all of them hope for the reign

of law and cannot but reject aggression, threats and violence. It follows that, in the organization of world security, these nations without designs or plans for conquest can and must be regarded as a powerful force serving the peace-loving community of nations, the rules of international law, and the ethical and legal principles of civilization. As between what is just and what is unjust, they will choose justice; as between what is legitimate and illegitimate, they will choose law; and as between violence and security, they will choose the maintenance of peace.

28. To call upon geographically small and militarily weak countries to co-operate in the maintenance of international peace and security means to employ a new force to establish effective and solid guarantees for the achievement of the essential and supreme aim of the Organization: international peace and solidarity. The co-operation of all the nations, large and small, militarily weak or strong, whatever their creed, race or political organization, will make it possible to build a lasting world peace, a peace which will not consist merely of the absence of war, but which will be founded on justice, law, liberty and the well-being of all mankind. Those are the objectives of this draft resolution.

29. One point, however, deserves particular attention. While this draft resolution calls upon the small States to play an active part in maintaining peace and security, it also imposes upon them grave and weighty responsibilities already laid down in the Charter. In voting for this draft resolution, every one of us will shoulder a serious obligation, a heavy responsibility. Every one of us must return to his country conscious of his duty to do his utmost for the adoption of the legal, economic and military measures required to place our countries in a legal and material position to discharge, whenever necessary, the responsibility which we are assuming in this historic hour.

30. We have been called upon to participate in the organization of security because of the failure of the great countries brought about by the recalcitrant attitude of one of them. We must not let a security based on the co-operation of all the countries, large and small, fail because of the indifference, unconcern or inertia of the small countries. We have criticized the failure of the great Powers so much that we dare not fail ourselves. . . .

31. MR. DULLES (United States of America): The First Committee has brought us a proposal which we can accept as a good policy of insurance against a third world war. The terms of this proposal are in themselves nothing novel. It is the Charter programme of seeking to deter aggression by being able quickly to expose and to suppress aggression. That Charter programme in turn was based upon the experience of the world during the decade of the 1930's.

36. Today the aggressors are largely broken and we surely breathe more freely than we did on Sunday, 25 June. But our respite may be short if we go on trusting to luck. We must organize dependably the collective will to resist aggression. If the Security Council does not do so, then this Assembly

must do what it can by invoking its residual power of recommendation. That is what we shall do by adopting the first draft resolution submitted by the First Committee.

40. In addition to the principal draft resolution to which I have already referred, there is another important draft resolution which was initiated by Iraq and Syria and which recommends to the permanent members of the Security Council that they should meet and discuss, collectively or otherwise, problems likely to threaten international peace. That draft resolution was approved unanimously. The United States was happy to support it for, as Secretary of State Acheson said in the course of our general debate and as President Truman told us last week, the United States will always be ready and willing to negotiate with a sincere desire to solve problems.

41. It should, I think, be borne in mind that what this draft resolution refers to as the fundamental difference which now dangerously divides the world is not a difference of a kind on which the so-called great Powers can readily compromise, for that fundamental issue deeply concerns others, and most of all it concerns the smaller nations.

46. The basic problem, as we see it, is to create enough collective strength to protect the freedom of the people who want to be free. The United States is willing to contribute to that strength, and indeed we have already contributed largely. We do so because we do not believe in a "one world" of enforced conformity. We believe that peace does not depend upon forcibly ironing out differences, but that peace should permit people to respond in their own distinctive ways to their own distinctive needs and aspirations and, for example, to practise socialism, private enterprise or even communism, if they desire. The people of the United States feel a sense of common destiny with other free peoples, even though we disagree with them. That is the key to an understanding of our foreign policy.

47. Of course, when a materially strong Power like the United States contributes preponderantly to a common cause, that fact automatically exposes it to the charge of seeking to dominate and extend its power in the world. No one who knows the people of the United States, no one who takes into account our record as a major victor in two world wars, credits those charges. But many do not know of their own knowledge, and they are misled by false propaganda.

48. That fact is an added reason why the United States wants the new conditions which would be created by the main draft resolution now before the General Assembly. Under that resolution, if implemented, the defensive power of the free world will be more evenly distributed, so that there will not be so great a dependence upon one or two; each Member nation will maintain some forces available to serve as United Nations units. Of course, in many cases that force would be small, but the total would be large and its composite character would itself bear eloquent testimony to the collective will behind it.

49. Then, too, under that resolution, the direction of concerted action

will be more securely lodged in the United Nations, so as to reduce the risk that force might be used to promote distinctly national ambitions. As the world moves in the path that this resolution defines, it will move nearer and nearer to the Charter ideal, the ideal of impressing armed force, with a trust, so that it will not be used, as our Charter says, save in the common interest, a common interest as found by a body that is responsive to the moral judgment of mankind.

50. The step marked by this draft resolution is along a path that is as yet untravelled. We are explorers, but we can proceed, confident that we are taking a historic step towards reaching the great goal of a peace that will be both durable and just.

51. GENERAL ROMULO (Philippines): Few draft resolutions have been debated so minutely and exhaustively in committee as the first draft resolution now before the General Assembly. This is only as it should be. I doubt whether any single act of the United Nations, other than the adoption of the Charter, will loom so large and vital as this in the history of the Organization.

52. The draft resolution now before the General Assembly has been attacked on legal and constitutional grounds. The argument that, by the terms of the resolution, the General Assembly would usurp the functions and powers of the Security Council, was advanced in the First Committee with great force and skill by Mr. Vyshinsky and others. I am sure it will be repeated here again. That argument was met with the explanation that no such usurpation is intended or, indeed, will ever take place, and that the sole aim and purpose of the proposal is to enable the United Nations, through its most representative organ—the General Assembly—to consider breaches of the peace and acts of aggression and to make suitable recommendations thereon whenever the Security Council is prevented from taking action by reason of the veto.

53. The principle bears repeating: while the Security Council has primary responsibility for the maintenance of peace and security, this responsibility is not exclusive, and the General Assembly may, in default of a decision by the Security Council, make appropriate recommendations to the Member States to curb a breach of the peace or an act of aggression. This authority springs from the broad powers of the General Assembly under the Charter, from the United Nations' inherent right of survival and from its supreme responsibility to all the world's peoples to preserve the peace. No legal technicality, however brilliantly advanced, can prevail against the overriding force of this threefold principle.

54. The argument based on the principle of the inviolability of the Charter must be rejected as a pretext once it can be shown, as indeed it has been shown, that the proposal before us, far from nullifying the Charter, seeks rather to give it life and to make it work. The whole purpose of this proposal rests upon a reasonable interpretation of our fundamental law.

55. The struggle which has become familiar in the political histories of

most countries, between a strict and a liberal interpretation of the constitution, is now being re-enacted among us with equal bitterness and tenacity of purpose. However, reason and common sense must prevail, for growth is the genius of life, and those who stultify life are sundered and broken in the end.

56. Among nations, as among men, the first law is the law of survival. Long ago, it was said that the Sabbath was made for man and not man for the Sabbath. We say, with equal conviction, that the nations were not made for the Charter but the Charter for the nations which desire peace with all their hearts. To hold a contrary view would be, as it was two thousand years ago, to betray a certain poverty of conscience and imagination, for it was intended from the very beginning that the Charter should be much more than a mere instrument for the adjustment of the rival political claims and ambitions of the great Powers, a tool to be cast aside at the first sign of disagreement among them. The Charter was and is a covenant among the peoples of the world, by which they have resolved to abolish the scourge of war.

57. We are committed to this world-embracing purpose, with the support of all the great Powers if possible, but without the sanction of any of them if necessary.

169. Mr. Michalowski (Poland): At the last stage of the discussion on what is known as the Acheson plan, we find ourselves almost at the same point where we were at the beginning of our long discussion in the First Committee.

170. The first draft resolution before us is bad. It not only violates the law, but it is illegal as well as harmful and dangerous for the future of our Organization.

171. Before the voting machine is put into motion and before you put the stamp of doubtful legality on this draft resolution, the Polish delegation deems it its duty to raise its voice once more in protest and in warning. We shall briefly reiterate our viewpoint because our arguments, in our opinion, prove irrefutably the unacceptability of this draft resolution, and explain our negative attitude to it.

172. We had the opportunity to state our arguments very extensively during the discussions in the First Committee. We heard there from many delegations crushing and irrefutable legal criticisms of the principles of the draft resolution. Even in the speeches of those representatives who on the last day mechanically raised their right hands in affirmation or cautiously retired behind the safe position of abstention, we could hear expressions of uncertainty and anxiety, expressions of doubt and reservations.

173. Our arguments have not been refuted by the sponsors of the draft resolution. The doubts have not been dispelled; they have merely been belittled through phraseology and false pathos. Anxieties have not been allayed, they have been silenced by pressure and strangled by threats. It could not be otherwise. This draft resolution was intended to heal our

Organization and to diminish the international tension, but if it is erroneous and illegal, it is so first of all because it is based on a false evaluation of the reasons of the political tension, and on a lack of correct diagnosis of the sickness which is to be cured.

174. The threat of a new war which hangs over mankind did not develop spontaneously. It was built up by the spreading of false ideas, for instance, the idea of the impossibility of political and economic co-operation between two different systems, namely, socialism and capitalism. It was built up by harmful myths, for instance, the myth that the "American way of life" must be imposed upon all the nations of the world. It was built up by the breaking of mutual understandings and agreements forged in the fires of the last just war; thus, for instance, the four-Power agreement for the control of Germany has been broken and the agreements on the liquidation of the consequences of the war, on demilitarization, on denazification and on democratization have been violated.

175. The spark of a new conflict has been fanned on by efforts to subordinate economically the major part of the world to one big Power, to one centre of political control. The Marshall Plan, the loans with political strings attached to them, the discrimination in international trade are well known facts. Furthermore, the creation of a military bloc, the North Atlantic Treaty and projects of new pacts, the enormous programme of armaments within the United States, the thrusting of armaments programmes on other nations, the promotion of war hysteria, warmongering, the threats to use the atomic and hydrogen bombs and, finally, the open aggression on Korea—all these are but a short enumeration, but a part of those facts and actions which have resulted in the tense situation in which we find ourselves at present.

176. Mr. Acheson did not remember—or rather he preferred not to remember—all those facts while drafting his resolution. . . .

301ST MEETING OF THE GENERAL ASSEMBLY*

33. Mr. Vyshinsky (Union of Soviet Socialist Republics): When the question included in the agenda of the General Assembly under the title "United action for peace" was considered by the First Committee, the USSR delegation stated that it was prepared to support a number of the provisions of the seven-Power draft, but that it also had some amendments and objections to put forward regarding the other provisions in the draft.

34. The delegation of the Soviet Union supports all proposals which are genuinely designed to strengthen international peace and security, which are directed towards the noble objective of averting the danger of new wars. The USSR has always supported, still supports, and will continue to support all measures for peace, even when these measures are incomplete and indecisive, and even if, on that account, they fall short of what we want. If,

* General Assembly, *Official Records,* 5th session, 301st meeting (November 2, 1950), pp. 324-335.

however, under these conditions, such measures are really directed towards strengthening peace, averting the threat of another war and ensuring the security of nations, the Soviet Union is always prepared to support them with firmness and decision.

35. When the USSR is faced with measures which are acceptable in principle, in substance, but which have certain shortcomings, the delegation of the Soviet Union considers itself bound—and will consider itself bound—to correct such mistakes, and to improve and strengthen the measures for peace, in order to achieve better and more positive results in that important task, which affects the vital interests of many millions of people.

36. When this question was discussed in the First Committee, therefore, the USSR delegation submitted a number of amendments to the seven-Power draft resolution. Some—unfortunately very few—were adopted, others were rejected. We are now submitting these amendments to the General Assembly once more, for we firmly believe that if the seven-Power draft resolution, which has now been submitted as a draft resolution of the First Committee, is adopted by the General Assembly without taking these amendments into account and without the requisite improvements, the resolution before us will not effectively ensure the strengthening of peace but, on the contrary, will seriously endanger the cause of peace and will thus do more harm than good. That is why it is absolutely essential to include in the text the various amendments on which the delegation of the Soviet Union, among others, is insisting. . . .

109. At first it was sought to by-pass the Security Council by establishing the Interim Committee. That did not work, and the Interim Committee seems to have had its day. Now another instrument is sought, and found—the General Assembly. But how are they to go about it? A pretext must be found. They therefore invented the paralysis of the Security Council—a paralysis which they brought about themselves and which they say consists in the failure of the Security Council to exercise its functions. There are among us jurists or would-be jurists, or, at any rate, interpreters of the Charter—for instance, the representative of Cuba—who actually state that where the Charter says "functions" it means "action"—some sort of action—and if somebody—meaning the Security Council—does not act, he is not exercising his functions.

110. Let us analyse this question. It is true that Article 12 of the Charter says that, while the Security Council is exercising its functions, the General Assembly shall not make any recommendations with regard to the questions involved. The conclusion is drawn that the Security Council must be doing something. That is quite true, it must. But what must it be doing?

111. Let us consider the Charter. In Chapter V of the Charter on the Security Council, there is a special section entitled "Functions and Powers," which comprises Articles 24, 25 and 26. There you have three articles on the functions of the Security Council. In addition, as Article 24 mentions Chapters VI, VII, VIII and XII, those chapters also relate to those functions.

All the provisions contained therein define the functions of the Council, and there is no need to guess or invent anything, as the Cuban representative has. The functions are defined in the Charter. What are they? These functions are: prompt and effective action, examination of any dispute arising between States or of any situation, investigation of disputes, recommendation of measures, study of these questions, adoption of measures to remove the danger of the situation, etc. Those are all its functions.

112. What would be your argument, then, in the following case? The Security Council is considering a question of aggression. Suppose State A is complaining about State B. Three members of the Security Council consider that A has committed aggression against B; but two members consider that B is the aggressor. So those members of the Security Council cannot settle the question at all. I ask you, is the Council carrying out its functions or not? The reply is that it is not carrying out its functions, because it has not found that either State is the aggressor. But the Council's function is not necessarily to find, in every case, that aggression has been committed. It is possible that someone accuses a State of aggression although there is at the time no reason to conclude that aggression has taken place. Perhaps someone accuses State X of aggression when in actual fact there are no grounds, or even any evidence that State X is the aggressor. However, one or two members of the Security Council insist that X is in fact the aggressor, while the remainder do not agree; or perhaps one of the remainder, as it is perfectly entitled to do, does not agree that there is aggression.

113. In such a case, according to the representative of Cuba and his colleagues, the Security Council is paralysed and inactive. Does that mean that if you, the majority, agree with this draft resolution, while several delegations, including mine, do not agree with it, I am inactive when I oppose you? Will you say that I am not carrying out my functions as a member of the General Assembly when I oppose you? Will you say that only you are carrying out your functions because you support that draft resolution, which you wish at all costs to have adopted here?

114. Is that logical? I think that the Cuban representative became so entangled that even Professor Kelsen could not help him to disentangle himself. I understand, of course, that the aim of any organ in exercising its functions should be to accomplish the tasks assigned to it. That is indisputable. However, this aim is achieved, when aggression is the issue, not only by removing a threat of aggression, but also by finding that no such threat exists. Of course the Council is discharging its functions in such a case too. Consequently, the fact that the Security Council has not found, in such a case, that there is a threat, although certain parties desired it to do so, does not mean that the Security Council is paralysed, or inactive, or not discharging its functions. You say that it is discharging its functions only when it finds that there is aggression. What if it does not find that there is aggression? This amounts to saying that the Security Council discharges its functions only when it acts in accordance with the will of the majority. But

where is such a provision laid down? On the contrary, it is stated in the Charter itself, in Article 27, paragraph 2, that any permanent member of the Security Council has the right to disagree with the majority and in such case there is no decision. Consequently that rule should be changed if you do not consider it appropriate. But while it remains in force, it must be observed; it must not be violated; it must not be set aside by recourse to all kinds of artifices and completely incomprehensible arguments such as those put forward here by the representative of Cuba.

115. I thus come to the conclusion that the sickness of the Security Council has been incorrectly diagnosed, since, in fact, that which is regarded at the sickness—paralysis—is neither sickness nor paralysis. What is regarded by some as non-discharge of functions is not non-discharge of functions, as the Council's function is not necessarily to accept the majority decision, however the majority may justify that decision; the Council's function is to consider the situation and take a decision on the question whether there is or is not aggression. If there is aggression, measures must be taken to combat it. If there is no aggression, nothing need be done. . . .

133. But what do you propose in your draft resolution? Do you not propose therein, starting with the preamble and proceeding through the various sections of the operative part, that armed forces should be transferred to the control of the General Assembly? Since Article 11, paragraph 2 also applies, do you not disregard Chapter VII of the Charter where, beginning with Article 43, it is expressly stated that only the Military Staff Committee shall be responsible under the Security Council for the direction of armed forces, and that they may be used only by decision of the Security Council and not of the General Assembly, since Article 11, paragraph 2 also applies?

134. Consequently, can it honestly be said that we deny the General Assembly the right to decide questions relating to the maintenance of peace and security? That is not true; we do not dispute that right. That right is laid down in Articles 10 and 11, since the General Assembly has the right to consider all questions relating to the maintenance of peace and security, and not only questions which do not relate to peace and security. But when the Security Council is considering such questions, then, in accordance with Article 12, the General Assembly may merely consider them and does not have the right to make recommendations; in the same way, when the measures envisaged call for action in the sense of enforcement action, particularly by means of armed forces, the General Assembly can do nothing, since the Charter does not give it the right to act.

135. That is how the matter stands under the law, under the Charter. But in reply to this we are told that we cannot permit the Council to be paralysed. But you say it is paralysed only when you fail to push your decisions through the Security Council. Only then is it "paralysed." But if it accepts your decisions, then it is not paralysed. Thus you wish to turn the Security Council into a tool, to make it an instrument, of your policy. As

you are unable to do that with the veto in existence, you attack the veto. But as you are afraid of destroying the veto because, first, you will not succeed in doing so without destroying this Organization, and, secondly, because you yourselves wish to preserve the veto for your own future use, you devise a means whereby you may remain apparently loyal to the Charter and at the same time gain all the advantages of not carrying out its requirements.

136. That is the simple philosophy of your whole policy. And it is idle to attempt to say that nothing is changed here, that the Charter remains as before, that the Security Council remains as before. Nothing remains as before, and in particular the basic principles of the Charter are being thrown on the scrap heap.

137. Consequently we cannot agree to the proposals contained in your draft resolution, which would destroy the Charter and obstruct the Security Council, place it somewhere in the background, remove it from the front line of the struggle for peace and make it possible to carry on that struggle exclusively through the General Assembly where you have a majority, where you are always able to twist any question whichever way you want whether you are acting legally or illegally.

138. I shall go even farther: you act more energetically when you violate the law by your proposals, than you act when you are obliged to observe the law. This is the defect, the basic defect in your draft resolution. We therefore consider that it is our duty, in conscience, and as Members of the United Nations, to insist that such a draft should be rejected, or at least that those parts of the draft which are incompatible with the law by which we must be guided—that is, the Charter—should be amended in the way we have proposed, guided solely by the true interests of our Organization, by respect for the law of our Organization and for its constitution—the Charter.

302ND MEETING OF THE GENERAL ASSEMBLY*

1. MR. PEARSON (Canada): As one of the sponsors of the first draft resolution which is now before the General Assembly, I should like to add a few words concerning it before the vote is taken, and also a few words— although it is tempting to say more than a few words—on the statements made to the General Assembly by the leader of the Soviet Union delegation.

2. When he spoke yesterday, Mr. Vyshinsky complained of the rattle and the thunder of our speeches in support of this draft resolution. . . .

3. Then what did he do in his own speech? When he came to the rostrum, he attempted to drag the debate down to the level of an attack on various individuals, and more particularly on Mr. Dulles.

10. This draft resolution has been attacked, and very vigorously attacked, as aimed against, for one thing, the unanimity of the great Powers. That, as I see it, is nonsense. No one has more to gain from such unanimity

* General Assembly, *Official Records,* 5th session, 302nd meeting (November 3, 1950), pp. 341-343.

than the smaller and middle-sized Powers. But what is the use of a unanimity which can be achieved only by doing nothing, which is used as a cloak for obstruction and reaction? That kind of unanimity is meaningless and will get us nowhere.

11. The draft resolution has also been attacked as a violation of the Charter. In this Assembly some honest doubts have been expressed about its constitutionality, and, as honest doubts, the sponsors of the draft resolution respect them. Nevertheless, we feel convinced that the draft resolution is within the terms of the Charter. We believe that the General Assembly has the power to make recommendations on the subjects dealt with therein, although it would not have the power to make decisions which would automatically impose commitments or enforcement obligations on the Members of the United Nations.

12. There has been a great deal of legal argument about this draft resolution, but I suspect that nothing that we can do or say on that subject will make any impression on the delegations of the Soviet bloc, which keep on repeating that it is a flagrant violation of the Charter.

16. In the first draft resolution, we are making further progress toward organizing collective security. That is our goal. It is a good goal, and it is one which we are determined to reach, especially we of the smaller and middle Powers who know that by no other means can our security be ensured against those who threaten it. What this resolution does has been, I think, sufficiently explained by previous speakers, but let me mention one or two things which it does not do.

17. It does not sabotage the Security Council. It merely establishes peace machinery under the General Assembly to supplement the Security Council when the latter body sabotages itself. If the Security Council can work effectively to defend the peace and defeat the aggressor, this resolution will never have to be invoked. And no one will be more pleased by that than its sponsors and supporters.

18. Also, this resolution does not, as some friendly critics in Asia have suggested, organize the Assembly for war. It merely lays down methods by which, through General Assembly action, Members of the United Nations can implement obligations already undertaken under the Charter.

19. Thirdly, this resolution does not set up an international force. It recommends that Members should place national contingents at the disposal of the United Nations to carry out obligations and recommendations which those Members accept. These contingents must be equipped, trained and ready to join in international police action, so that, if a 27 June 1950 occurs again, the United Nations will have forces from many of its Members ready to meet the aggression, and not from one or two alone. To make this provision effective—the provision in paragraph 8—it will not be enough for a few countries to take the action recommended. We must all, within the measure of our capacities, contribute to its implementation. That will be the

test of the sincerity of our words in favour of collective security, and that will be the test of the effectiveness of this new effort to put international force behind the collective will for peace of the United Nations.

20. Finally, this resolution, even if it is fully implemented, will not of itself bring peace. As section E indicates—and for that section we are indebted to the Chilean delegation—peace, in the long run, will be achieved only by establishing conditions of economic and social decency and security throughout the world. In the shorter run, peace will be achieved if the stronger Powers settle the problems which now so tragically divide them and which threaten to engulf us all in the tragic consequences of failure.

21. In this draft resolution we have made a bold step forward toward a genuine and effective system of collective security. This is our answer to those who would frustrate and make futile the efforts of the Security Council to carry out the task for which it has primary responsibility, namely, the maintenance of international peace and security. This draft resolution is also our warning to those who would threaten the peace and who are tempted to commit aggression. If they yield to this temptation, they will not only find opposed to them the collective conscience of the peaceful world, expressed through the United Nations, they will also find that this conscience can express itself through international forces organized and equipped to carry out the decisions of our world Organization, decisions which will have no other purpose than the defence of peace. We are organizing collective security not for war but to prevent war, not for the pursuit of national policy but for the defence of international peace. In this high endeavour, all men of good will everywhere and all nations which follow the policies of peace will be on our side. . . .

Editor's Note: After voting down the amendments proposed by the Soviet Union, the General Assembly adopted the report of the First Committee 52 votes to 5, with 2 abstentions, See General Assembly, *Official Records, 5th* session, 302nd meeting (November 3, 1950), pp. 345-347.

On the Interpretation of Treaties*

Myres S. McDougal and Richard N. Gardner

The Fallacy of the "Unambiguous Meaning"

. . . It is no longer revolutionary, however, to point out that the effort to impose upon any legal language—especially upon language of a complicated multilateral treaty like the United Nations Charter—an "absolute," "literal," "plain," or "natural" meaning puts an impossible burden on words. "The view that the verbal expression of a legal norm has only one 'true' meaning which can be discovered by correct interpretation," Professor Kelsen writes, "is a fiction, adopted to maintain the illusion of legal security, to make the law-seeking public believe that there is only one possible answer to the question of law in a concrete case." The main point was long ago generalized by Dean Wigmore:

> There can be, in the nature of things, no absoluteness of standard in interpretation. . . . The fallacy consists in assuming that there is or ever can be *some one real* or absolute meaning. In truth, there can be only *some person's* meaning. . . .

To this succinct statement, Dean Wigmore might well have added: not only *"some person's* meaning," but some person's meaning in *relevant context*. It is the principal lesson of contemporary semantics that all words, legal and otherwise, take their complete meaning from such a context. For understanding any communication the relevant and indispensable questions are: Who, says What, to Whom, for what Objectives, How, under what Conditions, and with what Effects. Omission of any element of this inquiry leaves an observer in that degree with inadequate or false orientation. It should need no further emphasis today that the words of an international agreement cannot be taken as timeless absolutes; apart from their uses in context,

* Myres S. McDougal and Richard N. Gardner, "The Veto and the Charter: An Interpretation for Survival," *Yale Law Journal,* Vol. 60, No. 1 (January 1951), pp. 262-292. Reprinted by permission of the authors and the copyright holder from the *Yale Law Journal.* Single issues, as well as back issues available at $2.50 from Fred B. Rothman, 57 Leuning Street, South Hackensack, New Jersey. Subscription $10.00 per volume available from Business Office, Yale Law Journal, 401-A Yale Station, New Haven, Connecticut 06520. Copyright © 1950, by the Yale Law Journal Company. Myres S. McDougal is currently Sterling Professor of Law at Yale University. He is the co-author of *Property, Wealth, and Land* (1948), *Studies in World Public Order* (1960), and *The Public Order of the Oceans* (1962). Richard N. Gardner was formerly Professor of Law, Columbia University and is currently Deputy Assistant Secretary of State for International Organization Affairs. He is the author of *Sterling-Dollar Diplomacy* (1963) and *In Pursuit of World Order* (1964).

such words, like other words, are but "shapes on paper" or "agitations in the air." This common sense insight, long accepted with respect to national constitutions and authoritative doctrine, is made fully explicit with respect to treaties by the *Harvard Research*:

[T]he bare words of a treaty have significance only as they may be taken as expressions of the purpose or design of the parties which employed them; they have a 'meaning' only as they are considered in the light of the whole setting in which they are employed. To purport to attribute a 'clear,' a 'natural,' or a pre-existing meaning to them apart from that setting is to ignore the fact that words may be given any meaning which the parties using them may agree to give them, and that few words have an exact and single meaning. 'Such is the inevitable imperfection and ambiguity of all human language, that the mere words alone of any writing, literally expounded, will go a very little way towards explaining its meaning.'

An observer who seeks to cloak his interpretation in some fanciful depersonalized, disembodied "literal" meaning which transcends context merely conceals from himself, and perhaps from others, his own active role, and the context he substitutes, in the choices he makes. The alleged canon that "it is not allowable to interpret what has no need of interpretation" or as otherwise stated, that "one cannot disturb a plain meaning," is little more than a myopic platitude which serves to maintain a primitive and irrational faith in the omnipotence of words.

A second, and only less vulnerable, form of the assumption of "unambiguous meaning" is that it is possible for contemporary interpreters to divine in detail the "true" or "real" *intention* of agreement makers of an earlier day. When an agreement of any importance is effected among two or more nation-states the relevant events include, at the minimum: a great variety of actors (negotiators, drafters, approvers, ratifiers), expressing agreement through verbal forms of all degrees of generality or precision, by all the methods known to international law, for implementation of a great variety of both short-run and long-term objectives, under the peculiar conditions and perspectives of their day, and with certain designed and undesigned effects upon the expectations of all the parties and the distribution of values among them. When at some later date decision-makers are confronted with the necessity of interpreting this agreement, the events relevant for understanding again include at a minimum: certain interpreters (located in value and institutional position), applying traditional criteria of interpretation, to the words and acts of the earlier day and to the subsequent practice of the parties under the agreement, for certain contemporary objectives, under the conditions and perspectives of their day, and with certain obvious effects upon the distribution of values among the parties. From this comprehensive perspective of the relevant events, it is wholly fantastic to assume either, first, that the framers of the original agreement can project their vision and anticipate all the more specific details of the evolving future or agree upon a common purpose with respect to all these details or draft so precisely as to remove all ambiguity with respect to such common purpose, or, secondly, that the later interpreters of the agreement working in a new total context, with their own contemporary objectives and conscious of many changes in conditions since the making of the agreement, can resurrect in detail the subjectivities of the original framers of the agreement and ascertain what was their clear intent concerning the new events confronting the interpreter. For an excellent statement of the general point in more traditional language we turn again to the *Harvard Research*:

The process of interpretation, rightly conceived, cannot be regarded as a mere mechanical one of drawing inevitable meanings from the words in a text, or of searching for and discovering some preexisting specific intention of the parties with respect to every situation arising under a treaty. It is precisely because the words used in an instrument rarely have exact and single meanings, and because all possible situations which may arise under it cannot be, or at least are not, forseen and expressly provided for by the parties at the time of its drafting that the necessity for interpretation occurs. In most instances therefore, interpretation involves *giving* a meaning to a text."

It is for these reasons, therefore, that each generation must, whatever its preference, in considerable measure interpret its legacy of agreements, as well as of other authoritative doctrine, in terms of contemporary conditions and objectives. Interpreters differ most strikingly only in the degree to which they are conscious of this necessity.

Interpretation by Major Purposes: The Rational Alternative

It is not intended, however, by this analysis to suggest that concern for the "intent" of framers of agreements is in all measure irrational or that contemporary interpreters can reasonably or legally remake or unmake agreements at their arbitrary pleasure. On the contrary, our concern is, like that of most commentators today, to clarify a mode of interpretation which can give the most rational effect to the intent of framers in so far as they can achieve a common intent and express it. Though it is beyond the competence of framers of agreements to anticipate in utmost detail the unfolding events of the future or to specify with exact precision the minute modalities of their projected cooperation with respect to events and conditions constantly changing, it is possible for them to project both a primary pattern of expectations with respect to their major general objectives, and, with varying degrees of precision, even a secondary pattern of the institutional means by which their objectives are to be effected. When the march of events inevitably lays bare ambiguities and alternatives of interpretation with respect to the secondary institutional means so prescribed, even the most modest deference to rationality must require that interpretation of such means which best promotes the major purposes for which they were established. Hence the principle of interpretation most widely supported by disinterested authorities today is that international agreements must be interpreted primarily in terms of the major, general purposes they are intended to serve. Thus, the *Harvard Research,* after insisting that the process of interpretation rightly conceived requires the *giving,* and not simply the finding, or a meaning, continues that the meaning to be given is "not just any meaning which appeals to the interpreter to be sure, but a meaning which, in the light of the test under consideration and of all the concomitant circumstances of the particular case at hand, appears in his considered judgment to be the one that is logical, reasonable, and most likely to accord with and to effectuate the larger general purpose which the parties desired the treaty to serve." In the blackletter of its proposed *Draft Convention on the Law of Treaties,* the *Research* is concise, comprehensive, and definitive:

A treaty is to be interpreted in the light of the general purpose which it is intended to serve. The historical background of the treaty, *travaux préparatoires,* the circumstances of the parties at the time the treaty was entered into, the change in these circumstances sought to be affected, the subsequent conduct of the parties in applying the provisions of the treaty, and the conditions prevailing at the time interpretation is being made, are to be considered in connection with the general purpose which the treaty is intended to serve.

In one form of statement or another, this principle is both of the most ancient lineage and, as indicated, is today accepted and honored by the overwhelming weight of authority, official and unofficial. Professor Lauterpacht has even summarized:

. . . The work of the Permanent Court has shown that alongside the fundamental principle of intepretation, namely, that effect is to be given to the intention of the parties, full use can be made of another hardly less important principle, namely, that the treaty must remain effective rather than ineffective. *Res magis valeat quam pereat.* It is a major principle, in the light of which the intention of the parties must always be interpreted, even to the extent of disregarding the letter of the instrument and of reading into it something which, on the face of it, it does not contain.

Fortunately, it is not necessary to do violence to the words of Article 27 (3) of the United Nations Charter in order to give those words a meaning which will promote, rather than defeat, the purposes for which the United Nations was established. . . .

"Uniting for Peace": The General Assembly Acts for Survival

The General Assembly has also, fortunately, gone on record . . . as in favor of liberal principles of interpretation by major purposes. Interpretation of the Charter in terms of its primary design as an instrument of collective security prevailed in recent meetings of the Assembly to strengthen the machinery of the United Nations for resisting aggression. The General Assembly overwhelmingly adopted the proposals for "United Action for Peace," framed to enable enforcement action by members in cases where the

Security Council is paralyzed by use of the veto. These proposals were also met by Soviet charges of "illegality" and it is worth examining these charges briefly to demonstrate the extremes to which advocacy of "strict" interpretation and single power domination can lead.

The heart of the resolutions of "United Action for Peace" passed November 3 by the General Assembly is the provision that an emergency meeting of the General Assembly can be held at 24 hours notice upon the vote of any seven members of the Security Council in the event that the Council is prevented by the veto from exercising its primary responsibility for international peace and security. Under this provision, the General Assembly would make "appropriate recommendation to members for collective measures, including in the case of a breach of the peace or act of aggression the use of armed force when necessary." Other provisions call for the establishment of a Peace Observation Commission working under the authority of the General Assembly to report on situations of international tension; a Collective Measures Committee to study methods for improving the machinery of collective security; and national contingents of member nations to be held ready to deal with cases of aggression. These resolutions represent the three elements basic to any system of collective security—a reliable means of information to apprehend aggression, a prompt and dependable central initiative to authorize enforcement measures, and a military power to carry out those measures. Since the veto prevents the Security Council from performing any of these functions, the General Assembly decided that it was necessary to organize new procedures under its own powers if such functions were to be carried out at all.

The same charge of "illegality" that followed the attempt to repel aggression in Korea was made against this new attempt to strengthen the capacity of the United Nations to resist aggression in the future. Mr. Vishinsky, in debates before the General Assembly, stated the position of his government simply and clearly. In his view, the Security Council had the exclusive authority to take enforcement action under the Charter. If, in the absence of unanimity among the great powers, the Security Council was unable to take collective measures against aggression, the General Assembly was precluded from making attempts of its own to restore peace and security. For these conclusions Vishinsky cited that section of Article 12 which provides that the General Assembly shall not make recommendations "while the Security Council is exercising in respect to any dispute or situation the functions assigned to it in the present Charter." He cited also the provisions of Article 11, paragraph 2 to the effect that questions relating to the maintenance of international peace and security "on which action is necessary shall be referred to the Security Council by the General Assembly either before or after discussion." The letter of the Charter and the "principle of unanimity," it was contended, combined to render the "United Action for Peace" proposals entirely illegal.

These arguments . . . represent attempts to find in the Charter a "meaning" both more restrictive than that which the words in context require and more limited than that which has been permitted in practice or that which is required to effectuate the purposes of the organization. In the first place, the Security Council was given "primary," not "exclusive" responsibility for the maintenance of international peace. Nothing in the Charter requires the conclusion that the Security Council is the only organ that can be used to implement that purpose. The Charter does preclude the General Assembly from making recommendations while the Council is exercising its functions. But an interpretation designed to promote the major purpose of the United Nations need not maintain, in oblivion to fact, that the Council is "exercising . . . the functions assigned to it" when a veto by a permanent member prevents it from doing so.

There is similarly little force in the reference to the necessity for the Assembly to refer to the Council questions relating to international peace "on which action is necessary." This has on a number of occasions been interpreted to refer only to mandatory acts of the Assembly, not to resolutions which rely only on the moral obligations of the members for their effectiveness. Such an interpretation is reinforced by reference to the requirement that these provisions "shall not limit the general scope" of the broad provisions of Article 10 enabling the General Assembly to "discuss any questions or any matters within the scope of the present Charter." It should be remembered that this provision was exacted by the small powers at San Francisco as the price of the veto.

The almost unanimous adoptions by the General Assembly of the "United Action for Peace" resolutions represents an encouraging example of interpretation of the Charter in terms of its major purposes. This interpretation does indeed reflect a change in emphasis regarding the procedures by which the United Nations will deal with threats to international peace and security. It was originally hoped that there would be sufficient unanimity among the great powers to enable the organization to require the mandatory action of all the members to repel aggression. In the absence of that unanimity resort has been made to other provisions of the Charter enabling the United Nations to achieve security by recommending the voluntary action of its members. There is nothing "illegal" about this change. It is simply a rational evolution, well within the words of the Charter, to meet new and unanticipated contingencies.

To call such a development a violation of the principle of unanimity is again to mistake the whole place of that principle in the United Nations system. This was effectively pointed out during the General Assembly debates by the delegate of Cuba:

The Organization of the United Nations is in existence, and it is to be justified, uniquely and solely, in the achievement of those aims for which it was set up. The Charter provides the procedures and means whereby it is possible to fulfill such aims. Among them is the principle of unanimity; it is a mere method, a means for the fulfillment of a function. When there is a dispute or a conflict between the means and the end, between the procedure and the function or aim which it tries to achieve, it is the first which loses its validity and it is the fundamental obligation of the Charter which prevails, namely, to seek by other means or other procedure, the achievement of the aims of the organization. . . .

Collective Defense Indispensable to World Order

The principal issue in interpreting relevant provisions of the Charter is therefore sharp and clear: it is whether the vast majority of the members of the United Nations can so read their Charter, despite unanticipated obstructions, as to make the organization an effective instrument for collective security and its other purposes or whether a single member can impose its will to bring the organization and its purposes to ruin. The choice is, in a blunt literality for once relevant, a choice between life and death, between survival and destruction—not for the organization alone, but also for the peace and freedom it was designed to secure. It is indeed unfortunate that the hoped-for unanimity among the great powers has not been forthcoming, that only a few years after the end of the Second World War the peoples of the free world are faced with a new threat of unprecedented magnitude. It would be the worst kind of folly, however, to think that any "principle of unanimity" stands in the way of meeting that threat through the organized procedures lawfully provided for in the United Nations Charter. Member states that do not hang together and combine their strength, will certainly hang separately. Although there is not at present enough order in the world community, or strength in its organization, to compel participation in collective measures, there is no reason why the principles of right and justice agreed to by a majority of the United Nations should not be enforced on a voluntary basis. So modest a step toward an enforceable international law cannot of itself insure peace and freedom. But it is indispensable to the other necessary measures. Without the protection against aggression that their combined strength can secure, member states cannot be expected to cooperate freely and fully for the promotion of human rights, enlightenment, health, wealth and other values. If the vast majority of the United Nations can, however, effectively organize their strength against aggression, international law, instead of being made to await an "order" which never arrives, may perhaps be made an instrument for that integration of many measures which is an essential prerequisite to lasting peace.

The Idea of Collective Security*

Roland N. Stromberg

"Emotion, not intellect, is the dynamic of history," as H. N. Brailsford has observed. Of the great ideas which have captured men's imaginations, in the modern democratic age at least, most have arisen from some urgent emotional need, not from a strictly rational analysis. This was remarkably true of the new concept of international relations that emerged from Versailles in 1919. The idea of collective security certainly did not come from the more experienced diplomats and statesmen, who were in the main quite sceptical about it. It came from journalists, moralists, popular politicians, from "the people"; it responded to a cry of protest against the intolerable existence of world war and a demand for reassurance that such wars be not permitted to happen again. This popular and unsophisticated call for the abolition of war insistently required some visible sign of a wholly new spirit. The planners of peace had to contrive some scheme to meet this demand, and they scurried about rather frantically trying to make reason match emotion. The League of Nations (a poetic rather than an accurate title, for nation is not a political term) was a mystical symbol born of the shattering experience of 1914-18, with little to do with logic. But it soon acquired great intellectual respectability, and the world has been struggling to make it practical ever since. It has had, indeed, a remarkable sanctity, criticism of it being almost an act of impiety in the United States.

This mystical emotion came mostly from the Anglo-Saxon peoples. There was a certain enthusiasm in France, but too much method could be detected in the French madness. Italy contributed little to the League except a very curious plan which indicated how differently a "proletarian" nation, as Italy called herself, looked at the problem: the new international organization should be a device for redistributing the good things of the earth. The defeated powers did not count, and Russia was disqualified. Yet if the League belonged primarily to Britain and America, to men like Wilson and Bryce and Smuts, all the world felt in some degree the spiritual need to assail the no longer tolerable notion that wars are inevitable. A considerable background of such thinking may be found in almost every country. No one

* Roland N. Stromberg, "The Idea of Collective Security," *Journal of the History of Ideas*, Vol. XVII, No. 2 (April 1956), pp. 250-263. Reprinted by permission of the author and the *Journal of the History of Ideas*. Roland N. Stromberg is Associate Professor of History at the University of Maryland. He is the author of *Republicanism Reappraised* (1952) and *Collective Security and American Foreign Policy* (1963).

had in mind a super-state. Nationalism was at a peak. President Woodrow Wilson himself soon thought better of his oratorical suggestions for an international army to be at the disposal of the new international organization, while all states disarmed; he agreed with his advisers that this was, on sober reflection, "unconstitutional and also impossible." Herbert Hoover had already announced that the United States Government "will not agree to any program that even looks like inter-Allied control of our resources after peace"—this in response to a suggestion for an international relief organization, and Hoover's reason was that this would not secure "proper appreciation" of *American* contributions. If America could not be altruistic, how much less the hate-ridden peoples of Europe. A world government, the abolition of national states, was out of the question. The war had increased nationalism almost everywhere. There was a good deal of loose talk about the evils of "selfish nationalism," but no really international spirit existed, and no one explained how you could have nationalism without it being selfish—indeed, no one recognized his own nationalism as selfish at all. Yet the people did want first assurance that war would be put in the way of elimination.

It was strongly if vaguely held that something had been terribly wrong about the old system, or lack of it. A symbol of hope had to be created. Hastily constructed, the League of Nations was established with due solemnity: "The tents have been struck," said General Smuts, "and the great caravan of humanity is once again on the march." But whither it was marching was unfortunately not very clear. The League was supposed to embody some wholly new formula for rendering war obsolete. The phrase was Collective Security. It has never been a clear idea, and those who remain its enthusiastic supporters still confess that they do not know what it means. The League of Nations subsequently "failed", war was not prevented. That the idea behind it has nevertheless not only survived but even gained strength may be a tribute to the desperate plight of the world—*faute de mieux*. Or it may only be a tribute to the force of a *mystique,* to the astonishing ability of the modern masses to engage in slogan-thinking, and to the weakness of reason when confronted with terrible fears and earnest hopes. In any case the logical weaknesses in the idea deserve to be reviewed more often than they have.

The Covenant of the League of Nations contained ideas drawn from various sources, thrown together without much regard for the whole. Of these the only very original one, which Wilson was to call the "heart of the Covenant," was apparently first broached by Lord Parker of Waddington; it was the principle of the hue-and-cry, in American parlance the vigilance committee. In communities where no organized system of law and police existed, a rough approximation to justice had been provided by—to use a less reputable phrase—the lynch gang. Citizens turned out and caught the criminal. The mob taking law into its own hands is a monstrosity where the law exists, but where it does not exist it may be a necessity. Some such system stands logically between anarchy and law, which is where the world of international relations stood at this moment. The League of Nations belonged to the frontier era of inter-state history. To seize thus upon a casual idea thrown into a parliamentary debate for the foundation of the solemn new world order illustrates perhaps the desperation to which men were reduced. The idea was based on an analogy; and all analogies are more or less false. Are estates like individuals? Is the world like Prairie Gulch? Are wars like the depredations of Billy the Kid? But here it was, embodied in the League Covenant, and of course its creators were prepared to admit its experimental nature.

The older idea of compulsory mediation was also incorporated into the League, and married to the hue-and-cry in a curious sort of wedding, appropriate perhaps to the frontier. We need not here review the details. Central to the war-preventing hopes of the League and its successor has been the theory that a peace-loving majority can coerce a criminal or war-loving minority. It is the function of the international machinery to determine when an act of aggression has taken place, and it is the duty of the member-states to act jointly to suppress this act. True, some have deprecated this coercive aspect and have preferred to think of the League of Nations or United Nations as merely moral agencies for the shaping of world opinion, providing machinery for the old-fashioned techniques of mediation or arbitration; but the great majority, at least in this country, have never had patience with such a modest conception of the new world order. They have nevertheless grown disillusioned from time to time, for they have expected a miracle and have thus far not received it.

In the fateful 1920s and 1930s the League failed to prevent deterioration towards war. The United States stayed out while the British Commonwealth joined with obvious reservations. The reason for this was clear: these important states would not accept in advance a binding commitment to go to war anywhere at someone else's behest. The word "sovereignty" may be a chimera, but the prospect of going to war for something its citizens might not be interested in fighting about was all too real, for any government. In these years France was the one good friend of collective security, but she was also in a way the worst, and the case is instructive. France was for obvious reasons the most enthusiastic advocate of collective defense of the 1919 boundaries and terms. But in addition to supporting the League she also built up alliance outside the League, sabotaged its commitment to secure a general reduction of armaments, and prevented some of those abatements of the peace terms which might have appeased the embittered victims of the settlement. To the French the League was simply a system of force against Germany, as such obviously in her interest; but it was only one possible system, perhaps not wholly reliable, and France had no intention of breaking other strings to the same bow. One cannot blame the French for pursuing their interests, but by the same token one cannot blame other powers for refusing to become the tools of the French interest.

Here is no place to discuss the tangled history of interwar diplomacy, but some confusions of thought surrounding the League's rôle in that history ought to be clarified. It has become common to argue that the League system of collective security failed only because the powers lacked faith in the principle. "The reason why the League failed (to prevent World War II)," says Arnold Toynbee, "was that the enforcement of the Covenant had been backed by insufficient armed power and insufficient resolution to use such power as was available." The statement is equally true, and much more to the point, if we substitute for the word "League" the words "British and French and American foreign policy" and for the words "enforcement of the Covenant" the words "their opposition to Germany and Japan." Their failure can be explained wholly without reference to the League. And indeed throughout the period the League played an obfuscatory rôle, confusing the issues at every opportunity. It had frightened the United States away, and served as a convenient foil for American isolationists, and if British opinion was, as Mr. Toynbee concedes, hopelessly muddled in its thinking about foreign affairs, that was in part because of the illusions fostered by collective security. It was fatally easy to push the terrible burdens of national responsibility onto the shoulders of the League: let Collective Security do it, while Britain and France disarmed. It is important to realize that nothing called collective security existed except as the sum of Britain and France and the United States, the great powers opposed to the Axis, and their ability to cooperate in particular policies. When realities of power are lost from view the result may be confusion and chaos in international affairs. We still read that the path to Nazi aggression was made possible by the failure of the League to coerce Japan in 1931 and Italy in 1935. We have the absurdity, to which collective security is always being reduced, of saying that war in 1931 would have prevented war in 1941. It is implied that had the Western states been fighting Japan in Asia they could have fought Germany better in Europe. The verdict of careful history might be that the ill-conceived effort to apply "sanctions" against Italy in 1935 weakened, not strengthened, the front against Germany, but collective security will have it exactly the opposite. The lamentable weakness of the powers opposed to Germany and Japan is of course the key to the period, but it has nothing to do with an abstraction called collective security. That dogma hardly helped them to find their way out of the darkness in the 1930s. On the contrary, it often enabled them to avoid their problems, and it sometimes increased their difficulties. At the end of its career the League of Nations was engaged in hurling moral thunderbolts at Russia, a power whose aid was vital in resisting Nazi Germany.

Rising on the ashes of the League, the United Nations accepted more frankly the apparent truth that collective security is no good against the Great Powers. It strengthened the powers of the organization to intervene anywhere against a "breach of the peace" but at the same time it necessarily strengthened the veto power of the Great Powers. It relied on Great Power unanimity. Of this it can of course be said that if the Great Powers are in accord there is not likely to be a major war anyway. The formula of collective security seems to become in the end either useless or redundant. In the absence of such idyllic unity among the Big Three or Four, which would have itself amounted to the achievement of utopia, with or without an international assembly, the United Nations has followed the same disillusioning course as the League: alliances have reappeared, diplomacy largely ignores the United Nations, the important decisions are taken elsewhere, conflict persists, and the "idealists" are in despair—or day-dreaming in the 21st century. There is this time perhaps a greater tendency to blame this failure not on the perversity and wickedness of human nature which will not see the light, but on radical defects in the idea of collective security itself. Let us try to state these defects logically.

The slipperiness of the idea of collective security is, as we said, frankly conceded by its defenders. It is neither a system of world government (manifestly impossible today) nor yet the old "international anarchy" following Canning's simple rule of "every nation for itself"; it is something in between, if that is possible, but just what is not clear. But a study of its literature and of its practical experience leads us to extract several basic assumptions upon which this "impalpable Something" appears to rest. Whatever the exact definition of collective security, there can be little doubt that these assumptions are strongly associated with it. They appear to be as follows:

(1) All international disputes are subject to peaceable, just, satisfactory settlement.

(2) Nations are for the most part inclined to peace, not war.

(3) The inclination to war is everything: war results only when at least one side is guilty of a deliberately aggressive action.

(4) Since wars are always caused by a deliberate aggressor, this must be checked in its first stages if it will lead on to ever greater aggression; the incipient criminal will certainly become a hardened one if not caught in time.

(5) As an inference from (3) and (4), all states have an obvious stake in a war no matter where it may occur, and will, if they understand their interests properly, join in helping to suppress it.

In regard to points 1 and 2: such has been the evident, optimistic bias of all the great supporters of collective security, from Wilson to Stimson, and a workable system of this sort seems to require that really troublesome disputes be few in number and susceptible of a "fair" solution. The advocates of collective security have tended to believe that some final and just world order is possible, a stable and reasonable *status quo* where everyone is happy; they have obviously felt that the coercive powers of the international organization would have to be used rarely and, as time goes on, hardly at all. If peace is the rule, and conflict is the exception; if wars are only the occasional deviation from the norm, like madness or chronic criminality in individuals, then the task of a United Nations becomes feasible. But history does not seem to support such a view. Conflict is, unhappily, real and constant in the world; it is not, alas, an irrational deviation, but is all too rationally rooted in facts of economics, of ethnology, of the struggle for existence and the clash of cultures. We need go no farther than modern Palestine, or the Istrian peninsula, or the Saar, or the vale of Kashmir, not to speak of larger quarrels, to find clashes too stubborn to yield readily to settlement and too puzzling to allow us to say that one side is "right" and the other "wrong." The problem is not, as the Wilsonians imagined, one of suppressing an infrequent case of diabolism, a clear case of law and decency *versus* the criminal aggressor.

Thus the first two points lead toward the third, which is clearly the heart of the matter. Wars are caused by "aggression." Collective security began with a theory based on an analogy with law and the criminal. But again, history does not show that most wars have been the result of calculated and cold-blooded aggression. Some were, but the vast majority leave the historian wondering how to apportion the blame and ending with the perhaps uncomfortable feeling that both sides were right and both were wrong. A distinguished historian has said of the coming of the Hundred Years War that each king seems aggressive when looked at from the other's view but "hesitating and reluctant" when looked at from his own; and this is a common conclusion about wars. No one exactly willed the World War, or the Thirty Years' War, or the French Revolutionary War. That neither Lincoln nor Davis deserves to be put in the dock now reserved for "war criminals" is grasped by most Americans, despite all the bitterness left by their Civil War; and that tragedy is far more typical than the examples of a Tamurlane or a Hitler.

It is notable that neither the League nor the United Nations, despite many efforts, ever arrived at a definition of "aggression." During 1953 a special committee of the United Nations labored in vain to draft an acceptable definition; apparently there will never be any. We may well wonder about a law which cannot be stated, and must be determined *ad hoc* after the crime, flouting the venerable principle *nulla poena sine lege*. Presumably even the members of the vigilante gang all had a clear understanding of what constituted crime. Aggression cannot be defined because there is no world government, because force inevitably exists in international affairs, and because the history of disputes and wars between nations is ordinarily far too complex to be judged easily. It is obvious that it cannot be that he who strikes the first blow is always the aggressor. "If A attacks B because he is afraid of B, the blame is shared." History is full of cases in which the technical aggressor was rather clearly no more guilty than the victim. France was the aggressor against Germany in 1870, though most people suppose that Bismarck laid the plot. Cavour was forced on a famous occasion to make Austria strike the first blow against Piedmont, which he contrived to do—for a man of his talents it was a trifle. One might consider that example for a moment: the aggressor was Austria, but Cavour tricked and provoked her into it, but Cavour's cause, that of Italian unification, many thought to be the "just" one—but of course Austria did not think this, nor everyone. The point is that definitions of aggression usually rest finally on a moral opinion which is distinctly subjective. An unbiased opinion is impossible, for no power can be neutral; oddly enough, this is one of the maxims of collective security itself.

In the recent United Nations discussion of the problem, one of the most interesting objections to any advance definition of aggression was that if such a decision were adopted the United Nations might then have to "adopt decisions which in certain cases might aggravate international tension instead of allaying it." Put in clearer language, this meant that a great power would not want to invoke sanctions against one of its own allies! If South Korea flagrantly attacked North Korea, would the United States, true to the demands of collective security, help the Russians subdue her? Such a case immediately reduces the idea to absurdity. An American would want to say, no doubt, that in a higher sense such aggression would serve the cause of anti-aggression; is an aggressor an aggressor when he attacks a former aggressor, or the greatest potential aggressor? But this is to end in utter sophistry, and we had better just say (what is a plain and even wholesome enough truth) that states have to be free to pursue their interests, to oppose their rivals by whatever means are most expedient. The definition of aggression loses itself in what can only be construed by normal people as a dismal fog of hypocrisy.

We must note that some advocates of collective security deny that such a definition is necessary. The United Nations Charter provides authority for action in case of a "breach of the peace." It is argued that the enforcing agency has no need to inquire into the merits or motives of an armed clash. Its job is to stop the fighting, that is all. It could then presumably either dictate a settlement or try to mediate one. But in any case it is no more necessary first to determine who was the aggressor than it is for the policeman on the beat to do so before he stops a fight. Unfortunately this answer will not do; it is again misled by a false analogy between collective security and world government. If the United Nations were a world-state, exercising sole police power, it could use its police power in the way a civil state does: the fight would be stopped, the belligerents hailed *into court,* and a decision ultimately reached about the merits of the quarrel. But the United Nations is not a super-state, and no responsible advocate of collective security thinks it is. It has not established a rule of law, but has assumed simply that, somehow, the peaceful majority may restrain a warlike minority. If we abandon the distinction between peaceful and aggressive states, and say merely that conflicts of interest arise, we must surely abandon collective security. We may still have *ad hoc* intervention for particular reasons, we may still have efforts at mediation—but this is not new at all, these things have been a part of international relations since time immemorial.

Certainly orthodox and thoughtful supporters of collective security worry most about the absence of a "judicial" procedure for determining aggression and complain that as it now stands "there is no law in the procedure at all"—it is entirely political. They seem to feel that this can be remedied in time; but clearly it cannot. If a world-state existed and could enforce the law against all violence or violent threats, there would not have to be any laws about "aggression"; the problem does not arise in ordinary law within states. Apparently the confused search for "rules of law to determine aggression" springs from a situation in which it is desired to prohibit some wars but not all. As if the law were to say, good people can carry arms and use them at their own discretion, but bad people cannot; then you would have to define "good" and "bad" legally. To determine the aggressor is really to decide which is a bad nation. And a general law can never do this. Collective security gets into this curious dilemma because it is not a superstate but (as it is hoped) a device for preventing war by setting some armed gangs (the good ones) against other armed gangs (the bad ones). It is the hue-and-cry, not the rule of law; and unfortunately the international hue-and-cry does not work so well as in Prairie Gulch.

The fourth of the assumptions we have listed is partly dependent upon the prior assumption that war results from the deliberately malevolent action of some state bent on a life of crime, obviously. But the maxim "peace is indivisible," which M. Litvinov used to proclaim, or the analogy used by Franklin D. Roosevelt in comparing war to a contagious disease which will spread if not "quarantined," might be taken as a simple statement that war, if not opposed, feeds on itself; regardless of who was to blame for it, all other states have an interest in checking the smallest war, because little wars grow into big ones. Obviously under certain circumstances they may. This is not a new idea, for the old diplomacy with its keen sensitivity to the balance of power always understood that some very small bone might create a very large crisis. Indeed collective security has not been notable for any keen awareness of potential sources of trouble; it has shown a rather lamentable tendency to wait until some breach of peace occurs and then pounce on it with "punitive" action. It has always been known that apparently trivial disputes *may* involve the danger of a big war. But collective security seems to assert dogmatically that this is true of every case. It is certainly true that every threat to peace ought to be a matter of concern to everyone, but it is hardly true that a general intervention is always the most desirable remedy. The latter approach may, of course, succeed not in preventing the growth of a small war but in helping to make a great war of a small one. The comparison of a war with a contagion to be stamped out lest it spread may be compared with the old view that war is an infection which must be localized by neutralizing the areas around it. But all such analogies are misleading. No one formula is likely to cover every case. It is certainly a mistake to think of "sanctions" as a universal panacea, at any rate. Force is not a universal panacea, but a dangerous remedy which ought to be reserved for certain rare and otherwise incurable maladies. Very probably the confusion here would vanish if we banished the illusion, chronic with collective security, that every war is, like a nursery quarrel (to use a phrase from R. G. Collingwood), the work of a wicked child, for whom spanking is the only proper treatment.

The last of the five assumptions confronts us with the formidable question whether collective security, whatever its theoretical inconsistencies, will or will not "work." It is a question hung about with the mists of confusion laid down by the doctrine itself. Clearly some states can wage war on others, and can find many allies if it is a case of opposing an "overmighty" and menacing power. In those exceptional cases in history when an overly powerful state developed an insatiable appetite for conquest, a form of "collective security" always came into existence. The lesser states of Europe, led by England, organized "collective security" against France in 1689 and again in Napoleon's time. But these were extraordinary measures taken against extraordinary dangers, and it did not then occur to men to enshrine them into dogma. There may be at any time, of course, a practical case for opposing an overmighty state by building what was then called a grand alliance. But it is quite another matter to state dogmatically that every war or threat of war is in the same category. The effort to treat them as if they were seems certain to fail. Not only does common sense assert itself to declare that many conflicts are not best handled in this way, but governments will simply refuse to risk war or join it for any save the most pressing and obvious reasons.

The United Nations itself of course commands no force. A United Nations army was discussed, for a moment, when the Big Three, flushed with their cooperative triumph over Hitler, imagined that they could never be parted. It was soon abandoned, as in 1919. Only with its own consent does any nation support what is (we think incorrectly) described as a "police action" of the United Nations, and only by voluntary contributions does it provide military aid for such actions. If the Great Powers are unanimous (or if as in the Korean affair one of them chooses to forego its veto), they may invoke sanctions and create some sort of *ad hoc* army. But no state with substantial military forces will sign them over in advance to the United Nations. Enthusiasts for collective security regard this as most regrettable, but it is an unalterable fact. The reasons for it are massive and multitudinous; they are, given the great fact of nationalism, sound. What is in question, then, is the degree to which states will agree on a particular occasion that there has been a breach of the peace, and that they will send their share of troops to suppress it. The United Nations is not a police force; it is a meeting-place where chiefs of police decide how far they will authorize the use of their men in case of war between the member-municipalities who belong to the organization. This decision can only be made with reference to the interests of the particular nation. If a national interest can be seen by a large number of states, all may be reasonably well with the United Nations action; but then we must suppose that in the wicked old days there would have been the same action under a different name. The United States did not go to war in Korea because of the bare doctrine of collective security, but because the American people had their interests and sentiments deeply engaged against Russia. We may safely predict that the abstract injunction to intervene where there is strife, just because it is strife, will never send a single soldier to war. National interest must still, as of old, determine action.

This is a profound point, because it involves collective security's confusion between nationalism and internationalism. If we are to expect nations to act in a disinterested and international way, we must expect them to cease to be nations. We imply the existence of that international community in which a resident of North America sees no difference in importance between those who live near him and those who live anywhere else in the world, politically and humanly speaking. If such a spirit existed, world government would be feasible. Since it does not, then it is doubtful whether collective security is more than occasionally and imperfectly feasible; better to say, doubtful whether it is anything more than a new name for a very old game, the game it thought rhetorically to condemn as "power politics" or "cynical nationalism."

If all the sloganizing about collective security has not really changed the character of international relations at all, but has only assigned new names to old processes, then we might conclude that it has done little harm, if little good. Hypocrisy is at least sin's tribute to virtue, and collective security, however unsatisfactory it is, may represent a valuable ideal pointing toward that internationalism everyone hopes to advance. Unfortunately this is not quite true.

Collective security by introducing confusion in a field where clarity is needed has done something to damage the world's affairs—how much it is difficult to say, for this doctrine is of a piece with other modern attitudes which the keenest students of international relations have deplored under such names as moralism, sentimentalism, totalism, utopianism, etc. All these criticisms may be perhaps boiled down to the masses' essential innocence about a most complicated area and their tendency to generalize and to moralize where both such processes are peculiarly dangerous. Clearly this sort of feeling has fostered dangerous illusions: thus the United States, as President Roosevelt and Secretary Hull both declared, entered the postwar era expecting no alliances, no "unilateral action," no balance of power, and indeed no problems, for collective security was to banish the "unhappy past" and usher in the golden age of international cooperation. This doctrine obscures issues and blinds us to realities; it reduces the whole of international relations to the infantile level of a conspiracy and has prevented us, for example, from having insight into the vast and complex Asian revolution, which Americans tend to see simply as a Communist conspiracy. It is related to our distaste for negotiations and the oft-noted inflexibility of American policy. Collective security has taught the people, unwisely, that all "appeasement" is bad, a conclusion which follows from the view that every act of national restlessness is "aggression" and potentially unlimited aggression. To issue periodic warnings against aggression and then wait for these to be violated, after which one considers whether to go to war, is not to practice the wisest means of keeping peace in the world. The assumption of superior righteousness involved in the procedure of hailing an aggressor before the bar to receive his punishment has proved an irritant. Thus we know that in 1932 the hand of the violent nationalists in Japan was strengthened, not weakened, by the League's condemnation of Japan, while in 1935 Mussolini welcomed with glee the effort to penalize Italy, for it made his originally dubious Ethiopian adventure far more popular with his people.

And so a considerable indictment can be drawn up against this idea which began as a search for peace but has ended by bringing anything but peace to the world. The essential trouble is that any such narrow and pedantic formula clouds over the real sources of conflict with the pale film of theory, and substitutes a vague slogan for that patient and concrete analysis which every situation demands. The bewilderment about foreign policy which has lately proved so fruitful a field for demagogues has perhaps come about because of a rather thorough disorientation in popular thinking about international affairs. The roots of neurosis are irrational ideas. For nearly forty years now, commentators have been talking about the "immaturity" of the American people in foreign affairs, or about the tendency of democracy to produce a muddled foreign policy. But the people are known to learn in other subjects; and if they have not made progress in this one, the fault may lie at least as much in wrong theoretical guidance as in their own obtuseness. In general the Wilson-Stimson-Roosevelt tradition has been the only alternative to a sterile, blind and discredited isolationism, and thus has prevailed without competition. But a thorough analysis should reveal the remarkable illusions and shortcomings of these ideas, clustered about the modern version of collective security with its world of heroes and villains, law and the criminal, its confusions between nationalism and internationalism, its overtones of a medieval moralism, its false analogies between international and civil society.

The idea of collective security has managed, through its Wilsonian and Rooseveltian associations, to become closely connected with the liberal tradition. But in conclusion it might be pointed out that a strong case can be made against its liberalism. In Western thought liberalism has held with Locke, and against Hobbes, that law derives not from force but from reason and consent; that a political community must grow, as a result of experience and the working of reason on the not utterly depraved human mind, rather than be imposed by the sword of the strongest. The United Nations as an instrument of education and a place where irrational national prejudices are gradually dissolved is in the liberal tradition; but the appeal to force involved in collective security seems to be Hobbesean: "covenants without the sword are but words and breath." The older approach was surely the more liberal—that which concentrated on the mitigation of war, taking its elimination to be impractical until, by a slow process of education, a sense of international community had time to develop. It is true that the United Nations is not a tyrant-state, far from it; but neither is it, in the collective-security philosophy, a place where habits of compromise are patiently learned. It is a place, rather, where groups of states denounce each other and try to organize coalitions for punishing each other. From time to time well-meaning friends of collective security deplore the fact that the United Nations has degenerated into an arena where the "selfish nationalisms" they had thought to exorcise intrigue and lobby against one another, and convert the halls of international idealism into a place of "power politics." But the very idea of collective security has helped make this inevitable. National interests must continue to exist, and it is not shocking that they should jostle one another and seek adjustments by means of expediency and compromise. But by refusing to adopt a frankly political purpose, by attempting to bring in a rule of law where none can exist, collective security lends to this process of national conflict an air of self-righteousness which is hostile to habits of compromise. The interests of other states appear not natural but criminal, not to be recognized but to be prosecuted. The spirit of liberalism is tolerance; the idea of collective security, as has been noticed from time to time, smacks of a medieval intolerance, the crusade and the "just war."

The idea of collective security has hardly received the critical analysis it requires, though it is beginning to receive more. A certain aura of sanctity has surrounded it, because it has seemed to carry the honorific cause of internationalism against nationalism, idealism against cynicism, peace against war. But we need no longer respect the pretensions to holiness of an idea which seems to issue in so much unholiness. For if good intentions were the sole test of an idea's value, then even the Marxian Communists might put in a claim to virtue. Their example illustrates above all else the pregnant truth that intellectual confusion may defeat virtuous intentions and lead one on a tortuous path to perdition.

Collective Security Reexamined *

Kenneth W. Thompson

From one standpoint it is a truism to say that collective security is something new under the sun. In past eras and especially in the eighteenth and nineteenth centuries, war was conceived of as a duel in which contestants should be isolated and restrained by the rest of international society. When nations engaged in armed conflict their neighbors sought to localize the struggle and alleviate its poisonous effects. However short-sighted their actions in not meeting the conflict directly and turning back aggression at its source, the nations pursuing these policies were sometimes successful for varying periods of time in preserving islands of peace in a warring world.

On August 8, 1932, however, Secretary of State Henry L. Stimson proclaimed the revolutionary fact that the modern state system was entering a new era in which warring powers were no longer entitled to the same equally impartial and neutral treatment by the rest of society. He announced to the New York Council of Foreign Relations that in future conflicts one or more of the combatants must be designated as wrong-doer and added: "We no longer draw a circle about them and treat them with the punctilios of the duelist's code. Instead we denounce them as lawbreakers."

This is the cornerstone of the universally recognized theory of collective security to which most Western statesmen profess loyalty today. It is said that Mr. Stimson's memoirs, *On Active Service*, have become the "bible" of the Department of State, and in Britain we have the word of *The Times* (London) in a recent editorial that collective security ". . . indeed, is the view to which this country, like most others, is committed by its membership in the United Nations. . . ."

How are we to account for this new form of international relations? Perhaps there are three keys to the radical transformation of Western thought and the more modest shift in Western practice. Approached in imaginary and figurative terms, collective security may be said to have found its soul in the revolution in beliefs, its body in the revolution in techniques, and its mind in the revolution in contemporary international

* Kenneth W. Thompson, "Collective Security Reexamined," *American Political Science Review*, Vol. XLVII, No. 3 (September 1953), pp. 753-772. Reprinted by permission of the author and the *American Political Science Review*. Kenneth W. Thompson, formerly a member of the political science faculties of the University of Chicago and Northwestern University, is Vice-President of the Rockefeller Foundation. His publications include *Political Realism and the Crisis of Foreign Policy* (1960) and *American Diplomacy and Emergent Patterns* (1962). He is co-editor with Joseph E. Black of *Foreign Policies in a World of Change* (1963).

institutions taking place in the last three-quarters of a century. The soul of collective security has been formed by the growth of practical morality. The chief characteristic of social behavior in the late nineteenth and early twentieth century has been the increasing attention paid to all forms of humanitarian projects. In medieval society the thought of eliminating war or poverty was rarely given serious attention. War and poverty were conceived of as abiding moral problems and defects and flaws in a universal moral order. So long as man continued in his present state and society could not be fundamentally transformed, war would never be eradicated. This philosophy, as well as the theological concepts undergirding it, was swept away by the Age of the Enlightenment. In its place the West seemed to accept the creed of democratic liberalism with its aim of abolishing all ills and diseases disturbing the body social. Voltaire in his pleadings for condemned men, Bentham in his views on prison reforms, and the various programs for the elimination or outlawry of war reflected the new spirit. War became a practical problem in social engineering. The belief in one moral universe had been shattered; the belief in one world community demanding a multitude of social and institutional reforms took its place.

Another contemporary change of unparalleled importance has been the revolution in techniques and economics. If one excludes the force of contemporary nationalism, the overwhelmingly most powerful force in producing revolutionary changes in both East and West has been industrialization. The consequences which follow from the shrinking of a large-scale atlas into a small-scale globe can be attributed largely to industrialism. Economically, it is obvious that the world is one world wherein ideally the activities and production of each part must be geared and meshed with the functions of all the others. Industrialism for historians like Arnold J. Toynbee displays the force on a massive oecumenical movement drawing the world together. Technological change, which progressed slowly enough for eighteen centuries, has suddenly exploded. Within our present century the change has been so staggering, the rate so accelerated that few fully comprehend and appreciate its scope. For eighteen centuries, ten miles an hour was the maximum speed of travel on sea and sometimes on land. In 1790 four days were required to travel the two hundred miles from Boston to New York. Today the same time permits travellers to circle the globe. The earth today is smaller and is more intricately and profoundly interdependent than the thirteen original states, and in consequence the technological basis for Wendell Willkie's one world is said to exist.

Since the technological basis of a single world is at hand, it is only logical that for many a single government should be indicated. The revolution in techniques and the transformation of beliefs have called for new institutions to enable the development of the mind of the West to keep pace with the growth of its body and soul. It was said that the interdependent and socially self-conscious international society lacked only rational controls and organization. It was shown that we suffer from a profound cultural lag.

It was argued that for nations to act in concert solely when their immediate interests in survival are at stake is not enough. The mind, the body and the soul of modern society have called for a universal system of collective security heralded as the final essential step in repudiating great power conflicts and in guaranteeing perpetual peace.

The Idea of Collective Security

It is important that we ask at the outset, then: What is collective security in theory? What are its precepts and main tenets? What, in simplest terms, is the philosophy of collective security? The rock bottom principle upon which collective security is founded provides that an attack on any one state will be regarded as an attack on all states. It finds its measure in the simple doctrine of one for all and all for one. War anywhere, in the context of Article 11 of the League of Nations, is the concern of every state.

Self-help and neutrality, it should be obvious, are the exact antithesis of such a theory. States under an order of neutrality are impartial when conflict breaks out, give their blessings to combatants to fight it out, and defer judgment regarding the justice or injustice of the cause involved. Self-help in the past was often "help yourself" so far as the great powers were concerned; they enforced their own rights and more besides. In the eighteenth and nineteenth centuries this system was fashionable and wars, although not eliminated, were localized whenever possible. In a more integrated world environment, a conflict anywhere has some effect on conditions of peace everywhere. A disturbance at one point upsets the equilibrium at all other points, and the adjustment of a single conflict restores the foundations of harmony at other points throughout the world.

This idea of collective security is simple, challenging and novel. It would do for the international society what police action does for the domestic community. If the individual is threatened or endangered in municipal society, he turns to the legitimate agents of law enforcement, the police. The comparatively successful operation of this system has meant relative peace and tolerable harmony for most local communities. Through the action of police or "fire brigades" on a world scale, collective security has as its goal two comparable objectives. It would *prevent* war by providing a deterrent to aggression. It would *defend* the interests of peace-loving states in war if it came, by concentrating a preponderance of power against the aggressor. These two ends have been the goals of both the League and the United Nations. Through power and persuasion, a collective system would seek to deter aggression, as in the case of the Soviet imperialist threat to Titoist Yugoslavia. A potential aggressor must know that Yugoslavia and other United Nations powers stand together under the same protective umbrella. If war comes, the security system by pooling resources defends its interests against any nation which threatens to undermine it by swallowing up one of its members.

The ideal of collective security nowhere has been taken more seriously than among responsible leaders in the United States. More than the other political leaders accountable for the conduct of their nations' policies during and following World War I, Woodrow Wilson assumed that national interests were rapidly being supplanted by the common enlightened purposes of mankind everywhere and, particularly at the outset of the peace talks, sought to act upon his convictions. But the moral and political foundations required for collective action vanished with the cessation of hostilities and Wilson himself was forced to turn from his principles. He was driven to accept postwar territorial settlements in the Balkans that were at best half-hearted compromises with the crusade he had led. The tragic march of events of the "Twenty Years' Crisis" following 1919, however, revived the flame of belief in the hearts of other American political leaders that better forms for the conduct of international relations must be discovered and instituted. An uneasy conscience over America's departure from collective security after World War I—when the Senate defeated the Covenant of the League of Nations—coupled with a more skillful marshalling of opinion in support of the United Nations, inspired internationalist and isolationist senators to join hands in support of the same principle after World War II.

In his first speech to the Senate, Harry S Truman of Missouri declared: "The breaking of the peace anywhere is the concern of peace-loving nations everywhere." Senator Arthur H. Vandenberg announced following the San Francisco Conference in a dramatic speech to the Senate that he would support the ratification of the Charter with all the resources at his command. For, he explained: "peace must not be cheated of its collective chance. . . . We must have collective security to stop the next war, if possible, before it starts; and we must have collective action to crush it swiftly if it starts in spite of our organized precautions." Thus, the American President whose course in foreign policy was to be charted boldly and unambiguously according to the abstract principles of collective security, and the reputed architect of the bipartisan foreign policy were from the beginning unequivocally committed by their words to support of the United Nations.

Indeed, American support for the new method of preserving international peace and order has gone far beyond the ritualism of pious affirmation of an inspiring ideal. Approval for the principles of collective security at the time of World War II was asserted even more eloquently in the actions and policies of its leaders. As a young man Franklin D. Roosevelt had argued against the annexation of Hawaii. For, he maintained: "before we bother about foreign coaling-stations and fortifications we should look to the defense of our own coasts." New York, Boston, and San Francisco were still at the mercy of an enemy, and rather than prepare far-reaching security plans, the United States ought to concentrate on its own national defenses. In his concrete policies, however, President Roosevelt rejected this youthful counsel. In the late nineteen thirties, it became obvious that American interests could be protected only if other nations were secure, and the Roosevelt foreign policy became one of collective self-help. "Suppose my neighbor's home catches fire, and I have a length of garden hose. . . . ," he remarked, in justifying Lend-Lease to the Senate and the American people. This neighborly analogy was a practical way of convincing the people that their security was intimately bound up with Britain in its struggle for survival.

To symbolize the collective effort involved in the conduct of World War II, the Grand Alliance was referred to as the Military United Nations, on which the Constitutional and Political United Nations was to be based. In June of 1950, President Truman enlisted American manpower and resources in a struggle which all responsible authorities agreed involved the survival of the United Nations and not the protection of American vital interests. Thus not only by words but more emphatically by policies and actions, recent American leaders have boldly approved and faithfully supported the ideal of collective security.

The Real Issue of Collective Security

This simple picture of the idea of collective security hardly furnishes a useful and realistic perspective on the way such a system operates in practice today. Nor are we helped by comparing the structure of the two historic experiments in collective security. The formal agencies for collective security after World War I were in several important respects unimpressive. Article 16 of the Covenant provided that any member resorting to war contrary to the Covenant had committed *ipso facto* an act of aggression against all other members. It was intended that first economic measures and then overt force should be applied against any offender. But although the international obligations of members were less ambiguous than in the Charter, there was no clear provision for their implementation or organization by a central enforcement agency. Each nation had full freedom to provide what troops it saw fit. The Council could then advise on additional measures. In contrast, Article 39 of the Charter of the United Nations commissions the Security Council to determine the existence of a threat to the peace or act of aggression and Articles 43-47 obligate the members, upon the completion of agreements, to supply troops to the Military Staff Committee. The agencies for partial collective security, as found in the constitutional provisions of the North Atlantic Pact and the practical steps undertaken under NATO, are even more impressive and formidable today.

From the beginning, however, the real issue concerning collective security has had little to do with charters or compacts. The real issue has been the question of why the implementation of a system logically so flawless, and enjoying such impressive official devotion and popular support, should have been accompanied by a period of virtually unprecedented collective insecurity. It is a sobering fact that the nineteenth century was perhaps the most peaceful of modern centuries; the twentieth, by contrast, has been an epoch of unparalleled bloodshed. From 1815 to 1914 a system of old-fashioned balance of power contributed to the achievement of nearly a full century of uninterrupted peace. The past forty years have witnessed in rapid succession two great wars which the historian Arnold J. Toynbee compares to the double wars of the Romans and the Carthaginians and the two struggles of the Peloponnesian War which wrecked Hellenic Civilization. He has observed that quite possibly we have dealt ourselves the same "knockout blows" that these wars represented for the older civilizations. There were only eighteen months in the nineteenth century when France, Russia, Austria, Prussia, England and Spain found themselves at war with one another (excluding the Crimean War as a colonial struggle). By contrast, our experience thus far with the novel machinery of collective security has hardly warranted the unqualified postwar optimism of men like Mr. Hull that, with the new international organization, power politics and war were being left far behind in our progress toward utopia.

Instead the recent decades have been years of unceasing war or threats of war. What are the causes of this state of affairs? What are the reasons for the enormous gap between the theory and practice, the promise and performance of collective security? The most popular and reassuring answer has been that the radical doctrines of National Socialism and Communism have undermined the ideal system, and that modern technology has shattered the earlier limitations on conflict. Yet an equally dynamic creed challenged peace and order in the nineteenth century and provided a fighting faith for imperialist France.

The serious observer must look more deeply at the substance of political reality. In so doing he will find that collective security yesterday and today has been viewed unrealistically, and that its executors have been asked to perform tasks which could be performed with complete success only if certain objective conditions were realized. The most vital questions regarding collective security have seldom been asked; the real problems have often been evaded. The fundamental issues and problems which should have been boldly and realistically confronted have been concealed and obscured in constitutional verbiage and formal legalistic arguments. The four basic problems responsible for the tragic predicament of collective security include the problem of its basic preconditions, the political problem, the psychological problem and the problem of peaceful change. The first is from one standpoint most basic, for the preconditions of collective security, being frequently misunderstood, have presented the most stubborn obstacle to the maintenance of international peace.

Preconditions of Collective Security. Manifestly, collective enforcement is unattainable in the absence of appropriate international machinery and binding obligations clearly set forth in recognized legal instruments. Yet every informed citizen knows from experience that a legal arrangement imposed upon political and social conditions incompatible with its fulfillment makes successful political action difficult. Therefore it is essential in considering the reality of collective security that we understand fully its assumptions and requirements.

First, collective enforcement assumes a status quo, or situation of peace, on which the nations with predominant strength agree. In practical terms, the peace which a collective system must defend is the territorial status quo existing at the time the system is brought into being. There is nothing in past experience to indicate that all nations, or even a combination sufficiently powerful to defy the rest, will agree on the meaning of a particular status quo. Following every war, the defeated powers who feel they have suffered most by the terms of peace come to oppose the established status quo. In the aftermath of World War II, however, the question of satisfaction or dissatisfaction with the status quo has largely been superseded by an earlier and prior question. Up to the present time, no practical arrangement has been worked out acceptable to the major powers, who in this case are primarily the Soviet Union and the United States, on which the postwar status quo could be founded. The unresolved conflict between East and West has prevented the establishment of peace. Consequently, the latest experiment in collective security presents us with the anomalous picture of a system created to defend a status quo which has not yet been brought into being.

Moreover, the absence of accepted conditions of peace has been interpreted by some as a positive virtue. The wartime Secretary of State Cordell Hull argued that the League had been destroyed on the floor of the American Senate because of its intimate relationship with the Peace Treaty of Versailles. Better to establish a general international organization, he urged, and then, with passions less inflamed, work out a just and reasonable peace. James F. Byrnes, one of Mr. Hull's successors as Secretary of State in the postwar period, said that he was convinced, based upon his studies as a congressman of the proceedings of the Paris Peace Conference, that a "new approach" was essential. The negotiators at Paris had tried to settle too many difficult problems when the spirit of conflict and revenge still dominated their counsels. Mr. Byrnes prescribed a schedule of discussions in which the less controversial treaties, such as the Italian and Balkan settlements, would be negotiated first. Then the negotiators might turn from their initial successes to the more difficult questions of a German and a Japanese settlement. All agreements arrived at in this order would be introduced in the United Nations, where great and minor powers might participate in considering and amending them. In order to prevent the historic division of the nations into opponents and supporters of the postwar status quo, Mr. Byrnes reached the ingenious conclusion that: "We had to devise a system that would facilitate agreement among the major powers and at the same time provide the smaller states with ample opportunities to express their views." The newly created collective organization would intervene directly in the establishment of the postwar status quo.

In retrospect the problem inherent in the "new approach" has become plain for all to see. Its author, Mr. Byrnes, has observed: "It was a good theory. But it was faulty in one assumption." It assumed that the claims of the Soviet Union could be more readily accommodated to the vital interests of the West than has been the case. While this faulty assumption was shared by the majority of those responsible for the conduct of Soviet-American relations, there were at least three prominent leaders who at various times expressed misgivings about the priority accorded the founding of the United Nations. In 1941 President Roosevelt declared that he "would not be in favor of the creation of a new Assembly of the League of Nations, at least until after a period of time had passed . . . ," during which the major powers, and Britain and the United States in particular, had been successful in establishing and maintaining peace.

Secretary of War Henry L. Stimson maintained, in opposition to Mr. Byrnes, that the breakdown of peace after World War I was due primarily to the lack of political foundations from which the League of Nations had suffered. He held that ". . . the mistake was made of not securing that guarantee [of French security] before the second step of creating the League of Nations. . . ." was taken. In the preparatory discussions on the United Nations Mr. Stimson accordingly warned: "we should not put the cart before the horse." He urged that attention not be diverted from the paramount need for a settlement among the major powers by too much premature concern over blueprints for world organization. For the international organization would gain power and authority only if outstanding political problems had been adjusted. He advised: "We should by thorough discussion between the three or four great powers endeavor to settle . . . fundamental problems." If a general settlement based on mutual guarantees could be worked out, the new instruments of international organization would stand on more viable foundations.

A third distinguished American statesman supported the views of Secretary Stimson. In the Senate debate in 1944 on postwar plans, Senator Arthur H. Vandenberg insisted that the United States must not subscribe to collective security ". . . until we know more about what the new status quo will be. It is my argument that we should go ahead and perfect a plan for collective security; but that we should make it wholly contingent . . . the new 'league' must be *contingent* upon the *character* of the *peace*."

Second, collective security demands that nations subscribing to the status quo be willing and able at all times to muster overwhelming strength for collective defense at successive points of conflict. In theory, the supporters of the status quo might be capable in particular emergencies of mobilizing effective and decisive power against the single aggressor who sought to defy them. Or, by pooling the resources of all the nations in a permanently organized international force, collective enforcement could be made automatic, instantaneous, and preponderant. The former condition, however, is practically impossible of fulfillment, inasmuch as the threat to the status quo comes historically from more than one dissatisfied power or aggressor. The second condition would call for the unprecedented practice of international contingents operating under an international agency empowered to decide conclusively when and how they should be used.

The United Nations Charter seems to take a long step toward this objective by providing that all members are "to make available to the Security Council, on its call and in accordance with a special agreement or agreements, armed forces, assistance and facilities. . . ." (Article 43, Paragraph 1.) Through this provision, the incurable weakness of decentralized enforcement by which past international systems have been rendered impotent is ostensibly rectified. For the Achilles' heel of the earlier experiments was the decentralized character of the enforcement process; separate nations retained the right to determine whether or not military forces would be made available to meet particular crises. In 1942, Cordell Hull had urged that "some international agency must be created which can—by force, if necessary—keep the peace. . . ." Yet Mr. Hull's proposition and Articles 43ff of the Charter, by which this historic difficulty apparently had been surmounted, in practice have remained a dead letter. No special agreements have been concluded by Members with the Security Council; talks in the Military Staff Committee soon reached an impasse. The Soviet Union has opposed proportionate contributions to an international air and naval force, which would leave it particularly vulnerable to forces overwhelmingly more powerful than its own. The United States has been concerned to make the United Nations Armed Force as strong as possible against the military preponderance of the Soviet Army in Europe and Asia, while the Russians have sought to keep it as weak as possible. The stalemate in the Military Staff Committee is fundamentally a symptom of the struggle between the two great powers and between supporters and opponents of the undefined status quo. In practice, the realization of the second condition of overwhelming strength for collective enforcement has constantly run afoul of special national demands for military security and supremacy.

There is a *third* and final prerequisite of collective security, however, to which we now turn, that was widely assumed to be in existence at the time preparations for the United Nations were first being made. It is essential to collective security in a world of unequal powers that at least the major powers enjoy a minimum of political solidarity and moral community. On October 13, 1944, Premier Stalin asked himself, in an article appearing in the Soviet *Information Bulletin*, if the world organization could be effective. He predicted that it would "be effective if the Great Powers, which have borne the brunt of the war against Hitler-Germany continue to act in a spirit of unanimity and accord."

The effectiveness of the United Nations and of the Security Council in particular was predicated upon the unanimity of the five great powers. It was an article of political faith in the Roosevelt Administration that trustworthiness and good will on the part of Americans would inspire the same qualities among the Russians. In a particularly revealing memorandum for President Harry S Truman dated September 11, 1945, Mr. Stimson explained: "The chief lesson I have learned in a long life is that the only way you can make a man trustworthy is to trust him; and the surest way to make him untrustworthy is to distrust him and show your distrust." Unanimity among the great powers which alien ideologies and conflicting interests might otherwise undermine would be secured through the application of a code of social ethics that had in general been effective within the United States.

By October of 1947, Mr. Stimson, writing in *Foreign Affairs,* had cause to reformulate his proposition and to say: "I have often said that the surest way to make a man trustworthy is to trust him. But I must add that this does not always apply to a man who is determined to make you his dupe. Before we can make friends with the Russians, their leaders will have to be convinced that they have nothing to gain, and everything to lose, by acting on the assumption that our society is dying and that our principles are outworn." Thus the preconditions of collective security under the United Nations have either been wanting from the beginning, or have been corroded and destroyed by the all-consuming forces of the "cold war."

The Political Problem. The chief practical obstacle to collective security is the political problem deriving from the conflict of independent foreign policies. The loyalties and interests of nations participating in international organizations and collective security systems are of a different order from those of individuals taking part in the more intimate communities of the family and nation. Both individuals and nations pursue their own interests, but in some areas and on certain occasions the individual may forsake his egotistic motives for loyalty to some higher institution or nobler cause. There are institutions in integrated societies which provide common standards under which the individual can realize his aspirations. There need be no inherent conflict between an individual's private interests and his national loyalties, for the latter can often promote the realization of the former. On the other hand, conflicts are often inevitable between national and supranational loyalties, and when the projected policy of an international organization conflicts with that of a particular nation, at all times and in all places the national interest prevails.

In the debate between the so-called realists and idealists, the latter have often assumed that the conflict between national and supranational policies and purposes need not take the form the realists give it. Idealists have maintained that if two sets of objectives should be in conflict, the clash could always be resolved by taking "the long view." It should not be surprising that statesmen have been more disposed to approach the foreign policies of *other* nations with this as their "rule of thumb." For example, on January 10, 1945, in his momentous speech to the American Senate, Arthur H. Vandenberg assessed the objectives of the Soviet Union. He announced that the Soviet leaders appeared to contemplate the engulfment, directly or indirectly, of a surrounding circle of states on the Russian borders. Their defense of this sphere of influence policy was on grounds of security against German aggression. While finding this a perfectly understandable claim, Senator Vandenberg observed: "The alternative is collective security. . . . Which is better in the long view, from a purely selfish Russian standpoint:

To forcefully surround herself with a cordon of unwillingly controlled or partitioned states, thus affronting the opinion of mankind . . . or to win the priceless asset of world-confidence in her by embracing the alternative, namely, full and whole hearted cooperation with and reliance upon a vital international organization."

Yet Senator Vandenberg and other American statesmen, while raising this standard for others, have by their actions and not infrequently their words appealed to another less lofty if more attainable political goal. Not all of our leaders have been as transparently candid as Senator Vandenberg in expressing the hope "that American spokesmanship at the peace table is at least as loyal to America's own primary interests as Mr. Stalin is certain to be in respect to Russian and Mr. Churchill . . . to the British Empire." Yet in his warning, the Senator appeared to employ a new "rule of thumb" based on the precept "that no one is going to look out for us . . . unless we look out for ourselves. . . ."

It is true that the ambivalence we have found in Senator Vandenberg's use of guides to action in foreign policy is sometimes accounted for by the role he played in American life. As a onetime arch-isolationist, he could be expected to cling to certain narrow standards and selfish nationalist principles. Yet Theodore and Franklin D. Roosevelt, who can hardly be placed under the same stricture, sensed instinctively the importance of American vital interests in the conduct of foreign policy. Theodore Roosevelt intervened to sustain a balance of power in Europe and Asia by offering American good offices at the Portsmouth Conference and by seeking to moderate the crisis over Morocco at the Conference of Algeciras in 1906. When asked at the time of the Russo-Japanese War of 1904-5 why he opposed England, though admiring its democracy, and why he favored Russia, though despising its despotism and mendacity, he replied: "Do you not understand that I am looking after America's interest, that and nothing more. . . . If anyone else views action taken in American interest from the standpoint of a foreign power, I shall be sorry, but it certainly will not alter my own conduct."

The nature of the first Roosevelt's concept of foreign policy may be less surprising than the private admission by Franklin D. Roosevelt that he approached foreign policy on essentially the same basis. In early 1941, when seeking a formula by which aid to Britain could be extended, Franklin Roosevelt received a letter from a well-known advertising man reporting that charges being made by the Nyes and Lindberghs that we were acting in foreign policy to save the British and not ourselves were taking a serious toll. The business man urged Mr. Roosevelt to tell the truth, namely, that we were not concerned primarily with the British Empire as such but with our own safety, the security of our trade, the future of our crops, the integrity of our continent, and the lives of our children in the next generation. The President replied: "That I think, is a pretty good line to take because it happens to be true and it is on that line itself that we must, for all the above purely selfish reasons, prevent at almost any hazard the Axis domination of the world." The American strategy of fighting World War II first on the Atlantic sea lanes and in Europe reflected the priority Mr. Roosevelt gave to our interests in Europe.

In short, it is untrue to imply that American statesmen have been free from concern for immediate strategic interests and have consistently taken "the long view." There is almost no evidence that in pursuing our national destiny we have been immune from the same basic considerations by which other members of the society of nations have been guided. When this principle has been disregarded, as in certain military decisions in 1945, American security has been gravely imperilled.

However, the pursuit of separate national interests by the various independent states presents the most troublesome issue we face in appraising collective security. The problem which impaired collective security under the League, and which was perhaps more decisive than the defection of the United States in causing its downfall, was the unresolved conflict in the foreign policies of the principal powers. The conceptions of the national interests of France and England clashed with one another and with the principles of the League. France had one overarching objective: the absolute security of its territory. In French eyes, the one conspicuous threat it faced was Germany, which bordered France and perpetually endangered its northeastern frontier. In 1935-36, the second attack on the integrity of the League was launched with Mussolini's cruel "Rape of Ethiopia," which Il Duce preferred to describe euphemistically as a "civilizing mission." The dilemma with which France was confronted provides us with the classic instance of the political problem.

For France the sole threat against which sanctions had been prepared was Germany. Italy's aggressive action represented the wrong threat, at the wrong time, at the wrong border. Italy was the natural ally of France for, aligned with the much publicized Italian army, France hoped to balance the preponderance of the land forces of Germany, especially after Germany had moved into the Rhineland. The character of French foreign policy made it highly improbable that France could support sanctions up to the point where French loyalty to the Covenant would cost France its recent *entente* with Italy against Germany. British opinion appeared to accept this fact and Mr. Churchill observed that "the Foreign Secretary [Mr. Eden] was *justified in going as far with the League of Nations against Italy as he could carry France;* but I added that he ought not to put any pressure upon France because of her military convention with Italy and her German preoccupations; and that in the circumstances I did not expect France would go very far." In simplest terms, the choice for France was between the long range precedent which effective action might provide against the likelihood of German expansion and the immediately tangible results of not losing an ally against Germany. France compromised and sanctions were applied only half-heartedly.

The political problem also presents itself in regard to actual enforcement. Who is to apply sanctions? Who is to carry the burden of overt military action? In 1935-36, Britain alone was in a position to cut Mussolini's lines of communication and isolate his army. If genuine sanctions and force had been applied, the British navy would have shouldered the main burden. Yet there were murmurings by admirals and statesmen that the navy was ill-prepared, that there was ammunition for only about thirty minutes of fighting. British foreign policy, in contrast to that of France, directed that a stand should be taken. But the military component for action was lacking. In any enforcement action, since states are unequal, someone must bear more than his share. For this the British were unready in 1935-36.

The political problem has returned to plague Western society in the actions of the United Nations. The foreign policies of some nations have clashed periodically with the resolutions of that body. France and England are probably second and third-rate powers. England in particular has sensed this and has sought to husband her resources. Her first duty has been to her interests in Europe. She has maintained that a threat to her survival could come only from Europe. Any new action that would drain off a single drop of strength for efforts not in the national interest has been viewed with alarm. Moreover, England's policy has been one of watchful waiting in China. Under present conditions, the hope has been fostered that wise diplomacy could drive a wedge between the USSR and China, so that they would cease to march as members of a well-drilled team. The later phases of the United Nations' Korean policy have conflicted at every point with British Far Eastern policy. Is it surprising, therefore, that she has been a reluctant partner? The foreign policies of the member states, including those of the West, have diverged within the United Nations precisely as they did in 1935-36. Only the overwhelming power and material and political influence of the United States, made possible by the decline and exhaustion of postwar European and Asian powers, have prevented a repetition of the earlier experience. Unless nations have a margin of power beyond that essential to their survival, they can hardly be expected to share in the defense of a principle.

The Psychological Problem. Collective security founders on other shoals. It sometimes breaks down because of collective resentments or hatreds and reactions which express certain features of a particular national character. In 1931, the Japanese spilled over into Manchuria. Why was it that more positive action was not taken? To be sure there were legal, economic, and political obstacles existing. "War" in international relations is a weasel-word, and debates which surround it easily become legal quagmires. Japan said it had not declared war, China had not done so, and therefore the bombs were a mere illusion. Behind this legal smokescreen the struggle went on and men were as dead as if they had fought in a legally more respectable war. Economically, the world was deep in a painful depression; politically, Manchuria seemed far away and of little immediate interest to

Western nations. There was in addition, however, a psychological factor. Certain groups in the West harbored deep resentments against the victims of Japanese imperialism. In particular, certain elements within the British trading community remembered private scores that had not been settled and the recent ingratitude of the Chinese toward the West. This sector of Western public opinion took a kind of vicarious pleasure in the punishment the Japanese were inflicting upon China which, with India, became a symbol of the heavy toll being taken economically and psychologically in Europe by Asia's revolt. The Japanese action was unconsciously viewed as a retaliation against the whole anti-foreign movement that was sweeping Asia.

Another psychological factor was the attitude of responsible naval and military experts in Britain. One major result of the Washington Treaties of 1921-22 had been to leave Japan supreme on all fronts in the Far East. Its strategic position made it virtually immune from any serious attack. This confronted the newborn collective system with a military and naval problem which was made more acute by the prospects of joint operations by British and American naval forces. To British naval experts, American admirals and naval leaders were a boisterous and unproven lot. They had emerged overnight as the one irresistible threat to British naval supremacy. As youngsters in naval warfare, they would as likely as not prove erratic and unreliable under fire. Therefore, for Britain to commit herself unqualifiedly to a policy of military and naval intervention in an area where the newly acquired American naval supremacy would prevail would be risky and hazardous to British national interests. The disdain in which British naval leaders held their American opposite numbers was a psychological factor of great importance in 1931.

In 1950-51, a new psychological obstacle appeared to block effective universal collective security. The British have had a Far Eastern policy for nearly a century-and-a-half. To them the policy of the United Nations, as influenced by the United States and especially by its spectacular and outspoken general, was from the first based on false assumptions. When General MacArthur's abortive thrust toward the Yalu River was turned back and the one action which all Western policy had sought to forestall—the intervention of the Chinese Communists—followed, the British reaction, however restrained, was clearly inevitable. Given the policy, the outcome was inescapable.

Peaceful Change. Collective security, as we have seen, depends upon agreed concepts of justice in international society shared by all or most of its members. In domestic societies this consensus is arrived at by public opinion's availing itself of the instruments of government in registering the majority will. If societies were characterized by ideal justice and perfect equilibrium among contending social groups, the problems of social change would perhaps disappear. Since the demands for social change are continuously asserted in the market place and resolved in legislative and electoral debates, the pursuit of abstract justice assumes less urgency than the claims for justice of particular social groups.

In every society two social forces inevitably exist in basic tension with one another. The one force comprises the groups supporting the status quo as stabilized and perpetuated in the political and legal order of the day. Another force made up of the groups sharing common opposition to the status quo seeks to change or overturn it. In the light of this conflict, the basic problem of government is to provide ways by which continuity is achieved and social change not prevented. Within organized and integrated societies, the courts historically have contributed continuity whereas legislatures have been the faithful agents of change. As Congress was the forum in which the claims and grievances of distressed groups were alleviated by New Deal laws and decrees in the 1930's, the British Parliament in the nineteenth century was the agency in which the middle-class revolt against feudalism was expressed and achieved.

It should be apparent, however, that the process of change in society is made possible by other agencies as well. The executive has provided an instrument through which opinion can be channeled and transformed into effective policy. Peaceful change thus involves the whole of society with its orderly machinery through which social groups seek support for their claims elevated into principles of justice that must be compatible with the society's fundamental values. It is the whole of domestic society, therefore, and not the legislature in isolation, that brings about social change. For while the making of new laws is the formal act of social change, the role of legislatures is essentially the ratification of the choices at which unorganized society has already arrived. This is made possible by the generally accepted framework of justice within which disputes can be settled.

It is obvious that the conditions and institutions which exist within domestic societies are absent or greatly weakened in international society. Legislative bodies with law-making powers capable of fulfilling the functions that Congress or any other legislature performs are conspicuously absent on the international scene. The General Assembly has the power to "make recommendations" on matters prescribed in the Charter; the Security Council may "decide" on measures to be taken and "call upon" members to act. While these powers appear to mark an advance, in practice they have hardly resulted in any especially decisive step toward international law-making. The basic defects in the structure of international society are nowhere more apparent than in connection with peaceful change. Some observers maintain that the least satisfactory provisions of both the Charter and the Dumbarton Oaks Proposals are those dealing with pacific settlement. At San Francisco, substantial criticism of these provisions was made. Chapter VIII, Section A of the Proposals dealing with peaceful settlement was subject to sufficient attack to require its revision by the Technical Committee and the Coordination Committee. If more time had been available, further changes no doubt would have been made. For example, it is unclear whether parties shall seek a solution only to those disputes "likely to endanger the maintenance of international peace" by the means specified in Article 33, and if so who shall decide if the dispute is likely to endanger the peace. A substitute phrase was offered toward the close of the conference which provided: "The parties to any international dispute shall, first of all, seek a solution by negotiation, etc. . . . so that the maintenance of international peace and security will not be endangered." In the time remaining at San Francisco, this change could not be instituted; exaggerated concern with collective enforcement at the expense of accommodation and adjustment as instruments of peace appears to have been largely responsible for this shortcoming in most of the preliminary discussions.

If the provisions contained in the Charter are not fully satisfactory, there is a more basic issue in connection with peaceful change. Collective security if pursued to its logical conclusion is probably incompatible with peaceful change. In the 1930's, the Far Eastern situation deteriorated to a point where serious observers maintained that only military intervention could restore a stable balance of power. It was plain for all to see that Japan by its invasion of Manchuria was guilty of aggression. By its action, Japan had flouted its treaty obligations under international law. Yet the Japanese action in another respect was only an overt recognition that the treaties had become mere "scraps of paper" not based on political realities.

The staunchest advocate of firmness in Asia, Henry L. Stimson, conceded that the test for collective security had come in the worst part of the world. For the issue there was not what the law was but what it ought to be. He said at the time: "The peace treaties of modern Europe made out by the Western nations of the world no more fit the three great races of Russia, Japan, and China, who are meeting in Manchuria, than . . . a stovepipe hat would fit an African savage." Yet the claims of these nations for justice and the need for safeguarding the integrity of the collective system became mutually incompatible. If collective security was to survive, every treaty would have to be defended or the structure's prestige would be undermined. Therefore, Mr. Stimson was forced to conclude: "Nevertheless, they are parties to these treaties and the whole world looks on to see whether the treaties are good for anything or not, and if we lie down and treat them like scraps of paper nothing will happen, and in the future the peace movement will receive a blow that it will not recover from for a long time." The dilemma of collective security has been that its major proponents have been driven to oppose social change in the name of the sanctity of treaties. And since the agencies of social change which are available on the domestic scene are not present in international society, the military redress of claims or grievances has often appeared to be the sole rational alternative to the allegedly aggrieved parties.

To the extent that peaceful change is provided for in the Charter itself, Article 14 grants power to the General Assembly to recommend "measures for the peaceful adjustment of any situation, regardless of origin." Yet although this principle is less concrete and specific than what Senator Vandenberg proposed, it has remained essentially a dead letter. For while it was invoked on the occasion of the Palestine dispute, it was subsequently abandoned and repudiated by the American delegation. Therefore the problem of peaceful change, which threatened and eventually destroyed the League and the Holy Alliance, has likewise imperilled and threatens to destroy the United Nations security system.

The Unreality of Two Approaches to Collective Security

In the face of the problems we have outlined and discussed, two approaches to the idea and the reality of collective security have vied with one another in recent years. The one demands in the name of a principle that all nations at all times resist aggression. Its adherents maintain that only in this way can the national interests of independent states be protected and served. This approach takes its stand on the abstract and uncorruptible ideal of collective security.

Another approach, based primarily on what we have denoted the reality of collective security, reaches other conclusions on the basis of opposing concepts and principles. In the present state of world affairs, we are told, a policy of collective security leads inevitably down the road of general war and universal catastrophe. The Founding Fathers of this Republic knew more clearly than their present day heirs the futility of seeking to coerce sovereign states. At the Constitutional Convention of 1787, it was argued that unless states were united in one sovereign government (which both approaches agree is absent from the international scene today), they could be coerced only through civil war. Alexander Hamilton declared to the New York State Convention, met to ratify the new Constitution: "to coerce the states is one of the maddest projects that was ever devised. A failure of compliance will never be confined to a single state. This being the case can we suppose it wise to hazard a civil war?" Writing in the same tradition, Hans J. Morgenthau has maintained: "Under a system of collective security operating under less than ideal conditions, war between A and B or between any other two nations anywhere in the world is of necessity tantamount to war among all or at best most nations of the world." Since ideal conditions are not presently in sight, collective security is tantamount to war.

Thus the West is presented, in theory at least, with a choice between almost equally hopeless and catastrophic alternatives. Through the fact of membership in the United Nations, Western nations are committed to a system of collective security embodied in the Charter. Confronted with reality, however, the staunchest champions of collective security are driven to invoke a dual standard as a guide for action. On the one hand, they must firmly resolve on principle to intervene to arrest aggression at its source. On the other hand, while unable to disavow the principle, in concrete actions they are required to apply it judiciously with immense self-restraint.

The gulf between principles and actions in 1935-36 and again in 1950 illustrates the irony of collective security in the real world for, under its dispensation, Mussolini's aggression in Ethiopia and the North Korean invasion of South Korea made intervention a foregone conclusion. Once aggression is identified, the duty of the nations espousing collective security is unequivocal. Yet since Britain and France were unprepared in 1935, it was doubtful that more could be accomplished than to drive Italy into the camp of Germany. Notwithstanding, the viewpoint prevailed that if the champions of collective security did nothing, other more dangerous acts of aggression would follow.

The perils in pursuing the idea of collective security to its logical conclusion are matched only by the hazards involved in abandoning it. It is tempting to say that since collective security against a great power is unworkable, since psychological and political obstacles exist, and since the requirements for peaceful change are quite frequently at odds with enforcement, the system should be scrapped and replaced. Yet the coalition of the Western nations has been aroused to the threat confronting it by the resolute stand that was taken in Korea, and the whole free world has been animated and inspired by our boldness, courage and, lately, our patience and restraint. In the struggle against Soviet imperialism, it is vital that we have firm friends and willing allies who recognize mutual interests. We can best assure their cooperation by preserving and strengthening the tenuous ties by which all are bound together within the United Nations.

Perhaps the supreme paradox of American foreign policy today is the necessity placed upon us to seize and employ the essentially utopian instruments of collective security in a brutally realistic power struggle. Its agencies furnish a political framework through which the broad coalition of the free world can be strengthened and a more stable equilibrium of world power be restored. Britain and France and the free powers of Asia are more likely to play their part and contribute to the restoration of a balance of power in Europe and Asia if we assure them of support through mutual guarantees and create confidence by discussions in the halls and anterooms of the United Nations.

Collective security, with its present foundations weakened and enfeebled, can contribute to peace and order if wisely and moderately employed. It has become clear in Korea that policies undertaken in the name of collective security are not necessarily tantamount to world war. Localized struggles are still possible if major powers are not confounded by the ideal or misled by a too absolute interpretation of the meaning of collective enforcement. Moreover, the influence of other nations more skilled in historic diplomacy has served within the United Nations as a kind of built-in restraint on the impulses of American foreign policy. Our partners in utopia have nudged us in the direction of what would appear to be a more realistic foreign policy. Beyond this, with the recent breakup of the simple bi-polar balance of power in the world, the practical uses for collective agencies may be multiplied indefinitely as the prospect of action by coalitions of members against independent if minor centers of power becomes a reality.

The uses of collective security are more modest and limited than its more ardent advocates appreciate. Yet if participants base their policies on enduring political principles and judge and measure each action by the interests and power involved, it need not be an inevitable blind alley. Between the scylla of blind acceptance and the charybdis of logical rejection we must aim to establish the intellectual foundations required for an empirical and pragmatic approach to the modern concept of collective security.

INTRODUCTION TO PARTS
FOUR AND FIVE

New Myth or Dynamic Design?

After the Korean episode, the political *raison d'être* of the United Nations changed. If its members refused to sponsor the conditions necessary for effective peacekeeping machinery, if the Korean conflict showed the futility of expecting joint leadership and direction from the great powers when aggression occurred, alternate techniques of maintaining world peace and security needed to be developed. The great United Nations venture, the late Dag Hammarskjold once said, had either to go forward or slip back. Standing still was not an alternative, and slipping backwards meant that there was a possibility of returning to international anarchy. The collective security system having been proved Utopian, preventive diplomacy became the organization's new approach to peace in our contempory era of virulent East-West disagreements, bipolarity of power, and fading nineteenth-century colonialism.

The idea of stationing multinational military units in areas outside those where the great powers were in conflict and of placing such troops under the control and flag of the United Nations developed without a clear design. Professor Inis L. Claude, Jr. has written that the world agency invented preventive diplomacy "half consciously at best." [1]

In the fall of 1956 the news from the Middle East was repetitiously grim. The steady insults and accusations that Egypt and Israel had been hurling at each other for years had grown increasingly menacing. Egypt's quarrel with the principal users of the Suez Canal had reached an impasse. London and Paris believed that Cairo's policies endangered peace in the entire Middle East region. Moscow announced that its security was threatened by the military preparations that Great Britain and France were believed to be planning. The Secretary-General was not able to negotiate a settlement of the Canal dispute, as the Security Council had authorized him to do.

On October 29 Israel invaded Sinai. The following day Britain and France vetoed the American cease-fire resolution, but only after issuing an ultimatum to both belligerents and demanding that an Anglo-French military force take over the canal. Simultaneously with the Egyptian crisis, the

---

[1] Inis L. Claude, Jr., *Swords into Plowshares,* 3rd rev. ed. (New York: Random House, 1964), p. 295.

Hungarian uprising took place. Both the Security Council and the General Assembly debated the Russian intervention, but without influencing to any extent whatsoever the brutal Soviet suppression of the revolution. To help resolve the Egyptian crisis, however, a United Nations Emergency Force (UNEF) was proposed, approved, assembled, and stationed all within a matter of days. *The New York Times* told its readers on November 11th that:

> We cannot assess the present importance of the United Nations until—and unless—this magnificent police experiment succeeds. There are still dangerous elements in the Near Eastern situation. This, however, can be said: it was better to take the risk than not to make the attempt. It was better to set up a true United Nations army even for peaceful police work than to give up hope that such an army was or could ever be possible.[2]

We have chosen to introduce the drama of both the Suez and the Hungarian crises by extracting portions of the debate that took place in the Council and the two Emergency Special Sessions of the General Assembly. The charges and countercharges of those actually engaged in the fighting, the arguments and rebuttals of other United Nations members, even the excitement and dramatic tempo of those anxious days come alive when the verbatim testimony of the delegates is reviewed.

Since these events mark the emergence of the preventive diplomacy concept as the main field of useful activity for the world organization, the Middle Eastern and Hungarian situations must be placed in larger prospective. Professor Stanley Hoffmann of Harvard University wrote in 1957 "Sisyphus and the Avalanche: the United Nations, Egypt and Hungary," which remains one of the most penetrating analyses of the double crises and significance to the future security activities of the organization. The "paradoxical balance sheet carries with it some important lessons," Hoffmann says, who thereupon proceeds to examine a number of engaging discrepancies and inconsistencies.

Secretary-General Dag Hammarskjold was the man most responsible for re-examining and redirecting the peacekeeping role of the United Nations. From 1956 until September 1961, when his plane crashed in the jungles of Rhodesia, he (aided by his imaginative staff) experiemented with the machinery of the organization. As the United Nations turned to the preventive diplomacy approach to peace, Mr. Hammarskjold became increasingly impressed with the capacity and strength of the organization to deal successfully with the Cold War. At a 1959 press conference he said, speaking of the future of the organization:

> The policy line as I see it, is that the United Nations simply must respond to those demands which may be put to it. If we feel that those demands go beyond the present capacity, from my point of view, that in itself is not a reason

[2] *The New York Times,* November 11, 1956, p. 12E.

why I, for my part, would say no, because I do not know the exact capacity of this machine. It did take the very steep hill of Suez; it may take other and ever steeper hills. I would not object beforehand unless I could say, and had to say in all sincerity, that I know it cannot be done. Then I would say it. So far, I do not know of any question that has been put to which I would have to give that very discouraging reply. For that reason, my policy attitude remains . . . that the United Nations should respond and should have confidence in its strength.[3]

Perhaps Hammarskjold had the United Nations evolution in mind when he wrote just two months before his death in his exciting book of meditations, *Markings,* the following:

> The seasons have changed
> And the light
> And the weather
> And the hour.
> But it is the same land.
> And I begin to know the map.
> And to get my bearings.[4]

Dag Hammarskjold's basic definition and analysis of the functions of preventive diplomacy as a feasible Cold War approach to peace is found in the next selection, his *Introduction to the Annual Report of the Secretary-General on the Work of the Organization, 16 June 1959-15 June 1960.* He acknowledges that the organization's peacekeeping activities are going to be severely limited because of the ideological-power conflict that has affected all international affairs. There are many peripheral regions that are not involved in the East-West disagreement, and he argues, they must remain outside of the bloc struggle. If the United Nations is prepared to dispatch an international police force to the fringe areas, the organization "exercises a most important, though indirect, influence on the conflicts between the power blocs by preventing the widening of the geographical and political area covered by these conflicts and by providing for solutions whenever the interests of all parties in a localization of conflict can be mobilized in favour of its efforts." Thus, preventive diplomacy, to again quote one of its most distinguished interpreters, Professor Claude, "aims not to threaten an expansionist state with defeat, but to offer the promise of assistance to competing states or blocs in limiting the scope of their competition. Helping all states to avoid war, rather than helping some states to resist attack, is the theme of preventive diplomacy." [5]

In the United Nations Congo operation preventive diplomacy was

[3] Quoted by Lester B. Pearson, "Keeping the Peace," *The Quest for Peace,* Andrew W. Cordier and Wilder Foote, eds. (New York: Columbia University Press, 1965), p. 100.

[4] Dag Hammarskjöld, *Markings,* Leif Sjöberg and W. H. Auden, trans. (New York: Alfred A. Knopf, 1964), p. 222.

[5] Inis L. Claude, Jr., *Swords into Plowshares,* 3rd rev. ed. (New York: Random House, 1964), p. 292.

given its greatest opportunity to date to contain the Cold War and prevent a widening of the ideological-power conflict between East and West. It was the misfortune of the Congo to be caught in a complex vortex of political forces. The era of Western colonialism was passing, but the establishment of Western type nation-states, never an uncomplicated development, was doubly perilous in Africa because of illiteracy, poverty, and tribalism. Further, the Soviet Union was not disinterested in the continent's ultimate political orientation. When the Congolese leaders appealed in July 1960 to the United Nations for aid, Hammarskjold convened the Security Council and told the delegates: "The difficulties which have developed in the Congo are well known to all members of the Council. They are connected with the maintenance of order in the country and the protection of life. But the difficulties have an important international bearing as they are of a nature that can not be disregarded by other countries." [6]

In the first of the two essays dealing with the Congo situation, Ralph Bunche reviews the Politico-Military aspects of the operation. As Under-Secretary for Special Political Affairs, he had been sent by the Secretary-General to represent the United Nations at the Congo's independence celebration. Political chaos erupted simultaneously with the raising of the new flag, and Bunche remained for some time in the Congo. Although his article shows that he refuses to gloss over functional problems, Mr. Bunche concludes: "The United Nations strengthened itself morally and won new prestige. And it also gave to itself, no doubt unknowingly at the time, a far wider role and meaning in world affairs than it had ever had, and made indispensable a much stronger position for the Secretary-General as the executive arm." Not to be overlooked are the interesting misconceptions that local Congolese leaders had concerning the peacekeeping functions of the United Nations before its June 1964 withdrawal.

Professor Harold Jacobson examines "another, less widely known facet" of the Congo operation. Following in the wake of the military forces came a United Nations army of civilian experts and technicians, whose assignment was no less important than the one given to the military troops. According to Jacobson's definitions, the civilians were called upon (1) to keep the infrastructure of the Congolese state and secure the level of modernity that had been achieved, and (2) create a viable structure to replace the precarious one that had been hastily contrived out of the remnants of the colonial regime. "ONUC'S Civilian Operations: State-Preserving and State-Building" is a perceptive survey of these two aspects of the operation. The author does not claim that the work of the civilian contingents has eliminated for all times the possibility of anarchy in the Congo, but finds that "there can be no question that the United Nations has made a significant contribution to de-colonization by its activities in this instance."

[6] Letter of July 13, 1960 from the Secretary-General to the President of the Security Council. Security Council, *Official Records,* 15th Year, 873rd meeting (July 13, 1960), p. 3.

Assessing Preventive Diplomacy

In politics, as in all other enterprises, nothing succeeds like success. The United Nations peacekeeping operation in the Middle East continues to function with distinction; its four-year operation in the Congo was an impressive action in an extremely difficult crisis area. Currently, as a recent editorial in *The Economist* noted, "Lipservice is everywhere paid to the ideal of international peace-keeping." [7] Has the United Nations in improvising the preventive diplomacy approach to peace come upon a new dynamic design, or are we seeking to institutionalize a politically unreliable scheme, one that despite its modern format will eventually prove to be as illusory as the classical collective security formula? How politically realistic is it to expect mixed contingents of national military forces to be placed at the disposal of the United Nations to help isolate the rivalries of the great nuclear powers?

In Chapter 9 the first reading is Dr. Gabriella Rosner's review of the many past attempts to establish an international police force. Beginning with early European history, she traces the evolution of a concept related to, but going beyond, classical collective security. Until the formation and deployment of UNEF, the multinational force idea has had but limited application in world affairs. History, Dr. Rosner implies, is no unfailing guide to the future. The world of thermonuclear super-powers, of course, has changed many facts of political life, but have we reached the point in the evolving development of international organization when "the continuous opposition of sovereign states to international control" of their military forces, of which the author speaks, no longer is applicable?

The next selection by Professors Goodrich and Rosner describes the emergence of "The United Nations Emergency Force." The organization's potentialities for future preventive diplomacy operations have to be developed, the authors believe, but they call attention to serious political, financial, and constitutional issues which must not be overlooked. Their concluding point is the key to the future. A stand-by military force may be designed to counter aggression, but plans to use the machinery must be discussed within the framework of the real and the possible.

The next three essays were selected because all analyze crucial problems that will govern the establishment and use of an international police force. In the first of the trilogy, Lester B. Pearson, who during the Suez crisis first proposed the UNEF idea, argues that since member governments are unable to give the United Nations a "fighting force ready and organized to serve it on the decision of the Security Council," they should be willing to earmark smaller contingents for the more limited duty of securing a cease-fire already agreed upon by the belligerents. The author, currently Prime Minister of Canada, considers a "Force for U.N." as a "half-way house at the cross-roads

[7] *The Economist*, December 19, 1964, p. 1329.

of war." After examining a number of controversial limitations concerning the composition, control, and leadership of such a force, Pearson states that "It would act as the United Nations' policeman and his watchdog."

John Holmes is another Canadian who scrutinizes the international security force idea. His essay emphasizes the need to enlist the collaboration of the great powers in future action because there are serious limitations on what can be accomplished unless they all are committed to the organization's operations. One of his comments brings us back full-circle to the original San Francisco security plan. "If we are working our way toward great power unanimity at least on fundamental attitudes to war and peace," he says, "then I think we should try to work our way back—or forward—to the basis of Article 43."

One clue to Mr. Holmes' analysis is provided by the concluding article in the chapter. "Who Pays?" by John G. Stoessinger and his associate authors explores the economics of peacekeeping and its constitutional aspects. As even the most casual student of world affairs realizes, the United Nations struggled throughout 1964 and 1965 with the financial consequences of its two major peacekeeping successes, but without agreeing on a satisfactory solution. The continuing argument over the organization's purse-strings is not primarily a financial crisis, the essay holds, but is political in its nature. Possible new sources of revenue for the organization may be forthcoming, "but the fact remains that, in our lifetime at least, most of these proposed sources of revenue will not offset the failure of states to pay their financial obligations. Moreover, the liberals must ask themselves whether, if large new sources of revenue were actually found, the conservatives would not discover other techniques of impeding the expansion of the United Nations. Once again, the problem of political consensus is central."

The terminal article is both an end and a beginning. In 1961 Dag Hammarskjold raised a question that will have to be answered within our lifetime. Is the United Nations to become a dynamic instrument of government or continue its historical role of conference machinery? His eloquent analysis of the two points of view of the United Nations is contained in the Introduction to his annual report for 1960-61.

PART FOUR

Preventive Diplomacy
and the Maintenance of Peace

I SUEZ AND HUNGARY

Extracts from Security Council Debate of "The Palestine Question" (October 30-31, 1956)

748TH MEETING OF THE SECURITY COUNCIL*

At the invitation of the President, Mr. Loutfi, representative of Egypt, and Mr. Eban, representative of Israel, took places at the Council table.

3. MR. LODGE (United States of America): We have asked for this urgent meeting of the Security Council to consider the critical developments which have occurred and which are unfortunately still continuing in the Sinai Peninsula as the result of Israel's invasion of that area yesterday.

4. It comes as a shock to the United States Government that this action should have occurred less than twenty-four hours after President Eisenhower had sent a second earnest personal appeal to the Prime Minister of Israel urging Israel not to undertake any action against its Arab neighbours, and pointing out that we had no reason to believe that those neighbours had taken any steps justifying Israel's action of mobilization.

5. Certain things are clear. The first is that, by their own admission, Israel armed forces moved into Sinai in force to eliminate the Egyptian *fedayeen* bases in the Sinai Peninusla. They have admitted the capture of El Qusaima and Ras el Naqb. Second, reliable reports have placed Israel armed forces near the Suez Canal. Third, Israel has announced that both the Egyptian and Israel armed forces were in action in the desert battle.

6. An official announcement in Tel Aviv stated that Egyptian fighter planes strafed Israel troops. We have a report that President Nasser has called for full mobilization in Egypt today, and that the Egyptian Army claims that it has halted the advance of major Israel forces driving across the Sinai Peninsula. The Secretary-General may receive more information from General Burns and the United Nations Truce Supervision Organization, and I am sure that we shall continue to be fully informed as we proceed with our deliberations here.

7. These events make the necessity for the urgent consideration of this item all too plain. Failure by the Council to react at this time would be a clear avoidance of its responsibility for the maintenance of international

---

* Security Council, *Official Records,* 11th year, 748th meeting (October 30, 1956), pp. 1-12.

peace and security. The United Nations has a clear and unchallengeable responsibility for the maintenance of the armistice agreements.

8. The Government of the United States feels that it is imperative that the Council act in the promptest manner to determine that a breach of the peace has occurred, to order that the military action undertaken by Israel cease immediately, and to make clear its view that the Israel armed forces should be immediately withdrawn behind the established armistice lines. Nothing less will suffice.

9. It is also to be noted that the Chief of Staff of the United Nations Truce Supervision Organization has already issued a cease-fire order on his own authority which Israel has so far ignored. Information has reached us also that military observers of the United Nations Truce Supervision Organization have been prevented by Israel authorities from performing their duties.

10. We, as members of the Council, accordingly should call upon all Members of the United Nations to render prompt assistance in achieving a withdrawal of Israel forces. All Members, specifically, should refrain from giving any assistance which might continue or prolong the hostilities. No one, certainly should take advantage of this situation for any selfish interest. Each of us here, and every Member of the United Nations, has a clear-cut responsibility to see that the peace and stability of the Palestine area is restored forthwith. Anything less is an invitation to disaster in that part of the world. This is an immediate responsibility which derives from the Council's obligations under its cease-fire orders and the armistice agreements between the Israelis and the Arab States endorsed by this Security Council. It derives, also, of course, from the larger responsibility under the United Nations Charter.

11. On behalf of the United States Government, I give notice that I intend at the afternoon meeting to introduce a draft resolution whereby the Council will call upon Israel to withdraw and will indicate such steps as will assure that it does. . . .

749TH MEETING OF THE SECURITY COUNCIL*

2. SIR PIERSON DIXON (United Kingdom): The situation which faces the Council in the Middle East is exceedingly grave. To place recent events in their proper perspective, I cannot do better than quote from the statement to which I referred this morning which was made earlier today in the House of Commons by the British Prime Minister. The full text is now being distributed. This statement was made after anxious and intensive consultation between Her Majesty's Government in the United Kingdom and the Prime Minister and Foreign Minister of France.

3. Sir Anthony Eden described how for some time past the tension on the frontiers of Israel had been increasing. He went on:

* Security Council, *Official Records,* 11th year, 749th meeting (October 30, 1956), pp. 1-35.

"The growing military strength of Egypt has given rise to renewed apprehension, which the statements and actions of the Egyptian Government have further aggravated. The establishment of a joint military command between Egypt, Jordan and Syria, the renewed raids by guerrillas, culminating in the incursion of Egyptian commandos on Sunday night had all produced a very dangerous situation.

"Five days ago news was received that the Israel Government were taking certain measures of mobilization. Her Majesty's Government at once instructed Her Majesty's Ambassador at Tel Aviv to make enquiries of the Israel Minister for Foreign Affairs and to urge restraint.

"Meanwhile, President Eisenhower called for an immediate tripartite discussion between representatives of the United Kingdom, France and the United States. A meeting was held on 28 October in Washington and a second meeting took place on 29 October.

"While these discussions were proceeding, news was received last night that Israel forces had crossed the frontier and had penetrated deep into Egyptian territory. Later, further reports were received indicating that paratroops had been dropped. It appeared that the Israel spearhead was not far from the banks of the Suez Canal. From recent reports it also appears that air forces are in action in the neighbourhood of the Canal.

"During the last few weeks Her Majesty's Government have thought it their duty, having regard to their obligations under the Anglo-Jordan Treaty, to give assurances both public and private of their intention to honour these obligations. Her Majesty's Ambassador in Tel Aviv late last night received an assurannce that Israel would not attack Jordan.

"[Mr. Selwyn Lloyd] discussed the situation with the United States Ambassador early this morning. The French Prime Minister and Foreign Minister have come over to London at short notice at the invitation of Her Majesty's Government to deliberate with us on these events.

"I must tell the House that very grave issues are at stake, and unless hostilities can quickly be stopped, free passage through the Canal will be jeopardized. Moreover, any fighting on the banks of the Canal would endanger the ships actually on passage. The number of crews and passengers involved totals many hundreds, and the value of the ships which are likely to be on passage is about £50 million [sterling], excluding the value of the cargoes. Her Majesty's Government and the French Government have accordingly agreed that everything possible should be done to bring hostilities to an end as soon as possible . . .

"In the meantime, as a result of the consultations held in London today, the United Kingdom and French Governments have now addressed urgent communications to the Governments of Egypt and Israel. In these we have called upon both sides to stop all warlike action by land, sea and air forthwith and to withdraw their military forces to a distance of ten miles from the Canal. Further, in order to separate the belligerents and to guarantee freedom of transit through the Canal by the ships of all nations, we have asked the Egyptian Government to agree that Anglo-French forces should move temporarily—I repeat, temporarily—into key positions at Port Said, Ismailia and Suez. The Governments of Egypt and Israel have been asked to answer this communication within twelve hours. It has been made clear to them that, if at the expiration of that time one or both have not undertaken to comply with these requirements, British and French forces will intervene in whatever strength may be necessary to secure compliance."

4. In order that the Security Council may have the fullest possible information before it, I shall read out the text of the communication which was handed to the *Chargé d'affaires* of Israel in London at 4.15 G.M.T. this afternoon by the Permanent Head of the Foreign Office and the French Foreign Minister:

"The Governments of the United Kingdom and France have taken note of the outbreak of hostilities between Israel and Egypt. This event threatens to disrupt the freedom of navigation through the Suez Canal, on which the economic life of many nations depends. The Governments of the United Kingdom and France are resolved to do all in their power to bring about the early cessation of hostilities and to safeguard the free passage of the Canal. They accordingly request the Government of Israel: (*a*) to stop all warlike action on land, sea and air forthwith, and (*b*) to withdraw all Israel military forces to a distance of ten miles east of the Canal.

"A communication has been addressed to the Government of Egypt requesting them to cease hostilities and to withdraw their forces from the neighbourhood of the Canal, and to accept the temporary occupation by Anglo-French forces of key positions at Port Said, Ismailia and Suez.

"The United Kingdom and French Governments request an answer to this communication within twelve hours. If at the expiration of that time one or both Governments have not undertaken to comply with the above requirements, United Kingdom and French forces will intervene in whatever strength may be necessary to secure compliance."

5. At 4.25 p.m., G.M.T., today—ten minutes after the communication was handed to the *Chargé d'affaires* of Israel—a similar communication was given to the Egyptian Ambassador in London.

6. I would draw the Security Council's attention to certain considerations which arise in the mind of my Government. The first consideration is that the fighting between Israel and Egypt must stop. The second consideration is that, unless hostilities can quickly be stopped, free passage through the Suez Canal will be jeopardized—that free passage on which the economic life of so many nations depends.

7. Both sides, in different ways, have shown such repeated disregard for the resolutions of the Security Council that we have felt confident that we should have the general support of the Council, and the United Nations as a whole, for what we are doing—namely, everything in our power to bring about the earliest cessation of hostilities and to safeguard the free passage of the Canal.

8. At this point, I would stress that the action which we have felt in duty bound to take—which involves the temporary action of having Anglo-French forces in key positions along the Canal—is of a temporary character. I do not believe that our motives are likely to be generally misconstrued, but they are certain to be misconstrued in some quarters. I recall the remarks made by the Foreign Minister of the Soviet Union when we were debating the Suez Canal problem. He then suggested that the Government of the United Kingdom and the French Government were seeking an occasion to settle our differences with Egypt about the Canal by force. At that time we treated the allegations with the contempt which they deserved. That is not our object, and it has never been our object. This morning Mr. Sobolev insinuated something of the same kind and alleged that certain Powers had prompted the Israel Government to take action against Egypt. The contrary is, of course, the truth.

9. We have done everything in our power to lower tension in the Middle East, and if tension has increased, it is because unhappily neither Israel nor its Arab neighbours have seen fit to listen to our advice and to that of our friends. Since this advice has not been heeded, the present explosive situation has arisen. How can we have confidence, much as we should like to, that some future injunction by the Security Council would in fact prove effective to deal, in time—and time is of the essence—with a situation which is rapidly getting out of control?

10. I need hardly remind the Council that unfortunately those provisions of the Charter which provided that the Council should have a military arm have never been put into effect. I need not go into the reasons why. The roadblocks have been placed by a permanent member of the Security Council, whose persistent misuse of the veto has done much to complicate the situation in the Middle East and to bring us to the extremely grave situation which we now face. This is not, of course, to say there is nothing that the Security Council can do in this situation. I believe that a correct judgement on the situation, which I am confident that the Council will reach, can materially aid the cause of peace. I would remark that as soon as the news of the developments on the Israel-Egyptian border reached us here in New York yesterday afternoon, I took immediate steps with the representative of the United States and the representative of France, who is also President of the Security Council, to make it clear that in my view the Council should be seized of this situation today, and my Government confirmed to me this morning that that was also its view.

11. I trust that the great majority of the members of the Council will agree that the action which the French Government and Her Majesty's Government have taken is in the general interest and in the interest of security and peace. As I have explained, the communications were made a few hours ago to the Governments of Israel and Egypt. It seems to me that for the moment there is no action that the Security Council can constructively take which would contribute to the twin objectives of stopping the

fighting and safeguarding free passage through the Suez Canal. In view of these new developments, of which neither I nor my colleagues were aware when we began our meeting this morning, I hope that the United States representative will agree that in the circumstances nothing would be gained by pressing on with the consideration of his draft resolution today.

32. THE PRESIDENT (Mr. Bernard Cornut-Gentille of France): Since no members of the Council wish to speak at the moment, it remains for the Council to hear the parties, as it agreed at the beginning of this meeting.

33. Mr. EBAN (Israel): At this morning's meeting I defined the objective of the security measures which the Israel defence forces have felt bound to take in the Sinai Peninsula in the exercise of our country's inherent right of self-defence. The object of those operations is to eliminate the Egyptian *fedayeen* bases from which armed Egyptian units, under the special care and authority of Mr. Nasser, invade Israel's territory for purposes of murder, sabotage and the creation of permanent insecurity to peaceful life.

34. World opinion is naturally asking itself what these *fedayeen* units are, what their activities imply for Israel's security, whether their actions in the past and their plans for the future are really full of peril for Israel, and whether this peril is so acute that Israel may reasonably regard elimination of the danger as a primary condition of its security and indeed of its existence.

35. The Government of Israel is the representative of a people endowed with a mature understanding of international facts. We are not unaware of the limitations of our strength. We fully understand how certain measures might at first sight evoke a lack of comprehension even in friendly minds. Being a democracy, we work under the natural restraints of a public opinion which compels us to weigh drastic choices with care and without undue precipitation. It is therefore a Government which governs its actions by its single exclusive aim of ensuring life, security and opportunities of self-development for the people whom it represents, whilst also safeguarding the honour and trust of millions linked to it by the strongest ties of fraternity.

36. In recent months and days the Government of Israel has had to face a tormenting question: Do its obligations under the United Nations Charter require us to resign ourselves to the existence of uninterrupted activity to the south and north and east of our country, of armed units practising open warfare against us and working from their bases in the Sinai Peninsula and elsewhere for the maintenance of carefully regulated invasions of our homes, our lands and our very lives, or, on the other hand, are we acting in accordance with an inherent right of self-defence when having found no other remedy for over two years, we cross the frontier against those who have no scruple or hesitation in crossing the frontier against us?

37. Members of the Security Council may be in a better position to evaluate this choice and to identify themselves with this situation if they hear something about the *fedayeen* movement, of its place in the total pattern of Egyptian belligerency, of its extension, under Egyptian direction,

to other Arab countries falling under Nasser's sway, and of what would happen if we made no attempt at this time to resist that movement in its drive towards total conflict. The system of waging war against Israel by *fedayeen* units is the product of Mr. Nasser's mind. It is one of his contributions to the international life and morality of our times. After intensive preparation during the spring and summer of 1955, this new weapon was launched in August of that year, breaking a period of relative tranquillity on the Egyptian front, and indeed coming at a time when Egypt and Israel were engaged in hopeful negotiations with the Chief of Staff of the United Nations Truce Supervision Organization looking towards the integral implementation of the 1949 General Armistice Agreement. The Government of Egypt made no secret of these activities or of its responsibility for them.

38. Between 30 August and 2 September last year the following were amongst the official statements made by Egyptian governmental authorities and agencies.

41. On 31 August the official Cairo radio informed the Egyptian people of this new military technique:

"Egypt has decided to despatch her heroes, the disciples of Pharaoh and the sons of Islam, and they will cleanse the land of Palestine. Therefore, ready yourselves; shed tears; cry out and weep, O Israel, because near is your day of liquidation. Thus we have decided and thus is our belief. There will be no more complaints and protests, neither to the Security Council, nor to the United Nations, nor to the Armistice Commission. Nor will there be peace on the border because we demand vengeance and the vengeance is Israel's death."

42. On 31 August, another official radio *communiqué* stated:

"The Egyptian *fedayeen* have begun their activities inside the territory of Israel after repeated clashes on the border during the past week. The Egyptian *fedayeen* have penetrated into Jewish settlements spread out in the Negev until Beersheba and Migdal Ashqelon at a distance of forty kilometres, from the Egyptian border, and have taught the aggressive Israelis a lesson that they will not forget. The Egyptian *fedayeen* sowed fear and consternation among the citizens of Israel."

44. On 2 September the following official statement was broadcast in Cairo:

"The forces of the Egyptian *fedayeen* moved toward Israel, reached her capital Tel Aviv and caused heavy casualties to Israel along the border between Gaza and Tel Aviv. Apparently this was necessary to make it clear to Israel that we are able to pay back and to move the battle into the very heart of Israel, and that the attack on Palestinians is considered an attack on Egypt itself. It is possible that because of that, Israel approached General Burns after a prolonged crying, and asked him to inform Egypt about her readiness to finally stop the fighting. May it be a lesson she will never forget."

45. These, then, are the documents which mark the origin, over a year

ago, of the *fedayeen* movement. United Nations authorities repeatedly condemned these activities; designated them as aggressions; held the Egyptian Government responsible for them; called for their cessation. As an example, I quote a statement at that time by General Burns. In his report to the Security Council, he wrote:

"The episode of 22 August was soon after followed by an organized series of attacks on vehicles, installations and persons, carried out by gangs of marauders in Israel territory which, according to my information, resulted in the deaths of eleven military and civilian personnel and the injury of nine.

"The number and nature of these acts of sabotage perpetrated well within Israel territory are such as to suggest that they are the work of organized and well trained groups. Investigations so far completed by United Nations military observers tend to support this view. The sudden resumption of this type of incident after they had practically ceased for three months is significant."

46. This, then, was the first wave of *fedayeen* activity opening in the summer of 1955. In the spring of 1956 the activities of the *fedayeen* groups took on a new scope and intensity. This was the period during which the arms race, initiated by Mr. Nasser with external help, was running most drastically to Israel's disadvantage. Members of the Security Council will recall how close we were then to the threshold of general war, while these units came in and out of Israel every day on their missions of murder and plunder, accompanied by the official exhortations of Mr. Nasser and his officials, and by exuberant shouts of triumph in all the media of Arab territory.

47. It was during this agonizing spring and summer that Israel was called upon to display its greatest capacities of restraint, going far beyond the normal obligations of a sovereign State endowed with the inherent right of self-defence. The Security Council records should, in all historic justice, at this grave hour contain some chronicle of *fedayeen* attacks upon Israel since April 1956. The Council will recall that by that time the *fedayeen* plague had spread to other Arab countries as a direct result of the spread of Nasserist hegemony to those countries. Thus, any one of these invading units might spring upon us from any of three quarters.

48. While other Arab Governments shared the responsibility for sheltering, feeding and training these units on their soil, we never doubted for a single moment that the original guilt and the active responsibility of command rested with Nasser. It is he who presses the button; it is others who suffer the impact of the explosion.

91. Throughout the whole of this period, the activities of the United Nations organs concerned with security on our frontier were devoted very largely to this problem of the *fedayeen*. On 8 April 1956, the Chief of Staff of the United Nations Truce Supervision Organization had addressed a

letter to the Foreign Minister of Israel. This letter includes the following passages. General Burns wrote:

"I am dispatching to the Foreign Minister of Egypt a protest against the action of the *fedayeen,* assuming it to have been authorized or tolerated by the Egyptian authorities, and requesting the immediate withdrawal of any persons under Egyptian control from the territory of Israel.

"This follows my attempt on 6 April to get an assurance that the Egyptian authorities were not contemplating allowing these terrorists to infiltrate into Israel.

"I strongly urge that Israel refrain from any attempt at reprisal for the Egyptian action."

92. We did so refrain. In a significant passage, General Burns said:

"I consider that if Egypt has ordered these *fedayeen* raids, it has now put itself in the position of an aggressor."

94. It cannot be seriously suggested that these activities are not the direct responsibility of the Government of Egypt. In recent months it has become apparent to us that the Arab Governments, and especially Egypt, have come to regard the *fedayeen* weapon as an instrument not for mere harassment but for Israel's destruction. The Commander-in-Chief himself, Mr. Nasser, defined their mission on 28 May of this year when he said:

"The *fedayeen,* the Palestine army, which started as a small force of 1,000 men last year, is today great in number and training and equipment. I believe in the strength, the ability, the loyalty and the courage of this army. Its soldiers will be responsible for taking revenge for their homeland and people."

97. The Security Council will observe that this was merely the spearhead of Egyptian belligerency. It was a new device for making war, and for making it with safety. The doctrine was that of unilateral belligerency. The Egyptian-Israel frontier is to be a one-way street; it is to be wide open for these armed Egyptian units to penetrate as deeply into Israel as they like, to accomplish their mission and then return; it is to be closed in their favour against any defensive response.

98. I have spoken of these penetrations into Israel by armed units under the responsibility and control of Mr. Nasser. No one ever called a session of the Security Council to condemn these penetrations or to call for their withdrawal or to threaten Egypt with the consequences of non-compliance. Can Israel be required to reconcile itself with a situation in which any Arab country which chooses to send units into Israel, to murder its population, to plunder and to destroy, should be able to rely upon a large measure of international apathy?

99. It is one thing to present resolutions for protecting the *fedayeen* against the risk that they might not be safe in their abodes. It is a fact that there have never been any resolutions adopted by the Security Council designed specifically to protect the Israel civilian population against the

encroachments and the depredations of the *fedayeen* units. The people of Israel are not able to understand the meaning of this distinction. They do not know why the shelter of the Charter should not be spread over innocent workers tilling their fields, over women in their homes, over children in the sacred hour of religious observance who were mowed down and killed by *fedayeen* encroachments, and why this protection should apply only to those who, across the frontier, organize these penetrations for death and destruction. Would it not be a paradox if these *fedayeen* units, the greatest plague to security in the Middle East, were to become inadvertently the beneficiaries of international protection?

100. In discussing the Suez Canal case on a previous occasion, I referred to this paradox of unilateral belligerency. I ask leave to recall what I said in that context:

"At the root of these tensions lie a theory and practice of belligerency. Egypt considers and proclaims that there is 'a state of war'. In the name of that 'state of war', Egypt asserts a 'right' to perform hostile acts of its choice against Israel. On the other hand, Egypt claims immunity from any hostile response emanating from Israel. This is the doctrine of unilateral belligerency, and it has no parallel or precedent in the jurispurdence of nations."

101. The Government of Israel had ample reason to fear that this activity was to be renewed on a scale unprecedented even during the first wave of *fedayeen* invasion in August 1955 or during its recrudescence in the spring of 1956. Following the meeting of the Chiefs of Staff of Egypt, Syria and Jordan in Amman, we had stronger reason than ever before to believe that this recrudescence would take place. We duly gave this information to many Governments concerned with the maintenance of peace and security in the Middle East. They very day after we gave notice of this apprehension, the *fedayeen* units began to arrive. Three of them entered our territory on Sunday, two of them being captured, the other retreating to one of their bases in the Sinai Peninsula.

103. In these circumstances, both the position and the attitude of the Israel Government are clear. The attitude is based upon our fundamental concept of reciprocity. If the frontier between Egypt and Israel is to protect Egyptian territory against Israel entry, then it must protect Israel territory against Egyptian entry. We hold it as a self-evident truth that the lives of Israel men, women and children are not less sacrosanct or less worthy of international protection than are the lives of these hired *fedayeen* gangs which are the main instrument of Nasserism in its assault upon the peace and the decencies of Middle Eastern life.

104. Behind these incidents, grave as they are, we discern issues of even greater moment. World opinion must choose between two candidates for its confidence: on the one hand, the farmers and workers, the men, women and children of Israel; on the other hand, these fanatic warriors of the *fedayeen* groups. Behind this confrontation, there stands the broader alignment between Israel and Nasser. A small people build its society and culture in its

renascent homeland. In the early days of its independence, it is set upon by the armed might of all its neighbours, who attempt to wipe it off the face of the earth.

105. My memory tells me that it took something like eight weeks for the Security Council to secure the withdrawal of Egyptian and other Arab armies from the sovereign soil of Israel. The effort to secure that withdrawal was, perhaps, not marked by a sufficient urgency or zeal. In the following years of the conflict, Israel's neighbours have continued to assault her with warlike acts of their own choice, to attempt her destruction by armed intervention, by blockade and boycott. They sent armed units into her territory to murder and plunder. They strive by every means to ensure that nowhere in Israel shall there be tranquillity for peaceful pursuits. They blare forth the most violent threats for Israel's destruction. They accumulate vast armaments for bringing about that result. They announce, as they did last week from Cairo, that it is they who will choose the time and the place for the final assault, and that it is for us to wait passively for that selection. They proclaim that a state of war with Israel already exists. They seize the greatest of the world's international waterways and convert it into an instrument for unilateral national pressure, while maintaining a constant violation of international maritime law.

106. Across Africa and Asia, wherever Nasserism spreads its baneful influence it works actively to subvert all peace and progress and to establish an ambitious and insatiable hegemony. Now, having considered that it has humbled the international community and maritime Powers, Mr. Nasser's action returns to his first target, Israel, which is to be swamped from three sides with a new wave of *fedayeen* violence.

107. Accordingly, while studying with attention all proposals for strengthening security in the Middle East, we reject with vehement indignation the charges of aggression launched against us. There is aggression, there is belligerency in the Middle East; but we are its victims and not its authors. That is what I mean when I say that world opinion must decide whom to trust. Shall it be a small, free people establishing its homeland in peace and constructive progress, or shall it be the dictatorship which has bullied and blustered and blackmailed its way across the international life of our times, threatening peace in many continents, openly avowing belligerency, placing its fist on the jugular vein of the world's communications, bringing the Middle East and the world ever nearer to the precipice of conflict, intimidating all those who stand in its path—all except one people, at least, which will not be intimidated, one people which no dictator in history has ever intimidated, a people which has risen up against all the tyrants of history, a people which knows that the appeasement of despots yields nothing but an uneasy respite and that a Government which allowed its citizens to be murdered daily in their homes would lose the essential justification for which Governments are instituted among men?

108. This is the background, and these are the issues which have guided

my Government's choice. We have faced them alone, and we made a decision to invoke for this purpose, and no other, our sovereign rights of self-defence. Israel is not out to conquer any new territory, but is determined to wipe out the bases in the Sinai wilderness from which murder and death and destruction are launched against it.

109. We believe, as we have always believed, in our destiny of peace, and for that we are ready now, but it must be a real peace—peace by agreement, peace without boycott or blockade, peace without murdering *fedayeen* gangs, peace, in short, within a framework of a reciprocal regard for the ideals and the principles of the United Nations Charter.

110. Mr. LOUTFI (Egypt): I do not propose to reply to Mr. Eban, for a simple reason. Mr. Eban talked to us at length about the *fedayeen*. So far as I know, the item we are discussing today, which was submitted by the United States representative, is worded: "Steps for the immediate cessation of the military action of Israel in Egypt."

111. As for the offensive terms and insults which Mr. Eban has seen fit to direct at Egypt's leaders in connexion with the armed aggression committed by Israel, I shall not follow the example he has set. I shall not even answer him.

112. May I take this opportunity to draw the Council's attention to the fact that I have today submitted a request for the inclusion on the agenda of a new item concerning the Franco-British ultimatum which has exposed Egypt to the threat of aggression. What is involved is nothing less than the occupation of three Egyptian towns, Ismailia, Port Said and Suez.

113. Since the ultimatum expires tomorrow morning at 6 a.m., Egyptian time, my delegation requests that the Security Council should meet this evening to consider this question.

Editor's note: In a later meeting of the Security Council on October 30, the Soviet Union introduced a draft resolution calling for a cease-fire and the withdrawal of the Israeli armed force behind the established lines. The negative votes of Great Britain and France defeated its passage. The vote was 7 to 2, with 2 abstentions. See Security Council, *Official Records,* 11th year, 750th meeting (October 30, 1956), p. 5.

751ST MEETING OF THE SECURITY COUNCIL*

71. Mr. BRILEJ (Yugoslavia): At the close of yesterday's night meeting, as the Council stood apparently powerless in the face of a rapidly worsening situation, I suggested the possibility of an emergency session of the General Assembly. The tragic developments that have since taken place have given an added emphasis and a new sense of urgency to the necessity of finding other forms of United Nations action to deal with the deepening crisis. My delegation therefore formally proposes that an emergency special session of

---

* Security Council, *Official Records,* 11th year, 751st meeting (October 31, 1956), pp. 12-15.

the General Assembly be called in accordance with rule 8 (*b*) of the rules of procedure of the General Assembly. The text of the draft resolution which I am submitting to the Council is as follows:

"*The Security Council,*

"*Considering* that a grave situation has been created by action undertaken against Egypt,

"*Taking into account* that the lack of unanimity of its permanent members at the 749th and 750th meetings of the Security Council has prevented it from exercising its primary responsibility for the maintenance of international peace and security,

"*Decides* to call an emergency special session of the General Assembly, as provided in General Assembly resolution 377A (V) of 3 November 1950, in order to make appropriate recommendations."

I hope the text of this draft will be circulated as soon as possible.

81. SIR PIERSON DIXON (United Kingdom): The representative of Yugoslavia has just submitted a draft resolution calling for an emergency special session of the General Assembly under General Assembly resolution 377A (V) entitled "Uniting for peace."

82. I submit that the procedure proposed is quite out of order and not in accordance with the clear terms of the "Uniting for peace" resolution itself. I shall explain why.

83. It is quite clear that the "Uniting for peace" resolution may be invoked only when certain conditions are fulfilled. The relevant passage of the resolution provides for the calling of an emergency special session of the General Assembly: ". . . if the Security Council, because of lack of unanimity of the permanent members, fails to exercise its primary responsibility for the maintenance of international peace and security in any case where there appears to be a threat to the peace, breach of the peace, or act of aggression . . .". Thus, a pre-condition of invoking the procedure is that a lack of unanimity of the permanent members of the Security Council should have prevented the Council from taking a decision.

84. This clearly presupposes that a draft resolution on the substance of the item before the Council has been submitted, circulated and voted upon, and until that has been done, it cannot be determined that the Security Council has failed to take a decision owing to the lack of unanimity of the permanent members. But no such text has been circulated or voted upon on the item now before the Council, namely, the letter dated 30 October from the representative of Egypt.

85. Furthermore, the two draft resolutions which we voted upon yesterday under another item are not within the compass of the "Uniting for peace" resolution and, therefore, in my submission they cannot be invoked to support the Yugoslav proposal.

86. A further consideration in my mind is that it is quite true that two draft resolutions, advanced successively by the United States delegation and then by the Soviet Union delegation, failed yesterday to carry because of the

lack of unanimity of the permanent members of the Council, but the reason for that is simple and must be well known to all the members of the Council. It was because my Government and the French Government were and are convinced that action on the lines proposed by the United States delegation would not be an effective method for maintaining international peace and security in the present case. That is very evidently true of the truncated version of the same draft which subsequently was put to the vote at the request of the Soviet delegation. On the contrary, our two Governments believed yesterday and believe today that the action undertaken by them as an emergency temporary measure was then and is a more effective course.

87. Finally, I would add that in the present circumstances the calling of an emergency special session of the General Assembly on this subject would clearly have serious implications.

88. MR. BRILEJ (Yugoslavia): I am sorry, but it is impossible for me to accept the arguments submitted by the representative of the United Kingdom. It seems to me that some of his arguments are not at all relevant to the draft resolution, such as, for instance, the reasons for which the two permanent members of the Security Council used the veto yesterday. They used the veto twice on two draft resolutions calling for a cease-fire.

89. It seems to me that the representative of the United Kingdom will agree with me that there exists not only a threat to the peace but also a breach of the peace. I hope that he will agree with me that the landing of armed forces on the territory of an independent country and the bombarding of its cities are certainly a breach of the peace. The Security Council failed to agree on that because of the veto.

90. The third argument the representative of the United Kingdom introduced is that on the item now under discussion no draft resolution has been vetoed, and that, therefore, the "Uniting for peace" resolution cannot be applied. Both aspects of the problem in respect of which we propose that an emergency special session should be convened are covered by the United States draft resolution, which was submitted yesterday. The question of the intervention in Egypt of forces other than Israel forces is covered by paragraph 2 (a) of that draft resolution. . . .

92. It seems to me, therefore, that the provisions of the General Assembly resolution entitled "Uniting for peace" are in full accordance with the draft resolution which I presented this evening.

95. THE PRESIDENT: I should like to speak as the representative of France.

96. I cannot agree with Mr. Brilej's interpretation of the juridical background of his draft resolution. I note that this draft resolution does not specify the question which would be brought before the General Assembly. There have been no manifestations today of a lack of unanimity among the permanent members of the Security Council. If the Yugoslav representative is referring to the voting which took place yesterday, I must point out to

him that the item to which those votes related, that is to say, the United States complaint, is not on the agenda of this meeting.

97. Moreover, the resolution entitled "Uniting for peace" provides that the Council may bring before the General Assembly cases of threats to the peace, breaches of the peace or acts of aggression. Now—and I am still speaking of the United States complaint—neither the text of the complaint nor the draft resolutions proposed yesterday by the United States and the Soviet Union delegations respectively came within the terms of the General Assembly resolution, in other words within the terms of Chapter VII of the Charter. A specific decision would have been necessary for that purpose.

98. For both these reasons, the Yugoslav draft resolution seems to me to be inconsistent with the texts on which it is based.

99. I would add, with regard to substance, that if such a draft resolution were adopted this evening, the consequences might be most serious.

100. MR. LODGE (United States of America): The United States has always been a strong supporter of the "Uniting for peace" resolution. I personally remember that in 1950, when I was a representative, Mr. Dulles, who is now Secretary of State, represented the United States in the First Committee. He played a very active part in the drafting of that resolution and, as a matter of fact, is somewhat of an expert on its spirit and on its letter.

101. We believe in exhausting every remedy that is open to us in the interests of peace. Much as we dislike to disagree with our friends, we do think that the Yugoslav draft resolution is clearly relevant and clearly applicable in the present circumstances, and we shall therefore vote in favour of it.

Editor's note: The British motion to the effect that the draft resolution submitted by Yugoslavia should be ruled out of order was rejected 6 to 4 with 1 abstention. The Yugoslavia draft proposal was thereafter adopted 7 to 2 with 2 abstentions. See Security Council, *Official Records,* 11th year, 751st meeting (October 31, 1956), p. 22.

Extracts from General Assembly First Emergency Special Session
Debate of "The Palestine Question" (November 1, 1956)

561ST MEETING OF THE GENERAL ASSEMBLY*

Statement by the President

4. THE PRESIDENT (Mr. Rudecindo Ortega of Chile) : These are not only hours of suspense and anxiety for people everywhere. These are times of drama and tribulation which trouble the conscience. Peace has been disturbed in the Middle East, and the first attempts to restore it have failed. People all over the world are turning anxiously towards the United Nations, which bears the heavy responsibility of finding a solution for the problems which have brought about this serious situation of belligerency, and of reconciling the divergent views of the parties. Is it still possible for the United Nations to do that? Every Member State bears the grave responsibility, the historic responsibility, of answering that question in the affirmative.

5. This first emergency special session, which I, as chairman of the delegation of Chile, have the honour to open, has been convened for the purpose of examining the problem in all its aspects. . . .

24. MR. LOUTFI (Egypt) : I sincerely thank the members of the Security Council who voted yesterday for the draft resolution presented by Yugoslavia, and also those Member States which have informed the Secretary-General that they support that draft resolution and have voted for its inclusion in our agenda today. They have given me an opportunity to address the world forum of the General Assembly in this hour of trial for my country.

25. You all know what the issue is. I shall therefore be brief. As I stated yesterday before the Security Council, this is no time for speeches. My country has been subjected to bloody aggression. More blood is being shed every minute as the result of that aggression.

26. During the night of 29 October 1956, Israel committed the most serious act of unprovoked armed aggression that has taken place since the conclusion of the armistice agreements. This time, it was not a reprisal raid. It was a premeditated, carefully prepared armed attack for the purpose of occupying part of Egyptian territory and provoking war in that area.

27. On 30 October, during the day, a note from the British Government was handed to the Egyptian Ambassador in London, serving an ultimatum on the Egyptian Government and calling upon it, first, to cease all hostilities

* General Assembly, *Official Records*, First Emergency Special Session, 561st meeting (November 1, 1956), pp. 1-12.

on land, sea and air; secondly, to withdraw all Egyptian military forces ten miles from the Suez Canal; and thirdly, to agree to the occupation by French and British forces of part of Egyptian territory, including the towns of Port Said, Ismailia and Suez.

28. The ultimatum called for a reply by 6.30 a.m., Cairo time, on 31 October, failing which the Governments of the United Kingdom and France would intervene as they deemed necessary in order to obtain satisfaction of their demands.

29. Since that date, the Franco-British air force has begun to bomb Egypt from bases in Cyprus, where it is stationed against the will of the inhabitants of the island. Several raids took place yesterday, including raids on Cairo. According to information I have received, three air raids were carried out yesterday by British and French jet bombers, at 7 p.m., 8.45 p.m. and 10.30 p.m. respectively, against the military academy, a mosque, a hospital at Almaza, Cairo airport, some military airfields and several points in the Shubra district. Nine lives were lost.

30. Throughout last night, British and French bombers carried out non-stop raids against all the Egyptian airports. The French air force joined Israel aircraft in their attacks on Egyptian troops in the Sinai peninsula.

31. Today, 21 raids took place over Egypt, 9 of them on Cairo, 3 on Ismailia, 3 on Port Said, 3 on Suez and 3 on Alexandria. In the raid on Alexandria, dwellings at Montaza, near Alexandria, were destroyed. The number of casualties is not yet known.

32. Furthermore, the Commander-in-Chief of the Franco-British forces attacking Egypt declared today, at Nicosia: "Aerial bombing will continue until Egypt sees reason. Length of the operation depends on how quickly Egypt accepts our terms. The sooner Egypt sees reason, the less damage will occur. We have considerable strength to deal severe blows." This cynical *communiqué* calls for no comment.

33. Egypt is thus the victim of combined premeditated aggression by Israel, the United Kingdom and France. It is now clear that the aggressors conspired together to commit this act of war.

34. In order to justify the armed attack they have just perpetrated, the Governments of the United Kingdom and France have presented arguments which it is very difficult to find words to describe.

35. Sir Pierson Dixon said yesterday in the Security Council that he regretted that Egypt had rejected the British ultimatum. I was amazed that the United Kingdom representative could have thought for a single moment that Egypt would agree to Franco-British forces landing on its territory against its will, after unprovoked aggression had been committed against it.

36. The United Kingdom representative has alleged that the main purpose of this intervention is to safeguard the Suez Canal and to restore peace in the Middle East. But no danger threatened the Suez Canal before the Franco-British interventions.

37. According to our information, the aircraft of the aggressors have

sunk an Egyptian vessel in the Canal. This act of war committed by France and the United Kingdom in the Canal zone is a violation of the United Nations Charter, the Constantinople Convention of 1888, and the principle of free passage, even in time of war, guaranteed to all States under article 4 of that Convention.

38. Apart from all this, who gave the United Kingdom and France the right to intervene in order to safeguard the Canal? The 1888 Convention gives Egypt alone the right to take measures for the defence of the Canal. Has there been a decision by the United Nations, a resolution of the Security Council, giving the United Kingdom and France the right to resort to force, with the alleged purpose of safeguarding the Canal and ensuring the free passage of vessels? Many other States use the Canal, yet no one else thought for a moment of resorting to force or of joining the French and the British in occupying the Canal zone.

39. What makes the situation even more strange, as was stressed by Mr. Brilej, the representative of Yugoslavia, at the meeting of the Security Council in the afternoon of 30 October 1956, is that:

"This threat of force is primarily directed against the country which is the victim of aggression. Egypt is being enjoined to waive its inherent right of self-defence as set forth in Article 51 of the United Nations Charter. Egypt is also being summoned to acquiesce in the occupation of part of its territory by two foreign Powers. It is confronted with a rigid time-limit in the worst tradition of what we had hoped had become an obsolete policy of ultimatums."

40. Moroever, the United Kingdom representative claims that one of the purposes of the Franco-British intervention is to put an end as soon as possible to any act of war on land, at sea and in the air. If that is really the purpose of the Franco-British intervention, why did the representatives of those two countries use the veto against two draft resolutions containing stipulations for a cease-fire?

41. An argument advanced by the French and United Kingdom representatives which struck my delegation forcibly was their allegation that the occupation was merely a "temporary measure." History has taught us that the words "temporary measure" as used by the United Kingdom representative have a very different meaning from their usual one. The occupation of Egypt in 1882 was a "temporary measure," according to the British leaders at that time. It lasted seventy-four years.

42. But the bad faith of the aggressors hardly needs further proof. It is self-evident that the aggressive action of France and the United Kingdom in trying to settle, on their own account and in a unilateral manner, a question which has been submitted to the United Nations, is a flagrant violation of the Charter. We thought the United Nations Charter had put an end to the reign of force and that the era of the ultimatum and the *diktat,* of bitter memory, had vanished with the signing of the Charter at San Francisco.

Resort to force may now take place only in accordance with the principles and provisions of the Charter.

43. France and the United Kingdom, in violating the Charter, have assumed a heavy burden of responsibility before the world. This act will have incalculable repercussions, and France and the United Kingdom will have to bear the consequences.

44. In this grave ordeal which my country is undergoing while attempts are being made to invade Egypt and to trample its sovereignty under foot, one thing only comforts us—the condemnation of this act of aggression by world public opinion, and the fact that two of the great Powers which are members of the Security Council, the United States and the Soviet Union, have censured the use of force by France and the United Kingdom.

45. No less a person than President Eisenhower, and the Soviet leaders also, have clearly stated that they oppose the use of force in the settlement of this dispute. Many other leaders have made similar statements, among them Marshal Tito, the Head of State of Yugoslavia, and Mr. Nehru, the Prime Minister of India. I should have liked to quote their statements, and others as well, but I shall leave this to the representatives of the countries concerned.

46. Even in the United Kingdom, the members of the Opposition, the Labour Party, have condemned the policy of the present British Government in no uncertain terms. Mr. Gaitskell, the leader of the Opposition, made the following statement in the House of Commons yesterday:

"All I can say is that, in taking this decision, in the view of the Opposition, the Government has committed an act of disastrous folly, whose tragic consequences we shall regret for years . . . I can only say that any impartial observer must recognize that this is a clear breach of the Charter of the United Nations . . . There are millions and millions of British people—as we believe a majority of the nation—who are deeply shocked by the aggressive policy of the Government and who still believe that it is both wise and right that we should stand by the United Nations, the Commonwealth and the United States alliance."

The conclusion to be drawn from these quotations is that, even in the United Kingdom, public opinion by no means approves of the policy of Sir Anthony Eden's Government.

47. As I have already told the Security Council, until such time as the necessary measures are taken by the Council or the General Assembly, the Egyptian Government has no other choice but to defend itself and to protect its rights against this armed and unprovoked attack. We stand by this attitude.

48. This act of war committed by two permanent members of the Security Council is a heavy blow to the United Nations, world peace and all mankind.

49. By using their right of veto against the draft resolutions presented

in the Security Council, France and the United Kingdom have paralysed the Council's action. In these circumstances, it is for the General Assembly to follow up the adoption of the Yugoslav draft resolution in the Security Council, and, in accordance with resolution 377 (V), to take the necessary measures for the prevention and removal of threats to the peace, and for the suppression of acts of aggression and other breaches of the peace.

50. The Assembly is called upon to take very grave decisions, which will affect the future of our Organization and the principles governing the world in which we live. Egypt is defending itself and will continue to do so. The matter is in your hands. Denounce the aggressors, and put an end to aggression.

65. Sir Pierson Dixon (United Kingdom): Before I enter into the substance of the matter for which this emergency session of the General Assembly has been called, I feel bound to point out, as has already been done by the representative of France, and as I did in the Security Council yesterday, that the procedure under resolution 377 (V) of the General Assembly, "Uniting for peace," has, in our view, been improperly invoked on this occasion. . . .

67. Her Majesty's Government in the United Kingdom has nevertheless decided to attend this session, for an important reason. It is because it believes that the United Nations can and should do what it can to make effective contributions in the present grave situation in the Middle East.

68. The situation in the Middle East is indeed grave. I do not believe that it has been fully realized by those who may not be as intimately concerned with Middle Eastern affairs as we are how explosive the situation in the Middle East was a few days ago, when the United Kingdom and French Governments took the drastic steps which they felt obliged to take.

69. From all the information at our disposal, we had reason to judge that a major clash, whose consequences would have been incalculable, between Israel and its Arab neighbours was more imminent than at any time since the signing of the armistice agreements in 1949. The sudden Israel mobilization and incursion into Egypt made it imperative to take very speedy and effective measures to prevent a war between Israel and Egypt which could only lead to a general conflagration throughout the Middle East and which would, in its train, have involved prolonged disruption of free passage through the Suez Canal, the canal which is of such vital interest to so many nations.

70. It has long been the declared policy of the United Kingdom to do everything in its power to lower tension in the Middle East in order to bring about conditions favourable for the conclusion of a final peace settlement between Israel and its Arab neighbours. Unhappily, neither Israel nor the Arab States has seen fit to listen to our advice or to that of our friends. It is as a consequence of this that we are now faced with the present situation which culminated in the Israel incursion into Egypt. I think it is fair to say that the United Nations has done everything that it could do to

promote the prospects of a final settlement and, in the meantime, to uphold the fabric of the armistice régime.

72. Then let us look for a moment at the history of this question in the Security Council. As those representatives who have served in recent years on the Council will know, the Security Council has devoted a very great part of its activities to a continuous effort to uphold the armistice régime and to support the United Nations Chief of Staff. It is my impression—and I should be interested to hear whether my present and past colleagues in the Council disagree with me on this—that the attitude of all the parties has been getting more and more refractory, and less and less inclined to take serious account of the Council's views in so far as these seem to them inconvenient.

73. In these circumstances, how could we have confidence, much as we should have liked to, in view of the past disregard shown by all parties for the United Nations wishes and injunctions and, indeed, disregard for their treaty obligations to one another, that any fresh injunctions by the Security Council would be effective to deal in time—and time was of the essence—with a situation which was getting so clearly out of control?

74. With regret, I say that the Security Council, in our opinion, could have provided no effective remedy in time.

75. I need not here go into the reasons why those provisions of the Charter which were designed to provide the Council with a military arm have remained in abeyance. It is well known that it is because a permanent member of the Security Council, by a persistent misuse of the veto, has seen fit to thwart the intentions of the Charter. The result has been that the world has not been able to rely on the United Nations for the collective security which the Organization was designed to provide. Least of all, in view of the intransigence of the parties and the cynical misuse of its veto power by the Soviet Union, could we expect swift and effective action from the United Nations in an emergency in the Middle East.

76. It is hard to say these things, but I fear they are true. It is precisely because of this unhappy limitation in the effective powers of the Security Council to deal with such an emergency that the United Kingdom and French Governments were compelled to intervene at once, as they were fortunately in a position to do.

77. It was through no wish of ours that a situation arose in which we were compelled to act independently of the United Nations. . . .

78. We did not, however, consider that the course of action proposed by the United States, without consultation with Her Majesty's Government, could effectively achieve the twin objectives of separating the belligerents at once and of safeguarding free passage through the Canal.

79. It was in these circumstances that we were obliged to cast our negative votes in the Security Council. The action which we and the French Government have taken is essentially of a temporary character, and, I repeat it, designed to deal with a unique emergency. Our intervention was swift

because the emergency brooked no delay. It has been drastic because drastic action was evidently required. It is an emergency police action. The situation is not dissimilar to that which obtained at the time of the North Korean invasion. On that occasion the Member of the United Nations which had forces on hand and was in a position to intervene at once courageously did so. By a happy chance—and I mean the absence of the Soviet representative from the Security Council on that occasion—the Council was able to endorse the United States action. The same fortunate chance was not ours. I cannot, however, believe that the United States would not, in any case, have acted, and rightly so, in the circumstances.

82. It would be a profitless task to attempt to apportion the blame between Israel and the Arab States. It may be, but I am not sure, that in terms of border incidents Israel has infringed the armistice agreements more seriously than have the Arab States. An increasingly serious situation culminated a few days ago in the partial mobilization by Israel of its forces, and a large-scale incursion into Egyptian territory in violation of the armistice agreements. But we must not lose sight of the fact that Israel has felt its very life to be threatened, in particular by Egypt, whose Government has proclaimed, again and again, that its aim is the total destruction of Israel.

83. Let us not forget that Egypt stands today in open defiance of the United Nations. It has deliberately maintained the exercise of belligerent rights against Israel and has refused to afford free passage to Israel ships and cargoes through the Suez Canal, thereby flouting the express injunctions of the Security Council. It is unrealistic to think that, in searching for a peaceful solution of the Palestine problem, we can ignore the declared aspirations of the Egyptian Government to establish an Egyptian hegemony throughout the Middle East, after having eliminated the State of Israel.

84. That is what has been happening, and it is essential to understand this background if we are to deal constructively with the present situation. For it is from these Egyptian policies in particular that much of the present crisis has sprung. I submit that to ignore them is to shun reality.

85. So grave, indeed, is the present situation that it would be wrong for this Assembly to turn a blind eye on the malevolent activities of a country, outside the area, which are no less pernicious for being partially concealed.

86. The Soviet Union bears a heavy burden of responsibility for the present situation. Having extended its domination over a number of ancient and civilized countries of Europe by overt aggression and by covert subversion, the Soviet Union had until recently been able to keep those great nations in subjection by such means of terrorism as the execution, on orders from Moscow, of sincere national patriots, and by the dreaded and hated secret police.

87. It then looked round for further areas to subjugate, and turned its attention to the Middle East. The Soviet Union has repeatedly intervened in Middle Eastern affairs with the scarcely concealed purpose of discomforting the Western Allies and profiting from the disorder which it itself has helped

to create. Both inside and outside the United Nations, Soviet influence has been used to incite the extremists in the Arab countries and to thwart all attempts to achieve a peaceful solution of the Palestine problem.

89. Not content with thus inciting the Egyptian extremists to follow out expansionist aims in the Middle East, the Soviet Union, by methods of propaganda and subversion, has sought to undermine the establishment of the other Arab States. I do not believe that Egypt would have dared defy the United Nations or forcibly seize the Suez Canal if it had not thought that it would never be brought to book because the Soviet Union could be relied upon to frustrate any efforts by the United Nations to establish peaceful conditions and the rule of law.

90. It was, above all, the Soviet Union's irresponsible exploitation of the privileges of a great Power that had made it impossible for the Security Council to mete out impartial justice as between Israel and its Arab neighbours. Who can deny that, as a consequence, the Security Council has been working under impossible conditions in attempting to maintain the peace in the Middle East?

91. It has indeed been for me ironical, in these last few days, to see the Soviet Union posing—and, it would seem, being accepted—as the apostle of peace, and to see the motives of the United Kingdom and France being maligned and misunderstood. It is more ironical if one pauses for a moment to consider the record of my country in the Middle East.

96. The Assembly must acknowledge that, by our swift intervention, the Israel advance has already been halted and this threat to the Canal has been averted. I do not know of any alternative steps which could have achieved this result.

97. It is absurd to suggest—as it has, I regret, been suggested—that our intervention was part of a long-prepared plot concerted with Israel. Such allegations are not only absurd, they are false. It is common knowledge, I think, that, over the past few months, our relations with Israel have been difficult and strained, precisely because of our efforts to restrain Israel from retaliation against its Arab neighbours.

98. Between Egypt and Israel the attitude of Her Majesty's Government remains quite impartial. We do not and could not condone this Israel action, which is clearly in violation of the Armistice Agreement and aimed at the occupation of positions in Egyptian territory. It was indeed precisely because of this very serious Israel violation that we judged it necessary ourselves to intervene. It is, of course, our view that Israel should withdraw its forces from its present positions as soon as this can be arranged.

99. Let me, at this stage, towards the end of my speech, briefly restate the objectives of the Anglo-French intervention. The overriding purposes are: the safeguarding of the Suez Canal and the restoration of peaceful conditions in the Middle East. Let me say with all the emphasis at my command that neither we nor the French Government have any desire whatever that the military action which we have taken should be more than

temporary in its duration. It will be terminated as soon as the emergency is over. It is our intention that our action to protect the Canal, to terminate hostilities and to separate the combatants should be as short as possible in duration.

100. The action taken by my Government and by the Government of France has been called an act of aggression against Egypt. This is a charge which we emphatically deny. There is much debate about what constitutes aggression, but it is certainly not true to say that every armed action constitutes aggression. Every action must clearly be judged in the light of the circumstances in which it has taken place and the motives which have prompted it.

101. The action of France and the United Kingdom is not aggression. We do not seek the domination of Egypt or of any part of Egyptian territory. Our purpose is peaceful, not warlike. Our aim is to re-establish the rule of law, not to violate it; to protect, and not to destroy. What we have undertaken is a temporary police action necessitated by the turn of events in the Middle East and occasioned by the imperative need not only to protect the vital interests of my own and many other countries, but also to take immediate measures for the restoration of order.

102. Our action is in no way aimed at the sovereignty of Egypt, and still less at its territorial integrity. It is not of our choice that the police action which we have been obliged to take is occurring on Egyptian territory. We have taken the only action which we could clearly see would be effective in holding the belligerents apart and which would give us a chance to re-establish peace in the area. By entering the Suez Canal area, we would only be seeking to protect a vital waterway, and it is also the only practicable line of division between the combatants.

103. Finally, on this point, I cannot help contrasting the motives of this police action undertaken by France and the United Kingdom in the Middle East with the armed action of the Soviet Union aimed at perpetuating its domination of Hungary.

104. I suggest that there is a great need for realism about this situation. After all, the fighting in which Israel is involved is taking place in Egypt, and it is therefore only in Egypt that it can be stopped. When two house-holders have committed a breach of the peace, the policeman has no option but to attempt to separate them where it is taking place.

105. Although my Government was obliged to disagree with the measures which it was proposed that the Security Council should take to meet this emergency, because they would have been too late to be effective, I trust that, in the light of what I have said, this Assembly will recognize that the Anglo-French intervention has been justified and is indeed in the best interests of all concerned.

106. I can well understand that the emotional shock naturally created by the fast-moving pattern of events may have obscured the realities behind the events in the Middle East. In the light of what I have said about the

ambitions of Egypt and the policies of the Soviet Union, I hope that the true situation will now be clearer.

107. It is indeed ironical to see today in the United Nations the two Powers which have contributed so much to the world Organization being arraigned in certain quarters for actions which they have taken in the interests of the world community and of the United Nations itself.

108. We believe that the United Nations now has a unique opportunity to bring peace to the Middle East. It is our hope that the emergency action we have taken to protect the Canal, to terminate hostilities and to separate the belligerents will result in a setttlement which will prevent such a situation from arising in the future. We must speedily work for a settlement of the whole Middle East question which takes account of the legitimate interests of the Arab countries as well as those of Israel.

109. I am not making any precise proposals—it would be inappropriate on such an occasion—but I should like to throw out the suggestion that one method of achieving this would be to convene a suitably constituted conference to consider how best to promote a permanent settlement.

110. I realize that there may at this moment be a temptation for this Assembly to take no effective action but merely to call upon all parties to cease hostilities and withdraw, but I must solemnly state—and I say this with great emphasis—that, if that were the only action which the United Nations was prepared to take at this time of crisis, we would merely revert to the continuation of the chaos in the Middle East which we have endured in the last eight years. We should thus inexorably be drawing nearer to the time when the growing threat of war became a reality.

111. The first urgent task is to separate Israel and Egypt and to stabilize the position. That is our purpose. If the United Nations were willing to take over the physical task of maintaining peace in the area, no one would be better pleased than we. But police action there must be, to separate the belligerents and to stop the hostilities.

112. In my sober submission, all Members of the United Nations should earnestly bend their efforts to bring about a lasting settlement which can replace the armistice agreements which have now proved to be too fragile for their task of preserving peace and order in the Middle East.

132. Mr. Dulles (United States of America): I doubt that any representative ever spoke from this rostrum with as heavy a heart as I have brought here tonight. We speak on a matter of vital importance, where the United States finds itself unable to agree with three nations with which it has ties of deep friendship, of admiration and of respect, and two of which constitute our oldest and most trusted and reliable allies.

133. The fact that we differ with such friends has led us to reconsider and re-evaluate our position with the utmost care, and that has been done at the highest levels of our Government, but even after that re-evaluation we still find ourselves in disagreement. And, because it seems to us that that disagreement involves principles which far transcend the immediate issue,

we feel impelled to make our point of view known to you and, through you, to the world.

134. This is the first time that this Assembly has met pursuant to the "Uniting for peace" resolution which the General Assembly adopted in 1950. I was a member of the United States delegation and had the primary responsibility for handling that proposal in committee and on the floor of this Assembly. It was then the period of the communist attack upon the Republic of Korea, and at that time surely we little thought that the resolution would be invoked for the first time under the conditions which now prevail.

135. What are the facts that bring us here? There is, first of all, the fact that there occurred, beginning last Monday, 29 October 1956, a deep penetration of Egypt by Israel forces. Then, quickly following upon that action, there came action by France and the United Kingdom in subjecting Egypt first to a twelve-hour ultimatum, and then to an armed attack, which is now going on from the air with the declared purpose of gaining temporary control of the Suez Canal, presumably to make it more secure. Then there is the third fact that after the matter had been brought to the Security Council, it was sought to deal with it by a draft resolution which was vetoed by the United Kingdom and France, which cast the only dissenting votes against the draft resolution.

136. Thereupon, under the provisions of the "Uniting for peace" resolution, the matter was brought before the Assembly upon a call from the Secretary-General instituted by a vote of seven members of the Security Council requiring that this Assembly convene in emergency special session within twenty-four hours.

137. The United States recognizes full well that the facts which I have referred to are not the only facts in this situation. There is a long and sad history of irritations and provocations. There have been armistice violations by Israel and against Israel. There have been violations by Egypt of the Treaty of 1888 governing the Suez Canal, and disregard by Egypt of the Security Council resolution of 1951 calling for the passage through that Canal of Israel ships and cargoes. There has been a heavy rearmament of Egypt in somewhat ominous circumstances. There was the abrupt seizure by Egypt of the Universal Suez Canal Company which, largely under British and French auspices, had been operating that Canal ever since it was opened ninety years ago. There had been repeated expressions of hostility by the Government of Egypt towards other Governments with which it ostensibly had and should have friendly relations.

138. We are not blind to the fact that what has happened within the last two or three days has emerged from a murky background. We have, however, come to the conclusion that these provocations—serious as they were—cannot justify the resort to armed force which has occurred during these last two or three days and which is continuing tonight.

139. To be sure, the United Nations has perhaps not done all that it should have done. I have often—and particularly in recent weeks—pointed

out that Article 1, paragraph 1, of the United Nations Charter calls for the settlement of these matters in conformity with the principles of justice and international law; that it calls not merely for a peaceful but also for a just solution. The United Nations may have been somewhat laggard, somewhat impotent, in dealing with many injustices inherent in this Middle Eastern situation. I think that we should, and I hope that we shall, give our most earnest thought—perhaps at the next regular session of the General Assembly—to the problem of how we can do more to establish and implement the principles of justice and international law. We have not done all that we should have done in that respect, and on that account part of the responsibility for the present events lies at our doorstep.

140. If, however, we were to agree that the existence in the world of injustices which this Organization has so far been unable to cure means that the principle of the renunciation of force should no longer be respected, that whenever a nation feels that it has been subjected to injustice it should have the right to resort to force in an attempt to correct that injustice, then I fear that we should be tearing this Charter into shreds, that the world would again be a world of anarchy, that the great hopes placed in this Organization and in our Charter would vanish, and that we should again be where we were at the start of the Second World War, with another tragic failure in place of what we had hoped—as we still can hope—would constitute a barrier to the recurrence of world war, which, in the words of the preamble to the Charter, has twice in our lifetime brought untold sorrow to mankind.

141. This problem of the Suez Canal, which perhaps lies at the basis of a considerable part of the forcible action now being taken, has been dealt with over the past three months in many ways and on many occasions. I doubt whether, in all history, so sincere and so sustained an effort has been made to find a just and peaceful solution.

142. When, on 26 July 1956, the Universal Suez Canal Company was abruptly seized by the Egyptian Government, all the world felt that a crisis of momentous proportions had been precipitated. Within, I think, three days after that event, representatives of the Governments of the United States, the United Kingdom and France met together in London to see what could be done about the situation. Already at that time voices were raised in favour of an immediate resort to force in an attempt to restore the *status quo* before the Egyptian seizure. But it was the judgment of all three of our Governments that such resort to force would be unjustified—certainly under the conditions existing at the time—and that efforts should first be made to bring about a peaceful and just solution.

143. Instead of any resort to force at that critical moment, the three Governments agreed to call a conference. Invitations were issued to twenty-four nations—including nations which were clearly surviving signatories of the Convention of 1888, nations which were the principal users of the Canal, and nations whose pattern of traffic showed a particular dependence upon the Canal. And twenty-two of those twenty-four nations met. Egypt de-

clined to attend the conference. Out of the twenty-two nations at the conference, eighteen agreed upon what they regarded as sound principles for arriving at a peaceful solution which would be just and fair and which would secure for the future the open use of this waterway.

144. That agreement of the eighteen was sent to Cairo as a proposal. It was presented to President Nasser, who rejected it. Then, the eighteen met again in London and considered a proposal for creating an association, a co-operative group, of the users of the Canal. We felt that it might be possible to work out, with the Egyptian authorities, on some practical, provisional basis, an acceptable arrangement for ensuring the operation of the Canal in a free and impartial way. While that association was in the process of being organized, the question was brought to the Security Council of the United Nations by France and the United Kingdom.

145. In the Security Council, six principles were unanimously adopted. Egypt, which participated in the proceedings, although it is not a member of the Council, concurred. Those principles were, in essence, the ones which had been adopted by the eighteen nations which met in London. A second part of the draft resolution which was presented to the Security Council looked forward to the implementation of the principles. That part was not adopted—owing, in that case, to a veto by the Soviet Union.

146. Despite that fact, there occurred under the auspices of the Secretary-General—to whom I should like to pay a tribute for his great contribution to the efforts at a just and peaceful solution of this problem—exchanges of views on how the six principles could be implemented. I do not think it is an exaggeration to say something which I am quite sure the Secretary-General would confirm—that is, that very considerable progress was made and that it seemed that a just and peaceful solution, acceptable to all, was near at hand. It was hoped that those negotiations would continue.

147. I would remind the Assembly that, at the close of that series of Security Council meetings, I made a statement, which was acquiesced in by all present, to the effect that the Security Council remained seized of the problem and that it was hoped that the exchanges of views by the three countries most directly concerned—Egypt, France and the United Kingdom —with the assistance of the Secretary-General, would continue. They did not continue, although I am not aware of any insuperable obstacle to their continuance.

148. Instead, there occurred the events to which I have already referred: the resort to violence, first by Israel and then by France and the United Kingdom—the events which again brought the matter to the Security Council and which, in the face of the vetoes cast there, have brought the matter before the General Assembly tonight.

149. Surely, I think that we must feel that the peaceful processes which the Charter requests every Member of the United Nations to follow had not been exhausted. Even in the case of Israel—which has a legitimate complaint, since Egypt has never complied with the Security Council's 1951

resolution recognizing Israel's right to the use of the Canal—there was a better prospect, because the principles adopted at the series of Security Council meetings on the Suez Canal, and adopted with the concurrence of Egypt, called for the passage of ships and cargoes through the Canal without discrimination and provided that the Canal could not be used or abused for the purposes of any nation, including Egypt.

150. Thus, peaceful processes seemed to be at work. As I have said, it appeared—at least to us—that those peaceful processes had not run their course. While I should be the last to say that there can never be circumstances where force may not be resorted to, and certainly there can be resort to force for defensive purposes under Article 51 of the Charter, it seems to us that, in the circumstances which I have described, the violent armed attack by three Members of the United Nations upon a fourth cannot be treated as anything but a grave error inconsistent with the principles and purposes of the Charter; an error which, if persisted in, would gravely undermine this Organization and its Charter.

151. The question then is: what shall we do? It seems to us imperative that something should be done, because what has been done, in apparent contravention of our Charter, has not yet gone so far as irretrievably to damage this Organization or to destroy it, and indeed, our "Uniting for peace" resolution was designed to meet just such circumstances as have arisen. It is still possible for the united will of this Organization to have an impact upon the situation and perhaps to make it apparent to the world, not only for the benefit of ourselves but for all posterity, that there is here the beginning of a world order. We do not, any of us, live in a society in which acts of disorder do not occur, but all of us live in societies where, if such acts do occur, something is done by the constituted authority to deal with them.

152. At the moment, we are the constituted authority, and while, under the Charter, we do not have the power of action, we do have a power of recommendation, a power which, if it reflects the moral judgment of the world community, world opinion, will be influential upon the present situation.

153. It is animated by such considerations that the United States has introduced a draft resolution which I should like to read out:

"*The General Assembly,*

"*Noting* the disregard on many occasions by parties to the Israel-Arab armistice agreements of 1949 of the terms of such agreements, and that the armed forces of Israel have penetrated deeply into Egyptian territory in violation of the General Armistice Agreement between Egypt and Israel of 24 February 1949,

"*Noting* that armed forces of France and the United Kingdom of Great Britain and Northern Ireland are conducting military operations against Egyptian territory,

"*Noting* that traffic through the Suez Canal is now interrupted to the serious prejudice of many nations,

"*Expressing* its grave concern over these developments,

"1. *Urges* as a matter of priority that all parties now involved in hostilities in the area agree to an immediate cease-fire and, as part thereof, halt the movement of military forces and arms into the area;

"2. *Urges* the parties to the armistice agreements promptly to withdraw all forces behind the armistice lines, to desist from raids across the armistice lines into neighbouring territory, and to observe scrupulously the provisions of the armistice agreements;

"3. *Recommends* that all Member States refrain from introducing military goods in the area of hostilities and in general refrain from any acts which would delay or prevent the implementation of the present resolution;

"4. *Urges* that, upon the cease-fire being effective, steps be taken to reopen the Suez Canal and restore secure freedom of navigation;

"5. *Requests* the Secretary-General to observe and promptly report on the compliance with the present resolution to the Security Council and to the General Assembly, for such further action as they may deem appropriate in accordance with the Charter;

"6. *Decides* to remain in emergency session pending compliance with the present resolution."

154. I recognize full well that a recommendation which is merely directed towards a cease-fire, to getting back to the armistice lines the foreign land forces in Egypt which, so far as we are aware today, are only those of Israel, to stopping the attacks by air and to preventing the introduction of new belligerent forces in the area, and which puts primary emphasis upon that and upon the opening, as rapidly as possible, of the Suez Canal, is not an adequate and comprehensive treatment of the situation. All of us, I think, would hope that out of this tragedy there should come something better than merely a restoration of the conditions out of which this tragedy arose. There must be something better than that, and surely this Organization has a duty to strive to bring that betterment about. If we should fail to do that, we, too, would be negligent and would have dealt only with one aspect of the problem.

155. I have said, and I deeply believe, that peace is a coin which has two sides—one is the avoidance of the use of force and the other is the creation of conditions of justice. In the long run you cannot expect one without the other. I do not by the from of this draft resolution want to seem in any way to believe that this situation can be adequately taken care of merely by the steps provided therein. There needs to be something better than the uneasy armistices which have existed now for these eight years between Israel and its Arab neighbours. There needs to be a greater sense of confidence and sense of security in the free and equal operation of the Canal than has existed since three months ago, when President Nasser seized the Universal Suez Canal Company. These things I regard as of the utmost importance.

156. But if we say that it is all right for the fighting to go on until these difficult and complicated matters are settled, then I fear that such a situation

will be created that no settlement will be possible, that the war will have intensified and may have spread, that the world will be divided by new bitterness and that the foundation for peace will be tragically shattered. These things that I speak of need to be done, and I believe that they are in the process of being done because the Security Council is already seized of these matters and has been working upon them in a constructive way.

157. We must put first things first. I believe that the first thing is to stop the fighting as rapidly as possible, lest it becomes a conflagration which endangers us all—and that is not beyond the realm of possibility. As President Eisenhower said last night, the important thing is to limit and to extinguish the fighting in so far as it is possible and as promptly as possible. I hope, therefore, that this point of view, reflected in the draft resolution, will prevail, because I fear that if we do not act, and act promptly and with sufficient unanimity of opinion so that our recommendations carry real influence, there is great danger that what has started and what has been called a police action may develop into something which is far more grave; and that, even if that does not happen, the apparent impotence of this Organization to deal with this matter may set a precedent which will lead other nations to attempt to take into their own hands the remedying of what they believe to be their injustices. If that happens, the future will be dark indeed.

158. When we wrote the Charter at San Francisco in 1945, we thought that we had perhaps seen the worst in war and that our task was to prevent a recurrence of what had been. Indeed, what then had been was tragic enough. But now we know that what can be will be infinitely more tragic than what we saw in the Second World War. I believe that at this critical juncture we owe the highest duty to ourselves, to our peoples, and to posterity to take action which will ensure that this fire which has started shall not spread but shall be promptly extinguished; and then to turn with renewed vigour to curing the injustices out of which this trouble has risen.

Editor's note: At a second session of the General Assembly held later that day the United States resolution was adopted. The vote was 64 to 5 with 6 abstentions. See General Assembly, *Official Records*, First Emergency Special Sessions, 562nd meeting (November 1, 1956), p. 35.

On the following day, November 2, the uprising in Hungary and its brutal suppression by Soviet forces was brought to the attention of the United Nations. The Security Council was called into emergency session to consider "The situation in Hungary." The American representative introduced a resolution urging the Soviet Union to stop interfering, and in particular with armed forces, in the internal affairs of Hungary and to make appropriate arrangements with the Hungarian Government for withdrawal of all Soviet forces from the country without delay. Also, the resolution requested the Secretary-General to investigate as a matter of urgency, the needs of the Hungarian people for food and medicine and other similar supplies and to report to the Security Council as soon as possible. See Security Council, *Official Records,* 11th year, 753d meeting (November 3, 1956), p. 4.

At the 3:00 A.M. meeting of the Security Council on November 4, the American resolution was rejected. The vote was 9 to 1 with Yugoslavia abstaining. Immediately after, the United States used the "Uniting for Peace" resolution to convene the second emergency session of the General Assembly in order to take up "The situation in Hungary." See Security Council, *Official Records,* 11th year, 754th meeting (November 4, 1956), pp. 12-14.

Extracts from General Assembly Second Emergency Special Session Debate of "The Situation in Hungary" (November 4-9, 1956)

564TH MEETING OF THE GENERAL ASSEMBLY*

9. THE PRESIDENT: The item which appears on the provisional agenda of the second emergency special session is entitled "The situation in Hungary." Is there any objection to its inclusion in the agenda?

10. MR. SOBOLEV (Union of Soviet Socialist Republics): The Soviet Union delegation objects to the inclusion in the agenda and to any discussion of the item entitled "The situation in Hungary," on the ground that such a discussion would be a gross breach of Article 2 of the United Nations Charter, which prohibits any intervention by the Organization in the domestic affairs of Member States.

11. For the same reasons, the Soviet delegation opposed the discussion of this question in the Security Council. It is regrettable that the majority of the members of the Council, acting in contravention of the United Nations Charter, tried to impose a discussion of this question on the Council. And now attempts are being made to impose the discussion of this question on the General Assembly.

12. It must be pointed out that the Security Council's decision to raise the question of the situation in Hungary was adopted in spite of the statement issued on 28 October 1956 by the legal government of the Hungarian People's Republic, categorically protesting against the discussion of any matters relating to the domestic affairs of Hungary in the United Nations, since the discussion of such questions in the United Nations would be a serious violation of the sovereign rights of the Hungarian People's Republic.

* General Assembly, *Official Records,* Second Emergency Special Session, 564th meeting (November 4, 1956), pp. 1-20.

13. With regard to Mr. Nagy's communications to the United Nations, it must be borne in mind that these were unconstitutional, and are therefore invalid. The Nagy government has in fact collapsed, and a Revolutionary Workers' and Peasants' Government has been formed, which includes several ministers of the Nagy cabinet who have remained loyal servants of the Hungarian people. This Workers' and Peasants' Government has sent the Secretary-General a telegram to the effect that all communications from Mr. Nagy are invalid. The Government of Hungary, this declaration states, objects to any discussion of the situation in Hungary in the United Nations, either in the Security Council or in the General Assembly, since this is a matter within the domestic jurisdiction of Hungary.

14. Thus, the proposal for placing on the agenda and discussing the question of the situation in Hungary is motivated not by a desire to promote a return to normal conditions in the Hungarian People's Republic but, on the contrary, by a desire to aggravate the situation and to support fascist elements which have risen against the Hungarian people and its lawful government. Nor would such a step contribute in any way to furthering the high purposes and principles proclaimed in the United Nations Charter. This provocative move is really aimed not at the maintenance of international peace and security, in accordance with the Charter, but at aggravating the international situation.

15. The reasons for the attempt to involve the General Assembly in a discussion of the situation in Hungary just at this particular time are quite clear. The initiative in raising this issue was taken by the United Kingdom and France, which are engaging in open aggression against the Egyptian people, and by the United States, where certain groups have done everything in their power to prepare the way for the criminal attacks of fascist elements against the Hungarian people. By imposing a discussion of the item entitled "The situation in Hungary" on the General Assembly, they are hoping to distract the attention of the United Nations and of world public opinion from the aggressive action undertaken by the United Kingdom and France against Egypt. The Governments of the United Kingdom and France have rejected the General Assembly's cease-fire decision, thus flouting the wishes of the sixty-four States which resolutely supported the demand for the cessation of military operations.

16. Only yesterday, our Organization adopted a new decision calling for an immediate halt to military action against Egypt. By trying, in contravention of the Charter, to involve the General Assembly in a discussion of the situation in Hungary, the United Kingdom and France, together with the United States, are attempting to gain time and to enable the British-French forces to settle accounts with the Egyptian people.

17. The Soviet delegation expresses the hope that those who are genuinely concerned for the immediate cessation of British and French aggression against Egypt will refuse to allow the attention of the General Assembly and of our Organization as a whole to be distracted from the neces-

sity of ensuring the implementation of its decision on the cessation of military activities against Egypt, or to authorize United Nations intervention in the domestic affairs of the Hungarian People's Republic.

56. MR. LODGE (United States of America): At dawn this morning, Soviet troops in Hungary opened fire in Budapest and throughout the country. We learn from Vienna that the Soviet artillery was firing incendiary phosphorus shells at centres of civilian population. These are the shells which set fire to buildings and which burned the flesh of women and children and other civilian non-combatants.

57. The Hungarian Prime Minister, Mr. Nagy, has appealed to the United Nations for help—and I must say we can understand it. After several days of ominous reports, the situation in Hungary has become all too clear. What is revealed is the sickening picture of duplicity and double-dealing. While this wholesale brutality by the Soviet Government was being perpetrated, the Soviet representative here in this hall was praising peace and non-aggression and raising his hands in horror against bloodshed in the Middle East. Those of us who were striving with every fibre of our being for peace in the Middle East can never forget this unutterable cynicism.

58. For the last few days, Soviet troop movements in Hungary have been reported. These reports have been accompanied by Soviet assurances to the United Nations and to the Hungarian Government that Soviet troops in Hungary had not and would not be reinforced. The reported movements were pictured as the redeployment of soviet forces stationed in the country. As late as 10 o'clock last night, Soviet representatives began negotiations—or what were described as negotiations—with Hungarian representatives, ostensibly for the withdrawal of Soviet troops from Hungary pursuant to Hungary's decision to renounce its membership in the Warsaw Pact.

59. The Soviet Union has made little pretence lately of its urge to dominate Hungary by the power of its military machine. It talked about a new relationship with its satellites, based on sovereign equality and independence and non-intervention in internal affairs. It spoke of negotiations under the Warsaw Pact for the withdrawal of its troops from some of these countries, particularly Hungary, where it admitted that the further presence of its army units could "serve as a cause for an even greater deterioration of the situation"—a deterioration which has, of course, so tragically occurred.

60. What a picture of deception we have had. After Mr. Nagy had formed his government, here was how *Pravda,* the Soviet Government organ, described the Nagy government on 28 October 1956:

"Today Budapest Radio announced the formation of a new national government of the Hungarian People's Republic on a broad democratic basis, led by Comrade Imre Nagy. The new Government immediately took up its duties. The Hungarian Government, guided by a desire to ensure that no one of the honest but misguided people should be punished, declared an amnesty for all who voluntarily laid down their arms."

61. On 30 October, Moscow Radio, which, of course, as in all totalitarian States, is an official government radio station—something which we do not have here—was telling its listeners in Europe: "Fortunately, under the leadership of Imre Nagy's Government, life is gradually returning to normal."

On the same day, Moscow Radio told its own people:

"The Hungarian working people have welcomed with satisfaction the statement made yesterday by Imre Nagy, which was approved by the Hungarian Workers Party and which announced the programme of action of the Government."

That is what Moscow Radio and *Pravda* said at that time. Today, *Pravda* calls erstwhile "Comrade" Nagy an "accomplice of reactionary forces."

68. That is what they were saying on 28 and 29 October 1956. Now what could have changed the situation in so short a time? The desire of Prime Minister Nagy to govern Hungary for the Hungarians? Does the Soviet Union fear this? The constant, deceitful reinforcement of the Soviet troops in Hungary during these fateful days says that it does.

69. It is now reliably reported that Soviet forces occupied the Parliament building in Budapest. The Prime Minister, Mr. Nagy, and other members of his Government, are now under arrest. Pal Maleter, the Minister of Defence and heroic defender of the Maria Theresa barracks against Soviet assault, who only yesterday was engaged in negotiations with Soviet military representatives for troop withdrawal, is also under arrest. A Soviet ultimatum was issued calling for the capitulation of Budapest by noon, and threatening the bombing of the city if it did not capitulate.

71. Let us not be deceived by this cynical and wanton act of aggression against the Hungarian people and its Government. A small group of Soviet strawmen announced their own formation as a government at the moment that Soviet troops began their attack. We have seen no passage of governmental authority from one Hungarian Government to another, but only the creation of a puppet clique and the overthrow of a liberal socialist government responsive to popular will in its desire to see these troops go.

72. Two hours after the attack began, the new puppet group appealed to the Soviet Union to come to its assistance. It cannot be maintained, therefore, that the Soviet action is undertaken in response to any request for assistance. The "assistance"—and I put that word in quotes—arrived long before the call.

73. This is how General Janos Kadar, the Communist puppet installed by Soviet military intervention this morning, spoke of Mr. Nagy when the Prime Minister first took over the Government: "I am in wholehearted agreement with Nagy, an acquaintance and friend of mine, my esteemed and respected compatriot." Wonderful friend. He was with him up to the hilt.

74. We must take drastic and decisive action here in this Assembly to

answer the appeal of the Hungarian Government. The United States delegation, therefore, is submitting a draft resolution which we believe should be promptly put to the vote and which I would now like to read:

"*The General Assembly,*

"*Considering* that the United Nations is based on the principle of the sovereign equality of all its Members,

"*Recalling* that the enjoyment of human rights and of fundamental freedom in Hungary was specifically guaranteed by the Peace Treaty between Hungary and the Allied and Associated Powers signed at Paris on 10 February 1947 and that the general principle of these rights and this freedom is affirmed for all peoples in the Charter of the United Nations,

"*Convinced* that recent events in Hungary manifest clearly the desire of the Hungarian people to exercise and to enjoy fully their fundamental rights, freedom and independence,

"*Condemning* the use of Soviet military forces to suppress the efforts of the Hungarian people to reassert their rights,

"*Noting moreover* the declaration by the Government of the Union of Soviet Socialist Republics, of 30 October 1956, of its avowed policy of non-intervention in the internal affairs of other States,

"*Noting* the communication of 1 November 1956 of the Government of Hungary to the Secretary-General regarding demands made by that Government to the Government of the Union of Soviet Socialist Republics for the instant and immediate withdrawal of Soviet forces,

"*Noting further* the communication of 2 November 1956 from the Government of Hungary to the Secretary-General asking the Security Council to instruct the Government of the Union of Soviet Socialist Republics and the Government of Hungary to start the negotiations immediately on withdrawal of Soviet forces,

"*Noting* that the intervention of Soviet military forces in Hungary has resulted in grave loss of life and widespread bloodshed among the Hungarian people,

"*Taking note* of the radio appeal of Prime Minister Imre Nagy of 4 November 1956,

"1. *Calls upon* the Government of the Union of Soviet Socialist Republics to desist forthwith from all armed attack on the peoples of Hungary and from any form of intervention, in particular armed intervention, in the internal affairs of Hungary;

"2. *Calls upon* the Union of Soviet Socialist Republics to cease the introduction of additional armed forces into Hungary and to withdraw all of its forces without delay from Hungarian territory;

"3. *Affirms* the right of the Hungarian people to a government responsive to its national aspirations and dedicated to its independence and well-being;

"4. *Requests* the Secretary-General to investigate the situation, to observe directly through representatives named by him the situation in Hungary, and to report thereon to the General Assembly at the earliest moment, and as soon as possible suggest methods to bring an end to the existing situation in Hungary in accordance with the principles of the Charter of the United Nations;

"5. *Calls upon* the Government of Hungary and the Government of the Union of Soviet Socialist Republics to permit observers designated by the Secretary-General to enter the territory of Hungary, to travel freely therein, and to report their findings to the Secretary-General;

"6. *Calls upon* all Members of the United Nations to co-operate with the Secretary-General and his representatives in the execution of his functions;

"7. *Requests* the Secretary-General in consultation with the heads of appropriate specialized agencies to inquire, on an urgent basis, into the needs of the Hungarian people for food, medicine, and other similar supplies, and to report to the General Assembly as soon as possible;

"8. *Requests* all Members of the United Nations, and invites national and international humanitarian organizations to co-operate in making available such supplies as may be required by the Hungarian people."

75. Our draft resolution is aimed at securing speedy action to cope with this grave situation. We do not believe that it is sufficient only to call upon the Soviet Union to desist from any further intervention in the internal affairs of Hungary and to withdraw all its troops without delay. We urge also that the Secretary-General should investigate the situation in Hungary directly and without delay and report to the Assembly as soon as possible. We call upon the USSR and Hungary to admit representatives of the Secretary-General to Hungarian territory, and if there is nothing to hide they have nothing to fear from the visit of impartial observers.

78. We cannot stand idly by while Hungarians are dragged bodily into servitude, even as they were re-emerging to independence and freedom. The principles set forth in the Charter of the United Nations are at stake. The basic and fundamental right of self-determination, which so many in this hall have endorsed time and again, is in grave danger. If we fail to act, it will constitute a base betrayal of the people of Hungary, who have appealed to us for aid. The Hungarian people can be sure that the United Nations will accept their cause as its own.

91. Mr. Sobolev (Union of Soviet Socialist Republics): In its first statement at this session of the General Assembly, the Soviet delegation gave its reasons for opposing the inclusion of the item on the situation in Hungary in the agenda.

92. As we have already pointed out, this item has been included in the agenda of the Security Council and of this session of the General Assembly in violation of the United Nations Charter, and there are no grounds whatever for its discussion.

93. However, in view of the fact that the real situation and the course of events in Hungary have been distorted in the statements of the representative of the United States and of other delegations, the Soviet delegation feels obliged to dwell on some of the facts relating to the situation in Hungary.

94. The course of events in Hungary has shown that the Hungarian workers, who have made great strides under the popular democratic system, rightly raised the question of eliminating certain serious shortcomings in the economic organization of their country and of further promoting the material well-being of the population.

95. Like most, if not all countries, the Hungarian People's Republic has had and still has its own difficulties, its own unresolved problems, resulting from a variety of causes. There is no doubt, however, that the workers of Hungary can very quickly overcome these difficulties if no artificial obstacles are created.

96. Many facts show that the legitimate and progressive movement of the workers in Hungary was rapidly joined by the dark forces of reaction and counter-revolution, which tried to use the discontent of sectors of the workers to undermine the foundations of the popular democratic system in Hungary and to re-establish the former landowners' and capitalists' order. Counter-revolutionary elements, taking advantage of the mistakes that had been made, using demagogical slogans and passing themselves off as fighters for freedom, tried to delude the working masses into following them. They took up arms against the legitimate government of the Hungarian People's Republic and succeeded in associating with their venture some of the Hungarian workers who had been deceived by their false propaganda.

97. The activities of the counter-revolutionary forces in Hungary, as is convincingly borne out by many facts, are to a great extent the result of the continuous subversive activities of the Western Powers, particularly the United States, against the popular democratic system. The examples we adduced in the Security Council make it abundantly clear that one of the guiding principles of United States policy is flagrant interference in the domestic affairs of the peoples' democracies and the instigation and financing of counter-revolutionary elements for subversive activities against the legitimate governments of the Soviet Union and the peoples' democracies, including Hungary.

98. I have already had an opportunity to draw attention to the existence in the United States of an unprecedented law, promulgated in 1951, called the Mutual Security Act, which openly proclaims that the United States Government undertakes to give administrative and financial support to spies and diversionists engaged in subversive activities against the Soviet Union, Hungary and the other peoples' democracies. It should also be noted that on 16 April 1956, only six months ago, the United States House of Representatives adopted a resolution containing an open appeal for the so-called libera-

tion of the peoples' democracies, which cannot be interpreted as anything but an appeal by the United States for the forcible overthrow of the legitimate governments of those countries.

99. There can be no doubt that the activities of the reactionary forces in Hungary are also the result of lengthy subversion by the imperialistic Powers. The members of the former Arrow Cross movement and the Horthyists, entrenched in Western Germany and Austria, have been carrying on their activities with the support of generous funds from the imperialists. These funds were also used for a slanderous campaign against the Hungarian peoples' democracy, for sending many balloons with propagandist literature, for inflammatory radio broadcasts and for creating and strengthening a reactionary underground movement. It is these reactionary forces which committed unlawful acts in Hungary, destroyed the socialist enterprises set up by the labour of the people, sacked State and social institutions and newspaper publishing houses all last week, killed workers and carried out fierce reprisals against Hungarian Communists and progressive leaders.

100. At the request of the Hungarian People's Government, the Soviet Government agreed to send Soviet military forces to Budapest in order to help the Hungarian peoples' army and the Hungarian authorities to restore order in the city. On 25 October 1956, the Hungarian Government declared that the introduction of Soviet troops had become essential to the vital interests of our socialist system. Although the head of that government, Mr. Nagy, said that he recognized the danger presented by the counter-revolutionary instigators, as he called them, he in fact showed himself to be assisting those reactionary forces, and this, of course, was bound to aggravate the situation in Budapest and the whole country.

101. The Soviet Government, considering that the continued presence of Soviet armed forces in Hungary might serve as a pretext for an even further aggravation of the situation, ordered its military command to withdraw the Soviet troops from Budapest. Subsequent events showed, however, that the reactionary forces in Hungary had become bolder still, taking advantage of the open tolerance of Mr. Nagy's cabinet. The bloody terror unleashed against the workers assumed unprecedented proportions. In those circumstances, it became absolutely clear that Mr. Nagy could not and did not wish to fight against the dark forces of reaction. The Nagy government fell apart, and gave way before the anti-popular elements.

102. As a result, conditions in the country became chaotic. Industrial enterprises and railways came to a standstill. Various reactionary groups, masking themselves behind high-sounding names, alluring programmes and demagogical slogans, advanced their claims to power in the country. It is known, for example, that a group of Horthyist fascist elements has gathered at Györ and directs the activities of counter-revolutionary forces in Hungary.

103. This situation was clearly bound to arouse legitimate anxiety and

concern among the real Hungarian patriots for the future of their country. On 4 November, a number of democratic Hungarian statesmen demanded the removal of the Nagy cabinet and took the government of the country into their own hands, forming a Hungarian Revolutionary Workers' and Peasants' Government. . . .

104. The new legitimate government of Hungary appealed to the Soviet troops which were in Hungary under the Warsaw Pact, for assistance in suppressing the counter-revolutionary elements which were trying to inflame the counter-revolutionary rebellion in Hungary.

105. The most recent reports from Hungary show that order is beginning to be restored there and that the Hungarian workers support the removal of Mr. Nagy from power and the formation of the new Workers' and Peasants' Government.

106. Attempts have also been made here to give a distorted interpretation of the facts relating to the presence of Soviet troops in Hungary. As everyone knows, in the years which have elapsed since the Second World War close ties of friendship and co-operation in all spheres of life have been established between the Soviet Union and the peoples' democracies, including Hungary. In the military sphere, an important foundation of the mutual relations between the Soviet Union and the peoples' democracies is the Warsaw Pact, under which the parties undertook certain military obligations, including that of taking any concerted action necessary for strengthening their capacity for defence in order to protect the peaceful work of their peoples, to guarantee the integrity of their frontiers and territories and to ensure defence against possible aggression.

107. The presence of Soviet forces in Hungary is determined by the provisions of the Warsaw Pact, and serves the general interests of the security of all the States parties to the pact. This was a response to the militarization of Western Germany and to the conclusion of military agreements of an aggressive kind between it and the United Kingdom, France and the United States.

108. It has been asserted here that the measures taken in Hungary against fascist elements constitute a violation of the human rights guaranteed under the Treaty of Peace with Hungary. We feel obliged to point out that these assertions are not only absolutely unfounded, but that the Hungarian Government, in taking measures to put an end to the criminal activities of counter-revolutionary elements, has acted in full conformity with article 4 of the Treaty of Peace, under which Hungary agreed not to allow the existence or operation of organizations of a fascist character pursuing the aim of depriving the Hungarian people of their democratic rights.

109. In the light of the facts to which I have referred, there can be no doubt as to the reason why the United States, the United Kingdom and France are determined at all costs to involve the United Nations in the

discussion of the so-called Hungarian question, in spite of the protests of the legitimate Hungarian government, which has clearly stated in its communications to the Secretary-General that the interference of the United Nations in the domestic affairs of Hungary is inadmissible.

110. The attempts of the representatives of the United States, the United Kingdom and France to set themselves up as defenders of the rights of the Hungarian people are ludicrous, to say the least. There can be no doubt—and indeed, it is absolutely self-evident—that they are concerned not with the rights of the Hungarian people, but with the restoration of the former corrupt capitalist régime in Hungary. That is why they give every support to the anti-popular elements which are attacking the legitimate Hungarian government.

111. At the same time, by imposing on the General Assembly the discussion of the question of the situation in Hungary, in contravention of the United Nations Charter, the representatives of the United States, the United Kingdom and France are trying to distract the attention of international public opinion from the merciless suppression of popular movements directed towards national independence and democratic freedoms which is taking place in Algeria, Cyprus, Malaya and other parts of Africa and Asia.

112. Moreover, by bringing the question of the situation in Hungary before the United Nations, they are seeking, as we have already said, to create a smoke-screen in order to divert attention from the armed aggression undertaken by the United Kingdom and France against Egypt. It is not by accident that it is the United Kingdom, France and the United States which have been urging so insistently for a discussion of the Hungarian question in the General Assembly, just when the Assembly has before it the urgent task of taking effective and rapid steps to halt the British-French aggression in Egypt.

113. The situation in Hungary cannot and should not be discussed in the United Nations, since it is the domestic affair of the Hungarian people. The United Nations cannot interfere in the exercise by a people of their inalienable right to determine the future of their country and to defend their historic achievements against the blows dealt by fascist elements to the popular democratic system.

114. We have just heard a statement from Mr. Lodge. This statement can only be regarded as a direct incitement to the fascist elements in Hungary to continue their nefarious subversive activities against the Hungarian people and their legitimate government. This statement is an expression of the frenzied efforts of certain circles in the United States, now and in recent years, to tear Hungary away from the camp of socialism and democracy. But this attempt has been thwarted by the Hungarian people. The Hungarian People's Republic is living through a period which will have a decisive influence on its further development. The victory of the democratic forces, headed by the working class, ensures for Hungary real independence,

full democratic freedoms for the whole people, and co-operation with other countries on the basis of the principles of equal rights and respect for national sovereignty.

116. . . . The Hungarian people themselves must be given an opportunity to build up their State and to overcome the difficulties which have existed and still remain in their path. That is why the Soviet delegation will object emphatically to any attempts to impose on the Assembly any decision concerning the so-called Hungarian question, since such a decision would constitute interference in the domestic affairs of Hungary.

170. Sir Pierson Dixon (United Kingdom): The United Nations has found itself during these last few days in an extraordinary position, which must, I think, cause all of us the greatest uneasiness. On two different problems, each of great importance, the majority of Members—both in the Security Council and in the General Assembly—has found itself in opposition to the actions of permanent members of the Security Council. As the representative here of one of the Governments concerned, I can assure my colleagues that the difference that has arisen between the United Nations and my Government has caused my Government very great concern.

171. The news of the Soviet attack on Budapest reached us early this morning. Reports of heavy fighting have continued to come in all day. These developments are known to all—though not, I fear, in all their terrible detail. . . .

181. In his speech this afternoon, the Soviet representative has again compared—as he did in the Security Council earlier today—the intervention of Hungary and the events which are now taking place in the Middle East. I will only say again very briefly, that there is no comparison. Even before the full-scale invasion of Hungary which has just started, Soviet troops had interfered in the internal affairs of Hungary to repress the people of Hungary in their struggle to assert their rights. The action of the United Kingdom and France in Egypt is none of these things. It is intended to stop the spread of war in the Middle East and to restore international law and order.

182. Furthermore, I feel obliged to point out that Her Majesty's Government and the French Government have supported a proposal that a United Nations force should take over the task of keeping the peace in the area of the Middle East in which fighting has been taking place. I hope the Soviet Government—and, to the extent to which it is permitted to express its will, the Hungarian Government—will be prepared to accept similar United Nations mission.

183. The first necessity is to secure an end to the bloodshed, to the carnage, in Hungary. With this end in view, I would urge the Assembly to call for an immediate cease-fire by Soviet land and air forces in Hungary and the withdrawal of all Soviet troops.

184. This would be only the first step. Our ultimate aim must be to secure to the Hungarian people the exercise of the rights which they have been guaranteed both by the Charter and by the Peace Treaty of 1947

between the Government of Hungary and the Allied and Associated Powers.

185. Furthermore, the Hungarian people must have the right to choose their own government by means of free elections.

186. This Assembly should also, in my view, accord formal recognition to Hungary's new-found independence. We recall that Mr. Nagy has twice declared the Hungarian Government's intention to establish the neutrality of his country. In a statement in the House of Commons yesterday, the British Foreign Secretary has welcomed this declaration on behalf of Her Majesty's Government in the United Kingdom. I therefore urge that, in addition to calling for an immediate cease-fire, the Assembly should forthwith meet Hungary's request for the recognition of the neutrality which it has proclaimed.

187. I give my full support to the draft resolution submitted by the United States delegation and in conclusion I would say that our word from this place will not go out in vain to the gallant Hungarian people, and it will, I trust, give them renewed hope in their heroic struggle for independence and liberty.

Editor's note: The American resolution was approved 50 votes to 8, with 15 abstentions. See General Assembly, *Official Records*, Second Emergency Special Session, 564th meeting (November 4, 1956), p. 20.

569TH MEETING OF THE GENERAL ASSEMBLY*

107. MR. VITETTI (Italy): The task of the Assembly is too important and too urgent, and its time too precious, for me to make a speech. This is not the moment for eloquence, but the moment for action.

108. Four days have elapsed since the Assembly adopted the resolution condemning the intervention of Soviet armed forces in Hungary. During those four days the masacres in Hungary have continued. Deaf to the decision of the Assembly and to the humanitarian appeal which came from it, Soviet troops have been fighting and killing Hungarian workers, peasants and students.

109. The news which comes from Hungary is appalling. Even though Hungary seems blacked out so that the world is kept in the dark about what is really happening, we have sufficient information to understand and realize that the heroic Hungarian people has been resisting with whatever forces it could in face of a violent and bloody repression.

110. The struggle now seems to be coming to its tragic end. Soviet armed forces are strangling the revolt of the Hungarian people, and now we are told that order has been restored. A Mr. Kadar, who styles himself "Prime Minister of the Revolutionary Workers' and Peasants' Government," has sent the Secretary-General a telegram saying that he objects categorically

* General Assembly, *Official Records*, Second Emergency Special Session 569th meeting (November 8, 1956), pp. 41-42.

to any discussion of Hungarian events because that question is within the exclusive jurisdiction of the Hungarian People's Republic.

111. That telegram is really a tragic farce. It is a farce for the Hungarian Government to style itself "the Workers' and Peasants' Government," when the peasants and workers are massacred in Hungary by the Soviet soldiers, who imposed that government on them. It is a farce to deny the right of the United Nations to discuss events in Hungary when those events represent a brutal, cynical and murderous violation of the Charter. It is a farce to call events in Hungary domestic affairs when there is a foreign army which has taken possession of Hungary and is in complete control of its affairs.

112. We cannot rely on any statement whatever which comes or may come in the future from the so-called Hungarian Government. That Government has been created under the thunder of Soviet guns and the terror of Soviet invasion. It is not a governmemt: it is a Soviet agency, and its voice is not the voice of the Hungarian people. The voice of the Hungarian people is the voice of the workers, the peasants and the students dying in their desperate struggle. It is not our right, but our duty to ignore the utterances of Mr. Kadar, whoever he is. It is our duty to continue along the road which we have chosen, and on that we must be resolute and firm.

113. Soviet troops must leave Hungary, and they must leave Hungary immediately. A foreign army which has been committing the crime of decimating the Hungarian population to such an extent that it must be considered an act of genocide can no longer be allowed to remain in Hungary. Hungary must be free. The Hungarian people must be given the right to choose its own government through free elections, as is done in every civilized country. That is what we must demand, and demand now.

114. On those lines, my delegation, together with the delegations of Cuba, Ireland, Pakistan and Peru, has prepared a draft resolution which I shall now read out to the General Assembly:

"*The General Assembly,*

"*Noting with deep concern* that the provisions of its resolution of 4 November 1956 have not as yet been carried out and that the violent repression by the Soviet forces of the efforts of the Hungarian people to achieve freedom and independence continues,

"*Convinced* that the recent events in Hungary manifest clearly the desire of the Hungarian people to exercise and to enjoy fully their fundamental rights, freedom and independence,

"*Considering* that foreign intervention in Hungary is an intolerable attempt to deny to the Hungarian people the exercise and the enjoyment of such rights, freedom and independence, and in particular to deny to the Hungarian people the right to a government freely elected and representing their national aspirations,

"*Considering* that the repression undertaken by the Soviet forces in Hungary constitutes a violation of the Charter of the United Nations, of the Peace Treaty between Hungary and the Allied and Associated Powers and of the Convention on Genocide,

"*Considering* that the immediate withdrawal of the Soviet forces from Hungarian territory is necessary,

"1. *Calls again upon* the Government of the Union of Soviet Socialist Republics to withdraw its forces from Hungary without any further delay;

"2. *Considers* that free elections should be held in Hungary under United Nations auspices, as soon as law and order have been restored, to enable the people of Hungary to determine for themselves the form of government they wish to establish in their country;

"3. *Reaffirms* its request to the Secretary-General to continue to investigate, through representatives named by him, the situation caused by foreign intervention in Hungary and to report at the earliest possible moment to the General Assembly;

"4. *Requests* the Secretary-General to report in the shortest possible time to the General Assembly on compliance."

115. In my opinion, it is imperative that the United Nations should state in a clear, definite and precise way the necessity for and urgency of the withdrawal of Soviet troops from the scene of their crimes. It is imperative that we should provide for free elections in Hungary. It is imperative that we should help the Hungarian people to reconstruct its free life, to be what it wants to be: a free people among free peoples.

116. I am not unaware of the grave difficulties which must be met. We shall face them. We shall explore the possibility of further action. The conditions in Hungary are appalling, and the help of the United Nations will be necessary. The Italian delegation considers, above all, that it will be necessary to provide for a United Nations commission to proceed to Hungary, and that it will be necessary, in order to protect peace and order, to establish a United Nations police force. We reserve the right to present, at a later stage, definite proposals on these lines.

117. What I can say now is that my Government is not only prepared but determined to do everything in its power to promote whatever international action is possible for the achievement of Hungarian freedom.

570TH MEETING OF THE GENERAL ASSEMBLY*

1. MR. LODGE (United States of America): In almost four years at the United Nations, I do not think that I have ever heard a higher degree of eloquence or a more genuine expression of feeling than I did when I listened, at this special session yesterday, to the speeches on the question of the

* General Assembly, *Official Records,* Second Emergency Special Session, 570th meeting (November 9, 1956), pp. 47-53.

Soviet Union outrages in Hungary—and I have heard some very eloquent speeches here in the past.

2. It is some measure of the deep sadness which is in our hearts that the speeches here have had some of the quality of funeral orations. I say "some" because, however sad we are, we cannot believe that this is, in fact, the end of Hungarian independence. We refuse to admit that the glorious dead of these past weeks have died in vain.

3. The Soviet Union has already paid an immense price for this bullying of a defenceless people. In Western Europe the newspapers tell us that people are leaving the Communist Party in droves; Communist headquarters are being burned; angry crowds of working people are parading and demonstrating against these 1956 models of totalitarian imperialism.

4. We must, therefore, not let the memory of this outrage die. Let the world never forget that the Soviet Union is in open defiance of the General Assembly's call to desist from armed attack on the people of Hungary. Let it also be remembered that, since the resolution [of November 4, 1956] was adopted, the Soviet Union has actually stepped up its attack.

5. The Hungarian people have been fighting with small arms, pitchforks and bare hands against massive formations of Soviet tanks. We hear that Soviet tanks have taken over bridges and roads, blocking all movement, even the movement of food and medical supplies; hospitals are ablaze; Red Cross units on their missions of mercy have been attacked; other legitimate Red Cross activities have been halted on Soviet orders. Such interference with the flow of medical aid, of all things, is proof of a horrifying callousness to human suffering.

6. All reports of the fighting of the past few days in the streets of Budapest use the word "savage" in describing the fury and speed of the Soviet army's attack against the people of Hungary, and even now, when resistance is broken, there are reports of heavy shellings still going on. Pathetic appeals for help were coming even yesterday from radio stations remaining in the hands of the Hungarian people. The Hungarian people, unlike the young man who claims to represent them here at the United Nations, are asking: when will the United Nations observers come?

7. Nothing can blot from human memory the sickening spectacle of Soviet tanks firing upon a literally unarmed population. Nothing can wipe out the black memory of military assaults on hospitals. Nothing can cleanse the stain of indiscriminate mass arrests or violent vengeance against a whole population. The action of the Soviet Government on the one hand in speaking of sending food to Hungary while, on the other, part of its military action is aimed at starving out the citizens of Budapest, is utterly revolting.

8. We have seen with interest the Secretary-General's report on the initial steps he has undertaken pursuant to the Assembly's resolution of 4 November. We hope he will press forward with his work. We want to know at the earliest possible moment the response of the Soviet Union and of the

present government of Hungary to his cablegram. We ask, will the Soviet Union and the government it has put in power in Hungary comply with the expressed wishes of the Assembly and co-operate with the Secretary-General in the execution of his responsibilities under the resolution?

9. Pending the outcome of the further efforts of the Secretary-General, this Assembly can appropriately address itself to the plight of the unfortunate people of Hungary. We now hear of repressive measures against whole segments of the population, and of mass deportations. There is widespread hunger, misery and suffering. There are also the thousands of Hungarian refugees who have fled across Hungary's borders to the West.

10. These are cogent reasons why it is important not only to obtain a first-hand account of events in Hungary, as contemplated by the Assembly resolution, but also to take immediate further steps towards meeting the urgent problem facing the gallant Hungarian people.

11. The United States has proposed, in a draft resolution which is now before the Assembly, to help meet their immediate needs. The draft resolution reads as follows:

"*The General Assembly,*

I

"*Considering* that the military authorities of the Union of Soviet Socialist Republics are interfering with the transportation and distribution of food and medical supplies urgently needed by the civilian population in Hungary,

"1. *Calls upon* the Union of Soviet Socialist Republics to cease immediately actions against the Hungarian population which are in violation of the accepted standards and principles of international law, justice and morality;

"2. *Calls upon* the Hungarian authorities to facilitate, and the Union of Soviet Socialist Republics not to interfere with, the receipt and distribution of food and medical supplies to the Hungarian people and to co-operate fully with the United Nations and its specialized agencies, as well as with other international organizations such as the International Red Cross, to provide humanitarian assistance to the people of Hungary;

"3. *Urges* the Union of Soviet Socialist Republics and the Hungarian authorities to co-operate fully with the Secretary-General and his duly appointed representatives in the carrying out of the tasks referred to above.

II

"*Considering* that, as a result of the harsh and repressive action of the Soviet armed forces, increasingly large numbers of refugees are being obliged to leave Hungary and seek asylum in neighbouring countries.

"1. *Requests* the Secretary-General to call upon the United Nations High Commissioner for Refugees to consult with other appropriate international agencies and interested Governments with a view to making speedy and effective arrangements for emergency assistance to refugees from Hungary;

"2. *Urges* Member States to make special contributions for this purpose."

12. We urge every Member State to do all in its power to aid in this vital humanitarian task. . . .

14. The United States draft resolution is aimed at immediate needs, and we believe it should be adopted and carried out in the shortest possible time.

15. The draft resolution submitted by the delegations of Cuba, Ireland, Italy, Pakistan and Peru deals with longer-range objectives. We shall vote for it also.

16. The Assembly has already called for the immediate withdrawal of Soviet troops from Hungary, where they remain clearly against the will of the people of that unhappy nation—people whose only crime was their desire for basic human rights, which in many of our countries are taken for granted. Only a week ago, a declaration by the Soviet Union explicitly promised withdrawal of Soviet forces from Hungary. That declaration lent an air of credibility to the claim, which is now proved to have been infamously deceitful, that negotiations on withdrawal were in fact actually under way.

17. We need action on the part of the Soviet Union in conformity with the expressed will of this Assembly. In the light of the attitude of the Soviet Union, we can consider what further United Nations action can be undertaken which is both constructive and feasible. Let us see how much support the Soviet Union is prepared to give to the words in the United Nations Charter which pledge all Members to respect "fundamental human rights" and "the dignity and worth of the human person." Let us see what the force of world opinion, supported by our United Nations observers, can do to achieve the objectives of this Assembly. We have set machinery in motion. Let us give it a chance to work. If the desired results are not achieved, then, of course, we must reappraise the situation and determine our further action. We will not let this heartbreaking tragedy drop. We will not forget.

26. Mr. Kuznetsov (Union of Soviet Socialist Republics): I should now like to make a few remarks on the statements made yesterday, and to refer to the Soviet Union's position with regard to the two draft resolutions that have been presented.

27. In previous statements made at this session of the General Assembly, the USSR delegation has already stressed that the inclusion of the question of the so-called "Situation in Hungary" in the agenda of this session of the General Assembly is a violation of the United Nations Charter. The Hungarian Government protests against the discussion of the so-called Hungarian question in the United Nations because it regards this as interference in the domestic affairs of the country. This is a fact which the United Nations cannot disregard.

28. It is now evident that the motives behind the discussion of the so-called Hungarian question are quite alien to the interests of the Hungarian

people and the principles of the United Nations Charter. What has happened and what is happening at these meetings of the General Assembly in connexion with events in Hungary is, I think, unprecedented in the history of the United Nations. The delegations of the United States, the United Kingdom, France and a number of other countries are using the forum of the United Nations in an attempt to incite reactionary fascist groups to use violence against the popular democratic system in Hungary and to mobilize the reactionary forces which are still dreaming of restoring the old land-owner-capitalist order in Hungary. Another reason why the Western Powers have introduced the so-called Hungarian question is to divert public attention from the armed attack that they have organized against Egypt.

29. The unsavoury task which these delegations have undertaken is being carried out, as might be expected, to the accompaniment of various fabrications and lying attacks against the Soviet Union, Hungary and all the countries where the popular-democratic system prevails. The political aim of these statements is absolutely clear and is neither original nor new, as far as either Hungary or the Soviet Union is concerned. We in the Soviet Union have been hearing our enemies calling for the overthrow of our State for the past thirty-nine years.

45. The collapse of the counter-revolutionary rising in Hungary has infuriated certain circles in the United States, the United Kingdom and France, as it represents the failure of their attempt to restore capitalism in one of the countries of Eastern Europe and the loss of the considerable resources which they had spent on organizing diversionist activities in that country. Those circles are now trying to use the United Nations to slander the Hungarian people, who are acting in defence of their democratic rights, and to slander also those who are giving the Hungarian people all possible support in strengthening their popular-democratic system.

46. From this exalted forum of the General Assembly speeches are being made with a view to fomenting hostility among nations, and all kinds of fabrications and insinuations are being bandied about concerning the events in Hungary and in other countries whose policy is displeasing to the West. All possible means are being used to delude the peoples of the world and to conceal from them the truth about Hungary.

50. As the entire course of the debate on the so-called Hungarian question shows, the sponsors of the item have yet a second objective in mind. They are trying by this provocative method to divert the attention of world public opinion from the armed aggression carried out by the United Kingdom, France and Israel, with the encouragement of the United States, in Egypt and throughout the Middle East.

51. No talk of a so-called Hungarian question will succeed in hiding the fact that the United States Government has embarked upon the course of openly encouraging the aggressors in their efforts to enslave the Egyptian people. At the same time, it has no objection to taking advantage of the present situation in the Middle East for its own predatory purposes, and

fishing in troubled waters. As is known, the United States is well versed in tactics of this kind, which it has used in Indochina and certain other parts of South-East Asia, for example.

52. It was therefore not surprising that when the Soviet Government proposed certain practical measures with a view to putting an immediate halt to the aggression against Egypt, the United States not only refused to support them, but, together with the United Kingdom and French delegations, prevented their consideration by the Security Council. What could be more hypocritical and treacherous towards the Egyptian people than a policy of this kind?

53. The ruling groups in the United Kingdom and France, having launched a war of aggression in Egypt, are at the same time cynically denouncing the measures which have been taken by the democratic forces of Hungary in defence of their people's democratic régime; their object in so doing is to divert attention from their crimes in Egypt. Ignoring the decisions of the General Assembly, which called for the cessation of hostilities in Egypt, United Kingdom and French armed forces have savagely bombed peaceful Egyptian communities, killed women and children, and destroyed the material and cultural fruits of the Egyptian people's labours. The object in view was to seize the Suez Canal.

54. United Kingdom and French forces are ruthlessly suppressing the legitimate national liberation movements of the peoples of Malaya, Singapore, Kenya, Cyprus, Algeria and other territories and colonies. Yet at the same time United Kingdom and French representatives are hypocritically trying to pose as defenders of the rights of the Hungarian people, vainly hoping that by manoeuvres of this kind they will succeed in deluding world public opinion and diverting attention from the aggressive activities of the British and French armed forces in the Middle East, Africa and other areas of the world.

58. The representatives of the United States, the United Kingdom and France, and certain other representatives who have spoken here, have tried to call in question the Soviet Union's firm adherence in its foreign policy to the principle of the peaceful coexistence of peoples, and to challenge the position of the Soviet Union with respect to the principles adopted by the Bandung Conference and to many other aspects of its domestic and foreign policies. These attempts will fail. No matter what reactionary groups do to hide the truth about the Soviet Union, it will find its way to the peoples of the world.

59. The Soviet Union has always pursued and will unswervingly continue to pursue a policy of peace; it will continue to strive for the relaxation of international tension and for the realization of the principle of peaceful coexistence, and will fight with all its might for the maintenance and strengthening of peace. The Soviet people have always welcomed and sympathized with the national liberation movements of the peoples for their freedom, their democratic rights and their national independence. Since it

pursues this policy, the Soviet Union is entitled to expect other States to see it as it is. Those who count on the Soviet Union renouncing its principles as a result of its increased contacts and co-operation with other countries, are making a serious mistake. Nothing can deflect the Soviet Union from this course, for such a policy serves the fundamental interests not only of the Soviet people, but of ordinary people throughout the world; that is, it serves the cause of world peace.

60. So far as the question of the presence of Soviet forces in Hungary is concerned, the Soviet delegation wishes to emphasize that these troops are stationed in Hungary in pursuance of the Warsaw Treaty and at the request of the legal Hungarian government. The Hungarian Government asked for assistance to the Hungarian people in its effort to suppress the dark forces of reaction and counter-revolution, to re-establish the people's socialist system and to restore order and tranquillity in Hungary. The Hungarian Government also declared that when order and tranquillity had been restored in Hungary it would enter into negotiations with the Soviet Government and the other parties to the Warsaw Treaty on the subject of the presence of Soviet forces on Hungarian territory.

61. Thus the question of the withdrawal of Soviet forces from Hungary is a matter exclusively within the jurisdiction of the Hungarian and Soviet Governments.

62. Attempts have been made here to discredit the collective security system created under the Warsaw Treaty. The Warsaw Treaty, as everybody knows, was concluded as a measure essential to the security of the contracting parties, and necessitated by the fact that the Western Powers were re-arming the Federal Republic of Germany and recreating the former Hitler *Werhmacht* in that country; by the fact that they were encircling the peoples' democracies and the USSR with large numbers of military bases and established the North Atlantic Treaty Organization, an aggressive military bloc directed against the peoples' democracies, the USSR and other countries.

63. The Soviet Union and the other parties to the Warsaw Treaty, as is well known, have stated that they would agree to the abrogation of the Warsaw Treaty, provided that NATO also was dissolved. However, the Western Powers have rejected that proposal. It should also be noted in this connexion that the question of the existence and implementation of a regional agreement such as the Warsaw Treaty is exclusively within the jurisdiction of the contracting parties, and any attempt to turn this question into a subject for discussion by the United Nations is illegal and a violation of the Charter.

66. The Governments of the USSR and a number of other countries friendly to Hungary have responded to the appeal addressed by the new government of Hungary to the Governments of the fraternal socialist countries to co-operate with Hungary in restoring the country to normal and healing its wounds as quickly as possible. The USSR Government, for its

part, is sending foodstuffs, medicines, building materials, fuel and other goods to Hungary. The Hungarian people will undoubtedly succeed in overcoming the present difficulties and rapidly restoring the country to normal.

67. All that is required of the United Nations at the present time is that it should prevent any attempts to hinder the Hungarian people in their peaceful creative work and reject the pretensions of the United States, the United Kingdom, France and certain other countries to interfere in the internal affairs of Hungary for the purpose of restoring the former capitalist system.

68. However, the initiators of the slanderous campaign against the Hungarian People's Republic, the Soviet Union and all the peoples' democracies are trying to aggravate the situation in Hungary. Before the ink of the previous General Assembly resolution, adopted on 4 November, has had a chance to dry, before the Secretary-General of the United Nations has been able to say a single word about the measures taken in connexion with that General Assembly resolution, further draft resolutions are submitted.

69. One draft resolution, proposed by Cuba, Ireland, Italy, Pakistan and Peru, constitutes yet another attempt to rob the Hungarian people of their legal right to free democratic elections free of outside interference. Its other provisions are similarly designed to extend further and to increase interference in the internal affairs of Hungary, in order to stir up the campaign of slander against the countries enjoying democratic régimes. For the reasons I have stated, the Soviet delegation opposes this draft resolution and will vote against it.

70. With respect to the second draft resolution, proposed by the United States delegation, the Soviet delegation feels it necessary to make the following statement. The Soviet Government has already decided to send assistance to Hungary in the form of 50,000 tons of grain and flour, 3,000 tons of meat, 2,000 tons of butter, 3 million tins of milk, 5,000 tons of sugar, and large quantities of building materials and other goods. The Soviet Union has already begun to dispatch these goods. It is reported that the Hungarian People's Republic is receiving help from the People's Republic of China, Czechoslovakia, Romania and other peoples' democracies. Any Governments and organizations that want to help Hungary can also, given the desire to do so, easily find a way of establishing direct contact with the Hungarian Government in this matter.

71. The draft resolution proposed by the United States representative contains a number of slanderous allegations about the Soviet Union, allegations intended to deceive the Hungarian people and world public opinion. The Soviet delegation will therefore vote against it.

72. If we look into the events taking place in Hungary objectively, the only conclusion we can reach is that the so-called Hungarian question should be removed from the agenda of this session of the General Asembly, as the Hungarian Government has requested, as a violation of the United

Nations Charter and a threat to the authority of the United Nations. Any attempt to pursue the discussion of this question in the United Nations can only be regarded as reflecting a desire to support the reactionary underground movement in Hungary and to hamper the task of restoring Hungary's domestic life to normal, a task that is being carried out under the direction of the new government.

73. The removal of the Hungarian question from the agenda of the United Nations will be in the interest of the Hungarian people, who want not interference in their internal affairs but the opportunity of strengthening the people's democratic system in their country. It will also serve the cause of maintaining and strengthening peace.

571ST MEETING OF THE GENERAL ASSEMBLY*

100. MR. SUDJARWO (Indonesia): Yesterday, I set forth my Government's basic attitude towards this question of Hungary which is now being dealt with by the General Assembly in emergency special session. Delegations are prone to state the high and noble principle on which the policies of their Governments are based. This is a good thing, and my delegation has followed this practice, also.

101. I believe that, so far as declared principles are concerned, there is not much disagreement among delegations to the General Assembly. Indeed, the very fact of being a Member of this Organization entitles each of us here to claim that, in our policies, we uphold the noble principles expressed in the Charter.

102. My delegation has clearly stated the principles involved in this question of Hungary. What is important now is the fact that we must solve the problem, that we must seek a solution to a grave and serious situation which presents itself to us, but even more to the people and country of Hungary. I should like to repeat what I said here yesterday:

"Whatever we do, at this crucial time in the history of the Hungarian people, we should do in the real interests of the Hungarian people as a whole, for the country as a whole, and thereby assist the Hungarian Government to carry out such objectives, taking into account, however, the need for a country, especially a small one, to maintain friendly relations with its neighbours."

103. We must seek a peaceful solution in the interests of the Hungarian people. We must contribute to the cessation of fighting and destruction in that country. We must do that in the real interests of the country and its people, but also, I believe, in the interests of peace in that entire area of the world. My delegation will view every draft resolution in that light, basing its final position on the usefulness or the effectiveness of the draft resolution in paving the way for a rapid and peaceful solution of the problem.

* General Assembly, *Official Records,* Second Emergency Special Session, 571st meeting (November 9, 1956), pp. 68-74.

104. Sentiments of sympathy, of anger and of condemnation of one another have been expressed. Everyone is, of course, free to state his views and to express his feelings. We respect all those sentiments and feelings, many of which, indeed, we share. If, however, we ask the Assembly to take a decision, the prime consideration should be whether, after the adoption of the first resolution on 4 November, the adoption of another draft resolution would really contribute further to the solution of the situation, even though it might satisfy our sentiments and feelings.

105. Moreover, we are dealing here with a Member State, a sovereign State with a government of its own—whether we like it or not—which, according to the Charter, has its own rights and obligations. Nothing, in fact, can be solved now without the co-operation of the Hungarian Government. Only yesterday, the Secretary-General communicated to that Government an *aide-mémoire,* which was also circulated to delegations here, bringing to the attention of the Hungarian Government the provisions of the Assembly resolution of 4 November and seeking that Government's co-operation in implementing the provisions. Thus, we are in fact at this moment awaiting the Hungarian Government's answer to and comments on the *aide-mémire.* Now, a five-Power resolution has been submitted which seeks to make further demands of that Government and contains further expressions of condemnation. I do not know whether such a draft resolution will be helpful at a time when we are seeking, through the Secretary-General, the co-operation of the Hungarian Government in many matters. I do not want to challenge or to question the principles involved in this draft resolution. In fact, my delegation supports the idea of the withdrawal of Soviet forces from Hungary; this is a matter to be negotiated by the Hungarian Government with the Soviet Union.

106. We also support the idea of free elections in Hungary, but, again, let this be their own choice, the choice of the people of Hungary. With all respect to the sentiment and principles which are expressed in this draft resolution, in all fairness we do have honest doubts whether this draft resolution, if adopted, would have the effect it seeks to achieve. Therefore, the Indonesian delegation will be unable to support this draft resolution because of the considerations I have mentioned. The difference between my delegation and the sponsors of this draft resolution is not, I believe, on matters of principle, but rather on the conduct of policy at a certain moment in seeking a peaceful solution of a certain situation.

107. My Government believes in the kind of approach I have described dealing with a difficult and delicate situation such as the one before us. Exploring persistently the possibilities for a just but peaceful solution, we will continue to conduct ourselves in that way.

108. In regard to the second draft resolution presented by the United States delegation I think its intention is to carry out the humanitarian tasks recommended in the resolution of 4 November as quickly and as smoothly as possible. This endeavour certainly has my delegation's support. This

morning we heard with satisfaction the announcement of the Government of the Soviet Union that it, too, has already begun to send medical supplies, food and so on to alleviate the plight of the Hungarian people.

109. The United States draft resolution, however, unforunately is couched in terms which are rather controversial and which will therefore, I am afraid, make its implementation only more difficult. This certainly would not be helpful in serving the purpose intended. My delegation would like to see this draft resolution confined to the humanitarian tasks, that is, couched in terms which would make its implementation easier rather than more difficult. If the harsh or accusing phrasing were taken out, my delegation would be able to support it whole-heartedly. The question of phrasing is important in this kind of endeavour.

110. If one wants a resolution to be adopted by the greatest possible majority, one can, without relinquishing one's principles, permit or acquiesce in the use of a kind of terminology in a resolution which, while not wholly meeting with one's sentiments, still is most appropriate to meet the need for general support. In the case of the Middle East question, for instance, or rather in the case of the aggression of the United Kingdom and France against Egypt, my delegation and all the Asian and African delegations acquiesced in terming this United Kingdom and French aggression against Egypt just "military operations against Egyptian territory." This term did not fully meet our sentiments, but we agreed to it for the sake of attaining general support, taking into account the different positions of several delegations towards the United Kingdom and France, positions we wished to understand. While for us, indeed, for the great majority of the Assembly there was the fact of clear-cut aggression against Egypt by the United Kingdom, France and Israel, the word "aggression" or even the phrase "deploring such aggression or such actions," let alone condemning them, was not introduced in the draft resolution submitted by the United States delegation. The word used in the preamble was merely *"Noting"* and the draft resolution only expressed the grave concern of the General Assembly over the developments.

111. We indeed gave much consideration to the objections of some Powers against using those harsh words in a resolution. We acquiesced in this moderation and incorporated words in the resolution only in the most business-like way. Therefore, we hope that in this question of Hungary also the same considerations can prevail without, I must say again, compromising anybody's principles. Accordingly, with regard to the United States draft resolution I should like to suggest that it be amended in such a way as to read as follows:

"The General Assembly,

I

"Considering that distribution of food and medical supplies is urgently needed by the civilian population in Hungary,

"1. *Requests* the Hungarian authorities to facilitate the receipt and distribution of food and medical supplies to the Hungarian people and to co-operate fully with the United Nations and its specialized agencies, as well as other international organizations such as the International Red Cross, to provide humanitarian assistance to the people of Hungary;

"2. *Urges* the Hungarian authorities to co-operate fully with the Secretary-General and his duly appointed representatives for the carrying out of the tasks referred to above.

II

"*Considering* that large numbers of refugees are leaving Hungary,

"1. *Requests* the Secretary-General to call upon the United Nations High Commissioner for Refugees to consult with other appropriate international agencies and interested Governments with a view to making speedy and effective arrangements for emergency assistance to refugees from Hungary;

"*Urges* Member States to make special contributions for this purpose."

112. Amendments to this effect will be formally submitted by the delegations of Ceylon, India and Indonesia. I believe that so amended the draft resolution would maintain its essence of obtaining the speedy carrying out of the needed humanitarian work which is indeed a very urgent matter and one which should be viewed in the most objective manner in order to secure its success.

114. MR. KRISHNA MENON (India): The General Assembly has before it a number of draft resolutions, the amendments to one of the draft resolutions presented by the delegations of Ceylon and Indonesia together with my own delegation, and there is also pending the resolution of 4 November 1956. I should like to deal with the resolutions which are before us today in the order in which they have been submitted.

115. There is first of all the five-Power draft resolution which deals in substance with the situation in Hungary. With regard to that draft resolution, the position of most delegations has already been stated, because that draft resolution deals with the subject matter covered by the resolution of 4 November.

116. I should like to reiterate what I said from this rostrum yesterday. Having considered the position in Hungary, the Assembly [on November 4, 1956—Ed.] passed a resolution which requested the Secretary-General to make certain investigations and report to it. That resolution is still pending. We are told and the Secretary-General has informed us that he is not in a position to make that report. It appears to me in the normal course of things entirely an unusual proceeding to go on to other decisions. The decision of the Assembly of 4 November is, on the face of it, a clear indication that the Assembly wants information. The Assembly wants to know what the Secretary-General is able to do in these matters.

117. It is quite true that my delegation abstained on this resolution for the reasons I set out yesterday. But even though a delegation abstains on the

vote, when a resolution is adopted it becomes the resolution of the Assembly. In our opinion, there is a duty cast upon the Assembly at least to conform to its own resolution passed only a few days ago. Therefore, we think that the five-Power draft resolution apart from all other considerations, to which I shall refer in a moment, is misconceived. We are not able to support it, and shall vote against it.

118. Secondly, in making this approach to the problem, my delegation desires to submit with respect that we are not giving sufficient thought and attention to the resolving of the problems and the difficulties that exist in Hungary at the present moment. There was no one here who does not appreciate that there has been fighting, suffering and unsettlement and that there is not the stability required. Any decisions that we adopt here must be directed to the improvement of those conditions. Furthermore, my delegation cannot subscribe at any time to any phraseology or proposals before the Assembly which disregard the sovereignty of States represented here. For example, we cannot say that a sovereign Member of this Assembly, admitted after due procedures, can be called upon to submit its elections and everything else to the United Nations without its agreement. Therefore, any approach that we make as though this is a colonial country which is not represented at the United Nations, is not in accordance either with the law or the facts of the position.

119. With regard to the subject matter, it disturbed our minds and caused my Government and people a great deal of anxiety; as I said yesterday on this rostrum, we have, as a Government, as all Governments do, the right to exert what influence we have and make such approaches as are possible to assist in resolving this problem and to bring about a situation where the Hungarian people will be able to settle down to constructive tasks and enjoy their national independence.

120. I am to say that in the correspondence between the Prime Ministers of the Soviet Union and India, the last part of which was communicated from New Delhi and received here this afternoon, the Soviet Government informed us of a determination to deal with its relationships with their neighbouring socialist States on the principles of mutual respect of their sovereignty, territorial integrity, and friendship, co-operation and non-interference in the internal affairs of each other. This appears in the declaration of the Soviet Government of 30 October, and it is reiterated.

121. There is the problem of the Soviet troops. The Government of India is informed that Soviet troops are to be withdrawn from Budapest in agreement with the Hungarian Government as soon as order is restored. And the Russian Government intends to start negotiations with the Hungarian Government in regard to Soviet-Hungarian relations in conformity with this declaration.

122. It is entirely up to the Assembly to make its own decision with regard to these matters. As far as our Government is concerned, we have made efforts in this direction with a view to attaining the ends that are put

forward in these resolutions. In agreement with Yugoslavia, Poland and other countries, who are very near to Hungary and whose problems though not identical are of a similar character, we think that we should not do things here merely out of emotion or other reactions or out of our political predilections, forgetting the interests of the Hungarian people and of the Hungarian State. Therefore, any attitude which is taken which will retard this process of the withdrawal of troops and the settling down of the Hungarian people will be contrary to our general purposes.

123. For those reasons, we think that the five-Power draft resolution is not one which we can support. We consider that it will not assist in the purposes in which the Assembly has interested itself. We also think it is not consistent with the requests we have made to the Secretary-General and the tasks assigned to him. What we are really doing is asking the Secretary-General to make an investigation and to report; and then, before we hear from him, proceeding to take decisions. Either our first decision was wrong and we do not want information—in which case we should say so—or we ask the Secretary-General to do something and then we disregard that. There is also the *aide-mémoire* which he submitted yesterday, in which he informed the Assembly that he had taken steps in this direction and that he is awaiting a reply. He also points in that *aide-mémoire* that nothing of this kind can be done without the co-operation of the Hungarian Government. In his communication, the Secretary-General says that there is a Hungarian Government with which he is in correspondence. I think that *aide-mémoire* should be regarded as expressing the view of the United Nations, because no one has challenged it so far.

124. We come now to the second draft resolution before us, which stands in the name of the United States of America. This draft resolution is of an entirely different category, and I would like to say that we are in agreement with its purposes. If I am right, the purposes of this draft resolution are humanitarian, that is, the relief of suffering. But a purpose always gets rather distorted when material that is relevant to other purposes is imported into it. Therefore, my delegation, while agreeing with the purposes as being in conformity with the general approach towards relieving suffering whatever may be the causes, has tried to remove from the United States draft resolution such parts as make it unacceptable to us, and to retain all the rest, even though we might not have phrased it in that way; that is to say, if my delegation and those who co-sponsored these amendments had to submit a draft resolution *de novo*, we might not have adopted this phraseology. But we are anxious to retain as much of this draft resolution as we can and to take away from it only those things that have no relevance at all or may come in the way of its purposes.

125. It is our submission that the draft resolution as we seek to amend it meets the purposes which the United States draft resolution has in view, without importing into it other considerations and that it will achieve the

end to which my colleague from Indonesia has just referred, namely, to bring to this draft resolution a larger degree and wider extent of support.

126. In regard to the whole question of the relief of suffering in conditions of war or conditions of civil disturbance, I should like to draw the attention of the Assembly to the fact that these matters have been taken into consideration by the nations of the world and have led to the formulation of the Geneva Convention in regard to a disturbance of this character, whether the disturbance be a civil disturbance, a civil commotion, internal might be said—and therefore as coming within Article 2 paragraph 7 of the United Nations Charter—or an international war. It is the submission of my delegation that these matters of relief should be dealt with in accordance with the Geneva Convention. If it is dealt with in accordance with the Geneva Convention, the channelling of aid should be through organizations of a character which do not call into question the nature of that aid or its purposes or whether, in a packet containing medicaments, arms are going in, or anything of that kind. Therefore, in these circumstances, the aid should go to the International Red Cross which would decide the local organs through which their further transmission should take place.

127. I am sure that the Assembly will share the feeling of my delegation that we were glad to hear this morning from the representative of Yugoslavia that the International Red Cross has not met with any resistance from any party concerned, and that the International Red Cross is functioning through the Hungarian and Yugoslav Red Cross missions. Therefore, it is the appropriate international authority free from political or national bias which conforms to the terms of the Geneva Convention, and is the appropriate authority to deal with this matter.

128. While we have no desire to have a specific mention of this apart from what appears in the draft resolution, half the troubles arising from political controversy would disappear if we would separate the humanitarian aspects from our own political objectives. That is why my delegation has moved these amendments, and I hope that after the statement that the representative of Indonesia has made and that I have made—and that I am sure those who speak after me will make—it will be seen that we are in agreement with the purposes and the motives that lie behind the United States draft resolution. But we cannot agree with its formulation; however, we are in agreement with the main purposes. We hope, therefore, that these amendments will find favour with the sponsor of the draft resolution.

129. I will not follow one of the preceding speakers into a discussion of topics that are not before us now. This is the second emergency session of the Assembly dealing with the problem of Hungary. The first one dealt with the problem of Egypt and, normally speaking, it would be out of order, I suppose, to deal with the topic of the first emergency session in the second emergency session; but it would not be out of order to deal with what has been said in the second emergency session by someone else if the President

did not rule him out of order. Therefore, it is necessary to state that it is a little inconsistent to try and tell us at this time that the aggression committed by the Anglo-French alliance on Egyptian territory is in defence of peace and has any relation to this problem whatsoever. Therefore, in view of that fact having been mentioned, my delegation wants its expression of opinion to be placed on the record.

134. Mr. GUNEWARDENE (Ceylon): I stated yesterday in categorical terms that as regards the Government of Ceylon, we would only be too prepared to accede to any request for a cease-fire. . . .

135. In the same way that we registered our protest against the United Kingdom and France for their armed intervention in Egypt, we certainly protest even in stronger language against the action of Soviet forces in Hungary.

136. The point was made by Sir Pierson Dixon, my very esteemed friend and distinguished colleague from the United Kingdom, that the United Kingdom and France have accepted the cease-fire and have freely undertaken to withdraw their forces from Egyptian territory. We are certainly grateful for that statement. At the same time, although there was no reason for bringing up the Egyptian question in connexion with this debate, the statement was also made that they were willing to do so and that Soviet Russia was not so willing. I should like to remind Sir Pierson Dixon that in spite of the resolution adopted by the General Assembly, Anglo-French forces landed in Egypt in defiance of the resolution. I believe that such action may sometimes set a bad example for others.

137. Soviet Russia seems to be carrying out the same policy, at least for the time being, of retaining its forces in spite of the resolution adopted by the Assembly. I hope that Soviet Russia will have the same realism and practical wisdom which were displayed by the United Kingdom and France, and agree to remove their forces from Hungary forthwith and promptly. As a rule I do not like such qualifications as "as soon . . . as order is restored." It can take many years before order is restored. Also, of course, it depends on one's definition of "order."

138. In these circumstances, I would rather adopt the phraseology that was used in the case of the resolutions relating to the United Kingdom and France "promptly," "without delay," "immediately." I trust that Soviet forces will be withdrawn from Hungary so that the people of Hungary may be able to settle their own affairs.

139. We certainly denounce armed intervention in the affairs of a country, whichever that country may be. I freely admit that there was a Warsaw Treaty, under which Soviet troops had the right to be in Hungary, a reason which certainly could not cover the action of the United Kingdom and France in Egypt. If comparisons are being made, however odious it may be, it is sometimes necessary to point out such facts.

140. My Government holds the view that, whether for reasons of restoring order or in the name of peace, we do not want foreign forces to

interfere in the internal affairs of a country, whatever pacts there may be. The Government of Ceylon does not believe in military pacts and has always denounced them. These actions are sometimes the results of military pacts. We do not believe in military pacts. I hope that Soviet Russia will not plead the Warsaw Pact in order to keep its forces in Hungary.

142. We in Asia believe in a philosophy of life; we do not believe in making political capital out of human suffering. In the name of humanity and in the furtherance of humanitarian causes we do not try to make use of such occasions for the expression of our political views, even for purposes that are supposed to be noble. Believing as we do in a philosophy of life, we deplore the fact that political considerations should be brought into humanitarian work.

143. There is no denying the fact that Hungary needs assistance. Hungary needs aid, medical supplies and all the sympathy and good will that people can give. However, let that be given in the spirit of humanitarian work, in the spirit of humanity, in the spirit of understanding. This is not the occasion for vindictiveness, for revenge or for the gospel of hatred. In the name of humanity, let there be no gospel of hatred. Whatever one's views may be, they have been expressed on the political issue. On the humanitarian issue, however, let us get rid of such considerations.

144. In these circumstances, I have no alternative but to express my strong disapproval of the United States draft resolution in its present wording. I should certainly wish to applaud the United States for the noble objectives which it has in view, for the very real interest in its expressions of sympathy and support and for the declaration that the United States is prepared to spend so much money. However, even in a good cause, words sometimes matter—language counts.

145. Therefore, together with the delegations of India and Indonesia, and with the support of the delegation of Burma, we concluded that the humanitarian objective should be the primary motive of the draft resolution. I hope that it will be possible, therefore, to accept unanimously the amendments that we have proposed. This question should not be a subject of debate, because the relief of human suffering is not a matter for debate. There is not one of us who is not moved by the suffering in Hungary. Let us therefore take a unanimous stand on this question. It is in order that we might be able to take a unanimous stand that our amendments have been placed before the Assembly, and I hope that they will be received in that spirit.

146. As regards the political issues, I state again in categorical language that we are pledged to the upholding of the democratic ideal. We who believe in democracy would like to see the right of self-determination be given to every country of the world. We believe in the freedom of speech, we believe in the freedom of assembly, we believe in the freedom of the people to vote a government out of office. We believe that it is the right of a people to determine what their future should be.

147. Therefore, we would always welcome free elections. But in the name of free elections I would certainly not support the five-Power draft resolution because it serves no practical purpose. I certainly would like to have free elections—in the way I think they are free—in Russia, in Poland, in Romania, in Eastern Germany, in Hungary, in all countries of the world, and even in some of those other democratic countries with different political ideologies. There are also others with the name of democracy, with the name of freedom, who do not have the same concept of democracy as I have. There are countries in the world who believe that sometimes the bullet is superior to the ballot. But we who believe in the supremacy of the ballot would like to have seen free elections.

148. The mere moving of a resolution to the effect that we should like to have free elections in Russia, in Poland, in Hungary and in these countries will not secure the result. It may have excellent propaganda value, but I am not a party to that business. We are not aligned with any power politics. We are not aligned with any power blocs. We only deal with questions as and when they arise. With regard to the present occasion, the bringing into this resolution something in connexion with elections and asking the United Nations to interfere with the sovereign rights of peoples is a dangerous principle. On the present occasion is may sometimes suit the fancies and the wishes of several Members. But they must visualize the time when such interference may be possible even in the domain of their own affairs.

149. Therefore, on principle, I would not have the United Nations interfering in elections. How are elections to be held? Surely elections must be held on the basis of a constitution. Did it not take Pakistan eight years to draft a constitution? Are we going to say that elections are to be held pending a constitution? Are we going to wait for eight years for it? No, I certainly do not say so. Elections therefore must be based on a constitution, and a constitution can be drafted only after peoples have expressed their wishes. It is a long process. The mere saying that elections must be held means nothing.

150. Let us get down to practicalities. It is all very well to talk of free elections. I believe in free elections. My country believes in free elections and all of us believe in free elections. But the mere adoption of a draft resolution in this form does not bring about free elections. Therefore, I have no alternative but to say that I cannot understand how this should be interposed in the draft resolution, asking the United Nations to do something which is impossible of achievement. Of course, I have no doubt that it is also premature, because we have already assigned to the Secretary-General a task of first-class importance, of great magnitude, to survey the position and to submit a report to us. It is only after the observers have gone in, if they do go there—and that must be at the express wish of the Government of the country—and it is only after the submission of a report that we can get down to the practical business of what we should do: whether elections are to be held, what elections should be held, and what should be done next. It is like putting the cart before the horse. I am not prepared, therefore, in the

name of propaganda, or in the name of revenge, or in the name of anything else, to subscribe to something that is utterly futile. In those circumstances I have no alternative but to oppose that draft resolution, though with much regret.

151. I have already commented on the two draft resolutions before the Assembly and I hope that we will be able to take a unanimous stand on this affair. Believe me, we feel very deeply about the sufferings of the people of Hungary. All Asian countries feel very strongly about it, and it is a pity that even the Hungarian sufferings should have brought to the political arena the injection of a discussion on the Egyptian issue, which is quite apart. I do deplore these tendencies. Let us discuss issues as and when they come and express our verdict on the issues before us.

182. MR. LODGE (United States of America): I am sorry that I am constrained to differ with the representatives of Ceylon, India and Indonesia as regards their amendments to the United States draft resolution. I appreciate the courteous frankness with which they disclosed their views, and I shall try to be equally frank and, I may say, equally courteous.

183. It seems to me that we would be making a great mistake if we were to strike out the various phrases which these three delegations suggest that we strike out. I should like to read what these phrases are. First, we are asked to strike out the words "the military authorities of the USSR are interfering in the transportation and," in the preamble to section I, before the words "distribution of food and medical supplies . . .". Well, we know it to be a fact that the authorities of the USSR are so interfering. Do we want to go on record as voting that something is not a fact when we know that it is a fact?

184. The next amendment would strike out paragraph I of the operative part: "1. *Calls upon* the Union of Soviet Socialist Republics to cease immediately actions against the Hungarian population which are in violation of the accepted standards and principles of international law, justice and morality." We have absolutely first-hand information—we in the United States from our own legation, and many in this hall from other sources—that that is precisely what is happening. Do we want to vote that it is not happening, when we know that it is?

185. Then the word *"Request"* would be substituted for the words *"Calls upon"*, and the words "and the USSR not to interfere with" would be deleted in paragraph 2 of Section 1. Well, the same objection holds to that amendment and to amendments to other places where "the Union of Soviet Socialist Republics" would be struck out.

186. Then, in section II of the draft resolution, the words "as a result of the harsh and repressive action of the Soviet armed forces, increasingly . . . being obliged to leave . . . and seek asylum in neighbouring countries" would be struck out from the preambular paragraph. Well, that is what is going on. We have heard from a number of countries which were volunteering to take as many as 1,000 of these refugees each. President Eisen-

hower is moving to take 5,000 of them here. There is no use saying that these dreadful things—unpleasant and tragic though they are—are not happening, when in fact they are.

187. We have no interest in propaganda. We have no interest in revenge. But we do not see that there is a distinction that can be drawn between the intent of these words which would be stricken out and the other passages relating to medicines and food. We think that both these provisions are humanitarian.

188. We think that it is humanitarian to take a step which may free a man from being oppressed. We think that it is just as humanitarian to take steps to provide people with international law, justice and morality as it is to take steps which will put food in their stomachs and give them medicines to cure their illnesses.

189. The fact is—and we sometimes forget it—that the United Nations is a moral organization. The United Nations has a moral standard. The United Nations Charter does distinguish between right and wrong. The United Nations was never intended to be a mere sordid cockpit in which the values of the criminal and the values of the law-abiding were indiscriminately scrambled up, and it is not that and should not become that.

190. That being true, it follows that there cannot be a double standard of international morality in the world. If discrimination is bad in one part of the world, as it is, then it is bad in another part of the world. If we deplore injustice here, we must deplore injustice there. If we are against prejudice in one area, we should be against prejudice in another area. If we resist brutality in one region, we must resist brutality in the other. And if we are going to raise our voices against oppression, if we are going to raise our voices against occupation by foreign troops in one part of the world, then we must be equally steadfast, we must be equally stalwart, with regard to other parts of the world.

191. So, in that spirit and for those reasons, I hope that the amendments offered by my friends from Ceylon, India and Indonesia will not prevail, and that our draft resolution will be adopted as written.

Editor's note: When the three major resolutions were voted by the General Assembly, the delegates adopted the Five Power resolution, as amended, 48 votes to 11, with 16 abstentions. The United States resolution was approved 53 votes to 9, with 13 abstentions. The resolution of Ceylon, India, and Indonesia was rejected 45 votes to 18, with 12 abstentions. See General Assembly, *Official Records,* Second Emergency Special Session, 571st meeting (November 9, 1956), pp. 77-80.

Sisyphus and the Avalanche: The United Nations, Egypt, and Hungary*

Stanley Hoffmann

The gods had condemned Sisyphus to push a rock up the top of a mountain, from which the rock kept rolling down. International organization seems to be a modern illustration of an old myth. After each crisis, new attempts are made to push the rock of peace up again, and no crisis has revealed the frustrating task of international organization more sharply than the recent shock of the Middle Eastern and Hungarian explosions.

First, the crisis has revealed that, in spite of multiple efforts, the mechanisms which the United Nations had established for the prevention and repression of threats to peace did not work well enough to save the organization from having once again to improvise in an emergency. Secondly the crisis has shown that in its policies also, the United Nations was limited to a Sisyphus-like role; the United Nations could not prevent a return to the *status quo* of Soviet control of Hungary, and in the Middle East the strenuous efforts of the organization have not been able to achieve much more than a restoration of a slightly amended but still unsatisfactory *status quo*. Thirdly, the crisis has thrown a strong light over some of the deeper reasons for these procedural and political shortcomings. Fourthly, the split among the leading western powers over the Middle East and the embarrassment provoked in the west by the simultaneity of the Middle Eastern and Hungarian affairs have shown the need for a political strategy common to the western nations (the United States as well as western Europe) for their relations with the United Nations in matters concerning peace and security.

The present article is an attempt to examine briefly the four aspects of the crisis of last fall.

Institutional Weaknesses

Just as after each disappointment the horse in Orwell's *Animal Farm* thought that the happy days would come at last if it only did more work, so after each major incident the statesmen of the world have deplored the chinks in the armor of international organization and have striven for more

* Stanley Hoffmann, "Sisyphus and the Avalanche: The United Nations, Egypt and Hungary," *International Organization*, Vol. XI, No. 3 (Summer 1957), pp. 446-469. Reprinted by permission. Stanley Hoffmann is Professor of Government at Harvard University. His publications include *Le Mouvement Poujade* (1956), *Organisations Internationales et Pouvoirs Politiques des Etats* (1954), and *Contemporary Theory in International Relations* (1960).

and better institutional engineering. Thus, the "Uniting for Peace" resolution tried to institutionalize the Korean miracle so that despite the big powers' split, future threats to peace or aggressions would again be handled effectively by the United Nations. The resolution created an impressive series of procedures and organs for preventive and repressive purposes. A more limited but complementary system of alarm bells had been established in such dangerous parts of the world as the Middle East and Kashmir. In last year's crisis, most of these mechanisms proved useless—either because they were simply not used by the very nations that had created them, or because they had been allowed to decay, or because they were not adapted to the circumstances of last fall.

1. Let us look first at the preventive arsenal. The "Uniting for Peace" resolution had established a Peace Observation Commission to "observe and report on the situation in any area where there exists international tension the continuance of which is likely to endanger the maintenance of international peace and security." This Commission has been singularly neglected. It has been used only with reference to the Balkans, where a subcommission was appointed in 1951 by the General Assembly to succeed the United Nations Special Committee which was being discontinued. The subcommission did send a few observers to Greece; they reported back to the subcommission, which submitted no reports of its own—as indeed, there was no need for any, since Greece was now a quiet NATO member. Since 1954, the Peace Observation Commission has been totally lethargic. Thailand requested a subcommission shortly before the end of the Indochina war, but no decision was taken. The Commission was not used in the crisis over the nationalization of the Suez Canal Company. The Security Council, when it discussed the matter in October 1956, was politically in no position to do so. The Egyptian complaint against English and French threats of force and mobilization measures was put on the agenda but never taken up, and Egypt, whose consent or invitation was required under the terms of the 1950 resolution, never asked for a subcommission to be sent into its territory. Indeed, since the threats came from across the sea, a system patterned after Korea was somewhat inappropriate. Thus, only the Anglo-French complaint against Egypt was discussed, and it was dealt with as an ordinary dispute. The whole emphasis was put on diplomacy and conciliation, not on alarm and prevention.

The Peace Observation Commission was not used in connection with the Arab-Israel dispute either. And why should it have been? Was not this dispute taken care of by an elaborate international machinery? The trouble is that this machinery was in pitiful condition. The Palestine Conciliation Commission was left without instructions ever since the General Assembly, at its seventh session, failed to agree on any resolution. The Commission has long ago acknowledged the impossibility of reconciling the various parties on the fundamental issues (borders, refugees, and Jerusalem) with which it had been asked to deal in those earlier days when the young international organization was setting its hopes very high indeed. The Commission had turned to more modest tasks: the question of Arab accounts blocked in Israeli banks and compensation for abandoned Arab lands in Israel. Such efforts were sure neither to stir nor to calm the troubled waters of Arab-Israel relations.

With no prospect of global settlement, the whole burden of preserving peace in the area fell upon the Truce Supervision Organization (UNTSO). But no mechanism of observers and mixed armistice commissions could forever bear the weight that was put on the UNTSO by the failure to achieve a lasting settlement. Inevitably, a system whose organs could pass judgments on armistice violations but whose condemnations and proposals were ineffective if the parties did not want to accept them was bound to wear down. The strain was increased by a frequently used and complicated circuit. The more important violations were sent by their victims before the Security Council, which in turn called for the Chief of Staff (or his deputies, the chairmen of particular armistice commissions) to report or to appear in person; then after "condemning," "taking note" or "endorsing," the Council dumped the whole matter back into the commanders' laps.

Even more striking, however, was the extraordinary fragility of the mechanism itself, and the passivity of the members of the United Nations who were presiding over its decay. There were so few observers—at one point only five for the whole Israel-Jordan border—that they could intervene only *after* the incidents, waste their energies in post-mortems, and merely maintain a score-board. Ever since the days of the much more numerous truce observers of 1948 the grievances of United Nations representatives in the field have been the same: "the uncooperative attitude" displayed by local authorities, the huge number of complaints by both sides, the violation of the armistice provisions which called for reciprocal reduction and with-drawal of forces, the attempts at limiting the freedom of movement of the observers. Year after year, the Security Council resolutions and the reports of the Chiefs of Staff have monotonously referred to the same sore spots.

The deterioration of the mechanism accelerated in 1955 and 1956. After the Israeli raid into the Gaza Strip in February 1955, General Burns restated a previous proposal for joint patrols, a barbed wire fence, and the manning of outposts by regulars; the Security Council endorsed his suggestions, but no agreement was reached. A new incident occurred in August; the Chief of Staff asked again for an effective physical barrier along the demarcation line. Once more the Security Council backed him. What followed was a series of incidents on the eastern front of Israel. Sisyphus went to work anew; in April 1956, the Security Council asked the Secretary-General to go to the Middle East. Mr. Hammarskjold, when he returned one month later, seemed to believe that he had consolidated the truce mechanism. He had formulated the doctrine of absolute, unconditional observance of each provision referring to the armistice lines; he had obtained an agreement (limited to October 31 by Israel) for the stationing of observers on both sides of the Gaza Strip, and he had hopes for a prompt agreement on the separation of forces, the erection of physical obstacles, and a clearer delimitation of the line. However, he noted that "there is not in all cases an adequate functioning machinery for resolving disputes" over the armistice agreements, and that "no procedure has been established for the handling of conflicts covered by the *general* clauses of the armistice agreements," conflicts over which the mixed commissions had no jurisdiction and which were not usually referred by the parties to the Security Council. He emphasized both the need for such procedures and the impossibility of making any proposals acceptable to the parties. In spite of a new endorsement by the Security Council, which nodded itself back to sleep, the machinery was not repaired and storm signals accumulated.

The hopes of the spring did not materialize, as General Burns reported early in September. Twice the mixed commissions broke down. Mr. Hammarskjold issued a warning to all Middle Eastern states—and not only to them. He stressed that there were limits to what the United Nations could do if the governments concerned did not want to cooperate, and with the same discretion as in his May report he added that "these matters . . . can in no way excuse the United Nations from resolutely pursuing its efforts." The United Nations did not do anything about it, and when the crisis came, the alarm bell was out of order: the Truce Supervision Organization was prevented from investigating the incidents that preceded Israel's attack, and Israel's mobilization and invasion of Egypt came before the United Nations could wake up.

In the weeks that separated Mr. Hammarskjold's warning from Israel's move, and especially after Israel's statement on the Suez Canal blockade, Mr. Ben Gurion's denunciation of Colonel Nasser and Mr. Eban's statements in the Security Council during the discussion of the Jordanian complaint on October 25, the United Nations still had at its disposal one big preventive weapon which could theoretically have been used for the first time: Part A of the "Uniting for Peace" resolution, which provided for an emergency session of the Assembly when "there appears to be a threat to peace," and when the Security Council is paralyzed. But this provision was not used for the same obvious reason which accounts for the failure of Mr. Hammarskjold's warning; the states were either not listening, or they did not want to listen. If a resolution asking for emergency measures had been brought before the Council, an Anglo-French (or French) veto might well have paralyzed the Council, and thus created the conditions for a resort to the 1950 procedure. But no such resolution was introduced or contemplated; on the 25th of October, further debate in the Council was postponed to the 30th.

Thus, the preventive mechanisms had failed. The arsenal was, on the whole, rich enough; but both its exploitation and the repair of those of its weapons that were in bad shape depended on the will and alertness of the United Nations Members. No foolproof set of procedures could ever automatically oblige states to take measures once a certain danger point is reached; and no system would have alerted either the Council or an emergency session of the Assembly about the gravity of the Suez crisis just before the Anglo-French intervention. The Anglo-French ultimatum came at a moment when the dispute apparently had entered a cooler period of bargaining and compromises under the auspices of the Secretary-General. The preventive parts of the "Uniting for Peace" resolution, modelled on the Korean example, can only be operative in cases where the tension is building up gradually and where no party succeeds in concealing its plan to use force. For similar reasons, there was no mechanism which could have prevented the Hungarian crisis.

2. Let us turn next to the repressive equipment of the United Nations. What we find here, paradoxically, is both a poorer and a more useful arsenal. The weapon which was used with great speed and efficiency, contrary to the expectations of the British and the French, was that very Part A of the "Uniting for Peace" resolution which had not been invoked preventively. At the request of the Security Council, two emergency sessions of the Assembly were summoned.

Now, Part C of the 1950 resolution had asked states to take certain initiatives which would facilitate the resort to "collective measures" (including armed force once peace has been broken); and it had established a Collective Measures Committee to study methods of maintaining and strengthening peace. After the failure of the system of Chapter VII, after the watering-down of Mr. Trygve Lie's proposal for "an internationally recruited police force," Sisyphus had been trying again. But this time the rock did not get pushed very high. The states did not react very enthusiastically to the requests of the 1950 resolution, nor to those of the resolution of January 1952 which embodied some suggestions of the Collective Measures Committee's first report. Indeed, the way in which these suggestions were emasculated by the Sixth Assembly was remarkable enough: imperative exhortations for advance preparation (including if necessary legislative changes) were turned into soft recommendations studded with reassuring grants of liberty. The key idea of getting Members to earmark certain elements of their armed forces for service as United Nations units quietly got lost.

The Committee itself based its work on two principles which were probably unavoidable and certainly unfortunate from the point of view of last fall's crisis. First, entrusted with what amounted to a general study of collective security, and realizing that advance commitments to "particular procedures or specific contributions" were unlikely, it tried to design measures that could fit as many circumstances as possible. One of the requirements of collective security is anonymity, but the price one has to pay is vagueness. It is therefore not too astonishing that the efforts of the Committee "were sterile." Secondly, what made them still more surely useless for the Assembly in 1956, even as a mere guide, was the way in which the Committee, just like the "Uniting for Peace" resolution itself, had taken the Korean case as a model—both in order, no doubt, to have at least one island of reference in an ocean of generalities, and because of the permanent tendency of statesmen and generals to prepare meticulously for the previous crisis. This principle had two consequences. The whole effort of the Committee was oriented toward collective enforcement against a transgressor. The Committee thus neglected the cases in which there would be a need for a supervisory force but not for a shooting one, and of course all its efforts were superfluous for a case such as Hungary where what was going to be decided was collective blame without enforcement. Also, the work of the Committee, almost from the first page of its first report, as based on the hypothesis of a clear-cut case of aggression; the other hypothesis (a "breach of peace" which is not a clear-cut aggression) got lost. Now, in the fall of 1956, the United Nations was faced with two baffling situations. One was an armed intervention in a civil war, opposed by one revolutionary government, but called for by the previous cabinet. The other case was a breach of peace composed of two separate invasions. About each of them one could argue endlessly as to whether it constituted a naked aggression, a partly provoked aggression, or a use of force devoid of "aggressive intention" which a well-known international lawyer once stated to be a necessary part of any definition of aggression and then refused to define abstractly. Indeed, the flaw of the Commission's decision to study the suppression of acts of aggression is well indicated by the failure of a host of international bodies to agree on any legally or politically satisfactory definition of aggression. Surely the apex of confusion is reached when a group as serious as the International Law Commission decides that all acts of aggression are crimes against mankind, after having failed to define aggression. Politico-legal concepts should not be defined by lawyers and cannot be adequately defined by politicians either.

At any rate, when the challenge came, the Members of the United Nations had once again to improvise a response in the heat of the moment. Nations condemned to improvisation are rarely willing to go beyond what is immediately needed to save peace, except perhaps for vague promises to think about more stable structures once the danger has receded. Indeed, the history of international organizations is like a graveyard of specialized commissions, or *ad hoc* representatives, who have been more or less gracefully allowed to fade away after finishing their temporary job.

The Policies Followed

We turn now to a brief discussion of the way in which the United Nations used its freedom last fall.

Ever since 1945, the organization has been faced with a series of disputes which were not the traditional quarrels of a stabilized period—quarrels of limited scope which do not challenge the international *status quo* or the internal regimes of states. The United Nations has had to deal with the explosions of a revolutionary period—disputes tainted by violence or at least accompanied by threats of violence. In such circumstances, the neat categories provided for by the Charter ("disputes," "situations," "aggression") often make little sense, and the United Nations has felt free to discard them and to select its course empirically. Last fall the Assembly decided to take a middle road between the two following extremes. On the one hand there is the policy which we might call "pure coercion"; it tries through injunctions, threats or collective enforcement to oblige the transgressors to give up any gains obtained through violations of the Charter; it refuses to subordinate a return to law to concessions asked or conditions raised by the transgressors. On the other hand, there is what might be called a policy of "pure conciliation"; it treats all parties to a dispute as equals and tries to reach a compromise through accommodation without any pressure being put on either side. Of course these two extremes are ideal types, but they have at times been realized. Thus, "pure coercion" was the United Nations policy in Korea, and "pure conciliation" was used during much of the Palestine crisis of 1948, during the first Indonesian conflict (1947-1948), and in the Kashmir stalemate. Now in the case of the Suez crisis, the middle road taken by the Assembly proved to be an increasingly narrow path, and in the case of Hungary, the road soon led to a dead end.

1. In the Middle Eastern crisis, there were excellent reasons for eliminating the two extremes. First, any policy that aimed merely at coercing France, England and Israel back into compliance with the Charter, even if it was not initially accompanied by collective enforcement measures, was risky. If the violators did not choose to obey the injunctions of the United Nations any more than the north Koreans had observed the provisions of the resolution of June 25, 1950, the United Nations would have either to lose face or to turn to sanctions, just as it had on June 27, 1950. Sanctions were both dangerous and questionable. The draft resolution introduced by the United States in the Security Council after the beginning of the Israeli attack was almost a replica of the resolution of June 25, 1950; England and France were right in pointing out the differences between the cases of north Korea and Israel. After the English and French intervention, any attempt at treating the crisis as a new Korea disappeared. No one was called an aggressor. Consequently, the United Nations on the one hand refused to take up the Soviet appeal for an international mandate to an American-Russian expedition against the invaders—an appeal made, significantly enough, not to the Assembly, where it might have been well received, but to the Security Council, where it was sure to die fast. On the other hand, the United Nations also decided to offer to the parties an instrument that belongs not to the coercive but to the conciliatory arsenal of international organization: the United Nations Emergency Force (UNEF). UNEF is the sort of procedural guarantee which has in previous cases led belligerents to accept a cease-fire. States unwilling to lose face by obeying purely and simply a United Nations call because they do not want to appear to give in to their

enemy in the field have often proved more ready to bow to an international mechanism. Seen in this light, UNEF has been playing a role comparable to the role of United Nations commissions and truce organizations in Palestine, Kashmir and Indonesia.

Secondly, however, there were good reasons for discarding a policy of mere conciliation. An organization committed to the defense and illustration of certain principles of international behavior could not accept as *faits accomplis* a series of moves which, however explainable by previous failures of the United Nations itself to redress certain wrongs, nevertheless violated the ban on the use of force against the territorial integrity or political independence of states. Israel had a strong case. The situation that existed before October 29, when Egypt claimed to be still at war with its neighbor but wanted to be protected against it ("unilateral belligerence") was indeed absurd. The need for Israel to defend itself, even through retaliation, against armed Egyptian attacks and against Colonel Nasser's plans for encirclement cannot be dismissed lightly either. But there remain enough arguments on the other side, such as the perils of preventive war, the well established principle that retaliation should not be disproportionate, and the idea that violations of the Charter presented as justified by the opponent's own breaches of treaties can only lead to international anarchy. Mr. Hammarskjold's firm decision to refuse to "condone a change of the *status juris* resulting from military action contrary to the provisions of the Charter" cannot be seriously challenged. Furthermore, in previous cases of disputes in which one side had resorted to military action and which the United Nations had tried to solve through purely conciliatory techniques, the organization had come close to failure; it had been able to remain in control of events only by coming around to Mr. Hammarskjold's doctrine. Consequently, the Assembly aimed some sharp recommendations at the invaders of Egypt; the resolution of November 2 called for their prompt withdrawal. This call had few precedents in the history of the United Nations, outside of the plain collective security case of Korea.

Now, once the two extreme policies had been eliminated, there remained a very broad range of possible "middle roads." Coercion and conciliation can be combined in infinitely varying doses. The crucial question is whether the mixture used after the resolution of November 2 was the best one. The course followed by the Assembly became rather like collective security, with moral and negative political sanctions (the denial of certain claims) substituted for the positive political, economic or military sanctions envisaged by the Collective Measures Committee. In other words, the Assembly and the Secretary-General moved further and further from the pole of "pure conciliation" and closer and closer to the pole of "pure coercion." Instead of achieving both an elimination of illegally obtained advantages and a peaceful settlement of the problems that had led to a violation of the law, the United Nations allowed the first aspect to obliterate the second. In the first place, the issue of "cease-fire and withdrawal" was separated from the underlying substantive issues; consideration of the Suez nationalization problem and of an over-all Arab-Israel settlement was postponed until after the first issue had been disposed of. The two United States draft resolutions which aimed at removing the fundamental causes of tension were shelved. Now, neither during the second Indonesian conflict nor when the Security Council invoked Chapter VII against the Arabs in the summer of 1948 had a policy of strong pressure against one side ruled out consideration of the deeper political issues which explained the breach of peace. In the second place, the elimination of the breach of peace and the restoration or quasi-restoration of the *status quo* became synonymous; Mr. Hammarskjold refused to permit Israel's withdrawal to be accompanied by guarantees over what one might call the "intermediate" issues—issues half way between the return to the *status quo* and a general political negotiation: Gaza, the Gulf of Aqaba, and passage of Israeli ships through the Suez Canal. These two decisions really condemned the United Nations to play the role of Sisyphus; for the crisis had its origins in the precariousness of a *status quo* which was never supposed to last eight years, at least as much as in the bad will of the parties.

Mr. Hammarskjold stated that his proposals tended to restore not the *status quo,* but the *status juris.* But the distinction is a fragile one: indeed, what *is* the *status juris?* The parties disagree, and this disagreement itself explains in part the collapse of the armistice agreements. For the Israelis, the law includes not only the end of border raids, or the scrupulous observance of articles VII and VIII of the Israel-Egypt armistice agreement, dealing with the armistice lines, but also the end of the blockade of the Suez Canal and of the Gulf of Aqaba. For the Egyptians, this is not the case, and in his report of January 24 the Secretary-General (who has constantly refused to answer Israel's questions concerning Egypt's policy of belligerency) was only able to say about the Gulf of Aqaba that "any possible claims of belligerent rights . . . if asserted, should be limited to clearly non-controversial situations." In his report of January 24, he defined the return to the *status juris* as "a withdrawal of troops, and . . . the relinquishment or nullification of rights asserted in territories covered by the military action and depending upon it." The *status juris* is a return to the *status quo* accompanied by hopes that the parties would in the future respect the law.

A policy should be judged by its results. Mr. Hammarskjold's policy led to an impasse. The Assembly resolution of February 2—the last document adopted by the United Nations—merely endorsed his report of January 24. It asked, as he had done, for a stationing of UNEF "on" the armistice lines— with no length of time suggested. It also called for "the implementation of other measures as proposed in the Secretary-General's report with due regard to the considerations set out therein with a view to assist in achieving situations conducive to the maintenance of peaceful conditions in the area." "It seems very pretty," said Alice in Wonderland after she had read the poem "Jabberwocky," "but it is *rather* hard to understand." If one goes back to Mr. Hammarskjold's report, what one finds is the hope that the parties will let UNEF take over the functions of the Truce Supervision Organization and the familiar wish that the parties will accept at long last "such supporting measures as would guarantee a return to the state of affairs envisaged in the armistice agreement and avoidance of the state of affairs into which conditions, due to a lack of compliance with the agreement, progressively deteriorated." This year's hope for a mined fence replaces last year's hope for a barbed wire one. Sisyphus trusted that the rock would stop rolling down the next time. The Secretary-General, in answer to Israel's request, also stated in his report that "if it is recognized that there is such a need for such an arrangement," UNEF units could be stationed at the entrance of the Gulf of Aqaba. If this was a hint for specific Assembly endorsement, the Assembly, by its wholesale endorsement of Mr. Hammarskjold's "other measures," did not in turn do much more than hint back that it did not mind Mr. Hammarskjold's own hint. It was a tie. It became a deadlock when Israel persisted in asking for more, and Mr. Hammarskjold refused because "adherence to principle and law must be given priority and cannot be conditioned"—an admirable statement that would be even more perfect if the meaning of the law were clear and if Egypt had not, in one instance, defied successfully a principle affirmed by the Security Council.

Therefore, the United States, which until then had left the Secretary-General in charge of all the discussions with Egypt and Israel, had to intervene and to take the matter, in effect, out of the Secretary-General's hands. But it could not, at that stage, contradict him too vigorously. Hence the twists and turns of an "unconditional withdrawal" nevertheless subordinated not to conditions, but to "assumptions," to "hopes and conditions that are not unreasonable." Both because these "assumptions" went a little beyond Mr. Hammarskjold's doctrine, and because they had to be so obscure in order not to clash with it, they became controversial enough to make impossible the drafting of any resolution that would embody them.

It is instructive to establish a sort of balance sheet. By way of documents, we have only the United Nations resolution of February 2, the Secretary-General's report to which it refers, and the "assumptions" of Israel as qualified by the United States and interpreted by Mr. Hammarskjold. (a) On the Egyptian side of the former armistice line the United Nations has a police force tolerated by Egypt, but whose mission has not been clearly spelled out. The appeal for a stationing "on" the line, still unheeded by Israel, gives Egypt a most useful political weapon, in addition to Egypt's legal right to ask the Force to leave. (b) In the Gaza Strip, Israel's expectations (which Mr. Hammarskjold never encouraged) have proved in great part wrong. The temporary period of United Nations civilian control has been short indeed. Egyptian troops have not returned but they have the legal right to do so. (c) At the entrance of the Gulf of Aqaba, a UNEF unit has been stationed. But its duration is shaky, its mission most obscure, and the only solid guarantee seems to be Israel's solemn warning that any inter-ference with free navigation will be considered as an attack giving rise to the right of self-defense. (d) As to passage through the Suez Canal, Egypt has not renounced its belligerency. (e) Nothing new, except more hatred, has happened with reference to a general settlement between Israel and its neighbors. (f) The Suez Canal Company issue has been handled after the Anglo-French withdrawal, and has ended in a *de facto* acceptance of a unilateral Egyptian declaration—with no United Nations pronouncement of any kind.

An abundance of texts calling for a cease-fire and withdrawal had been succeeded by a stunning dearth of authoritative documents covering the present and the future. The interplay between public international debates and secret diplomacy has produced a series of stop-gap agreements differently interpreted by the parties. Some of the multilateral gobbledygook which has replaced the elegant obscurity of nineteenth century diplomacy is still with us—but not much of the authority attached to previous United Nations pronouncements, an authority which has often offset their obscu-rity. The course followed through the United Nations seems to have led to little more than a temporary reinforcement of the truce system at the Israel-Egypt border. Egypt's present informal acceptance of UNEF can hardly be seen as a big concession. UNEF might prevent new raids, but it also pro-tects Egypt from Israel; and Egypt made sure that the Force would be absolutely weightless in the political balance of power in the Middle East; UNEF is not, as Egypt had feared, an "occupation force," it had served far more, as Egypt wished, as a "fire brigade" called to the rescue of Egypt. Indeed, in an area where all issues *are* linked, the elimination of the breach of peace does not merely restore Egypt's position in the supposed "next phase" (the discussion of the underlying issues). The position has improved. Egypt's right of veto over UNEF provides Colonel Nasser with an instru-ment of blackmail against any attempt at a solution that he would dislike. We must therefore ask whether another "middle road," a different combina-tion of coercion and conciliation, might not have been *tried* (this is not to say that it would have *succeeded*). For it is one thing to condone violations of the Charter, but it is quite another to refuse to follow a course that makes new violations timely.

It seems that there remained a choice between the Secretary-General's policy of proceeding step-by-step, so that no new issue would be considered before the previous one had been disposed of, and the policy outlined by Mr. Pearson. The Canadian foreign minister wanted to continue the tradition, often used with success, of having the political organs of the United Nations take without delay a stand on all issues involved in the crisis, i.e. suggest procedures for settlement of the deeper underlying problems and define a policy concerning the "intermediate" issues. This would still have upheld the principle that gains obtained by force should not be kept. But it would also have taken into account the fact that the issues raised by Israel's, France's and the United Kingdom's action were linked. After all, the trouble in the Middle East did not begin on October 29, 1956.

It might be argued on legal and on political grounds that Mr. Pearson's "middle course" was not realistic, and that Mr. Hammarskjold's line was the only possible one—except for appeasement or collective enforcement. The legal objections do not seem decisive. One could argue that under international law Egypt's consent was needed at every stage. But Mr. Pearson's proposals did not overlook this requirement. They merely invited the United Nations *first* to define a line of policy and *then* promote negotiations with the parties to get this line adopted. Maybe Egypt's consent would have been hard to get; but Egypt, which had been rescued by the United Nations, which was still partly occupied by a victorious enemy, and which was economically as badly shaken as its opponents, was in no strong position to resist pressure, had it come. One could also object that the resolutions of the Assembly did not leave much leeway to the Secretary-General. Nevertheless, we can observe that Israel did not withdraw "forthwith." Furthermore, the key resolution of November 2 mentioned the problem of raids and the need for observance of "the armistice agreements"—terms which left the door open for arrangements over the "intermediate" issues, as, for instance, Egypt's claiming of belligerency rights, which the Security Council had declared to be in contradiction to the armistice agreements.

In fact, both legal objections do raise far more serious political problems. How could the Secretary-General *himself* exert pressure on Egypt? How much *political* leeway did he have in interpreting the resolutions? It is not enough to state that he probably had much to say in the drafting of the instructions he received from the Assembly, and that the Assembly was unlikely to overrule him if he decided to follow Mr. Pearson's course, at a time when American policy was to praise, paraphrase, and propose whatever Mr. Hammarskjold suggested. For even if he had obtained from the Assembly directives in accordance with Mr. Pearson's program, the success of such a policy depended on one major criterion, which was missing: the willingness of the United States to exert pressure on Egypt in order to gain Egyptian consent. Pressure by the Assembly in the form of resolutions, recommending certain measures was not enough. It had to be accompanied by pressure outside of the United Nations. It was the combination of United Nations and United States pressure which obliged the Dutch to give in in Indonesia—and the Israelis to evacuate Egypt. When it came to the second aspect of the Middle Eastern crisis (the settlement of the deeper and "intermediate" issues) the United States was willing to support the Secretary-General in the Assembly, but Mr. Hammarskjold, had he selected a more vigorous course, would have needed the United States in front of him, in Cairo, so to speak, and not merely behind him in New York.

This objection cannot be dismissed. The decisions of the Assembly and the silence of the United States did condemn the Secretary-General to the following dilemma. He had to take political initiatives that belong to an independent executive rather than to an official with little political power. Or else he had to zigzag between the question marks of ambiguous resolutions. However, it seems to this writer that Mr. Hammarskjold resigned himself to the latter course with such skill, caution and good grace that the dangers of the dilemma were too easily overlooked; the members of the Assembly were encouraged to travel a road which has justly been called a "reversion to the abnormal." Finally, if Mr. Hammarskjold's policy was the inevitable product of the Assembly's feelings and of United States inaction, it becomes necessary to transfer the blame, but not to whitewash the policy.

2. One can argue whether it is Egypt or the United Nations which has been the master in the Middle Eastern crisis. No argument, alas, is possible in the Hungarian one. The road which the Assembly tried to travel was different from the Middle Eastern one; it amounted to an attempt at pure coercion through mere dictation. No collective measures were undertaken, but Soviet military action was condemned far more severely and directly than the Israeli, French and British operation. The call to desist "forthwith" and to withdraw "without any further delay" was not accompanied by the offer of a face-saving international mechanism such as a truce or "non-shooting" police force, or by the offer of a conciliatory device such as a commission of mediation between Hungary and the Soviet Union (such as, for instance, the Balkan Commission). The United Nations merely offered its Secretary-General and observers designated by him, not as peacemakers or mediators, but as investigators, and soon thereafter decided that free elections should be held under United Nations auspices. Conciliation was ruled out. However, when dictation failed, as had all previous attempts in similar circumstances (in the Balkans, in Korea before June 1950, and in Berlin during the United Nations phase of the dispute), the United Nations had to reconsider its policy and to face the dilemma: retreat or toughness. Some Members would have liked the United Nations to introduce a certain dose of conciliation, by offering its services and by avoiding unilateral definitions of policy. Hence India protested against the call for free elections, and appealed for negotiations with the Soviet and Hungarian governments the sort of discussion of underlying political issues that was being avoided in the Middle East because it seemed to some that such a negotiation would be a reward for aggression! However, the United Nations remained consistent and did not follow Mr. Menon; but it did not change the nature of the pressure exerted on the Soviet Union either. No sanctions of any kind were decided; even one rather mild sort of collective measure that had been suggested was not taken up: the appointment as observers of diplomatic representatives serving in Hungary. The United Nations margin of action was thus quite small. The United Nations could solemnly condemn the violation of the Charter, try to post observers outside of the iron curtain and create an investigation committee which by necessity operated outside of Hungary, but these measures amount to solemn protests, and the formal

condemnation has more in common with the Stimson doctrine than with the branding of Red China as an aggressor, which was accompanied by sanctions.

Thus, in effect, the *status quo* was restored everywhere, but it was the Hungarian revolution which was contained, and the Israelis who were rolled back. This apparently paradoxical balance sheet carries with it some important lessons.

Political Limitations of the United Nations

1. The first lesson seems to be that the assumptions of the drafters of the Charter have been vindicated: international organization can operate with maximum effectiveness, i.e. both preserve the political independence and territorial integrity of its members and settle international disputes, only if big power unity is preserved and if the claims to be reconciled do not involve the existence of states or the nature of regimes.

The first of these assumptions was contradicted by the "Uniting for Peace" resolution, which was based on the thought that the organization should not be paralyzed by the cold war and that collective security could be organized even against big powers. Now, it is to a large extent the breakdown of the negative Russian-American concert in the Middle East which led to last year's explosion; between 1947 and the death of Stalin, neither the Soviet Union nor the United States was actively involved in Middle Eastern politics. The Soviets had not intervened in the Iranian oil crisis, and a long series of Security Council resolutions from 1948 to 1953 proved that the two great powers were not on opposite sides of the fence in matters concerning the "Palestine problem." The first Soviet veto came in January 1954—at a time when the British were trying to convince Colonel Nasser to join a Middle Eastern defense organization. What followed is familiar enough: the Baghdad Pact, the Egyptian arms deal, the Aswan Dam affair, and the Soviet veto of the second part of the western resolution over Suez submitted to the Security Council in October. Inversely, it is to a large extent the temporary return to a big power concert which explains the success of the United Nations in getting a Middle Eastern cease-fire and withdrawal without resort to sanctions. The carrot of UNEF was accompanied by the stick of combined (although antagonistic) Soviet and American pressure. Soviet threats of resort to "collective measures" increased in effect the weight of American pressure. Finally, it is of course the existence of a "bi-polar" world which explains the failure of the United Nations to achieve any comparable result in Hungary.

The "Uniting for Peace" resolution provided only a procedure for acting in an emergency such as the Hungarian one. The success of the Korean experiment in collective action was misleading; there, the Russian armed forces were not *directly* involved, and the Chinese were not a military power of the first magnitude. It has been said quite rightly that the "Uniting for Peace" resolution, to be effective, supposes that the world is "divided for war" and ready to fight. To fight north Korea, indeed; far less ready to fight Red China and not at all to fight the Soviets. On the one hand, in 1950 and again in 1956 certain small or medium-size Members of the United Nations have been most unwilling to go beyond the original Charter and to envisage any form of coercion (even purely verbal) against a great power. On the other hand, the United States itself adopted toward the Soviet Union a policy which in effect does not have much use for the United Nations. The doctrine of massive retaliation "by means and at places of our own choosing" implies that when the United States decides to strike at the Soviet Union, the main American action will take place outside of the United Nations, which is too slow, militarily unprepared, and anyhow heavily compelled by its own principles to fight on the field chosen by the enemy. The doctrine also means that, when the United States decides that there is no point in striking back, as it did last October, the United Nations can only hurl rhetorical thunderbolts at the Soviets.

As for the other original assumption of the Charter, it seems that the very inability of the United Nations to do much more than restore the *status quo* in the Middle East shows the limitations of the policy of collective assertion, parliamentary debates and majority votes with which the United Nations has tried to tackle the problem of change and the anticolonial revolution. Various factors contribute to the deadlock. In the first place, if the majority tries to accelerate the process, the nation whose sovereignty is infringed by United Nations policies still has the legal power to resist—as the Union of South Africa has shown and as Israel shows now in connection with the stationing of UNEF. In the second place, if, on the contrary, nations adversely affected by the nationalist revolutions try to reverse the trend, the states that owe their existence to these revolutions, those that stand to gain by encouraging the trend and those that are afraid of resisting it are numerous enough in the Assembly to prevent any such move. The new nations of Asia and Africa can therefore save the territorial *status quo* of any one of them, when it is threatened from the outside. They tend to favor or accept a measure such as the nationalization of the Suez Canal Company because it is presented politically as a victory over colonialism and legally as the mere exercise of territorial sovereignty. (Far less concern is shown over matters involving persons.) Thus, the "new United Nations" can operate as a boomerang against countries like England, France or Israel —a western bridgehead in the Arab world.

Thirdly, there is a deeper reason which explains why it is so difficult for international organization to provide peaceful change in a revolutionary world. Most of the causes of trouble and change are completely beyond the reach of the United Nations. The United Nations in this respect is both restricted and anachronistic. It approaches dynamic forces such as pan-Arabism or communism with nineteenth century concepts such as the duty of non-intervention of states. It approaches the crucial problem posed by the different behavior of different regimes—dictatorships, totalitarian governments, democracies—with the old liberal concept according to which the type of government has to be discounted in international affairs, as if ideologies and national politics really did stop at each border or at "the water's edge." It ignores the submerged part of the iceberg of world politics, such as the techniques of subversion or the struggle for control of raw materials and sources of energy. By its occasional attempts at concentrating on the technical aspects of a dispute so as to make it less explosive, the United Nations can be led to underestimate such imponderable elements as those without which the Suez crisis can hardly be understood: the issue of national prestige, the fear of humiliation, the defensive nationalism of France and England (a reaction to the triumphant nationalism of Asia and Africa) the Anglo-French instinctive Munich reaction in the summer of 1956, or the fear of colonialism which explains why Asian countries reacted more violently to Suez than to Budapest. The United Nations tries to play Hamlet with Fortinbras alone.

2. Even though the original assumptions of the Charter have been vindicated, the United Nations has to operate in a world in which those assumptions simply do not apply. Hence there has appeared in the debates and policies of the United Nations a number of inequities and discrepancies which the last crises have put into clear focus and which weaken the influence of the organization. There is first of all the problem of the use of force. The ban of the Charter seems either too rigid or too narrow; it has led in practice to a different treatment of *faits accomplis* without armed violence, or of the subtler forms of pressure or subversion, and of "coups" accomplished by armies. Now, if the first category is tolerated, the ban on the second cannot be interpreted as an absolute. The Charter was an attempt at providing states with a better alternative to the solution of international disputes. If this alternative does not work, if states' claims of great emotional or political importance are either not taken into account by international mechanisms or are merely dragged or gradually compromised away from one conference to the next, we will have more Suez expeditions. The alternative to collective adjustment is certainly not collective sainthood and it cannot be individual suicide. The successful suppression by the United Nations of a big scale attempt at solving disputes by armed force in the Middle East might merely encourage states caught in such a dilemma to resort to all kinds of force except armed force, or to attack anything (through subversion, blockade, embargoes, etc.) as long as it is not someone's territory. Even the resort to armed force has often been successful. It has been unpunished when it was decided by the Soviet Union within its zone of influence; it has also been unpunished when the dose of force used each time has been small although it was administered frequently, such as in armistice line violations, or when the theater of operations was not a vital one in world politics (such as in the case of Hyderabad and to some extent Kashmir), or when the plea of domestic jurisdiction still has some authority (as in Algeria).

Inconsistencies in United Nations attitudes have also been criticized with reference to the power of the states which the United Nations has challenged. Messrs. Pineau, Lloyd and Spaak have complained about the differences between the United Nations' "kindness" toward the Soviets and harshness toward England, France and Israel. Here some distinctions must be made. If one looks at the documents, this accusation is quite unfair. It is not the United Nations which has treated the transgressors differently; it is the transgressors who have reacted differently to United Nations resolutions; to whitewash violations of the Charter in one part of the world because they cannot be remedied elsewhere is a policy of chaos. Similarly, if one looks at the problem from the point of view of the preservation of world peace, it could be argued that the failure of the United Nations in Hungary and its success in Egypt contributed equally to the safeguarding of peace. Those who would have liked the United Nations to send a UNEF to Hungary forget among other things that UNEF was sent to Egypt with the consent of all parties and that any other kind of force would be not a supervisory unit but an international fighting army. As for non-military sanctions (economic reprisals or the suspension or expulsion of Mr. Kadar's United Nations delegates), they would merely have assuaged the nerves of United Nations members—and further demonstrated the lack of effective United Nations power in that area. However, if one looks at the problem from the point of view of "justice" rather than of "peace," and if one considers the actual amount of pressure that was put respectively on the Soviets and on Britain, France, and Israel, rather than the texts voted upon, Messrs. Pineau, Lloyd, and Spaak do have a very real point. The contrast in the amount of pressure, however justified by power considerations, is shocking precisely because the principles of the Charter are supposed to apply equally to all. "Two wrongs don't make one right," said Mr. Eisenhower. In a way, this is true; but in another way, one wrong (the Soviet refusal to budge) and one right (Israel's unconditional withdrawal) do finally make two wrongs: the Soviet immunity and the difference in pressure. Through some perverse law, it also seems that the more a state resists the United Nations, the more this state gets away with: the Soviets, and Egypt on the issue of the Suez blockade, have emerged scot free; Israel has finally saved a bit more than England and France, which agreed faster to withdraw.

A final discrepancy was alluded to by Barbara Ward, when she defined international agencies as "mechanisms for making other nations do what one would not do oneself." There have been admirable examples of this during the recent crises. The Israelis have insisted that UNEF should not be stationed on Israeli soil or on any territory controlled by Israel, but at the same time they have protested against the Secretary-General's reminder that all the requests made by Israel concerning Gaza or UNEF required the consent of Egypt. Yugoslavia refused to accept United Nations observers who would investigate about Hungary because this would be "a dangerous precedent," whereas for years similar investigations were conducted about the Union of South Africa's *apartheid* policies. India protested against mere "propaganda" resolutions condemning the Soviets, but she also wanted to see maximum pressure put on Israel, as though blame became propaganda only when the recipient was not easily influenced by outside pressure. The states which have used the United Nations most effectively as an instrument for the advancement of their cause are the ones which have insisted most constantly upon the limited and temporary role of UNEF. The main common bond among the members of the United Nations is the defense rather than the moderation of their sovereignty; that there should be growing cynicism or skepticism as a result is not surprising.

The West and the United Nations

Nevertheless, the United Nations is here to stay, and western powers should adopt a policy or strategy toward the United Nations. The Soviets have one; so do the new nations. We have just mentioned some inconsistencies; we could add here the example of the United States, which last summer showed no enthusiasm whatsoever toward bringing the Suez Canal issue to the United Nations, and which after October 30 emphasized vehemently its reliance on the United Nations in all Middle Eastern problems except the fight against "international communism."

1. An obvious starting point would be the fact that the western nations cannot put the United Nations at the center of their foreign policies. This is as true with reference to the competition for the "uncommitted" world as it is in relation to straight east-west issues. The predominance of small states in the Assembly and the sort of "bloc veto" or diluting power of the African-Asian nations when they are allied with the Soviet group have somewhat tarnished Mr. Morganthau's vision of "new United Nations" as a field in which the United States could multilateralize its national interest. On the contrary, given the rules of the Assembly, the interests of the Africans and Asians (and, at times, through the intermediary of these nations, the interests of the Soviet group) might receive American naturalization. When the weight of multilateral restraint on American or western interests is such that these interests emerge quite unrecognizable, how acceptable is such a restraint, and how useful the mechanism in which this alchemical process takes place. In certain cases, a tail constituted by a few small states, whose support is needed, can wag the American dog.

But there is a second and equally obvious starting point. The west has a tremendous interest in keeping the United Nations alive and in good health —even in political matters. The United Nations provides the west with an indispensable, although too lofty, set of ideals and with a necessary, although too narrow, set of procedures. It is not merely because the United Nations has defended the national sovereignty of non-western countries that so many of the latter have applauded the American attitude in the crisis of last fall. It is also, as Hugh Gaitskell has recognized, because the Charter constitutes the only hopeful international ideal for most nations of the present world, as well as a code of behavior which represents the maximum that anyone has a right to expect. The way in which the Soviets have in turn exploited this ideal and this code in the Middle Eastern crisis should be a warning.

The crisis of last fall demonstrated that the United Nations plays a legitimizing role of increasing importance—at least negatively. The United Nations does not quite have the strength to *initiate,* but it has the authority to prevent certain things and to stop others, and it has enough moral force to legitimize what it endorses. Consequently, actions (other than the construction of regional or functional organizations, or action aimed directly at the Soviet bloc) which are undertaken outside and without the *imprimatur* of the United Nations risk losing part of their value. The two London conferences over Suez last summer suffered somewhat from that risk. It is easy to show how shaky this international legitimacy is and to denounce "international majoritarianism." But every state today, however grudgingly, gropes for the former and wants the benefits of the latter. It was a majority which England and France were trying to get behind their (and Mr. Dulles') scheme at the first London conference. When Mr. Dulles stated that "it is one thing for a nation to defy one or two nations but it is quite another thing to defy the sober and considered judgment of many nations," England and France approved, since the defiant nation, then, was Egypt. The Menzies mission did its best to impress Colonel Nasser with the importance of majority rule. In September and October, when England and France first began to lose that majority, then decided to go it alone, the fact that an overwhelming number of nations decided against them did influence their policy. The legitimacy of the United Nations is bound to be fragile, given the political limitations and inconsistencies imposed by a revolutionary period, as well as such structural defects as the right of veto and the egalitarian voting formula. But any kind of legitimacy in such a period is a blessing and a guide for future stabilization.

No western nation can afford to define the national interest so narrowly that such an asset would be left to others. Nor can any western nation afford deliberately to put the United Nations to a test which the organization will lose, so as to use this failure as a pretext for Charter violations; for if this nation's bold attempt should go wrong, it will be only too happy if there is an international mechanism available to rescue it from the mess. "In an inflammable world, it is no mean achievement of international organization to serve as a candle snuffer so as to minimize the necessity for relying upon an unreliable fire department." If there were no United Nations that could offer a United Nations Emergency Force to a suspicious Egypt, the alternative would be a clash between Soviet "volunteers" and Anglo-French "policemen." The nations' almost hysterical emphasis on sovereignty explains both why the candle snuffer can do so little and why only an international organization can be the candle snuffer. Anything else would smell of "intervention," neo-colonialism, or gunboat diplomacy.

2. With these two opposed starting points, we can at least suggest certain lines of policy. No doubt, it is uncomfortable for the west to have to live in two rather conflicting eras at the same time: The traditional era of "power politics," sovereignty, and unilateral action, which is still with us, and the emergent era of the "rule of law," symbolized more by ideals than by acts. The Soviets have the advantage of living almost exclusively in the first. The underdeveloped nations are carried by a "wave of the future" or "stream of history" which allows them to use quite naturally the principles and purposes of the Charter as a tool of national policy. The west has done the same thing in the cold war but finds it far more difficult with respect to the anti-colonial revolution; nevertheless, a way must be found to bridge the gap between the two eras.

A first precept would be to avoid any head-on clash with the ideals which the west professes (and profits from). This involves, first of all, in cases where attempts at conciliation or peaceful change have failed, the duty to defend one's interests by methods which are not internationally regressive. The use of armed force, except for collective security, in self-defense and perhaps in circumstances as tragic as Israel's position after years of encirclement and insecurity, is to be avoided. Israel itself has not brought lasting peace any nearer either by its former massive retaliatory raids or by last fall's war. The case of England and France is even clearer. It could be shown quite persuasively that Colonel Nasser's nationalization of an international public service accompanied by statements which expressed a will to use this service for national purposes and which presented the move as an act of retaliation was going against the direction which international society is bound to take if complete disintegration is to be avoided. Thus, England and France had a number of perfectly "progressive" arguments. Legally, Egypt could exploit the letter of international law and invoke the narrowest interpretation of rather ambiguous provisions, but the western powers could resort to an interpretation in which the spirit and purposes of the law rather than the textual arguments served as criteria. In fact, a number of Asian and African nations did agree with the western reasoning in the first London conference. If a special session of the United Nations Assembly had been summoned at the time instead of the Conference, as the British Labor Party had suggested, the west might have obtained the legitimizing seal of the United Nations. However, this "progressive" case was destroyed by the use of military force in circumstances that seemed to combine the perils of a plot and the imprudence of an improvization. Such a move immediately provoked a clear opposition by Asia and Africa against the invaders—the very kind of alignment that threatens to wreck both the United Nations and the international politics of the west, and that had been miraculously avoided in the Suez crisis until then. The only justification is that the wavering of Mr.

Dulles seemed to shut out all the more subtle forms of pressure on Egypt. But perhaps Mr. Dulles would have been less anxious to stress "peace" so absolutely if there had been fewer war noises in Paris and London. The arsenal of coercion is rich enough for western states to find in it other weapons than bombers and tanks.

Our precept also involves the duty to prevent situations in which a head-on clash between the Charter and western nations seems like a lesser evil. Whenever the United Nations is unable to provide adequate procedures of peaceful adjustment, or whenever the only possible decisions of the United Nations would conflict with western interests, other mechanisms must be tried. The United Nations as a set of procedures is not necessarily the best means toward the ideals for which these procedures stand. In such cases to avoid the United Nations altogether is far more respectable than the tactic which consists in finally bringing to the United Nations disputes which many previous attempts have failed to solve and which have reached such a temperature that they can only explode in the faces of the United Nations Members. The United Nations should be a hospital, not a morgue. Nor can western policy-makers let it become a force which would weaken or increase the weaknesses of the west in world affairs. A second precept would be to use the United Nations in such a way that United Nations ideals and western interests would be brought together without too much strain. This involves, first of all, the need to strengthen as much as possible those very alarm bells and mechanisms whose weaknesses we have deplored in the beginning. The more fragile the *status quo* and the smaller the chance of peaceful adjustment, the more necessary it becomes to repair the institutional deficiencies described last year by the Secretary-General and to equip the Assembly with devices which will allow it, should the crisis recur, to react more smoothly instead of staggering "from crisis to crisis improvising in haste."

Our precept involves, secondly, the need at least to try to find ways in which the United Nations could play a more active role in efforts toward peaceful change. The hope is dim, as recent failures in Kashmir have confirmed. However, attempts at substituting small negotiating bodies for unruly parliamentary debates or at restoring the League of Nations system of rapporteurs might be fruitful. As the Assembly works now, it is far more capable of creating subsidiary organs than of providing conciliation, and it would be good to use more of the former in order to gain more of the latter.

Our precept also requires a thorough effort at leadership by western nations in the United Nations in order to obtain the necessary two-thirds majority for proposals which are in the interest of the west. The crisis of last fall has shown that only such political leadership can produce results. For a great power such as the United States to "leave to the United Nations" matters of great concern to itself or to its allies is a mistake, whenever it means that this great power has no policy of its own to propose to the United Nations. Abandoned without such leadership to the free play of voting blocs, the Assembly will inevitably tend to pass the buck to the Secretary-General, and no civil servant, national or international, however subtle and dedicated, will ever tend to take bold initiatives in a political vacuum. Mr. Acheson has wisely reminded us that in the minds of the authors of the "Uniting for Peace" resolution, the Assembly was supposed to execute, not to frame, policy. Such leadership should imply a will to refuse excessive dilution of vital proposals for the sake of getting a text on the books, and a readiness to take matters out of the United Nations if necessary (as last February). The alternative to a "bloc veto" in the Assembly does not have to be a weak compromise where important interests are lost and only sponsors gained. Western nations have enough voting power of their own to block any proposals that would conflict with their policies; chess can be played by more than one group. In the long run no non-communist member of the United Nations has anything to gain either by refusing institutional improvements or by opposing efforts at coping with the problem of change in areas where the *status juris* has all the marks of a powder keg.

Our precept means, finally, that such leadership must not only be exerted within the United Nations but must also be extended outside of the United Nations. Precisely because many factors in world affairs are beyond the control of the organization, and because it is not a world government with an executive branch entrusted to the Secretary-General (even though the Assembly tries to act as a legislature), the Members of the United Nations have the duty to supplement and not just to echo the calls of the United Nations for peaceful adjustment. This is another major lesson of the crisis.

To sum up, the tragic events of Hungary have confirmed the powerlessness of the United Nations in the zone under Soviet control; there, a change of the *status quo* cannot be obtained by the United Nations and it is anyhow hard to see how other mechanisms can obtain it at a price acceptable to the west. In the Middle East a general settlement satisfactory to all parties was and still is probably impossible either in or outside the United Nations; but no efforts were made at all. A considerable "intermediary" improvement was probably far less impossible; but it was not achieved. Diplomatic efforts that might have been aimed at a settlement will have to be devoted instead to a consolidation and improvement of the *status quo*. Because of the very limitations and inequities revealed by the crisis it is not possible to expect the United Nations itself to contribute much in the future to a settlement of the more explosive Middle Eastern issues. This imposes upon the statesmen of the west the triple duty to see that such a settlement be attempted within or outside the United Nations by all means compatible with the Charter; to avoid moves and maneuvers that imperil the principles upon which the United Nations rests; and to strengthen those United Nations techniques whose purpose it is to postpone or to limit explosions until a deeper settlement has been achieved.

Already the Middle East in the United Nations has become disturbingly similar to the Turkish question in the Concert of Europe. There too, the main powers of the world had for years agreed only on the maintenance of the *status quo* and on the need to prevent the peoples of the area from disturbing peace by trying to settle their own fate violently. When the hands-off policy of the big powers disappeared and when the nationalities so long contained began to lift the lid and to exploit their guardians' rivalries, the first world war put an end to the game. The Concert was institutionally and politically too weak to prevent the catastrophe. A war temporarily averted or repressed is not a world restored—it might simply mean a bigger blast prepared.

Thus Sisyphus has survived the avalanche. He will have to stay on the job. To be sure, if other mortals do not come to help him, his rock will never remain on top of the mountain and the next landslide might crush him. But if he does not try again, however clumsily, with their help, the gods of war and want will have won a remarkable victory.

II REFLECTIONS OF THE SECRETARY-GENERAL

Introduction to the Annual Report of the Secretary-General on the Work of the Organization, 16 June 1959-15 June 1960 *

Dag Hammarskjold

II

The African developments are putting the United Nations to a test both as regards the functions of its parliamentary institutions and as regards the efficiency and strength of its executive capacity.

The considerable increase in the membership of the United Nations stemming from a region with short independent experience in international politics has led to doubts regarding the possibility of the General Assembly and its committees to work expeditiously and in a way which truly reflects considered world opinion. In this context the question of the voting system has again been raised.

In previous reports to the General Assembly I have touched on this problem, indicating as my conviction that there is no practical alternative in

* Dag Hammarskjold, "Introduction to the Annual Report of the Secretary-General on the Work of the Organization, 16 June 1959-15 June 1960," General Assembly, *Official Records,* 15th Session, Supplement 1A, pp. 1-8. Also in *United Nations Review,* Vol. VII, No. 4 (October 1960), pp. 20-28.

keeping with the basic tenets of the Charter to the present system of equal votes for all sovereign Member States. Naturally it may be said that the irrationality of such a system is demonstrated when a new voting balance can be achieved through a sudden expansion of the number of Members by some 20 per cent. However, this fails to take into account realities to which reference has likewise been made in previous reports.

The General Assembly is a body which reflects in its decisions on major questions the results of long and careful negotiations and consideration. During this process, common lines are elaborated and compromises reached which give to the decisions the character of a confirmation of a negotiated approach rather than of a solution achieved through the mechanics of voting. Furthermore, the background of the decisions of the General Assembly, which, of course, anyway have the character of recommendations, should be analysed in order to arrive at a true evaluation of their significance. A voting victory or a voting defeat may be of short-lived significance. What is regarded as responsible world opinion as reflected in the voting and in the debates is in many respects more important than any formally registered result.

There is in the views expressed in favour of weighted voting an implied lack of confidence in the seriousness and responsibility with which newly independent States are likely to take their stands. Such a lack of confidence is not warranted by the history of the United Nations and must be rejected as contrary to facts. Neither size, nor wealth, nor age is historically to be regarded as a guarantee for the quality of the international policy pursued by any nation.

It is my conviction that the addition of a great number of new Member States will widen the perspectives, enrich the debate and bring the United Nations closer to present-day realities. I also believe that this development will exercise a sound influence in the direction of a democratization of proceedings by lessening the influence of firm groupings with firm engagements.

However, the widened membership does create certain practical problems. It may tend to lengthen debates, and it may make the General Assembly proceedings seem too cumbersome in cases where speed and efficiency are of the essence. For that reason, the development directs attention again to the possibilities for improving the methods applied in the parliamentary institutions of the Organization. Thus, I feel that Member nations may wish to consider a greater role for the General Committee, so that it can assume a wider responsibility for the conduct of the work of the General Assembly and eventually ease the burden of the Assembly and its substantive committees.

If and when the question of Charter revision comes up for consideration, the evolution of the General Assembly also is likely to add weight to the question of the role, composition and procedures of the Security Council.

During the Suez and Hungary crises, a development took place through which increased responsibilities were temporarily transferred from the Security Council to the General Assembly. Since it is difficult for the General Assembly to act expeditiously if it is required to engage in detailed consideration of complicated legal and technical problems, the Assembly found that the most adequate way to meet the challenges which it had to face was to entrust the Secretary-General with wide executive tasks on the basis of mandates of a general nature.

Especially in the Suez crisis, when all the executive work was entrusted to the Secretary-General, this put the Secretariat to a severe test. However, it proved possible, in close interplay between the General Assembly and the Secretary-General, assisted by the Advisory Committee appointed by the General Assembly, to work smoothly and swiftly towards a speedy achievement of the established aims. The value and possibilities of the Secretariat as an executive organ were thus proved, a fact which has in significant ways influenced later developments. . . .

III

On various points the preceding observations have touched upon the ideological conflicts and the conflicts of power which divide our world of today.

There is no reason to elaborate here the way in which these major conflicts have influenced proceedings within the United Nations and even the constitutional pattern which has developed in practice. One word may, however, be said about the possibilities of substantive action by the United Nations in a split world.

Fundamental though the differences splitting our world are, the areas which are not committed in the major conflicts are still considerable. Whether the countries concerned call themselves non-committed, neutral, neutralist or something else, they have all found it not to be in harmony with their role and interests in world politics to tie their policies, in a general sense, to any one of the blocs or to any specific line of action supported by one of the sides in the major conflict. The reasons for such attitudes vary. That, however, is less important in this special context than the fact that conflicts arising within the non-committed areas offer opportunities for solutions which avoid an aggravation of big Power differences and can remain uninfluenced by them. There is thus a field within which international conflicts may be faced and solved with such harmony between the power blocs as was anticipated as a condition for Security Council action in San Francisco. Agreement may be achieved because of a mutual interest among the big Powers to avoid having a regional or local conflict drawn into the sphere of bloc politics.

With its constitution and structure, it is extremely difficult for the United Nations to exercise an influence on problems which are clearly and definitely within the orbit of present day conflicts between power blocs. If a specific conflict is within that orbit, it can be assumed that the Security Council is rendered inactive, and it may be feared that even positions taken by the General Assembly would follow lines strongly influenced by considerations only indirectly related to the concrete difficulty under consideration. Whatever the attitude of the General Assembly and the Security Council, it is in such cases also practically impossible for the Secretary-General to operate effectively with the means put at his disposal, short of risking seriously to impair the usefulness of his office for the Organization in all the other cases for which the services of the United Nations Secretariat are needed.

This clearly defines the main field of useful activity of the United Nations in its efforts to prevent conflicts or to solve conflicts. Those efforts must aim at keeping newly arising conflicts outside the sphere of bloc differences. Further, in the case of conflicts on the margin of, or inside, the sphere of bloc differences, the United Nations should seek to bring such conflicts out of this sphere through solutions aiming, in the first instance, at their strict localization. In doing so, the Organization and its agents have to lay down a policy line, but this will then not be for one party against another, but for the general purpose of avoiding an extension or achieving a reduction of the area into which the bloc conflicts penetrate.

Experience indicates that the preventive diplomacy, to which the efforts of the United Nations must thus to a large extent be directed, is of special significance in cases where the original conflict may be said either to be the result of, or to imply risks for, the creation of a power vacuum between the main blocs. Preventive action in such cases must in the first place aim at filling the vacuum so that it will not provoke action from any of the major parties, the initiative for which might be taken for preventive purposes but might in turn lead to counter-action from the other side. The ways in which a vacuum can be filled by the United Nations so as to forestall such initiatives differ from case to case, but they have this in common: temporarily, and pending the filling of a vacuum by normal means, the United Nations enters the picture on the basis of its non-commitment to any power bloc, so as to provide to the extent possible a guarantee in relation to all parties against initiatives from others.

The special need and the special possibilities for what I here call preventive United Nations diplomacy have been demonstrated in several recent cases, such as Suez and Gaza, Lebanon and Jordan, Laos and the Congo.

A study of the records of the conflicts to which I have just referred shows how it has been possible to use the means and methods of the United Nations for the purposes I have indicated. In all cases, whatever the immediate reason for the United Nations initiative, the Organization has moved so as to forestall developments which might draw the specific conflict, openly or actively, into the sphere of power bloc differences. It has done so by introducing itself into the picture, sometimes with very modest means, sometimes in strength, so as to eliminate a political, economic and social, or military vacuum.

The view expressed here as to the special possibilities and responsibilities of the Organization in situations of a vacuum has reached an unusually clear expression in the case of the Congo. There, the main argument presented for United Nations intervention was the breakdown of law and order, the rejection of the attempt to maintain order by foreign troops, and the introduction of the United Nations Force so as to create the basis for the withdrawal of the foreign troops and for the forestalling of initiatives to introduce any other foreign troops into the territory with the obvious risks for widening international conflict which would ensue.

Whether the Congo operation is characterized as a case of preventive diplomacy, or as a move in order to fill a vacuum and to forestall the international risks created by the development of such a vacuum, or as a policy aimed at the localization of a conflict with potentially wide international repercussions, is not essential. Whatever the description, the political reality remains. It is a policy which is justified by the wish of the international community to avoid this important area being split by bloc conflicts. It is a policy rendered possible by the fact that both blocs have an interest in avoiding such an extension of the area of conflict because of the threatening consequences, were the localization of the conflict to fail.

Those who look with impatience at present day efforts by the United Nations to resolve major international problems are inclined to neglect, or to misread, the significance of the efforts which can be made by the United Nations in the field of practical politics in order to guide the international community in a direction of growing stability. They see the incapacity of the United Nations to resolve the major bloc conflicts as an argument against the very form of international co-operation which the Organization represents. In doing so, they forget what the Organization has achieved and can achieve, through its activities regarding conflicts which are initially only on the margin of, or outside, the bloc conflicts, but which, unless solved or localized, might widen the bloc conflicts and seriously aggravate them. Thus the Organization in fact also exercises a most important, though indirect, influence on the conflicts between the power blocs by preventing the widening of the geographical and political area covered by these conflicts and by providing for solutions whenever the interests of all parties in a localization of conflict can be mobilized in favour of its efforts.

The Organization in this way also makes a significant contribution in the direction of an ultimate solution of the differences between the power blocs, as it is obvious that it is a condition for an improvement in the situation that the area to which those differences apply, as a minimum requirement, is not permitted to expand and, so far as possible, is reduced.

It is with this background that the initiative for United Nations intervention in the Congo conflict was taken under Article 99 of the Charter, for the first time applied fully, according to its letter and in the spirit in which it must have been drafted. It is also in this light that one has to view the fact that not only the first but also the subsequent decisions in the Security

Council regarding the Congo have been taken by votes in which the power bloc conflicts have not been reflected.

These observations are of special interest when we turn to the consideration of questions regarding which the power bloc interests openly clash. I have in mind especially disarmament. In general terms, it is not surprising that, in the case of problems so deeply related to the security of many nations and to the predominant powers within the different blocs, negotiations have presented extraordinary difficulties. On the other hand, it is also evident that there is a latitude within which a shared interest in avoiding an aggravation of the situation overrides the specific security interests of any one party and within which, for that reason, agreement may be possible.

De facto, we have seen such an agreement developing in the field of nuclear tests. I believe that there are also other questions within the field of disarmament regarding which success is possible for new efforts to reach agreement, on at least so much of a common *de facto* policy as is indicated by the mutual interest to avoid a widening of the substantive basis for the present day race towards a world crisis. Approached in this way, disarmament seems to offer important possibilities, still incompletely explored, of a gradual reduction of the area in which clashing security interests so far have rendered formal agreement impossible.

There is no contradiction between this application to the disarmament problem of the philosophy and practices successfully tried by the United Nations in specific conflicts and the view that there can be no solution to the disarmament problem short of the acceptance of total disarmament under satisfactory control by both sides. The pragmatic approach and the, so to say, global one are not at variance, for it is obvious that efforts to avoid a widening of the field of conflict and to reduce the area in which concrete agreement for the moment is impossible should at all events be integrated into a wider, more far-reaching plan under which the security interests of the parties can be balanced out against each other in ways that will make it possible for the parties to reach the ideal target of total disarmament.

It is certainly not productive to approach the disarmament problem solely on a pragmatic basis, without integration of the steps taken into a plan ultimately aiming at full disarmament. Likewise, however, it seems unrealistic to approach the total problem oblivious of the fact that all political experience and all previous negotiation show that the road to progress lies in the direction of efforts to contain and reduce the area of disagreement by mobilizing such common interests as may exist and as may override other and special interests tending in the opposite direction.

The Members of the General Assembly will excuse me for presenting these general observations on a problem to which the Assembly has devoted so much attention. I have done so only because it seems to me that the experiences from other political fields in which the United Nations has acted with success have a bearing also on a field like this one where, so far, the Organization has failed to achieve results.

IV

The responsibilities and possibilities of the Organization in the exercise of preventive diplomacy apply also to the economic sphere. Far less dramatic in their impact as the economic activities must be, they are of decisive long-term significance for the welfare of the international community. In the end, the United Nations is likely to be judged not so much by the criterion of how successfully it has overcome this or that crisis as by the significance of its total contribution towards building the kind of world community in which such crises will no longer be inevitable.

This aim, naturally, cannot be reached overnight, nor can it be considerably furthered by any institutional or constitutional reforms of the United Nations. It cannot even be achieved by the political resolution of the conflicts which today divide the major Powers. Essential though such a political resolution would be, it would not by itself ensure stability and peace in the face of the dangerous economic and social vacuum created and maintained by the enormous gap which separates countries at different stages of development.

In the enduring task of bridging the gulf between countries, all Member nations, whether developed or under-developed, whether in the East or the West, have a common interest. This common interest is recognized by everyone. It is clearly stated in the Charter of the United Nations, in which countries pledge themselves to take joint and separate action in co-operation with the Organization to promote "higher standards of living, full employment and conditions of economic and social progress and development." It is reflected in all of the debates of the Economic and Social Council as well as of the General Assembly on the relevant items. It has borne fruit in a host of activities within the United Nations and its sister institutions. And yet, in considering the rate of progress that has been made in relation to the task that remains to be achieved, it is difficult to escape a feeling of disappointment.

It is true that the mere recognition of the community of interest in the economic development of under-developed countries itself represents a major step forward. And the expressions of common interest in economic development are no lip service. The achievements of the United Nations family in the economic and social field, as generously supported by Member Governments, demonstrates their seriousness. However, it must, in the context of a newly emerging Africa, be registered, in a spirit of candid realism, that the rate of achievement is not at all commensurate with the needs.

The coincidence of interest in the economic field stems from the economic interdependence of the world community. The degree of interdependence has been increasing rapidly, partly as the inevitable outcome of an accelerating rate of advance in science and technology, partly owing to the emergence of the countries of the continents of Asia and of Africa to independence and full participation in the affairs of the world at large, but, to a significant degree, also as a result of economic forces making for a growing integration of the world community.

For the first time in history, the concept of a world economy has come to take on a significant meaning not only for the student of economics but also for the statesman and the layman.

Unfortunately, this growing interdependence has recently been reflected much less in efforts and activities within the United Nations than outside it. The United Nations can welcome regional arrangements among neighbouring or like-minded countries; as long as such arrangements are so designed as to reinforce rather than to supplant the common effort towards establishing conditions of economic and social progress, they have an important role to play. A real danger arises, however, when such regional arrangements are so envisaged as to make them fall within the sphere of bloc conflict. In that case, efforts which properly should embody and be supported by a common interest may instead lead to a weakening of the uniting force of that interest and aggravate the split. This, obviously, is the reverse of the major purpose and function of the United Nations in its efforts to provide for a growing measure of political stability.

Just as it is clearly within the interests of the entire world community to prevent the widening of the area of conflict in cases of political crises, so it must be in the interests of all constantly to seek to widen rather than to restrict the area of coincidence of economic interest within the United Nations. Unless this is done, the entire world, and not just one or the other side, is bound to lose. As I noted in my statement to the Economic and Social Council at its thirtieth session, "the United Nations Organization remains the only universal agency in which countries with widely differing political institutions and at different stages of economic development may exchange views, share their problems and experiences, probe each other's reactions to policies of mutual interest, and initiate collective action."

V

In the Introduction to my Report to the General Assembly at its fourteenth session I discussed the role of the United Nations. In that context I said:

"The work of today within and for the United Nations is a work through which the basis may be laid for increasingly satisfactory forms of international co-operation and for a future international system of law and order, for which the world is not yet ripe."

I continued:

"It has so often been said that the world of today is one which requires organized international co-operation on a basis of universality that one repeats it with hesitation. However, there are reasons to do so. It still seems sometimes to be forgotten that—whatever views may be held about the

United Nations as an institution—the principle of organized international co-operation on a basis of universality which is at present reflected in this Organization is one which has emerged from bitter experiences and should now be considered as firmly established."

In the previous parts of this Introduction I have tried to outline my views on some specific problems arising for the Organization at the present juncture, which may well, in the perspective of history, come to be regarded as a turning point. Especially, I have wished to draw the attention of the Members to the scope for possible diplomatic and political action by the Organization in a split world and to the desirability of the widening of that scope by patient and persistent action, using as the lever the community of interests which is created by the desire of everybody to limit the area of conflict, to reduce the risk of conflicts and to create a basis for joint action for solution, or at least localization, of conflicts.

Recent developments—reflected in a revolutionary technical evolution of arms for destruction, in the entry of new major regions of the world in full strength into international politics and in new and world-wide economic interdependence—have given to the Organization, and what it represents as an instrument in the hands of Member Governments, greatly increased responsibilities, but also increased usefulness.

The Organization and its activities can be viewed on different levels. It provides Member Governments with a highly developed, continuously operating conference and negotiation machinery. However, to a growing extent it has provided them also with an effective executive organ for joint action. In this latter respect, the evolution has taken a course somewhat different from the one envisaged in San Francisco, but, as recent developments have shown, the departure as to methods is not considerable and the conformity as to aims is complete. Finally, the Organization is also the embodiment of an ideal and the symbol of an approach to international life which recognizes the common interest of all in the rejection of the use of force, in any form, as a means for settling international disputes and in adherence to the principles of law, justice, and human rights.

The Organization has often in the past been faced, and is likely in its continued work again and again to be faced, with situations in which a compromise with these last-mentioned principles might seem to facilitate the achievement of results in negotiations or to promise an easier success for the Organization in its executive efforts to resolve a problem. It is for the Members themselves to judge to what extent the Organization, in particular cases, has accepted such compromises and to what extent it has remained faithful to the principles and ideals which it embodies.

It is my firm conviction that any result bought at the price of a compromise with the principles and ideals of the Organization, either by yielding to force, by disregard of justice, by neglect of common interests or by contempt for human rights, is bought at too high a price. That is so because a compromise with its principles and purposes weakens the Organization in a way representing a definite loss for the future that cannot be balanced by any immediate advantage achieved.

The United Nations has increasingly become the main platform—and the main protector of the interests—of those many nations who feel themselves strong as members of the international family but who are weak in isolation. Thus, an increasing number of nations have come to look to the United Nations for leadership and support in ways somewhat different from those natural in the light of traditional international diplomacy. They look to the Organization as a spokesman and as an agent for principles which give them strength in an international concert in which other voices can mobilize all the weight of armed force, wealth, an historical role and that influence which is the other side of a special responsibility for peace and security. Therefore, a weakening of the Organization, resulting from an attempt to achieve results at the cost of principles, is a loss not only for the future but also immediately in respect of the significance of the Organization for the vast majority of nations and in respect of their confidence in the Organization on which its strength in our present day world ultimately depends.

There are in the Charter elements of a thinking which, I believe, belongs to an earlier period in the development of the world community. I have in mind especially the concept that the permanent members of the Security Council should not only, as is natural, be recognized as carrying special responsibility for peace and security, but that, further, these permanent members, working together, should represent a kind of "built-in" directing group for the world community as organized in the United Nations.

The fifteen years which have passed since the founding of the United Nations have witnessed a different development. In the first place, we have seen a split among the permanent members which, in fact, has created the major war risk of today and considerably hampered the development of the Organization. But, further, we have experienced a growth into independence of a majority of States of two great continents, with other interests, other traditions, and other concepts of international politics than those of the countries of Europe and the Americas. Who can deny that today the countries of Asia or the countries of Africa, acting in a common spirit, represent powerful elements in the international community, in their ways as important as any of the big Powers, although lacking in their military and economic potential?

The United Nations is an organic creation of the political situation facing our generation. At the same time, however, the international community has, so to say, come to political self-consciousness in the Organization and, therefore, can use it in a meaningful way in order to influence those very circumstances of which the Organization is a creation.

It is impossible for anyone to say where the international community is heading and how the United Nations will change in the further course of the evolution of international politics. But it can safely be said that international co-operation will become increasingly essential for the maintenance of peace, progress and international justice. It can also safely be said that if the United Nations firmly adheres to its principles and purposes, with flexibility and intelligent adjustment to needs as regards procedure, Members engaged in this co-operation will increasingly turn to the Organization for assistance. Therefore, they will find it increasingly necessary to maintain its strength as an instrument for the world community in their efforts to reduce those areas of major conflict where the Organization so far has been powerless, as well as in efforts to resolve problems, arising outside or on the margin of these areas, in a spirit reflecting the overriding common interest.

This concept of the role and of the future of the United Nations may go beyond the conventional thinking which sees in the Organization only, or mainly, a machinery for negotiation, but I am convinced of its realism and I am convinced also that the Organization and its member nations would act rightly and wisely if they acted consistently with this concept in mind, even if temporarily it may seem to point out a road full of risks and of difficulties which they may doubt that the Organization is yet strong enough to overcome.

III THE CONGO

The United Nations Operation in the Congo*

Ralph J. Bunche

I have chosen as my topic in the Dag Hammarskjöld Memorial Lecture Series "The United Nations Operation in the Congo" (called ONUC for short), primarily because that operation meant so very much to Dag Hammarskjöld, and he far more to it, and also because I have been directly associated with the operation from its inception. Dag Hammarskjöld initiated the Congo operation in midsummer of 1960, encouraged it to become the biggest of all United Nations operations to date, and gave his major attention to it through many tense and unpleasant months until, in September, 1961, he gave his life while serving it.

* Ralph J. Bunche, "The United Nations Operation in the Congo." *The Quest for Peace*, eds. Andrew W. Cordier and Wilder Foote (New York: Columbia University Press, 1965), pp. 119-39. Reprinted by permission. Ralph J. Bunche, the recipient of the Nobel Peace Prize in 1950, has been the United Nations Under-Secretary for Special Political Affairs since 1958.

It is especially appropriate, I think, to introduce this particular lecture with a few remarks about Dag Hammarskjöld himself. It is, of course, never easy to talk about one's chief or former chief, and Dag Hammarskjöld was my hard-working and demanding "boss" for eight years. It is even less easy to present a balanced judgment about a man as remarkable and as remarkably complex as Dag Hammarskjöld.

One need not elaborate here on the widely accepted fact that he was one of the truly great men of our times; on his widely known and deserved reputation for being uniquely gifted in intelligence, wisdom, statesmanship, and courage; or on his literally total dedication to the causes of peace and human advancement and the United Nations efforts to promote them. We who worked with him came to know Dag Hammarskjöld also as bold, sometimes daring in his moves and approaches to problems, but not reckless. He was not given to acting without cool and thorough calculation, and was never one to act impulsively, although when an idea firmly commended itself to him he would pursue it doggedly. It is not suggested, however, that he was above anger, even fury, or other emotions. He could and at times did erupt. He had an uncanny and almost intuitive sense of political timing and this may have been one of his greatest assets throughout his years of devoted service to the United Nations. . . .

Dag Hammarskjöld was himself a dynamic person and he strove with, I believe, no little success to make the United Nations a dynamic force for peace and human advancement. Wherever in the world there was a conflict situation, actual or threatening, he believed the United Nations should actively seek to contain or avert it: by quiet diplomacy, when the circumstances permitted, in the form of good offices if the parties themselves demonstrated an inability to deal with the situation; and, if necessary, by overt United Nations action. He saw more clearly than any man I have known that the United Nations must do more than hold meetings and talk and adopt resolutions. It was good for the General Assembly to be the forum of the world, and to afford a unique opportunity for a meeting of statesmen from all over, and for those statesmen to exchange views. But this in itself, he knew, could never be enough to save the world. In his conception, the United Nations must play an ever more active role, must project itself into the very area of conflict.

It was in pursuance of this line of thought that under Dag Hammarskjöld came the numerous acts of quiet diplomacy and the establishment, for peace-making and peace-keeping purposes, of the United Nations "presence" in a number of places, whether by a representative of the Secretary-General, by the stationing of United Nations military observers, or by a United Nations peace force. It was his firm conviction that it was not only possible to conceive of but that there actually had been built up at the United Nations—at the very heart of world events—a body of thoroughly objective, if not "neutral," international officers who, under his leadership, when given opportunity and resources and the confidence of enough governments, could play a vital and at times even decisive role in averting conflict.

Thus Dag Hammarskjöld strengthened the United Nations truce and cease-fire operations in the Near East and Kashmir, which had begun under Trygve Lie, his predecessor, giving increasing attention particularly to the United Nations Truce Supervision Operation (UNTSO) in Jerusalem. At the time of the Suez crisis in 1956, even though it was an untried idea, without precedent and without any prior provision for its financing, Mr. Hammarskjöld helped to initiate and proceeded speedily to establish the United Nations Emergency Force (UNEF) in Gaza and Sinai, in pursuance of a resolution of the General Assembly. He made an enormous miscalculation in this instance, for he had anticipated that UNEF would be needed in the Near East for only a few months, and he could not have imagined how indispensable it would become. After almost six and a half years at an annual cost to the United Nations of approximately $19,000,000, that peace force is still deployed along the Gaza-strip armistice line and the international frontier between Israel and the United Arab Republic, and there is little prospect that it can be withdrawn in the foreseeable future without risking a new war.

The United Nations Operation in the Congo was mainly Hammarskjöld's in conception and reflected Hammarskjöld's boldness. From the beginning, it was apparent that this would be by far the largest and most costly operation ever undertaken by the United Nations, and it also soon became distressingly clear that it would be the most difficult and trying of all United Nations efforts. It began in mid-July, 1960, and still goes on, although, in accordance with General Assembly action, the United Nations Force is definitely scheduled to be withdrawn from the Congo at the end of June, 1964, which will be just short of four years after its arrival in the Congo.

In the three and a half years to date of the Congo operation, the United Nations has expended some $400,000,000 in its military and civilian assistance activities.

The Congo task posed the sort of stern challenge that brought out the imaginative and courageous best in Dag Hammarskjöld. He loved to rise to a challenge. He was never so stirred and inspired—or inspiring—as when entering the lists with a tough new issue.

Dag Hammarskjöld anticipated the possibility of trouble in the Congo after its independence, even before that independence was achieved on June 30, 1960. It was well known even then, of course, that the Congolese had had very little preparation for independence. How totally unprepared they were was to become fully and tragically revealed soon after independence day. In late May of that year, Mr. Hammarskjöld called me into his office to inform me that he wished me to go to the then Belgian Congo toward the end of June to represent the United Nations at the Congo's independence ceremony. He also informed me I was to stay on in the Congo for some time after independence to be of such assistance as might be required of me by the new government, bearing in mind, he added, that there might well be trouble in that new country.

His anxiety was justified. There was to be trouble in the Congo, profound and shattering trouble, and it came only a week after independence, when the ANC (the Armee Nationale Congolaise, which had been the Force Publique under Belgian rule) mutinied in early July and arrested or chased away all of its Belgian officers, which at that time meant quite literally *all* of its officers.

Soon after the mutiny of his troops, Patrice Lumumba, the Congo's first Prime Minister, who only a few months later was to come to such a tragic end, called me into a meeting of his Cabinet members to make the government's first request for assistance from the United Nations. At that time the government was thinking only of military technical assistance and not a military force. When, however, only a few days later, the Belgian troops, to protect Belgian nationals, moved outside of their bases in the Congo without the consent of the Congolese government, Mr. Lumumba, on July 12, 1960, urgently called on the United Nations for military assistance in getting the Belgian troops to withdraw and in helping to protect the country's territorial integrity.

There was not at this time very much understanding on the part of any Congolese official about the nature of the United Nations, or about what it could or could not do, its functioning and structure, and particularly about the meaning and status of the United Nations Secretariat. Indeed, even today, one could wish for much more understanding along these lines. The feeling in Leopoldville in July, 1960, seemed to be that the United Nations would quickly respond with everything that was wanted and needed and that the United Nations personnel, military and civilian alike, would be constantly at the bidding of Congolese government officials, even at times to serve most petty personal aims. Mr. Lumumba bluntly stated in his bitter letter of August 14, 1960, to Mr. Hammarskjöld, that the Security Council, by its resolution of August 9, 1960, "is to place all its resources at the disposal of my government." Congolese officials holding such views have naturally suffered profound disillusionment.

The United Nations experience in the Congo has demonstrated, sometimes painfully, the serious difficulties that will inevitably be encountered by a United Nations peace force stationed in a country under a specific mandate to provide the government with military assistance in preserving its integrity and in maintaining internal law and order, without clear, precise, and full directives about its function and authority in relation to the government of the country in which it is to be deployed, and prior agreement about these with the government concerned.

In July and August of 1960 I was seeing Patrice Lumumba almost daily. He was an electric figure; his passionate oratory could entrance an audience and, as it sometimes appeared, even himself; he was indefatigable; he was quickly perceptive and shrewd; also he was deeply suspicious of almost everyone and everything. He may have been subject to leftist influence but I did not regard him as anyone's stooge and felt that he was not greatly concerned with ideology. Mr. Lumumba, it must be said, was one of the few Congolese who seemed to grasp the vital necessity of national unity in a new nation and he strove against all the divisive forces of tribalism and special interest to promote this unity. Unfortunately, however, he and most of his colleagues in his Cabinet had little knowledge of and apparently no deep interest in government and administration as distinct from crude politics and political maneuver. It was this, combined with the mutiny of the ANC, the inability, which was all too clear from the beginning, of Kasavubu and Lumumba to reconcile their differences, the extraordinary atmosphere of rumor, fear, suspicion, and violence which pervaded the Congo at that time, that soon brought the Congo to near chaos.

It must be said that the Belgian decision to move their troops out of their Congo bases against the will of the Congo government, or, at least, the manner in which it was done, was a disastrous step. Some in Leopoldville at that time, including myself, had advised Belgian authorities that it would likely be so, before the fateful move was undertaken. I had suggested that a wiser tactic than unilateral military action would have been an appeal to the Security Council for assistance in protecting the thousands of Belgian nationals remaining in the Congo. The move of the Belgian troops left Mr. Lumumba furious and desperate, and led him to broadside appeals for outright military aid to the United States (President Eisenhower advised him to turn to the United Nations), to the USSR, and, only as a last resort, to the United Nations. In response to this second appeal, I assured Mr. Lumumba that the United Nations would most likely respond sympathetically, but even with my deep faith in the United Nations I could not have imagined at that time that the United Nations response to Mr. Lumumba's call would be as rapid and as immense as it turned out to be.

It developed that virtually the entire international community was sympathetic to the cries from this newly emerged country in the very heart of Africa, and wished to help. As mentioned earlier, the second appeal was received at the United Nations on July 12, 1960, and the first Security Council resolution in response to it, promising assistance, was adopted in the before-dawn hours of July 14, 1960. The follow-up action by the United Nations was unbelievably rapid, for the first United Nations troops—the Tunisians, quickly followed by Moroccans, Ethiopians, and Ghanaians—landed at Ndjili airport in Leopoldville on July 15, 1960. For this swift and effective response, my friend and former colleague in the Secretariat, Dean Andrew Cordier, deserves major credit.

The United Nations had no reasonable alternative to its favorable response to the Congo's appeal—the appeal of a weak government in a new state. In so doing, the United Nations strengthened itself morally and won new prestige. And it also gave to itself, no doubt unknowingly at the time, a far wider role and meaning in world affairs than it had ever had, and made indispensable a much stronger position for the Secretary-General as the executive arm. An unfettered executive with authority to act is imperative to the effective conduct of a peace-keeping field operation.

The Congo issue, when it came before the United Nations, was not in the context of the East-West conflict or of the Cold War. This accounted for the unanimity and spontaneity of the early support for the Congo's appeal, the Security Council resolutions, and ONUC. But it was not long before this changed and the United Nations Operation in the Congo came to be an issue between East and West, with Dag Hammarskjöld caught squarely in the cross-fire because of his responsibility, as Secretary-General, for the conduct of the operation. In any case, the United Nations, by having ONUC on the spot without delay, was able to fill what otherwise, because of the collapse of government in the Congo, would have been an inviting and most dangerous vacuum of authority in the heart of Africa, with obvious implications for rival East-West interests.

As soon as the July 12th appeal was received from the Congolese government, Dag Hammarskjöld began intensive consultations, particularly with the representatives of a number of African governments. He had seen immediately, with his usual keen perception, that the solid support of the Africans would be a decisive factor in getting the Congo operation launched. It was from these discussions that the idea—and the necessity—of a United Nations force which should be basically although not exclusively African in composition emerged.

The African Members, although they later became much less of one view on questions relating to the Congo operation than at first, have continued to exercise a decisive influence on matters affecting the operation. It was their unified voice, for instance, that led the General Assembly last fall to respond favorably to the appeal of Prime Minister Adoula to extend the stay of the United Nations Force in the Congo from the end of December, 1963, when it was originally scheduled to be withdrawn, to the end of June, 1964.

The near anarchy and chaos which occurred in the Congo so soon after independence and continued for so long led to a most unfortunate if unavoidable diversion to military assistance of the major part of the United Nations resources for the Congo from the hoped-for program of massive *technical* assistance, designed to help the country get on its feet after the departure of the Belgians who had been doing just about everything in the government, in administration, and in the economy. This military assistance was provided to help induce, as it did, Belgian troops to return to their bases and ultimately to leave the country, and to assist the government in maintaining law and order and preserving its territorial integrity. For the United Nations, this really meant undertaking for some time virtually the entire responsibility of holding things together in the Congo, while not trespassing on the authority of the government, at a time when governmental machinery was just about nonexistent owing to lack of experienced officials and the incessant quarrels of the politicians, and when the ANC was not only weak but dangerous, owing to lack of officers and discipline.

In a United Nations operation which, in both its military and its civilian aspects, must be in such close and daily contact with a government which has to lean so heavily on United Nations assistance, the problem of relations with that government is a most serious one. The operation, obviously, must meticulously avoid any interference in the internal political affairs of the country or any appearance of such interference, although many persons unconnected with the operation seem to take it for granted that there is such interference. The government, on its part, requests and is dependent upon the assistance the operation can afford, but many of its officials actually resent the need for it, or at least having to seek and ask for it. The government also, of course, would resent any United Nations political intervention unless it could be directed against the opposition, when it would, naturally, be entirely welcome.

Considering all the delicate circumstances, the relations between the Congolese government and the United Nations by and large have been tolerable, although they have seldom been really happy. They are, in truth, none too good at this very moment, although there has been no change in the policy of the United Nations or Secretary-General U Thant toward the Congo, which is to afford that country the maximum assistance possible with the resources available. The difficulties leading to strained relations usually arise when the United Nations, most likely for reasons of sound principle, finds it impossible to grant one or another request of the government. In this regard, I cannot help but recall my own experience with Mr. Lumumba, Mr. Gizenga, and other members of the Lumumba Cabinet back in August, 1960, when I was rejecting almost daily demands from them that elements of the United Nations Force be put instantly at the disposal and under the command of the Congolese government, which would then dispatch them to Katanga to fight Mr. Tshombe, or to Kasai or to Kivu to fight someone else—the ANC itself being unable to do so for lack of officers, retraining, and discipline.

I suppose one cannot speak of the United Nations Operation in the Congo without some reference to the attempted secession of Katanga, which has, perhaps more than any other single factor, the ANC mutiny excepted, complicated and bedeviled the post-independence history of the Congo. I say "attempted" advisedly because Katanga's secession never actually took place, and, indeed, Moise Tshombe, from his retreat in Spain, was recently avowing without a smile that, after all, the secession of Katanga was never his intention.

Although Mr. Tshombe had attended the Brussels Conference before independence and had agreed with the other Congolese leaders on the arrangements for independence, including the provisional constitution, it seems certain that the idea of secession was actively on his mind, possibly for a combination of personal political and financial reasons. I first met Mr. Tshombe in my suite at the Stanley Hotel in Leopoldville a few days after Congo independence. He was peeved, rather justifiably I think, at having been ignored by Messrs. Lumumba and Kasavubu. Mr. Tshombe at that time also expressed great dissatisfaction that the concept of a centralized government had been adopted, and informed me, with a surprising knowledge of the United States Articles of Confederaton, that he favored a loose (and weak) federation in the Congo along those lines. He seemed only to be encouraged when I protested strongly that the United States Articles of Confederation had failed woefully to work.

A few days later, Mr. Tshombe returned to Katanga and proclaimed secession. This declaration of July 11, 1960, was about the only basis Katangese secession ever had, and it would have had little or no meaning if Mr. Tshombe had not acquired disputed access to very large financial resources as well as the support of the European community in Katanga and of mining interests in and outside of that province. He was thus able to raise a Katangese army and employ non-African mercenary officers to lead it. Even so, Mr. Tshombe and Katanga and the mercenaries would not have been able to cause nearly as much trouble as they did had it not been for the utter incapacity of the Central Government and its army.

It deserves passing mention that Mr. Tshombe had at his bidding throughout the secession effort a quite formidable propaganda apparatus which was very active in the Western world and had especially strong impact in the United States. In this country, strangely, it succeeded in blinding a surprisingly large number of people, including some in public position, to the verities of the Katanga situation particularly and the Congo situation generally, and led them to oppose the policy of the United States government on the Congo.

The specter of Katanga and Mr. Tshombe always had highest priority in the thoughts of Congolese government officials, sometimes to an obsessive and paralyzing degree. Although this may be less the case today than it was three years ago, it could become so again very quickly should Mr. Tshombe emerge onto the active scene, as he may well do, once the United Nations troops are withdrawn from the Congo at the end of June. In fact, at this very time we are receiving a number of increasingly disturbing reports from reliable sources of a renewed concentration of the relics of Tshombe's army and of the mercenary officers' corps along the Angolan-Congolese border.

I recall an evening in Leopoldville in August, 1960, at Patrice Lumumba's home when he was vigorously lodging a series of complaints against ONUC until, in sheer self-defense, I took out of my case a cable that I had just received from Dag Hammarskjöld, giving the text of the long message he had recently sent to Mr. Tshombe firmly rejecting the latter's claim for Katanga's membership in the United Nations. Mr. Lumumba's face lighted up with near ecstasy when he read the message. He immediately dropped the subject of his complaints and asked only that he be permitted to make a copy of that message.

It is a most difficult situation for any government, and particularly for a new and proudly sensitive one, to have a right to a certain line of action, and a desperate need to take it, as in the case of the Congo's opposition to the attempted secession of Katanga, but to lack completely the means to launch the action, while at the same time there is in their country an international agency which they think has the right, as well as the means, to undertake the action for them, but which refuses to do it except in its own way and time. The resulting emotions and frustrations lead to many unrealistic attitudes. For example, on one of his visits to the Congo, Mr. Hammarskjöld informed Mr. Gizenga, who was Acting Prime Minister in the absence of Mr. Lumumba, and his colleagues, of his intention to send me to Katanga to prepare the way for the entry of the United Nations Force into Katanga. This was in early August, 1960. Mr. Gizenga was insistent that several members of the Congolese government should accompany me on the flight, although he knew very well that the only possible result of this would be that all of us would be promptly arrested on landing at Elisabethville, if not shot down before landing there. Mr. Gizenga was furious when Mr. Hammarskjöld decided that only United Nations personnel would take this trip. We went alone and got into trouble anyway.

While it was apparent that Katanga had no military force of consequence at that time, Mr. Tshombe was appealing by every means to the people of Katanga to resist United Nations entry. It would clearly put the United Nations Force in an untenable position if it had to fight the people of Katanga to enter that province and to remain there, for this would give it the posture of an army of occupation. Therefore I advised Mr. Hammarskjöld not to send the force to Katanga for the time being. I greatly doubt that a United Nations peace force could be stationed for very long in any country if, even in self-defense, it would have to turn its guns on civilians rather than military forces. The political realities of the United Nations, I imagine, would not long permit a peace force to be in the posture of an army of occupation.

Subsequently, the Secretary-General, with characteristic decisiveness and courage, decided to go himself to Katanga to talk with Mr. Tshombe, following a quick visit to New York to report to the Security Council. He went and succeeded in convincing Mr. Tshombe that the United Nations troops should be permitted to come into Katanga without resistance, and this they promptly did. Far from pleasing Mr. Lumumba, however, this accomplishment infuriated him, and on Mr. Hammarskjöld's return to Leopoldville from Katanga he received some incredibly angry and insulting letters from Mr. Lumumba about his trip to Katanga and his interpretation of Security Council resolutions. In fact, from that time on, Mr. Lumumba rejected all normal relations with the United Nations.

Before concluding this lecture I feel in duty bound to take advantage of the opportunity to try to clear up or dissipate certain misconceptions and myths about the Congo operation.

The United Nations Operation in the Congo at no time has had any executive authority there, or any share in executive authority. Its role has been exclusively that of assstance and advice. We do not participate in governing the country and have no responsibility for the actions of government. There are those, for example, who still say that the United Nations made a fatal mistake in the early days of the operation in that it did not disarm the mutinous ANC. It is quite possible that if the United Nations could have done this at the time—although to do it would almost certainly have involved considerable fighting—the course of events in the Congo might have been considerably different. But the United Nations had no authority to do this except the request of the Congolese government, and that request never came, although it had been made clear to the government that the United Nations would also undertake this type of assistance upon request of the government.

There has been much talk also, and some still persists, about United Nations "offensives" in the Congo, about the United Nations thwarting secession, conquering Katanga and returning it to the Congo, and otherwise using force to achieve its ends. The United Nations Force in the Congo has always adhered strictly to the principle that it is a peace force and that its arms are for defensive purposes only, although they may be used for its protection when it is discharging responsibilities assigned to it by Security Council resolutions, such as the prevention of civil war or the removal of mercenaries. In its three and a half years in the Congo the United Nations Force has had to use its arms on remarkably few occasions. It has *not* undertaken any offensive actions in Katanga. If it had, it could very easily have dealt with the problem of Katanga secession in 1960, or at any other time in the last three and a half years. It did, in pursuance of directives from United Nations Headquarters based upon Security Council action, undertake to round up Tshombe's mercenaries in Katanga. In September, 1961, this led to fighting in Elisabethville, with the United Nations troops being on the defensive. The attempt of the mercenaries, now admitted in various memoirs, to liquidate the United Nations Force in Elisabethville in December, 1961, led to heavier fighting, which stopped the moment the security and freedom of movement of the United Nations Force had been restored.

In the classic manner of propaganda, naturally, the Katangese Information Service asserted on both these occasions that Tshombe's troops were the victims of "an offensive," and this distortion received credence in quite a wide circle.

The decisive fighting in Katanga occurred in December-January, 1962-63. Then, it may be said quite frankly, the Katangese troops, led by mercenaries, played into the hands of the United Nations Force by launching an attack on United Nations positions in Elisabethville and continuing that attack for several days with no reaction from the United Nations troops. Finally, however, when Mr. Tshombe's own cease-fire orders to his troops were disregarded by them, the United Nations Force was commanded to react firmly and it then proceeded to clean out all threatening pockets once and for all, and also to assert and realize fully for the first time its undoubted right, under an agreement with the Congolese government, to freedom of movement throughout the Congo, including Katanga. Tshombe, however, remained as President of Katanga Province and was even at times given physical protection by the United Nations when it seemed that his personal security might be in danger.

We speak of the Congo, but the unhappy fact is that at the time of its independence, and to a considerable degree still, there was not, and there is not, a true national spirit or wide sense of national statehood and government in the Congo. The divisive factors of tribalism and sectional, or even personal, interests are still very strong, and there are too few leaders who stanchly believe in and well understand the concepts of centralization, central government, and national loyalty.

While there are some who charge that the United Nations Operation in the Congo has not taken a strong enough line and has failed to exercise the necessary authority, there are others who have from the early days of the operation used the unkind expression of "neo-colonialism" to describe United Nations action in the Congo. In truth, the United Nations Operation has bent over backwards to avoid most scrupulously the least basis for any such charge and has carefully refrained from any interference in Congolese internal affairs except upon the specific request of Congolese authorities. Thus, for example, the United Nations in 1961 at the request of such authorities as there were, in a situation in which there was no constitutional government, undertook to find, transport, and protect the members of Parliament throughout the country, many of whom were in fear of their lives and in hiding, in order that the Congolese Parliament might convene in Leopoldville and establish a new government. The successful search for its members and the protection of the reconvened Parliament prevented the country from falling into anarchy. In brief, the United Nations Operation has been criticized most unjustly by groups who, in theory at least, are at the opposite poles of political thought, the one crying "Communist agent" and the other crying "neo-colonialist." This testifies to the genuine objectivity and impartiality of the United Nations in the Congo.

One still hears it said occasionally that Dag Hammarskjöld took an unnecessary risk in going to the Congo in 1961, on a trip that tragically proved to be his last. There was always a risk, of course, when he went to the Congo, as there was when he went to a number of other places, but to say that there was an unnecessary risk is to say that it was not necessary, or at least not important, for him to go to the Congo when he did, and even to imply that he was acting recklessly in doing so. In view of the situation and of what Dag Hammarskjöld had in mind, his trip to the Congo in September, 1961, was of major importance. He went on the eve of the sixteenth session of the General Assembly, knowing that the issue of the Congo was likely to arouse a bitter and divisive debate in the Assembly.

Dag Hammarskjöld did not go to the Congo in gracious response to a polite and not at all pressing invitation received from Prime Minister Adoula, but for more compelling reasons. He had it definitely in mind to try to induce Mr. Tshombe to enter into talks with Mr. Adoula, preferably in Leopoldville. He knew that if this could be achieved it might well relieve the Assembly of the necessity of extensive and poisonous debate on the subject of the Congo, which would do neither the Congo nor the United Nations any good. In this regard, I wish to present a passage never before published from a message which Mr. Hammarskjöld addressed to me from Leopoldville on September 15, 1961, two days before his death. I had informed him of certain criticisms of the operation, and he replied:

However, the key question is this one: What have our critics done in order to bring Mr. Tshombe to his senses? . . . It is better for the United Nations to lose . . . support . . . because it is faithful to law and principles than to survive as an agent whose activities are geared to political purposes never avowed or laid down by the major organs of the United Nations. It is nice to hear . . . parties urge . . . that we do everything in our power to bring Adoula and Tshombe together after having gone, on our side, to the extreme point in that direction without any noticeable support at the crucial stages from those who now complain.

It was Mr. Hammarskjöld's misfortune that a totally unanticipated fighting situation should have developed in Elisabethville at the very time of his arrival in the Congo. While there were standing instructions to the United Nations people in Katanga to seek to round up and evacuate all mercenaries, Dag Hammarskjöld had not authorized any specific action involving fighting and was indeed surprised and shocked to learn about it. This is established beyond a doubt by another passage from the message just mentioned, one of the last he sent from Leopoldville before his fatal trip. He said the following with reference to the fighting that had broken out in Elisabethville on September 13, 1961: "It belongs to the history . . . that the first I knew about this development, I learnt by a tendentious Reuters report in Accra on my way to Leopoldville."

The "tendentious Reuters report," by the way, was a press story to the effect that Conor Cruise O'Brien, the United Nations representative in Elisabethville, had announced the end of Katangese secession, a statement which O'Brien subsequently denied to the United Nations that he had ever made. One can readily imagine Mr. Hammarskjöld's feeling at such a report in the light of his intention to try to bring Tshombe and Adoula together.

Because of the success that has attended the deployment of the United Nations peace forces in Gaza-Sinai and in the Congo, there has been a recent tendency to regard a United Nations peace force as a panacea for conflicts. It has happened increasingly, lately, that whenever a conflict situation is brought to the United Nations there will be some automatic suggestions that a United Nations force should be organized and dispatched. This is a misconception which overrates the true possibilities in the employment of a peace force, which are, in fact, limited.

First of all, a peace force is a very expensive device. The Congo force, for example, at its peak strength of 20,000 was costing over $10,000,000 a month; and the small UNEF—just over 5,000 officers and men—has been costing approximately $19,000,000 per year.

The locus of responsibility for the cost is a controlling factor in determining ability to obtain contingents for a force. If the United Nations is able to defray all extra expenses, the force can be recruited rather easily and quickly; otherwise not.

The composition of such a force has to be most carefully selected in the light of the particular conflict situation and the political considerations that apply to it. A basic determinant is the definition of acceptable contingents by the government of the country on whose territory the force is to be stationed. This is a serious and built-in limitation which has also vital implications for the extent to which the troops of a standing force could be used in a particular situation, as, for example, in Cyprus.

The nature of the conflict situation with which the force is to be involved also affects the ability to obtain contingents, for naturally the countries providing the contingents never fail to examine carefully the situation in which their troops will be placed before they agree to make them available to the United Nations. The states providing contingents also wish to know in advance the extent of danger for their troops, the likelihood that they would have to fight, and particularly the prospect that they might become embroiled in fighting with the civilian population or segments of it, or be charged with intervening in the internal affairs of a country.

Such considerations have all come very much to the fore in establishing the United Nations Peace-keeping Force in Cyprus in response to the decision of the Security Council in its resolution of March 4, 1964, not the least the financial restriction and the limitation on acceptable contingents. Here was to be found the reason for the delay in constituting the Cyprus force. All necessary preparations—transport, logistics, etc.—had been made; only the contingents were lacking.

The United Nations Operation in the Congo, in the light of its mandates, has certainly had great success; it may even be considered the most successful operation the United Nations has undertaken when measured in terms of what it was called upon to do and has in fact done. Striking evidence of the success of the operation is found in the almost complete cessation of organized attacks on it from whatever source, West or East. It is especially noteworthy that some governments that had been most critical of the military aspect of the operation became the strongest voices in urging the retention in the Congo of the United Nations Force.

There is very, very much still to be done in the Congo, of course, particularly in the realm of civilian assistance. The anxious question now is what will happen when the United Nations troops are withdrawn. Will much of what has been done over four years be then undone? Since the United Nations Force in the Congo could be extended beyond the end of June of this year only through action of the General Assembly called in special session for this purpose—and this seems next to impossible—we may only wait and see—and hope. Not much encouragement can be derived from the barbarous raids of the Jeunesse rebels in Kikwit Province in recent weeks, which have taken many lives. The raiders have encountered only feeble opposition by the ANC. It is good to be able to say that ONUC has succeeded in rescuing many of the victims or potential victims of these youthful terrorists. The Congo operation thus displays vividly the problem which we also have with UNEF in Gaza-Sinai: how can a successfully functioning United Nations peace force ever be withdrawn without disastrous consequences?

In concluding this talk with a look to the future, it may be said that there is clear need for a critical but honest appraisal of the United Nations and its present effectiveness in peace making, not only in the Congo but elsewhere. Improvements in existing practices, even new methods, may be found. On the one hand, we see that the interdependence of countries and situations in the modern world makes the United Nations essential as a last resort in critical emergencies when all other efforts at a solution have failed, as in Cyprus now. By the very nature of things, the tough problems come to the United Nations when they have been found insoluble by others, and this is especially true when these problems, as in the case of Cyprus, may be fraught with the gravest danger for the wider peace. At the same time, it is becoming a way of life for the United Nations, though by no means a happy way, that there is a vast and increasing discrepancy between the peace aims and responsibilities of the United Nations and, on the one hand, what is called upon to do about them by the Security Council or the General Assembly and, on the other hand, its resources, its authority, and its support, both political and material. The "tin cup" approach to financing provides a most uncertain and insecure financial basis for a peace operation. Except for a rare and exceptional set of circumstances, such an arrangement cannot fail to affect adversely the efficiency, expedition, and effectiveness of the operation.

The United Nations is a young organization in the process of developing in response to challenges of all kinds. In its peace making it operates, notoriously, not only largely by improvisation but on a shoestring. This has been seen in the Congo where a force, which is now less than 5,000 men and at its largest was only 20,000, was given the task of assisting a weak government to restore law and order out of chaos in a country the size of the subcontinent of India. This is being seen again with regard to Cyrpus where there have been great difficulties in establishing an international force on that island, although failure to do so could well mean war in the eastern Mediterranean.

Serious people everywhere should cogitate on this, the indispensability of the United Nations in our present world, in situations where it alone affords the chance to avoid war, measured against its present meager resources of money and authority. It bears emphasis that, while most governments in the end give the United Nations their warm and loyal support in critical situations, the Organization (and the world) sometimes find themselves on the very brink of disaster of incalculable dimensions before the essential support is forthcoming.

Dag Hammarskjöld left a great legacy of high idealism wedded to great political and practical wisdom and imagination. The United Nations and the world have been fortunate in having a man with the devotion, wisdom, and courage of U Thant to inherit, carry on, and expand the aim of the United Nations in a strong and dynamic enough manner to meet its great challenges.

ONUC'S Civilian Operation: State-Preserving and State-Building*

Harold Karan Jacobson

The United Nations involvement in the Congo crisis can be viewed in various perspectives. It is a significant example of the United Nation's peace-keeping activities and a formidable test of Secretary-General Dag Hammarskjöld's concept of preventive diplomacy. From the viewpoint of legal analysis, it shows the flexibility of the Charter. In terms of the United Nation's institutions, it demonstrates both the potentialities and the perils of the development of the executive capacity of the Secretary-General. In addiion, the Civilian Operations of the United Nations Operation in the Congo (abbreviated as ONUC, the initials of *Organisation des Nations Unies au Congo*), it has another, less widely known facet. Alongside efforts to contain, ease, and ultimately eliminate the political-military crisis in the Congo, the United Nations has undertaken through ONUC's Civilian Operations

* Harold Karan Jacobson, "ONUC's Civilian Operations: State-Preserving and State-Building," *World Politics*, Vol. XVII, No. 1 (October 1964), pp. 75-107. Reprinted by permission. Harold Karan Jacobson is Associate Professor of Political Science at the University of Michigan. He is the author of *The U.S.S.R. and the U.N.'s Economic and Social Activities* (1963) and the editor of *America's Foreign Policy* (1960).

emergency and longer-term functions which can most appropriately be called "state-preserving" and "state-building."

These terms need to be defined and their relationship to the more commonly used term "nation-building" explained. Decolonization left the formal structure of a modern state in the Congo, sovereignty and all of its manifestations, the machinery of state, and a complex economic and social structure. State-preserving involved keeping this heritage intact, protecting it against the danger of imminent collapse. It meant maintaining the infrastructure of the state and the level of modernity that had been achieved. In performing this function, ONUC's Civilian Operations filled a crucial gap in the administrative structure of the Congo, assumed important educational and medical functions, and provided vital emergency relief. One could also think of state-preserving in a wider sense as including protection of the territorial integrity of the state, and in an instance such as this, where secession was attempted, a strong case could be made for the broader definition. However, since that aspect of the United Nation's activities was so complicated and since its character was essentially different from that of the Civilian Operations, the narrower definition was chosen for purposes of this analysis.

State-building in the Congo involved the creation of a viable structure to replace the precarious one which had hastily been contrived out of the remnants of the colonial regime; the formal structure of the state had to be given substance and revised in relation to the realities of independence. This meant training Congolese cadres for executive, administrative, and professional positions and assisting the Congo in adjusting its inherited institutions so that they would fit its independent resources and new status as a sovereign state. Nation-building, on the other hand, is a broader concept than state-building. It involves the development of a cohesive spirit, a sense of national identity, as well as the instruments of modern government. Obviously the three concepts are related. State-preserving is a prerequisite for state-building and nation-building, unless one is to start with a different basic unit. State-building cannot ultimately succeed without nation-building occurring; in the end the structure of the state cannot function without a degree of cohesiveness. Conversely, state-building contributes in various ways to nation-building. The creation of institutions is a vital part of nation-building, and these institutions can be used to develop national consciousness. But for analytical purposes, and in practice, the three tasks can be separated. Among other things, it is much easier for external actors to contribute to the first two.

The activities undertaken by ONUC's Civilian Operations were unprecedented in several respects. In no other place had the United Nations undertaken such extensive tasks. A unified administrative structure had never been attempted before. United Nations personnel had never exercised as significant authority as some did in the Congo. For these reasons alone ONUC's Civilian Operations are worthy of study. Moreover, an analysis of this facet of the United Nations' involvement in the Congo could have more than historical importance. State-preserving and state-building tasks comparable to those faced in the Congo cannot be ruled out in speculation about the process of decolonization in the southern third of Africa. Another Congo crisis, albeit with special permutations, is a distinct possibility. An examination of this case may yield some guidelines for future policy. . . .

The United Nations had anticipated the Congo's needs to a certain extent; it had, after all, been forewarned in April.* A small group of technical assistance officials had been sent to the Congo at the time of independence, and Sture Linner of Sweden had been named Resident Representative of the Technical Assistance Board. By July 10, however, it was apparent that the Congo's needs exceeded this modest mission, and a request for assistance was urgently transmitted to the Secretary-General through Ralph Bunche, who was in the Congo to represent the United Nations at independence ceremonies and to constitute a United Nations presence during the transition period. The request stressed the need for military technical assistance to aid the Congolese government in reorganizing the *Force publique*. The Secretary-General treated this request as a matter falling within his own competence and the following day instructed Mr. Bunche to report his agreement in principle. The Secretary-General circulated the request on an informal basis to the members of the Security Council, and on July 12 he discussed it, as well as the plan which Mr. Bunche had worked out with the Congolese government for the administration of security, with the representatives of the nine African states that were then members of the United Nations.

That same day the problem was thrown into a new perspective by the Congo's request for the dispatch of a United Nations military force. In the ensuing debate in the Security Council on July 13 and 14, the problems of state-preserving and state-building tended to be submerged by the seemingly more urgent questions surrounding the creation and deployment of a United Nations Force (UNF). Some delegates in passing endorsed the Secretary-General's action with respect to the request for technical assistance, but there was no detailed substantive discussion of this issue.

The resolution which the Security Council adopted mentioned state-building only in the following paragraph:

2. *Decides* to authorize the Secretary-General to take the necessary steps, in consultation with the Government of the Republic of the Congo, to provide the Government with such military assistance as may be necessary, until, through the efforts of the Congolese Government with the technical assistance of the United Nations, the national security forces may be able, in the opinion of the Government, to meet fully their tasks.

* In April 1960 the Abako party sent a mission to the United States to seek out possible aid from the United Nations, the International Bank for Reconstruction and Development, and Washington—Editor.

In presenting the Congolese request to the Security Council, the Secretary-General appeared to regard the role of a UNF as that of a temporary instrument which could be used to restore and maintain order while the longer-term training program was being implemented, and the resolution confirmed this concept.

In the following days, the United Nations' perception of the Congo's needs in the area of state-preserving and state-building broadened swiftly. On July 18 the Secretary-General reported that he had asked eight countries for food supplies to alleviate the shortages (especially acute in Léopoldville) which had been caused by the breakdown of transportation and public services, and that seven of the eight—including the Soviet Union and the United States—had already responded affirmatively. Maurice Pate, Executive-Director of the United Nations Children's Fund (UNICEF), arrived in the Congo on July 17 to ascertain what his agency could contribute and to direct the emergency food supply. The World Health Organization (WHO) began to take action to supply doctors and other medical personnel.

When the Security Council met on July 20 to resume its consideration of the Congo crisis, the Secretary-General presented this broader picture. To facilitate his dealing with the many emergency and longer-term problems, he asked the Council to request the Specialized Agencies to give him their assistance, and such a request was written into the resolution which the Council adopted.

On August 11 the Secretary-General outlined an overall plan for ONUC's Civilian Operations, which had been worked out in consultation with and approved by the Republic of the Congo. His scheme was ambitious. He envisaged activities which would follow the established patterns of the United Nations' technical assistance and Operational and Executive Personnel (OPEX) programs. (Under the latter, United Nations specialists serve as staff members of the administrative services of the beneficiary governments.) In addition, he foresaw the need for "activities on a level of higher administrative responsibility, for which the experts employed must receive a new and so far untried status." These officials would "be available at the call of the government to give advice on various problems and provide the government with such studies as it may request for the planning of its activities and its decisions." Formally having functions only within the United Nations orbit, and without being accredited to the Ministries, they "would *de facto* be able to serve, with senior responsibility, at the request of the Government, the various Ministries and departments." This group of officials would carry the title "Consultants to the Chief of the Civilian Operations," would be responsible to him, and would comprise a "Consultative Group." The group would consist of consultants in (1) agriculture; (2) communications; (3) education; (4) finance; (5) foreign trade; (6) health; (7) instruction (national security forces); (8) labor market; (9) magistrature; (10) natural resources and industry; and (11) public administration. Most of the officials would be appointed by the Specialized Agencies as their representatives in the Congo and then be appointed by the Secretary-General to the Consultative Group. This structure would give ONUC's Civilian Operations an unprecedented unity, since the relationship between Specialized Agency personnel and the United Nations Resident Representative of the Technical Assistance Board has normally been much looser. This has at times resulted in relationships between the United Nations and the Specialized Agencies in the field being marked more by competition than cooperation. Whether or not the members of the Consultative Group would have unprecedented powers within the Congolese administration would depend upon the arrangements which were worked out in practice. Sture Linner was appointd Chief of ONUC's Civilian Operations (in addition to his position as Resident Representative) with rank and authority equivalent to that of the Supreme Commander of the United Nations Force. The plan was partially implemented by the time that the Secretary-General presented it and, in accordance with his original interpretation, he never asked for nor received the formal approval of the plan by the Security Council or any other United Nations body.

The resemblance betewen the Secretary-General's plan and the activities which the United Nations actually undertook and the assistance requested by M. Yumbu's mission is significant, although the conditions prevailing at the time of the United Nations' involvement were much more difficult than had been envisaged. In considering future contingencies, it may well be wise to reflect about the extent to which the Congo crisis could have been averted had the United Nations been involved more substantially at an earlier stage. . . .

The Secretary-General's early request for food supplies indicated that the Congo would need material assistance as well as advisory and operational personnel. The United Nations Children's Fund, the only United Nations agency which could readily supply funds for such purposes, entered the situation immediately and has made frequent material contributions. In September 1960, when it became apparent that the Congolese government would also need budgetary and foreign exchange assistance, the Secretary-General asked the Security Council to establish a fund to be raised by voluntary contributions and to be used under the control of the United Nations for such purposes. Although a Soviet veto blocked the Council's taking such action, the General Assembly, acting in Emergency Session, established the United Nations Fund for the Congo on September 20, 1960. Grants of $5,000,000 and $10,000,000 for import support were given to the Congo from this fund in 1960 and 1961 respectively. Beyond that, the fund has been used to finance several of the technical assistance programs of ONUC's Civilian Operations, and in 1964 those costs which were formerly charged to ONUC's *Ad Hoc* Account began to be charged to the fund.

Finally, as a result of agreements worked out in 1961, the United Nations has been given some control over certain counterpart funds resulting from bilateral grants to the Congo. Committees have been established in

Léopoldville consisting of representatives of the Congolese government, ONUC, and the donor country and unanimous agreement is necessary for the utilization of the funds.

Two other matters relating to the establishment and framework of ONUC's Civilian Operations need to be considered before turning to substantive activities. The first is the Soviet Union's disaffection. As early as July 21, 1960, the USSR lodged the caveat that it did not regard the Security Council's initial resolution "as endowing the United Nations with the right to interfere in the domestic affairs of a State and to assume responsibility for a country's domestic laws and regulations." The Soviet view was that the fundamental purpose of the United Nations' intervention should be to secure the withdrawal of the Belgian forces; beyond that, matters should be left to the government of the Republic of the Congo.

A month later this demurrer became a strong dissent. In a letter to the Secretary-General on August 20 and in a vituperative statement in the Security Council the following day, V. V. Kuznetsov, First Deputy Minister of Foreign Affairs of the USSR, attacked the plan outlined in the Secretary-General's memorandum of August 11. He asserted that the plan involved "the limitation of the sovereignty of the Republic of the Congo," and in effect meant "the placing of the Congo in the position of a Trust Territory, which is contrary to the Charter of the United Nations." Secretary-General Hammarskjöld's response that the position of the members of the Consultative Group in relation to the Congolese government was a "weaker one than that of technical assistance in the conventional sense" failed to still Soviet criticism. In view of the role that at least some of the members of the Consultative Group were expected to play, and that some in fact did play, the explanation seems rather disingenuous.

The Secretary-General appeared to be somewhat more sympathetic to a second aspect of the USSR's criticism of ONUC's Civilian Operations. Kuznetsov pointed out that 21 of the 65 individuals in the field as of August 15, occupying the posts of key significance, were nationals of the United States or countries aligned with it, and that the staff included no nationals of Eastern European (i.e., Soviet bloc) countries. He went on to assert that because of these facts, and the dominant role of citizens of Western countries in the United Nations Secretariat (the USSR had already been critical of the prominent position of Ralph Bunche in ONUC and of his activities), "the implementation of the proposed plan would mean that the development of the Congo would be conducted along lines satisfactory to the United States, and this might in fact not only jeopardize the independence of the Republic of the Congo but also create a dangerous precedent for the future." In the debate the Secretary-General agreed that the geographical distribution of personnel on ONUC's Civilian Operations was not satisfactory. He attempted to explain the existing situation by referring to the necessity of quick recruitment and to the fact that he had had to rely to a large extent for recruiting on the services of the Specialized Agencies, thereby inadvertently implying—perhaps correctly—that the Agencies were less impartial in the cold war than the United Nations.

A more fundamental issue, though, was really at stake. The core of the Soviet position was that state-preserving and state-building were not and could not be treated as apolitical tasks. This issue was never joined.

The other matter relating to the framework of ONUC's Civilian Operations that must be considered at this point also involved the Soviet Union, although it affected several other states as well. It concerned the relationship between bilateral aid programs and the United Nations program. Whether because of its perception of the way in which ONUC's Civilian Operations were developing, or because it preferred this method to any other, the Soviet Union soon began a bilateral program of assistance to the Congo. Actually this program was rather short-lived, for immediately after his coup in mid-September 1960 Colonel Joseph Mobutu expelled all Soviet bloc technicians. A modest Soviet bilateral program was reinstated somewhat later in Stanleyville, but it was of insignificant proportions. By virtue of the pre-independence arrangements, Belgium had a large bilateral program from the outset. After the Congo's independence, various African states also dispatched several semi-technical advisers to one or another faction of the government. The United States in contrast, although it continued a modest bilateral program planned prior to independence that involved 300 training and scholarship grants, once the crisis began almost ostentatiously eschewed taking further independent action, and for some time channeled the major portion of its aid through the United Nations and carefully cleared the remainder with the world organization.

Despite its short life, the Soviet program provoked the initial debate and decision in the United Nations on this matter. The circumstances surrounding the Soviet program are somewhat obscure, but the initial shipments appear to have left the USSR in late July or early August 1960. One hundred trucks were involved and some tehnical personnel—exactly how many is not clear. The medical part of the program had a loose connection with ONUC, but the other aspects did not. The issue became prominent when the Soviet aid was used to facilitate the movement of forces of the *Armée nationale congolaise* (ANC—the new name for the *Force publique*) to Kasai. The purpose of this movement was apparently to quash Albert Kalonji's *"état autonome"* in South Kasai and to prepare for an attack against Katanga. While in Kasai, in late August 1960, the disorganized ANC units apparently killed hundreds of Balubas in actions which the Secretary-General asserted had "the characteristics of the crime of genocide."

When he reported these incidents to the Security Council in early September, Secretary-General Hammarskjöld asked the Council to request that *all* assistance to the Congo "should be channeled through the United Nations, and only through the United Nations." The Secretary-General was obviously disturbed by the massacre in Kasai. Moreover, the Soviet assistance had enabled Prime Minister Patrice Lumumba to attempt to solve by force constitutional problems which the Secretary-General felt should be solved by negotiations. Finally, the Secretary-General clearly feared the development of competitive intervention, following the pattern of the Spanish Civil War. In his appeal, he also alluded to the problems caused by the Belgian assistance in Katanga.

The debate on this matter was carried on at length in the Security Council and then, after a Soviet veto, continued in the General Assembly. The USSR met the Secretary-General's point head on. It asserted, as it had previously in an exchange of correspondence, that the Security Council resolutions did not contain any provisions restricting the right of the Congolese government to request assistance directly from other states, or the right of other states to render assistance to the Congo. Indeed, the USSR even implied that by aiding the Central Government of the Congo it was actually doing more to comply with the intent of the Security Council resolutions than ONUC. The USSR extended its concept to the logical conclusion by proposing that, rather than create a United Nations Fund for the Congo, the Security Council should merely ask governments to provide financial and economic assistance directly to the government of the Congo. Only Poland supported the Soviet proposal. On the other hand, during the debates, only Australia, Norway, and the United Arab Republic argued, as the Secretary-General had, that *all* assistance to the Congo should be channeled through the United Nations.

The resolution which the General Assembly finally adopted, 1474 (ES-IV), contained this prohibition:

6. Without prejudice to the sovereign rights of the Republic of the Congo, *calls upon* all States to refrain from the direct and indirect provision of arms or other material of war and military personnel and other assistance for military purposes in the Congo during the temporary period of military assistance through the United Nations, except upon the request of the United Nations through the Secretary-General for carrying out the purposes of this resolution and of the resolutions of 14 and 22 July and 9 August 1960 of the Security Council.

Obviously it left many loopholes. The initial phrase—"without prejudice to the sovereign rights"—reflected a general concern for sovereignty and also doubt, felt especially by several newly independent African states, about the wisdom of restricting the right of a government to request and receive assistance. Limiting the prohibition to military assistance and to a temporary period was another expression of these concerns. Furthermore, during the last days of August, a group of African political leaders, meeting in Léopoldville, had explicitly urged African states to supply more bilateral assistance to the Congo.

As indicated by the innuendoes of the USSR in justifying its own policy, the question of confidence in ONUC's policies was also at stake. These debates occurred while the quarrel between Prime Minister Lumumba and Secretary-General Hammarskjöld was at its height. It would have been difficult for states which seriously disagreed with ONUC's policies to grant it an exclusive right to supply assistance to the Congo. It is significant that the Assembly went as far as it did in limiting bilateral assistance.

By September 20, when the General Assembly adopted Resolution 1474 (ES-IV), the Soviet technicians had already left the Congo. From the long-run point of view, the problem of Belgian bilateral activities and Belgian technicians was much more troublesome than the Soviet program. The involvement of Belgians in the Katanga imbroglio is well-known. In addition, after Colonel Mobutu's coup and the establishment of the College of Commissioners-General, a large number of Belgians returned, or were re-cruited, for service as technicians in the government of the Republic of the Congo. A special recruiting agency was established in Brussels. Senior United Nations officials felt that many, if not most, of these Belgians were hostile to ONUC and charged that they sought to block cooperation between the Congolese government and the United Nations. Therefore the resolution which the Security Council adopted on February 21, 1961, urging "that measures be taken for the immediate withdrawal and evacuation from the Congo of all Belgian and other foreign and para-military personnel and political advisers not under the United Nations command, and mercenaries," was aimed at the whole of the Congo, not only Katanga, although its application was confined almost exclusively to that province. This resolution broadened the exclusion established in General Assembly Resolution 1474 (ES-IV), so that it covered foreigners who exercised an undesirable (that is, anti-United Nations) political influence as well as the narrower category of military personnel. The resolution also made the exclusion apply to individuals in the named categories who had come to the Congo on their own initiative rather than as a result of governmental agreements.

Through these two resolutions, the United Nations sought to debar bilateral aid which might be used for military purposes (a neat problem of definition—the USSR asserted that it had only supplied civil trucks and aircraft) and also personnel who might complicate ONUC's tasks. In actual practice, the United Nations Secretariat went beyond these legal restrictions and sought to have *all* aid to the Congo channeled or cleared through the United Nations. The United States strongly supported the Secretariat's position. The Secretariat did not alter its attitude until early 1963, after Katanga's secession had been ended. In his report of February 4, 1963, Secretary-General U Thant allowed that it might be "advisable and desirable to envisage . . . an increase in bilateral aid." The United States began to shift its position somewhat earlier. Although it continued to obligate the major portion of its assistance via the United Nations through fiscal year 1963, in late 1962 it began to administer the import program on a more direct basis with the Congolese government, and a United States Agency for International Development Mission was formally established in Léopoldville in October 1962.

Instead of examining ONUC's Civilian Operations in the Congo in considerable detail, it may be sufficient here simply to establish certain categories of action and to cite a few illustrative examples.

A large number of the tasks performed by ONUC's Civilian Operations can best be described as emergency operations. Examples include the reactivation of the ports and the railway system; the distribution of food and medical supplies; the provision of temporary care and the facilitation of the resettlement of refugees (principally Balubas); and the initiation of public works for unemployment relief.

Secondly, the United Nations has provided, from the United Nations Fund for the Congo, financial assistance to meet urgent foreign exchange needs. Grants amounting to $15,000,000 were made during the first year of ONUC.

Thirdly, the United Nations has performed a number of operational tasks. It has supplied most of the technical staff to man the airports and the telecommunications systems. In addition, it has provided teachers and medical and legal personnel. At the end of 1963, the United Nations was supplying 801 secondary-school teachers, nearly 200 doctors and other medical technicians, and 47 jurists and legal experts.

Fourthly, the United Nations has provided the services normally encompassed in its technical assistance programs. During the first year of operations, nearly 1,000 Congolese were enrolled in training courses organized within the Congo by ONUC, and 84 were given fellowships by the United Nations for study abroad. By the end of 1962, 9,464 Congolese had enrolled in various ONUC training courses within the Congo and 332 students had been sent abroad by the United Nations. ONUC has also been instrumental in the creation of various permanent training institutes within the Congo, including the National School of Law and Administration. Among other things, the United Nations has provided a number of fellowships for study at these institutes.

Fifthly, members of the Consultative Group and other ONUC personnel have given high-level policy advice and have served in executive capacities. The Consultant in Finance has served as President of the Congolese Monetary Council since its creation. This body was established on the advice of ONUC, and it has extensive powers over the Congo's economy. The Consultant in Education has assisted in the preparation of far-reaching programs for revising the Congolese educational system. In 1962 four United Nations experts prepared a draft of a new constitution for the Congo. United Nations experts played a vital role as assistants to Prime Minister Cyrille Adoula in his negotiations in early 1964 with Belgian Foreign Minister Paul-Henri Spaak concerning the Congo's pre-independence public debt and the shares that the Belgian colonial administration held in private companies operating in the Congo.

Finally, ONUC's Civilian Operations have cleared, coordinated, and to some extent controlled bilateral aid. The system of tripartite control over counterpart funds has already been mentioned. At a very early stage a Fellowship Service was established to centralize the processing of applications by Congolese for overseas training. At the United Nations' suggestion, a Bureau of Economic Coordination was established in the Prime Minister's office. This organ, headed by a United Nations official, has the express function of attempting to coordinate external assistance to the Congo. Of course, the degree of collaboration between ONUC's Civilian Operations and bilateral programs has varied greatly. As has been mentioned, there was little contact between ONUC and the Soviet program. Relationships with the Belgian program have been severely strained at times, and even though there has been gradual improvement since the coming to power of the Christian Social-Socialist coalition in Belgium in May 1961, the connection is still far from tight and cordial. On the other hand, the United States has always worked very closely with ONUC.

The speed with which ONUC's Civilian Operations were established, the extent of the tasks which have been undertaken and their coherence, and the quality of some of the key personnel have been most impressive. There can be no question that ONUC's Civilian Operations have been vital to the continuation of the administrative, economic, and social structure of the Congo since its independence.

The accomplishments of the Civilian Operations, however, have extended beyond this. Had the former metropole been the predominant source of post-independence assistance, given both the extent to which the Congolese lacked training and the nature of the arrangements which had been made prior to independence, it probably would have been difficult to alter the habits of the past, particularly the pattern of paternalism. Unencumbered by this heritage, ONUC's Civilian Operations have been able to give the Congolese a new sense of dignity. This is of course not to say that all Belgians were paternalistic or that all United Nations personnel have treated the Congolese as equals, for there have certainly been exceptions on both sides. It is rather to attempt to assess the cumulative impact. Moreover, because of its multinational composition, the Civilian Operations have opened new vistas for the Congolese, have made them aware of alternative ways of viewing problems and of alternative techniques for attempting to resolve them. Perhaps this has been most evident in the sphere of education, where the system has been significantly revamped on the basis of United Nations recommendations. Moves have been made toward the secularization of the school system, greater emphasis has been put on secondary education, and curricula have been reworked, adjusting them to the needs of a newly independent country. For example, the teaching of Greek and Latin has been deemphasized and greater stress has been placed on technical training. In 1963-1964, there were almost three times as many children enrolled in secondary schools as in 1959-1960 and, in contrast to the earlier year, most of the students were Congolese. This increase would have been impossible without the secondary school teachers supplied by ONUC. Although the evidence may be less striking, the same phenomenon has occurred in other fields.

On the other hand, there are certain things that ONUC's Civilian Operations have not been able to accomplish. Although the United Nations has been able to prevent the disintegration of the administrative, economic, and social structure of the Congo, it has not been able to prevent severe deterioration in these sectors. This is partly attributable to insufficient resources.

The funds at the United Nations' disposal have been sharply limited. . . . These [i.e. monetary disputes] have had some effect on the Civilian Operations since, as has been mentioned, some of the activities have been financed on this budget, and because they have engendered a general opposition to large expenditures for the Congo. The United Nations Fund for the Congo has fallen disappointingly short of the $100,000,000 target set by the Secretary-General when it was created. As of January 1964, less than half that amount had been contributed and the United States had given more than 75 per cent of the total. The idea of using the United Nations Fund for the Congo for import support grants had to be dropped after the first year because of the limited resources of the Fund and the predominance of the American contribution. Meeting this need through bilateral grants appeared to be a simpler and more direct technique, and also made it easier for the United States to impose conditions to protect its balance-of-payments position.

On balance, it has proved more difficult to raise funds for the Civilian Operations than for the United Nations Force. ONUC's political-military functions have seemed more urgent than its state-preserving and state-building tasks to a majority of the United Nations' members. In addition, a number of newly independent states have felt that their economic and social problems are equally as grave as the Congo's and have privately expressed some resentment about the relative magnitude of the United Nations' assistance to the Congo. Significantly, there has been no discussion of making contributions to the budget for ONUC's Civilian Operations obligatory. The financial pressures reached a climax during the planning of the program for 1964. A severe cut had to be made in the "minimal" program planned by ONUC, and even the reduced program could only be sustained by a substantial grant from the Congo.

Financial limitations, however, have been only part of the problem. It has also been difficult to obtain sufficient and adequate personnel for ONUC's Civilian Operations. Although the Civilian Operations team totaled 1,149 on December 31, 1962, ONUC's plans envisaged a staff at least 300 larger and at that time financing was available for these posts, but the United Nations could not find suitably qualified individuals for appointment. The requirement that the experts have a working command of French was one obstacle. The French-speaking parts of the developed world are not as numerous as the English-speaking areas, and France itself was deeply committed to assisting its own former colonies in Africa and less than enthusiastic about the United Nations' involvement in the Congo. The problem was compounded by the chaotic security conditions in the Congo, which discouraged interest in volunteering for ONUC. It is possible that deeper motivational problems were also involved. The United Nations could not draw on the same patriotic motives that a national effort could. At the same time, ONUC had too many political ramifications to appeal to purely humanitarian motivations. The problem of recruitment could have been eased had the United Nations been more willing to hire Belgians, and had more Belgians been willing to work for the United Nations, but as of December 31, 1962, only 15 Belgians were employed in the Civilian Operations. In view of the tradition of Belgian colonial policy, and the special way in which the Civilian Operations assisted in decolonization, the United Nations' reluctance to hire Belgians is understandable. However, it is possible that some United Nations officials were as doctrinaire in their opposition to Belgians as some Belgians were in their opposition to ONUC, and one wonders whether it would not have been possible to develop appropriate screening mechanisms so that more Belgians could have been used. Short of the actual hiring of Belgians, perhaps more effective means for coordinating ONUC activities with Belgian bilateral programs could have been found. Of course, this would have required efforts on both sides. With respect to the quality of personnel, some deterioration has been noticed as the proportion of individuals on permanent United Nations contracts has declined, as it has since the first year of operations. The United Nations employee may feel a greater stake in the outcome of the operation and beyond that, by virtue of his affiliation, in most cases he has a better background for making policy decisions. In addition to these general problems, the United Nations has also found it especially difficult to recruit vitally needed financial experts.

The United Nations' inability to prevent the deterioration of the administrative, economic, and social structure of the Congo is also attributable to its lack of power. The position of ONUC's Civilian Operation vis-à-vis the Congolese government was defined in the relevant sections of the resolutions of the Security Council and the General Assembly and in a series of agreements between the Secretary-General and representatives of the Congo. Although these guaranteed ONUC freedom of movement, and gave its personnel the requisite privileges and immunities, they did not give the United Nations power to take executive action. The mandate of the Civilian Operations was to serve in an advisory capacity. When individuals performed tasks that went beyond this, it was at the invitation of the Congolese government. In some cases, even though the Central Government asked an expert to serve in an executive capacity, the provincial authorities in the area involved refused to concur, and the mission consequently could not be executed. The division of the Congo into twenty-three provinces rather than the original six obviously multiplied these problems. Finally, the United Nations was enjoined not to become a party to internal conflicts, constitutional or otherwise, or in any way to intervene or attempt to influence their outcome.

Almost all individuals connected with ONUC's Civilian Operations, from the Secretary-General down, at one time or another have felt severe frustration because of these limitations. Innuendoes—and often direct complaints—about the unwillingness or inability of Congolese officials to take what appeared to ONUC personnel as obviously necessary action can be found throughout the Progress Reports of the Civilian Operations. This passage from the report covering the month of February 1961 is an example: "Preoccupied with political issues, neither the Central nor the Provincial Authorities have seemed to pay sufficient attention to the economic situation under their respective control. In spite of repeated warnings and recommendations by ONUC's advisers, no practical measures have been taken so far to check or alleviate the danger of further disintegration." In private conversation, United Nations personnel have spoken in even stronger terms.

The Congolese were extremely sensitive about their sovereignty, and thus quick to assert their prerogatives. At the same time, they were untrained and inexperienced. Ralph Bunche has asserted that Congolese officials resented the need for United Nations assistance, "or at least having to seek and ask for it." Moreover, these officials were often much more deeply concerned about their political futures than about the maintenance of the modern sector of the Congolese economy, in which they may not have played much part prior to independence. To compound the situation, from September 1960 until August 1961 there was no legally constituted Central Government. As a consequence of all these factors, at times there were no officials with whom ONUC could deal. At other times, contacts between ONUC personnel and Congolese officials were limited as a consequence of ONUC's refusal to grant full recognition to the College of Commissioners and Joseph Ileo's government. Even when these problems were not involved, the extent to which United Nations recommendations would be implemented was problematical. Given the visible deterioration in the administrative, economic, and social structure of the Congo, for the United Nations to be limited to giving advice was inevitably frustrating.

The United Nations' lack of power has stemmed not only from its formal, legal position, but also from its inability to use informal techniques. One method of attempting to secure the implementation of recommendations is to make granting assistance conditional upon the fulfillment of specified actions. Although the United Nations has attempted to do this to some extent, its efforts have at best had only limited success. One explanation is that the resources at the United Nations' disposal have been extremely limited; thus the reward for compliance has not been very large. Further, the debate on the United Nations Fund for the Congo suggests that the imposition of stringent conditions on grants of aid from the United Nations would not win majority approval in the Assembly. Most delegates were extremely sensitive about questions involving the Congo's sovereignty and sought to avoid any action that might prejudice it. In addition, many delegates from newly independent countries appeared to desire to avoid creating precedents which conceivably could cause difficulties for their own countries in future contingencies. Finally, since one purpose of ONUC's Civilian Operations was to forestall bilateral intervention, to take actions which might make the Congo prefer bilateral assistance would be self-defeating.

The deterioration in the administrative, economic, and social structure of the Congo has been most noticeable in places other than Léopoldville and Elisabethville. In outlying areas the various inabilities of ONUC's Civilian Operations have combined with cumulative effect. Other than technical assistance personnel, the staff in the field has typically consisted of a Chief ONUC Civilian Officer posted in the capital of each of the six original provinces and possibly one other ONUC Civilian Officer posted either in the capital or in some other urban center. These individuals have often been confronted with overwhelming problems, yet their resources and powers have been extremely limited. Their situation became even more difficult when the Central Government's authority in the provinces declined. At times ONUC's Civilian Operations have had virtually no contact with large sectors of the Congo. The inauguration of a series of air missions to remote areas in early 1962 did much to improve the situation, but contact was still sporadic.

Beyond this broad incapacity to prevent the deterioration of the administrative, economic, and social structure of the Congo, there are also certain specific things that ONUC's Civilian Operations have been unable to accomplish. Very little has been achieved in the field of military and internal security, although providing training in these areas was originally regarded as one of the most important functions of the Civilian Operations and ONUC personnel have continued to have a sense of urgency and disquiet about Congolese inabilities in these matters. The United Nations has found it impossible to launch significant programs, and those which have been put into operation have not had outstanding results.

General Ben Hamou Kettani of Morocco was named ONUC Consultant for Military Instruction at an early stage, and he remained in the Congo through January 1961. His activities were limited to preparing plans which were accepted in principle by the Commander-in-Chief of the *Armée nationale congolaise,* but never put into effect, and to assisting in the preparatory training of one para-commando battalion. The Consultantship in Military Instruction has remained unfilled since General Kettani's departure, except for the brief appointment in August 1961 of General Mengasha Iyassu, who was able to accomplish even less than his predecessor. After the secession of Katanga was ended, ANC forces stationed in Katanga were placed under ONUC command, but this was done for security reasons rather than as part of a training program.

According to Ralph Bunche, at one stage the United Nations would have been willing to disarm the ANC forcibly and to impose a training program, but only at the request of the Congolese government. Such a request was never made. At that time—late August and early September 1960—Major General H. T. Alexander, commander of the first United Nations Ghana contingent, argued that the United Nations should take this action even over the objections of the Congolese government, but Mr. Bunche insisted that from a legal standpoint such a course would be out of the question.

Since it proved impossible for ONUC and the ANC to implement a training program, in the winter of 1962-1963 Prime Minister Cyrille Adoula proposed a modernization program for the ANC involving bilateral assistance from Belgium (army), Canada (communications), Italy (air force), Israel (paratroops), Norway (navy), and the United States (equipment), with the United Nations serving in a coordinating capacity. The Secretary-General's Advisory Committee on the Congo balked at the choice of countries, there being objections to the fact that all of the donors were Western and particularly to the inclusion of Belgium and Israel. The Advisory Committee refused to approve the program and also refused to agree that if the Congo proceeded to implement the program without United Nations participation it would not violate paragraph 6 of General Assembly Resolution 1474 (ES-IV), barring bilateral assistance for military purposes. Despite this, the Congolese government attempted to put the program into effect; however, Canada and Norway refused to participate without the United Nations' sanction. So far, Belgium, Israel, and the United States have gone farthest in implementing the program.

The United Nations' difficulties in this area have partly been attributable to its failure to establish a firm working relationship with General Mobutu. The difficulties started with ONUC's refusal to recognize the legality of his military coup and the College of Commissioners-General. Probably more fundamental factors have also been involved. Training a military force is obviously one of the most crucial aspects of state-building; it goes to the core of sovereignty and also can have significant international ramifications. The state involved will naturally want to maintain a high degree of freedom, and external forces will attempt to intervene, overtly and covertly. It is therefore understandable that so little has been accomplished with respect to the ANC. Bilateral programs in this area in other countries have also encountered severe difficulties.

The United Nations has been somewhat more successful in implementing programs for police training. Programs in this area have been in operation since February 1961. Over 1,500 police officers have received some training, but the effects of it can be questioned. The Léopoldville police mutinied in May 1963 and had to be replaced by ANC forces. It is perhaps significant that in 1963 Nigeria was asked and agreed to provide police training on a bilateral basis. Subsequently this arrangement was altered, and the United States agreed to finance a program that would be conducted under United Nations auspices.

ONUC's Civilian Operations have also been able to do very little to assist in the political development of the Congo. Although the United Nations provided experts to prepare a draft constitution, there has been no way that it could force the Congolese to accept this or any other constitution. Thus until July 1964 there was no agreement in the Congo about the basic legal framework of the state. Moreover, while some United Nations personnel have served as advisers to leading Congolese politicians, and while the United Nations could facilitate the convening of parliament, ONUC's Civilian Operations have legally and practically been unable to do much to teach the Congolese the political skills necessary for the operation of a modern state. On the other hand, by strengthening the bureaucracy through its training programs, the effect of the Civilian Operations may well have been to strengthen authoritarian and centralizing tendencies in the Congo. It should be noted, however, that bilateral programs in other parts of the world have also done little to transmit political skills, and that their effect often appears to have been an augmentation of centralizing and authoritarian tendencies.

In reviewing the achievements of ONUC's Civilian Operations, one is impressed by the closeness of the connection between these relatively technical activities and the United Nations' more publicized involvement in the political-military aspects of the Congo crisis. Perhaps the Katanga imbroglio provides the best broad illustration of this point. It is widely known that the failure of *Union Minière du Haut Katanga* to pay taxes to the Central Government contributed to the Republic of the Congo's budgetary crisis. However, the secession of Katanga also contributed to the budgetary crisis in another way. There was universal agreement among ONUC personnel and other external observers that the Congo did not need as extensive a military force as the ANC and that the ANC was taking too large a share of the national budget. Congolese officials were of the same opinion, but it was politically impossible for them to contemplate reducing the size of the ANC as long as the Katanga secession continued.

In view of the interlocking nature of the several aspects of the United Nations' involvement in the Congo, ONUC has wisely refrained from attempting to maintain a rigid separation in its own administrative arrangements. ONUC has operated from a central headquarters in the Hotel Royal in Léopoldville, where close contact between various branches of the operation has always been possible. There has also been a considerable interchange of personnel. Chief ONUC Civilian Officers in the provinces have been responsible for all ONUC activities in their territories. On the other hand, such division as has existed has allowed a measure of cooperation at the technical level even when relationships between ONUC's high command and the *de facto* government of the Congo were severely strained.

There is also a broader sense in which the connection between the technical and the political aspects of the United Nations' activities is evident. In many ways Mr. Kuznetsov's prediction that the outcome would be the one desired by the United States has been proved correct. One need only take the testimony of various Americans. On several occasions, official spokesmen have praised the United Nations for keeping the cold war out of the Congo, and in their more candid moments they have substituted "communism" for the "cold war." ONUC's Civilian Operations have contributed to this result. State-preserving and state-building are tasks which have very wide political ramifications; the external actors involved in giving assistance cannot help but influence the future political orientation of the recipient. Surely this has been the case in the Congo. While ONUC's Civilian Operations may not have done much to advance the goals of democracy, they certainly have done nothing to advance the goals of communism and their influence has been basically Western.

Since ONUC's Civilian Operations are still in process and there is no way of knowing how lasting their effects will be, it is much too early for any definitive evaluation. Some conclusions, however, can be drawn.

On balance, as of the moment it appears that the United Nations has performed its state-preserving and state-building tasks creditably and with a fair degree of success. The Congo has been preserved as an administrative entity and as a functioning state, and there has been no sharp lapse from the level of modernity achieved prior to independence. In the realm of state-building, a number of Congolese have received training to equip them for executive, administrative, and professional positions. Steps have been taken to increase vastly the number of secondary school graduates, and thus the pool of manpower available for semi-technical positions and further training. Some progress has been made in adjusting the Congo's institutions. Admittedly there have been areas—most notably, the field of internal security—where the United Nations' accomplishments have been less than might have been hoped, and whether or not the overall gains achieved thus far will stand once the United Nations force is withdrawn remains to be seen.

Although the United Nations has been able to do a great deal in the Congo in the realm of state-preserving and state-building, its contribution to nation-building—which presumably is the ultimate goal of both the Congolese and the majority of the international community—has been minimal. Nation-building involves the development of a cohesive spirit, a sense of national identity, as well as the development of the instruments of modern government. Insofar as state-building affects the latter aspect of nation-building, ONUC's Civilian Operations have made some contribution. Government is more than administration, however, and the farther removed the United Nations' achievements have been from pure administration, the more they have generally diminished. Perhaps through its work in the fields of telecommunications and, more importantly, education ONUC may have done something to aid the Congo in developing a sense of national identity, but this cannot be measured. Beyond these things there is little that the United Nations has or could have done. Nation-building is, after all, at its core a domestic process. It might be argued that the United Nations should have attempted to do more in the area of political development, but quite apart from the inherent difficulties of working in this field, one wonders about the extent to which a universal international organization composed of widely varying regimes could engage in such activities.

It is doubtful that as much could have been accomplished in the Congo through any other technique than ONUC's Civilian Operations. In the circumstances which prevailed it is hard to conceive of feasible bilateral programs. Certainly, in mid-July 1960 the Congolese were in no mood to rely principally on the former metropole. Whether or not they would have been willing to accept a European consortium arrangement—for example, on the part of the European Economic Community (EEC)—is questionable, and it is also doubtful that EEC would have been able to mount the effort. Had the Organization for Economic Cooperation and Development been in existence, it might have been a better vehicle, but as an exclusively Western institution it would have had many of the same liabilities as EEC. Since the United States has provided the bulk of the resources for the United Nations' program, presumably it could have undertaken the effort alone, and the Congolese, as their early entreaties to President Eisenhower indicated, might have been willing to accept this. However, this would have raised ticklish problems for American relations with its NATO ally, Belgium, and surely at least some Asian and African states would have raised the cry of neo-colonialism. Moreover, there would have been the problem of possible Soviet competitive intervention. On the other side, it is doubtful that the Soviet bloc could or would have committed the resources that the United Nations has, and the West certainly would not have allowed the Soviet Union to assume a dominant role in state-preserving and state-building in the Congo without putting up strenuous opposition. The Asian and African states obviously did not have the resources to spare, nor did the Latin American. On another level, it is doubtful that a Western program or a United States bilateral program would have made as far-reaching recommendations as the United Nations has. Thus, assuming that the changes have been in the interests of the Congolese, they have fared better under ONUC's Civilian Operations than they would have otherwise.

Whether or not the United Nations could again undertake a task of the magnitude of ONUC's Civilian Operations is problematical. To do so, the financial and personnel problems which have proved so troublesome in this instance would have to be solved. Although many aspects of the record with respect to these issues are discouraging, there are some grounds for encouragement.

The establishment of tripartite control over counterpart funds, involving representatives of the United Nations, the donor country, and the Congo; the use of the United Nations as a means of channeling and coordinating bilateral fellowship assistance; and the financial arrangements mooted for the Civilian Operations in 1964, whereby countries would give money to the Congo, which would in turn give it to the United Nations, all suggest that the problems of raising money for activities like the Civilian Operations should not be viewed simply as those of obtaining direct contributions to the United Nations. Perhaps in the future greater use could be made of indirect methods of raising financial support, and this difficulty consequently might be eased somewhat.

The Congo experience indicates that the United Nations' ability to respond to state-preserving and state-building tasks is partly a function of the reservoir of personnel available on its own staff. One way of increasing this reservoir would be to place a greater portion of the United Nations' technical assistance personnel on "program appointment," a form of permanent contract. At present the number of such appointments is limited to a very small percentage of the total number of experts serving under the United Nations. ONUC's Civilian Operations evidenced a serious need for individuals who could perform a variety of functions in outlying areas, resembling in many ways those performed under colonial rule by district officers. These tasks were generally best performed by United Nations headquarters personnel. Among other things, they were intimately familiar with United Nations procedures and traditions. The need to have individuals available who could perform such functions may well be an argument for some overstaffing at United Nations headquarters. The personnel problems encountered in ONUC's Civilian Operations might be eased if appropriate screening techniques were found so that more citizens of the former metropole could be utilized. Greater coordination with bilateral programs might provide an indirect technique for resolving the personnel problem. A somewhat more flexible attitude on this question than the Secretariat maintained during the early stages of ONUC would facilitate efforts in this area.

If tasks similar to those performed by ONUC's Civilian Operations were contemplated again, the question of the United Nations' powers vis-à-vis the host government would surely be raised. Numerous individuals connected with the Civilian Operations have said in private conversation, "If only the United Nations had had a trusteeship. . . ." In their analysis of the UNF, Arthur Lee Burns and Nina Heathcote have considered the related possibility of the United Nations' being given internal policing powers and have found much to commend it. Although it is possible that a host government might accept such an arrangement with respect to the UNF, it is questionable whether in other areas the United Nations could or should attempt to gain considerably more extensive powers than it has had in the Congo. There would first of all be legal and political barriers. Article 78 of the Charter prohibits the application of the trusteeship system to United Nations Member States, and the tendency has been for states to become

United Nations Members almost immediately after they have gained independence. This article is important not only because of its legal effect, but also because it symbolizes the intense desire of newly independent states to protect their sovereignty. The history of ONUC's Civilian Operations provides further documentation of this desire. Secondly, it is extremely doubtful that the United Nations could muster sufficient resources to undertake much more extensive responsibilities than it has had in the Congo. Finally, since the United Nations' purpose in undertaking state-preserving and state-building functions is to prepare the host government to stand alone as quickly as possible, it can be argued that the sooner that government is forced to assume responsibility for its own affairs—though with guidance and assistance—the better.

To maintain that the United Nations could not and should not attempt to establish anything as extensive as a trusteeship, however, is not to argue that the United Nations should not have more powers than it had in the Congo. Clearly some modifications in the agreements which have been in force in the Congo would be useful and desirable. It would be helpful if United Nations officials in outlying areas had greater powers. This would be beneficial in itself, and might lead to the stationing of greater numbers of United Nations officials in such areas, which would also be useful. In addition, Civilian Operations could benefit from the United Nations' having greater powers in the realm of internal security. This might ease the problem of personnel recruitment and would also facilitate the implementation of training programs in these areas. Whether or not giving the United Nations greater powers in this respect would involve totally or partially disarming the indigenous security forces is moot.

The internal administrative arrangements for ONUC's Civilian Operations appear to have been quite successful. The pattern of the Consultative Group gave the United Nations' activities an unprecedented unity. ONUC's pattern could be repeated in another emergency, and perhaps ought to be considered for broader application to the United Nations' normal technical assistance activities.

If, then, under certain conditions the United Nations could undertake functions similar to those performed by ONUC's Civilian Operations, it may also be useful to consider whether or not it should do so. This question can be answered only in terms of one's values. It is clear that ONUC's Civilian Operations have served to implement American objectives and that, from the American viewpoint, the tactic of first relying on a multilateral agency as a channel for United States and other aid and then shifting to more normal bilateral patterns once the crisis has eased has proved rewarding. Soviet influence has been checked and Western influence preserved. Beyond that, Belgium's resentment at having at least some of the props knocked out from under its paternalistic plans has largely fallen on the United Nations rather than the United States. Given the nature of this case, it is difficult to believe that a bilateral or exclusively Western program would have served American interests as well. On the other hand, there are grounds for arguing that the United States ought to be cautious in calling on the United Nations to perform such tasks. The USSR's dissent is a warning signal. State-preserving and state-building do have serious political implications, and to overload the United Nations with tasks of this nature might well jeopardize the organization's usefulness as an East-West meeting place.

Whether or not the United Nations will ever again be called upon to perform state-preserving and state-building tasks and the ultimate success of those that it has performed in the Congo remain to be seen. However, even if ONUC's Civilian Operations stand as a unique case and time proves that some of the United Nations' accomplishments in the Congo were less substantial than they now appear, there can be no question that the United Nations has made a significant contribution to decolonization by its activities in this instance. It has facilitated and eased a radical change, which could easily have been even more disruptive and painful than it was, not only for the Congo, but also for the surrounding territories and for the international community generally. Beyond that, ONUC's Civilian Operations have at least made it possible for the Congolese to take, and have assisted them in taking, the first steps toward nation-building.

The International Military Force Idea: A Look at Modern
History*

Gabriella Rosner

Early Proposals for an International Military Force

A look at modern history shows great concern with the concept of
international police, but no success in its firm and continued establishment
in reality. As early as the year 1000, French princes of the Church declared
their willingness to make "war against war" by the intervention of collective
military forces under religious leadership. A little later, Archbishop Aimon
of Bourges who "may, in fact, be considered as the earliest predecessor of
the commander of a modern international armed force," led a number of
punitive expeditions with an international army of priests against groups of
recalcitrant knights. In the thirteenth century, the Church Council of Tou-
louse passed a strong resolution ordering every person over fourteen years of
age to solemnly renounce war, and proclaiming that any violator of this
pledge would be immediately punished by collective action.

The ideal of universal peace, the notion of war as fundamentally evil,
came to the fore at the beginning of the fourteenth century. Thereafter, a
great number of proposals—among them those of Dante, the Duc de Sully,
William Penn, the Abbé de Saint-Pierre, and J.-J. Rousseau—began to be
made as to the best means of achieving this aim. Most of these projects
envisaged a system of world government or a stringent order of collective
security backed by an international army. But from these larger principles
would inevitably emerge the concept of a small international force, useful
for limited purposes, functioning in the aid of peace. The idea of a large
world army and the idea of a small police force are fundamentally linked.

Actual practical arrangements were also instituted. For example, dissen-
sion in the Low Countries between Britain, Austria, and the States General
in 1715 came to be regulated by a treaty which designated a section of the
Austro-French frontier where Dutch soldiers, functioning as international
police, would buttress the peace. The Concert of Europe was perhaps the
"most elaborate attempt at peace preservation prior to the twentieth cen-

* Gabriella Rosner, *The United Nations Emergency Force* (Columbia University Studies in
International Organization No. 2: New York: Columbia University Press, 1963), pp. 207-222.
Reprinted by permission. Gabriella Rosner Lande currently is associated with the Center of
International Studies, Princeton University.

tury"; an international army was not instituted during the "Era of Metternich" but national forces were made to act in the name of the whole alliance. And, at the time of the Boxer Rebellion in 1900, an allied force of 18,600 men, representing five countries, was sent to the aid of foreign legations in Peking. Authority over these forces was in the hands of the commanders of the national contingents; cooperative conferences were held, however, and decisions were taken by majority vote.

The question of international police as an instrument in the machinery of peace enforcement claimed the attention of innumerable statesmen, military authorities, and scholars throughout the first part of the twentieth century. This was the Hague Period, a time when the idea of peace enforcement was strong. Theodore Roosevelt spoke often about the desirability of an international system of collective security. T. W. Kinkaid, Commander of the United States Navy, declared in 1911: "The criticism that the Hague Tribunal has no military support need not always exist. The object of this brief paper is to suggest that the leading nations of the world unite for the formation and maintenance of an international navy." Fundamentally supporting the views of his colleague, U.S. Rear Admiral C. F. Goodrich wrote an article entitled: "Wanted—An International Police." Nicholas Murray Butler and Andrew Carnegie espoused the cause of a police force, drawn from many countries, to act as international sheriff in keeping the peace. And the United States Congress passed a joint resolution in June 1910, appointing a five-member commission to consider, among other things, the expediency "of constituting the combined navies of the world an international force for the preservation of universal peace."

In many parts of the world these ideas were voiced. Urging the Dutch government in 1910 to make a positive and masterful contribution to the Third Peace Conference at the Hague by formulating a new "Deed" for a world organization, C. Van Vollenhoven, Professor of Law in the University of Leyden, discussed an international army in all its aspects of *pro* and *con*. During a public debate on international police in May 1913, the Dutch professor elaborated his views in terms that seem quite "modern" today, although inordinately optimistic:

As long as the current view was—as in Grotius's days and a long time afterwards—, that quarrels between states could only be peacefully settled by the other states themselves, the question of impartial international arbitration was indeed insolvable. But it has become easy, since it has proved possible to have international differences settled by a separate tribunal, created, it is true, by the states themselves, and therefore in accordance with their sovereignty, but composed not of states, but of independent individuals. The same thing exactly applies to an impartial international police. This institution will only be possible, if directed by a board, created by sovereign states and maintained by them, but consisting of independent individuals, and therefore withdrawn from the influence of national interests and national secretaries of foreign affairs.

Rafael Erich of Finland likewise urged creation of an army composed of forces from several nations, independent as far as possible from the authority of particular states, and exercising its function in the name of the "Community of States." The army would operate only upon appeal from a state needing protection, an independent authority would decide upon such an appeal, and an international agreement would settle the terms by which the international executive force would be used:

The circumstance that the different States would make unequal contributions to the international force, would make no difference in their claim upon it, as it would be in no wise at the service of individual States; but at that of their Community. Although the force, put together in this way, would form a power, independent of the States lending national contingents to it, yet, upon general principles of justice, it follows that the portion of the force contributed by a State would never be used against that State.

But the first decade of the twentieth century failed to see either a police force or a workable system of peace established. A whirlwind of armament races and international crises gained sway and the peace projects which had been so earnestly forwarded were swept away in the course of events. After the commencement of the First World War, however, proposals for an international *gendarmerie* or a multi-national police force became even more numerous: for, the horrors of war and the destruction perpetrated, engendered a belief that "If we do not try to end war, war will end us"; and one of the means of eliminating war was peace enforcement. Lord Bryce and David Davies in England, the British League of Nations Society, and the American League to Enforce Peace (supported by President Wilson, William Howard Taft, Charles E. Hughes, among others), the American League of Free Nations Association, the Fabian Society of England, and many more persons and groups in Europe and in the United States formulated explicit plans for the avoidance of war and each, in one way or another, envisaged the use of military sanctions or an international police. Likewise, the great majority of drafts for the Covenant of the League of Nations—the proposals of Phillimore, Smuts, Cecil, and Hurst Miller and the programs of the German and Italian governments—contained provisions for the use of international military forces.

One of the most carefully formulated and advanced proposals on this matter was submitted by the French government during the discussions in Paris on the drafting of the League Covenant. The French plan entrusted the execution of military sanctions to an international force or to one or more Powers of the League. It was envisaged that the troops, distributed over the globe and commanded by a permanent staff, would be directly responsible to the "International Body," although the Member States themselves would supply the force with adequate strength to uphold League decisions. The "International Body" would determine the total magnitude and the composition of the force and would be empowered to control the activities of the national armies.

In 1919, however, neither the British nor the Americans favored the organization of such military measures. Indeed, President Wilson was firm in his avowal that "the United States would never ratify any treaty which put the force of the United States at the disposal of such a group or body." Consequently, an international armed force to guarantee compliance with League decisions was not directly authorized in Articles 10 and 16 of the Covenant; and in no way was the Council expressly empowered to employ military sanctions for definitive purposes or under deliberate conditions.

Proposals and Uses During the League Period

Nevertheless, after the Polish-led occupation of Vilna in 1920, the League attempted to establish an international police force, not for purposes of peace enforcement, but "to ensure a well-ordered and fair expression of opinion" in the impending plebiscite. The force, instituted by a Council resolution of November 21, 1920, was to have consisted of 1,800 men composed of Belgian, British, Spanish, French, Danish, Dutch, Norwegian, and Swedish troops supplied by the contributing states. But the entire project was abandoned by the Council on March 3, 1921, when it became evident that a plebiscite could not be expected while Polish occupying forces were still in the area, while disagreement between the parties remained rife, and while Russia objected to settlement of the question by the League. The dispatch of troops to Vilna by the League of Nations would, according to the Soviet Union, have constituted a danger to Soviet security and, had Lithuania let such forces enter, Russia would have considered it an unfriendly act.

In 1934 the League Council again created an international force which operated, with the consent of France and Germany, to ensure order before, during, and after the plebiscite in the Saar Territory. This time the endeavor was a success and, indeed, presaged the experiment of UNEF. Authorized by a resolution of November 11, the Saar Force was primarily intended as an emergency reserve exercising by its mere presence a restraint on any use of violence by the interested parties. Effective policing of the Territory during the plebiscite constituted a problem which had caused concern in many quarters. Diverse political groups were maneuvering for position during the pre-plebiscite campaign; rumors of a *Putsch* were abundant. Observers expected that by the time of the election itself, political fervor would be raised to fever pitch. For, hatred between political adversaries in the Territory was exceptionally acute, complaints of boycott, pressure and terrorism on the part of political extremists were often voiced, and paramilitary organizations were numerous. The idea of a neutral police force, primarily intended as an emergency reserve to keep the peace, evolved in discussions on the plebiscite.

A Committee of Three, appointed by the League Council and assisted by a sub-committee, formulated specific recommendations concerning the functions, composition, organization, and finances of the police force which was placed under British Command and was directly responsible to the Governing Commission of the Saar Territory. National contingents totaling 3,300 men were contributed by the United Kingdom, Italy, the Netherlands, and Sweden.

The main task of the international force was to uphold order in the territory and to keep peace between the contending parties in the plebiscite. In the early stages of the operation, the soldiers were asked to show themselves to the local population, and to be ready to appear immediately, if necessary, at any spot where disturbances threatened. At five different times mobile parties were dispatched to areas where trouble appeared to be brewing, but it seems that the mere show of force dampened overzealous spirits and, in effect, no military action had to be taken. On the day of the vote, members of the international force were asked to guard polling stations and urns, to escort lorries carrying the ballot boxes, and to be on hand in the event of conflict.

Colonel A. H. Burne, an officer of the British contingent, reported that not a single shot was fired while the Force operated in the Saarland. Whether orders were or were not given to use weapons in the event of trouble is not known. We do know that the same general principles of action were observed throughout:

(1) To make an imposing parade of force *before* the trouble breaks out.

(2) To keep the troops hidden away during the actual period of tension, leaving the maintenance of order, in the first instance, to the Police. . . .

(3) To maintain a large mobile reserve.

Carefully coordinated and imposed by Headquarters, this "British Method" of troop employment was adopted in place of the "Continental Method" (also propounded at the time), which "consisted in the main of placing machine guns, etc., at street corners." If necessary, however, would machine guns have been used? There is no record that the League Council actually discussed or authorized enforcement measures.

After having attained the consent of Germany, France, and the contributing states to the operation, the League Council remained the ultimate source of creation and control; the Council decided when the Force should enter the Territory, what it would do there, who would command, and when withdrawal would be effectuated. The troops were thus truly international soldiers serving the interest of the world community; for, the Governing Commission of the Saar Territory continued as the responsible authority for the maintenance of order and the Force was subject to its rules and decisions, while emergency powers were vested in the commander-in-chief, who controlled the staff officers of each national unit.

It was a well-organized and carefully planned force. Each contingent consisted of infantry, armored cars, and ancillary troops, and Member States were asked to grant every facility for the transit through their territory of the soldiers and their supplies. Furthermore, the League Council authorized the Governing Commission

to enact the legislation necessary to exempt the international force and its members from all responsibility for any act accomplished in the performance of their mission and to confer on itself in case of need the power of requisition for the accommodation, maintenance and transport of the said force.

Exemption from the jurisdiction of the courts of the Saar was granted to the command of the Force, its organs and services and members. Only the Supreme Plebiscite Tribunal (a League creation) was declared "competent to judge breaches of penal law committed against the international force or its members. . . ."

In regard to the financing of the Force, the principle adopted by the Council, just as in the plans for the Vilna project, was that the contributing states would be reimbursed for the cost of all expenditures which exceeded those sums normally spent by them for maintenance of their contingents—that is, the costs of transport and costs of maintenance resulting from expatriation. These expenses would be charged to a fund for expenditures in connection with the plebiscite.

On June 4, 1934, the Council had decided that the German and French governments were to advance five million French francs respectively and the Governing Commission of the Saar was to advance one million French francs as immediate advances to cover the expenses of the plebiscite. These sums were to be placed in a special account, apart from the ordinary funds of the League. The future government of the Saar, to be established as a result of the plebiscite, was to incur the obligation for compensation of lost or damaged material belonging to the international force as well as payment of death or invalidity pensions "which may have to be paid in respect of the death or invalidity of members of the international force as a result of their service, in accordance with the most favorable rules embodied in the legislation in force in the four participating countries. . . ." It was firmly decided that in no case were the resources proper of the League to be drawn upon "either for payments which are not reimbursable, or for advances from the Working Capital Fund." These financial arrangements were very different indeed from those made in 1956 for UNEF.

However, the fiscal principles adopted were in line with general League policy, for many of the League's Commissions and special projects were not directly supported by the Organization but were charged to those states for whom the expenses of the programs had been incurred. This was true, for example, of the Manchurian Commission, the Chaco Commission, and the High Commissioner for Danzig. It was true as well for the two peace and security operations planned by the League—operations which, perhaps, represent significant precedents to those Members of the United Nations today who would like to see UNEF and ONUC financed solely by the countries benefiting directly from the existence of the two police forces.

The multinational Force for the Saar worked efficiently and effectively. Colonel A. H. Burne, a participant and close observer, asked whether the International Police was in fact justified by the results obtained and whether the experience promoted the acceptability of a permanent police force. The answer to the first question was emphatic: the "experiment was a complete and unqualified success"; the League's prestige was raised; since tension between Nazi and *status quo* parties was high, the local police would have been inadequate to meet the situation and, if French troops had been called upon to deal with the mounting pressures, would certainly have been exacerbated; indeed, "in the opinion of many, this would have led to open conflict between the French and Germans. The expressed opinion of many prominent Germans on the Saar that the presence of the Saar Force averted a European war may therefore not be devoid of substance."

But Colonel Burne found it difficult to answer the second question pertaining to a permanent force. He attributed the success of the Saar experiment mainly to the British character of the High Command, to the personality of the Force Commander, the good personal relations between Headquarters and the contingents, the short period that the Force was in existence, the adoption of British methods, and the personality of one of the Englishmen leading the Force. These factors were unlikely to be duplicated in a future situation. Commenting on Colonel Burne's remarks, Captain B. H. Liddell Hart was especially struck by the difficulty of drawing many conclusions from the Saar policing episode:

It is a fact that the Force as organized fulfilled its task without trouble, and so we can at least draw the conclusion that a force of this kind is practicable in conditions that do not develop into war or an armed outbreak.

But any deductions as to difficulties which a force of different composition or one acting under different conditions might suffer from are necessarily speculative.

As a truly international force created and controlled by a world organization, the Force, however, may be considered as a precursor of the United Nations Emergency Force. Like UNEF, the Saar Police Force had no coercionary powers and functioned mainly as an international representative, keeping order by its mere presence and prestige. Consent of the parties concerned was considered a strict prerequisite to the formation of both groups and an advisory committee assisted in their creation and organization. Similarities in the legal regulation of the two groups, their structure and control, are many. The difference lies primarily in the scope of the two operations, the nature of the crises, and the functions performed. The aim of the Saar Force was to keep order during a time when a plebiscite was in progress. UNEF was entrusted with much more delicate and responsible tasks: to supervise a cease-fire, to guide the withdrawal of powerful military forces from foreign territory, and to oversee an armistice. The political situation of 1956 in regard to the Middle East was decidedly more disturbed and incendiary than that of 1934 in respect to the Saarland. And the UNEF operation may be considered, in its entirety, not only more extensive and vital than that of the Saar Force, but more closely planned and organized. However, by propagating the idea of an international police, by demonstrating its success even in limited circumstances, the Saar expeditionary force of the League may have furthered in a small way the entire concept of a military force for the international community of states and may have provided a precedent in a general way for the organization of the Emergency Force in 1956.

Military Forces and the United Nations

Even before the time of the Saar plebiscite, another plan for the creation of a permanent police force to prevent war was proposed by France at the Disarmament Conference in 1932. The police force was to be always on hand "with complete freedom of passage to occupy in times of emergency areas where a threat of war has arisen"; each of the contracting parties was to furnish contingents "in a proportion to be determined," while command arrangements were to be made by the League. A primary contingent of mobile forces was to bring immediate assistance to any victim of aggression. For, the new era of air power required advance planning which aimed toward the *immediate* use of aircraft and personnel when it should be needed. The First World War days of military planning, focusing upon supremacy on the seas, had passed. As a result, France also made concrete proposals for placing civil aviation, bombing aircraft, and certain matériel of land and naval forces at the disposal of the League. Although coolly received at the time, these suggestions later formed the essence of Articles 43 and 45 of the Charter of the United Nations.

Indeed the Disarmament Conference, accompanied as it was by Hitler's swift rise to power, perhaps marked the beginning of the end of the League; and no real efforts toward military enforcement of peace by world organization were made again until the Dumbarton Oaks Conference in 1944. Multinational armed forces were harnessed during the Second World War and their experience and organization provided (as did later the NATO experience) a precedent upon which the creators of UNEF could lean. But the war operations were not executed by international military forces serving a world organization, but of one or the other party to the war. And, actually, there is no indication that these were "precedents," relied upon by UNEF's architects.

At Dumbarton Oaks, the United States submitted proposals not unlike those of the French government in 1932, which were accepted in substance by the other delegations at the conference, and later formed Chapter VII of the United Nations Charter. By the terms of this chapter the Security

Council "may take such action by air, sea, or land forces as may be necessary to maintain or restore international peace and security."

In order that the Security Council may operate effectively, Article 43 of the Charter commits Members of the United Nations to make available to the Council "armed forces, assistance, and facilities, including rights of passage," in accordance with special agreements, for the purpose of maintaining international peace and security. A Military Staff Committee, composed of the Chiefs of Staff of the permanent members of the Council or their representatives, is to advise and assist the Council on all questions relating to these military requirements and on the employment and command of forces placed at its disposal. The permanent members of the Council, however—particularly the Soviet Union and the United States—were unable to come to terms on the basic principles to govern an international force and, as a result, agreements were never concluded between Member States and the Security Council. The impasse was a political rather than a technical one: although the members of the Military Staff Committee wrangled over the various ideological and practical aspects of an international military force, it was the growth of the "cold war" which helped to produce the fundamental deadlock. The debates in the committee revealed the extent to which each major power would endeavor to obtain maximum influence over a United Nations army and hence compete on the questions of organizing and of stationing such a force. The problem of creating an international military operation cannot be divorced from the unified political purpose it is to serve. Deadlock, then, prevented the Security Council from obtaining the military means to enforce its decisions. And one of the essential provisions of the Charter remained unfulfilled.

Since there was no immediate hope of agreement between the Great Powers on the establishment of an enforcement army, a number of schemes for a small armed force outside the framework of Article 43 of the Charter and without enforcement powers were considered at the United Nations. Upon the request of the United Nations Mediator in Palestine, more than a hundred military officers from the armed forces of Sweden, Belgium, France, and the United States were sent to the Middle East as military observers in 1948. During July of the same year, Secretary-General Trygve Lie proposed the creation of "a small United Nations Guard Force" of 1,000 to 5,000 men "which could be recruited by the Secretary-General and placed at the disposal of the Security Council and the General Assembly." The "primary positive purpose" of the Guard was "to be representative of United Nations authority in support of United Nations Missions in the field and to provide a limited protection to United Nations personnel and property." Mr. Lie stated that "such a force would not be used as a substitute for the Force contemplated in Articles 42 and 43. It would not be a striking force, but purely a guard force. It could be used as a constabulary under the Security Council or the Trusteeship Council in cities like Jerusalem and Trieste during the establishment of international regimes. It might also be called upon by the Security Council under Article 40 of the Charter, which provides for provisional measures to prevent the aggravation of a situation threatening the peace."

Faced with considerable opposition in the Assembly to the Guard Force, Secretary-General Lie initiated a more modest plan which the Assembly accepted, on November 22, 1949, by the establishment of a United Nations Field Service of 300 communication technicians and guards to form a normal unit of the Secretariat and aid the operation of United Nations Field Missions. This was undoubtedly a useful institution, but fell far short of being a police force of international military units whose aid the United Nations could enlist for functions of pacific settlement or for enforcement action to prevent or suppress acts of aggression.

Thus military forces were not immediately available for use by the world organization when the Security Council on June 25, 1950, determined that a breach of the peace had been committed in Korea. Unable to act under Article 42, the Council recommended that Member States "furnish such assistance to the Republic of Korea as may be necessary to repel the armed attack" and invited the United States to establish a unified command. Fortunately, the United States government had substantial forces in close proximity to the area of the North Korean attack and favored their immediate use to repel the invasion. "If it had not been for this special juxtaposition of circumstances, it is quite unlikely that assistance would have been rendered to the Republic of Korea in time to halt the North Korean attack."

Indeed, the Korean operation undoubtedly demonstrated the weakness of the United Nations system of enforcement action, without advance preparation by governments to place their forces at the disposal of the United Nations and without adequately training, organizing, and equipping them for this specific use. Members of the United Nations other than the United States acted slowly in contributing military assistance to the United Nations Command in Korea. Difficulties were encountered in regard to the strategic direction of the international force. And it became apparent that

when one state assumes a major responsibility initially for aiding the victim of aggression, largely on its own and not as part of a prepared plan of collective action, the whole operation fails to acquire a truly collective character, because the state bearing the major responsibility almost necessarily exercises a dominant control over the whole operation.

The drawbacks inherent in the improvised and unilateral procedure of the Korean operation were important factors in leading Members of the United Nations to pass the "Uniting for Peace" resolution of November 3, 1950, in which the Assembly recommended that "each Member maintain within its national forces elements so trained, organized and equipped that they could promptly be made available . . . for service as a United Nations unit or units, upon recommendation by the Security Council or the General Assembly." The resolution also established a Collective Measures Committee which would undertake the preparation of basic principles and plans of action to guide and facilitate the application of collective measures. Although this Committee made extensive studies of the question and submitted a number of significant proposals on the matter to the General Assembly, it was soon evident that most Member States were unwilling to undertake specific commitments for the future. The failure of the Security Council to establish an effective system of collective security had caused many of them to provide for their mutual defense by means of special arrangements for collective self-defense and hence they were anxious to determine their future course of action in the light of these commitments and the circumstances of the particular situation. Leland Goodrich and Anne Simons assert that the efforts of the Collective Measures Committee and the Assembly's deliberations and resolutions did not seem to "have had any direct or immediate effect on preparatory measures taken by Members to strengthen 'international peace and security.'" Actually, those states whose response was most favorable never "indicated any intention of taking new steps on the basis of this institution alone."

Thus efforts to earmark military forces for United Nations use, although persistently made in the past, had not matured at the time of the Suez crisis in November 1956. The reasons for this are many and probably lie most fundamentally in the continuous opposition of sovereign states to international control. "Broadly speaking, international (or better, supernational) ways of thinking, feeling, and acting cannot be simply superimposed on national ways. The larger mode will not embrace the smaller; it must replace it by means of a thorough permeation." In the period since the establishment of the United Nations, the postwar world—with its bipolar-power system, cold war, emphasis on regional alliances, and lack of trust in world organization—has been so constituted as to engender profound differences between the Great Powers on the basic considerations to govern an international military force. Yet developments in atomic and hydrogen weapons, space and intercontinental ballistic missiles have made the fear of war so overwhelming that keen attention has been paid to every situation which might, if left unchecked, lead to global disaster. Consequently, "What we faced in the Assembly last November [1956] was the necessity of organizing quickly a force, not to fight but to ensure that fighting would not be resumed." There was no attempt during the Middle Eastern emergency to establish a large army with coercionary powers. But even the establishment of a small para-military group required considerable foresight and planning. The few limited experiences of the past, as well as the myriad schemes for an international military force, were probably more valuable in their function of furthering and spreading the idea of international policing than in their practical nature as precedents to guide the architects of UNEF. Hence, the United Nations Emergency Force emerges as a distinct pioneering effort.

The United Nations Emergency Force*

Leland M. Goodrich and Gabriella E. Rosner

When the Charter of the United Nations was being written and put into effect, the feature that was most emphasized by its supporters was the provision for the use of collective forces to keep the peace. It was the failure of this particular feature of the Charter system to become effective which was mainly responsible for the subsequent decline of confidence in the United Nations as a peace organization. For a time, hopes were rekindled by the role of the United Nations in meeting aggression in Korea. Recent events in the Middle East, particularly the establishment of the United Nations Emergency Force (UNEF), have revived interest in the possibility of strengthening the United Nations as an organization to maintain international peace and security. Because of the hopes aroused as well as the results achieved, it is important to analyze objectively what UNEF is, what its role has been, and to what it may lead.

The Creation of UNEF

UNEF came into being as the result of action taken by the General Assembly and the Secretary-General, acting in agreement with Members of the United Nations. It was a part—and an essential part—of the total response of the United Nations and its Members to the military invasion of Egyptian territory by Israel, France and the United Kingdom, beginning October 29, 1956.

In some respects the situation facing the United Nations in late October and early November was similar to that which faced the Organization at the time of the north Korean attack in June 1950. The Israeli military attack on Egypt was open and deliberate. The United Nations was not at the time equipped with armed forces of its own which it could use to restrain or suppress the attacks or take other appropriate measures to restore peace. Finally, certain of the major powers, the United Kingdom and France, claimed to have special interests in and responsibilities for the maintenance of peace and security in the area and had made military preparations which permitted them to act in case their interests required it.

In other respects, however, the situation in the Middle East was quite different from that in Korea in 1950. The Israeli attack, though overt and

* Leland M. Goodrich and Gabriella E. Rosner, "The United Nations Emergency Force," *International Organization*, Vol. XI, No. 3 (Summer 1957), pp. 413-430. Reprinted by permission.

deliberate, was quite widely viewed as provoked and as an understandable reaction to Egyptian threats and acts. Though the governments of the United Kingdom and France sought to justify their military intervention as a necessary step to maintain peace and security in the area, their action was clearly directed toward strengthening their position in the Suez Canal negotiations, and, in the case of France, toward eliminating one source of support for the Algerian independence movement. For different reasons, both the United States and the Soviet Union were strongly opposed to their action. Thus there was not in this case the agreement among the western anti-communist powers that had existed in 1950. With the permanent members of the Security Council present and in disagreement, there was no possibility of getting any action by the Security Council. However, the "Uniting for Peace" resolution made action by the General Assembly possible without undue delay.

The Assembly began consideration of the matter on November 1, the day following the veto by France and the United Kingdom of the Soviet draft resolution in the Security Council calling for a cease-fire and the withdrawal of forces. This resolution was an adaptation of the United States proposal which had been vetoed the day previously. Thus General Assembly consideration began three days after the Israeli attack, two days after the Anglo-French ultimatum, and the day following the Anglo-French bombing of Egyptian airfields.

In the course of General Assembly discussion, it became clear that some delegations, in addition to being concerned over the attack on Egypt, were particularly alarmed over the breach that had developed between the United States and the United Kingdom and France as the result of the failure of the latter governments to consult Washington. Furthermore, as has been noted, there was considerable sympathy with Israel, though not necessarily approval of the methods used. There was also a feeling on the part of some delegations that the United Kingdom and France had legitimate grievances against Egypt, which should not be wholly overlooked in the action taken by the Assembly. Consequently, on the floor of the Assembly and outside, there was support for two quite different approaches to the situation which the Assembly faced.

The majority, including the Afro-Asian bloc and the communist bloc, desired to condemn the Israeli attack and the subsequent Anglo-French military actions, to bring hostilities to an end, and to secure the prompt withdrawal of invading forces, without concern for face-saving or the satisfaction of grievances. On the other hand, the older Commonwealth countries and the western European Members, while not approving the methods used, particularly by the United Kingdom and France, were unwilling to envisage the use of collective measures against them, were anxious to restore the unity of the western powers, and sought to achieve the termination of hostilities and the withdrawal of forces on terms which took some account of the grievances of the attackers and which would contribute to satisfactory political settlements. Lester Pearson described Canadian policy in these words:

. . . instead of indulging then or since in gratuitous condemnation we expressed our regret and we began to pursue a policy, both here by diplomatic talks and diplomatic correspondence, and later at the United Nations, which would bring about peace in the area on terms which everybody would accept. Our policy, then, in carrying out these principles was to get the United Nations into the matter at once; to seek through the United Nations a solution which would be satisfactory to all sides.

In line with this policy, after the adoption of the Assembly's first resolution of November 2 calling on the parties to cease fire and withdraw their forces, Mr. Pearson suggested that the Secretary-General begin to make arrangements with Member States for a United Nations force large enough to keep "these borders at peace while a political settlement is being worked out." On November 3, the Secretary-General reported to the General Assembly that the Governments of the United Kingdom and France had informed him that "They would most willingly stop military action" as soon as three conditions had been satisfied: (1) Egyptian and Israeli acceptance of a United Nations force to keep the peace; (2) constitution and maintenance of such a force until an Arab-Israeli peace settlement had been reached and satisfactory arrangements regarding the Suez Canal had been agreed to; and (3) acceptance by both parties of the stationing of limited detachments of Anglo-French forces until the United Nations force was constituted. While these conditions were not acceptable to the General Assembly, they did suggest the possibility of United Nations action which would be consistent with Charter principles and which at the same time might be acceptable to the interested parties.

Later the same day Mr. Pearson introduced a draft resolution requesting the Secretary-General, as a matter of priority, to submit, within forty-eight hours, a plan for the setting up, with the consent of the nations concerned, of an emergency international United Nations force. This proposal was adopted by the General Assembly early in the morning of November 4, and later that day the Secretary-General submitted his first report. In his report the Secretary-General proposed the appointment of Major-General E. L. M. Burns, Chief of Staff of the United Nations Truce Supervision Organization, as Chief of Command of a United Nations force, and outlined a plan for recruiting staff and additional officers. These suggestions were approved by the Assembly in its resolution of November 5 which established a "United Nations Command for an emergency international Force to secure and supervise the cessation of hostilities in accordance with all the terms of the General Assembly resolution 997 (ES-I) of 2 November 1956".

The November 2 resolution had urged "that all parties now involved in hostilities in the area agree to an immediate cease-fire and, as part thereof, halt the movement of military forces and arms into the area". It had urged "the parties to the armistice agreements promptly to withdraw all forces behind the armistice lines, to desist from raids across the armistice lines into neighboring territory, and to observe scrupulously the provisions of the armistice agreements". It recommended that no military goods be introduced into the area by any Member state. It urged "that, upon the cease-fire being effective, steps be taken to reopen the Suez Canal and restore freedom of navigation". The resolutions of November 2 and 5 furnished the basis for the establishment and for the operation of UNEF.

On November 6, 1956, after Israel, France, the United Kingdom and Egypt had unconditionally accepted a cease-fire, the Secretary-General submitted a second and final report to the Assembly in which he set forth the basic principles to govern the functions, size, organization, financing and recruitment of the Force. Moreover, Mr. Hammarskjold indicated that the governments of Canada, Colombia, Denmark, Norway, Pakistan and Sweden had expressed their willingness to contribute contingents to the new military organization. On the following day, November 7, the Assembly adopted a resolution approving these principles. It invited Mr. Hammarskjold "to continue discussions with the Governments of Member States concerning offers of participation in the Force . . ." It requested the Chief of Command, in consultation with the Secretary-General, to proceed forthwith with the full organization of the Force, and established an Advisory Committee consisting of Brazil, Canada, Ceylon, Colombia, India, Norway and Pakistan "to undertake the development of those aspects of the planning for the Force and its operation not already dealt with by the General Assembly and which do not fall within the area of the direct responsibility of the Chief of Command". It authorized the Secretary-General to issue all regulations and instructions which might be considered essential to the effective functioning of the force after consultation with the Advisory Committee.

What was particularly notable in connection with the establishment of the United Nations Emergency Force was the extent of the responsibility which the Secretary-General and his staff were asked to assume. In addition to proposing a plan for the Force, the Secretary-General was asked to negotiate with Member states regarding national contributions, to advise the Chief of Command with respect to organization, and to issue all regulations and instructions essential to effective functioning, subject only to consultation with the Advisory Committee. Furthermore, the Secretary-General was expected to arrange with the parties to the hostilities for a cease-fire and for the withdrawal of forces, and to make necessary arrangements with them to permit UNEF to enter into the performance of its functions.

In discharging these responsibilities, the Secretary-General and his staff were without the advantage of an established practice. . . . The Charter provisions for such a force remained a dead letter. To repel the north Korean attack in 1950, it had been necessary to rely primarily on the initiative and armed forces of one Member, the United States. The Collective Measures Committee had made a detailed study of ways of strengthening collective security, but its conclusions were not wholly relevant to the November 1956 situation in the Middle East. Proposals made by Secretary-General Lie in 1948 for "a small United Nations Guard Force" of 1,000 to 5,000 men to be placed at the disposal of the General Assembly or the Security Council were unacceptable to Members at the time, and the resolution in which the Assembly actually adopted in 1949 provided only for a United Nations Field Service of technicians. There had been experience with the use of military observers, notably in Kashmir and in Palestine, where the United Nations Truce Supervision Organization had been functioning since 1949.

In the Middle East situation, therefore, it was necessary to do much improvising, and to do so under the pressure of great anxiety as to the future course of events. The Secretary-General received the fullest cooperation from Member governments. By direct contact with their representatives at Headquarters, he was able to cut red tape and to work out detailed arrangements which made it possible for the Force to enter upon its duties within a surprisingly short time. At the time it appeared that the establishment of this Force was the necessary prerequisite to the withdrawal of British, French and Israeli forces, and the lessening of the dangerous tension which had gripped the Middle East. The threat of introducing Soviet volunteers to defend Egypt in case the invading forces were not withdrawn made the situation even more serious.

Legal Basis of UNEF

While the establishment of UNEF was an action determined by political considerations, it was also an action which in the minds of its supporters had a sound legal basis. It is desirable to examine this basis, both because the matter is of some importance so far as UNEF is concerned, and more importantly, because of its bearing on the possibilities of establishing a permanent United Nations force in the future.

Speaking generally, the legal basis for the Force is to be found in the Charter, in the decisions of the principal organs, in the consent of Members, and in the general principles of international law. In seeking further to ascertain the nature and extent of this legal basis, it is well to concentrate on two particular aspects of the problem: (1) the extent of the powers of the General Assembly and the other organs of the United Nations; and (2) the legal basis of the activities of the Force itself.

It is commonly stated that the General Assembly acted under the terms of the "Uniting for Peace" resolution of November 3, 1950, in establishing the Force and defining its functions. While the "Uniting for Peace" resolution enabled the General Assembly to meet in special emergency session to deal with the situation, the powers that the Assembly exercised were derived directly from the Charter. In the debate leading up to the adoption of the "Uniting for Peace" resolution, proponents pointed to the "residual responsibility" of the General Assembly for dealing with breaches of the peace and acts of aggression. But they were forced to admit that, unlike the Security Council, it could only recommend.

In addition, the Charter gives the Assembly power to establish such subsidiary organs as it may consider necessary to the performance of its functions. This power the Assembly has frequently exercised. When the General Assembly, by its resolution of November 5, established a United Nations Command for an emergency international force, and subsequently on November 7 approved the principles governing the organization and functioning of such a force, it thereby set up a subsidiary organ to assist it in carrying out its functions. It could not confer upon this organ any powers which it did not have itself. What the Assembly in effect did was to prepare and approve a plan for a force and to recommend to Members that they cooperate in making the force an actuality. Whatever power the Assembly might have to send the force into the territory of a Member to perform specific functions could only be based on the consent of the Members directly concerned, a consent, however, which need not be given for each specific situation but which may be given in general terms.

In this connection the exchanges between the Secretary-General and the Egyptian government with respect to UNEF are extremely significant. Before consenting to the actual arrival of the Force, the Egyptian government insisted on clarifications. Discussions between the Secretary-General and the Egyptian government led to understandings which were summarized in an *aide mémoire* approved by the General Assembly on November 24. The Egyptian government agreed to the arrival of UNEF in Egyptian territory and declared that in the future exercise of its sovereign rights "it will be guided, in good faith", by its acceptance of the General Assembly's resolution of November 5, 1956.

While the General Assembly itself is not authorized, except with the consent of the states concerned, to direct that an international force be stationed or operate on the territory of a particular state, the Charter does not exclude the possibility of a force being so used by the Security Council. It is clear, however, that UNEF, which has been established for a particular purpose and for use in a certain way, with contingents contributed by Members on that understanding, cannot be used by the Security Council for the wider purposes and with the degree of authority provided in Chapter VII of the Charter.

The question of the legal basis of the activities of the Force is, of course, closely related to that of the authority of the organs of the United Nations. Since the General Assembly can only recommend, it follows that the Force, in its operations, is limited "to the extent that consent of the parties concerned is required under generally recognized international law". Egypt agreed to be guided "in good faith" by its acceptance of the General Assembly resolution of November 5. By the terms of its agreement of February 8, 1957, with the Secretary-General regarding the status of the United Nations Emergency Force in Egypt, the Egyptian government accorded to the Force a definite legal status, and agreed that the Force and its personnel should have those privileges and immunities considered necessary to the performance of their functions. Certain understandings were reached in the discussions between the Secretary-General and Member governments regarding conditions under which national forces were made available for service in UNEF. In this connection, note should be made of the statement of Mr. Krishna Menon in the General Assembly on November 7 of the conditions formulated by the Indian government for the participation of its forces and of the Secretary-General's acceptance of these conditions.

While there can be no question regarding the requirement of consent for UNEF operations, there still remains the need of interpreting the limits and meaning of this consent. On this point, serious disagreement is possible with respect to the future of the Force. Can India withdraw its contingent if its interpretation of the conditions governing participation is, in its opinion, violated? Can the General Assembly order the use of the Force for a purpose not specifically approved by Egypt? Would Egypt be bound by the General Assembly's decision? Questions of interpretation have not thus far led to any fatal fissure in the consent on which UNEF is based, thanks to the skillful diplomacy of the Secretary-General and his staff.

Functions and Powers

The tasks and powers of UNEF are defined generally by the Charter and the Assembly's resolutions of November 2 and 5. These resolutions, however, required interpretation and elaboration as the Force was organized and entered into the performance of its duties. In this development, the Secretary-General has played an important part.

In his second report to the Assembly on the plan for an emergency United Nations force, the Secretary-General explained at some length his understanding of the tasks and powers of the Force as envisaged in the Assembly's resolutions. According to his interpretation, the Assembly's intention was "that the force should be of a temporary nature, the length of its assignment being determined by the needs arising out of the present conflict." He did not regard the Force "as part of an enforcement action directed against a Member country." "There is an obvious difference," he observed, "between establishing the force in order to secure the cessation of hostilities, with a withdrawal of forces, and establishing such a force with a view to enforcing a withdrawal of forces." According to his interpretation of the terms of reference, there was "no intent in the establishment of the force to influence the military balance in the present conflict." Thus, though "para-military in nature," it was not a combat force "with military objectives."

More specifically, the Secretary-General indicated that the functions of the Force would be to enter Egyptian territory with the consent of the Egyptian Government, in order to help maintain quiet during and after the withdrawal of non-Egyptian troops, and to secure compliance with the other terms established in the resolution of 2 November 1956. The Force obviously should have no rights other than those necessary for the execution of its function, in cooperation with local authorities. It would be more than an observers' corps, but in no way a military force temporarily controlling the territory in which it is stationed; nor, moreover should the Force have military functions exceeding those necessary to secure peaceful conditions on the assumption that the parties to the conflict take all necessary steps for compliance with the recommendations of the General Assembly. Its functions can, on this basis, be assumed to cover an area extending roughly from the Suez Canal to the armistice demarcation lines, established in the Armistice Agreement between Egypt and Israel.

These views of the Secretary-General were approved by the General Assembly in its resolution of November 7. Thus UNEF was viewed from the beginning as having a quite different role from the United Nations forces which were contributed under the Security Council resolutions of June 25 and 27, 1950, to repel the north Korean attack and "to restore international peace and security in the area." In many respects the functions and powers of the Force were to be more akin to those of the United Nations Truce Supervision Organization established by the Security Council to supervise the implementation of the Palestine armistice agreements.

In the Secretary-General's discussions with the representatives of Member governments, the exact nature of the functions and powers of the Force was further explored and clarified. The Indian representative, on instructions from his government, raised certain questions regarding the conditions and circumstances under which the Force would function. In reply, the Secretary-General gave his understanding that the Force would be set up in the context of the withdrawal of the Franco-British forces from Egypt and on the basis of the call to Israel to withdraw behind the armistice lines, that the Force could not in any sense be a successor to the invading Franco-British forces or in any sense take over their functions, and that its purpose was to separate the combatants, Egypt and Israel, with the latter withdrawing as required by the November 6 resolution. These assurances the Indian government considered necessary in light of the conditions earlier set by the British and French governments for the cessation of military action, the ambiguity of certain provisions of the Assembly's resolutions, and the insistence of Israel that the armistice agreement was no longer in force.

The initial steps in the organization of the Force were successfully completed in a remarkably short time and on November 15, following agreement of the Egyptian government to receive units of the Force on its soil, the first transport of troops took place. UNEF units took up positions in buffer zones between Egyptian and Anglo-French forces, and between Egyptian and Israeli forces. They maintained order and performed temporary administrative duties which they took over from the occupying forces and in turn relinquished to the Egyptian authorities.

The withdrawal of Anglo-French forces from Egypt was completed on December 22, but evacuation of Israeli troops proceeded more slowly and more doubtfully. Notwithstanding the General Assembly's request that Israeli troops be withdrawn back of the armistice line, and the best efforts of the Secretary-General to secure this result, Israel had not by the end of January withdrawn its forces from the Gaza Strip or the Sharm el-Sheikh area along the Gulf of Aqaba.

The Israeli position, generally speaking, was that the withdrawal of forces from these areas should not be undertaken without an assurance from Egypt that she would cease belligerent acts against Israel and respect Israel's right of navigation in the Straits of Tiran and the Gulf of Aqaba. More specifically, the Israeli government proposed that it should be the function of UNEF to see that freedom of navigation was maintained and belligerent acts avoided in the Gulf of Aqaba and the Straits of Tiran until an effective guarantee of freedom of navigation was provided by agreement of the parties. With respect to the Gaza Strip, the Israeli government did not indicate what the specific function of UNEF would be.

In his report to the General Assembly on January 24, the Secretary-General made it clear that he did not accept the Israeli view. Emphasizing that United Nations action "must be governed by principle and must be in accordance with international law and valid international agreements," he thought it was "generally recognized as non-controversial" that "the United Nations cannot condone a change in the *status juris* resulting from military action contrary to the provisions of the Charter," that "the use of military force by the United Nations other than that under Chapter VII of the Charter requires the consent of the states in which the force is to operate," and that such use of force must respect legal rights and must be impartial "in the sense that it does not serve as a means to force settlement, in the interest of one party, of political conflicts or legal issues recognized as controversial." Referring specifically to the Sharm el-Sheikh area, the Secretary-General observed that the "duties of the Force in respect of the cease-fire and the withdrawal will determine its movements. However, if it is recognized that there is a need for such an arrangement, it may be agreed that units of the Force (or special representatives in the nature of observers) would assist in maintaining quiet in the area beyond what follows from this general principle." The Secretary-General hastened to repeat, however, that the Force should not be used "to prejudge the solution of the controversial questions involved" nor "to protect any special position on these questions, although, at least transitionally, it may function in support of mutual restraint in accordance with the foregoing." Thus it was clear that though the Secretary-General was attempting to leave open an area for negotiation, he nevertheless refused to accept the Israeli position.

In the General Assembly discussion following the Secretary-General's report, some delegations, notably those of Australia, the United Kingdom, and France, supported the Israeli claim. The attitude of the great majority, however, seems to have been expressed by Krishna Menon of India, who insisted that UNEF should not become an army of occupation or a means of supporting one side in a political negotiation. The two resolutions adopted by the Assembly on February 2 called upon Israel to complete its withdrawal of forces "without delay," called upon the governments of Egypt and Israel "scrupulously to observe" the provisions of the armistice agreement, and considered that,

after the full withdrawal of Israel from the Sharm el-Sheikh and Gaza areas, the scrupulous maintenance of the armistice agreement requires the placing of the United Nations Emergency Force on the Egyptian-Israel armistice demarcation line and the implementation of other measures as proposed in the Secretary-General's report, with due regard to the considerations set out therein with a view to assist in achieving situations conducive to the maintenance of peaceful conditions in the area.

In his efforts to implement the Assembly's two resolutions and more particularly to get the two parties to agree to "other measures" proposed in his report, the Secretary-General found Israel less cooperative than Egypt. The Israeli government continued to insist on guarantees as the condition of complete withdrawal, insisted that the armistice agreement was no longer in force, and refused to permit UNEF units to be stationed on its side of the demarcation line. On the basis of discussions, the Secretary-General expressed confidence in the "willingness and readiness [of the Egyptian government] to make special and helpful arrangements with the United Nations and some of its auxiliary bodies, such as UNRWA and UNEF." In the end, however, the Israeli government yielded to pressure, particularly by the United States government, on the matter of withdrawal. On March 1 the Israeli foreign minister announced in the Assembly the decision of her government to withdraw Israeli forces completely from the Gaza Strip and the Sharm el-Sheikh area. Withdrawal was carried out during March 7 and 8.

Upon the withdrawal of Israeli forces UNEF units moved in and took over responsibilitiy for the maintenance of order and for patrolling the demarcation line with respect to the Gaza Strip. There apparently was some hope on the part of the Secretary-General and his staff that the Egyptian government would refrain, for the time being, from any active assumption of administrative responsibilities in the Gaza Strip. However, President Nasser's suspicions were apparently aroused by press reports that an international administration was being planned. On March 12 he appointed Major-General Mohammed Hassan Abdel Latif, who arrived in Gaza two days later, as Administrative Governor. Notwithstanding, UNEF, as the only armed force in the area, continued to be responsible for the maintenance of order and for patrolling the demarcation line. Functions of the Truce Supervision Organization have been placed under the operational control of the

Force. The United Nations Relief and Works Administration, in cooperation with UNEF, continued to discharge its responsibilities for providing food and other services.

Composition, Organization and Control

When the Secretary-General was asked by the General Assembly in the early morning of November 4 to prepare a plan for a United Nations emergency force, he was in the position where he had to make the best use of what was readily available. First of all, however, he had to choose among various concepts of such a force. As in Korea, one country could have been charged with the responsibility of organizing and directing such a force. If this had been done, it might have been difficult to make United Nations control effective. A second alternative would have been to allow the international force to be set up and used on the basis of agreement among a group of states. This was what the United Kingdom and France in effect proposed, which made this concept wholly inadmissible to the majority of Members. The third alternative, and the one proposed by the Secretary-General and approved by the Assembly, was that the chief officer should be appointed by the United Nations and directly responsible to the United Nations, and that his authority should be so defined as to make him fully independent of the policies of any one nation.

Recruitment by the Chief of Command of a limited number of officers from the observer corps of the United Nations Truce Supervision Organization or directly from various Member states other than Britain, France, the United States, the Soviet Union and China, was authorized by the Assembly resolution of November 5. Mindful of the need "to avoid the loss of time and efficiency," the Secretary-General proposed in his second report that self-contained national contingents, "drawn from countries or groups of countries which can provide such troops without delay", be utilized for the Force. Individual recruitment of troops on an emergency basis would entail, Mr. Hammarskjold believed, considerable time and effort, "unavoidable when new units are set up through joining together small groups of different nationalities." Furthermore, the Secretary-General was of the opinion that, for obvious political reasons, contingents should not be accepted from the permanent members of the Security Council. "It is my endeavour in the approaches to Governments", stated Mr. Hammarskjold, "to build up a panel sufficiently broad to permit such a choice of units as would provide for a balanced composition in the Force. Further planning and decisions on organization will to a large extent have to depend on the judgment of the Chief of Command and his staff."

Twenty-four Members on their own initiative offered to contribute to the Force. Ten of these offers were accepted to form a force of about 5,200 men. In determining the offers to be accepted, the Secretary-General was influenced by a variety of considerations, such as the need of an operationally well-rounded and balanced force including the necessary supporting units, the desirability of wide geographical representation on political grounds, and the wisdom of taking account of the sensitivities of the parties directly concerned, particularly Egypt, on whose territory the Force would operate. The suggestion has been made that Egypt exercised a veto over the inclusion of contingents from certain countries. The Secretary-General's position from the beginning was that Egypt, by agreeing to the Assembly's resolution of November 5, undertook to admit the Force as constituted by him and his staff, acting in consultation with the Chief of Command. Any right of veto was therefore denied in principle. In the case of Canada, the offer of supporting units was readily accepted, but the Canadian government was asked to hold in reserve the infantry battalion which it offered. There appear to have been two reasons for this: (1) General Burns at the time did not need foot soldiers but rather reconnaissance, air, transport, administration, signal, engineering and medical units and forces of that nature; and (2) the Egyptian government had warned that because of the similarity of the dress of the Canadian battalion (the Queen's own) to that of British units, there might be instances of mistaken identity on the part of the Egyptians and resulting incidents. In the case of Pakistan, the offer was apparently not accepted because it was felt that this would be unwise in view of some official utterances at the time which were highly critical of the Egyptian government. While the attitude of the Egyptian government in these two cases was undoubtedly a factor influencing the Secretary-General's decision, his position would appear to have been that with many more offers made than were needed, it was unwise to accept an offer which might jeopardize the success of the whole operation unless it was the only way of meeting a particular need.

In addition to the armed forces, other important contributions of services, facilities, and supplies have been made. Besides providing the staging area for the troops (Capodichino near Naples), the Italian government supplied accommodations, "mountains of spaghetti and cooperation of a sort that is rare even in wartime". Brazil, Canada, Italy, Switzerland, the United States and Yugoslavia donated airlift and other transport. At the Secretary-General's request, normal flight services were curtailed by Swissair during the early days of recruitment and were made available for UNEF transport. After November 15, this airline flew a regular service to Abu Suweir, the airfield near Ismalia which had been chosen by General Burns, in agreement with Egypt, for the preliminary landing of forces.

As we have seen, the responsibility placed upon the Secretary-General for the organization and direction of the Force was very great. By resolution 1001 of November 7, 1956, he was authorized to issue all regulations and instructions essential to the functioning of UNEF and "to take all other necessary administrative and executive actions." On February 20, 1957, after consultation with the Advisory Committee, the Secretary-General issued Regulations for UNEF in the exercise of this authority. In exercising his extensive powers, the Secretary-General acts subject to the authority of the

Assembly, and in consultation with an Advisory Committee composed of one representative from Brazil, Canada, Ceylon, Colombia, India, Norway and Pakistan. In addition to assisting Mr. Hammarskjold in his plans for the Force, this Committee is empowered to solicit reports from the Secretary-General and "to request, through the usual procedures, the convening of the General Assembly." It may also give notice to the Assembly "whenever matters arise which, in its opinion, are of such urgency and importance as to require consideration by the General Assembly itself".

"Full command authority" in respect to the operations of the Force is vested in the Chief of Command, Major-General E. L. M. Burns of Canada. He has "direct authority for the operation of the Force and for arrangements for the provision of facilities, supplies, and auxiliary services". In the exercise of this authority, however, he must act "in consultation with the Secretary-General". He has authority to designate the chain of command for the Force, and general responsibility for its good order and discipline.

Assisting the Secretary-General, his staff, and the Chief of Command in technical questions of logistics, supply and transportation, is a UNEF Military Staff comprising the military representatives of those states whose offers of troops for the Emergency Force were initially accepted by the Secretary-General—Canada, Colombia, Denmark, Finland, India, Norway, Sweden, and Yugoslavia. Having established headquarters in New York City, this group works in close cooperation with members of the Secretariat.

Legal Status of the Force

Agreement on the legal status of the Force was reached by an exchange of letters on February 8 between the Secretary-General and the government of Egypt. Article 23 of the agreement provides that the United Nations Emergency Force, as a subsidiary organ of the United Nations, is entitled under Article 105 of the Charter to all privileges and immunities necessary for the fulfillment of its purposes in the territories of Member states. Enumeration of these rights and prerogatives is set forth in the General Convention on the Privileges and Immunities of the United Nations to which Egypt acceded on September 17, 1948. Furthermore, provisions of Article II, section 2, are declared to apply to "the property, funds and assets of Participating States used in Egypt in connection with the national contingents serving with the United Nations Emergency Force". The right of the Force to import, free of duty, equipment, provisions and supplies is recognized.

The Commander of UNEF and his family enjoy "the privileges and immunities, exemptions and facilities accorded to diplomatic envoys, in accordance with international law". Officers serving with the United Nations Command are entitled to coverage of Article VI of the Convention which applies to "experts performing missions for the United Nations". To these officers are extended "such privileges and immunities as are necessary for the independent exercise of their functions during the period of their missions. . . . In particular they shall be accorded: (a) immunity from personal arrest or detention . . . ; (b) in respect of words spoken or written and acts done by them in the course of the performance of their mission, immunity from legal process of every kind . . ." Members of the Secretariat serving with the Force are entitled to protection under Articles V and VII, which designate them as "officials of the United Nations" and grant them, *inter alia,* immunity from all legal processes connected with their official work.

The Regulations for UNEF stress the international character of the Force. Although members of UNEF remain in their national service, they are, during the period of their assignment to the United Nations Command, international personnel under the authority of Major-General Burns. Therefore, members of the Force are called upon to discharge their functions and regulate their conduct with the interest of the United Nations only in view. This requires members of the Force to "exercise the utmost discretion in regard to all matters relating to their duties and functions" and to refrain from communicating "to any person any information known to them by reason of their position with the Force which has not been made public, except in the course of their duties or by authorization of the Commander". It also entails the duty "to respect the law and regulations of a Host State and to refrain from any activities of a political character in a Host State".

Members of the UNEF are subject to the exclusive jurisdiction of their respective national states in respect of any criminal offenses which may be committed by them in Egypt. . . .

The February 8 agreement also provides that no member of UNEF is subject to the civil jurisdiction of the Egyptian courts or to other legal process in any matter relating to his official duties. "In those cases where civil jurisdiction is exercised by Egyptian courts with respect to members of the Force, the Egyptian courts and authorities shall grant members of the Force sufficient opportunity to safeguard their rights."

Areas for headquarters and camps and other premises necessary for the accommodation and fulfillment of the function of the Force are provided by the Egyptian government in agreement with the Commander. "These premises remain Egyptian territory but inviolable and subject to the exclusive control and authority of the Commander, who alone may consent to the entry of officials to perform their duties." Use of roads, waterways, port facilities, airfields, and railroads by the Force is allowed without the payment of dues, taxes or tolls.

Financing the Force

The total expense incurred by the operation of UNEF is not inconsequential. Salaries and equipment of individual soldiers are paid and supplied by their national governments but UNEF itself is responsible for providing a certain amount of gear, transport, fuel, currency and food. A daily overseas allowance of one dollar a day for all members of the Force is provided by the United Nations.

In his report of November 21, 1956, on administrative and financial arrangements for UNEF, the Secretary-General recommended that the finances of the Force be handled under a Special Account outside the normal budget and "that the expenses of the Force be allocated to Member States on the basis of the scale of assessments to be adopted for the United Nations budget for 1957". Moreover, Mr. Hammarskjold suggested that the Assembly, as an initial assessment, appropriate the amount of $10 million to the Special Account. In order to meet the immediate cash needs of the Force, the Secretary-General requested Assembly approval "to advance monies from the United Nations Working Capital Fund to the Special Account and, should the necessity arise, to seek other means of providing for cash needs". The General Assembly established the Special Account in the initial amount of $10 million on November 26, 1956, and requested the Secretary-General to issue such rules and regulations to govern it as he deemed necessary. . . .

In the Fifth Committee a number of delegates, including the United States representative, voiced the opinion that since UNEF had been established by overwhelming vote of the Assembly, Member states must assume full responsibility for its effective functioning. In consequence, they believed that the expenses of UNEF could be considered as a United Nations expenditure within the general scope and spirit of Article 17 of the Charter to be shared in conformity with the scale of assessments applied to the regular budget.

Other delegations, as for example the Danish, expressed the view that the position of those countries which had contributed troops to the Emergency Force should be taken into consideration and their financial contributions reduced accordingly. The financial burden involved for other members was "small compared to the huge damages that would have been suffered by all countries throughout the world in the case of a major conflict. It would be of importance in the future if the United Nations assumed responsibility for the expenses of the Emergency Force."

Another suggestion was that a part of the costs should be borne by the five permanent members of the Security Council, considering their primary responsibility for the maintenance of peace, and the remainder by all Members of the Organization, including the five permanent members. Still other proposals entailed financing on the basis of voluntary contributions.

The delegates of the "Soviet bloc" insisted that the collective sharing of the costs of the Emergency Force was neither right nor proper and that therefore reference to Article 17 of the Charter was irrelevant to the point at issue. They maintained that all the material costs of the operation should be borne by those governments which had precipitated the crisis; they would thus not consider themselves bound by any resolution which provided that UNEF costs should be borne by the United Nations.

The draft resolution which was finally recommended by the Committee by a vote of 57 in favor, 8 against and 9 abstentions, and adopted by the Assembly on December 21, 1956, provided "that the expenses of UNEF, other than for such pay, equipment, supplies, and services as may be furnished without charge by Member Governments, shall be borne by the United Nations and shall be apportioned among Member States to the extent of $10 million in accordance with the scale of assessment adopted by the General Assembly for contributions to the annual budget of the organization for the financial year 1957; . . . [that] this decision shall be without prejudice to the subsequent apportionment of any expenses in excess of $10 million which may be incurred in connection with UNEF." A Committee composed of Canada, Ceylon, Chile, El Salvador, India, Liberia, Sweden, the Soviet Union and the United States was established to examine the question of apportionment of expenses of the Force in excess of $10 million.

The initial appropriation of $10 million to cover UNEF expenses amounted to a 20 percent increase in the normal budget of the United Nations and a corresponding increase in each nation's contribution. Since this original estimate, the United Nations has been obliged to budget an additional $6,500,000 to meet expenses during 1957. To cover this additional appropriation the Assembly on February 26 invited voluntary contributions from Member states.

Future of UNEF

Diverse opinions have been expressed with respect to the future of UNEF. Mr. Munro of New Zealand, for example, stated in the Assembly that "the Force, in the performance of its functions of securing and supervising the cessation of hostilities, should remain in the area at least until the Suez and Aqaba issues are settled and some progress is made towards an overall settlement". He believed that the decision to withdraw the Force should be a matter for the United Nations to decide, not Egypt or any other country. According to the Israel delegate, UNEF's term of assignment will not be completed until a final settlement is obtained between Israel and Egypt. The representative from France would have the Force "used as long as the situation may require it and at any place where the complete implementation of the resolution of 2 November would make its presence useful in the maintenance of peace". On the other hand, the Soviet Union and the members of the Soviet bloc have maintained that following the withdrawal of foreign forces from Egypt, United Nations units have no further function to perform in the country. The Ukrainian delegate insisted on February 2 that "the United Nations Emergency Force as a whole carried out its task, and any continuation of its presence in Egypt would only aggravate the situation because certain circles are striving to utilize these forces for their own interests and advantage and against the interests of the Egyptian people."

. . . For the time being the situation in the Middle East is relatively quiet. UNEF units patrol the demarcation line between Egypt and Israel and along the Gulf of Aqaba. They are the only armed forces in the Gaza Strip, and in most of the Sinai Peninsula. For the time being their presence in

Egyptian territory and the performance of their duties under Assembly resolutions are accepted by the Egyptian government. Nevertheless there are unresolved problems that may create difficulties. The Israeli government does not admit that the armistice agreement is in force nor will it agree to the stationing of UNEF units on its side of the demarcation line, as recommended by the Assembly. If the Egyptian government comes to feel that the present arrangement no longer serves its interests and demands the withdrawal of the Force, it is unlikely that this demand will be resisted for long. Furthermore, there is strong likelihood that if such a demand is made or Egyptian dissatisfaction is expressed, some of the contributing Members will withdraw their contingents. While their legal right to do so may not be admitted by United Nations organs, the chances are that no effective resistance to such action will be made. Finally, there is the financial problem. If maintaining the Force means a substantial increase in the United Nations assessment of each Member, there is likely to be a decline of enthusiasm for it. The best chance of its continuation pending a satisfactory political settlement between Israel and Egypt would seem to lie in getting Israel to accept the validity of the armistice agreement and in merging UNEF with the Truce Supervision Organization in a system of more effective implementation.

The UNEF experience may well prove, however, to be of permanent consequence. As the Secretary-General has observed, "this force, although modest in size and, for constitutional reasons, also modest in aim, broke new ground which inevitably will count in future efforts to preserve peace and promote justice." Responsible and serious thought is being given to the establishment of a permanent United Nations force which will be available at all times to assist in the maintenance of international peace. What kind of force can reasonably be envisaged in the light of UNEF experience, against the background of over ten years of relative frustration, is a question that deserves serious consideration.

It would seem reasonably clear that if such a force is to be established it will be done on the basis of a resolution of the General Assembly. That being the case, the general approval and consent of the United Nations membership becomes vitally important. It would seem quite unrealistic to envisage a force with enforcement responsibilities. Any force that will be widely acceptable will in all likelihood be restricted to the performance of functions similar to those of UNEF—securing a cease-fire, supervising an armistice, patrolling a frontier, maintaining order in a plebiscite area. While there are appealing arguments for a force composed of persons individually recruited, equipped, trained and maintained by the United Nations itself, the practical difficulties in the way of organizing and maintaining such a force seem prohibitive. There would be the necessity of a permanent base or bases and a larger budget than probably would be politically possible, to mention only two of the difficulties that would be encountered. It probably will be necessary to settle for a force composed of national contingents maintained and supported, when not on United Nations missions, as units of national armed forces. These contingents should preferably be contributed by members other than the permanent members of the Security Council.

In what sense would this be a permanent United Nations force? The commander and his staff would be permanent United Nations officials, appointed by the Secretary-General. They would have responsibility for preparing plans for the use of the force, including model agreements on member contributions, the conditions of entry of the force into the territory of a state, and the status of the force within the territory of a state. They would advise the Secretary-General on military aspects of his responsibilities and would be available to assist in the interpretation and implementation of cease-fire, truce and armistice agreements. They would assume command responsibilities when it became necessary to organize and use a force for specific purposes. While the force other than staff would consist of national contingents, Members would be expected in advance to pledge the use of these contingents for the purposes of the force. The pledges would provide a panel from which the Secretary-General, acting on the advice of the commander and his staff, could draw, in organizing a force for a particular purpose defined by the General Assembly or the Security Council.

It is clear that a force of this nature is a far cry from an international police force capable of enforcing peace wherever or whenever it may be threatened or disturbed. Rather, following the example of UNEF, it would be a force used in discharge of the United Nations' responsibilities for creating conditions favorable to achieving a peaceful settlement. It would make available "an intermediate technique between merely passing resolutions and actually fighting."

Force for U.N.*

Lester B. Pearson

Peace, one might think, is not the sort of human occupation which should normally require supervision. Yet the United Nations, instead of concentrating on more positive and progressive activities, has ever since its inception been engaged in supervising a kind of peace which has been not much more than the absence of fighting—and not always even that. Now policing a peace—or an armistice—can be an essential international function,

* Lester B. Pearson, "Force for U.N.," *Foreign Affairs,* Vol. 35, No. 3 (April 1957), pp. 395-404. Reprinted by permission. Lester B. Pearson, currently the fourteenth Prime Minister of Canada, is a recipient of the Nobel Peace Prize (1957). He has served as Canada's Ambassador to the United States and Delegate to the United Nations. His books include *Democracy in World Politics* (1955) and *Diplomacy in the Nuclear Age* (1959).

at times a dramatic one. It cannot be denied that the United Nations has been successful in this function in some important cases. However, action in this field has been largely pragmatic and ad hoc. I believe—and recent events have strengthened my belief—that the time has come when we should seek ways to enable the United Nations to pursue this work in a more organized and permanent way. . . .

As we have seen, however, hopes for ensuring collective security were not fulfilled. The Security Council remained powerless to provide such security and the Assembly was unorganized for this purpose. In view of the undiminished threat from the Soviet Union, which had a preponderance in armed forces and pursued aggressive policies, certain members of the United Nations sought for a regional means of providing for their mutual defense within the framework of the organization. The North Atlantic Treaty, for example, was created and exists only because of the failure to attain a really effective system of collective security on a universal basis.

The search for means to establish a universal system nevertheless continued. Against the sombre background of events in Korea, members of the United Nations reviewed again the collective security machinery available, with the result that in the autumn of 1950 the Assembly adopted a resolution which potentially was of great importance. The Uniting for Peace Resolution, as it came to be called, meant simply that the General Assembly had decided to provide machinery for utilizing certain powers which it already possessed. The resolution did not itself constitute any revolutionary departure in interpreting the Charter; it was conceived simply as a practical measure designed to meet certain situations in which the purposes of the United Nations might be frustrated by the negative attitude of a permanent member of the Security Council. The General Assembly was to be used for security purposes only when the Security Council failed to perform, or was prevented from performing, its primary function. If the Council acted, nothing in the resolution would interfere with its action.

But if the Security Council did not act, what then? Were we to admit frankly the failure of our United Nations peace machinery and fall back entirely upon regional collective security arrangements such as NATO? While filling a gap, these obviously were limited in scope or character. Surely, it was thought, some way could be found for the United Nations to provide a force which would at least halt a drift to war by helping to carry out an Assembly recommendation when the Security Council failed to act. True, according to the Charter the Assembly had no legal power of enforcement and could act only by recommendation. Nevertheless, in terms of persuasiveness and moral force, the Assembly's recommendations, if responsibly conceived and generally accepted (two very weighty provisos), would carry as much weight as those of the Security Council—perhaps more. So why not at least make available some machinery which might carry them out?

Such was the background of the Uniting for Peace Resolution. It provided, among other things, that an emergency session of the Assembly might be called on 24 hours' notice for the purpose of making recommendations if the Security Council had failed to agree on means of resisting a breach of the peace or an act of aggression. It also called for the establishment of a Collective Measures Committee to study methods which might be used to strengthen the collective security machinery. . . .

As a whole, the efforts of the Collective Measures Committee were sterile. With the General Assembly's adoption of its third report on November 4, 1954, it concluded its work. Another series of studies had been accumulated and now were laid away in files and vaults. The United Nations, nine years after its founding, still had no force at its disposal to implement its decisions—even to "secure and supervise" a cease-fire and armistice.

Nevertheless, the Uniting for Peace Resolution remained on the books; and almost six years later, in November 1956, in circumstances very different from those contemplated by its authors, it enabled the General Assembly to meet and discuss in emergency special session the serious situation in the Middle East. The Assembly still was ill-prepared to take on responsibilities for "peace supervision" through police action. The Uniting for Peace Resolution recommended the earmarking of forces for its use in peace and police action, but nothing had been done. When the need for these forces was upon us we had to embark on an improvised experiment, starting literally from nothing. There was neither precedent nor organization available to the Assembly in carrying out the new responsibility thrust upon it.

In a sense this was due to the unexpected nature of this responsibility. With fighting actually going on and threatening to spread, quick action was required. In the crisis, an Assembly resolution set up a United Nations Emergency Force and authorized the Secretary-General to organize it within 48 hours. Due largely to the devotion, energy and intelligence of the Secretary-General and his assistants, the Force was in fact brought into being at once. This amazing example of international improvisation showed what can be done by the United Nations when the collective will to action is strong and united. Moreover, the Force has so far proved effective for the purpose it was meant to achieve, the securing and supervising of a cease-fire.

Nevertheless, these purposes were very different from those originally contemplated in the Charter. What we faced in the Assembly last November was the necessity of organizing quickly a force, not to fight, but to ensure that fighting would not be resumed. We were trying to implement, if not a new concept of United Nations supervisory action, certainly an enlarged one.

Such a concept has already stirred interest and hope and optimism. Some of this optimism is exaggerated, because it does not take sufficiently into consideration the limitations under which the Assembly must act. There can be no certainty that the UNEF will complete successfully the tasks that have been or may be given to it. It may fail, either because it does not secure the right kind of collective backing in the Assembly or because it becomes the victim of Middle Eastern politics. If so, the failure will extend far beyond the immediate situation. It will destroy confidence in the effectiveness of the United Nations in the whole field of security. On the other hand, its success might well lead to further steps in developing means to supervise the peace.

Whatever may be the ultimate result, the intervention of the United Nations through an Emergency Force in November 1956 was certainly an indispensable prerequisite to the acceptance of a cease-fire and the subsequent withdrawal of Anglo-French and Israeli forces from Egyptian territory. Its action also emphasized, however, the need to be better prepared to meet future situations of a similar kind. Even if governments are unable to give the United Nations a "fighting" force ready and organized to serve it on the decision of the Security Council, they should be willing to earmark smaller forces for the more limited duty of securing a cease-fire already agreed upon by the belligerents. We might in this way be able to construct a halfway house at the crossroads of war, and utilize an intermediate technique between merely passing resolutions and actually fighting.

The first step would seem to be to create a permanent mechanism by which units of the armed forces of member countries could be endowed with the authority of the United Nations and made available at short notice for supervisory police duties. It is not suggested that the present Emergency Force should become a permanent force or, indeed, that its functions should be extended beyond those laid down in the relevant Assembly resolutions. We should, nevertheless, build upon the experience of this enterprise. Otherwise, I repeat, we shall only go back again to the situation in which we found ourselves last November, when everything had to be improvised, when there was no precedent for making units available, no administrative and financial procedure and no organization to which the Secretary-General could turn in the task given him by the Assembly of putting a United Nations force into a dangerous and delicate situation. We improvised successfully then. We cannot reasonably expect the same degree of success a second time.

We now have at our disposal a body of experience from which can be developed some tentative principles governing the establishment of United Nations machinery and, as required, a Peace Supervision Force. Among these principles—some of which I have already referred to—the following strike me as forming an essential minimum.

Member governments, excluding the permanent members of the Security Council, should be invited to signify a willingness in principle to contribute contingents to the United Nations for purposes that are essentially noncombatant, such as, for example, the supervision of agreed cease-fires and comparable peace supervisory functions.

Since the Security Council is charged with the primary responsibility for the maintenance of peace, members who have sought and secured election to the non-permanent seats on it would normally be expected to be among those signifying a willingness to contribute contingents to such a force.

For effective organization, there would have to be some central United Nations machinery. The Secretary-General should have a permanent Military Adviser who, with a small staff, might assume responsibility for the direction of other truce supervision arrangements which have been or might be agreed on.

If at any time a Peace Supervision Force were constituted, the Secretary-General would require an advisory committee similar to that which now assists him in connection with the UNEF in Egypt.

While such a force is not primarily a fighting force, it must be capable of defending itself once it is in the field, since the inherent duty of a commander is to preserve the safety of his men. It should also include the necessary administrative and supporting elements to enable it to function effectively as an entity.

A force to deal with a particular situation could be established by a resolution either of the Security Council or of the General Assembly. Presumably it would be associated with efforts made by the United Nations towards assisting in the settlement of the dispute. These efforts in turn could be furthered by a revitalized Peace Observation Commission given real responsibility to investigate disputes. In a sense, a Peace Supervision Force would be an extension in space of the Peace Observation Commission and the subordinate bodies it was expected to produce.

By its very nature such a force would not be expected to fight its way into a country. Indeed, since it would be deployed upon recommendation of the United Nations, it could enter a country only with the consent of the government of that country. This consent would normally take the form of an agreement between the government concerned and the Secretary-General acting on behalf of the United Nations. To facilitate the negotiation of such agreements, and also to expedite the creation of a force when required, the Secretary-General should be requested to draw up model agreements regarding the financial, administrative and legal procedures which would govern the operations of a Peace Supervision Force. The agreement recently negotiated between the United States and Egypt on arrangements concerning the status of the UNEF in that country would provide a very useful example of what can be done in this regard.

It is my firm conviction that the sort of machinery I have outlined, and the kind of United Nations force that would be expected to function through it, are practicable, are within the competence of the General Assembly, and might be of great value in avoiding, ending or limiting hostilities. The early arrival of a United Nations force of this kind at a scene of emergency would give assurance to the fearful and hope to the despairing. It would act as the United Nations policeman and his watchdog.

How these arrangements would function would, of course, depend on the circumstances of the particular emergency to be met. Actually, there is nothing so very new in all this. The United Nations has on more than one occasion provided teams of truce observers or supervisors and has now set up an emergency force to enlarge that activity where the danger of renewed fighting, pending the working out of a settlement, required it. A synthesis and systemization of these two concepts would provide a base of departure for the future.

As always, in the last resort, individual governments must determine whether the best laid plans of the United Nations are to succeed or fail. If a plan anything like that which I have outlined is to succeed, governments must, both within and outside the United Nations, follow policies consistent with its objectives and its capabilities. The very least each of our governments can now do, it seems to me, is to draft, in accordance with our respective constitutional processes, whatever measures are required to place us in a better position to support agreed decisions of the United Nations in an emergency. Are we to go on from crisis to crisis improvising in haste? Or can we now pool our experience and our resources, so that the next time we, the governments and peoples whom the United Nations represents, will be ready and prepared to act?

The Political and Philosophical Aspects of U.N. Security Forces*

John W. Holmes

. . .

One is faced at the beginning with a problem of definition. Our principal interest is in the Gaza and Congo forces, but the product of United Nations experience has been not a single kind of international force but rather a variety of supervisory armies, observer corps, border patrols, ranging from small groups of officers to military units numbering thousands. Much of their virtue lies in their diversity. It is hard to identify what they have in common except that they are all "forces" which accomplish their missions not really by force at all but by the persuasion of their presence. As is known from the Congo experience, there is still need to limit the use of force to accord with varying situations. This kind of intervention is most effective when the military force is associated with a United Nations mediatory presence. It is more closely related in kind to the non-military

* John W. Holmes, "The Political and Philosophical Aspects of U.N. Security Forces," *International Journal*, Vol. XIX, No. 3 (Summer 1964), pp. 292-307. Reprinted by permission. John W. Holmes currently is President, Canadian Institute of International Affairs.

mediation of the United Nations between Cambodia and Thailand, for example, than to the United Nations single effort at collective security action in Korea. This is not collective security action in the proper sense of the term at all. The force, as an instrument of the United Nations, armed or unarmed, interposes rather than enforces, develops the United Nations role neither as a policeman nor an avenging fury but as an objective entity. The United Nations accepts as inevitable the quarrelsomeness of its members and seeks in this way only to get them to agree. The pure objectivity of the force, however, is far from absolute. The United Nations often does not pretend to be neutral in these disputes. It may provide a force as in Yemen without any commitment on the merits of the case, and it may seek to be uncommitted in internal disputes as in Lebanon or the Congo. However, over Congo or Suez, United Nations bodies adopted moral positions on aspects of the issues at stake. In the light of United Nations opposition to certain parties in the Suez and Congo cases, some element of enforcement was implicit in the very United Nations presence, even if the military power was by no means adequate to impose a United Nations will.

There is no generalization which accurately fits all these things. The function of these bodies is adapted and adjusted to accord with the moral and military strength the United Nations musters in the particular situation and in the certainty of its convictions about the rights and wrongs of the case. The certainty of its convictions, needless to say, is determined not just by the validity of the respective arguments of the disputants but also by the weight which their partisans can throw about in United Nations councils. The power and authority are affected by the degree of unanimity which exists in the United Nations—and particularly among the leading powers.

A perceptive explanation of the function of United Nations peace-keeping forces as now developed is given by Inis Claude in his *Power and International Relations:*

This . . . is not a device for defeating aggressors—and certainly not for coercing great powers determined to expand the sphere of their control—but for assisting the major powers in avoiding the expansion and sharpening of their conflicts and the consequent degeneration of whatever stability they may have been able to achieve in their mutual relationships. The best hope for the United Nations is not that it may be able to develop a military establishment which will enable it to exercise coercive control over great powers, but that it may be able to continue the development of its capability to serve the interests of the great powers—and of the rest of the world—by helping them to contain their conflicts, to limit their competition, and to stabilize their relationships. The greatest political contribution of the United Nations in our time to the management of international power relationships lies not in implementing collective security or instituting world government, but in helping to improve and stabilize the working of the balance of power system, which is, for better or for worse, the operative mechanism of contemporary international politics. The immediate task, in short, is to make the world safe for the balance of power system, and the balance system safe for the world.

Professor Claude's definition sets out United Nations security forces in their place in the history of international relations. We might at this point look at our accumulated United Nations peace-keeping experience in relation to two concepts of international forces: first, the persistent anticipation of an "international police force" capable of enforcing world law or agreed international decisions anywhere in the world; and secondly, the San Francisco plan embodied in the United Nations Charter for a security force composed of national contingents placed at the disposal of the United Nations and acting on the basis of great power consensus.

With the concept of an "international police force" this United Nations peace-keeping has little in common. It is generically different because it is based on a quite different view of the relations among peoples. The "international police force" assumes a delegation of supreme authority to a world federal government or at least to some authority with supreme security functions. Such a force, to exercise unquestioned power, would have to operate in a virtually disarmed world. Our kind of peace-keeping assumes the necessity of acting in a world in which military power is controlled by states, although the states may on occasions delegate military force for international assignments. That this is the kind of world we are going to live in for a long time to come—unless we expire in it—is the most prudent assumption. It is not likely to be changed merely by imprecations against the wickedness of national sovereignty, because the disorders which trouble us have their roots not in the petty stubbornness of nation states but in the disorderly contours of the earth's surface and the multiplicity of tribes who inhabit it. Inter-tribal conflicts would outlive the destruction or sublimation of national sovereignty. My own view is that for an inherently disorderly universe a flexible array of sovereign states of varying shapes and sizes is probably the safest system of government, and the world is less likely to blow up if we have a United Nations of a non-federal kind and peace-keeping methods which are essentially diplomatic in character. The difference between these two concepts—our peace-keeping and the international police force—seems to me so clear I hesitate to labour the obvious. The only real question is whether or not we should see in the Gaza and Congo forces the nucleus of an "international police force." One can be misled by seeing too much significance in what have been reasonably successful experiments with polyglot military units. It is not, however, the composition of the international force but the control of it which is crucial. We are not within far distant sight of an international authority capable of mounting and directing an international police. It is, in fact, too early to say whether the "international police force" is our goal at all. In the meantime, assuming that it is, could lead us into experiments which are bound to fail and destroy with them the sound precedents which have been established.

Although it is customary to decry the illusions of the constitution-makers at Yalta, Dumbarton Oaks, and San Francisco, they were closer to earth than are those who dream of the "international police force." If we want to make progress from where we stand we might better set as our target the kind of force envisaged in Article 43, approaching it, however, enriched by the variety of experience we have had in United Nations peace-keeping by means never envisaged in 1945. The kind of peace-keeping we have developed did not, of course, have its roots in Article 43; it developed when the effort by the Military Staff Committee to implement Article 43 failed. The essence of the San Francisco principle of security was the delegation by member states, especially the great powers, of forces to serve the purposes of the United Nations. Those purposes would be enforceable because they would be supported by the great powers—or if not supported by all of them, at least not actively opposed by any great power. The principle broke down, not because it was intrinsically unsound, but because the great powers moved rapidly away from consensus.

The kind of peace-keeping functions the United Nations has developed did not come as a conscious alternative to Article 43; they just evolved out of necessity. The experiment started before, and was resumed after, the Korean experience convinced most people that, although the Korean effort was by no means a failure, it was *sui generis* and did not provide a precedent for United Nations collective security action which could be followed again. The early experience of United Nations intervention in Greece, Indonesia, Kashmir, Palestine were steps on the way to the much bolder experiment of UNEF, and the remarkable success of UNEF set a pattern for the plunge into the Congo. These achievements were pragmatic. I don't believe anyone, scholar or bureaucrat, had articulated in advance this particular kind of middle power operation, although Mr. Trygve Lie certainly deserves credit for adumbrating, in his early proposals for a United Nations Guard Force, the concept of a limited United Nations body of a military kind capable of maintaining in troubled areas the agents of United Nations mediation. Now, of course, we have a great deal of theory being expounded about this kind of peace-keeping, but it is a codification of what has taken place and a projection of past experience into the future—and all the sounder for being that. There was never a deliberate intention in setting up United Nations forces as we know them to set the United Nations off on a different course from that which had been contemplated in the Charter. It was an effort to cope as well as possible with the dangerous situations which flared all over the world during a period of great power disunity. It was in fact the United Nations groping, with lesser powers as its agents, to take advantage of the elemental but tacit consensus which did exist among the great powers, the consensus of fear of uncontrollable conflict. That consensus was neither strong nor explicit enough for the great powers to act directly by combination of their own forces, but they were prepared to let others act. Some of the great powers viewed these events with, to say the least, very little enthusiasm, but their fear of conflict and their deference to a United Nations majority have held them back from bold enough opposition to wreck the operations.

The kind of United Nations security forces we are talking about, in which lesser rather than great powers make personnel available for United Nations purposes, is a great deal closer in kind to the San Francisco concept than to the idea of an "international police force." The difference, which is admittedly great, lies in the scope of action which can be envisaged without great power participation. We must be extremely wary of assuming that the rudimentary peace-keeping we have been able to develop could, in the absence of a far larger degree of great power consensus than now exists, be pushed to fulfil the collective security function which the framers of the Charter had in mind. It should not be forgotten, however, that it was not the intention of the great powers who drafted the essential principles of the Charter that the United Nations security provisions should be implemented against any of them; that denial was implicit in the provision for the veto on which they all insisted. It is the extent of great power consensus rather than any fundamental difference between the principle of Articles 42 and 43 on the one hand and the principle of UNEF or ONUC on the other which determines whether or not United Nations security forces can expand the area of their competence.

There is much reason for gratification with the results so far achieved. Fighting was stopped in Greece, Indonesia, Kashmir. Relative stability was established in the Middle East. The Congo has a chance. The fact that all this has been achieved to a considerable extent by diplomatic pressures of the great powers outside the United Nations is no reason for despondency about the United Nations role. The United Nations is essentially a broad framework. It is a purpose of United Nations peace-keeping to be associated with or to be an agent of the direct negotiation between disputants or their intermediaries. What, it might be asked, is outside the United Nations if it contributes to a reasonable settlement of disputes? In addition to these specific achievements in various parts of the planet has been the experience of international collaboration. Brian Urquhart, who should know, put it this way:

The thousands of soldiers from some twenty countries who accepted the challenge in the Congo have begun to learn to apply the arts of war to the infinitely subtle and difficult problems of maintaining the peace—this may be a development of more lasting importance than what eventually does or does not happen in the Congo itself.

The accomplishments of United Nations peace-keeping should not be underestimated; and yet they raise certain difficult questions not only about the future of United Nations peace-keeping but about the record.

The basic thesis of these enterprises is that our object is to stop the fighting to provide an opportunity for negotiated settlement. A settlement was achieved in Indonesia, although it may have set a precedent for a later United Nations role in West Irian that was more a face-saving than a peace-keeping operation. There is no settlement after fifteen years in Kashmir or

Palestine. The United Nations Military Observer Group in India and Pakistan (UNMOPIG) and United Nations Truce Supervision Organization (UNTSO) look like being permanent establishments. UNEF has provided a framework for a temporary peace, but lasting peace seems no nearer. The United Nations Observer Group in Lebanon (UNOGIL) did help to make possible a transition of political power in Lebanon, although some might argue that this was achieved by the intervention of the U.S. Marines. A final verdict on the accomplishment of ONUC cannot yet be given with assurance. It is said, of course, that the cost of maintaining these establishments is relatively small in an armed world and well worth while. Fighting has been contained, although the aim of promoting settlement has all too seldom been achieved.

A more disturbing question is whether the intervention of the United Nations made a lasting settlement more difficult. We live in a world in the throes of violent change, of old discontents, new and unstable governments, empires in fission and drastic inequalities. Is the achievement of a new stability dependent on the completion of violent solutions whether they are in the abstract good or bad? Would the sub-continent, for instance, be more or less tranquil if the situation had been frozen after rather than before the Pakistanis secured a solution by force? Would there be less ferment in the Middle East if the Israelis had been able to consolidate their positions on the old borders of Palestine; or in Central Africa if some strongman had had a chance to establish his authority by force over the whole of the Congo before the United Nations arrived on the scene in 1960? Or consider the obverse argument: how happy would we be if the United Nations, in accordance with peace-keeping precedents, had established a United Nations presence with force to promote a peaceful settlement in Goa before the Indians took direct action? Without United Nations intervention in Palestine or Congo there would of course have been bitterness and continuing tension; but would the rough arbitrament of the violent solution have provided a better base for progress in the area than the perpetuation of uncertainty and the immobility imposed by the United Nations presence? And the cost of this is that the United Nations is involved indefinitely in financial drains which threaten its health and have led its major members into an impasse that could wreck the organization. Should we not at least have tied the continuing presence of a costly United Nations force to a commitment of the disputants to serious negotiation?

Of course, I think the answer to these questions is no. It seems to me that although the second and major half of our aim has not been accomplished, it was still worth while to stop the fighting. The fighting may not have spread, and the great powers may not have become involved as we feared, but the risk of these things happening was too great to be taken. History is long, and fifteen years is not an excessive period in which to wait for peace to come when the grudge is ancient. We ought to show the same patience with small cold wars as we are learning to show over the big one.

This is how it appears to me but I have been too much involved in these things ever to see them objectively. Nor has my country ever been tranquillized or paralyzed by United Nations peace-keeping. We can never know what might have happened, and we dare not assume that the way history worked itself out was the right way. We have to keep these hypothetical but nasty questions before us if for no other reason than to recognize that we must be discriminating in the application of this kind of United Nations force. There is no generally valid answer. The intervention of United Nations forces may have been wrong in some past cases and right in others.

We tend too early to accept as categorical the distinctions between disputes in which the great powers are and those in which they are not directly involved. We tend to dismiss the Korean crisis of 1950 by explaining that it has nothing to do with our kind of peace-keeping. Well, it may not belong to this chapter of the book, but it was a very real crisis. There is no guarantee that there will not be more like it, and the United Nations will not be able simply to declare it out of bounds. On the other hand, would it have been better to try in Korea our more conventional kind of United Nations peace-keeping? Would it have been better for the United Nations to remain uncommitted as a belligerent and keep itself available for good offices in the settlement? If the United Nations had left the fighting to the immediate parties and their great and small power friends, might it have had a better chance to be the *deus ex machina* when the truce was in sight? Would we thereby have avoided the Chinese argument that the United Nations, as a belligerent, had forfeited any right to an arbitral role in the reunification of Korea? As one who was present at Lake Success in the summer of 1950, I do not see how we could have acted otherwise. We were still perhaps beguiled by the collective security concept of the United Nations function, and this looked like a challenge to United Nations authority before which it would be fatal to fail. The implications of the balance of terror had not yet been absorbed. Nevertheless, the hypothetical questions about Korea we must ask ourselves in retrospect so that we shall calculate wisely in the next crisis.

A final and quite unrelated question is whether we may now be in danger of letting the United Nations become a mere service agency, hiring out policemen to maintain agreements in which it plays no part. In West Irian and Yemen the United Nations had no real say at all in the truces or settlements agreed on by the parties with the good offices or pressure of great powers; and yet it has organized the supervision. As I have suggested earlier, one must not under present circumstances reject reasonable settlements reached off the United Nations premises. However, the United Nations must be sure they are reasonable before it accepts responsibility for maintaining them. While avoiding the pretension to settle all disputes by its captious majorities, the United Nations must at the same time avoid the humiliation of being used by powers, great or small, for their private purposes.

Each of these questions could be exhaustively argued, and there is no final answer. However, we ought not to let our enthusiasm for accomplishments prevent us from keeping these doubts in the back of our minds.

We are confronted now, and particularly since July, 1960, with a conflict between political and practical realities. The United Nations has been conducting military operations which defy every rule of good soldiering. The world political situation, however, is such that another United Nations force is likely to be required at any time, but a direct attack on the military problems seems impossible.

The argument for a nucleus of a permanent force, at the very least a considerable military establishment in the Secretariat, the training of standby forces, perhaps even United Nations bases and a United Nations intelligence network seems to this layman incontrovertible. It is clear, however, that for international political reasons a standing United Nations force is out of the question. The consensus does not exist which would authorize us to go very far beyond Dag Hammarskjold's recommendation of a force formed *ad hoc* from standby forces in contributing countries, and it is politically unwise for a westerner to push. The political advantages of spontaneous improvisation are great, and it is tempting for statesmen, diplomats, and theorists like me to be complacent, to say that it always has been worked out somehow and will the next time. But the history of ONUC provides too much proof of what a near thing it was—so much luck, so much depending on heroic improvisation and the availability of remarkable men. We must press hard and with as sound a diplomatic base as possible to achieve at least minimal improvements: extension of Secretariat functions, establishment of precedents and procedure, reliable financial provisions, training of experts—if not undertaken by the United Nations itself, possibly by some unofficial international institution growing out of this conference.

Aside from improving the machinery, is there any way we can extend the applicability of present procedures? The formal definition of bolder theories of peace-keeping by any United Nations sub-committee would be as futile as the attempt to define aggression. Every step forward has been taken in the pressure of necessity when the consensus enlarges. Still, we can in private think about the direction in which progress might move.

All plans for the future must be based on a recognition of the slender resources available—personnel and material, as well as financial. We shudder at the prospect of another crisis, because those in which we are still involved absorb all the people we can get. How could the Secretariat cope with another operation like ONUC? I hasten to recognize that I would have asked the same question before Congo, a challenge which revealed extraordinary resources from African states. Diplomats should not assume the United Nations cannot cope with another such challenge, but they should not forget that United Nations forces do not spring fully armed out of thin air.

Need we accept as permanently desirable that only middle and small powers—preferably uncommitted—should participate in United Nations security forces? The arguments for doing so are strong. Not only has this practice been good for the United Nations, it has been good for the middle powers. We of the middle powers have all felt that our contributions to United Nations forces have given us a purpose in the world which justified our existence. We have even been tempted into smugness *vis-à-vis* the quarrelsome and predatory great powers. It had been good, practical United Nations politics to emphasize the objectivity of the United Nations forces and attribute it to the chastity of the weak powers which manned them, forgetting that lesser powers can have even more vigorous special interests in disputes than remoter great powers. We have conveniently forgotten also the part the great powers have actually played in the operations. The United States role in UNEF and ONUC may have been confined to transport and general servicing, but it has been indispensable. Britain and the Soviet Union have also made facilities and transport available. I recognize of course, that the part the Soviet Union played may not be considered a contribution, and that it can be argued that the United States and Britain have pursued special interests. So have many of the lesser powers involved in the United Nations Force. Great powers can be neutral enough in some controversies. Consider, for instance, the role the United States is playing in the disputes involving Indonesia—and, I add hopefully, the role France might play in Asia.

In staffing international forces, we might be less absolute in our thinking. If we have to cope with new situations, we shall almost certainly have again to call on the Americans for help. If the trouble should come in the Western Hemisphere it would be better to ask the British and French. It would be much better, of course, if we could also make use of Soviet services. Despite the obvious disadvantages, the advantages of including the Russians could be much greater than merely helping with the logistics. It could assist in winning them from an attitude of mistrustful toleration of exercises in which no members of their camp participate to positive collaboration in United Nations peace-keeping. The extending United States-Soviet dialogue could conceivably make this possible. The inclusion of Soviet or Eastern European personnel in United Nations forces would be primarily a reflection of rather than a cause of changing great power relations. We should recognize, however, that the broadening of the composition of United Nations forces is something to be anticipated rather than avoided, even though the United Nations cannot safely move too far ahead of the great powers in a policy based on *détente*.

Only if there is collaboration among the great powers in peace-keeping can we ever hope to apply this United Nations function to the great issue of our time. I am not suggesting we could then enforce the principles of collective security on all powers. I am thinking only of peace-keeping roles extended, for instance, to Berlin. It would not be wise for the United Nations to venture in its councils to impose a settlement on Berlin, even if it were not prevented from doing so by Article 107. Nevertheless, if the great powers concerned were to reach an agreement which required neutral supervision, it is conceivable that the United Nations could fulfil that function. There are strong cases for and against the occupying powers doing any such thing, or the United Nations accepting an assignment not of its own making. We must, however, contemplate the possibility that such a role for the United Nations might be found helpful. I do not want to argue here the case for and against zones of disengagement or nuclear disarmament in Europe or elsewhere, but these, too, are possibilities for United Nations service, possibilities which would be useful experiments in testing United Nations supervision of disarmament provisions. They would almost certainly require participation not only of uncommitted forces but also of forces committed to both East and West. It should be borne in mind also, that United Nations supervision was part of the formula on which President Kennedy and Premier Khrushchev found a way out of the impasse in Cuba, even though this was not carried out for reasons which did not seem to involve the validity of United Nations supervision in principle. It is not as certain as commonly stated that United Nations security forces as we know them have no role to play in controversies between the great powers.

It is usually forgotten that we have had for a decade in Indo-China a reasonably successful example of a peace-keeping operation comparable to United Nations missions, established by the great powers and operating in an area where their interests clash dangerously. This precedent is largely ignored by writers on this subject, presumably because it is outside the United Nations. Here we have an example of the great powers, faced in 1954 with the imminent catastrophe of uncontrollable conflict, negotiating a truce even though two of the great powers were not speaking to each other. Supervisory commissions for Viet-Nam, Laos and Cambodia were authorized on the troika principle of one communist country, Poland; one Western country, Canada; with a neutral chairman, India. These commissions were surprisingly effective in the disengagement of troops and populations in the first year or so of the truce and since then in serving as a reminder of international concern in its maintenance. It goes without saying that the troika arrangement often produced deadlock and has seemed more intractable than an entirely neutral body would have been. However, it does represent the real facts of power in the area in a way a neutral commission would not have done. It is fatuous to hanker after a supervisory commission homogeneous enough to reach agreement if such a commission has no influence on the disputants. The truces have been roughly maintained by the equilibrium of those external pressures which were represented in the commissions. It is unfortunate that the deterioration of the truces has diverted attention from a peace-keeping experiment which would be a pilot project for the United Nations—a pilot project which provides warnings as well as precedents. It was at least one step forward from the formula of two Communist states and two neutral states which the United Nations established to supervise the truce in Korea and which resulted in total deadlock. Whether it would have been more effective as a United Nations project rather than remaining responsible to a conference of powers is an argument with much significance for our discussion. Certainly the participants would have welcomed United Nations acceptance of the burden of logistics and administration. The lack too of an objective international entity like the United Nations Secretariat meant that the commissions were less coherent or singleminded. On the other hand, this inchoate international mechanism aptly reflected the minimal consensus among the powers. It reflected also the unwillingness of the great powers, even with their veto rights, to concede to a United Nations body the right to interfere in an area of such crucial importance to their vital interests. It was not merely the need to include the Peking government in the arrangements that kept this operation outside the United Nations. Even if the great powers in future are disposed to leave supervision of their settlements to the United Nations, they are likely to keep the United Nations as far removed as possible from the politics of the settlement.

For the time being we shall have to improve our United Nations peace-keeping forces on the accepted basis—with the Secretariat and the middle powers in the foreground and the great powers in the background. There are limitations, however, to what can be accomplished unless participation becomes more nearly universal and all the great powers are committed. Even if the fifth great power, sitting sullenly outside, shows no inclination to participate, and one of the lesser great powers holds such activities in contempt, concurrence of the other three would greatly extend the area of operation.

I do not think the kind of peace-keeping developed in Gaza and the Congo is incompatible with the basis of security envisaged at San Francisco. If we are working our way towards great power unanimity at least on fundamental attitudes to war and peace, then I think we should try to work our way back—or forward—to the basis of Article 43. If we do so, we could resume the effort to implement the Charter, a great deal wiser, on the one hand, from the United Nations' experience with collective security over Korea and, on the other hand, from its success with procedures of truce-keeping, tranquillization, and prevention adapted to the rudimentary state of international organization. It is to be hoped also that the great powers would have acquired a broader appreciation than they had in 1946 of the role lesser powers can play in the maintenance of peace.

It is only by this path that we could ever find our way to the international force which is expected to operate while the world disarms. How this international force would work I do not yet comprehend. That we cannot have disarmament without some kind of international force is a dogma now accepted by the two superpowers and most other people. The United States in its disarmament proposals of April, 1963, envisaged by the end of the disarming process a United Nations force with "sufficient armed forces and armaments so that no state could challenge it." Most students of international security measures discourage belief in the foreseeable possibility of such a force based on a monopoly of military powers under the control of a world authority responsible to the peoples of the world. Nevertheless, this utopian vision appears in the formal proposals of a hard-headed government. (The cynic could say that this is the American way of making sure that there will never be a state of total disarmament, but the cynic is never more than partly right when he talks about American policy.) On such a conception I remain agnostic. I cannot believe in it as a foreseeable goal, any more than I can believe that a federal state could ever be fitted safely to the jagged geography of this universe. At the same time I recognize that we cannot rule out the possibility of some day coming to these answers. I am inclined to think, however, that too many minds are frozen in the assumption that progress must be found in steps which lead towards the international police force and the world federation, thereby limiting the range of invention. It could lead us up constant blind alleys instead of more promising approaches.

In a recent report on *Disarmament and European Security* prepared for the Institute for Strategic Studies appears the following comment on the world authority required for a disarmed world:

In the end, it is possible that such an authority might be created through the commitment of national forces to a unified command in the manner foreseen by paragraph 8 of the Nassau Agreement, for the more limited purposes of the North Atlantic Treaty Organization. This system allows countries such as the United States and the United Kingdom to take part in a unified system while remaining secure in the knowledge they have in the hands of their own officers weapons which can, if necessary, be used under the orders of their own chiefs of staff. To rely on a peacekeeping authority constituted on this basis (a system much closer to what the Russians are proposing than what the West appears to be proposing) is to give the appearance of disarmament without for many years abandoning the reality of national power. But with this security national military systems would erode away, like the methods of personal and local self-protection in the old American West. The political framework of a disarmed world could be created and could through custom and acceptance be relied on increasingly to carry the burden of security.

This kind of thinking seems to me more profitable than the concoction of constitutions for international armies rooted to no feasible political institution. It is closer to our United Nations experience and it is closer to the intentions of the Charter on which there was great power agreement in 1945. Apocalyptic pronouncements that a world moving fast to destruction requires drastic measures are hard to deny, but they don't get us over the steps to Utopia. We must rather keep our eyes on the world as it exists and the progress that has been made, hoping that the moderation of international relations because of the dread facts of power and growing habits of collaboration will enable us to keep the peace more effectively and more reliably.

Who Pays? *

John G. Stoessinger, et al.

The financial crisis of the United Nations has aroused acute anxiety among many observers who see it as the unmistakable symptom of an early death of the Organization. They point to the history of the League of Nations and maintain that, in its case, financial atrophy was the first harbinger of doom. They claim that the same omens, the penury of states and the mounting deficits of the Organization, are gathering now over the United Nations.

On closer scrutiny, this analogy does not hold up. Many of the symptoms are similar, to be sure, but the causes are quite different. The fiscal plight of the League was a symptom of a struggle over its very existence. Many states had questioned the *raison d'être* of the League; others had tolerated it; certainly no state had wanted it to move beyond the concept of a "static conference machinery." In that sense, the League's chronic weakness was the result of a struggle between nihilists and conservatives: those who would deny its existence altogether, and those who would relegate it to the peripheries of their national policies. The former attitude had led to active hostility, the latter to political neglect and indifference.

Summary of Major Problem Areas

The financial plight of the United Nations is not the expression of a struggle over the Organization's existence. All states have accepted its presence. The struggle is being waged between the strict constructionists of the Charter and those who wish to interpret the basic document more liberally: those who wish to maintain the United Nations as a "static conference machinery," and those who wish to give it increasing strength and executive authority. Viewed in this light, the financial crisis of the United Nations does not indicate that the Organization has fallen into political collapse, but rather that the membership has not yet been willing to ratify and sustain its rise to a higher plane of evolutionary development.

The above does not deny the existence of a major crisis. But the crisis is more constitutional and political than financial. At its heart is not so much the problem of economic incapacity to pay the rising costs, but of unwillingness to pay for politically controversial operations. The overall costs of

* John G. Stoessinger et al., *Financing the United Nations System* (Washington, D.C., The Brookings Institution, 1964), pp. 293-306. Reprinted by permission. John G. Stoessinger has been Professor of Political Science at Hunter College since 1963. He is the author of *The Might of Nations: World Politics in Our Time* (1963), which received the Bancroft Prize from Columbia University, and *The United Nations and the Superpowers* (1964).

membership have risen across the board from $50 million in 1946 to $500 million in 1963. But when considered in a broader context, these amounts are a pittance. National incomes and national budgets have also risen almost everywhere. Nations have called on the United Nations to assume increasingly greater responsibilities. In that sense, the rising costs indicate the Organization's growing vitality. Moreover, nations save money because the United Nations exists. A host country like the United States absorbs a substantial sum as feedback into its economy because it houses the United Nations. In a more fundamental sense, what would have been the costs to governments if there had been no United Nations during the Suez crisis of 1956? Or even if the crisis had been permitted to continue for several days or weeks before the Organization became involved? There are, of course, so many variables that there are no answers to these questions. But they point up the fact that any discussion of the costs of the United Nations, if divorced from the broader role that it plays in world politics, has an air of unreality.

Of all the activities of the United Nations, those subsumed under the regular budget have been the least controversial—or were until 1963, when France refused to pay for principal and interest on United Nations bonds and the Soviet bloc countries not only followed suit but also refused to pay for certain minor peace-keeping operations that heretofore had been financed through the regular budget without much difficulty.

The regular budget has risen gradually in a gentle upward curve. In 1963, it was $86 million. The most significant changes over the years have been the downward adjustment of the United States assessment percentage and the upward revision of the Soviet share. Under the present assessment pattern, a small minority of the membership still bears most of the burden: sixty countries constituting over half of the membership pay only 3 percent of the budget while twenty countries constituting less than 20 percent of the membership contribute almost 90 percent of the total. The Big Five pay almost two-thirds, the United States close to one-third.

There has been no major crisis over the regular budget. The heart of the tension lies in the area of peace-keeping. Here the United Nations has truly ventured into uncharted territory. For the first time in history, an international organization has created and financed peace forces as a collective responsibility of the world community. UNEF and ONUC have been the most controversial of these. They have raised opposition both on financial and on political grounds. The problem of relative capacity to pay has pitted the "developed" countries against the large majority of "economically less developed" members. The former group, comprising twenty-six nations in 1964, has had most of the wealth, but the latter group, comprising eighty-seven nations, has controlled most of the votes. The conflict between them has resulted in a succession of "rebate" formulas under which the richer countries have made voluntary contributions to make up the deficits created by the reductions granted the poorer ones. While each assessment since 1956 has been *ad hoc,* and no formula was ever institutionalized, these "rebate" formulas in effect have come close to establishing special assessment scales for UNEF and ONUC.

By far the most serious problem, of course, has been posed by the political attitude of the strict constructionists toward the peace-keeping functions. In oversimplified terms, they wish to deny the peace-keeping role to the United Nations while the liberals desire to extend it. The strict constructionists, however, do not always say "no" with equal sonority. The Soviet Union objected to, but until 1963 paid for, a considerable number of minor peace-keeping operations that were financed through the regular budget; it acquiesced in the establishment of the United Nations Emergency Force; and it permitted the creation of the Congo Force and only later wished to destroy it. Hence, the strict constructionist position itself ranges from reluctant acquiescence through passive resistance to active obstruction. Moreover, these categories are in constant flux. The tempering of Soviet hostility toward the Congo operation after 1962 is a case in point.

Similarly, among the liberals, "yes" is not always said with the same degree of enthusiasm. Some states support the political resolutions authorizing the establishment of the peace forces, then vote for the financing resolutions and make payment. Others have second thoughts at the second stage and abstain or even vote against payment. And some that vote "yes" in the first two stages refuse to make payment after all. The range of liberalism, therefore, also extends along a fluid continuum of three points: enthusiastic support, moral support, and tacit consent. The more cautious form of liberalism and the permissive form of conservatism often meet in voting terms, if not in principle, on the common ground of abstention.

The financial crisis over UNEF and ONUC is first and foremost a political crisis over the proper role of these two peace forces. Only secondarily is it a crisis over money. The Soviet bloc does not oppose UNEF and ONUC and France does not oppose ONUC because they do not want to pay for them; they refuse to pay for them because they oppose them. Both liberals and strict constructionists have responded to specific cases in terms of national interest, rather than abstract principle. From the United States' point of view, UNEF and ONUC sealed off a "no man's land" in the cold war from a possible East-West military confrontation and reduced the likelihood of unilateral intervention by the Soviet Union. The Soviet Union reasoned in the same manner and therefore arrived at opposite conclusions. From its point of view, UNEF and ONUC prevented Soviet bridgeheads in the Middle East and Africa. Since, in the latter case, a bridgehead had already been established and had to be liquidated under United Nations pressure, Soviet opposition to ONUC took a more active form.

The United States has never yet had to respond to the creation of a United Nations peace force that it might have regarded with ambivalence or with outright hostility. What, for example, would American policy have been toward ONUC if Kasavubu had been killed instead of Lumumba? Or what would the United States reaction have been if the General Assembly in 1961 had recommended a peace force to help forestall an American-sponsored invasion of Cuba? It would be foolhardy to suggest easy answers to questions such as these. Yet the strong pressure that the United States delegation brought to bear on the other members of the Governing Council of the United Nations Special Fund in January 1963 to cancel an agricultural assistance project in Cuba may be a straw in the wind. The point here is not to indict the policies of the two superpowers, but to suggest that it is incorrect always to associate the United States with the liberal view in the abstract and the Soviet Union with the opposite.

While it is true in principle that the United States has been fundamentally committed to the basic purposes of the United Nations Charter, and the Soviet Union, as a minority power, has been deeply suspicious of the Organization, the two superpowers have tended to react to the Suez and Congo peace-keeping challenges primarily in terms of their own national interests. The only general difference that might be postulated is the United States tendency, when there is a choice between genuine United Nations neutralization and no United Nations action, to prefer the former and for the Soviet Union to prefer the latter. But this difference too is probably the result of the specific experiences of the two superpowers.

The purely fiscal factor has assumed far greater importance in the attitudes of most of the middle and smaller powers. On the one hand, the fear that "it could happen here," has led to support for the peace forces. On the other hand, the cost of these extraordinary expenses has militated in the opposite direction. The interaction between these two conflicting pressures has led to the admixture of political support and financial delinquency that has marked the behavior of so many of these member states.

To sum up, the positions of the United States, the United Kingdom, and the Soviet Union have had relatively little to do with finances *per se*. Neither has the policy of France, which accepted and helped pay for UNEF, but not for ONUC. In the case of China and the bulk of the middle and smaller powers, money played a far larger, in some instances, even a decisive role. In terms of national income, more than one-third of the member states have borne a heavier burden than the two superpowers. Hence, while the financial crisis of UNEF and ONUC is caused primarily by the political attitudes of the few, it has deepened considerably through the financial limitations of the many.

In its two major attempts to surmount the crisis, the General Assembly has tended to embrace the liberal position. The bond issue which—at least in a single instance—endowed the Organization with major borrowing powers was an important milestone in the evolution of the United Nations. Significantly enough, the bonds were purchased not only by liberals, but also by a considerable number of middle-of-the-roaders. Similarly, the Assembly's request for an Advisory Opinion from the International Court was in essence an invitation to the Court to declare itself on the nature of the

Organization. The majority opinion and its acceptance by the Assembly were clear vindications of the liberal position and acknowledged legally the Assembly's virtually unlimited fiscal authority. Yet neither the bond issue nor the Advisory Opinion provided a solution. The former was a stop-gap emergency device, and the latter did not move the majority of delinquent states to change their policies. Nor was the problem resolved by the two Working Groups or by the Special Session of the General Assembly in 1963. The mood of the Eighteenth General Assembly was definitely against any further massive appropriations for controversial peace-keeping operations. The 1964 cash appropriations for UNEF and ONUC amounted to less than one-fourth of the funds appropriated for the two forces during the previous year. ONUC was scheduled for termination in mid-1964. The total United Nations debt by the end of 1963 approached the $140 million mark. The political crisis continued unabated, with France and the Soviet bloc continuing their refusal to pay. At the heart of this crisis was the fact of international life that no power, least of all a great power, would adopt, or pay for, a policy that it considered inimical to its national interest.

In the economic and social activities of the United Nations, the dialogue between liberals and strict constructionists has taken a somewhat different form. The political division has fallen less along East-West lines than between the industrialized and the developing countries. Unlike peace and security operations, which have been unpredictable and sporadic, the economic and social activities of the United Nations have been stable and long-term commitments. The issue has not been whether they should exist but how rapidly they should grow.

Altogether, these activities, not including the International Monetary Fund and the International Bank for Reconstruction and Development, account for approximately two-thirds of the total annual expenditures of the United Nations system. The bulk of this money is raised through voluntary contributions from governments and is channeled into the special voluntary programs: United Nations Children's Fund (UNICEF), United Nations High Commissioner for Refugees (UNHCR), United Nations Relief and Works Agency for Palestine Refugees in the Near East (UNRWA), Expanded Programme of Technical Assistance (EPTA) and the Special Fund. The remainder is raised primarily by assessment for nine specialized agencies and the International Atomic Energy Agency. The IMF, the IBRD, and their affiliated bodies depend neither on annual assessments nor on voluntary contributions.

Commitments to the special voluntary programs have risen steadily, but the bases of support have been comparatively uneven. UNICEF, EPTA, and the Special Fund have won close to universal support, but the responses to UNHCR and UNRWA have been far more modest, largely because these programs had been set up for the benefit of a particular region or social group.

Comparison of the voluntary programs with the regular budget shows that most of the developing countries of Africa, Asia, the Middle East, and Latin America contribute in slightly higher proportion to the former than to the latter. The reason for this is quite obvious: most of the voluntary programs exist primarily for the benefit of the new and developing nations. The United States' contribution is financially controlling in all the voluntary programs and extends from 40 percent in EPTA and the Special Fund to 70 percent in UNRWA. The United Kingdom contributes in approximately the same proportion as to the regular budget; France, China, and the Soviet Union in far smaller proportions.

The assessments pattern in the specialized agencies has followed that of the regular budget rather closely. All the budgets have risen at a moderate rate. This expansion has taken place in the face of considerable resistance from some member states. As in the voluntary programs, the position of the United States is financially controlling although its percentge contribution has been declining over the years. Some of the agencies have experimented with novel schemes for raising additional revenue and several have attempted to invoke sanctions against nations in arrears on their assessments.

On the whole, a vigorous consensus already exists on the further expansion of the economic and social operations of the United Nations. This consensus, rather than any budget consolidation or fund-raising technique, is the best guarantor of a hopeful future for these activities.

If the overall patterns of financing the peace-keeping are compared with the economic and social operations of the United Nations, it seems paradoxical that the latter, on which there exists almost universal agreement on principle, should be funded primarily by voluntary contributions, while the former, which has divided the Organization against itself, has been financed primarily through compulsory assessments. Logically, the financing principles should perhaps be reversed. In practice, however, the economic and social programs have been so diversified in their character, appeal, and membership that voluntary support probably offered the only realistic basis on which most of them could get started. By now, the pattern is firmly entrenched. Nevertheless, the question may legitimately be raised whether the expenses of bringing economic and social welfare within the reach of all mankind ought to be considered any less binding on the United Nations membership than the task of keeping the peace.

There is yet another connection between the peace-keeping operations and the economic and social programs. The implication of the World Court Advisory Opinion was clearly that the General Assembly had the power to make legally binding decisions in the financial realm. Against the background of the Development Decade and a massive majority of economically less developed nations in the United Nations, it would not be inconceivable that the eighty-seven nations in the latter group could use the precedent of the opinion to vote large funds for economic and social operations as legally binding assessments on the membership. In view of this possibility, the importance of building consensus between those who control the votes and those who control the funds will become increasingly apparent in the future. Unless this problem of political control of funds is resolved, the great power of the Assembly could be employed by impatient majorities eager to push large economic and social programs to impose heavy assessments on a reluctant minority by deciding that such expenditures were "expenses of the Organization." Justice Fitzmaurice warned against such a possibility in 1962. It is a warning not to be taken lightly by the membership. Majority rule per se does not guarantee the healthy evolution of the United Nations.

Proposals for the Future

The analysis of proposals to surmount the financial crisis proceeds on the assumption that any meaningful evaluation of fiscal policy proposals must take into account the political context of the Organization. Indeed, the political aspects of United Nations financing are so all-pervasive that there is really no such thing as an exclusively fiscal question. The truth is that virtually all questions of finance are discussed and voted on as political questions only thinly disguised as fiscal. Hence, this analysis must be concerned not only with what is fiscally desirable but also with what is politically possible.

In the regular budget, further "controlled expansion" is likely. But the positions of France and the Soviet bloc in 1963 suggest mounting resistance to this trend. The inclusion of the costs of minor peace-keeping operations and bond amortization payments in the regular budget no longer makes it possible to insulate the normal day-to-day activities of the Organization from political controversy.

The strengthening process may begin with some modest improvements. First, the various fiscal years of member states might be coordinated with the United Nations fiscal period. This would put the Organization in a better cash position. Second, while it may not be possible to increase the Working Capital Fund much above the present figure of $40 million, it may be feasible to set aside the "miscellaneous income" of roughly $6 million every year and to use it as a contingency fund under proper controls of the General Assembly. This might be easier to accomplish than an increase in the "unforeseen and extraordinary expenditures" item because the money is in existence and could accumulate every year. A sizable peace and security fund or another bond issue would meet with stiff resistance.

In the area of peace and security operations, the two toughest problems are those of cost apportionment and of unwillingness to pay. Leaving aside for the moment the problem of the politically motivated deficits, the obstacles are still formidable. The main tension is between the industrialized and the developing nations. The former feel, on the whole, that the regular scale, which makes allowances for low-income nations, is an adequate basis for cost apportionment. They are willing to give further reductions to the new nations, but hesitate to go along with a new special scale for peace-keeping purposes. The United States in particular leans toward an *ad hoc* approach, arguing that each case should be dealt with as it arises. The majority of the developing nations, on the other hand, hold that they can ill afford peace-keeping payments according to the regular scale and that the great powers, which have a primary responsibility for the maintenance of peace and security, should bear the main financial burden under a special scale.

The discussion over relative capacity to pay clearly reveals that a meeting ground between those who control the funds and those who control the votes must be found. All economic indicators suggest that the twenty-six "developed" countries were able to absorb UNEF and ONUC expenses without much difficulty. Specifically, the congressional ceiling of 33⅓ percent imposed on the United States does not accurately recognize American capacity to pay. While there is merit in the argument that the United Nations should not become financially dependent on any one great power, the United States was in effect paying close to 50 percent for UNEF and ONUC until 1963 and close to 40 percent thereafter. A revision of the congressional ceiling to 40 percent would not change the *de facto* picture much, but would get rid of the cumbersome device of applying for additional voluntary contributions from the United States and, most important, would place that country on record as willing to assume a leading role in further extending the peace-keeping function of the United Nations.

Most economic indicators also suggest that, while peace-keeping expenses have often imposed a hardship on the developing nations, this hardship in most instances has certainly not been extreme. Rather, most of the developing nations have tended to give the peace-keeping operations fairly low priorities in their foreign policy calculations. An upward revision of the American ceiling might well set an encouraging example and generate better payment records in the developing parts of the world.

There seem to be four possibilities of a special scale for peace-keeping operations. These try to deal with the problem of economic incapacity to pay, but do not come to grips with the politically motivated deficits. A first such type of scale might simply institutionalize the 1963 rebate formula governing UNEF and ONUC assessments, under which reductions of up to 55 percent are granted to the poorer states, and continue to rely on voluntary contributions to make up the deficit created by these reductions. This is not a dependable formula since there is no assurance that voluntary contributions will always be forthcoming. A second type of scale would use the rebate formula but apportion the deficit among the richer states not eligible for rebates. This would avoid dependence on voluntary contributions, but would in turn increase politically motivated deficits since some of the richer powers refuse to pay. A third type of scale would use the same formula and try to make up the deficit out of regular budget items such as "special missions and related activities," "unforseen and extraordinary expenditures," and possibly "miscellaneous income." Fourth, the cumbersome rebate system might be abandoned altogether in favor of a completely new scale based primarily on GNP and GNP per capita figures.

A completely new scale would probably be the best solution since GNP figures are least permeated with political considerations and are recognized throughout the world as one index of a nation's capacity to pay. A sliding scale might be built into this or any other plan that would permit the percentages of the wealthier states to rise as the costs rise beyond certain norms, and the percentages of the poorer states to be lowered. But since agreement on such a scale would not be easy to reach, an interim solution may have to be devised. The meeting of deficits created by the rebate system through the regular budget items indicated above may provide such a transitional formula.

It may be prudent to build four safeguards into any special arrangement for the financing of peace-keeping operations. First, any special scale of contributions that might be established should have minimum and maximum percentages of contributions. Second, a sliding scale as indicated above should be a feature. Third, time limits should be fixed for review purposes by the General Assembly. And finally, it might be wise to link a future peace-keeping operation to a payment plan by including in the initial authorizing resolution a section clearly setting forth the terms under which the program would be financed.

None of the above proposals, however, comes to grips with the problem of politically motivated deficits. One way to face up to that challenge completely would be to use a system which permitted a member to refuse payment for a peace-keeping operation that it opposed. Such a solution would ignore the message of the Advisory Opinion that all member states should pay, but it would face up to the political reality that no power, certainly no great power, can be coerced into payment. In this connection, it is important to recall the distinction between passive opposition and active obstruction. If opposition remains limited to nonpayment, as was the Soviet Union's opposition to UNEF, supporters may find it prudent to override it provided they are ready to pay the share of the recalcitrant power. But if they override active opposition, they may find the operation endangered, as in the Congo, or they might even drive the obstructionist power out of the United Nations altogether. The central truth which emerges is that the launching of an operation in the face of either passive or active opposition is in fact to ask for financial crisis and any state that asks for such a crisis ought to be prepared to bail out the Organization.

The dilemma of the use of sanctions against delinquent states is a formidable one. Not to invoke Article 19 would flaunt the Charter as interpreted by the World Court in the Advisory Opinion of July 1962. On the other hand, the use of sanctions might increase the stubbornness of the politically motivated delinquents and perhaps even drive them out of the Organization.

Whether one believes that Article 19 is sufficiently clear-cut in its language to make its application unavoidable when the conditions for its application exist, it seems that the best chance of avoiding a confrontation with the issue lies in the mobilization of a broad and strong consensus that all members have an obligation to contribute to peace-keeping costs. In this respect, the United States has sacrificed a good deal of its potential for leadership toward this end because of its unwillingness to accept a commitment for the future to carry a share of peace-keeping costs greater than its contribution under the regular scale. Clearly, such a commitment could expose the United States to the risk of having to support or acquiesce in peace-keeping operations that it may find questionable in terms of its own national interest. But this is what the United States has demanded of the Soviet Union and other recalcitrant members when it has asserted the General Assembly's power to tax and the automatic application of Article 19. In the last analysis, American willingness to raise its contribution may help prevent what the majority of the membership fears most: a major constitutional and political showdown with the Soviet Union over sanctions under Article 19.

Should such a showdown be unavoidable, it should be remembered that the sanction will not be invoked *against* a given state, but *for* the law. The record of the United Nations demonstrates that the Organization has grown most as a peace-keeping mechanism when the membership has emphasized boldness rather than caution, even when such boldness temporarily strained the political consensus to the breaking point. Institutions, like people, gain in strength and depth by facing a challenge squarely.

The above discussion demonstrates that the opposition of the strict constructionists to peace and security operations to which they object has not been entirely unsuccessful. In consequence, liberals have increasingly turned to new sources for additional revenue for the United Nations.

Private support so far has been limited to the economic and social activities of the United Nations and even there the contributions, while sometimes significant, have not made possible any decisive new breakthroughs. The most generous amounts from private sources have gone to the voluntary programs for refugees and children. It is fairly safe to predict that such support will remain for a considerable time to come a modest supplement to the contributions of governments.

Some efforts have also been made in connection with the exploration of new sources of revenue. The income from these new sources would be meant to strengthen the hand of the United Nations in both the peace and security as well as the economic and social fields.

All of these proposals are based on the assumption that the United Nations has become an integral "organ of society" which is the producer of a "public good" and hence deserving of some additional revenue. Opponents maintain, on the other hand, that the Organization does not render its services free. Member states are already assessed for them. The proposals themselves fall into three major categories: income from United Nations service charges; levies on international activities; and long-range possibilities.

A systematic exploration of these potential sources of revenue leads to mixed conclusions. It becomes evident, on closer scrutiny, for example, that service charges could hardly become a significant source of additional income. In most cases, the returns would be small and the resistance great. Of the three types of levies on international activities that could be contemplated—mail, shipping, and travel—only the first shows real promise. A United Nations stamp surcharge scheme has a chance of adoption. Levies on shipping and travel would be discriminatory and might not yield enough to make the effort worthwhile. The long-range possibilities include the exploitation of the resources of Antarctica, the sea-beds, and outer space. Of these, the only one which is not hopelessly remote, economically as well as politically, is the sea-bed. Specifically, the petroleum resources discovered in the Gulf of Mexico and perhaps those in the North Sea are a possibility for potential United Nations revenue. Antarctica and outer space would necessitate huge capital investments before any returns could be realized.

The opening of these new vistas is impressive. But the fact remains that, in our lifetime at least, most of these new sources of revenue will not provide substitutes for the failure of states to pay their financial obligations. Solutions must be found now. Moreover, the liberals must ask themselves the question whether, if large new economically and politically feasible sources of revenue were found, the majority of states would be prepared to release the right to collect them to an international organization so long as there is serious controversy over its role. Once again, the problem of political consensus is central.

The vital importance of political consensus is also the lesson gleaned from a survey of the financing patterns of regional organizations. Where there is absence of consensus, there usually is penury. Where there is consensus, there usually prevails a wholesome financial climate as well. The formal structure of the organization seems to be of little relevance to the issue of financial health.

In the struggle over what the member states want the United Nations to be, it is certain that the tension between liberals and strict constructionists will continue. The progression from the League of Nations to the United Nations and the development of the United Nations itself suggest, however, that the historical trend is in the direction of the dynamic, evolutionary conception of international organization. When seen in this historical perspective, the financial crisis of the United Nations does not indicate that the Organization has fallen as low as many fear. It merely shows that it has not yet been allowed to rise as high as many had hoped.

Historical perspective also teaches that political consensus—that vital precondition for financial health—is not found. It is made. It is made primarily through a constant probing of its limits and the readiness to raise the search to a higher plane. Realism and idealism are needed in equal measure if the financial crisis is to be surmounted and if the United Nations is to move toward a better world of international order.

PART FIVE

*International Organization
in Transition*

CHAPTER 10 *Static Conference Machinery*
or Dynamic Instrument of Government?

Introduction to the Annual Report of the Secretary-General on
the Work of the Organization, 16 June 1960–15 June 1961 *

Dag Hammarskjold

Debates and events during the year since the publication of the last
report to the General Assembly have brought to the fore different concepts
of the United Nations, the character of the Organization, its authority and
its structure.

On the one side, it has in various ways become clear that certain Members conceive of the Organization as a static conference machinery for resolving conflicts of interests and ideologies with a view to peaceful coexistence, within the Charter, to be served by a Secretariat which is to be
regarded not as fully internationalized but as representing within its ranks
those very interests and ideologies.

Other Members have made it clear that they conceive of the Organization primarily as a dynamic instrument of governments through which they,
jointly and for the same purpose, should seek such reconciliation but
through which they should also try to develop forms of executive action,
undertaken on behalf of all Members, and aiming at forestalling conflicts
and resolving them, once they have arisen, by appropriate diplomatic or
political means, in a spirit of objectivity and in implementation of the principles and purposes of the Charter.

Naturally, the latter concept takes as its starting point the conference
concept, but its regards it only as a starting point, envisaging the possibility
of continued growth to increasingly effective forms of active international
cooperation, adapted to experience, and served by a Secretariat of which it is
required that, whatever the background and the views of its individual
members, their actions be guided solely by the principles of the Charter, the
decisions of the main organs, and the interests of the Organization itself.

The first concept can refer to history and to the traditions of national
policies of the past. The second can point to the needs of the present and of
the future in a world of ever-closer international interdependence where
nations have at their disposal armaments of hitherto unknown destructive
strength. The first one is firmly anchored in the time-honored philosophy of

* General Assembly, *Official Records* (16th session), Supplement 1A, pp. 1-8. Also in
United Nations Review, Vol. 8, No. 9 (September 1961), pp. 12 ff. and in *International
Organization*, Vol. 15, No. 4 (Autumn 1961), pp. 549-563.

sovereign national states in armed competition of which the most that may be expected in the international field is that they achieve a peaceful coexistence. The second one envisages possibilities of intergovernmental action overriding such a philosophy, and opens the road toward more developed and increasingly effective forms of constructive international cooperation.

It is clearly for the governments, Members of the Organization, and for these governments only, to make their choice and decide on the direction in which they wish the Organization to develop. However, it may be appropriate to study these two concepts in terms of the purposes of the Organization as laid down in the Charter and, in this context, also to consider the character and the significance of the decisions of the Organization as well as its structure.

II

The purposes and principles of the Charter are set out in its Preamble and further developed in a series of articles, including some which may seem to be primarily of a procedural or administrative nature. Together, these parts of the Charter lay down some basic rules of international ethics by which all Member States have committed themselves to be guided. To a large extent, the rules reflect standards accepted as binding for life within states. Thus, they appear, in the main, as a projection into the international arena and the international community of purposes and principles already accepted as being of national validity. In this sense, the Charter takes a first step in the direction of an organized international community, and this independently of the organs set up for international cooperation. Due to different traditions, the state of social development and the character of national institutions, wide variations naturally exist as to the application in national life of the principles reflected in the Charter, but it is not too difficult to recognize the common elements behind those differences. It is therefore not surprising that such principles of national application could be transposed into an agreed basis also for international behavior and cooperation.

In the Preamble to the Charter, Member nations have reaffirmed their faith "in the equal rights of men and women and of nations large and small," a principle which also has found many other expressions in the Charter.

Thus, it restates the basic democratic principle of equal political rights, independently of the position of the individual or of the Member country in respect of its strength, as determined by territory, population, or wealth. The words just quoted must, however, be considered as going further and imply an endorsement as well of a right to equal economic opportunities.

It is in the light of the first principle that the Charter has established a system of equal votes, expressing "the sovereign equality of all its Members," and has committed the Organization to the furtherance of self-determination, self-government, and independence. On the same basis, the

Charter requires universal respect for and observance of human rights and fundamental freedoms for all "without distinction as to race, sex, language or religion."

It is in the light of the latter principle—or, perhaps, the latter aspect of the same basic principle—that the Charter, in Article 55, has committed the Members to the promotion of higher standards of living, full employment, and conditions of economic and social progress and development, as well as to solutions of international economic and related problems. The pledge of all Members to take joint and separate action, in cooperation with the Organization, for the achievement of these purposes has been the basis for the far-reaching economic and technical assistance channelled through or administered by the Organization, and may rightly be considered as the basic obligation reflected also in such economic and technical assistance as Member governments have been giving, on a bi-lateral basis, outside the framework of the Organization.

It would seem that those who regard the Organization as a conference machinery, "neutral" in relation to the direction of policies on a national or international basis and serving solely as an instrument for the solution of conflicts by reconciliation, do not pay adequate attention to those essential principles of the Charter to which reference has just been made. The terms of the Charter are explicit as regards the equal political rights of nations as well as of individuals and, although this second principle may be considered only as implicit in the terms of the Charter, they are clear also as regards the demand for equal economic opportunities for all individuals and nations. So as to avoid any misunderstanding, the Charter directly states that the basic democratic principles are applicable to nations "large and small" and to individuals without distinction "as to race, sex, language and religion," qualifications that obviously could be extended to cover also other criteria such as, for example, those of an ideological character which have been used or may be used as a basis for political or economic discrimination.

In the practical work of the Organization these basic principles have been of special significance in relation to countries under colonial rule or in other ways under foreign domination. The General Assembly has translated the principles into action intended to establish through self-determination a free and independent life as sovereign states for peoples who have expressed in democratic forms their wish for such a status. Decisive action has in many cases been taken by Member governments, and then the United Nations has had only to lend its support to their efforts. In other cases, the main responsibility has fallen on the Organization itself. The resolution on colonialism, adopted by the General Assembly at its fifteenth session, may be regarded as a comprehensive restatement in elaborated form of the principle laid down in the Charter. Results of developments so far have been reflected in the birth of a great number of new national states and a revolutionary widening of the membership of the Organization.

The demand for equal economic opportunities has, likewise, been—

and remains—of special significance in relation to those very countries which have more recently entered the international arena as new states. This is natural in view of the fact that, mostly, they have been in an unfavorable economic position, which is reflected in a much lower per capita income, rate of capital supply, and degree of technical development, while their political independence and sovereignty require a fair measure of economic stability and economic possibilities in order to gain substance and full viability.

In working for the translation into practical realities in international life of the democratic principles which are basic to the Charter, the Organization has thus assumed a most active role and it has done so with success, demonstrating both the need and the possibilities for such action.

Further, in the Preamble to the Charter it is stated to be a principle and purpose of the Organization "to establish conditions under which justice and respect for the obligations arising from treaties and other sources of international law can be maintained." In these words—to which, naturally, counterparts may be found in other parts of the Charter—it gives expression to another basic democratic principle, that of the rule of law. In order to promote this principle, the Charter established the International Court of Justice, but the principle permeates the approach of the Charter to international problems far beyond the sphere of competence of the Court. As in national life, the principle of justice—which obviously implies also the principle of objectivity and equity in the consideration of all matters before the General Assembly or the Security Council—must be considered as applicable without distinction or discrimination, with one measure and one standard valid for the strong as well as for the weak. Thus, the demand of the Charter for a rule of law aims at the substitution of right for might and makes of the Organization the natural protector of rights which countries, without it, might find it more difficult to assert and to get respected.

The principle of justice can be regarded as flowing naturally from the principles of equal political rights and equal economic opportunities, but it has an independent life and carries, of itself, the world community as far in the direction of an organized international system as the two first-mentioned principles. It has deep roots in the history of the efforts of man to eliminate from international life the anarchy which he had already much earlier overcome on the national level, deeper indeed than the political and economic principles which, as is well known, were much later to get full acceptance also in national life. Long before the United Nations and long before even the League of Nations, governments were working toward a rule of justice in international life through which they hoped to establish an international community based on law, without parliamentary or executive organs, but with a judicial procedure through which law and justice could be made to apply.

The Charter states and develops the three principles mentioned here as a means to an end: "to save succeeding generations from the scourge of war." This adds emphasis to the concept, clearly implied in the Charter, of an international community for which the Organization is an instrument and an expression and in which anarchic tendencies in international life are to be curbed by the introduction of a system of equal political rights, equal economic opportunities, and the rule of law. However, the Charter goes one step further, drawing a logical conclusion both from the ultimate aim of the Organization and from the three principles. Thus, it outlaws the use of armed force "save in the common interest." Obviously, the Charter cannot, on the one side, establish a rule of law and the principle of equal rights for "nations large and small," and, on the other hand, permit the use of armed force for national ends, contrary to those principles and, therefore, not "in the common interest." Were nations, under the Charter, to be allowed, by the use of their military strength, to achieve ends contrary to the principle of the equality of Members and the principle of justice, it would obviously deprive those very principles of all substance and significance. One practical expression of this approach, which may be mentioned here, is that the organs of the United Nations have consistently maintained that the use of force, contrary to the Charter as interpreted by those organs, cannot be permitted to yield results which can be accepted as valid by the Organization and as establishing new rights.

In the Charter, the right to the use of force is somwhat more extensive than may seem to be the case from a superficial reading of the phrase "save in the common interest." Thus, apart from military action undertaken pursuant to a decision of the Security Council for repression of aggression—that is, for upholding the basic Charter principles—the Charter opens the door to the use of armed force by a nation in exercise of its inherent right to resist armed attack. This is a point on which, both in theory and in practice, the development of international law is still at a very early stage. As is well known, no agreement has been reached on a definition of aggression, beyond that found in Article 2, paragraph 4, of the Charter, and the Organization has several times had to face situations in which, therefore, the rights and wrongs in a specific case of conflict have not been clarified. It would be a vitally important step forward if wider agreement could be reached regarding the criteria to be applied in order to distinguish between legitimate and illegitimate use of force. History is only too rich in examples of armed aggression claimed as action in self-defense. How could it be otherwise, when most cases of armed conflict are so deeply rooted in a history of clashes of interests and rights, even if, up to the fatal moment of the first shot, those clashes have not involved recourse to the use of armed force?

In recognition of this situation and in the light of historical experience, the Charter makes yet another projection into international life of solutions to conflicts tested in national life, and establishes the final principle that the Organization shall "bring about by peaceful means and in conformity with the principles of justice and international law, adjustment or settlement of international disputes or situations which might lead to a breach of the peace." This principle, as quoted here from Article 1 of the Charter, is further developed specifically in Article 33, which requires parties to any dispute, the consequence of which is likely to endanger the maintenance of international peace and security, to "seek a solution by negotiation, enquiry, mediation, conciliation, arbitration, judicial settlement, resort to regional agencies or arrangements, or other peaceful means of their own choice." It is in this sphere that the Security Council has had, and is likely to continue to have, its main significance, both directly as a forum before which any dispute threatening peace and security can be brought up for debate and as an organ which directly, or through appropriate agents, may assist the parties in finding a way out and, by preventive diplomacy, may forestall the outbreak of an armed conflict. It seems appropriate here to draw attention especially to the right of the Security Council under Article 40 to "call upon the parties concerned to comply with such provisional measures as it deems necessary or desirable" for the prevention of any aggravation of a situation threatening peace and security, and to the obligation of Members to comply with a decision on such measures.

It is in the light of the approach to international coexistence in our world today, which is thus to be found in the Charter, that judgment has to be passed on the validity of the different conceptions of the Organization which in recent times have become increasingly apparent. As already pointed out, the basic principles regarding the political equality of nations and their right to equal economic opportunities are difficult to reconcile with the view that the Organization is to be regarded only as a conference machinery for the solution, by debate and joint decisions, of conflicts of interest or ideology. It seems even more difficult to reconcile these principles with a view according to which equality among Members should be reflected in the establishment of a balance between power blocs or other groupings of nations. The same difficulty is apparent as regards the principle of justice and the principle prohibiting the use of armed force. It is easier to apply the conference concept to the principle of prevention of conflict through negotiation, but also on this point the difficulties become considerable if it is recognized that such solutions as may be sought by the Organization should be solutions based on the rules of equality and justice.

III

The General Assembly, the Security Council, and other collective organs of the United Nations have features in common with a standing international diplomatic conference, but their procedures go beyond the forms of such a conference and show aspects of a parliamentary or quasi-parliamentary character.

While decisions of a conference, in order to commit its participants, must be based on their subsequent acceptance of the decisions, the organs of the United Nations act on the basis of voting, with the decisions being adopted if supported by a majority. However, the decisions of the Assembly have, as regards Member States, only the character of recommendations (except for financial assessments and certain other types of organizational action) so that obligations like those arising out of an agreement, coming into force after a conference, do not normally flow from them. But although the decisions, legally, are only recommendations, they introduce an important element by expressing a majority consensus on the issue under consideration.

Naturally, such a formula leaves scope for a gradual development in practice of the weight of the decisions. To the extent that more respect, in fact, is shown to General Assembly recommendations by the Member States, they may come more and more close to being recognized as decisions having a binding effect on those concerned, particularly when they involve the application of the binding principles of the Charter and of international law.

Both those who regard a gradual increase in the weight of decisions of the General Assembly as necessary, if progress is to be registered in the direction of organized peaceful coexistence within the Charter, and those who oppose such a development, have to recognize that, with certain variations in individual cases, the practice still is very close to the restrictive Charter formula. Experience shows that even countries which have voted for a certain decision may, later on, basing themselves on its character of merely being a recommendation, refuse to follow it or fail to support its implementation, financially or in other respects.

What has been said applies generally to the collective organs of the Organization, but, as is well known, the Charter has gone one step further beyond the conference concept, in the direction of the parliamentary concept, in the case of the Security Council. In Article 25, Member States of the United Nations have agreed to "accept and carry out the decisions of the Security Council in accordance with the present Charter," thus, by agreement, making the decisions of the Council mandatory, except, of course, when such decisions take the form of "recommendations" within the terms of Chapter VI or certain other articles of the Charter. They have further, in Article 49, undertaken to "join in affording mutual assistance in carrying out the measures decided upon by the Security Council."

This agreed mandatory nature of certain Security Council decisions might have led to a demand for unanimity in the Council, a unanimity which was the rule for the Council of the League of Nations. Even so, however, the arrangement would have gone beyond the conference principle with its requirement that no decision reached in an international organ should be binding on an individual Member short of his agreement. With the present arrangements, requiring a majority of seven and the concurring votes of the permanent members, a bridge between the traditional conference approach and a parliamentary approach is provided by the commitment in Article 25 to agree to the carrying out of the decisions in the Council which should be considered as giving the Council its authority by general delegation as indeed stated in Article 24, paragraph 1.

What clearly remains within the Council of the traditional conference and agreement pattern is the condition that its decisions of a nonprocedural character must be supported by the unanimous vote of the five permanent members, thus avoiding for those members the risk of being bound by a decision of the Council which has not met with their agreement. It may be observed that this special position for the permanent members, apart from other reasons, has the justification that, without such a rule, the other Members of the Organization, in complying with a Security Council decision, might find themselves unwillingly drawn into a big power conflict.

In spite of the delegated authority which the Council may be considered as exercising, and the condition that decisions must be agreed to by the permanent members, the experience of the Organization, as regards the implementation of Council decisions, is uneven and does not indicate full acceptance in practice of Article 25. In this case also, examples can be given of a tendency to regard decisions, even when taken under Chapter VII, as recommendations binding only to the extent that the party concerned has freely committed itself to carry them out; there is here a clear dichotomy between the aims of the Charter and the general political practice at its present stage of development. Such cases refer not only to Members outside the Council, or, perhaps, Members inside the Council, who have not supported a specific decision, but also to Members within the Council who have cast their votes in favor of a decision but who later on are found to reserve for themselves at least a right to interpret the decision in ways which seem to be at variance with the intentions of the Council. The ambiguity of this situation emerges with special force in cases where such attitudes have been taken by permanent members of the Council, who are considered to shoulder the responsibility for the maintenance of peace and security which is reflected in the special position they hold within the Council. Obviously, the problem whether the intended legal weight is given to decisions of the Security Council arises in practice not only in cases of noncompliance but also in cases of a refusal to shoulder the financial consequences of a decision of the Council.

These observations—which have been limited to a reminder of the Charter rules and a factual reminder also of the experiences in practice— point to a situation which in any evaluation of the United Nations must be given the most serious consideration by Members. For the judgment on the various concepts of the United Nations which are put forward, it is one thing to note what the Charter stipulates; it is an entirely different but ultimately more important question as to what the situation is in practice and what, in fact, is the weight given to decisions of the Organization when they go beyond the conference pattern of agreement.

For those who maintain the conference concept of the Organization, it is natural to side-step the mandatory nature of decisions by the Security Council. For those who take a different view, it is equally natural and essential to work for a full and general acceptance of the Charter rules. Were those to be right who hold that the Charter on the points discussed here, and, maybe, also as regards the five basic principles discussed in the first part of this Introduction, is ahead of our time and the political possibilities which it offers, such a view still would not seem to justify the conclusion that the clear approach of the Charter should be abandoned. Rather, it would indicate that Member nations jointly should increase their efforts to make political realities gradually come closer to the pattern established by the Charter.

In the light of such considerations, the significance of the outcome of every single conflict on which the Organization has to take a stand, and the weight given to its decisions in such a conflict stand out very clearly. A failure to gain respect for decisions or actions of the Organization within the terms of the Charter is often called a failure for the Organization. It would seem more correct to regard it as a failure of the world community, through its Member nations and in particular those most directly concerned, to cooperate in order, step by step, to make the Charter a living reality in practical political action as it is already in law.

Were such cooperation, for which the responsibility naturally rests with each single Member as well as with all Members collectively, not to come about, and were the respect for the obligations flowing from Article 25 of the Charter to be allowed to diminish, this would spell the end of the possibilities of the Organization to grow into what the Charter indicates as the clear intention of the founders, as also of all hopes to see the Organization grow into an increasingly effective instrument, with increasing respect for recommendations of the General Assembly as well.

What this would mean for the value of the Organization as protector of the aims, principles and rights it was set up to further and safeguard, is obvious. The effort through the Organization to find a way by which the world community might, step by step, grow into organized international cooperation within the Charter, must either progress or recede. Those whose reactions to the work of the Organization hamper its development or reduce its possibilities of effective action may have to shoulder the responsibility for a return to a state of affairs which governments had already found too dangerous after the First World War.

IV

The growth of the United Nations out of the historic conference pattern—which, as observed earlier in this Introduction, at all events naturally remains the starting point in all efforts of the Organization—is clearly reflected in what, in the light of experience, may seem to be a lack of balance in the Charter. While great attention is given to the principles and purposes, and considerable space is devoted to an elaboration of what may be called the parliamentary aspects of the Organization, little is said about executive arrangements. This does not mean that the Charter in any way closes the door to such arrangements or to executive action, but only that, at the state of international thinking crystallized in the Charter, the conference approach still was predominant, and that the needs for executive action, if the new Organization was to live up to expectations and to its obligations under the Charter, had not yet attracted the attention they were to receive in response to later developments.

The key clause on the executive side may be considered to be Article 24 in which it is said that "in order to assure prompt and effective action by the United Nations, its Members confer on the Security Council primary responsibility for the maintenance of international peace and security." On that basis the Security Council is given the right, under Article 29, to establish such subsidiary organs as it deems necessary for the performance of its functions, the right under Article 40 to decide on so-called provisional measures, the right to use, for the purposes of the Charter, under certain conditions, armed forces made available to the Council, the right under Article 48 to request from governments action on the Council's behalf, as well as the right to request of the Secretary-General to "perform such . . . functions as are entrusted to him" by the Council.

The various clauses here briefly enumerated open a wide range of possibilities for executive action undertaken by, and under the aegis of, the Security Council. However, no specific machinery is set up for such action by the Council, apart from the Military Staff Committee, with planning responsibilities in the field of the possible use of armed force by the Security Council under Chapter VII of the Charter. In fact, therefore, the executive functions and their form have been left largely to practice, and it is in the field of the practices of the Organization that cases may be found in the light of which it is now possible to evaluate the ways in which the Organization may develop its possibilities for diplomatic, political, or military intervention of an executive nature in the field.

The forms used for executive action by the Security Council—or when the Council has not been able to reach decisions, in some cases, by the General Assembly—are varied and are to be explained by an effort to adjust the measures to the needs of each single situation. However, some main types are recurrent. Subcommittees have been set up for fact-finding or negotiation on the spot. Missions have been placed in areas of conflict for the purpose of observation and local negotiation. Observer groups of a temporary nature have been sent out. And, finally, police forces under the aegis of the United Nations have been organized for the assistance of the governments concerned with a view to upholding the principles of the Charter. As these, or many of these, arrangements require centralized administrative measures, which cannot be performed by the Council or the General Assembly, Members have to a large extent used the possibility to request the Secretary-General to perform special functions by instructing him to take the necessary executive steps for implementation of the action decided upon. This has been done under Article 98, as quoted above, and has represented a development in practice of the duties of the Secretary-

General under Article 97. The character of the mandates has, in many cases, been such that in carrying out his functions the Secretary-General has found himself forced also to interpret the decisions in the light of the Charter, United Nations precedents, and the aims and intentions expressed by the Members. When that has been the case, the Secretary-General has been under the obligation to seek guidance, to all possible extent, from the main organs; but when such guidance has not been forthcoming, developments have sometimes led to situations in which he has had to shoulder responsibility for certain limited political functions, which may be considered to be in line with the spirit of Article 99 but which legally have been based on decisions of the main organs themselves, under Article 98, and thus the exclusive responsibility of Member States acting through these organs. Naturally, in carrying out such functions the Secretariat has remained fully subject to the decisions of the political bodies.

This whole development has lately become a matter of controversy, natural and, indeed, unavoidable in the light of differences of approach to the role of the Organization to which attention has been drawn earlier in this Introduction. While the development is welcomed by Member nations which feel a need of growth as regards the possibilities of the Organization to engage in executive action in protection of the Charter principles, it is rejected by those who maintain the conference concept of the Organization. The different opinions expressed on the development are only superficially related to this or that specific action and the way in which it is considered to have been carried through. They are also only superficially related to the choice of means used for translating decisions into action. The discussion regarding the development of executive functions is basically one confronting the same fundamentally different concepts of the Organization and its place in international politics, which could be seen also in the different attitudes toward the legal weight of decisions of the Organization.

It is in this context that the principle embodied in Article 100 of the Charter is of decisive significance. This principle, which has a long history, establishes the international and independent character of the Secretariat. Thus, it is said that the Secretary-General and the staff of the Secretariat "shall not seek or receive instructions from any Government or from any other authority external to the Organization," and that they "shall refrain from any action which might reflect on their position as international officials responsible only to the Organization." In the same Article, the Members of the United Nations undertake to respect "the exclusively international character of the responsibilities of the Secretary-General and the staff and not to seek to influence them in the discharge of their responsibilities."

The significance of the principle stated in Article 100 is a dual one. It envisages a Secretariat so organized and developed as to be able to serve as a neutral instrument for the Organization, were its main organs to wish to use the Secretariat in the way which has been mentioned above and for which Article 98 has opened possibilities. But in doing so, the principle also indicates an intention to use the Secretariat for such functions as would require that it have an exclusively international character.

In the traditional conference pattern, participants in a meeting are mostly serviced by a secretariat drawn from the same countries as the participants themselves, and constituting a mixed group regarding which there is no need to demand or maintain an exclusively international character. It is therefore natural that those who favor the conference approach to the United Nations tend to give to Article 100 another interpretation than the one which the text calls for, especially in the light of its historical background and its background also in other clauses of the Charter.

There is no reason to go more deeply into this special problem here. Suffice it to say that, while the Organization, if regarded as a standing diplomatic conference, might well be serviced by a fully international Secretariat but does not need it, the other approach to the Organization and its role cannot be satisfied with anything less than a secretariat of an exclusively international character, and thus cannot be reconciled with a secretariat composed on party-lines and on the assumption that the interests represented in the main organs in this manner should be represented and advocated also within the Secretariat. Thus, again, the choice between conflicting views on the United Nations Secretariat is basically a choice between conflicting views on the Organization, its functions, and its future.

In order to avoid possible misunderstandings, it should be pointed out here that there is no contradiction at all between a demand for a truly international Secretariat and a demand, found in the Charter itself, for as wide a "geographical" distribution of posts within the Secretariat as possible. It is, indeed, necessary precisely in order to maintain the exclusively international character of the Secretariat, that it be so composed as to achieve a balanced distribution of posts on all levels among all regions. This, however, is clearly something entirely different from a balanced representation of trends or ideologies. In fact if a realistic representation of such trends is considered desirable, it can and should be achieved without any assumption of political representation within the ranks of the Secretariat, by a satisfactory distribution of posts based on geographical criteria.

The exclusively international character of the Secretariat is not tied to its composition, but to the spirit in which it works and to its insulation from outside influences as stated in Article 100. While it may be said that no man is neutral in the sense that he is without opinions or ideals, it is just as true that, in spite of this, a neutral Secretariat is possible. Anyone of integrity, not subjected to undue pressures, can, regardless of his own views, readily act in an "exclusively international" spirit and can be guided in his actions on behalf of the Organization solely by its interests and principles, and by the instructions of its organs.

V

. . . the Organization has now reached a stage in its development where Member nations may find it timely to clarify their views on the direction in which they would like to see the future work of the Organization develop.

*The Covenant of the League of Nations**

The High Contracting Parties,

In order to promote international cooperation and to achieve international peace and security
> by the acceptance of obligations not to resort to war,
> by the prescription of open, just and honorable relations between nations,
> by the firm establishment of the understandings of international law as the actual rule of conduct among Governments, and
> by the maintenance of justice and a scrupulous respect for all treaty obligations in the dealings of organized peoples with one another,
> Agree to this Covenant of the League of Nations.

Article 1
MEMBERSHIP AND WITHDRAWAL

1. The original members of the League of Nations shall be those of the Signatories which are named in the Annex to this Covenant and also such of those other States named in the Annex as shall accede without reservation to this Covenant. Such accessions shall be effected by a declaration deposited with the Secretariat within two months of the coming into force of the Covenant. Notice thereof shall be sent to all other Members of the League.

2. Any fully self-governing State, Dominion or Colony not named in the Annex may become a Member of the League if its admission is agreed to by two-thirds of the Assembly, provided that it shall give effective guaranties of its sincere intention to observe its international obligations, and shall accept such regulations as may be prescribed by the League in regard to its military, naval and air forces and armaments.

3. Any Member of the League may, after two years' notice of its intention so to do, withdraw from the League, provided that all its international obligations and all its obligations under this Covenant shall have been fulfilled at the time of its withdrawal.

---

* The texts printed in italics indicate amendments adopted by the League.

Article 2
EXECUTIVE ORGANS

The action of the League under this Covenant shall be effected through the instrumentality of an Assembly and of a Council, with a permanent Secretariat.

Article 3
ASSEMBLY

1. The Assembly shall consist of representatives of the Members of the League.

2. The Assembly shall meet at stated intervals and from time to time, as occasion may require, at the Seat of the League or at such other place as may be decided upon.

3. The Assembly may deal at its meetings with any matter within the sphere of action of the League or affecting the peace of the world.

4. At meetings of the Assembly each Member of the League shall have one vote and may have not more than three Representatives.

Article 4
COUNCIL

1. The Council shall consist of representatives of the Principal Allied and Associated Powers [United States of America, the British Empire, France, Italy and Japan], together with Representatives of four other Members of the League. These four Members of the League shall be selected by the Assembly from time to time in its discretion. Until the appointment of the Representatives of the four Members of the League first selected by the Assembly, Representatives of Belgium, Brazil, Greece and Spain shall be Members of the Council.

2. With the approval of the majority of the Assembly, the Council may name additional Members of the League, whose Representatives shall always be Members of the Council; the Council with like approval may increase the number of Members of the League to be selected by the Assembly for representation on the Council.

2. *bis. The Assembly shall fix by a two-thirds' majority the rules dealing with the election of the non-permanent Members of the Council, and particularly such regulations as relate to their term of office and the conditions of re-eligibility.*

3. The Council shall meet from time to time as occasion may require, and at least once a year, at the Seat of the League, or at such other place as may be decided upon.

4. The Council may deal at its meetings with any matter within the sphere of action of the League or affecting the peace of the world.

5. Any Member of the League not represented on the Council shall be

invited to send a Representative to sit as a member at any meeting of the Council during the consideration of matters specially affecting the interests of that Member of the League.

6. At meetings of the Council, each Member of the League represented on the Council shall have one vote, and may have not more than one representative.

Article 5
VOTING AND PROCEDURE

1. Except where otherwise expressly provided in this Covenant or by the terms of the present Treaty, decisions at any meeting of the Assembly or of the Council shall require the agreement of all the Members of the League represented at the meeting.

2. All matters of procedure at meetings of the Assembly or of the Council, including the appointment of Committees to investigate particular matters, shall be regulated by the Assembly or by the Council and may be decided by a majority of the Members of the League represented at the meeting.

3. The first meeting of the Assembly and the first meeting of the Council shall be summoned by the President of the United States of America.

Article 6
SECRETARIAT AND EXPENSES

1. The permanent Secretariat shall be established at the Seat of the League. The Secretariat shall comprise a Secretary-General and such secretaries and staffs as may be required.

2. The first Secretary-General shall be the person named in the Annex; thereafter the Secretary-General shall be appointed by the Council with the approval of the majority of the Assembly.

3. The secretaries and the staff of the Secretariat shall be appointed by the Secretary-General with the approval of the Council.

4. The Secretary-General shall act in that capacity at all meetings of the Assembly and of the Council.

5. *The expenses of the League shall be borne by the Members of the League in the proportion decided by the Assembly.*

Article 7
SEAT, QUALIFICATIONS OF OFFICIALS, IMMUNITIES

1. The Seat of the League is established at Geneva.

2. The Council may at any time decide that the Seat of the League shall be established elsewhere.

3. All positions under or in connection with the League, including the Secretariat, shall be open equally to men and women.

4. Representatives of the Members of the League and officials of the

League when engaged on the business of the League shall enjoy diplomatic privileges and immunities.

5. The buildings and other property occupied by the League or its officials or by Representatives attending its meetings shall be inviolable.

Article 8
REDUCTION OF ARMAMENTS

1. The Members of the League recognize that the maintenance of peace requires the reduction of national armaments to the lowest point consistent with national safety and the enforcement by common action of international obligations.

2. The Council, taking account of the geographical situation and circumstances of each State, shall formulate plans for such reduction for the consideration and action of the several Governments.

3. Such plans shall be subject to reconsideration and revision at least every 10 years.

4. After these plans shall have been adopted by the several Governments, the limits of armaments therein fixed shall not be exceeded without the concurrence of the Council.

5. The Members of the League agree that the manufacture by private enterprise of munitions and implements of war is open to grave objections. The Council shall advise how the evil effects attendant upon such manufacture can be prevented, due regard being had to the necessities of those Members of the League which are not able to manufacture the munitions and implements of war necessary for their safety.

6. The Members of the League undertake to interchange full and frank information as to the scale of their armaments, their military, naval and air programs and the condition of such of their industries as are adaptable to warlike purposes.

Article 9
PERMANENT MILITARY, NAVAL AND AIR COMMISSION

A permanent Commission shall be constituted to advise the Council on the execution of the provisions of Articles 1 and 8 and on military, naval and air questions generally.

Article 10
GUARANTIES AGAINST AGGRESSION

The Members of the League undertake to respect and preserve as against external aggression the territorial integrity and existing political independence of all Members of the League. In case of any such aggression or in case of any threat or danger of such aggression the Council shall advise upon the means by which this obligation shall be fulfilled.

Article 11
ACTION IN CASE OF WAR OR THREAT OF WAR

1. Any war or threat of war, whether immediately affecting any of the Members of the League or not, is hereby declared a matter of concern to the whole League, and the League shall take any action that may be deemed wise and effectual to safeguard the peace of nations. In case any such emergency should arise the Secretary-General shall on the request of any Member of the League forthwith summon a meeting of the Council.

2. It is also declared to be the friendly right of each Member of the League to bring to the attention of the Assembly or of the Council any circumstance whatever affecting international relations which threatens to disturb international peace or the good understanding between nations upon which peace depends.

Article 12
DISPUTES TO BE SUBMITTED FOR SETTLEMENT

1. The Members of the League agree that, if there should arise between them any dispute likely to lead to a rupture, they will submit the matter either to arbitration *or judicial settlement* or to inquiry by the Council, and they agree in no case to resort to war until three months after the award by the arbitrators *or the judicial decision,* or the report by the Council.

2. In any case under this Article the award of the arbitrators *or the judicial decision* shall be made within a reasonable time, and the report of the Council shall be made within six months after the submission of the dispute.

Article 13
ARBITRATION OR JUDICIAL SETTLEMENT

1. The Members of the League agree that, whenever any dispute shall arise between them which they recognize to be suitable for submission to arbitration *or judicial settlement,* and which can not be satisfactorily settled by diplomacy, they will submit the whole subject-matter to arbitration *or judicial settlement.*

2. Disputes as to the interpretation of a treaty, as to any question of international law, as to the existence of any fact which, if established, would constitute a breach of any international obligation, or as to the extent and nature of the reparation to be made for any such breach, are declared to be among those which are generally suitable for submission to arbitration *or judicial settlement.*

3. *For the consideration of any such dispute, the court to which the case is referred shall be the Permanent Court of International Justice, established in accordance with Article 14, or any tribunal agreed on by the parties to the dispute or stipulated in any convention existing between them.*

4. The Members of the League agree that they will carry out in full good faith any award *or decision* that may be rendered, and that they will not resort to war against a Member of the League which complies therewith. In the event of any failure to carry out such an award *or decision,* the Council shall propose what steps should be taken to give effect thereto.

Article 14
PERMANENT COURT OF INTERNATIONAL JUSTICE

The Council shall formulate and submit to the Members of the League for adoption plans for the establishment of a Permanent Court of International Justice. The Court shall be competent to hear and determine any dispute of an international character which the parties thereto submit to it. The Court may also give an advisory opinion upon any dispute or question referred to it by the Council or by the Assembly.

Article 15
DISPUTES NOT SUBMITTED TO ARBITRATION OR
JUDICIAL SETTLEMENT

1. If there should arise between Members of the League any dispute likely to lead to a rupture, which is not submitted to arbitration *or judicial settlement* in accordance with Article 13, the Members of the League agree that they will submit the matter to the Council. Any party to the dispute may effect such submission by giving notice of the existence of the dispute to the Secretary-General, who will make all necessary arrangements for a full investigation and consideration thereof.

2. For this purpose the parties to the dispute will communicate to the Secretary-General, as promptly as possible, statements of their case with all the relevant facts and papers, and the Council may forthwith direct the publication thereof.

3. The Council shall endeavor to effect a settlement of the dispute, and, if such efforts are successful, a statement shall be made public giving such facts and explanations regarding the dispute and the terms of settlement thereof as the Council may deem appropriate.

4. If the dispute is not thus settled, the Council either unanimously or by a majority vote shall make and publish a report containing a statement of the facts of the dispute and the recommendations which are deemed just and proper in regard thereto.

5. Any member of the League represented on the Council may make public a statement of the facts of the dispute and of its conclusions regarding the same.

6. If a report by the Council is unanimously agreed to by the Members thereof other than the Representatives of one or more of the parties to the dispute, the Members of the League agree that they will not go to war with

any party to the dispute which complies with the recommendations of the report.

7. If the Council fails to reach a report which is unanimously agreed to by the members thereof, other than the Representatives of one or more of the parties to the dispute, the Members of the League reserve to themselves the right to take such action as they shall consider necessary for the maintenance of right and justice.

8. If the dispute between the parties is claimed by one of them, and is found by the Council, to arise out of a matter which by international law is solely within the domestic jurisdiction of that party, the Council shall so report, and shall make no recommendation as to its settlement.

9. The Council may in any case under this Article refer the dispute to the Assembly. The dispute shall be so referred at the request of either party to the dispute, provided that such request be made within 14 days after the submission of the dispute to the Council.

10. In any case referred to the Assembly, all the provisions of this Article and of Article 12 relating to the action and powers of the Council shall apply to the action and powers of the Assembly, provided that a report made by the Assembly, if concurred in by the Representatives of those Members of the League represented on the Council and of a majority of the other Members of the League, exclusive in each case of the Representatives of the parties to the dispute, shall have the same force as a report by the Council concurred in by all the members thereof other than the Representatives of one or more of the parties to the dispute.

Article 16

SANCTIONS OF PACIFIC SETTLEMENT

1. Should any Member of the League resort to war in disregard of its covenants under Articles 12, 13 or 15, it shall *ipso facto* be deemed to have committed an act of war against all other Members of the League, which hereby undertake immediately to subject it to the severance of all trade or financial relations, the prohibition of all intercourse between their nationals and the nationals of the covenant-breaking State, and the prevention of all financial, commercial or personal intercourse between the nationals of the covenant-breaking State and the nationals of any other State, whether a Member of the League or not.

2. It shall be the duty of the Council in such case to recommend to the several Governments concerned what effective military, naval or air force the Members of the League shall severally contribute to the armed forces to be used to protect the covenants of the League.

3. The Members of the League agree, further, that they will mutually support one another in the financial and economic measures which are taken under this Article, in order to minimize the loss and inconvenience resulting from the above measures, and that they will mutually support one another

in resisting any special measures aimed at one of their number by the covenant-breaking State, and that they will take the necessary steps to afford passage through their territory to the forces of any of the Members of the League which are cooperating to protect the covenants of the League.

4. Any Member of the League which has violated any covenant of the League may be declared to be no longer a Member of the League by a vote of the Council concurred in by the Representatives of all the other Members of the League represented thereon.

Article 17
DISPUTES INVOLVING NON-MEMBERS

1. In the event of a dispute between a Member of the League and a State which is not a Member of the League, or between States not Members of the League, the State or States not Members of the League shall be invited to accept the obligations of membership in the League for the purposes of such dispute, upon such conditions as the Council may deem just. If such invitation is accepted, the provisions of Articles 12 to 16, inclusive, shall be applied with such modifications as may be deemed necessary by the Council.

2. Upon such invitation being given, the Council shall immediately institute an inquiry into the circumstances of the dispute and recommend such action as may seem best and most effectual in the circumstances.

3. If a State so invited shall refuse to accept the obligations of membership in the League for the purposes of such dispute, and shall resort to war against a Member of the League, the provisions of Article 16 shall be applicable as against the State taking such action.

4. If both parties to the dispute when so invited refuse to accept the obligations of Membership in the League for the purposes of such dispute, the Council may take such measures and make such recommendations as will prevent hostilities and will result in the settlement of the dispute.

Article 18
REGISTRATION AND PUBLICATION OF TREATIES

Every treaty or international engagement entered into hereafter by any Member of the League shall be forthwith registered with the Secretariat and shall as soon as possible be published by it. No such treaty or international engagement shall be binding until so registered.

Article 19
REVIEW OF TREATIES

The Assembly may from time to time advise the reconsideration by Members of the League of treaties which have become inapplicable, and the consideration of international conditions whose continuance might endanger the peace of the world.

Article 20
ABROGATION OF INCONSISTENT OBLIGATIONS

1. The Members of the League severally agree that this Covenant is accepted as abrogating all obligations or understandings *inter se* which are inconsistent with the terms thereof, and solemnly undertake that they will not hereafter enter into any engagements inconsistent with the terms thereof.

2. In case any Member of the League shall, before becoming a Member of the League, have undertaken any obligations inconsistent with the terms of this Covenant, it shall be the duty of such Member to take immediate steps to procure its release from such obligations.

Article 21
ENGAGEMENTS THAT REMAIN VALID

Nothing in this Covenant shall be deemed to affect the validity of international engagements, such as treaties of arbitration or regional understandings like the Monroe doctrine, for securing the maintenance of peace.

Article 22
MANDATORY SYSTEM

1. To those colonies and territories which as a consequence of the late war have ceased to be under the sovereignty of the States which formerly governed them and which are inhabited by peoples not yet able to stand by themselves under the strenuous conditions of the modern world, there should be applied the principle that the well-being and development of such peoples form a sacred trust of civilization and that securities for the performance of this trust should be embodied in this Covenant.

2. The best method of giving practical effect to this principle is that the tutelage of such peoples should be intrusted to advanced nations who by reason of their resources, their experience or their geographical position can best undertake this responsibility, and who are willing to accept it, and that this tutelage should be exercised by them as Mandatories on behalf of the League.

3. The character of the mandate must differ according to the stage of the development of the people, the geographical situation of the territory, its economic conditions and other similar circumstances.

4. Certain communities formerly belonging to the Turkish Empire have reached a stage of development where their existence as independent nations can be provisionally recognized subject to the rendering of administrative advice and assistance by a Mandatory until such time as they are able to stand alone. The wishes of these communities must be a principal consideration in the selection of the Mandatory.

5. Other peoples, especially those of Central Africa, are at such a stage

that the Mandatory must be responsible for the administration of the territory under conditions which will guarantee freedom of conscience and religion, subject only to the maintenance of public order and morals, the prohibition of abuses such as the slave trade, the arms traffic and the liquor traffic, and the prevention of the establishment of fortifications of military and naval bases and of military training of the natives for other than police purposes and the defense of territory, and will also secure equal opportunities for the trade and commerce of other Members of the League.

6. There are territories, such as Southwest Africa and certain of the South Pacific islands, which, owing to the sparseness of their population, or their small size, or their remoteness from the centers of civilization, or their geographical contiguity to the territory of the Mandatory, and other circumstances, can be best administered under the laws of the Mandatory as integral portions of its territory, subject to the safeguards above mentioned in the interests of the indigenous population.

7. In every case of mandate, the Mandatory shall render to the Council an annual report in reference to the territory committed to its charge.

8. The degree of authority, control or administration to be exercised by the Mandatory shall, if not previously agreed upon by the Members of the League, be explicitly defined in each case by the Council.

9. A permanent Commission shall be constituted to receive and examine the annual reports of the Mandatories and to advise the Council on all matters relating to the observance of the mandates.

Article 23
SOCIAL AND OTHER ACTIVITIES

Subject to and in accordance with the provisions of international conventions existing or hereafter to be agreed upon, the Members of the League:

(*a*) will endeavor to secure and maintain fair and humane conditions of labor for men, women and children, both in their own countries and in all countries to which their commercial and industrial relations extend, and for that purpose will establish and maintain the necessary international organizations;

(*b*) undertake to secure just treatment of the native inhabitants of territories under their control;

(*c*) will intrust the League with the general supervision over the execution of agreements with regard to traffic in women and children, and the traffic in opium and other dangerous drugs;

(*d*) will intrust the League with the general supervision of the trade in arms and ammunition with the countries in which the control of this traffic is necessary in the common interest;

(*e*) will make provision to secure and maintain freedom of communications and of transit and equitable treatment for the commerce of all Members of the League. In this connection, the special necessities of the regions devastated during the war of 1914-1918 shall be borne in mind; (*f*) will endeavor to take steps in matters of international concern for the prevention and control of disease.

Article 24
INTERNATIONAL BUREAUS

1. There shall be placed under the direction of the League all international bureaus already established by general treaties if the parties to such treaties consent. All such international bureaus and all commissions for the regulation of matters of international interest hereafter constituted shall be placed under the direction of the League.

2. In all matters of international interest which are regulated by general conventions but which are not placed under the control of international bureaus or commissions, the Secretariat of the League shall, subject to the consent of the Council and if desired by the parties, collect and distribute all relevant information and shall render any other assistance which may be necessary or desirable.

3. The Council may include as part of the expenses of the Secretariat the expenses of any bureau or commission which is placed under the direction of the League.

Article 25
PROMOTION OF RED CROSS AND HEALTH

The Members of the League agree to encourage and promote the establishment and cooperation of duly authorized voluntary national Red Cross organizations having as purposes the improvement of health, the prevention of disease and the mitigation of suffering throughout the world.

Article 26
AMENDMENTS

1. Amendments to this Covenant will take effect when ratified by the Members of the League whose Representatives compose the Council and by a majority of the Members of the League whose Representatives compose the Assembly.

2. No such amendment shall bind any Member of the League which signifies its dissent therefrom, but in that case it shall cease to be a Member of the League.

APPENDIX TWO
The Charter of the United Nations

We the Peoples of the United Nations Determined

to save succeeding generations from the scourge of war, which twice in our lifetime has brought untold sorrow to mankind, and

to reaffirm faith in fundamental human rights, in the dignity and worth of the human person, in the equal rights of men and women and of nations large and small, and

to establish conditions under which justice and respect for the obligations arising from treaties and other sources of international law can be maintained, and

to promote social progress and better standards of life in larger freedom,

And for These Ends

to practice tolerance and live together in peace with one another as good neighbors, and

to unite our strength to maintain international peace and security, and

to ensure, by the acceptance of principles and the institution of methods, that armed force shall not be used, save in the common interest, and

to employ international machinery for the promotion of the economic and social advancement of all peoples,

Have Resolved to Combine Our Efforts to Accomplish These Aims

Accordingly, our respective Governments, through representatives assembled in the city of San Francisco, who have exhibited their full powers found to be in good and due form, have agreed to the present Charter of the United Nations and do hereby establish an international organization to be known as the United Nations.

CHAPTER I. PURPOSES AND PRINCIPLES

Article 1

The Purposes of the United Nations are:

1. To maintain international peace and security, and to that end: to take effective collective measures for the prevention and removal of threats to the peace, and for the suppression of acts of aggression or other breaches of the peace, and to bring about by peaceful means, and in conformity with the

531

principles of justice and international law, adjustment or settlement of international disputes or situations which might lead to a breach of the peace;

2. To develop friendly relations among nations based on respect for the principle of equal rights and self-determination of peoples, and to take other appropriate measures to strengthen universal peace;

3. To achieve international cooperation in solving international problems of an economic, social, cultural, or humanitarian character, and in promoting and encouraging respect for human rights and for fundamental freedoms for all without distinction as to race, sex, language, or religion; and

4. To be a center for harmonizing the actions of nations in the attainment of these common ends.

Article 2

The Organization and its Members, in pursuit of the Purposes stated in Article 1, shall act in accordance with the following Principles.

1. The Organization is based on the principle of the sovereign equality of all its Members.

2. All Members, in order to ensure to all of them the rights and benefits resulting from membership, shall fulfil in good faith the obligations assumed by them in accordance with the present Charter.

3. All Members shall settle their international disputes by peaceful means in such a manner that international peace and security, and justice, are not endangered.

4. All Members shall refrain in their international relations from the threat or use of force against the territorial integrity or political independence of any state, or in any other manner inconsistent with the Purposes of the United Nations.

5. All Members shall give the United Nations every assistance in any action it takes in accordance with the present Charter, and shall refrain from giving assistance to any state against which the United Nations is taking preventive or enforcement action.

6. The Organization shall ensure that states which are not Members of the United Nations act in accordance with these Principles so far as may be necessary for the maintenance of international peace and security.

7. Nothing contained in the present Charter shall authorize the United Nations to intervene in matters which are essentially within the domestic jurisdiction of any state or shall require the Members to submit such matters to settlement under the present Charter; but this principle shall not prejudice the application of enforcement measures under Chapter VII.

CHAPTER II. MEMBERSHIP

Article 3

The original Members of the United Nations shall be the states which, having participated in the United Nations Conference on International Organization at San Francisco, or having previously signed the Declaration by the United Nations of January 1, 1942, sign the present Charter and ratify it in accordance with Article 110.

Article 4

1. Membership in the United Nations is open to all other peace-loving states which accept the obligations contained in the present Charter and, in the judgment of the Organization, are able and willing to carry out these obligations.

2. The admission of any such state to membership in the United Nations will be effected by a decision of the General Assembly upon the recommendation of the Security Council.

Article 5

A Member of the United Nations against which preventive or enforcement action has been taken by the Security Council may be suspended from the exercise of the rights and privileges of membership by the General Assembly upon the recommendation of the Security Council. The exercise of these rights and privileges may be restored by the Security Council.

Article 6

A Member of the United Nations which has persistently violated the Principles contained in the present Charter may be expelled from the Organization by the General Assembly upon the recommendation of the Security Council.

CHAPTER III. ORGANS

Article 7

1. There are established as the principal organs of the United Nations: a General Assembly, a Security Council, an Economic and Social Council, a Trusteeship Council, an International Court of Justice, and a Secretariat.

2. Such subsidiary organs as may be found necessary may be established in accordance with the present Charter.

Article 8

The United Nations shall place no restrictions on the eligibility of men and women to participate in any capacity and under conditions of equality in its principal and subsidiary organs.

CHAPTER IV. THE GENERAL ASSEMBLY

Composition

Article 9

1. The General Assembly shall consist of all the Members of the United Nations.

2. Each Member shall have not more than five representatives in the General Assembly.

Functions and Powers

Article 10

The General Assembly may discuss any questions or any matters within the scope of the present Charter or relating to the powers and functions of any organs provided for in the present Charter, and, except as provided in Article 12, may make recommendations to the Members of the United Nations or to the Security Council or to both on any such questions or matters.

Article 11

1. The General Assembly may consider the general principles of cooperation in the maintenance of international peace and security, including the principles governing disarmament and the regulation of armaments, and may make recommendations with regard to such principles to the Members or to the Security Council or to both.

2. The General Assembly may discuss any questions relating to the maintenance of international peace and security brought before it by any Member of the United Nations, or by the Security Council, or by a state which is not a Member of the United Nations in accordance with Article 35, paragraph 2, and, except as provided in Article 12, may make recommendations with regard to any such questions to the state or states concerned or to the Security Council or to both. Any such question on which action is necessary shall be referred to the Security Council by the General Assembly either before or after discussion.

3. The General Assembly may call the attention of the Security Council to situations which are likely to endanger international peace and security.

4. The powers of the General Assembly set forth in this Article shall not limit the general scope of Article 10.

Article 12

1. While the Security Council is exercising in respect of any dispute or situation the functions assigned to it in the present Charter, the General Assembly shall not make any recommendation with regard to that dispute or situation unless the Security Council so requests.

2. The Secretary-General, with the consent of the Security Council, shall notify the General Assembly at each session of any matters relative to the maintenance of international peace and security which are being dealt with by the Security Council and shall similarly notify the General Assembly, or the Members of the United Nations if the General Assembly is not in session, immediately the Security Council ceases to deal with such matters.

Article 13

1. The General Assembly shall initiate studies and make recommendations for the purpose of:

a. promoting international cooperation in the political field and encouraging the progressive development of international law and its codification;

b. promoting international cooperation in the economic, social, cultural, educational, and health fields, and assisting in the realization of human rights and fundamental freedoms for all without distinction as to race, sex, language, or religion.

2. The further responsibilities, functions, and powers of the General Assembly with respect to matters mentioned in paragraph 1 (*b*) above are set forth in Chapters IX and X.

Article 14

Subject to the provisions of Article 12, the General Assembly may recommend measures for the peaceful adjustment of any situation, regardless of origin, which it deems likely to impair the general welfare or friendly relations among nations, including situations resulting from a violation of the provisions of the present Charter setting forth the Purposes and Principles of the United Nations.

Article 15

1. The General Assembly shall receive and consider annual and special reports from the Security Council; these reports shall include an account of the measures that the Security Council has decided upon or taken to maintain international peace and security.

2. The General Assembly shall receive and consider reports from the other organs of the United Nations.

Article 16

The General Assembly shall perform such functions with respect to the international trusteeship system as are assigned to it under Chapters XII and XIII, including the approval of the trusteeship agreements for areas not designated as strategic.

Article 17

1. The General Assembly shall consider and approve the budget of the Organization.

2. The expenses of the Organization shall be borne by the Members as apportioned by the General Assembly.

3. The General Assembly shall consider and approve any financial and budgetary arrangements with specialized agencies referred to in Article 57 and shall examine the administrative budgets of such specialized agencies with a view to making recommendations to the agencies concerned.

Voting

Article 18

1. Each member of the General Assembly shall have one vote.

2. Decisions of the General Assembly on important questions shall be made by a two-thirds majority of the members present and voting. These questions shall include: recommendations with respect to the maintenance of international peace and security, the election of the non-permanent members of the Security Council, the election of the members of the Economic and Social Council, the election of members of the Trusteeship Council in accordance with paragraph 1 (*c*) of Article 86, the admission of new Members to the United Nations, the suspension of the rights and privileges of membership, the expulsion of Members, questions relating to the operation of the trusteeship system, and budgetary questions.

3. Decisions on other questions, including the determination of additional categories of questions to be decided by a two-thirds majority, shall be made by a majority of the members present and voting.

Article 19

A Member of the United Nations which is in arrears in the payment of its financial contributions to the Organization shall have no vote in the General Assembly if the amount of its arrears equals or exceeds the amount of the contributions due from it for the preceding two full years. The General Assembly may, nevertheless, permit such a Member to vote if it is satisfied that the failure to pay is due to conditions beyond the control of the Member.

Procedure

Article 20

The General Assembly shall meet in regular annual sessions and in such special sessions as occasion may require. Special session shall be convoked by the Secretary-General at the request of the Security Council or of a majority of the Members of the United Nations.

Article 21

The General Assembly shall adopt its own rules of procedure. It shall elect its President for each session.

Article 22

The General Assembly may establish such subsidiary organs as it deems necessary for the performance of its functions.

CHAPTER V. THE SECURITY COUNCIL

Composition

Article 23

1. The Security Council shall consist of eleven Members of the United Nations. The Republic of China, France, the Union of Soviet Socialist Republics, the United Kingdom of Great Britain and Northern Ireland, and the United States of America shall be permanent members of the Security Council. The General Assembly shall elect six other Members of the United Nations to be non-permanent members of the Security Council, due regard being specially paid, in the first instance to the contribution of Members of the United Nations to the maintenance of international peace and security and to the other purposes of the Organization, and also to equitable geographical distribution.

2. The non-permanent members of the Security Council shall be elected for a term of two years. In the first election of the non-permanent members, however, three shall be chosen for a term of one year. A retiring member shall not be eligible for immediate re-election.

3. Each member of the Security Council shall have one representative.

Functions and Powers

Article 24

1. In order to ensure prompt and effective action by the United Nations, its Members confer on the Security Council primary responsibility for the maintenance of international peace and security, and agree that in carrying out its duties under this responsibility the Security Council acts on their behalf.

2. In discharging these duties the Security Council shall act in accordance with the Purposes and Principles of the United Nations. The specific powers granted to the Security Council for the discharge of these duties are laid down in Chapters VI, VII, VIII, and XII.

3. The Security Council shall submit annual and, when necessary, special reports to the General Assembly for its consideration.

Article 25

The Members of the United Nations agree to accept and carry out the decisions of the Security Council in accordance with the present Charter.

Article 26

In order to promote the establishment and maintenance of international peace and security with the least diversion for armaments of the world's human and economic resources, the Security Council shall be responsible for formulating, with the assistance of the Military Staff Committee referred to in Article 47, plans to be submitted to the Members of the United Nations for the establishment of a system for the regulation of armaments.

Voting

Article 27

1. Each member of the Security Council shall have one vote.

2. Decisions of the Security Council on procedural matters shall be made by an affirmative vote of seven members.

3. Decisions of the Security Council on all other matters shall be made by an affirmative vote of seven members including the concurring votes of the permanent members; provided that, in decisions under Chapter VI, and under paragraph 3 of Article 52, a party to a dispute shall abstain from voting.

Procedure

Article 28

1. The Security Council shall be so organized as to be able to function continuously. Each member of the Security Council shall for this purpose be represented at all times at the seat of the Organization.

2. The Security Council shall hold periodic meetings at which each of its members may, if it so desires, be represented by a member of the government or by some other specially designated representative.

3. The Security Council may hold meetings at such places other than the seat of the Organization as in its judgment will best facilitate its work.

Article 29

The Security Council may establish such subsidiary organs as it deems necessary for the performance of its functions.

Article 30

The Security Council shall adopt its own rules of procedure, including the method of selecting its President.

Article 31

Any Member of the United Nations which is not a member of the Security Council may participate, without vote, in the discussion of any question brought before the Security Council whenever the latter considers that the interests of that Member are specially affected.

Article 32

Any Member of the United Nations which is not a member of the Security Council or any state which is not a Member of the United Nations, if it is a party to a dispute under consideration by the Security Council, shall be invited to participate, without vote, in the discussion relating to the dispute. The Security Council shall lay down such conditions as it deems just for the participation of a state which is not a Member of the United Nations.

CHAPTER VI. PACIFIC SETTLEMENT OF DISPUTES

Article 33

1. The parties to any dispute, the continuance of which is likely to endanger the maintenance of international peace and security, shall, first of all, seek a solution by negotiation, enquiry, mediation, conciliation, arbitration, judicial settlement resort to regional agencies or arrangements, or other peaceful means of their own choice.

2. The Security Council shall, when it deems necessary, call upon the parties to settle their dispute by such means.

Article 34

The Security Council may investigate any dispute, or any situation which might lead to international friction or give rise to a dispute, in order to determine whether the continuance of the dispute or situation is likely to endanger the maintenance of international peace and security.

Article 35

1. Any Member of the United Nations may bring any dispute, or any situation of the nature referred to in Article 34, to the attention of the Security Council or of the General Assembly.

2. A state which is not a Member of the United Nations may bring to the attention of the Security Council or of the General Assembly any dispute to which it is a party if it accepts in advance, for the purpose of the dispute, the obligations of pacific settlement provided in the present Charter.

3. The proceedings of the General Assembly in respect of matters brought to its attention under this Article will be subject to the provisions of Articles 11 and 12.

Article 36

1. The Security Council may, at any stage of a dispute of the nature referred to in Article 33 or of a situation of like nature, recommend appropriate procedures or methods of adjustment.

2. The Security Council should take into consideration any procedures for the settlement of the dispute which have already been adopted by the parties.

3. In making recommendations under this Article the Security Council should also take into consideration that legal disputes should as a general

rule be referred by the parties to the International Court of Justice in accordance with the provisions of the Statute of the Court.

Article 37

1. Should the parties to a dispute of the nature referred to in Article 33 fail to settle it by the means indicated in that Article, they shall refer it to the Security Council.

2. If the Security Council deems that the continuance of the dispute is in fact likely to endanger the maintenance of international peace and security, it shall decide whether to take action under Article 36 or to recommend such terms of settlement as it may consider appropriate.

Article 38

Without prejudice to the provisions of Articles 33 to 37, the Security Council may, if all the parties to any dispute so request, make recommendations to the parties with a view to a pacific settlement of the dispute.

CHAPTER VII. ACTION WITH RESPECT TO THREATS TO THE PEACE, BREACHES OF THE PEACE, AND ACTS OF AGGRESSION

Article 39

The Security Council shall determine the existence of any threat to the peace, breach of the peace, or act of aggression and shall make recommendations, or decide what measures shall be taken in accordance with Articles 41 and 42, to maintain or restore international peace and security.

Article 40

In order to prevent an aggravation of the situation, the Security Council may, before making the recommendations or deciding upon the measures provided for in Article 39, call upon the parties concerned to comply with such provisional measures as it deems necessary or desirable. Such provisional measures shall be without prejudice to the rights, claims, or position of the parties concerned. The Security Council shall duly take account of failure to comply with such provisional measures.

Article 41

The Security Council may decide what measures not involving the use of armed force are to be employed to give effect to its decisions, and it may call upon the Members of the United Nations to apply such measures. These may include complete or partial interruption of economic relations and of rail, sea, air, postal, telegraphic, radio, and other means of communication, and the severance of diplomatic relations.

Article 42

Should the Security Council consider that measures provided for in Article 41 would be inadequate or have proved to be inadequate, it may take such action by air, sea, or land forces as may be necessary to maintain or restore international peace and security. Such action may include demonstrations, blockade, and other operations by air, sea, or land forces of Members of the United Nations.

Article 43

1. All Members of the United Nations, in order to contribute to the maintenance of international peace and security, undertake to make available to the Security Council, on its call and in accordance with a special agreement or agreements, armed forces, assistance, and facilities, including rights of passage, necessary for the purpose of maintaining international peace and security.

2. Such agreement or agreements shall govern the numbers and types of forces, their degree of readiness and general location, and the nature of the facilities and assistance to be provided.

3. The agreement or agreements shall be negotiated as soon as possible on the initiative of the Security Council. They shall be concluded between the Security Council and Members or between the Security Council and groups of Members and shall be subject to ratification by the signatory states in accordance with their respective constitutional processes.

Article 44

When the Security Council has decided to use force it shall, before calling upon a Member not represented on it to provide armed forces in fulfillment of the obligations assumed under Article 43, invite that Member, if the Member so desires, to participate in the decisions of the Security Council concerning the employment of contingents of that Member's armed forces.

Article 45

In order to enable the United Nations to take urgent military measures, Members shall hold immediately available national air-force contingents for combined international enforcement action. The strength and degree of readiness of these contingents and plans for their combined action shall be determined, within the limits laid down in the special agreement or agreements referred to in Article 43, by the Security Council with the assistance of the Military Staff Committee.

Article 46

Plans for the application of armed force shall be made by the Security Council with the assistance of the Military Staff Committee.

Article 47

1. There shall be established a Military Staff Committee to advise and assist the Security Council on all questions relating to the Security Council's

military requirements for the maintenance of international peace and security, the employment and command of forces placed at its disposal, the regulation of armaments, and possible disarmament.

2. The Military Staff Committee shall consist of the Chiefs of Staff of the permanent members of the Security Council or their representatives. Any Member of the United Nations not permanently represented on the Committee shall be invited by the Committee to be associated with it when the efficient discharge of the Committee's responsibilities requires the participation of that Member in its work.

3. The Military Staff Committee shall be responsible under the Security Council for the strategic direction of any armed forces placed at the disposal of the Security Council. Questions relating to the command of such forces shall be worked out subsequently.

4. The Military Staff Committee, with the authorization of the Security Council and after consultation with appropriate regional agencies, may establish regional subcommittees.

Article 48

1. The action required to carry out the decisions of the Security Council for the maintenance of international peace and security shall be taken by all for Members of the United Nations or by some of them, as the Security Council may determine.

2. Such decisions shall be carried out by the Members of the United Nations directly and through their action in the appropriate international agencies of which they are members.

Article 49

The Members of the United Nations shall join in affording mutual assistance in carrying out the measures decided upon by the Security Council.

Article 50

If preventive or enforcement measures against any state are taken by the Security Council, any other state, whether a Member of the United Nations or not, which finds itself confronted with special economic problems arising from the carrying out of those measures shall have the right to consult the Security Council with regard to a solution of those problems.

Article 51

Nothing in the present Charter shall impair the inherent right of individual or collective self-defense if an armed attack occurs against a Member of the United Nations, until the Security Council has taken the measures necessary to maintain international peace and security. Measures taken by

Members in the exercise of this right of self-defense shall be immediately reported to the Security Council and shall not in any way affect the authority and responsibility of the Security Council under the present Charter to take at any time such action as it deems necessary in order to maintain or restore international peace and security.

CHAPTER VIII. REGIONAL ARRANGEMENTS

Article 52

1. Nothing in the present Charter precludes the existence of regional arrangements or agencies for dealing with such matters relating to the maintenance of international peace and security as are appropriate for regional action, provided that such arrangements or agencies and their activities are consistent with the Purposes and Principles of the United Nations.

2. The Members of the United Nations entering into such arrangements or constituting such agencies shall make every effort to achieve pacific settlement of local disputes through such regional arrangements or by such regional agencies before referring them to the Security Council.

3. The Security Council shall encourage the development of pacific settlement of local disputes through such regional arrangements or by such regional agencies either on the initiative of the states concerned or by reference from the Security Council.

4. This Article in no way impairs the application of Articles 34 and 35.

Article 53

1. The Security Council shall, where appropriate, utilize such regional arrangements or agencies for enforcement action under its authority. But no enforcement action shall be taken under regional arrangements or by regional agencies without the authorization of the Security Council, with the exception of measures against any enemy state, as defined in Paragraph 2 of this Article, provided for pursuant to Article 107 or in regional arrangements directed against renewal of aggressive policy on the part of any such state, until such times as the Organization may, on request of the Governments concerned, be charged with the responsibility for preventing further aggression by such a state.

2. The term enemy state as used in Paragraph 1 of this Article applies to any state which during the Second World War has been an enemy of any signatory of the present Charter.

Article 54

The Security Council shall at all times be kept fully informed of activities undertaken or in contemplation under regional arrangements or by regional agencies for the maintenance of international peace and security.

CHAPTER IX. INTERNATIONAL ECONOMIC AND
SOCIAL COOPERATION

Article 55

With a view to the creation of conditions of stability and well-being which are necessary for peaceful and friendly relations among nations based on respect for the principle of equal rights and self-determination of peoples, the United Nations shall promote:

a. higher standards of living, full employment, and conditions of economic and social progress and development;

b. solutions of international economic, social, health, and related problems; and international cultural and educational cooperation; and

c. universal respect for, and observance of, human rights and fundamental freedoms for all without distinction as to race, sex, language, or religion.

Article 56

All Members pledge themselves to take joint and separate action in cooperation with the Organization for the achievement of the purposes set forth in Article 55.

Article 57

1. The various specialized agencies, established by intergovernmental agreement and having wide international responsibilities, as defined in their basic instruments, in economic, social, cultural, educational, health, and related fields, shall be brought into relationship with the United Nations in accordance with the provisions of Article 63.

2. Such agencies thus brought into relationship with the United Nations are hereinafter referred to as specialized agencies.

Article 58

The Organization shall make recommendations for the coordination of the policies and activities of the specialized agencies.

Article 59

The Organization shall, where appropriate, initiate negotiations among the states concerned for the creation of any new specialized agencies required for the accomplishment of the purposes set forth in Article 55.

Article 60

Responsibility for the discharge of the functions of the Organization set forth in this Chapter shall be vested in the General Assembly and, under the authority of the General Assembly, in the Economic and Social Council, which shall have for this purpose the powers set forth in Chapter X.

CHAPTER X. THE ECONOMIC AND SOCIAL COUNCIL

Composition

Article 61

1. The Economic and Social Council shall consist of eighteen Members of the United Nations elected by the General Assembly.

2. Subject to the provisions of Paragraph 3, six members of the Economic and Social Council shall be elected each year for a term of three years. A retiring member shall be eligible for immediate re-election.

3. At the first election, eighteen members of the Economic and Social Council shall be chosen. The term of office of six members so chosen shall expire at the end of one year, and of six other members at the end of two years, in accordance with arrangements made by the General Assembly.

4. Each member of the Economic and Social Council shall have one representative.

Functions and Powers

Article 62

1. The Economic and Social Council may make or initiate studies and reports with respect to international economic, social, cultural, educational, health, and related matters and may make recommendations with respect to any such matters to the General Assembly, to the Members of the United Nations, and to the specialized agencies concerned.

2. It may make recommendations for the purpose of promoting respect for, and observance of, human rights and fundamental freedoms for all.

3. It may prepare draft conventions for submission to the General Assembly, with respect to matters falling within its competence.

4. It may call, in accordance with the rules prescribed by the United Nations, international conferences on matters falling within its competence.

Article 63

1. The Economic and Social Council may enter into agreements with any of the agencies referred to in Article 57, defining the terms on which the agency concerned shall be brought into relationship with the United Nations. Such agreements shall be subject to approval by the General Assembly.

2. It may coordinate the activities of the specialized agencies through consultation with and recommendations to such agencies and through recommendations to the General Assembly and to the Members of the United Nations.

Article 64

1. The Economic and Social Council may take appropriate steps to obtain regular reports from the specialized agencies. It may make arrangements with the Members of the United Nations and with the specialized agencies to obtain reports on the steps taken to give effect to its own recommendations and to recommendations on matters falling within its competence made by the General Assembly.

2. It may communicate its observations on these reports to the General Assembly.

Article 65

The Economic and Social Council may furnish information to the Security Council and shall assist the Security Council upon its request.

Article 66

1. The Economic and Social Council shall perform such functions as fall within its competence in connection with the carrying out of the recommendations of the General Assembly.

2. It may, with the approval of the General Assembly, perform services at the request of Members of the United Nations and at the request of specialized agencies.

3. It shall perform such other functions as are specified elsewhere in the present Charter or as may be assigned to it by the General Assembly.

Voting

Article 67

1. Each member of the Economic and Social Council shall have one vote.

2. Decisions of the Economic and Social Council shall be made by a majority of the members present and voting.

Procedure

Article 68

The Economic and Social Council shall set up commissions in economic and social fields and for the promotion of human rights, and such other commissions as may be required for the performance of its functions.

Article 69

The Economic and Social Council shall invite any Member of the United Nations to participate, without vote, in its deliberations on any matter of particular concern to that Member.

Article 70

The Economic and Social Council may make arrangements for representatives of the specialized agencies to participate, without vote, in its deliberations and in those of the commissions established by it, and for its representatives to participate in the deliberations of the specialized agencies.

Article 71

The Economic and Social Council may make suitable arrangements for consultation with non-governmental organizations which are concerned with matters within its competence. Such arrangements may be made with international organizations and, where appropriate, with national organizations after consultation with the Member of the United Nations concerned.

Article 72

1. The Economic and Social Council shall adopt its own rules of procedure, including the method of selecting its President.

2. The Economic and Social Council shall meet as required in accordance with its rules, which shall include provisions for the convening of meetings on the request of a majority of its members.

CHAPTER XI. DECLARATION REGARDING NON-SELF-GOVERNING TERRITORIES

Article 73

Members of the United Nations which have or assume responsibilities for the administration of territories whose peoples have not yet attained a full measure of self-government recognize the principle that the interests of the inhabitants of these territories are paramount, and accept as a sacred trust the obligation to promote to the utmost, within the system of international peace and security established by the present Charter, the well-being of the inhabitants of these territories, and, to this end:

a. to ensure, with due respect for the culture of the peoples concerned, their political, economic, social, and educational advancement, their just treatment, and their protection against abuses;

b. to develop self-government, to take due account of the political aspirations of the peoples, and to assist them in the progressive development of their free political institutions, according to the particular circumstances of each territory and its peoples and their varying stages of advancement;

c. to further international peace and security;

d. to promote constructive measures of development, to encourage research, and to cooperate with one another and, when and where appropriate, with specialized international bodies with a view to the practical achievement of the social, economic, and scientific purposes set forth in this Article; and

e. to transmit regularly to the Secretary-General for information purposes, subject to such limitation as security and constitutional considerations may require, statistical and other information of a technical nature relating to economic, social, and educational conditions in the territories for which they are respectively responsible other than those territories to which Chapters XII and XIII apply.

Article 74

Members of the United Nations also agree that their policy in respect of the territories to which this Chapter applies, no less than in respect of their metropolitan areas, must be based on the general principle of good-neighborliness, due account being taken of the interests and well-being of the rest of the world, in social, economic, and commercial matters.

CHAPTER XII. INTERNATIONAL TRUSTEESHIP SYSTEM

Article 75

The United Nations shall establish under its authority an international trusteeship system for the administration and supervision of such territories as may be placed thereunder by subsequent individual agreements. These territories are hereinafter referred to as trust territories.

Article 76

The basic objectives of the trusteeship system, in accordance with the Purposes of the United Nations laid down in Article 1 of the present Charter, shall be:

a. to further international peace and security;

b. to promote the political, economic, social, and educational advancement of the inhabitants of the trust territories, and their progressive development towards self-government or independence as may be appropriate to the particular circumstances of each territory and its peoples and the freely expressed wishes of the peoples concerned, and as may be provided by the terms of each trusteeship agreement;

c. to encourage respect for human rights and for fundamental freedoms for all without distinction as to race, sex, language, or religion, and to encourage recognition of the interdependence of the peoples of the world; and

d. to ensure equal treatment in social, economic, and commercial matters for all Members of the United Nations and their nationals, and also equal treatment for the latter in the administration of justice, without prejudice to the attainment of the foregoing objectives and subject to the provisions of Article 80.

Article 77

1. The trusteeship system shall apply to such territories in the following categories as may be placed thereunder by means of trusteeship agreements:

a. territories now held under mandate;

b. territories which may be detached from enemy states as a result of the Second World War; and

c. territories voluntarily placed under the system by states responsible for their administration.

2. It will be a matter for subsequent agreement as to which territories in the foregoing categories will be brought under the trusteeship system and upon what terms.

Article 78

The trusteeship system shall not apply to territories which have become Members of the United Nations, relationship among which shall be based on respect for the principle of sovereign equality.

Article 79

The terms of trusteeship for each territory to be placed under the trusteeship system, including any alteration or amendment, shall be agreed upon by the states directly concerned, including the mandatory power in the case of territories held under mandate by a Member of the United Nations, and shall be approved as provided for in Articles 83 and 85.

Article 80

1. Except as may be agreed upon in individual trusteeship agreements, made under Articles 77, 79, and 81, placing each territory under the trusteeship system, and until such agreements have been concluded, nothing in this Chapter shall be construed in or of itself to alter in any manner the rights whatsoever of any states or any peoples or the terms of existing international instruments to which Members of the United Nations may respectively be parties.

2. Paragraph 1 of this Article shall not be interpreted as giving grounds for delay or postponement of the negotiation and conclusion of agreements for placing mandated and other territories under the trusteeship system as provided for in Article 77.

Article 81

The trusteeship agreement shall in each case include the terms under which the trust territory will be administered and designate the authority which will exercise the administration of the trust territory. Such authority, hereinafter called the administering authority, may be one or more states or the Organization itself.

Article 82

There may be designated, in any trusteeship agreement, a strategic area or areas which may include part or all of the trust territory to which the agreement applies, without prejudice to any special agreement or agreements made under Article 43.

Article 83

1. All functions of the United Nations relating to strategic areas, including the approval of the terms of the trusteeship agreements and of their alteration or amendment, shall be exercised by the Security Council.

2. The basic objectives set forth in Article 76 shall be applicable to the people of each strategic area.

3. The Security Council shall, subject to the provisions of the trusteeship agreements and without prejudice to security considerations, avail itself of the assistance of the Trusteeship Council to perform those functions of the United Nations under the trusteeship system relating to political, economic, social, and educational matters in the strategic areas.

Article 84

It shall be the duty of the administering authority to ensure that the trust territory shall play its part in the maintenance of international peace and security. To this end the administering authority may make use of volunteer forces, facilities, and assistance from the trust territory in carrying out the obligations towards the Security Council undertaken in this regard by the administering authority, as well as for local defense and the maintenance of law and order within the trust territory.

Article 85

1. The functions of the United Nations with regard to trusteeship agreements for all areas not designated as strategic, including the approval of the terms of the trusteeship agreements and of their alteration or amendment, shall be exercised by the General Assembly.

2. The Trusteeship Council, operating under the authority of the General Assembly, shall assist the General Assembly in carrying out these functions.

CHAPTER XIII. THE TRUSTEESHIP COUNCIL

Composition

Article 86

1. The Trusteeship Council shall consist of the following Members of the United Nations:

a. those Members administering trust territories;

b. such of those Members mentioned by name in Article 23 as are not administering trust territories; and

c. as many other Members elected for three-year terms by the General Assembly as may be necessary to ensure that the total number of members of the Trusteeship Council is equally divided between those Members of the United Nations which administer trust territories and those which do not.

2. Each member of the Trusteeship Council shall designate one specially qualified person to represent it therein.

Functions and Powers

Article 87

The General Assembly and, under its authority, the Trusteeship Council, in carrying out their functions, may:

a. consider reports submitted by the administering authority;

b. accept petitions and examine them in consultation with the administering authority;

c. provide for periodic visits to the respective trust territories at times agreed upon with the administering authority; and

d. take these and other actions in conformity with the terms of the trusteeship agreements.

Article 88

The Trusteeship Council shall formulate a questionnaire on the political, economic, social, and educational advancement of the inhabitants of each trust territory, and the administering authority for each trust territory within the competence of the General Assembly shall make an annual report to the General Assembly upon the basis of such questionnaire.

Voting

Article 89

1. Each member of the Trusteeship Council shall have one vote.

2. Decisions of the Trusteeship Council shall be made by a majority of the members present and voting.

Procedure

Article 90

1. The Trusteeship Council shall adopt it own rules of procedure, including the method of selecting its President.

2. The Trusteeship Council shall meet as required in accordance with its rules, which shall include provision for the convening of meetings on the request of a majority of its members.

Article 91

The Trusteeship Council shall, when appropriate, avail itself of the assistance of the Economic and Social Council and of the specialized agencies in regard to matters with which they are respectively concerned.

CHAPTER XIV. THE INTERNATIONAL COURT OF JUSTICE

Article 92

The International Court of Justice shall be the principal judicial organ of the United Nations. It shall function in accordance with the annexed Statute, which is based upon the Statute of the Permanent Court of International Justice and forms an integral part of the present Charter.

Article 93

1. All Members of the United Nations are *ipso facto* parties to the Statute of the International Court of Justice.

2. A state which is not a Member of the United Nations may become a party to the Statute of the International Court of Justice on conditions to be determined in each case by the General Assembly upon the recommendation of the Security Council.

Article 94

1. Each Member of the United Nations undertakes to comply with the decision of the International Court of Justice in any case to which it is a party.

2. If any party to a case fails to perform the obligations incumbent upon it under a judgment rendered by the Court, the other party may have recourse to the Security Council, which may, if it deems necessary, make recommendations or decide upon measures to be taken to give effect to the judgment.

Article 95

Nothing in the present Charter shall prevent Members of the United Nations from entrusting the solution of their differences to other tribunals by virtue of agreements already in existence or which may be concluded in the future.

Article 96

1. The General Assembly or the Security Council may request the International Court of Justice to give an advisory opinion on any legal question.

2. Other organs of the United Nations and specialized agencies, which may at any time be so authorized by the General Assembly, may also

request advisory opinions of the Court on legal questions arising within the scope of their activities.

CHAPTER XV. THE SECRETARIAT

Article 97

The Secretariat shall comprise a Secretary-General and such staff as the Organization may require. The Secretary-General shall be appointed by the General Assembly upon the recommendation of the Security Council. He shall be the chief administrative officer of the Organization.

Article 98

The Secretary-General shall act in that capacity in all meetings of the General Assembly, of the Security Council, of the Economic and Social Council, and of the Trusteeship Council, and shall perform such other functions as are entrusted to him by these organs. The Secretary-General shall make an annual report to the General Assembly on the work of the Organization.

Article 99

The Secretary-General may bring to the attention of the Security Council any matter which in his opinion may threaten the maintenance of international peace and security.

Article 100

1. In the performance of their duties the Secretary-General and the staff shall not seek or receive instructions from any government or from any other authority external to the Organization. They shall refrain from any action which might reflect on their position as international officials responsible only to the Organization.

2. Each Member of the United Nations undertakes to respect the exclusively international character of the responsibilities of the Secretary-General and the staff and not to seek to influence them in the discharge of their responsibilities.

Article 101

1. The staff shall be appointed by the Secretary-General under regulations established by the General Assembly.

2. Appropriate staffs shall be permanently assigned to the Economic and Social Council, the Trusteeship Council, and, as required, to other organs of the United Nations. These staffs shall form a part of the Secretariat.

3. The paramount consideration in the employment of the staff and in the determination of the conditions of service shall be the necessity of

securing the highest standards of efficiency, competence, and integrity. Due regard shall be paid to the importance of recruiting the staff on as wide a geographical basis as possible.

CHAPTER XVI. MISCELLANEOUS PROVISIONS

Article 102

1. Every treaty and every international agreement entered into by any Member of the United Nations after the present Charter comes into force shall as soon as possible be registered with the Secretariat and published by it.

2. No party to any such treaty or international agreement which has not been registered in accordance with the provisions of Paragraph 1 of this Article may invoke that treaty or agreement before any organ of the United Nations.

Article 103

In the event of a conflict between the obligations of the Members of the United Nations under the present Charter and their obligations under any other international agreement, their obligations under the present Charter shall prevail.

Article 104

The Organization shall enjoy in the territory of each of its Members such legal capacity as may be necessary for the exercise of its functions and the fulfillment of its purposes.

Article 105

1. The Organization shall enjoy in the territory of each of its Members such privileges and immunities as are necessary for the fulfillment of its purposes.

2. Representatives of the Members of the United Nations and officials of the Organization shall similarly enjoy such privileges and immunities as are necessary for the independent exercise of their functions in connection with the Organization.

3. The General Assembly may make recommendations with a view to determining the details of the application of Paragraphs 1 and 2 of this Article or may propose conventions to the Members of the United Nations for this purpose.

CHAPTER XVII. TRANSITIONAL SECURITY ARRANGEMENTS

Article 106

Pending the coming into force of such special agreements referred to in Article 43 as in the opinion of the Security Council enable it to begin the exercise of its responsibilities under Article 42, the parties to the Four-Nation Declaration, signed at Moscow, October 30, 1943, and France, shall, in accordance with the provisions of Paragraph 5 of that Declaration, consult with one another and as occasion requires with other Members of the United Nations with a view to such joint action on behalf of the Organization as may be necessary for the purpose of maintaining international peace and security.

Article 107

Nothing in the present Charter shall invalidate or preclude action, in relation to any state which during the Second World War has been an enemy of any signatory to the present Charter, taken or authorized as a result of that war by the Governments having responsibility for such action.

CHAPTER XVIII. AMENDMENTS

Article 108

Amendments to the present Charter shall come into force for all Members of the United Nations when they have been adopted by a vote of two thirds of the members of the General Assembly and ratified in accordance with their respective constitutional processes by two thirds of the Members of the United Nations, including all the permanent members of the Security Council.

Article 109

1. A General Conference of the Members of the United Nations for the purpose of reviewing the present Charter may be held at a date and place to be fixed by a two-thirds vote of the members of the General Assembly and by a vote of any seven members of the Security Council. Each Member of the United Nations shall have one vote in the conference.

2. Any alteration of the present Charter recommended by a two-thirds vote of the conference shall take effect when ratified in accordance with their respective constitutional processes by two thirds of the Members of the United Nations including all the permanent members of the Security Council.

3. If such a conference has not been held before the tenth annual session of the General Assembly following the coming into force of the present Charter, the proposal to call such a conference shall be placed on the agenda of that session of the General Assembly, and the conference shall be held if so decided by a majority vote of the members of the General Assembly and by a vote of any seven members of the Security Council.

CHAPTER XIX. RATIFICATION AND SIGNATURE

Article 110

1. The present Charter shall be ratified by the signatory states in accordance with their respective constitutional processes.

2. The ratifications shall be deposited with the Government of the United States of America, which shall notify all the signatory states of each deposit as well as the Secretary-General of the Organization when he has been appointed.

3. The present Charter shall come into force upon the deposit of ratifications by the Republic of China, France, the Union of Soviet Socialist Republics, the United Kingdom of Great Britain and Northern Ireland, and the United States of America, and by a majority of the other signatory states. A protocol of the ratifications deposited shall thereupon be drawn up by the Government of the United States of America which shall communicate copies thereof to all the signatory states.

4. The states signatory to the present Charter which ratify it after it has come into force will become original Members of the United Nations on the date of the deposit of their respective ratifications.

Article 111

The present Charter, of which the Chinese, French, Russian, English, and Spanish texts are equally authentic, shall remain deposited in the archives of the Government of the United States of America. Duly certified copies thereof shall be transmitted by that Government to the Governments of the other signatory states.

IN FAITH WHEREOF the representatives of the Governments of the United Nations have signed the present Charter.

DONE at the city of San Francisco the twenty-sixth day of June, one thousand nine hundred and forty-five.